BLAME IT ON

CW00350592

Blame it on the WTO?

A Human Rights Critique

SARAH JOSEPH

OXFORD
UNIVERSITY PRESS

Great Clarendon Street, Oxford, OX2 6DP,
United Kingdom

Oxford University Press is a department of the University of Oxford.
It furthers the University's objective of excellence in research, scholarship,
and education by publishing worldwide. Oxford is a registered trade mark of
Oxford University Press in the UK and in certain other countries

Published in the United States of America by Oxford University Press
198 Madison Avenue, New York, NY 10016, United States of America

British Library Cataloguing in Publication Data
Data available

ISBN 978–0–19–956589–4
978–0–19–968976–7 (Pbk.)

Printed in Great Britain by
CPI Group Ltd, Croydon, CR0 4YY

Foreword

When the World Trade Organisation (WTO) was established in 1995, few human rights lawyers at the time realized the significance of this event for their discipline. In part, this may have been because the creation of the WTO followed more than a decade of neoliberal policies characterized by deregulation and the removal of barriers to trade and investment in many regions. Although it strengthened the system originally established under the General Agreement on Tariffs and Trade in 1947, the WTO was not seen to represent a seismic shift: it was the final stage of a gradual evolution, rather than the beginning of something radically new.

The relative indifference of human rights lawyers also stemmed from a lack of understanding of the consequences of this ambitious overhaul of the global trade system. The WTO was deliberately placed outside the remit of the United Nations. With its establishment, the international trade system included for the first time a dispute settlement mechanism of a quasi-judicial nature, binding upon the WTO Members, and which could allow economic sanctions to be imposed on States that failed to comply with the disciplines imposed on them. Indeed, in retrospect, it is this aspect of the WTO Agreement that appears both the most novel and that has the most far-reaching consequences. Most notably, it created an imbalance between the commitments of States under the WTO framework and their other international obligations, including those under human rights treaties: should conflicts emerge between the two sets of obligations, States may be tempted systematically to prioritize their duties under the WTO, because of the sanctions attached to non-compliance, leaving aside the comparatively 'softer' commitments made under human rights treaties.

As this important book by Sarah Joseph shows, things are now changing. The problems arising from the fragmentation of international law are increasingly being acknowledged, and solutions are being explored to overcome them. Due to the 'special nature' of human rights treaties, which are irreducible to exchanges of undertakings between States,[1] merely to state that these treaties are paramount, will not suffice. We need to work towards practical ways of avoiding conflicts whenever possible, and of solving conflicts when they emerge, in ways that do not lead to the sacrifice of human rights on the altar of increased trade, even for the sake of economic growth.

And progress is being made. Increasingly, human rights treaty bodies—in particular, the Committee on Economic, Social, and Cultural Rights—insist that States comply with their 'extraterritorial obligations'. That is, States must ensure that the measures they adopt unilaterally or the international agreements

---

[1] Inter-American Court of Human Rights, *Case of the Sawhoyamaxa Indigenous Community v Paraguay*, Judgment of 29 March 2006, Series C No 146, para 140.

they negotiate, have no adverse impact on the human rights of persons outside their national territory; and that they protect human rights outside their borders by appropriately regulating non-State actors over which they are able to exercise influence.[2] As this book goes to print, a group of international experts are seeking to restate the existing international law in this area, focusing on economic, social, and cultural rights. The obligations of international assistance and cooperation have further strengthened the need for imposing a broad range of extraterritorial obligations, extending beyond cases in which a State directly influences a situation abroad through the activities of its agents. The emergence of extraterritorial obligations in human rights discourse will, of course, help to redefine the relationship between trade and human rights. First, it will restrain States from concluding trade agreements that may have a negative impact on the enjoyment of human rights by populations under the jurisdiction of the other party. Second, it will prohibit States from implementing trade policies liable to have such a negative impact, including, among others, practices of dumping and the use of trade dispute settlement mechanisms in order to force the other party to renounce the adoption of certain policies by which it seeks to protect the human rights of its own population.

At the same time, following the recommendations made by a number of human rights treaty bodies and the special procedures developed by the Human Rights Council,[3] the practice of human rights impact assessments of trade agreements is underway. The European Commission is preparing sustainability impact assessments of the agreements concluded between the European Union and third countries on a systematic basis since 2002. It has now acknowledged that, in order to take into account the binding status of the EU Charter of Fundamental Rights

---

[2] Committee on Economic, Social, and Cultural Rights, General Comment No 12 (1999), *The right to adequate food* (art 11), E/C.12/1999/5, paras 19 and 36 ('States parties should, in international agreements whenever relevant, ensure that the right to adequate food is given due attention'); Committee on Economic, Social, and Cultural Rights, General Comment No 14 (2000), *The right to the highest attainable standard of health (article 12 of the International Covenant on Economic, Social and Cultural Rights)*, E/C.12/2000/4 (2000), para 39 ('In relation to the conclusion of other international agreements, States parties should take steps to ensure that these instruments do not adversely impact upon the right to health'); Committee on Economic, Social, and Cultural Rights, General Comment No 15 (2002), *The right to water (arts 11 and 12 of the International Covenant on Economic, Social and Cultural Rights)*, UN Doc E/C.12/2002/11 (26 November 2002), paras 31 and 35–6 ('States parties should ensure that the right to water is given due attention in international agreements and, to that end, should consider the development of further legal instruments. With regard to the conclusion and implementation of other international and regional agreements, States parties should take steps to ensure that these instruments do not adversely impact upon the right to water. Agreements concerning trade liberalization should not curtail or inhibit a country's capacity to ensure the full realization of the right to water').

[3] See, eg, Committee on Economic, Social, and Cultural Rights, Concluding Observations regarding Ecuador, 7 July 2004, E/C.12/1/Add.100, para 56; Committee on the Rights of the Child, Concluding Observations regarding El Salvador, 30 June 2004, CRC/C/15/Add.232, para 48; Committee on the Elimination of Discrimination against Women, Concluding Observations regarding Colombia, 2 February 2007, CEDAW/C/COL/CO/6, para 29; Committee on the Elimination of Discrimination Against Women, Concluding Observations regarding Philipines, 25 October 2006, CEDAW/C/PHI/CO/6, para 26; Committee on the Elimination of Discrimination Against Women, Concluding Observations regarding Guatemala, 2 June 2006, CEDAW/C/GUA/CO/6, para 32; Report of the Special Rapporteur on the right to food, Addendum: Mission to the World Trade Organization, 4 February 2009, A/HRC/10/5/Add.2, paras 37–8.

within the EU legal order, the impact of trade agreements on fundamental rights should be systematically assessed in the future.[4] In order to provide guidance to States in preparing such human rights impact assessments, I have presented a draft set of guiding principles on human rights impact assessments of trade and investment agreements, in my official capacity as the UN Special Rapporteur on the right to food. The draft guiding principles—still under discussion at the time of writing this Foreword—define the preparation of human rights impact assessments as an obligation of States, which are bound by pre-existing human rights treaty obligations and are therefore prohibited from concluding any agreements that would impose inconsistent obligations on them. This measure, the guiding principles argue, imposes on States a duty to identify and resolve any potential inconsistency between pre-existing human rights treaties and subsequent trade or investment agreements. The draft guiding principles also refer to the right of every citizen to take part in the conduct of public affairs, recognized under the International Covenant on Civil and Political Rights;[5] the implication is that no trade or investment agreement should be concluded in the absence of a public debate, which should be informed precisely by human rights impact assessments.

Yet, as attempts are being made to reconcile trade agreements—particularly commitments made by States within the WTO framework—with human rights, three major difficulties emerge.

The first difficulty stems from the fact that economic, social, and cultural rights, while they do impose certain immediate obligations, are also subject to progressive realization, depending on the resources available to each State. Therefore, in order for the conclusion of trade agreements to be compatible with a State's human rights obligations, it is not sufficient simply to ensure that such agreements do not impose directly conflicting obligations on that State. The State must preserve a certain 'policy space' that will allow it to take measures whereby it discharges its obligation to 'fulfil' human rights: for instance, by enlarging access to certain public services, such as health or education, or by supporting access to basic necessities, such as food and housing. In order to ensure that a State is never prohibited from moving in this direction because of commitments—such as restrictions on subsidies liable to be trade distorting—made under previously agreed trade agreements, a general safeguard clause would be desirable. Such a clause would assert that the trade agreement is never to be interpreted as imposing a prohibition or creating an obstacle to the ability of a State to comply with its human rights obligations.

However, even that may not be enough. When a State moves towards the realization of human rights by choosing to implement certain policies that seek to improve the accessibility of goods or services conducive to the enjoyment of such rights, it is generally encouraged—but not, strictly speaking, obliged—to do so. In the area of human rights, States should be seen as having to score as high as they

---

[4] Communication from the Commission to the European Parliament, the Council, the European Economic and Social Committee and the Committee of the Regions, 'Smart Regulation in the European Union', COM(2010) 543 final of 8 October 2010, 7.

[5] International Covenant on Civil and Political Rights, GA res 2200A (XXI), 21 UN GAOR Supp (No 16) at 52, U.N Doc A/6316 (1966), 999 *UNTS* 171, art 25 (a).

can on a scale, and a 'violations' approach is not particularly apposite to effecting this situation: therefore, identifying 'conflicting' commitments made under trade agreements may not be sufficient. What is needed is an assessment of the ability of the State, in the mid- to long-term—and not only at the time when it enters into a trade agreement—to implement certain policies in a wide range of areas that can support the full realization of economic, social, and cultural rights. The further we move in this direction, the less a purely legal approach—comparing different obligations with one another to assess whether or not they are 'compatible'—will lead to satisfactory results, and the more economic modelling will be required. In my view, one way out of this difficulty may be to insist on States adopting a multi-year strategy for the realization of the various human rights they are bound to implement (or, perhaps, one single human rights action plan covering the full range of these obligations): only the trade agreements that would facilitate the implementation of the said strategies should be considered compatible with the human rights obligations of the State. The adoption of human rights national strategies, and making trade agreements conditional upon their contribution to such strategies, would be one way to ensure that the benefits expected from trade—such as economic growth and an increase in export revenues—would be treated as means that should serve the fulfilment of human rights, rather than—as is too often the case—as ends in themselves, to which human rights may even be subordinated.

But we encounter a second difficulty in the tension between the short- and long-term considerations that guide States in the commitments they make to remove barriers to trade. That is, that the deepening of the international division of labour, which may bring about certain immediate benefits, may however not work in favour of the long-term development of poor countries, and thus of their ability to promote the full realization of human rights. As already noted by the United Nations Economic Commission for Latin America under the leadership of Raúl Prebisch in the 1950s, countries that export raw commodities need to export increasing volumes in order to import the manufactured products, with a higher added technological value, that they are unable to produce themselves. Thus, *in the long term*, the removal of barriers to trade, which accelerates the specialization of each country in the kind of production in which it has a comparative advantage, will not benefit the least industrialized countries: while trade liberalization may bring them short-term advantages—they will increase their exports of agricultural products and pay less for their imports of manufactured goods than if they had to produce such goods themselves—the long-term consequences will be a widening of the gap between rich and poor countries, and an inability on the part of the latter to climb up the ladder of development.

That, in essence, is what has come be known as the Prebisch-Singer thesis of deteriorating terms of trade. It leads to the idea that international trade, replicating the patterns of colonialism, may in fact accentuate the dependency of developing countries on the former colonial powers, and make it impossible for these countries to overcome the obstacles to development. These views are currently being revived, with some variations, by economists such as Ha-Joon Chang or Erik Reinert, who note that rich countries have become rich thanks to the protection of their nascent industries, and that they now preach free trade to developing nations simply because, having climbed up the ladder of development, free trade is now in their interest.[6] Globalization, they remark, has benefited the countries—such as, for example, Brazil, China, South Korea, or India—which carefully sequenced trade liberalization, and which built an industry and a services sector behind trade barriers before opening up to trade. But for the developing countries that had not diversified their economies and whose industrial sector was still too weak at the time when the economies opened, it has meant the relegation to a permanent status of underclass nations.[7]

These views pose a clear challenge to the assessment of the impacts of trade liberalization on human rights: how to rank the immediate benefits against the long-term development impacts? How can the dimension of sustainability enter into the human rights equation? Should we say, to take the idea of sustainability at its word, that policies that seek to promote human rights today (as trade is sometimes alleged to do), should not be at the expense of the ability of States to promote human rights in the future? It is of course ironic that, in general, the tables are turned in exactly the opposite direction: in discussions about the relationships between human rights and trade, the free traders typically argue that the benefits of trade will be visible in the long term—that is, once the economic actors have adjusted to the new conditions it creates—even though there may be negative impacts in the short term—the so-called 'transition (or adjustment) costs'. That the positions are thus so easily exchanged shows the considerable degree of confusion that is now clouding the debate.

Finally, and linked to the previous point, there is the problem of trade-offs. Trade agreements will typically benefit certain groups, making them better off, and hurt others, whose situation will be made more fragile as a result. In particular, trade agreements may contribute to economic growth and thus may facilitate the ability of the State to mobilize budgetary resources allowing it to finance certain public goods in the areas of health, education, or housing. At the same time, they may negatively affect the situation of certain groups, such as workers in the least efficient sectors of the economy or local producers affected by dumping of imported products on the local markets. In such cases, difficult choices will have to be made about the priorities that the State seeks to pursue. Human rights impact assessments seek to clarify the nature of such choices, and to ensure that they are made on the basis of the best information available.

The question of which trade-offs are acceptable is to be decided at the level of each country, through open and democratic processes, informed by human rights

[6] See Ha-Joon Chang, *Kicking Away the Ladder. Development Strategy in Historical Perspective* (Anthem Press, London, 2002) ; Ha-Joon Chang, *Bad Samaritan. The Guilty Secrets of Rich Nations & the Threat to Global Prosperity* (Random House, London, 2007); Erik S Reinert, *How Rich Countries Got Rich and Why Poor Countries Stay Poor* (Constable, London, 2007).
[7] See also Joseph E Stiglitz and Andrew Charlton, *Fair Trade for All. How Trade Can Promote Development* (Oxford University Press, Oxford, 2005, rev edn 2007) 17 ('To date, not one successful developing country has pursued a purely free market approach to development. In this context it is inappropriate for the world trading system to be implementing rules which circumscribe the ability of developing countries to use both trade and industry policies to promote industrialization').

impact assessments. Yet, the process of setting priorities and managing trade-offs, as well as the substance of the outcome, must comply with certain conditions. First, the process of setting priorities must involve effective participation of all stakeholders, including the poorest and most vulnerable segments of the population. The institutional mechanisms through which impact assessments are prepared and which feed into political decision-making must therefore allow for the views of these stakeholders to be fully taken into account, either directly or through their legitimate representatives. Second, the principles of equality and non-discrimination rule out any trade-offs which would result in or exacerbate unequal and discriminatory outcomes such as, for example, giving priority to providing health and education services to the more affluent parts of society, rather than to the most disadvantaged and marginalized groups. Third, any trade-off that results in a retrogression in the level of protection of a human right should be treated as highly suspect: trade-offs whereby one right suffers a marked decline in its level of realization would need to be subject to the most careful consideration and to be fully justified by reference to the totality of human rights.

The issues above are only some of the difficult and highly contentious questions that are raised in the emerging dialogue between trade and human rights. Building on her unparalleled knowledge of human rights, Sarah Joseph makes an important contribution to this dialogue, at a particularly propitious time—a time when global capitalism is being reshaped in fundamental ways, and when human rights lawyers are developing tools to ensure that the choices that are made will move us in the right direction. I am grateful to her for not evading any difficult question, and for her continued commitment to this dialogue.

Olivier De Schutter
United Nations Special Rapporteur on the right to food
Professor at the University of Louvain
Visiting Professor, Columbia University

Preface

This book is the culmination of my work on an Australian Research Council grant on 'The WTO and Human Rights'. Most of it was written at the end of 2009 during a period of sabbatical at the Lauterpacht Centre for International Law, Cambridge University, and a lot of its ideas gleaned in two prior stints at the Lauterpacht in 2006 and 2007. I can thoroughly recommend the Lauterpacht as a lively and friendly place to write and share research. In that regard I must thanks its directors and staff at the time, James Crawford and Roger O'Keefe, Anne Skinner, Katie Hargreaves, Anita Rutherford, and Karen Fachechi, for their help and hospitality. And also all the other researchers and visiting scholars. . . . I won't name you all because I'll undoubtedly, inadvertently, leave someone out.

Some writing was also done, because 'I had to get this finished lest I go mad', during a retreat at The Last Villa in Sandy Bay in Hobart in early 2010. Again, that place is recommended for anyone who has to 'get away' to punch out a chapter (or just to relax in fine surrounds). Thanks also to Elise Histed in Hobart (and of course Libscombe Larder).

As a human rights lawyer, it was very difficult to wrap my head around the intricacies of WTO law and free trade theory. So of course I had a lot of help, and, in that respect, I must thank Jürgen Kurtz, Andrew Lang, Gig Moon, Amrita Narlikar, Jeff Waincymer, and also my brother Rob, especially for providing the missing link in my understanding of 'comparative advantage' ('opportunity cost', for the record). And also, for their invaluable feedback on my chapters: Olivier De Schutter (thanks too for his thought-provoking foreword), Chip Pitts, Frank Garcia, Scott Coleman, Adam McBeth, Melissa Castan, and Jenny Schultz (the latter being the person who first introduced me to the WTO over a decade ago). And there were many others who helped me with ideas and conversations, including Lorand Bartels, Iain Byrne, Rowena Cantley Smith, Thomas Cottier, Patrick Emerton, Joanna Gomula, Robert McCorquodale, James Harrison, David Kinley, Aileen Kwa, Justin Malbon, Gabrielle Marceau, Justine Nolan, Thomas Pogge, Margot Salomon, Sigrun Skogly, and Margaret Young. Of course, any errors in the text are my own.

Special thanks also to Susie Talbot, who was a meticulous and proactive researcher on this book. It was great knowing that I could email my chapters across the sea to have them returned on time exactly as I needed them. Thanks of course goes to Oxford University Press, who were patient with my lateness and then very diligent in getting this out for the Northern summer. So thanks to John Louth, Merel Alstein, and Ela Kotkowska. And also I must thank the Monash University Faculty of Law, especially its support with teaching-free periods of research, and its library and computer staff.

And finally thanks to friends and family, apart from those already mentioned above, for their support, especially during my crankier moments!

Sarah Joseph
Castan Centre for Human Rights Law
Monash University, Melbourne
February 2011

Preface to the Paperback Edition

In advance of the paperback edition, I make the following brief comments on developments since original publication in 2011. Little progress has been made with the Doha round negotiations, which continue to sputter.

The most positive development concerns TRIPS and the least developed countries. The deadline for their full compliance with TRIPS was extended from 2013 to 2021. Furthermore, the prohibition on the rolling back of existing intellectual property rules for LDCs was excluded in this new extension, which seems to give them much-needed flexibility. Beyond that initiative, none of the concerns raised in this book have been addressed.

Pascal Lamy will end his term as the WTO Director-General on 1 September 2013. His successor will be Brazil's Roberto Carvalho de Azevêdo.

New members have joined the WTO, namely Vietnam, Laos, Samoa, Montenegro, Tajikistan and, most importantly due to the size of its economy, Russia. Interestingly, the Ukraine, which only joined the WTO in 2008, is seeking to renegotiate the terms of its accession protocol, as it argues that its commitments were made in the expectation of a swift end to the Doha Round.

Concerns over spiraling global food prices, discussed in Chapter 6, have returned. There have also been interesting WTO cases. It has been confirmed that the Agreement on Technical Barriers to Trade (the TBT, discussed in Chapter 4) can apply to restrict mandatory labeling requirements. Challenges to Canadian subsidies on renewable energy, as well as a US ban on clove cigarettes, have succeeded, again confirming the real impact of WTO rules on "non-trade" areas such as health and the environment. Two ongoing cases will also shed light in this area: a challenge to the European Union's ban on seal products and a challenge to Australia's laws which mandate plain packages for tobacco products to reduce their consumer appeal.

I thank the wonderful staff at Oxford University Press for their marketing efforts with this book, and their demonstration of faith in it by proceeding to a paperback edition. And thanks too to all who have read it and sent feedback.

Sarah Joseph
June 2013

Contents

Table of Cases

EUROPEAN COURT OF HUMAN RIGHTS

UNITED NATIONS

Human Rights Committee

INTERNATIONAL COURT OF JUSTICE

WORLD TRADE ORGANIZATION/GATT

OTHER

Table of Conventions, Declarations, and other Instruments

Abbreviations

AMS	Aggregate Measures of Support
AoA	Agreement on Agriculture
ASEAN	Association of South East Asian Nations
ATC	Agreement on Textiles and Clothing
BITs	bilateral investment treaties
CAFOD	Catholic Agency for Overseas Development
CAFTA	Central American Free Trade Agreement
CAP	Common Agricultural Policy
CAT	Convention against Torture and other Cruel, Inhuman and Degrading Treatment or Punishment 1984
CBD	Convention on Biological Diversity 1992
CEDAW	Convention on the Elimination of All Forms of Discrimination against Women 1979
CERD	International Convention on the Elimination of all Forms of Racial Discrimination 1965
CPC	central product classification
CPRD	Convention on the Rights of Persons with Disabilities 2006
CRC	Convention on the Rights of the Child 1989
DFQF	duty-free and quota-free
DRD	Declaration on the Right to Development 1986
DRIP	Declarations of the Rights of Indigenous Peoples 2007
DSB	Dispute Settlement Body
EBA	Everything but Arms
EC	European Communities
ECHR	European Convention on Human Rights 1951
EPAs	European Partnership Agreements
EPZs	export processing zones
EU	European Union
FAO	Food and Agricultural Organization
FTA	free trade agreement
GA	General Assembly
GATS	General Agreement on Trade in Services
GATT	General Agreement on Tariffs and Trade 1947
GDP	gross domestic product
GMOs	genetically modified organisms
GNI	gross national income
GSP	General System of Preferences

HRC	Human Rights Committee
HRIAs	human rights impact assessments
IAAKSTD	International Assessment of Agricultural Knowledge, Science and Technology for Development
IBRD	International Bank for Reconstruction and Development
ICC	International Criminal Court
ICCPR	International Covenant on Civil and Political Rights 1966
ICESCR	International Covenant on Economic, Social and Cultural Rights
ICJ	International Court of Justice
IFIs	international financial institutions
ILO	International Labour Organization
IMF	International Monetary Fund
IP	intellectual property
ISO	International Standards Organization
ITO	International Trade Organisation
KEI	Knowledge Ecology International
LDCs	least developed countries
MDGs	Millennium Development Goals
MFN	Most Favoured Nation
MNCs	multinational corporations
MWC	International Convention on the Protection of the Rights of All Migrant Workers and Members of their Families 1990
NAFTA	North American Free Trade Agreement
NAMA	non-agricultural market access
NGOs	non-governmental organizations
PPMs	production or process methods
PSE	production support estimate
PVA	polyvinyl alcohol fibres
PwC	PricewaterCoopers
SCM	Agreement on Subsidies and Countervailing Measures
SDT	special and differential treatment
SIAs	Sustainability Impact Assessments
SPS	Agreement on the Application of Sanitary and Phytosanitary Measures
SSM	special safeguard mechanism
SVEs	small and vulnerable economies
TBT	Agreement on Technical Barriers to Trade
TED	turtle excluder device
TPRM	Trade Policy Review Mechanism
TRIMs	Agreement on Trade Related Aspects of Investment Measures
TRIPS	Agreement on Trade Related Aspects of Intellectual Property

UDHR	Universal Declaration of Human Rights
UN	United Nations
UNCTAD	United Nations Conference on Trade and Development
UNDP	UN Development Program
UPOV	International Union for the Protection of New Varieties of Plants
WHO	World Health Organization
WIPO	World Intellectual Property Organization
WTO	World Trade Organization

Introduction

It is well known that many human rights advocates are critical of the WTO. Is it possible that this enmity arises from 'regime envy', a mere bemoaning of the effectiveness of the WTO compared to the relative ineffectiveness, for example, of global human rights bodies? Or are the criticisms valid? This book is designed to explain and explore the validity of the main human rights concerns with the WTO.

Free trade advocates claim that free trade (and therefore the WTO given that it promotes free trade) promotes peace, cuts the cost of living, raises incomes, and promotes good government.[1] The WTO Director General, Pascal Lamy, has gone so far as to say: 'one could almost say that trade is human rights in practice'.[2] Lamy's statement echoes the conclusions of an expert panel which was set up to examine the future of the WTO. That report, colloquially known as the Sullivan Report after its chairperson, concluded:

[T]he notion that trade, investment, and the growth of business detracts from non-economic facets of human rights is the contrary of the truth.... In the end—and we accept that it may take time—the exposure of governments and citizens to an international institutional framework dedicated to openness will have its effects on much more than commerce.[3]

James Harrison has summarized the panel's conclusions thus:

there is no need directly to address the human rights impact of international trade on the protection and promotion of human rights, because it is in the very nature of the existing trade regime to enhance human rights protection.[4]

In stark contrast to the above rosy picture of the WTO, one of the first assessments of the human rights impact of the WTO by a United Nations human rights body was 'almost entirely negative'.[5] Global Exchange, a human rights non-governmental

---

[1] WTO, '10 benefits of the trading system' (2008) <http://www.wto.org/english/res_e/doload_e/10b_e.pdf> accessed 18 September 2010.

[2] Pascal Lamy, 'Towards shared responsibility and greater coherence: human rights, trade and macroeconomic policy' (Speech at the Colloquium on Human Rights in the Global Economy, Co-organized by the International Council on Human Rights and Realizing Rights, Geneva, 13 January 2010) <http://www.wto.org/english/news_e/sppl_e/sppl146_e.htm> accessed 18 September 2010.

[3] WTO, *The Future of the WTO: Addressing Institutional Challenges in the New Millennium* (Report by the Consultative Board to the former Director-General Supachai Panitchpakdi) (WTO, Geneva, 2004) 10.

[4] James Harrison, *The Human Rights Impact of the World Trade Organisation* (Hart, Oxford, 2007) 37.

[5] Ibid, 128, commenting on a report for the Sub-Commission on the Promotion and Protection of Human Rights by J Oloka-Onyango and U Deepika, 'The Realization of Economic, Social and

organization (NGO) focused on global economic justice, has asserted the following amongst its 'top reasons to oppose the WTO': it is fundamentally undemocratic, it tramples labour and human rights, it is increasing inequality and hunger,
it is destroying the environment, and it is killing people.[6] Lamy recently described
the opposition to his organization in the following terms:

> For many, trade is a villain. It is a symbol of mercantilism, capitalism, the tool through
> which powerful multinational corporations impose their law over human beings, impair-
> ing their economic, social and cultural rights.[7]

It is true that many human rights criticisms of the WTO are ill-conceived, and
based on misunderstandings including a failure to recognize the benefits of free
trade. At the same time, many trade experts are overly dismissive of human rights
critiques, blindly adhering to a belief in free trade as an undeniable good. As noted
by Joseph Stiglitz:

> Those who vilify globalization too often overlook its benefits. But the proponents of
> globalization have been, if anything, even more unbalanced.[8]

This book aims to explain the reasoning behind the main perceived human rights
'problems' with the WTO. These alleged shortcomings are explained and assessed
as to their validity. This book also aims to help break down the mutual ignorance
that exists in the relationship between trade and human rights. This reciprocal and
perhaps wilful ignorance[9] has fostered a relationship that is historically laced with
suspicion.[10] Hopefully this book will make some contribution to diminishing that
level of mutual misunderstanding.

The WTO in the global economy

The WTO is one component in the matrix of organizations and rules which regulate the global economy. It is not to be confused with the many other component
parts, which have also been accused of generating deleterious effects on human
rights. It is not, for example, responsible for the harm that has allegedly been caused
to client States by onerous loan conditions from the International Monetary Fund
(IMF), or the alleged funding for ill-conceived projects by the World Bank.[11] It is
not responsible for the behaviour of multinational corporations (MNCs) when they

---

Cultural Rights: Globalization and its Impact on the Full Enjoyment of Human Rights', UN doc.
E/CN.4/Sub.2/2000/13 (15 June 2000).

   [6] Global Exchange, 'Top Reasons to Oppose the WTO' (2008) <http://www.globalexchange
.org/campaigns/wto/OpposeWTO.html> accessed 18 September 2010.
   [7] Lamy, above n 2.
   [8] Joseph Stiglitz, *Globalization and its Discontents* (Penguin, London, 2002) 5.
   [9] Lamy has suggested that this ongoing ignorance is deliberate at Lamy, above n 2.
   [10] Ibid.
   [11] See, generally, on human rights and these international financial institutions: Adam McBeth,
International Economic Actors and Human Rights (Routledge, London, 2009); Mac Darrow, *Between
Light and Shadow* (Hart, Portland, 2003); and Sigrun Skogly, *Human Rights Obligations of the World
Bank and the International Monetary Fund* (Cavendish, London, 2001).

are accused of perpetrating grave human rights abuses with impunity.[12] It is not responsible for the rights conferred directly on foreign investors, largely MNCs, under the many hundreds of bilateral investment treaties (BITs) that criss-cross the world; it is feared that these rights constrain the ability of States to regulate foreign investors so as to protect human rights.[13] It is not responsible for the proliferation of bilateral and regional free trade agreements (FTAs), which impose more oner-ous obligations than the WTO agreements, allegedly to the detriment of human rights.[14] It is not responsible for the crippling debt loads, which in some cases force more money to flow from poor to rich countries than vice versa.[15] Finally, it is not responsible for the continual failure by rich States to honour their commitments in aid to poorer countries.[16]

However, just as the WTO cannot be directly blamed for the impact of other major actors or legal systems within the global economy, it cannot be viewed as an island with no connections to those other actors and systems.[17] For example, the WTO, in promoting foreign trade and in protecting intellectual property, undoubtedly enhances the power of MNCs, the major engines of free trade,[18] thus contributing to an environment that promotes 'permissive conditions for business-related human rights abuse',[19] especially if they are endowed with enforceable rights under BITs and FTAs. The constraints placed by WTO rules on the policy

---

[12] See, generally, on the relationship between human rights and the conduct of multinational corporations: the Business & Human Rights Resource Centre website at <http://www.business-humanrights.org> (which also maintains the portal for materials relating to the work of the United Nations Secretary General's Special Representative on Business and Human Rights); International Commission of Jurists (ICJ), *Report of the ICJ Expert Legal Panel on Corporate Complicity in International Crimes: Corporate Complicity & Legal Accountability* (2008) Vols 1–3. See also Michael Kerr, Richard Janda, and Chip Pitts in Chip Pitts (ed), *Corporate Social Responsibility: A Legal Analysis* (Butterworths/Lexis-Nexis, Canada, 2009).

[13] See, eg, Howard Mann, 'International Investment Agreements, Business and Human Rights: Key Issues and Opportunities' (Report prepared for Prof John Ruggie, UN Special Representative to the Secretary General for Business and Human Rights (International Institute for Sustainable Development, February 2008)) <http://www.iisd.org/pdf/2008/iia_business_human_rights.pdf> accessed 18 September 2010.

[14] See below Chapters 5 and 9.

[15] David Kinley, *Civilising Globalisation* (Cambridge University Press, Cambridge, 2009) 114–15. See, generally, on the key issues relating to the international debt crisis: the documents produced by the Debt and Finance Analysis Unit of the United Nations Conference on Trade and Development (available at <http://www.unctad.org>); the documents produced by the United Nations Secretary-General's Independent Expert on the effects of foreign debt and other related international financial obligations of States on the full enjoyment of all human rights, particularly economic, social, and cultural rights (available at <http://www2.ohchr.org/english/issues/development/debt/index.htm>).

[16] Less than six years away from the 2015 deadline to achieve the Millennium Development Goals, the United Nations warned that, despite many successes, overall progress has been too slow for most of the targets to be met by 2015; see United Nations, *Millennium Development Goals Report 2009* (DESA, New York, 2009) 4.

[17] See also UNGA, 'Report of the Special Rapporteur on the Right to Food, Olivier De Schutter', UN doc. A/63/278, 21 October 2008, para 23.

[18] Kinley, above n 15, 37–8. See also Mehdi Shafaeddin, 'Is Industrial Policy Relevant in the 21st Century?', *Third World Network Trade & Development Series No. 36* (TWN, Malaysia, 2008) 7.

[19] Human Rights Council, 'Report of the Special Representative of the Secretary-General on the issue of human rights and transnational corporations and other business entities: Business and human rights: mapping international standards of responsibility and accountability for corporate acts', UN doc. A/HRC/4/035, 19 February 2007, para 82.

space of developing States, that is the space in which they may flexibly choose among various strategic and tactical options to achieve the economic development, human rights, and other objectives affecting their people, are exacerbated if those same States are also subjected to arduous loan conditions by the IMF or onerous debt burdens. In short, the WTO is a key part of the governance of the global economy. Therefore, its human rights impact cannot be fairly assessed in isolation from that system of governance.[20]

Types of human rights arguments against the WTO

There are various types of human rights arguments raised against the WTO. The first is the risk that WTO law imposes obligations upon a State which conflict with its human rights obligations. In such a circumstance, compliance with WTO law would result in a breach of human rights law. On the basis of existing case law, it is difficult to identify such direct conflicts between the two areas of law. Indeed, the WTO dispute resolution bodies have addressed few cases of relevance to human rights. The relevant cases are addressed in this book, largely in Chapter 4. One area where human rights breaches might be mandated concerns the implementation of the Agreement on Trade Related Aspects of Intellectual Property (TRIPS), which is discussed in Chapter 7.

WTO case law has elaborated only the tip of the iceberg in terms of WTO obligations. For example, there are very few cases on a number of the WTO agreements, such as TRIPS, the Agreement on Technical Barriers to Trade (TBT), and the General Agreement on Trade in Services (GATS). Given the uncertainties that remain over the scope of WTO obligations, there is a danger of 'regulatory chill', in that a State might fear that the adoption of certain human rights measures will breach WTO law, and it may therefore fail to adopt them even if such a failure breaches its human rights obligations.[21] This second type of concern is addressed in Chapters 4 to 7.

Thirdly, WTO laws might constrain the ability of States to punish other States for violating human rights obligations through the use of trade sanctions. This concern is addressed in Chapter 4.

Fourthly, WTO laws might prompt abuses of human rights, even if they do not mandate them. As WTO law promotes the abolition of trade barriers, States might be tempted to adopt unconscionable methods to boost the competitiveness of their industries. Such a temptation could arise, for example, in the field of labour rights, where States might be tempted to attract foreign investment and boost competition by driving down labour costs.[22] This concern is addressed in Chapter 4.

---

[20] See also Joseph E Stiglitz and Andrew Charlton, *Fair Trade for All* (Oxford University Press, New York, 2005) 81.
[21] Olivier De Schutter, *International Trade and Agriculture and the Right to Food* (Dialogue on Globalization Occasional Paper No 46) (Friedrich Ebert Stiftung, Geneva, November 2009) 21; Harrison, above n 4, 180. [22] De Schutter, above n 21, 21.

Finally, the global implementation of WTO rules may diminish the capacities of certain States to implement human rights.[23] Chapters 5 and 6 examine arguments that WTO rules are eroding the relevant capacities of developing States, for example in relation to the right to food (discussed specifically in Chapter 6). Chapter 3 examines the argument that WTO negotiation and other internal processes further undermine the interests of developing States and other potentially disadvantaged constituencies.

Outline of the book

Chapter 1 explains the WTO regime and the international human rights regime. Greater attention is paid to the latter, while WTO law is fleshed out more in the following chapters. In particular, economic, social, and cultural rights are explained. In this author's experience, those rights are less well understood in the broader community, including trade lawyers and scholars, than civil and political rights.

In Chapter 2, the philosophical and normative relationship between the two regimes is examined. The philosophical issues essentially concern the extent to which the two regimes are driving towards the same, or different, ends. The normative relationship concerns the issue of how conflicts between the two systems are addressed in international law.

Chapters 3 to 7 then move to an analysis of the main alleged human rights problems with the WTO, and their validity. Chapter 3 focuses on the argument that WTO processes are unfair, and serve to marginalize certain constituencies, namely developing States and social justice interests, thus generating a democratic deficit which undermines human rights and generates unfair rules. Chapter 3 also examines the argument that WTO rules indirectly promote democratic rights and civil and political freedoms.

Relevant WTO provisions and case law are examined in Chapter 4, with a focus on the extent to which WTO law constrains the abilities of States to implement human rights measures. Such measures might consist of: (i) trade sanctions aimed at punishing States which breach human rights; (ii) trade sanctions aimed at products produced in a way that breaches human rights; and (iii) measures that regulate or prevent the entry of goods and services that might otherwise harm the human rights of the State's own population. The chapter focuses on the WTO treaties concerning trade in goods, trade in services, sanitary and phytosanitary standards, and technical standards. The pros and cons of a social clause within the WTO, which could provide extra protection for labour rights, are also discussed in Chapter 4. So too is the potential emancipatory effect of WTO rules, that is their potential to force States to permit trade in goods or services that improve the enjoyment of human rights by their populations. The WTO compatibility of China's internet restrictions is examined in that regard.

---

[23] Ibid, 22.

Chapter 5 examines the impact of WTO rules on poverty and development, particularly in developing States. The argument will be put that current WTO rules are biased against the interests of developing States. Furthermore, the orthodox argument that free trade alleviates poverty will be challenged. Unfair treatment of, and the prescription of inappropriate rules for, developing States within the WTO is not itself a human rights issue as States per se do not have human rights. However, such issues clearly bear an instrumental relationship with human rights protection as they impact on the capacity of developing States to discharge their human rights obligations.

In Chapter 6, the impact of WTO rules on the right to food is examined, including an analysis of the rules regarding trade in agriculture, as well as the impact of the Agreement on TRIPS. The difficult 'marriage' between trade and agriculture, and reasons for those difficulties, are outlined, along with proposals for reform.

Chapter 7 examines the impact of TRIPS on the right to health, particularly the debate regarding the impact of global patent rules on the prices of essential medicines. The arguments for and against patent regimes in the drug field will also be addressed in this chapter.

In Chapter 8, the issue of extraterritorial human rights obligations is discussed. Much of the material in Chapters 3 to 7 concerns conflicts between the interests of developed and developing States. Chapter 8 examines the extent to which States have duties to the people in other States. Such duties, if they exist, might signal that States have a duty under international human rights law not to enforce WTO rules which might harm the human rights of people in other States, or a duty to amend WTO rules to assist those in other countries, particularly the poor in developing countries.

In Chapter 9, recommendations for reform are summarized in light of Chapters 3 to 8. Current proposals for a new WTO deal are then examined in comparison to those recommendations, as is the advent of the proliferation of bilateral and free trade agreements outside the WTO.

Chapter 10 concludes the book.

1

Introducing the WTO and International Human Rights Law Regimes

In this opening chapter, the WTO and the international human rights regimes will be introduced and explained. Given that the following chapters will pay more detailed attention to WTO rules and processes, more space will be devoted in this introductory chapter to the basics of international human rights law. Particular attention is paid to economic, social, and cultural rights, as they are less well understood than other rights by those who lack human rights expertise.

A. The World Trade Organization

The origins of the WTO lie in the arrangements for the global economy that came into being after the Second World War. Representatives of the Allied Powers gathered at Bretton Woods in New Hampshire in 1944 to devise the blueprint for the post-War global economy. It was well recognized that economic instability during the global Great Depression of the 1930s had caused great human misery and had been a contributing factor to the advent of the War.[1] The Bretton Woods conference envisaged three pillars to stabilize and strengthen the new global economy comprised of the International Bank for Reconstruction and Development (IBRD), the International Monetary Fund (IMF), and the International Trade Organisation (ITO).

The IBRD was tasked with providing finance for reconstruction to the many war-devastated States. It has since evolved to become one of the five arms of the World Bank Group, with its current mission being to provide finance to fund development and combat poverty in developing States. The World Bank Group now generally promotes microeconomic reforms, largely in developing States, by funding initiatives such as infrastructure projects (for example, dams, pipelines) and anti-corruption and governance reforms.

The IMF's role was and is to promote macroeconomic stability in global exchange rates and balance of payments. It provides short term loans to States in economic crisis in order to stabilize those countries' economies and to prevent disruption to the global economy.

---

[1] James Harrison, *The Human Rights Impact of the World Trade Organisation* (Hart, Oxford, 2007) 9.

The ITO was intended to supervise international trading rules and promote free trade among nations, in order to guard against a return to the protectionist policies that had contributed to the Great Depression. Furthermore, the fostering of international trade linkages along with predictable, enforceable international trading rules would help to promote peaceful international relations. The Havana Charter establishing the ITO was concluded in 1948. The ITO however never came into being, largely due to the refusal by the United States to ratify the Havana Charter.[2]

One trade treaty, the General Agreement on Tariffs and Trade 1947 (GATT), did emerge as a comparatively modest agreement amongst member States. The GATT established a system whereby Contracting Parties committed to 'bound' tariffs with regard to named goods. Tariff bindings operated as ceilings above which a State's tariffs could not go. Each State had a different set of agreed tariff bindings in its Schedule of Concessions, and applied them to all imports from other Contracting Parties in accordance with the Most Favoured Nation (MFN) principle in Article I. MFN required a Contracting Party to treat the goods of all other Contracting Parties equally.[3] The complementary principle of 'National Treatment' in Article III obliged a Contracting Party to treat the goods of another Contracting Party the same as its own 'like' goods once the latter Party's goods had legitimately entered the former Member's market (for example, after they had complied with tariff or other border requirements). A third key principle was that of transparency, requiring Contracting Parties to publish their trade regulations.[4] Article XI prohibited quantitative restrictions, such as quotas, on imports and exports. Exceptions to the GATT applied, notably those in Article XX, which permitted trade restrictions in order to protect a limited set of social values. GATT also had a dispute settlement system whereby disputes were resolved by GATT Panels. Decisions of these panels had to be adopted unanimously, meaning that a losing Party could (and did on occasion) block adoption of Panel recommendations.[5]

With the demise of the ITO, the membership of the GATT became the forum for continued negotiation of free trade rules. These rules were developed over various 'rounds' of negotiations, culminating in the Uruguay round (1986–1994) which led to the creation of the WTO. The Marrakesh Agreement establishing the WTO of 1994 transformed the GATT from a negotiating forum held together by a multilateral treaty into the WTO, an international organization. At the time

---

[2] Amrita Narlikar, *The World Trade Organization: A Very Short Introduction* (Oxford University Press, New York, 2005) 11; David Kinley, *Civilising Globalisation* (Cambridge University Press, Cambridge, 2009) 39–40.

[3] MFN is subject to exceptions such as customs unions (eg the European Union) and free trade areas (see Article XXIV of GATT).

[4] Caroline Dommen, 'Raising Human Rights Concerns in the World Trade Organization: Actors, Processes and Possible Strategies' (2002) 24 *Human Rights Quarterly* 1, 11.

[5] Vázquez notes that there was a strong record of compliance with the GATT system despite its apparent weakness prior to the advent of the WTO, in Carlos Manuel Vázquez, 'Trade Sanctions and Human Rights—Past, Present and Future' (2003) 6 *Journal of International Economic Law* 797, 807–8.

of writing, there are 153 Member States of the WTO. The institution is based in Geneva, Switzerland.[6]

The Uruguay Round generated a series of Agreements to be monitored and supervised by the WTO. The Contracting Parties to the GATT became Members of the WTO, who were required to adhere to all WTO Agreements as a single undertaking without reservations.[7] Acceding Members are also required to sign up to the whole package deal, often with extra obligations.[8]

The WTO Agreements significantly expanded the mandate and strength of the WTO beyond that of its GATT predecessor. The GATT had focused solely on goods and largely on the dismantling of a single type of trade barrier, tariffs.[9] Tariff schedules under the WTO Agreements are more comprehensive than those under the GATT in terms of the number and types of goods covered. For example, trade in agricultural goods is now covered under the Agreement on Agriculture (AoA), while trade in textiles and clothing was regulated under the Agreement on Textiles and Clothing (ATC).[10] Furthermore, the WTO addressed non-tariff barriers. For example, the Agreement on the Application of Sanitary and Phytosanitary Measures (SPS) concerns domestic measures designed to protect human, animal or plant life or health. The Agreement on Technical Barriers to Trade (TBT) concerns mandatory domestic provisions regarding a range of matters, including labelling, packaging, production processes, and other product characteristics. The SPS and TBT regulate the extent to which such standards can restrict international trade.[11] Regulation of foreign investment is itself regulated to an extent under the Agreement on Trade Related Aspects of Investment Measures (TRIMs). The GATT itself was retained, including its key principles of MFN and National Treatment, and its principles and rules expanded and clarified in GATT 1994, and Agreements on Pre-Shipment Inspection, Rules of Origin, and Import Licensing Procedures. Agreements on Implementation of Article VI (concerning anti-dumping)[12] and Subsidies and Countervailing Measures specify the means by which States may counter certain unfair trade practices, while the Agreement on Safeguards recognizes some capacities for States to respond to unexpected import surges to protect home industries.

---

[6] The following commentary on the WTO is adapted from Sarah Joseph, 'Trade to Live or Live to Trade: The World Trade Organization, Development, and Poverty' in Mashood Baderin and Robert McCorquodale (eds), *Economic, Social and Cultural Rights in Action* (Oxford University Press, Oxford, 2007) 389–416.

[7] There are two plurilateral deals, which only bind States that voluntarily ratify them, concerning civil aircraft and government procurement; two further plurilateral deals on bovine meat and dairy produce have now expired. There are also some flexibilities in the main WTO deals, such as the ability of States to choose which services they will liberalize under the General Agreement on Trade in Services.

Some WTO treaties explicitly allow for reservations so long as all other parties consent to those reservations. This author is unaware of any reservations to WTO treaties.

[8] See Chapter 5, text at notes 89–100.

[9] Some regulation of non-tariff barriers applied on a plurilateral basis.

[10] This agreement expired on 1 January 2005. Textiles and clothing are now dealt with under the GATT 1994.

[11] See Chapter 4, Part D.

[12] 'Dumping' arises where goods are exported at a lower price than its normal value: States may take remedial measures if dumping harms competing local industries.

Furthermore, the WTO's jurisdiction has moved beyond issues regarding the trade in goods. The General Agreement on Trade in Services (GATS) adopts similar principles and exceptions to those in the GATT in respect of the international trade in services. However, its obligations are less strict than those in the GATT as Members are permitted to nominate the services to which GATS applies for the purposes of its National Treatment and market access obligations. Finally, WTO Members are also required to protect intellectual property rights under the Agreement on Trade-Related Intellectual Property Rights (TRIPS).

The WTO has a strong dispute settlement mechanism, established under the Understanding on Rules and Procedures Governing the Settlement of Disputes. The Dispute Settlement Body (DSB) is comprised of the totality of WTO Members. The first step in the dispute settlement process is the convening of consultations between disputing parties. If consultations do not lead to a settlement, the DSB will normally refer the matter to a WTO panel, which makes a decision on the merits of the dispute under WTO law. Appeals against panel decisions may be brought before the WTO Appellate Body on issues of law and legal interpretation.[13] As noted above, the decisions of GATT panels could only be enforced if endorsed by all GATT parties. In contrast, the DSB will adopt the decisions of a panel or the Appellate Body unless the decision is rejected by consensus; such rejection is not likely to happen as a victorious Member is unlikely to vote against its own victory. If a Member fails to satisfactorily implement the final decision within a reasonable period of time, the DSB will normally authorize retaliatory trade measures by the vindicated Member against the defaulting Member. A significant commercial price is therefore paid by a Member that fails to abide by DSB rulings. The dispute resolution system renders the commitments of WTO Members credible, as consequences attach to non-compliance.[14]

Like the GATT, the WTO is also a forum for its Members to negotiate further agreements on free trade. New agreements are to be reached by consensus, though facility is also made for majority vote.[15] All institutions within the WTO are open to representatives from all Members. The Ministerial Conference, the highest body within the WTO, formally meets to conduct negotiations every two years. The General Council oversees the everyday management of the organization, and also acts as the DSB. The General Council also meets as the Trade Policy Review Body which operates the Trade Policy Review Mechanism (TPRM), under which the trade policies of each Member are periodically reviewed in regard to their transparency and their effect on the international trading system. The TPRM process is not legalistic so it does not result in enforceable findings of 'violation',[16] though it can generate criticism of policies and recommendations for reform. There are also a number of specialist bodies within the WTO, which address different trade topics, such as the Councils on Trade Related Aspects of Intellectual Property Rights,

---

[13] No appeal provision existed under the old GATT arrangements.
[14] Martin Wolf, *Why Globalisation Works* (Yale Nota Bene, London, 2005) 91.
[15] Marrakesh Agreement Establishing the WTO (1994), 1867 UNTS, Article IX.
[16] Dommen, above n 4, 9.

Trade in Services, and Trade in Goods, and Committees which operate under those Councils, as well as Committees addressing broader issues such as the Committee on Trade and Environment and the Committee on Trade and Development. There is no Committee on Trade and Human Rights. Working Parties address various other issues such as the accession of new members.[17]

The WTO is serviced by a secretariat, headed by a Director-General, which provides administrative and technical support to the WTO institutions and the Members. The current Director-General is Pascal Lamy, the former European Commissioner for Trade.[18] It does not have an autonomous power of initiative, as all policies and decisions are made by the WTO Members.[19]

The current round of WTO negotiations has thus far failed to bear much fruit. A new round was intended to be launched at the Ministerial meeting in Seattle in 1999, but that meeting collapsed amidst recriminations inside the negotiating halls and outside on streets teeming with anti-globalization protestors. Members agreed two years later to establish a new negotiating round after the Doha Ministerial in 2001, known as the Doha Development Round. However, that round has foundered, with agreement proving elusive in Cancun in 2003, Hong Kong in late 2005 and in subsequent lower level meetings through to the present day. While Ministerial meetings are meant to be held every two years, there was a gap of four years between the Hong Kong Ministerial and the Geneva Ministerial in 2009. The Geneva Ministerial ultimately yielded only predictable calls for Members to endeavour to conclude the Doha round, and was essentially a 'housekeeping' exercise.[20]

Raison d'être of the WTO

The result of the globalization of trade, at least in the developed world and urban areas in many developing States, has been described by Martin Wolf:

We can buy food produced all over the world, which is then bought, processed, distributed and sold through a long chain of wholesalers and retailers to satisfy our varying tastes. The food will be extraordinarily safe [by historical standards]. One can buy clothing made by workers in China, India, Italy or Mexico, in a staggering number of different fabrics and styles. For personal transport, one can choose from many varieties of motor car; for entertainment, one can select a DVD player and flat-screen television; for work, leisure or personal bureaucracy, one can buy a personal computer. An army of competing investors, designers, producers, and distributors try to meet all these and many other demands. A

---

[17] See generally WTO, 'Understanding the WTO' (2007) Chapter 7: The Organization <http://www.wto.org/english/thewto_e/whatis_e/tif_e/utw_chap7_e.pdf> accessed 18 September 2010.

[18] Lamy became Director-General in 2005, and was re-elected by consensus in the General Council to a second four-year term, which commenced in 2009.

[19] Dommen, above n 4, 9. That is not to say that it has no influence: see Chapter 3, text at notes 80–86.

[20] See International Centre for Trade and Sustainable Development, 'WTO Ministerial Lifts Hopes for Doha, but Scepticism Lingers' (2009) 13 *Bridges Weekly Trade News Digest*, <http://ictsd.org/i/news/bridgesweekly/65367/> accessed 18 September 2010.

host of intermediaries takes money from households and supplies it to those who persuade them they can use it productively.[21]

Wolf could have added that these goods can be ordered via telephone or internet network services provided by foreign investors or offshore suppliers, and that the creators of the most innovative goods, or their assignees, benefit from global intellectual property protection.

The underlying rationale of the WTO is to preside over the reduction of trade barriers between nations, thereby promoting global free trade. As noted above, one reason behind the promotion of free trade is that the creation of trading relations between States alongside a peaceful and authoritative procedure for settling disputes will promote more harmonious international relations. After all, history is littered with trade disputes which escalated into wars.

Furthermore, the theory of comparative advantage, 'arguably the single most powerful insight into economics' according to the WTO website,[22] provides an important intellectual basis for arguments in favour of the benefits of free trade. Briefly, that theory holds that States should concentrate on producing what they are best at producing. To do otherwise generates inefficiency and opportunity costs. States should produce and export those goods, and import other goods. This practice, coupled with the removal of barriers to imports and exports, generates greater economic efficiency at both the domestic and global levels with all States producing what they are best at producing. Consumers are able to access goods at the best prices while industries are forced to innovate and become more efficient in order to survive in the globally competitive marketplace.

The theory of comparative advantage will be discussed further in Chapter 5. For now, it may be noted that the creation of greater global wealth is a laudable goal from a human rights point of view. In particular, greater wealth should facilitate the alleviation of poverty. Some characterize living in a state of poverty as a human rights abuse in itself.[23] At the least, human rights abuses often accompany a state of poverty.[24] The preamble to the Marrakesh Agreement establishing the WTO echoes the idea that free trade should constitute a means to desirable ends rather than an end in itself: 'trade should be conducted with a view to raising standards of living' and 'ensuring full employment', while 'allowing for the optimal use of the world's resources in accordance with the objective of sustainable development'. At first glance, the WTO's mission seems utterly compatible with the promotion, protection and enjoyment of human rights.[25] This issue, of course, is the subject matter of this book.

[21] Wolf, above n 14, 45.
[22] WTO, 'Understanding the WTO: The Case for Open Trade' (undated) <http://www.wto.org/english/thewto_e/whatis_e/tif_e/fact3_e.htm> accessed 18 September 2010.
[23] See, eg, Thomas Pogge, 'Recognized and Violated: the Human Rights of the Global Poor' (2005) 18 *Leiden Journal of International Law* 717.
[24] See Chapter 5, Part A.
[25] Frank Garcia, 'The Global Market and Human Rights: Trading away the Human Rights Principle' (1999) 7 *Brooklyn Journal of International Law* 51, 59. See also Adam McBeth, *International Economic Actors and Human Rights* (Routledge, Oxford, 2010) 87–8.

B. The International Human Rights Regime

UN standards

Prior to the Second World War, human rights were largely unrecognized in international law. Discrete exceptions existed, such as the early principles of international humanitarian law (the law of armed conflict) and certain protections for aliens.[26] However, a State's treatment of its own citizens was generally recognized as a sovereign matter of no international concern. The legal landscape changed in the aftermath of the Second World War, a conflict characterized by severe human rights atrocities which truly shocked the conscience of the international community. Just as the Bretton Woods conference was convened to address the economic catastrophes that pre-dated the war and the reconstruction which would be needed after the war, it was also decided that the post-war international legal system could no longer ignore the acts of inhumanity perpetrated by States against their own populations.

The promotion and encouragement of respect for human rights and fundamental freedoms was explicitly recognized as a purpose of the international organization set up to maintain international peace and security after the war, the United Nations (UN), in Article 1(3) of the UN Charter of 1945. Under Articles 55 and 56, UN Member States are committed to 'joint and separate action' to create 'conditions of stability and well-being' across the world, including the promotion of 'universal respect for, and observance of, human rights and fundamental freedoms for all without distinction as to race, sex, language, or religion'. Thus, from 1945, it was clear that human rights could no longer be characterized as a domestic issue hidden by the veil of State sovereignty.

'Human rights' and 'fundamental freedoms' were not defined in the Charter. The UN endorsed a list of recognized human rights in the Universal Declaration of Human Rights (UDHR). No State, either in 1948 or upon joining the UN, has ever denounced the UDHR.[27] The UDHR itself was reaffirmed in the Vienna Declaration and Programme of Action,[28] adopted after the World Conference on Human Rights in 1993, and remains the key expression of global human rights values. The UDHR was not adopted as a legally binding instrument. It is arguable however that its norms have now crystallized as customary international law.[29] Furthermore, it is arguable that the UHDR defines 'human rights' for the purposes of the human rights provisions of the UN Charter, such as Articles 1(3), 55 and 56, which are recognized as peremptory international norms.[30]

---

[26] See also Louis B Sohn, 'The new international law: protection of the rights of individuals rather than States' (1982) 32 *American University Law Review* 1, 2–9.

[27] Eight States abstained when the UN General Assembly adopted the UDHR: Byelorussia, Czechoslovakia, Poland, the Ukraine, the USSR, Yugoslavia, Saudi Arabia, and South Africa.

[28] Vienna Declaration and Programme of Action (1993), UN doc. A/CONF.157/23, para 2.

[29] See, eg, Sohn, above n 26, 15–17.   [30] Ibid, 16.

In 1966, most of the norms in the UDHR[31] were enshrined in two treaties, the International Covenant on Economic, Social and Cultural Rights (ICESCR) and the International Covenant on Civil and Political Rights (ICCPR). The three documents are often collectively called 'The International Bill of Rights'. An Optional Protocol to the ICCPR was also adopted in 1966, providing for a right of individual petition in respect of violations of the ICCPR against States that ratify that Protocol.

The first UN human rights treaty was in fact adopted a few months before the Covenants: the International Convention on the Elimination of all Forms of Racial Discrimination 1965 (CERD). The following UN treaties have been adopted since: the Convention on the Elimination of All Forms of Discrimination against Women 1979 (CEDAW), the Convention against Torture and other Cruel, Inhuman and Degrading Treatment or Punishment 1984 (CAT), the Convention on the Rights of the Child 1989 (CRC), the International Convention on the Protection of the Rights of All Migrant Workers and Members of their Families 1990 (MWC), the Convention on the Rights of Persons with Disabilities 2006 (CPRD) and the International Convention for the Protection of All Persons from Enforced Disappearance 2006 (Disappearances Convention).

There are also some important human rights declarations, concerning rights that have not yet attained treaty status, such as the Declaration on the Right to Development 1986 and the Declarations of the Rights of Indigenous Peoples 2007 (DRIP). Furthermore, many of the above treaties are supplemented by Optional Protocols which either add further substantive rights to their respective parent treaties,[32] or provide for new procedural mechanisms to hold States accountable for their treaty obligations.[33]

UN human rights institutions and enforcement machinery

A number of UN bodies have responsibilities for the enforcement of human rights. The main intergovernmental body is the Human Rights Council. The Council has a broad human rights mandate, including standard-setting and promotion. It may also authorize the investigation of particular human rights situations (for example, a particular human rights theme or the human rights situation in a particular State) by appointed expert bodies.[34] It also reviews the human rights performance of all States on a rolling basis under the process of Universal Periodic Review. Finally,

---

[31] Certain discrete rights are excluded, such as the right to seek and enjoy asylum (Article 14) and the right to property (Article 17).

[32] See, eg, Optional Protocol to the Convention on the Rights of the Child on the Sale of Children, Child Prostitution and Child Pornography (adopted 25 May 2000, entered into force 18 January 2002), 2171 UNTS 227.

[33] See, eg, Optional Protocol to the CEDAW (adopted 6 October 1999, entered into force 22 December 2000), 2131 UNTS 83, providing for a right of individual petition for alleged breaches of rights under CEDAW.

[34] These bodies are known by a variety of names, such as Special Rapporteurs, Special Representatives, Independent Experts, or (in the case of a group as opposed to an individual) a Working Group.

it may pass resolutions on any human rights matter. For example, its resolutions may endorse existing or proposed new human rights principles, or condemn the human rights record of a particular State. The Council is a political body made up of 47 State members, elected by the UN membership to serve three-year terms.

UN 'treaty bodies' are created to monitor and supervise implementation of each of the treaties. For example, the Human Rights Committee (HRC) is established under Article 28 of the ICCPR to perform various roles under that treaty. The treaty bodies are made up of independent human rights experts. They are not 'courts', so their decisions are not legally binding. However, their interpretations of their respective treaties have strong persuasive force, as they represent authoritative interpretations of legally binding documents.[35] The treaty bodies act as the quasi-judicial arm of the UN human rights machinery (in contrast to the political arm, represented by the Human Rights Council).

The treaty bodies have a range of functions. For the purposes of this book, the important functions are those that generate jurisprudence and authoritative human rights interpretations. Such interpretations can arise in making decisions with respect to individual complaints (for example, by the HRC under the Optional Protocol to the ICCPR). They can also arise under the 'reporting procedures', whereby each treaty body assesses the overall record of each State party to the relevant treaty and issues 'concluding observations' on the State. The concluding observations act as a human rights 'report card' for the relevant State and can also provide significant indicators as to the meaning of relevant human rights provisions. Finally, all treaty bodies may issue 'general comments', which address matters of relevance to all States parties to a particular treaty. Most general comments contain expanded interpretations of particular rights in a relevant treaty, though a general comment can address any issue of relevance to the implementation of a particular treaty.[36]

Both the charter bodies and treaty bodies are serviced by the Office of the High Commissioner for Human Rights, the bureaucratic arm of UN human rights machinery.[37]

The Achilles heel of the international human rights system lies in its enforcement, or lack thereof. No global body, apart from the UN Security Council[38] and

---

[35] See, eg, Human Rights Committee, 'General Comment No 33: The Obligations of States Parties under the Optional Protocol to the International Covenant on Civil and Political Rights', UN doc. CCPR/C/GC/33 (5 November 2008) paras 11–15.

[36] Eg, treaty bodies have issued General Comments on reporting guidelines, reservations to treaties, and denunciations of treaties.

[37] Sarah Joseph and Joanna Kyriakakis, 'United Nations and Human Rights' in Sarah Joseph and Adam McBeth (eds), *Research Handbook on International Human Rights Law* (Edward Elgar, Cheltenham, 2010) 18–20.

[38] The UN Security Council is one of the principal bodies of the UN. It has primary responsibility under the Charter for the maintenance of international peace and security. Its powers include the establishment of peacekeeping operations, and the authorization of international sanctions and even military action. Its resolutions under Chapter VII of the Charter are binding on UN Members under Article 25 of the Charter. There are 15 member States of the Security Council; 10 are elected to serve two-year terms and five (China, France, Russia, United Kingdom, and the United States) are

the International Court of Justice (ICJ),[39] is empowered to make legally binding decisions on human rights. The Security Council and ICJ rarely deal with human rights matters, though the number of human rights cases before the ICJ has increased in recent years.[40] Enforcement against recalcitrant States is largely promoted by the process of naming and shaming. While shame can prompt behavioural change by a State,[41] it is clearly a weak enforcement measure compared to the economic consequences that ensue from non-compliance with the rulings of dispute resolution bodies in the WTO.[42] The record of compliance with the rulings of UN human rights bodies such as the treaty bodies pales in comparison to the record of compliance by WTO members with the WTO dispute settlement bodies.

Regional systems

There are also regional human rights systems. The most successful human rights system, in terms of compliance and reputation, operates under the auspices of the Council of Europe. The European Convention on Human Rights 1951 (ECHR) and its Protocols largely protect civil and political rights, and is enforced by the European Court of Human Rights. The European Social Charter 1961 addresses economic, social and cultural rights and is enforced by a quasi-judicial European Committee on Social Rights. There are also single issue human rights treaties such as the European Convention against Torture 1987, again supervised by a quasi-judicial body.

Similar systems operate in the Americas and Africa, with the former system based on the American Convention on Human Rights 1969 and the latter based on the African Charter of Human and Peoples' Rights 1981. There are also separate treaties addressing economic, social, and cultural rights and other human rights issues. A new regional system is also emerging under the auspices of the Arab League, with the coming into force in 2008 of the Arab Charter on Human Rights 2004.

The regional systems are better equipped in terms of enforcement, as the decisions of regional courts are legally binding. Difficulties in enforcement nevertheless

---

permanent members who retain a right to veto any Security Council resolution apart from a procedural resolution.

[39] The ICJ is the principal judicial organ of the UN. It was established in June 1945; its constitution and powers are set out in the Statute of the ICJ, which is annexed to the UN Charter. The Court's role is to settle legal disputes submitted to it by States in accordance with international law and to issue advisory opinions on legal questions referred to it by authorized UN organs and specialized agencies. The Court is composed of 15 judges, who are elected for terms of office of nine years by the UN General Assembly and the Security Council.

[40] See, generally, Sandesh Sivakumaran, 'The International Court of Justice and Human Rights' in Joseph and McBeth (eds), above n 37, 299–325.

[41] See Joseph and Kyriakakis, above n 37, 26–8.

[42] See Philip Alston, 'Resisting the Merger and Acquisition of Human Rights by Trade Law: A Reply to Petersmann' (2002) 13 *European Journal of International Law* 815, 833; Vázquez, above n 5, 803–4.

remain, with States often opting to pay damages to an aggrieved individual, rather than undertaking the systemic change necessary to avoid future human rights abuses. Furthermore, not all regions are covered by regional human rights treaties, with no regional human rights system in Asia or Oceania.[43]

Another development regarding the regional protection of human rights is the extent to which other regional courts, such as the European Court of Justice under the auspices of the European Union,[44] or the ECOWAS Community Court of Justice established by the European Community of West African States,[45] have begun to enforce human rights norms. This circumstance is particular interesting for the purposes of this book given the genesis of the EU and ECOWAS as free trade regimes.

The ICCPR and the ICESCR

The key instruments for the purposes of this book are the two Covenants: the ICCPR and the ICESCR, though some reference will be made to other instruments, especially the UDHR and the Declaration on the Right to Development. The Covenants are of most relevance to this book due to their global (as opposed to regional) coverage, and the breadth of rights covered (as opposed to narrower instruments which are limited in terms of right-holders, such as the CEDAW, the CRC and the CPRD, or in terms of rights covered, such as the CAT and the Disappearances Convention).

The UDHR did not set up a hierarchy of rights, and it was initially intended that the follow-up treaty would not split the various UDHR rights. However, Cold War politics, as well as perceptions over fundamental differences between civil and political rights on the one hand, and economic, social, and cultural rights on the other, led to a decision to split the rights into two Covenants.[46] Nevertheless, the preamble to each Covenant proclaims both sets of rights as interdependent and indivisible. Formal equality is evidenced in that both Covenants came into force in 1977, and both have roughly the same number of States parties at September 2010. The equal importance and interdependence of both sets of rights was affirmed in the Vienna Declaration and Programme of Action of 1993.

---

[43] The Association of South East Asian Nations (ASEAN) established an ASEAN Human Rights Commission to promote human rights within ASEAN in late 2009. This Commission does not compare to the more mature regional systems discussed in this section. It is premature to assess its likely impact on human rights protection within the ASEAN region. See Yuval Ginbar, 'Human Rights in ASEAN—Setting Sail or Treading Water?' (2010) 10 *Human Rights Law Review* 504.

[44] See, eg, *Kadi and Al Barakaat International Foundation v Council of the European Union* (ECJ Grand Chamber, 3 September 2008) Cases C-402/05 and C-415/05 P.

[45] See, eg, *Mme Hadijatou Mani Koraou v The Republic of Niger* (2008) ECW/CCJ/JUD/06/08 (ECOWAS Community Court of Justice). See also Helen Duffy, 'Hadijatou Mani Koroua v Niger: Slavery Unveiled by the ECOWAS Court' (2009) 9 *Human Rights Law Review* 151.

[46] See, eg, Dominic McGoldrick, *The Human Rights Committee: Its Role in the Development of the International Covenant on Civil and Political Rights*, 2nd edn (Oxford University Press, New York, 1994) para 1.16.

The ICCPR protects civil and political rights.[47] It has 166 States parties at September 2010. A notable absentee is China, which has signed but not ratified the ICCPR.[48] Civil and political rights can be categorized as encompassing (1) rights of physical and spiritual integrity and autonomy; (2) rights of fair treatment; and (3) rights to participate meaningfully in the political process.[49] Category 1 includes the rights to life and freedom from torture and other ill treatment, freedom of movement and the right to privacy. Spiritual autonomy is ensured by rights such as freedom of religion, belief and thought. Category 2 encompasses fairness in a narrow procedural sense, such as the right to a fair trial, and in a broader sense, such as a general right of equal protection of the law and freedom from non-discrimination. Category 3 obviously encompasses the right to vote and to stand for election, and also includes rights which are essential for a healthy political process, such as the freedoms of assembly and association. These categories overlap considerably. For example, freedom of expression falls into all three categories. It is necessary for the preservation of one's spiritual autonomy to ensure that one is able to express one's own ideas, and to receive the ideas of others. It is also relevant to fair treatment: one cannot be treated fairly and equitably if one's needs and desires cannot be heard, or if one cannot access relevant information and ideas. Finally, freedom of expression is essential to a functional political system, so that there can be a free flow of communication between the elected and those whom they represent, and within society to ensure governmental accountability.

Most civil and political rights are qualified by permissible limitations. Very few ICCPR rights are absolute.[50] For example, the right to free expression in Article 19(2) does not entail the right to express any view at any time in any forum, though a State bears the burden of proof in establishing that limitations on that right are justified.[51] Most ICCPR rights can be limited by proportionate measures reasonably designed to achieve a legitimate end.

The ICESCR protects economic, social, and cultural rights, and has 160 parties. A notable absentee is the US, which has signed but not ratified the ICESCR. Economic rights are rights related to labour and employment, contained in

---

[47] The following commentary is adapted from Sarah Joseph, 'Civil and political rights' in Mashood Baderin and Manisuli Ssenyonjo, *International Human Rights Law: Six Decades after the UDHR* (Ashgate, Surrey, 2010) 89–106.

[48] Upon its succession to sovereignty over Hong Kong and Macau, China has agreed that the ICCPR continues to apply to those territories, as it had under their previous colonial rulers, the UK and Portugal. See, eg, *Kuok Koi v Portugal*, UN doc. CCPR/C/73/D/925/2000 (8 February 2002) (Human Rights Committee).

[49] See also Scott Davidson, 'Introduction' in Alex Conte, Scott Davidson, and Richard Burchill, *Defining Civil and Political Rights: The Jurisprudence of the United Nations Human Rights Committee* (Aldershot, Ashgate, 2004) 2.

[50] Examples of absolute rights are the right to be free from torture and other ill treatment (Article 7) and the right to be free from slavery and servitude (Article 8).

[51] Article 19(2) rights are limited by Article 19(3) which reads: 'The exercise of the rights provided for in paragraph 2 of this article carries with it special duties and responsibilities. It may therefore be subject to certain restrictions, but these shall only be such as are provided by law and are necessary: (a) For respect of the rights or reputations of others; (b) For the protection of national security or of public order (ordre public), or of public health or morals.'

Articles 6 to 8 of the ICESCR,[52] as well as the accrued benefits of labourers and social safety nets for those who cannot work, in Article 9 (the right to social security). Social rights are those needed to function adequately in society such as the right to family life (Article 10), the right to an adequate standard of living (Article 11), the right to health (Article 12) and the right to education (Articles 13 and 14). Article 15 covers cultural rights, including the right to participate in the cultural life of society and to benefit from scientific progress. Again, the distinction between the three categories is not watertight, and indeed is often ignored.[53]

The UN is committed to the formal equality of the two sets of rights. Furthermore, the two Covenants have similar numbers of States parties. And indeed, the rights are interdependent and mutually reinforcing. The right to life (Article 6 ICCPR) is closely linked to the right to health (Article 12 ICESCR). The right to education (Articles 13 and 14 ICESCR) helps to promote literacy, a key facilitator of freedom of expression (Article 19 ICCPR). The right to form trade unions (Article 8 ICESCR) is a sub-component of freedom of association (Article 22 ICCPR). The right to family life is reflected in Articles 17 and 23 of the ICCPR, and Article 10 of the ICESCR.

Differences between the ICCPR and the ICESCR

Nevertheless, the norms in the ICCPR are far more developed than those in the ICESCR. Civil and political rights have a longer legal pedigree, having generated much jurisprudence under domestic constitutional documents, such as the US Bill of Rights, for over 200 years. Therefore, there was significant source material from domestic law to aid the development of civil and political rights at the international level. In contrast, many economic, social, and cultural rights were first established in international law rather than domestic law.[54] As those rights lack a comparable history of domestic legal protection and justiciability, those norms are less legally developed.

Another 'advantage' for civil and political rights arises at the advocacy level. Those human rights non-governmental organizations (NGOs) that have most engaged in domestic and international political processes, such as Amnesty International and Human Rights Watch, have historically focused on civil and political rights. NGOs in the economic, social, and cultural rights arena have tended to be organizations that facilitated service delivery to disadvantaged groups, such as charitable organizations.[55] Thus, there has historically been greater agitation for States by human rights advocates to 'do something' about

---

[52] Articles 6–8 cover, respectively, the rights to work, to just and favourable conditions of work, and to join trade unions.

[53] Henry Steiner, Philip Alston, and Ryan Goodman, *International Human Rights Law in Context*, 3rd edn (Oxford University Press, New York, 2007) 276.

[54] Robert E Robertson, 'Measuring State Compliance with the Obligation to Devote the "Maximum Available Resources" to Realizing Economic, Social, and Cultural Rights' (1994) 16 *Human Rights Quarterly* 693, 694.

[55] J Oloka-Onyango, 'Beyond the Rhetoric: Reinvigorating the Struggle for Economic and Social Rights in Africa' (1995) 26 *California Western International Law Journal* 1, 38–9.

civil and political rights abuses, both at home and abroad, and less pressure to address deficiencies regarding economic, social, and cultural rights.[56] This distinction has been eroded in the last 20 years. For example, Amnesty International no longer ignores economic, social, and cultural rights.[57] And classical service NGOs like Oxfam and Médecins sans Frontières are far more politically active, and are responsible for some of the most sophisticated activism around human rights and trade.[58] Nevertheless, civil and political rights had a significant 'head start' over economic, social, and cultural rights in capturing the attention and shaping the agendas of human rights activists.

The infrastructure for civil and political rights established by the ICCPR was, and remains, superior to that in the ICESCR. The ICCPR established an independent expert body, the HRC, to oversee its implementation. No such body was established by the ICESCR, with oversight left initially to the United Nations Economic and Social Council (ECOSOC), a political body with political agendas. Only after eight years of inadequate performance did ECOSOC finally establish an independent expert body in 1985, the Committee on Economic Social and Cultural Rights, to supervise the implementation of the ICESCR.[59] Again, the theme of civil and political rights being 'ahead' of economic, social, and cultural rights is evident. The HRC had an eight-year head start over its ICESCR counterpart in developing its practices, procedures, institutional culture, and substantive jurisprudence.

Of even greater consequence are key differences between the respective obligations of States under the two Covenants. The key obligation provision in the ICCPR, Article 2(1), reads:

Each State Party to the present Covenant undertakes to respect and to ensure to all individuals within its territory and subject to its jurisdiction the rights recognised in the present Covenant, without distinction of any kind such as race, colour, sex, language, religion, political or other opinion, national or social origin, property, birth, or other status.

Therefore, the ICCPR requires States to immediately respect and ensure to all the enjoyment of the rights therein.

The parallel provision in the ICESCR, Article 2(1), reads:

Each State Party to the present Covenant undertakes to take steps, individually and through international assistance and co-operation, especially economic and technical, to the maximum of its available resources, with a view to achieving progressively the full realization of the rights recognized in the present Covenant by all appropriate means, including particularly the adoption of legislative measures.

---

[56] There has historically been much political agitation around economic and social issues, but not in terms of economic and social 'rights' beyond labour rights.

[57] See, generally, Amnesty International, 'Amnesty International action for economic, social and cultural rights: What is Amnesty International doing? (undated) <http://www.amnesty.org/en/economic-and-social-cultural-rights/ai-action-escr> accessed 18 September 2010.

[58] See, eg, Oxfam, *Rigged Rules and Double Standards* (Oxfam, London, 2002).

[59] ECOSOC Resolution 1985/17 (28 May 1985).

The obligation provision in the ICESCR is muddier than that in the ICCPR. The obligation is progressive rather than immediate, and is qualified by a State's 'available resources'. States are arguably required to 'try hard' in protecting ICESCR rights. The soft obligation makes it easier for States to evade findings of violation of the ICESCR. It is much easier to determine whether a State has or has not implemented a right, as is required for determinations under the ICCPR, than it is to determine whether a State has exercised sufficient endeavour in attempting to implement a right, as is the standard of obligation apparently dictated by the ICESCR.

Positive and negative rights

A key to the rationale behind the different obligations is the perception that civil and political rights are 'negative rights', requiring only that States refrain from rights violating behaviour, while economic, social, and cultural rights are 'positive', requiring States to take actions to fulfil the rights therein. Negative rights seem to require a State to do nothing. This inexpensive and simple obligation justifies the comparatively onerous ICCPR obligation. Positive rights are expensive and difficult to perform, justifying the leeway given to States under the ICESCR.

However, the reality is somewhat different. Civil and political rights are not wholly negative in nature. For example, the right to a fair trial in Article 14 of the ICCPR clearly requires the establishment of adequate judicial infrastructure. Article 25, covering the right to vote, entails the establishment of the necessary apparatus to run a fair election. Articles 23(1) and 24(1) explicitly require the adoption of measures by the State to protect families and children. Indeed, all human rights entail both positive and negative characteristics. Freedom from torture (Article 7 ICCPR) essentially requires States to refrain from torture, so it seems to be a quintessential negative right. However, a State cannot prevent torture by simply doing nothing. States must take positive steps to ensure that the opportunities for torture are minimized, that systems are in place to prevent torture, and that it is punished in the instances where it occurs. In General Comment 31, the HRC confirmed that Article 2(1), which specifies the duties upon States parties with regard to all ICCPR rights, 'is both negative and positive in nature'.[60]

The same is true of the ICESCR: its norms also entail both negative and positive aspects. For example, the right to housing, an aspect of the right to an adequate standard of living in Article 11, has a positive aspect in that States should make adequate provision for shelter for homeless people. It has a negative aspect in that a State should not arbitrarily evict people from their homes. One may note, for example, that arbitrary evictions and the destruction of homes are a human rights

---

[60] Human Rights Committee, 'General Comment No 31: Nature of the General Legal Obligation Imposed on States Parties to the Covenant' UN doc. CCPR/C/21/Rev.1/Add.13 (26 May 2008) para 6.

abuse that has reportedly been used in Zimbabwe against Robert Mugabe's political opponents.[61]

The tripartite nature of all human rights

States have duties to respect, protect, and fulfil all human rights, whether they be civil and political rights or economic, social, and cultural rights. The duty to *respect* is a duty to refrain from activities that harm human rights: it is the basic negative duty. The duties to protect and fulfil are positive duties. The duty to *protect* is the duty to take reasonable measures to protect people from harm to their human rights by other entities, such as individuals or corporations. Therefore, human rights certainly impact within the private sphere: States are required to regulate private entities in order to ensure, as far as is reasonably possible, that they do not harm the human rights of others. For example, the regulation of health and safety standards helps to ensure that workers' rights are not infringed by their employers. The duty to *fulfil* includes the duty to take the measures necessary to ensure that individuals enjoy their human rights. Examples of implementation of this obligation would be the provision of subsidies to ensure access by the poor to essential goods and services such as water, health care and education, and the implementation of an accessible vaccination programme to guard against threats to the rights to life and health.

The duties to respect and protect generally require fewer resources than the obligation to fulfil.[62] The duties to fulfil may be further categorized into duties to *facilitate*, *promote*, and *provide* for the implementation of a right. Facilitation obliges States to put appropriate structures in place to enable people to enjoy their rights. For example, facilitation of the right to education would include the adoption of a strategy to ensure a minimum level of quality in educational institutions. Promotion involves the raising of awareness about a particular right: an example would be dissemination of people's rights regarding their access to legal aid. Finally, the duty to provide involves the direct provision of rights to groups that are unable, for reasons outside their control, to enjoy a right under their own means. For example, legal aid has to be provided for those accused of serious crimes under Article 14(3)(d) of the ICCPR, if the accused cannot afford to pay for legal counsel. As a second example, a State should provide for the housing needs of those who are too poor to provide for their own shelter under Article 11 of the ICESCR.[63]

A final point to make about the tripartite nature of human rights duties is that the fulfilment of a human rights obligation does not automatically require that

---

[61] See Commission on Human Rights, 'Report of the Special Rapporteur on adequate housing as a component of the right to an adequate standard of living, Miloon Kothari: Summary of communications sent and replies received from Governments and other actors', UN doc. E/CN.4/2006/41/Add.1 (23 December 2005) paras 33–8.

[62] UN Economic and Social Council, 'Report of the United Nations High Commissioner for Human Rights', UN doc. E/2007/82 (25 June 2007) para 11.

[63] Ibid, para 12.

the government itself secure a right.[64] The duty to respect implies that the private sector be given the necessary space to play a role in, for example, growing food or providing housing. The duty to facilitate (part of the duty to fulfil) requires a State to provide an enabling environment for the fulfilment of a right, and thus can require the strengthening of the private sector in appropriate ways. For example, a State can facilitate and encourage the activities of private sector charitable organizations, which in turn help to provide for the enjoyment of ICESCR rights in the form for instance of low cost housing, by conferring tax advantages on such organizations.[65] Of course, national governments retain the primary obligation for guaranteeing all human rights: that obligation cannot be delegated or transferred to the private sector.

C. A Closer Look at Economic, Social, and Cultural Rights

The disadvantages of economic, social, and cultural rights compared to civil and political rights have begun to be redressed. For example, the Committee on Economic, Social and Cultural Rights has now issued 21 General Comments, which add considerable flesh to the bare bones of the text of the ICESCR. Thus, the lack of pre-existing definitions of the rights is being overcome.

Progressive obligations

The principle of progressive implementation of the obligations in Article 2(1) of the ICESCR requires that States must move forward in terms of their ability to guarantee a particular ICESCR right. Thus, its performance with regard to an ICESCR right should be better rather than worse in five years' time:[66] the expectations of a State increase over time. Progressive realization can be monitored, for example via the ICESCR's reporting procedures, through the use of indicators and benchmarks. Indicators comprise data, disaggregated on grounds such as race, sex, urban/rural divide, and socio-economic status, which helps to identify the actual performance of a State with regard to an ICESCR right. A benchmark is a goal set by the State to be achieved within a certain period of time: achievement of that benchmark is measured by indicators.[67] For example, an indicator can reveal

---

[64] Ibid, para 34.

[65] Commission on Human Rights, 'Realization of economic, social and cultural rights: Second progress report prepared by Mr Danilo Türk, Special Rapporteur', UN doc. E/CN.4/Sub.2/1991/17 (18 July 1991) para 188; Commission on Human Rights, 'The Realization of Economic, Social and Cultural Rights: Final report submitted by Mr Danilo Türk, Special Rapporteur', UN doc. E/CN.4/Sub.2/1992/16 (3 July 1992) para 192. See also Robertson, above n 54, 698–9.

[66] UNGA, 'Report of the Special Rapporteur on the right of everyone to the enjoyment of the highest attainable standard of physical and mental health, Paul Hunt', UN doc. A/61/338 (13 September 2006) para 55.

[67] Commission on Human Rights, 'Report of the Special Rapporteur on the right of everyone to the enjoyment of the highest attainable standard of physical and mental health, Paul Hunt', UN doc. E/CN.4/2006/48 (3 March 2006) para 34.

disaggregated information about the number of births across a country attended by a doctor. A benchmark would relate to a specified increase (for example, 50 per cent) in the percentage of such births across a certain time period (for example, three years). In setting benchmarks for progressive obligations, UN treaty bodies tend to defer to States parties, within reason, in determining reasonable and realistic targets.[68] Indicators and benchmarks help a State to monitor its own progress, and also help to ensure accountability for a State under the ICESCR.[69] States may be assisted in gathering the relevant data by international and civil society organizations. Furthermore, significant progress is being made within the UN Office of the High Commissioner for Human Rights in identifying appropriate human rights indicators, and how such indicators should be used and monitored by governments and the various UN treaty bodies.[70]

Given that progressive obligation implies that a State is continually moving forward in its implementation of ICESCR rights, there is a presumption that a State's performance will not go backwards. Hence:

deliberately retrogressive measures...would require the most careful consideration and would need to be fully justified by reference to the totality of the rights provided for in the Covenant and in the context of the full use of the maximum available resources.[71]

It is therefore possible for a State to take steps which are retrogressive in terms of the enjoyment of an ICESCR right, so long as such steps are justifiable in light of available resources (for example, a sudden economic crisis or catastrophic natural disaster) and the need to have regard to the overall implementation and enjoyment of the totality of ICESCR rights. A State however bears a heavy burden of proof in this regard, as indicated in General Comment 19, regarding retrogressive measures and the right to social security:

There is a strong presumption that retrogressive measures taken in relation to the right to social security are prohibited under the Covenant. If any deliberately retrogressive measures are taken, the State party has the burden of proving that they have been introduced after the most careful consideration of all alternatives and that they are duly justified by reference to the totality of the rights provided for in the Covenant, in the context of the full

---

[68] UN doc. E/2007/82, above n 62, para 54. There are procedural requirements in setting such benchmarks. Eg, they should be established according to a participatory and inclusive process at the national level. Therefore, a government cannot autocratically establish its own benchmarks.

[69] 'Report of the Special Rapporteur on the right of everyone to the enjoyment of the highest attainable standard of physical and mental health, Paul Hunt', UN doc. E/CN.4/2006/48 (3 March 2006), above n 67, para 35.

[70] See, eg, Office of the High Commissioner for Human Rights, 'Report on Indicators for Promoting and Monitoring the Implementation of Human Rights', UN doc. HRI/MC/2008/3 (6 June 2008). Eg, indicators may measure structures (they indicate whether or not key structures and mechanisms are in place within a state—eg has the State ratified a particular treaty?, has it adopted particular legislation?), procedures (monitoring the efforts being made by governments—eg does the State have a process in place to provide doctors for deliveries of babies in all parts of the country?), and outcomes (measuring the results of programmes and policies—eg what is the rate of maternal mortality?): see E/2007/82, above n 62, para 51.

[71] Committee on Economic, Social and Cultural Rights, 'General Comment No. 3: The Nature of States Parties' Obligations (Art. 2, Para. 1, of the Covenant)', UN doc. E/1991/23 (14 December 1990) para 9.

use of the maximum available resources of the State party. The Committee will look carefully at whether: (a) there was reasonable justification for the action; (b) alternatives were comprehensively examined; (c) there was genuine participation of affected groups in examining the proposed measures and alternatives; (d) the measures were directly or indirectly discriminatory; (e) the measures will have a sustained impact on the realization of the right to social security, an unreasonable impact on acquired social security rights or whether an individual or group is deprived of access to the minimum essential level of social security; and (f) whether there was an independent review of the measures at the national level.[72]

Maximum available resources

The ICESCR explicitly recognizes that a State's ability to fulfil ICESCR obligations, including the rate at which it progressively implements ICESCR rights, is subject to its available resources. Therefore, more is expected in terms of performance from richer States than from poorer States.[73] Financial resources are not the only resources of relevance to the ICESCR: there are also, for example, natural resources, human resources, information resources, and technological resources.[74]

One tool for assessing compliance with the obligation to use maximum available resources is to analyse State budgets. As noted by the High Commissioner on Human Rights in a 2009 report:

The budget is a useful source of information to evaluate which normative commitments are taken seriously by the State, because it provides a demonstration of the State's preferences, priorities and trade-offs in spending. For example, low apportionments in health care, education or social programmes when there are visible implementation gaps could show inadequate prioritization or insufficient estimation of the required funds to realize economic, social and cultural rights.[75]

For example:

If a significant percentage of the education budget is allocated to subsidizing private schools that cater for children from middle and high-income families compared with public schools serving low-income sectors of the population, the analysis would suggest that the Government's priorities may not be in line with its international obligations.[76]

Budget analysis could also reveal ICESCR violations in the form of clear instances of underfunding when there is a blatant disconnect between allocations and policy objectives, discrimination if there are manifest disparities in funding for particular groups or regions, and retrogression when there is a significant lessening of

---

[72] Committee on Economic, Social and Cultural Rights, 'General Comment No. 19: The right to social security (art. 9)', UN doc. E/C.12/GC/19 (4 February 2008) para 42.

[73] 'Report of the Special Rapporteur on the right of everyone to the enjoyment of the highest attainable standard of physical and mental health, Paul Hunt', UN doc. A/61/338 (13 September 2006), above n 66, para 55.

[74] See, generally, Robertson, above n 54.

[75] UN Economic and Social Council, 'Report of the High Commissioner for Human Rights on implementation of economic, social and cultural rights', UN doc. E/2009/90 (8 June 2009) para 46, and, generally, paras 44–54.

[76] Ibid, para 50.

funding for a particular programme in the face of ongoing need.[77] Furthermore, budget analysis must also be compared with actual spending. Underspending in areas of need would be another indication that resources are not being utilized in accordance with ICESCR requirements.[78]

Immediate obligations under the ICESCR

The Committee on Economic, Social and Cultural Rights has found that States have certain immediate obligations under the ICESCR. First, steps must actually be taken towards full realization of ICESCR rights immediately: a State is not entitled to do nothing or to regress. Rather, it must take 'deliberate, concrete and targeted measures'.[79] Secondly, Article 2(2) constitutes an immediate prohibition on discrimination in regard to the implementation of ICESCR rights on the grounds of 'race, colour, sex, language, religion, political or other opinion, national or social origin, property, birth or other status'.[80] Thirdly, certain ICESCR rights are, of their nature, capable of immediate implementation because they are not dependent on a State's resources, such as the right to form and join trade unions in Article 8.[81]

Finally, an implicit presumptive immediate obligation has been uncovered: States must guarantee a certain minimum core content of economic, social, and cultural rights unless they can prove that adequate resources are simply not available for that purpose. In General Comment 3 on 'The Nature of States Parties Obligations', the Committee stated at paragraph 10:

> [T]he Committee is of the view that a minimum core obligation to ensure the satisfaction of, at the very least, minimum essential levels of each of the rights is incumbent upon every State party. Thus, for example, a State party in which any significant number of individuals is deprived of essential foodstuffs, of essential primary health care, of basic shelter and housing, or of the most basic forms of education is, *prima facie*, failing to discharge its obligations under the Covenant. If the Covenant were to be read in such a way as not to establish such a minimum core obligation, it would be largely deprived of its *raison d'être*. By the same token, it must be noted that any assessment as to whether a State has discharged its minimum core obligation must also take account of resource constraints applying within the country concerned. Article 2 (1) obligates each State party to take the necessary steps 'to the maximum of its available resources'. In order for a State party to be able to attribute its failure to meet at least its minimum core obligations to a lack of available resources it must demonstrate that every effort has been made to use all resources that are at its disposition in an effort to satisfy, as a matter of priority, those minimum obligations.

Therefore, all States parties have a presumptive obligation to immediately guarantee the minimum core content of each of the ICESCR rights. States bear a heavy

---

[77] UN doc. E/2007/82, above n 62, para 65.　　[78] UN doc. E/2009/90, above n 75, para 54.
[79] Ibid, para 14.
[80] Committee on Economic Social and Cultural Rights, 'General Comment 20: Non-Discrimination in Economic, Social and Cultural Rights (art. 2, para. 2)', UN doc. E/C.12/GC/20 (2 July 2009) para 7.
[81] UN doc. E/2007/82, above n 62, para 16.

burden of proof in demonstrating that their lack of resources genuinely precludes such immediate implementation. The Committee's views on the minimum core content of the various ICESCR rights is elucidated in various General Comments, some of which are referenced in later chapters.

Justiciability of ICESCR rights

One of the biggest perceived differences between the two sets of rights is that civil and political rights are justiciable, while economic, social, and cultural rights are not. Their non-justiciable nature followed from the vague obligation provision, which hampered findings of violation, and the flawed positive/negative dichotomy. Civil and political rights have long been recognized as justiciable in a number of national courts, and may be the subject of individual complaints before the HRC under the Optional Protocol to the ICCPR. The existence of an individual complaints system under the ICCPR, and the absence of one under the ICESCR, has exacerbated the gap in normative material on the two sets of rights. While the HRC has decided over 1,500 cases,[82] which have helped concretize the meaning of ICCPR rights, the Committee on Economic Social and Cultural Rights has decided none.

The notion of indivisibility has nevertheless been underscored in the case law on civil and political rights. The HRC has identified numerous economic, social, and cultural rights issues that arise in the context of the ICCPR. For example, it has explicitly linked the right to life to the need for States to 'take all possible measures to reduce infant mortality and to increase life expectancy, especially in adopting measures to eliminate malnutrition and epidemics'.[83] Article 26 of the ICCPR, a broad guarantee against non-discrimination on various grounds such as race and sex, including the open-ended ground of 'other status',[84] has been interpreted as guaranteeing non-discrimination in regard to all rights, including economic social and cultural rights.[85] Thus, for example, discrimination in regard to the right to education on religious grounds in Canada (with Roman Catholics receiving funding privileges which were not available to Jews and other minority religions) was found to breach Article 26 in *Waldman v Canada*.[86] Hence, instances of discrimination in relation to economic, social, and cultural rights have long been justiciable under the ICCPR.[87]

---

[82] This number includes inadmissible cases, which can be instructive with regard to the normative content of a right.

[83] Human Rights Committee, 'General Comment 6: The right to life (art. 6)' (Sixteenth session, 1982) (30 April 1982) para 5.

[84] Sarah Joseph, Jenny Schultz, and Melissa Castan, *The International Covenant on Civil and Political Rights: Cases, Materials, and Commentary*, 2nd edn (Oxford University Press, Oxford, 2004) paras 23.20–23.30.

[85] See, eg, *Broeks v Netherlands*, UN doc. CCPR/C/29/D/172/1984 (9 April 1987) (Human Rights Committee).

[86] UN doc. CCPR/C/67/D/694/1996 (5 November 1999) (Human Rights Committee).

[87] Distinctions are permissible if made on reasonable and objective grounds. See generally, Joseph, Schultz, and Castan, above n 84, paras 23.41–23.67.

Furthermore, economic, social, and cultural rights per se have now been made justiciable in a number of national jurisdictions, such as South Africa, India, and various Latin American countries.[88] They are also justiciable under the regional human rights systems.[89]

For example, *Government of Republic of South Africa v Grootboom*[90] concerned the right to housing of a group that had been forced to squat on private land due to the appalling conditions in which they were living. The Constitutional Court of South Africa found that the government's housing programme breached the right to housing as it contained no apparent relief for those, such as the Grootboom group, who had no roof over their heads and were living in intolerable crisis conditions. The government was not however required to immediately provide the Grootboom group with shelter. Rather, it was required to adopt reasonable measures to make sure that persons in dire straits would have access to some form of shelter. Furthermore, the court left a wide latitude to the government in crafting the final remedy: it did not dictate budgetary outlays for housing programmes.

Minister for Health v Treatment Action Campaign[91] concerned a challenge, based on the right to health, to the restricted availability of nevirapine, a drug which restricted transmission of HIV-AIDS from mothers to babies ('MTCT transmission') in South Africa. Again, the decision was based on the concept of reasonableness: the restrictions were not reasonable in the circumstances so the government was required to devise a plan to expedite the availability of nevirapine at public health care facilities throughout the country. This decision may seem alarming to those who are concerned that justiciable economic, social, and cultural rights will lead to court decisions which impact severely on national budgets. However, such decisions are hardly unknown: court interpretations of many laws, such as taxation laws, can impact severely on government coffers.[92] Furthermore, several factors underlined the unreasonable nature of the impugned restrictions in *Treatment Action Campaign*. Nevirapine was made available for free to South Africa by the patent-holder. The drug was effective, and did not entail a complex consumption regime, so counselling and education of patients would not be onerous. The comparative health burden and associated costs entailed in not utilizing a proven method of combating MTCT transmission in South Africa would be enormous. Finally, the government had already committed substantial funds to fighting HIV in South Africa.

The South African cases prove that the justiciability of economic, social, and cultural rights is workable. In fact, they utilize techniques that are far from alien to the judicial process by using reasonableness as the touchstone for assessing violations of such rights. Assessments of the reasonableness of administrative action are a key component, for example, in administrative law in common law countries. Indeed,

---

[88] See generally, Malcolm Langford (ed), *Social Rights Jurisprudence: Emerging Trends in International and Comparative Law* (Cambridge University Press, New York, 2008) Part 2.
[89] Ibid, Part 3.   [90] (2000) 11 BCLR 1169 (South Africa Constitutional Court).
[91] (2002) 10 BCLR 1033 (South Africa Constitutional Court).
[92] Paul Hunt, 'Reclaiming Economic, Social and Cultural Rights' (1993) 1 *Waikato Law Review* 141.

reasonableness is often the test used for identifying violations of measures which interfere with civil and political rights. Furthermore, it has long been accepted that violations of negative rights are identifiable and justiciable. Both *Grootboom* and *Treatment Action Campaign* confirmed that positive obligations are also justiciable.

It is notable and perhaps ironic that many of the most sophisticated and influential decisions on economic, social, and cultural rights come from developing States, particularly from Africa and Latin America. This fact belies the presumed lesser abilities of poorer States to adequately address such rights.

In December 2008, the UN General Assembly adopted an Optional Protocol to ICESCR, which will provide for an individual complaints mechanism. That treaty will come into force when 10 States have ratified it. Its entry into force will usher in a new era of justiciable global economic social and cultural rights. It too adopts a standard of 'reasonableness' (in Article 8(4)) as the touchstone for assessing whether a State has taken sufficient steps in implementing a particular right, or whether it has violated a right. Article 8(4) also recognizes a margin of discretion for States by acknowledging that a 'State Party may adopt a range of possible policy measures for the implementation of' ICESCR rights.

It has been argued in a number of philosophical and political circles that economic, social, and cultural rights are not 'real' human rights,[93] and that they lack sufficient content to be useful in a trade context.[94] Such an argument ignores the fact that three quarters of the world's nations have committed to legal obligations under the ICESCR as a matter of international law, and that the non-justiciability argument has been proven wrong by numerous domestic courts[95] and was finally defeated with the adoption by consensus of the Optional Protocol in 2008. Such arguments are essentially ideological, or reflect a lack of understanding of international human rights law.[96]

D. Human Rights and Customary International Law

Customary international law is that core of international law that binds all States regardless of the treaties they have ratified.[97] States generate customary

---

[93] Harrison, above n 1, 26 (noting but not agreeing with the argument). See, eg, 'Human Rights Survey' *The Economist*, 5 December 1998, at 9, suggesting that economic, social, and cultural rights are issues that 'should be left to politics and the market'.

[94] See, eg, Gabrielle Marceau, 'WTO Dispute Settlement and Human Rights' (2002) 13 *European Journal of International Law* 753, 786–9; Jose E Alvarez, 'How not to Link: Institutional Conundrums on an Expanded Trade Regime' (2001) 7 *Widener Law Symposium Journal* 1, 10; Harrison, above n 1, 234.

[95] See Malcolm Langford, 'The Justiciability of Social Rights: From Practice to Theory' in Malcolm Langford (ed), above n 88, 3, 4.

[96] Robert Howse and Ruti Teitel, 'Beyond the Divide: The Covenant on Economic, Social and Cultural Rights and the World Trade Organization' in Sarah Joseph, David Kinley, and Jeff Waincymer, *The World Trade Organization and Human Rights: Interdisciplinary Perspectives* (Edward Elgar, Cheltenham, 2009) 40.

[97] There is an exception for 'persistent objectors'. According to the persistent objector doctrine, if a State persistently objects to an evolving rule of customary international law, it can avoid being

international law through State practice and *opinio juris*.[98] There is great controversy and speculation over the identity of the human rights that are protected under customary international law. This controversy is exacerbated by the general lack of binding decisions on the matter, so the topic is dominated by academic debate.[99]

The outer edge of likely customary international law seems to be the totality of rights in the UDHR,[100] though some commentators have claimed that rights in the Declaration on the Right to Development[101] and the DRIP[102] are customary too. A recent development in the UN Human Rights Council provides significant support to the notion that the UDHR in its entirety is part of customary international law. Under the new process of Universal Periodic Review, the human rights record of every State will be examined in accordance with the treaties it has ratified, voluntary pledges, the UN Charter as well as the UDHR.[103] Therefore, China, for example, has reported on its record regarding at least some civil and political rights, despite its failure to ratify the ICCPR.[104] The reporting by States of their record regarding rights based only on the UDHR, as well as the scrutinizing of that record by other States, constitutes significant State practice tending towards the customary status of the UDHR.[105]

The following seems to constitute the minimal position, in that there is little doubt the following rights are protected by custom: prohibitions on genocide, slavery, systemic racial discrimination, grave violations of international humanitarian law, murder, disappearance, torture and other cruel inhuman and degrading treatment or punishment, prolonged arbitrary detention, and consistent patterns of gross violations of internationally recognized rights, and the right of colonial peoples to self determination.[106]

That shorter list excludes economic, social, and cultural rights. However, Professor Philip Alston has convincingly argued that the inner core of economic, social and cultural rights captured within the Millennium Development Goals

bound by that rule. A State loses persistent objector status if it fails to object consistently over time once the rule is in place. See, generally, Jonathan I Charney, 'The Persistent Objector Rule and the Development of Customary International Law' (1985) 56 *British Yearbook of International Law* 1.

   [98] *Opinio Juris* constitutes a belief by States that a norm is legally binding.
   [99] See also, generally, Anthony E Cassimatis, *Human Rights Related Trade Measures under International Law* (Martinus Nijhoff, Leiden, 2007) 72–91.
   [100] See, eg, Sohn, above n 26, 17. See also above, text notes 29 and 30.
   [101] See, eg, Mohammed Bedjaoui, 'The Right to Development' in Mohammed Bedjaoui (ed), *International Law: Achievements and Prospects* (Martinus Nijhoff Publishers, Boston, 1991); Philip Alston, 'Making Space for New Human Rights: The Case of the Right to Development' (1988) 1 *Harvard Human Rights Year Book* 3.
   [102] See, eg, Megan Davis, 'Indigenous Struggles in Standard-setting: The United Nations Declaration on the Rights of Indigenous Peoples' (2008) 9 *Melbourne Journal of International Law* 439, 465–6, commenting on the arguments of others.
   [103] See Human Rights Council, 'Report to the General Assembly on the Fifth Session of the Council', UN doc. A/HRC/5/21 (7 August 2007) 4.
   [104] See Human Rights Council, 'National Report Submitted in Accordance with Paragraph 15(A) of the Annex to Human Rights Council Resolution 5/1: China', UN doc. A/HRC/WG.6/4/CHN/1 (10 November 2008) paras 42–62.
   [105] I am grateful to Professor Robert McCorquodale for sharing this idea.
   [106] See *Restatement of the Law Third, Foreign Relations Law of the United States* (American Law Institute, St Paul, 1987) para 702.

(MDGs) is now protected under customary international law. The MDGs are the eradication of extreme poverty and hunger, the attainment of universal primary education, the promotion of gender equality, the reduction of child mortality, improvements in maternal health, the combating of HIV/AIDS and certain other diseases, the achievement of environmental sustainability, and the development of a global partnership for development. These goals, the achievement of which are essential for the attainment of global human dignity, have been consistently 'affirmed, reiterated and restated' by governments,[107] which may constitute sufficient State practice and *opinio juris* to elevate them to customary status.

Customary international law is of course particularly important in the context of a State that has not ratified a relevant treaty which protects a particular human right: it provides an alternative source of obligation for that State with regard to that right. Where a State has ratified a treaty, it is bound under international law by the treaty anyway, regardless of the customary status of the norms therein. Most Member States of the WTO are parties to both Covenants. The huge majority are also parties to the CERD, CEDAW, and the CRC.

E. Conclusion

The above commentary has introduced relevant rules and concepts in WTO law and international human rights law. WTO law will be further elaborated, particularly in Chapter 4, so this chapter has focused more on international human rights law. Given that they are commonly misunderstood, and dismissed as idealistic goals rather than enforceable rights, this chapter has paid special attention to explaining economic, social and cultural rights. As highlighted in following chapters, particularly Chapters 5 to 7, economic, social, and cultural rights are particularly relevant to the debate regarding the human rights impact of the WTO.

---

[107] Philip Alston, 'Ships passing in the night: the current state of the human rights and development debate seen through the lens of the Millennium Development Goals' (2005) 27 *Human Rights Quarterly* 755, 774.

2

Relationship between the WTO and International Human Rights Law

Having introduced the two relevant international law regimes in Chapter 1, it is necessary to discuss the relationship between the two. First, the underlying philosophies of the two regimes will be compared, followed by an analysis of the normative legal relationship between these two areas of international law.

A. Underlying Values

Although they arguably have deeper and more universal, cross-cultural roots dating back to the earliest conceptions of law, modern notions of human rights are often traced back to Western liberal philosophies of the seventeenth and eighteenth centuries.[1] Specifically, John Locke's 'Second Treatise of Government' speculated that men in a 'state of nature' had 'natural rights' to life, liberty and property.[2] Similar ideas emerged in the Age of Enlightenment in France with the ideas of Rousseau, de Montesquieu and Voltaire, though the continental European theorists qualified rights more with limitations, duties, and ideas of fraternity and equality along with liberty.[3] Natural rights theorists argued that such rights were rooted in the inherent dignity and rationality of human beings (or rather, 'men'), a departure from the predominant but irrational religious dogma of the time.[4] In classical Lockean theory, societies were formed under a 'social contract', under which 'men' retained their natural rights subject to the qualification that they did not threaten or harm each other's rights. The role of government was minimal, and was essentially confined to enforcement of that social contract. Therefore, early conceptions of human rights construed them as a narrow range of civil and political freedoms from government action and protections from others, rather than entitlements to government-provided goods or services. These early

---

[1] The following commentary is adapted from Sarah Joseph, 'Civil and political rights' in Mashood Baderin and Manisuli Ssenyonjo, *International Human Rights Law: Six Decades after the UDHR* (Ashgate, Surrey, 2010) 89–106.

[2] John Locke, 'The Second Treatise of Government', reprinted in Peter Laslett (ed), *Locke, Two Treatises of Government*, 2nd edn (Cambridge University Press, Cambridge, 1988) 265ff.

[3] Mary Ann Glendon, *A World Made New: Eleanor Roosevelt and the Universal Declaration of Human Rights* (Random House, New York, 2001) xvii.

[4] See Burns Weston, 'Human Rights' (1984) 3 *Human Rights Quarterly* 257, 259.

conceptions of human rights law, which influenced the earliest Bills of Rights in the US and France, focused on libertarian negative rights rather than positive claim rights.

Despite numerous criticisms of natural rights theories from thinkers such as Karl Marx[5] and Jeremy Bentham,[6] natural rights theories endured and dominated the drafting and language of the UDHR in 1948.[7] However, by 1948, conceptions of natural rights had evolved far beyond their early libertarian roots to encompass rights for women and minorities, workers' rights, and rights to some minimum levels of material security in the form of welfare rights,[8] and the need for persons to function as members of society, rather than as mere individuals.[9]

The following values are articulated in the UDHR and encapsulate the values which underpin the modern international human rights system: universality, dignity, freedom (or liberty), justice, equality (or fairness, including distributive fairness), accountability (of governments), participation, empowerment, and brotherhood (or solidarity) amongst people.[10]

The Director-General of the WTO, Pascal Lamy, has proclaimed that trade rules, including WTO rules, are based on the same values as human rights: 'individual freedom and responsibility, non-discrimination, rule of law, and welfare through peaceful cooperation among individuals'.[11] The influential WTO scholar Ernst-Ulrich Petersmann has also stated that the WTO regime promotes freedom (in removing restrictions on trade), non-discrimination (in the form of MFN and national treatment), the rule of law (in committing WTO Members to transparent obligations and an enforceable rules-based international trading system), and economic efficiency leading to enhanced welfare.[12] All of those values, as proclaimed by Lamy and Petersmann, seem congruent with the promotion of human rights principles until subjected to greater scrutiny.

---

[5] Marx dismissed natural rights as egoistic and based on anti-social premises pitting man against man: see, eg, Karl Marx, 'On the Jewish question', reprinted in David McClellan (ed), *Marx: Selected Writings* (Oxford University Press, Oxford, 1977) 51–7.

[6] Bentham famously dismissed natural rights theories as 'anarchical fallacies' and 'nonsense upon stilts': see Jeremy Bentham, 'Anarchical Fallacies', reprinted in Jeremy Waldron (ed), *Nonsense upon Stilts: Bentham, Burke and Marx on the Rights of Man* (Methuen, London, 1987) 46ff.

[7] Johannes Morsink, 'The Philosophy of the Universal Declaration' (1982) 4 *Human Rights Quarterly* 391.

[8] See Henry Shue, *Basic Rights* (Princeton University Press, Princeton, 1980) 24–5; Matthew Craven, *The International Covenant on Economic Social and Cultural Rights* (Oxford University Press, Oxford, 1995) 13. Indeed, Morsink traces support for economic, social, and cultural rights to an early proponent of natural rights, Thomas Paine, at Morsink, above n 7, 326.

[9] Morsink, above n 7, 334.   [10] See UDHR, especially Preamble and Article 1.

[11] Pascal Lamy, 'Towards shared responsibility and greater coherence: human rights, trade and macroeconomic policy' (Speech at the Colloquium on Human Rights in the Global Economy, Co-organized by the International Council on Human Rights and Realizing Rights, Geneva, 13 January 2010) <http://www.wto.org/english/news_e/sppl_e/sppl146_e.htm> accessed 18 September 2010.

[12] Ersnt-Ulrich Petersmann, 'Time for a United Nations "Global Compact" for integrating human rights into the law of worldwide institutions: lessons from European integration' (2002) 13 *European Journal of International Law* 621, 636.

Freedoms and rights under trade law and human rights law

The freedoms promoted under the WTO lie exclusively in the international economic sphere, such as the rights of exporters to peaceful enjoyment of property and freedom of contract, non-discrimination in relation to other like industries (discussed below), and freedom of movement of goods and services across borders. This list of freedoms is very narrow compared to the freedoms promoted under human rights law. Furthermore, WTO law supports rights with respect to a few, namely foreign traders, while human rights law recognizes rights for all. The narrowness of the range of beneficiaries under the WTO gives rise to the danger that those beneficiaries are unduly privileged when their interests clash with those of others, such as, for example, local competitors or consumers, in a way that undermines the human rights of the latter.

As noted above, John Locke's theory of natural rights has profoundly influenced the development of human rights law. Locke was also one of the first modern philosophers to provide a justification for the right to private property. Nevertheless, in modern international human rights law, the right to property is heavily qualified. For example, Article 1(1) of the First Protocol to the ECHR outlines the right as follows:

Every natural or legal person is entitled to the peaceful enjoyment of his possessions. No one shall be deprived of his possessions except in the public interest and subject to the conditions provided for by law and by the general principles of international law.

The preceding provisions shall not, however, in any way impair the right of a State to enforce such laws as it deems necessary to control the use of property in accordance with the general interest or to secure the payment of taxes or other contributions or penalties.

The right is heavily qualified by the second paragraph, and by the fact that one can be deprived of one's property 'in the public interest' subject to domestic and international law.[13]

The right to property was not in fact transposed at the global level from the UDHR to either Covenant, largely due to the socialist bloc's opposition during the drafting thereof.[14] That is not to say that property rights are totally unprotected under the Covenants. The right to property must, for example, be enjoyed on a non-discriminatory basis. In a number of cases against the Czech Republic under the ICCPR, the HRC has found that the conferral of rights of restitution on citizens only, with regard to property confiscated by the previous communist regime, was a breach of the right of non-discrimination on the basis of nationality.[15] However, the right to property per se is not protected: no violation of the

---

[13] On relevant ECHR case law, see Pieter van Dijk, Fried van Hoof, Arjen van Rijn, and Leo Zwaak (eds), *Theory and Practice of the European Convention on Human Rights*, 4th edn (Intersentia, Antwerp, 2006) Chapter 17.

[14] See Audrey Chapman, 'Approaching intellectual property as a human right (obligations related to Article 15(1)(c))' (2001) XXXV *Copyright Bulletin* 4, 12.

[15] See, eg, *Simunek v Czech Republic*, UN doc. CCPR/C/54/D/516/1992 (19 July 1995) and *Adam v Czech Republic*, UN doc. CCPR/C/57/D/586/1994 (25 July 1996) (both Human Rights Committee).

ICCPR would have arisen in the Czech cases if no restitution rights had been granted to anybody.[16]

The promotion of property rights within the context of economic globalization (moving beyond the realm of the WTO) tends to focus on security of transactions and protection for foreign investors, rather than property rights as human rights enjoyed by all regardless of one's economic utility.[17] Ultimately, that lopsided promotion and protection of property rights can prompt the corrupt and forced transfer of lands to those who can pay more for that land, and/or those who can make the land more profitable, at the expense of indigenous peoples and the poor. While such transfers may be economically beneficial, at least in the short term,[18] they do not conform to international human rights norms. For example, land registration systems are generally designed to ensure secure property rights, and their introduction has been funded in some developing States by the World Bank. Unfortunately, such systems have on occasion fostered corruption and human rights abuses, whereby traditional land-owners such as indigenous peoples have been arbitrarily evicted, with their lands transferred to rich speculators and developers. For instance, a land titling project in Cambodia has entrenched inequality by exacerbating the vulnerability of poor householders in comparison with rich developers.[19]

There is no free-standing right to freedom of contract in international human rights law, apart from Articles 15(2) and 16 of the Charter of Fundamental Rights of the European Union. The commercial origins of the EU were undoubtedly influential in generating those provisions, which came into force in most EU countries on 1 December 2009.[20] At the domestic level, freedom of contract has had a chequered history under the Fourteenth Amendment to the US Bill of Rights. Notoriously, in *Lochner v New York*,[21] the Supreme Court of the United States struck down a New York law which limited the number of hours a baker could work in one day (10 hours) and in one week (60 hours). That law was designed to promote labour rights, but was found to undermine individual freedoms of contract. *Lochner* clearly demonstrated the tension that can exist between labour regulation, and indeed economic regulation, and the *laissez-faire* principle of freedom

---

[16] The ICCPR did not apply to the original confiscations, which discriminated against persons on the basis of their political opinion, as they predated the entry into force of the ICCPR for the Czech Republic.

[17] See also James Harrison, *The Human Rights Impact of the World Trade Organisation* (Hart, Oxford, 2007) 47.

[18] See, eg, Ha-Joon Chang, *Kicking Away the Ladder: Development Strategy in Historical Perspective* (Anthem Press, London, 2003) 82–3.

[19] See Natalie Bugalski and David Pred, 'Land Titling in Cambodia: Formalizing Inequality' (2010) 7 *Housing and ESC Rights Law Quarterly* 1. See also Nicola Colbran, 'Indigenous Peoples in Indonesia: at risk of disappearing as distinct peoples in the rush for biofuel?' (2010) *International Journal for Minority and Group Rights*, forthcoming, paper on file with the author, for a discussion of the eviction of indigenous peoples in Indonesia to make way for palm oil and jatropha plantations (partially for biofuel production), especially at 11–15.

[20] The Charter came into force with the Lisbon Treaty, which reformed the European Union. The Charter will not apply in full in the UK, Poland, or the Czech Republic.

[21] 198 US 45 (1905) (Supreme Court of the United States).

of contract.[22] Freedom of contract and other economic liberties can be abused where the relevant parties have unequal bargaining power.

The right to freedom of movement of goods and services is not per se relevant to human rights, as opposed to a right of freedom of movement of persons, which barely exists under the WTO.[23] Human rights attach to individuals and occasionally groups;[24] they do not attach to economic commodities. There has been robust debate over the merits of a 'right to trade', epitomized by the exchange of views between Petersmann and Philip Alston in 2002.[25] Such a right is of course heavily facilitated at the international level by the WTO. Indeed, a WTO panel has stated that 'one of the primary objectives of the GATT/WTO as a whole is to produce certain market conditions which would allow this individual [trading and business] activity to flourish'.[26] In contrast, no right to trade as such is recognized in human rights law.

Despite the comment in the WTO panel decision cited immediately above, the WTO does not confer property, contractual or trading rights as individual rights. Individuals do not have direct rights under the WTO; only Member States have rights (and duties). However, such rights are indirectly if not directly granted: States bring claims essentially on behalf of their traders. These claims are usually brought on behalf of large corporations; it seems doubtful that a State would engage in the time and expense of WTO litigation on behalf of small traders in an economically insignificant sector.[27] Corporations are not generally recognized as having human rights under international human rights law.[28]

The divergence of WTO values from human rights values is more profoundly illustrated by the differing purposes underlying the rights recognized. Alston has cogently argued that WTO rights are simply not analogous to human rights due to their fundamentally different rationale:

Human rights are recognized for all on the basis of the inherent human dignity of all persons. Trade-related rights are granted to individuals for instrumental reasons. Individuals

---

[22] *Lochner* has not been explicitly overruled, but has been wound back in cases such as *West Coast Hotel Co v Parrish* 300 US 379 (1937) (Supreme Court of the United States).

[23] Philip Alston, 'Resisting the Merger and Acquisition of Human Rights by Trade Law: A Reply to Petersmann' (2002) 13 *European Journal of International Law* 815, 825. The GATS presages some liberalization in the movement of mobile labour forces under Mode IV of GATS, but few commitments in this regard have been made. It may be noted that international human rights law rarely recognizes a right of human beings to enter a foreign State, except under international refugee law and systems of complementary protection.

[24] Most internationally recognized human rights attach to individuals, though some collective rights are also recognized, such as the right of self determination in Article 1 of both Covenants.

[25] See Petersmann, above n 12, and Alston, above n 23; see also Robert Howse, 'Human Rights in the WTO: Whose Rights, What Humanity? Comment on Petersmann' (2002) 13 *European Journal of International Law* 651.

[26] *United States—Sections 301–310 of the Trade Act of 1974*, WTO doc. WT/DS152/R (22 December 1999) (Report of the Panel) para 7.73.

[27] See also Caroline Dommen, 'Raising Human Rights Concerns in the World Trade Organization: Actors, Processes and Possible Strategies' (2002) 24 *Human Rights Quarterly* 1, 47.

[28] Exceptionally, artificial entities such as corporations may bring claims for human rights abuses before the European Court of Human Rights. See generally, Marius Emberland, *The Human Rights of Companies: Exploring the Structure of ECHR Protection* (Oxford University Press, New York, 2006). Corporations are recognized as having rights under some domestic Bills of Rights, such as those in Canada or the US.

are seen as objects rather than as holders of rights. They are empowered as economic agents for particular purposes and in order to promote a specific approach to economic policy, not as political actors in the full sense and nor as holders of a comprehensive and balanced set of individual rights. There is nothing *per se* wrong with such instrumentalism but it should not be confused with a human rights approach.[29]

Alston concedes that an exception to his proposition lies in the (indirect) intellectual property rights conferred under TRIPS, which arguably correlate with rights recognized under Article 15(1)(c) of the ICESCR. Ironically however, TRIPS has probably attracted the most sustained criticisms for its effects on human rights, as is discussed in Chapter 7.

The emphasis on freedom in WTO law is generally aimed at freeing trade from the constraints of government. Of course, much of human rights law is also aimed at freeing people from unreasonable government restrictions. However, as noted in Chapter 1, human rights obligations also entail positive duties to protect and fulfil which require action, regulation and intervention by States. Constraints (or perceived constraints) on State capacities to implement their positive human rights duties give rise to one of the biggest perceived challenges posed by WTO rules to human rights. As stated by Dr Andrew Lang:

> The international trade regime, it is said, has imposed new constraints on states' policy choices, so that they are now less able to intervene in the economy to fulfil their human rights obligations. The primary mechanism by which the human rights system achieves its objectives, the story goes, is losing its efficacy in the face of a newly powerful and newly dominant neoliberal international economic order.[30]

For example, States may wish to introduce price caps with regard to essential utilities, such as the provision of water or electricity, which limits the economic freedoms of water and electricity companies, in order to guarantee the right to an adequate standard of living for the poor under Article 11 of the ICESCR. There is a suspicion, the merits of which will be discussed in ensuing chapters, that WTO rules unduly undermine the ability of States to adopt such measures.[31]

Indeed, Petersmann has criticized the ICESCR for its 'neglect for economic liberty rights and property rights' as reflective of an anti-market bias.[32] However, Petersmann is possibly falling into the common trap of assuming that the ICESCR is solely premised on government control of the means to provide for economic and social rights. As noted in Chapter 1, governments have duties to respect ICESCR rights, and thus to refrain from measures which harm enjoyment of those rights, including unreasonable interferences with persons' livelihoods and abilities to improve their own economic situation.[33] As an example relevant to free trade, Oxfam has cited a high tariff by some African countries on mosquito nets

---

[29] Alston, above n 23, 826.

[30] Andrew Lang, 'Inter-regime Encounters' in Sarah Joseph, David Kinley, and Jeff Waincymer, *The World Trade Organization and Human Rights: Interdisciplinary Perspectives* (Edward Elgar, Cheltenham, 2009) 184. Ironically, intellectual property protection requires considerable state intervention: see also p. 293.

[31] See also Andrew Lang, 'The GATS and regulatory autonomy: a case study of social regulation of the water industry' (2004) 7 *Journal of International Economic Law* 801–38.

[32] Petersmann, above n 12, 628–9.   [33] See also Chapter 1, text at notes 64–5.

as a measure that costs lives by increasing the exposure of the poor to malaria, in breach of the right to health in the ICESCR (and probably the right to life in the ICCPR).[34] From a human rights point of view, the key is in part to ensure an appropriate balance between regulation and non-interference. Also from a human rights point of view, it is possible that the WTO dictates a sub-optimal balance which unduly impels the latter strategy.

'Freedom' in the WTO context is unbalanced and sometimes counterproductive from a human rights point of view. First, as noted above, it prioritizes freedoms that are not strictly recognized under human rights law. Secondly, under human rights law, it is well recognized that most of one's freedoms can be limited by the rights of others because freedoms and rights often clash. 'Freedom' in human rights law is rarely absolute and is normally necessarily constrained in order to protect the rights of others. For example, one's freedom of expression is limited by defamation of laws, which simultaneously protects the privacy and reputation rights of another. In WTO law, the freedoms of foreign traders are prioritized at the expense of the rights of local traders. As explained by James Gathii:

[E]very rule of international trade that opens trade up rests upon a corresponding act of limiting or controlling entitlements to other stakeholders.... After all, there is no liberty or freedom to trade that does not come with a simultaneous restriction or limitation of another freedom.[35]

Yet those countervailing freedoms are largely unrecognized by the WTO. Countervailing rights are not, for example, a recognized exception in the exception provisions such as Article XX of the GATT.[36] Furthermore, no compensation for the losers from free trade is mandated, and arguably (as explored in subsequent chapters), the capacity for States to provide for such compensation is constrained.

Non-discrimination

The non-discrimination rights in the WTO are very narrow, focused solely on the international economic realm, effectively protecting foreign businesses from discrimination in relation to other foreign businesses (under MFN) or local businesses (under National Treatment). In contrast, international human rights law recognizes rights of non-discrimination on a large (and open-ended) number of grounds with regard to all rights.[37]

The importance of the protection of foreigners should not be underestimated, given the very real temptations of governments to discriminate against

---

[34] Oxfam, *Rigged Rules and Double Standards* (Oxfam, London, 2002) 62.
[35] James Thuo Gathii, 'Re-Characterizing the Social in the Constitutionalization of the WTO: A Preliminary Analysis' (2001) 7 *Widener Law Symposium Journal* 137, 148.
[36] This exception provision is analysed in Chapter 4.
[37] Eg, Article 26 of the ICCPR guarantees equality before the law and equal treatment of the law with regard to the enjoyment of all rights without discrimination on a number of enumerated grounds, as well as 'any other status'.

non-nationals, perhaps in order to reap political capital amongst voting nationals. However, WTO non-discrimination provisions focus on 'equality in regulatory treatment of goods and services between different countries', rather than on discrimination against non-nationals per se.[38]

Furthermore, the goals of the non-discrimination provisions in WTO law and human rights law are very different. Discrimination in human rights law is linked to notions of substantive equality of people. For example, positive measures are required of States to 'redress the structural biases that lead to discrimination'.[39] Therefore, affirmative action to assist disadvantaged persons is permitted and occasionally required under international human rights law.[40] In contrast, WTO prohibitions on discrimination are meant to eliminate protectionism with respect to goods and services traded. For example, the WTO does not prohibit discrimination against local industry, nor does it seem to permit exceptions where certain local businesses might be disadvantaged compared to foreign competitors.[41] Indeed, part of the point of the WTO is to drive the less advantaged out of business on the basis that they are less efficient than the more advantaged. That ethos does not seem to support, for example, measures which favour subsistence farmers over agribusiness conglomerates, or not-for-profit educational charities ahead of commercial education providers.[42] Thus, the implementation of the non-discrimination framework of the WTO has great potential to entrench underlying inequalities in a way that undermines human rights non-discrimination principles. Harrison has described the differences between the two regimes regarding the principle of non-discrimination as 'probably the most problematic methodological difference between the two systems' given that a principle that at least uses the same wording is 'fundamental to both systems of law'.[43]

Rule of law

The WTO promotes the rule of law within its narrow field of international trading relations: this role is particularly important in constraining the use of trade

---

[38] See Adam McBeth, *International Economic Actors and Human Rights* (Routledge, Oxford, 2010) 96. See also Chapter 3, text at note 69, on how one WTO case against the US was effectively brought on behalf of a US investor.

[39] Commission on Human Rights, 'Analytical study of the High Commissioner for Human Rights on the Fundamental Principle of Non-Discrimination in the Context of Globalization', UN doc. E/CN.4/2004/40 (15 January 2004) para 26.

[40] HRC, 'General Comment No 18: Non-discrimination', UN doc. HRI/GEN/1/Rev.1 (10 November 1989) para 10; HRC, 'General Comment No 28: Equality of rights between men and women (article 3)', UN doc. CCPR/C/21/Rev.1/Add.10 (29 March 2000) para 3; *Stalla Costa v Uruguay*, UN doc. CCPR/C/30/D/198/1985 (9 July 1987) (Human Rights Committee). See also CERD, Articles 1(4) and 2(2); CEDAW, Articles 4 and 12(2).

[41] UNHCHR, above n 39, para 26. An example of such disadvantage might be that experienced by local small farmers in the case of agricultural trade, see para 35 and see also Chapter 6. See also McBeth, above n 38, 96–8. See also Joseph E Stiglitz and Andrew Charlton, *Fair Trade for All* (Oxford University Press, New York, 2005) 79.

[42] See Harrison, above n 17, 141.   [43] Ibid, 141.

measures as weapons by economically powerful States who would otherwise have few constraints on such power. Furthermore, the WTO's peaceful dispute settlement processes help to defuse the dangerous tensions that might be generated by trade disputes.

The rule of law within the WTO is focused on facilitating a more transparent and predictable environment for trade.[44] However, its concerns are again one-sided. It is not explicitly concerned where the rule of law might be bent to favour foreign traders over local people, as for example has been evidenced in the aforementioned land titling project in Cambodia.[45]

The rule of law is promoted in a different and much broader way under human rights law through numerous prohibitions on arbitrary and unpredictable exercises of power by governments, and requirements that limitations on rights be prescribed and circumscribed by clearly defined laws.[46] As noted by David Kinley, different global actors, such as commercial/economic actors and human rights actors, stress different aspects of the rule of law.[47]

Economic efficiency and enhanced welfare

The creation of greater net wealth by WTO rules is an outcome that plausibly promotes the capacity of States to protect and fulfil human rights obligations, and the capacities of beneficiaries of that wealth to enjoy human rights. However, an increase in net global wealth does not necessarily lead to the enhancement of individual welfare. WTO rules have nothing to say about the distribution of that wealth, whether between or within countries.[48]

The theory of comparative advantage holds that the removal of trade barriers is beneficial for all States by improving aggregate wealth, but it has little to say about distributional outcomes. From a human rights point of view, it is the effect of free trade on human beings that is important. The process of trade liberalization clearly creates 'winners' and 'losers' inside a State, that is those respectively employed in efficient and inefficient industries. The Committee on Economic, Social and Cultural Rights has made clear that the effects of policies on the most vulnerable

---

[44] See, eg, Article X of GATT relating to the publication and administration of trade regulations. See also Anne Orford, 'Beyond Harmonization: Trade, Human Rights and the Economy of Sacrifice' (2005) 18 *Leiden Journal of International Law* 179, 208.

[45] See above, text at note 19. See also, generally, Human Rights Council, 'Report of the Special Rapporteur on the Right to Food, Olivier De Schutter: Large-scale land acquisitions and leases: A set of minimum principles and measures to address the human rights challenge', UN doc. A/HRC/13/33/Add.2, 28 December 2009.

[46] Eg, Article 9(1) of the ICCPR demands that no instance of detention may be 'arbitrary' or 'unlawful', and one must have one's detention confirmed by a judicial body under Article 9(3), as well as the opportunity to challenge the lawfulness of detention under Article 9(4). Article 15(1) of the ICCPR protects the principle of legality; that is that the law must be clear, and no person may be charged with an offence for conduct that was not illegal at the time that it was perpetrated. Article 15(2) contains an exception to Article 15(1) in respect of international crimes, such as genocide and war crimes.

[47] David Kinley, *Civilising Globalisation* (Cambridge University Press, Cambridge, 2009) 131.

[48] See also Chapter 10, Part C.

are 'a particular preoccupation'[49] under the ICESCR.[50] Therefore, human rights law will be particularly concerned with the plight of the losers from free trade.[51]

Certainly, one might expect many of the losers from trade liberalization to change careers and move into more efficient production sectors. However, such options are not always available. As Professor Joel R Paul has noted:

> You cannot turn an automotive factory into a dairy farm; a 50 year old factory worker probably will not make a good computer engineer; and a factory town in Maine cannot grow oranges.[52]

These adjustments generate significant social costs, such as taxpayer costs to provide welfare payments to the unemployed, the decline of entire communities (for example, those built up around inefficient industries), and consequent social instability within those communities.[53] Of course, these costs include significant human rights costs, such as detriment to the right to work and the right to an adequate standard of living. However, those costs are arguably offset by the increased human rights enjoyment of the winners from globalization, those who gain jobs in the new industries which should eventually flourish more than the older less efficient industries. Furthermore, greater economic output within the State should generate greater revenues for the State, enhancing its ability to cater for these adjustment costs. However, those benefits may take considerable time to emerge, and human rights obligations do not countenance the automatic sacrifice of many to short term pain for (perhaps speculative) utilitarian long term gain.[54]

In particular, people cannot be left to fend for themselves after adjustments brought about free trade: the detrimental impact of liberalizing measures on the 'losers' should be cushioned by adequate compensatory measures.[55] However, as noted by Stiglitz and Charlton:

> The standard economic argument is that the net gains from trade liberalization are positive so the gainers can compensate the losers and leave the country better off overall. Unfortunately, such compensation seldom occurs.[56]

---

[49] Commission on Human Rights, 'The right of everyone to the enjoyment of the highest attainable standard of physical and mental health: Report of the Special Rapporteur, Paul Hunt: Mission to the World Trade Organization', UN doc. E/CN.4/2004/49/Add.1 (1 March 2004) para 26.

[50] See, eg, CESCR, 'General Comment 12: Right to adequate food (Art. 11)', UN doc. E/C.12/1999/5 (12 May 1999) para 13. See also UNECOSOC, 'Report of the United Nations High Commissioner for Human Rights', UN doc. E/2007/82 (25 June 2007) para 43(c).

[51] See also Human Rights Council, 'Report of the Special Rapporteur on the right to food, Olivier De Schutter: Mission to the World Trade Organization', UN doc. A/HRC/10/5/Add.2 (25 June 2008) para 8.

[52] Joel R Paul, 'Do International Trade Institutions Contribute to Economic Growth and Development?' (2003) 44 *Virginia Journal of International Law* 285, 300; see also Gathii, above n 35, 146.

[53] Paul, above n 52, 300.

[54] Margot Salomon, *Global Responsibility for Human Rights* (Oxford University Press, Oxford, 2007) 129–30.

[55] Harrison, above n 17, 45.

[56] Stiglitz and Charlton, above n 41, 28. See also Ha-Joon Chang, *Bad Samaritans: the Myth of Free Trade and the Secret History of Capitalism* (Bloomsbury Press, New York, 2008) 72–3.

Pascal Lamy has conceded that 'strong safety nets' are needed to 'correct... imbalances between winners and losers at the national level', and that States which lack that capacity need to be 'assisted by the international community' if trade is going to generate 'collective well-being'.[57] Yet the focus of WTO law is on aggregate rather than individual welfare, and it probably 'overestimates the capacity of States, [particularly] in the developing world, to operate such redistribution of gains'.[58]

Free trade is explicitly conceived of in the preamble to the Agreement establishing the WTO as being a means to desirable ends, notably sustainable development, equitable outcomes for the developing world, full employment, and raising standards of living for all. Trade is a means to desirable ends, rather than an end in itself. All of the above-mentioned ends boost the enjoyment of recognized human rights. Yet WTO rules are not generally directed towards such outcomes: it is largely presumed that free trade rules of themselves will generate those desirable outcomes,[59] or that they will in no way retard such outcomes.

Professor John Ruggie famously suggested in 1982 that the GATT regime was based on a premise of 'embedded liberalism', whereby GATT members agreed to reduce protectionist measures, whilst simultaneously promulgating domestic welfare policies to provide safety nets for the losers, such as those suddenly exposed to competition from imports.[60] Such a bargain was necessary: a State had to 'take care of its own through regulatory intervention in order to maintain its political ability to liberalize'.[61] However, while GATT rules explicitly dictated the dismantling of certain trade barriers, they did not explicitly require the provision of welfare benefits to individuals at the domestic level. Nor were such welfare obligations mandated with the advent of the WTO.

In any case, the ethos of the GATT had evolved so as to embrace, by the time of the WTO's birth, a neo-liberal commitment to free trade and letting the market sort things out, departing from the post-war focus on government intervention to soften the impact on disadvantaged individuals of free markets. The dominant 'neoliberal' economic philosophy since the 1980s has promoted economic efficiency through the invisible hand of the market free of government intervention.[62] This agenda was aided by the policies of other international economic institutions, such as the World Bank and the IMF, which aggressively championed the removal

---

[57] Lamy, above n 11.

[58] Report of the Special Rapporteur on the right to food, *Mission to the World Trade Organization*, above n 51, para 8.

[59] See also Kinley, above n 47, 43.

[60] John Ruggie, 'International Regimes, Transactions and Change: Embedded Liberalism in the Postwar Economic Order' (1982) 36 *International Organization* 379, 393–8. See also Jeffrey L Dunoff, 'The Death of the Trade Regime' (1999) 10 *European Journal of International Law* 733, 738–9, and Gathii, above n 35, 148–50.

[61] Joel Trachtman, 'Legal Aspects of a Poverty Agenda at the WTO: Trade Law and "Global Apartheid"' (2003) 6 *Journal of International Economic Law* 3, 8.

[62] See Yong-Shik Lee, *Reclaiming Development in the World Trading System* (Cambridge University Press, Cambridge, 2006) 52; Andrew TF Lang, 'Reflecting on "Linkage": Cognitive and Institutional Change in the International Trading System' (2007) 70 *Modern Law Review* 523, 529; Robert Howse, 'From Politics to Technocracy and back again: the Fate of the Multilateral Trading Regime' (2002) 96 *American Journal of International Law* 94, 98–103; Dunoff, above n 60, 736–7. See also Gathii, above n 35, 151.

of trade barriers along with other free market reforms such as privatization and reduced government spending in their lending programmes.[63] Fewer market regulations and lesser government spending means that there are fewer government redistribution schemes: markets will not redistribute by themselves. While embedded liberalism may have underlay the GATT in theory, concerns with individual welfare did not underpin the WTO.[64]

The WTO agenda based on economic efficiency ultimately has a utilitarian or consequentialist focus, aimed at increasing aggregate net welfare.[65] Such an approach sanctions the subordination of the rights of the few to the enjoyment of the many, and tolerates short-term pain for long-term gain. This focus does not gel well with the deontological focus in human rights law and policy on the rights of each and every individual, regardless of his or her utility.[66] For example, economic utilitarianism could theoretically justify torture or slavery on the basis that they are economically justifiable.[67] Human rights law dictates that the restoration or preservation of human dignity is an end in itself, which cannot be inherently compromised by utilitarian or consequentialist considerations. Certainly, limitations on rights for the purposes of promoting the rights of others are often tolerated under international human rights law. For example, the limitation of economic, social, and cultural rights according to resource availability means that one person cannot insist on his or her enjoyment of such rights being maximized and thus compromising access by others to those resources needed to enjoy their own ICESCR rights. Most civil and political rights may be limited by reasonable and proportionate measures designed to achieve a pressing social need, such as the preservations of public order, national security, public health, public morals, or the rights of others.[68] However, the routine limitation of human rights on utilitarian economic grounds is not envisaged under international human rights law.[69]

Finally, as argued in Chapters 5 to 7, the basic premise that WTO rules in fact facilitate economic growth and 'a bigger pie' is challengeable in the case of many developing States. In fact, WTO rules may restrict the capacities of some States to develop their economies and cater for the adjustment costs of the losers from free trade. WTO rules may be diminishing the economic capacities of some States, which impacts on their abilities to discharge their human rights obligations.

---

[63] See generally, World Bank, *Economic Growth in the 1990s: Learning from a Decade of Reform* (World Bank, Washington DC, 2005) <http://www1.worldbank.org/prem/lessons1990s/> accessed 19 September 2010.

[64] See also Dunoff, above n 60, 746–7; Gathii, above n 35, 152.

[65] Frank Garcia, 'The Global Market and Human Rights: Trading away the Human Rights Principle' (1999) 7 *Brooklyn Journal of International Law* 51, 67–9.   [66] Ibid, 62–73.

[67] Ibid, 72.

[68] See, eg, Articles 12 (freedom of movement), 18 (freedom of religion), 19 (freedom of expression), 21 (freedom of assembly) and 22 (freedom of association) of the ICCPR. Some civil and political rights are absolute, and cannot be compromised in any circumstances, such as the right to be free from torture (see Article 7 ICCPR, Article 2 CAT) and the right to be free from slavery and servitude (see Articles 8(1) and 8(2) ICCPR). See also Chapter 1, text at notes 50–1.

[69] Garcia, above n 65, 75. See also Daniel M Hausman and Michael S McPherson, 'Taking Ethics Seriously: Economics and Contemporary Moral Philosophy' (1993) 31 *Journal of Economic Literature* 671, 693–6.

Cultural and economic relativism

At this point, it is appropriate to mention the related challenges of cultural and economic relativism to international human rights law, and their relevance to the WTO/human rights debate. Cultural relativist arguments postulate that the application of human rights varies according to the different cultures of States. Such arguments generally emanate from non-Western States, which is perhaps unsurprising given the oft-accepted Western philosophical origin of human rights, particularly civil and political rights. For example, Colonel Ignatius Acheampong, former Head of State in Ghana, stated that 'one man, one vote' was 'meaningless unless accompanied by the principle of one man, one bread'.[70]

One prominent branch of cultural relativist argument relates more to *economic* rather than cultural differences, hence this author has termed the argument 'economic relativism'.[71] This theory postulates that economic development must be the first priority of developing States, so the implementation of human rights can be delayed while a State develops its economy to a satisfactory level. For example, this type of argument formed part of the rationale adopted by leaders of a number of Asian states during the 1990s against the applicability of 'Western' civil and political rights in the Asian context.[72] Acceptance of this argument would indicate that trade liberalization is justified, even if it leads to human rights abuses in the short term, so long as it is likely to lead to longer term prosperity.

The economic relativist argument tends to be made by undemocratic governments against civil and political rights more than economic, social, and cultural rights, suggesting that civil and political freedoms somehow undermine the promotion of economic development in vulnerable economies. For example, it might be argued that opposition groups with a free rein distract or undermine governments in managing and achieving their economic goals, and might prompt unhelpful u-turns in economic policy. Whilst developed States can withstand and absorb subsequent economic pressures, developing States do not have that luxury.

However, civil and political rights facilitate government accountability, which helps to guard against corruption and bad governance, both of which can have devastating economic effects.[73] Entrenched dictatorships, regardless of any initial benevolence, will inevitably succumb to the temptation to benefit their own elite interests.[74]

---

[70] As quoted in Rhoda Howard, 'The Full-Belly Thesis: Should Economic Rights take Priority over Civil and Political Rights? Evidence from Sub-Saharan Africa' (1983) 5 *Human Rights Quarterly* 467, 467.

[71] Sarah Joseph, Jenny Schultz, and Melissa Castan, *The International Covenant on Civil and Political Rights: Cases, Materials and Commentary*, 2nd edn (Oxford University Press, Oxford, 2004) para 1.92.

[72] For a brief outline of the 'Asian Values Debate', see Leena Avonius and Damien Kingsbury, 'Introduction' in Leena Avonius and Damien Kingsbury (eds), *Human Rights in Asia: A Reassessment of the Asian Values Debate* (Palgrave MacMillan, New York, 2008) 1–2.

[73] See Amartya Sen, 'Human Rights and Asian Values: What Lee Kwan Yew and Le Peng Don't Understand about Asia' (1997) 217 *The New Republic* 33–40. However, see the arguments of Ha-Joon Chang at Chapter 8, text at note 84.

[74] Howard, above n 70, 475–6.

The renowned economist Amartya Sen has persuasively argued that democratic and civil rights help protect against the continuance of disastrous economic policies. For example, he argues that the economic and humanitarian disaster of the Great Leap Forward in China, which caused the deaths of up to 30 million people from 1958 to 1961, lasted so long because China's authoritarian system of government provided for no correction of Mao's misguided policies: '[n]o democratic country with opposition parties and a free press would have allowed that to happen'.[75] A study by Daniel Kaufmann of the World Bank Institute has provided emphatic empirical support for Sen's thesis.[76] Similarly, Rhoda Howard has used examples of disastrous autocratic economic policies in Africa to argue that 'continued input by those affected is necessary to ensure that economic policies are effective'.[77] Suppression of such alternative inputs can also prompt a brain drain, as professionals who propose alternative economic policies are gaoled or exiled, rather than utilized.[78]

Another problem with suppressing civil and political rights is that it closes off peaceful options for opposition political forces, who are then tempted to turn to military options, leading to a vicious cycle of coups and counter-coups, as seen in some developing countries, particularly in Africa.[79]

Economic relativist proponents have tended not to target economic, social, and cultural rights or the right to development, and indeed are ardent supporters of such rights within UN human rights bodies such as the Human Rights Council. Such rights are not inconsistent with economic development. Certainly, they place a brake on the ability of a State to maximize certain financial outcomes by, for example, prohibiting the arbitrary eviction of people to make way for development projects. However, economic, social, and cultural rights help to ensure that development is equitable and sustainable. In any case, economic, social, and cultural rights are themselves economically relative, as the extent of a State's duties varies according to its level of resources.[80]

'Pure' cultural relativism, that is relativist arguments based on differing cultures, persists as a serious challenge to universality. The arguments for and against this type of argument will not be canvassed here.[81] One point however will be

---

[75] Amartya Sen, 'Human rights and economic achievements' in Joanne R Bauer and Daniel A Bell (eds), *The East Asian Challenge for Human Rights* (Cambridge University Press, New York, 1999) 93.

[76] Daniel Kaufmann, 'Human Rights and Governance: The Empirical Challenge' in Philip Alston and Mary Robinson (eds), *Human Rights and Development: Towards Mutual Reinforcement* (Oxford University Press, New York, 2005) 352–403.

[77] Howard, above n 70, 473. See also 471–4.   [78] Ibid, 474–5.   [79] Ibid, 474.

[80] In contrast, a State's underdevelopment does not justify failures to observe civil and political rights, as in the case of appalling prison conditions or undue court delays. See Joseph, Schultz, and Castan, above n 71, para 1.101.

[81] See, generally, Jack Donnelly, *Universal Human Rights in Theory and Practice*, 2nd edn (Cornell University Press, Ithaca, 2002). The cultural relativist issue is an important one in international human rights law. However, classical cultural relativist debates (eg regarding female genital mutilation, the rights of gays and lesbians, compulsory wearing of a veil for women in some countries) are not especially relevant in the trade/human rights debate: one area where it is possibly relevant in this book concerns the commentary on China's internet restrictions at Chapter 4, Part G.

made. It seems doubtful that the cultural impact of the implementation of human rights law is any greater than the cultural impact of trade liberalization, given that trade liberalization facilitates the greater exposure of peoples to products associated with foreign cultures (for example, clothing, movies, literature, music, food), and generates profound economic effects that will force many to fundamentally change their traditional ways of life.[82]

International human rights law generally embraces universality rather than relativism,[83] though some right limitations based on culture are permissible.[84] That does not mean that human rights law dictates cultural homogeneity. In fact, cultural practices are protected under human rights law under provisions such as Article 27 of the ICCPR, Article 15 of the ICESCR, and the requirement regarding the right to food in Article 11 of the ICESCR that food must be culturally appropriate.[85] Indeed, human rights law provides a buffer against the dangers of the erosion of vulnerable minority cultures posed by certain economic development projects.[86] However, human rights law also imposes minimum standards under which certain practices which are claimed to be based in a local culture, such as female genital mutilation, prohibitions on apostasy, and persecution of gays and lesbians, are simply unacceptable.

B. Normative Relationship between the WTO and International Human Rights Law

What is the normative relationship between WTO law and international human rights law? It is controversial to argue that the WTO itself, an international organization, has human rights duties, given that it is not a party to any human rights treaties.[87] Some human rights duties arguably arise under customary international law and *jus cogens*, or under the WTO Agreements themselves. A discussion of the

---

[82] See also Jack Donnelly, 'Human rights and Asian values: a Defense of "Western" Imperialism' in Joanne R Bauer and Daniel A Bell (eds), *The East Asian Challenge for Human Rights* (Cambridge University Press, New York, 1999) 69, 81–2.

[83] See, eg, Committee on Economic Social and Cultural Rights, 'General comment No 21: Right of everyone to take part in cultural life (art. 15, para. 1(a), of the International Covenant on Economic, Social and Cultural Rights)', UN doc. E/C.12/GC/21 (21 December 2009) paras 18, 25, 64.

[84] Eg, a number of civil and political rights, such as freedom of expression may be limited by proportionate measures designed to protect public morals (see Article 19(3) ICCPR). Public morals necessarily vary between States. See, eg, *Handyside v UK* (1976) (Application no 5493/72) Series A/24. On the other hand, States do not have unlimited rights to restrict rights on the basis of public morals: the measures must be found to be reasonable and proportionate: see, eg, *Toonen v Australia*, UN doc. CCPR/C/50/D/488/1992 (4 April 1994) (Human Rights Committee).

[85] Committee on Economic Social and Cultural Rights, 'General Comment 12: The right to adequate food (Art.11)', UN doc. E/C.12/1999/5 (12 May 1999) paras 8, 11, 39.

[86] See, eg, *Ominayak v Canada*, UN doc. CCPR/C/38/D/167/1984 (10 May 1990) and *Poma Poma v Peru*, UN doc. CCPR/C/95/D/1457/2006 (24 April 2009) (both Human Rights Committee).

[87] Exceptionally, it is anticipated at the time of writing that the European Union, a regional intergovernmental organization, will become a party to the ECHR.

human rights duties, or lack thereof, of the WTO is however beyond the scope of this book.[88]

The Member States of the WTO clearly have human rights obligations.[89] In the following chapters, I will examine the extent to which, if at all, WTO rules and processes undermine the ability of States to discharge their duties to respect, protect and fulfil human rights obligations.

Is there an applicable hierarchy in international law between international human rights law and WTO law? In the case of contradictory obligations, does one of these areas of law prevail over the other? This question gives rise to the issue of fragmentation, the subject of a 2006 report by a Study Group of the International Law Commission.[90] 'Fragmentation' refers to the phenomenon of States being subjected to specialist systems of international law, such as trade law and human rights law, which have developed largely in isolation from each other.

> The result is conflicts between rules or rule-systems, deviating institutional practices and, possibly, the loss of an overall perspective on the law.[91]

Treaties should be interpreted with an assumption that States parties do not mean to contradict other international legal obligations.[92] Therefore, WTO dispute settlement bodies should endeavour to interpret the WTO Agreements, if possible, so as to conform to the parties' human rights obligations, and human rights bodies should do the same in the reciprocal situation. The relevant interpretative practices of the WTO and human rights bodies are discussed below.

In the case of conflict between two international laws, Article 53 of the Vienna Convention on the Law of Treaties dictates that peremptory or *jus cogens* norms prevail over other norms. *Jus cogens* norms constitute the inner core of customary international law norms from which no derogation is permitted.

Given its club-like purpose of granting reciprocal rights and duties to Members, WTO norms cannot be part of *jus cogens* or even customary international law: non-Members surely cannot be bound by any of its rules without receiving the benefits of MFN and National Treatment. It is uncertain which human rights norms are recognized as *jus cogens*. Certainly, one may safely cite prohibitions on genocide,[93]

---

[88] See, McBeth, above n 38, Chapters 3 and 4. See also Commission on Human Rights, 'Report of the Special Rapporteur on the right to food, Jean Ziegler', UN doc. E/CN.4/2005/47 (24 January 2005) para 38. The CESCR Committee has certainly indicated that international organizations such as the WTO have human rights obligations, see, eg, CESCR, 'General Comment No. 19: The right to social security (art. 9)', UN doc. E/C.12/GC/19 (4 February 2008) para 53.

[89] Beyond the 150 Member States, Chinese Taipei, Hong Kong, and the European Communities are also parties to the WTO. Discussion of the existence of human rights obligations for those non-State entities is beyond the scope of this book.

[90] International Law Commission, 'Fragmentation of International Law: Difficulties Arising from the Diversification and Expansion of International Law. Report of the Study Group of the International Law Commission: finalised by Martti Koskenniemi', UN doc. A/CN.4/L.682 (13 April 2006).

[91] Ibid, para 8.

[92] See Vienna Convention on the Law of Treaties (adopted 23 May 1969, entered into force 27 January 1980), 1155 UNTS 331, Article 31(3)(c).

[93] *Armed Activities on the Territory of the Congo (New Application 2002)* (Democratic Republic of Congo v Rwanda) (Jurisdiction and Admissibility/Judgment) [2006], ICJ Rep 5, para 64.

torture, apartheid, and slavery as such norms.[94] However, beyond a small core list of the prohibitions on the most egregious human rights abuses, there is little consensus on the identification of *jus cogens* human rights norms.[95]

The European Court of Justice in *Kadi and Al Barakaat International Foundation v Council of the European Union* found that fundamental human rights in EC law prevailed over an EC regulation which implemented a Security Council resolution combating terrorism. It asserted that while obligations to the Security Council might allow divergence from the common market obligations of the Treaty establishing the European Community, those obligations did not permit derogation from 'the principles that form part of the very foundations of the Community legal order, one of which is the protection of fundamental rights'.[96] That Court clearly placed human rights high in the hierarchy of European Union law, even above the commercial obligations which originally gave birth to the regional grouping. The primacy of human rights law has also been repeatedly proclaimed by the various UN treaty bodies as well as the UN's intergovernmental human rights bodies.[97] In contrast, the European Court of Human Rights has been more deferential to other areas of international law, construing the ECHR in accordance with the rules of state immunity in *McElhinney v Ireland*[98] and *Al-Adsani v UK*,[99] and rules of jurisdiction and responsibility in *Bankovic v Belgium and others*.[100]

Some treaties explicitly address potential conflicts with other treaties. The UN Charter expressly prevails over other international law obligations under Article 103. As noted above, human rights promotion is an explicit purpose in Article 1(3) of the UN, and provides for some broad if vague human rights obligations for Member States in Articles 55 and 56. The Charter does not, in contrast, explicitly refer to the promotion of trade between nations.[101] Given the placement of human rights at the core of the Charter, Adam McBeth has argued that human rights should be recognized as having a pre-eminent status in international law.[102] Furthermore, it has been persuasively argued that the UDHR represents an

---

[94] Indeed, the entire 'short list' of customary norms cited in Chapter 1, Part D, probably classify as *jus cogens* norms.

[95] See the various iterations discussed by Dinah Shelton, 'Normative Hierarchy in International Law' (2006) 100 *American Journal of International Law* 291, 309–17. See also Gabrielle Marceau, 'WTO Dispute Settlement and Human Rights' (2002) 13 *European Journal of International Law* 753, 798, and Harrison, above n 17, 58.

[96] *Kadi and al Barakaat International Foundation v Council of the European Union* (ECJ Grand Chamber 3 September 2008) Cases C-402/05 and C-415/05 P, para 304.

[97] See, eg, Committee on Economic Social and Cultural Rights, 'Statement on Globalization and its impacts of economic, social and cultural rights', UN doc. E/1999/22 (11 May 1998) para 5.

[98] (2001) 34 EHRR 322.   [99] (2001) 34 EHRR 273.

[100] (2001) 11 BHRC 435. See International Law Commission, above n 90, paras 161–4.

[101] The references in Article 55 to the 'promotion of . . . conditions of economic and social progress and development' arguably refer, insofar as it focuses on economic progress, to the ends of free trade, but not free trade itself.

[102] Adam McBeth, 'Human rights in economic globalisation' in Sarah Joseph and Adam McBeth (eds), *Research Handbook on International Human Rights Law* (Edward Elgar, Cheltenham, 2010) 144–6.

authoritative interpretation of human rights for the purposes of the Charter, thus endowing its norms with the primacy of the Charter.[103]

When two conflicting international norms are equal in value, as may be the case with some and even most human rights norms compared to WTO norms, the available tools for resolving these conflicts in international law are unhelpful. One rule is that the more specific law will prevail over the more general law.[104] For example, international humanitarian law will prevail over international human rights law in times of armed conflict if the two should conflict.[105] However, that principle does not work when the two areas of law are not concerned with the same subject matter.[106] Human rights and WTO law are not the same subject matter, though they may intersect to simultaneously impact in a particular scenario. For example, in addressing the issue of patents on medicine, it is unconvincing to claim that TRIPS is the *lex specialis* in preference to the right to health in Article 12 of ICESCR, or vice versa. A similar difficulty arises with regard to another rule for resolving conflicts, that a later treaty will prevail over an earlier treaty: Article 30 of the Vienna Convention specifies that this rule applies with regard to treaties with 'the same subject matter'.

In conclusion on this point, it is submitted that it is far more likely that a human rights norm prevails over a WTO norm as a matter of international law than the reverse proposition. Furthermore, human rights are goals or ends in themselves, whereas free trade rules are means by which certain ends, including ends that are thoroughly compatible with and even equate with human rights (such as, according to the WTO preamble, sustainable development, raising standards of living and ensuring full employment), are to be achieved.[107] It would be odd for means to prevail over ends. Certainly, this author is unaware of arguments to the effect that trade law should trump human rights law. Pascal Lamy stated in a speech in 2006:

[T]he WTO is not more important than other international organisations and WTO norms do not necessarily supersede or trump other international norms.[108]

States themselves declared the primacy of their human rights obligations in the Vienna Declaration and Plan of Action of 1993.[109] Article 1 proclaims that human rights are 'the first responsibility of governments'. However, the alleged

---

[103] See, eg, Louis Sohn, 'The Human Rights Law of the Charter' (1977) 12 *Texas International Law Journal* 129. Some support for this proposition may be gleaned from *Advisory Opinion on Legal Consequences for States of the Continued Presence of South Africa in Namibia* [1971] ICJ Rep 16, para 131.

[104] International Law Commission, above n 90, paras 56–87.

[105] See, eg, *Legality of the Use by a State of Nuclear Weapons in Armed Conflict* (Advisory Opinion), [1996] ICJ Rep 266, para 25.

[106] International Law Commission, above n 90, paras 116–18.   [107] Kinley, above n 47, 2.

[108] Pascal Lamy, 'The WTO in the Archipelago of Global Governance' (Speech at the Institute of International Studies, UC Berkeley, 14 March 2006) <http://www.wto.org/english/news_e/sppl_e/sppl20_e.htm> accessed 19 September 2010.

[109] This Declaration was concluded after a major world conference on human rights in Vienna in 1993.

primacy of international human rights law has not generally been reflected in State practice.[110]

Certainly, some have asserted that in many instances, the norms are of equal value.[111] The relevant dispute settlement bodies in such an instance are likely to prioritize their own system, so WTO bodies will apply WTO law while human rights bodies will apply human rights law.[112] In such a case, there is a danger of a *de facto* hierarchy developing, with trade rules prevailing over human rights rules, due to the stronger enforcement system under the WTO compared to the global human rights system.[113] Alternatively, States perceive greater self interest in the trade system and are therefore predisposed to compliance with that regime compared to the human rights regime,[114] which might be perceived by States as an occasionally (or commonly) unwelcome constraint on power. Pascal Lamy has acknowledged this imbalance in the international system.[115] The disproportionate strength of the trade regime compared to the human rights regime can lead to prioritization of trade norms if they conflict with human rights norms, or regulatory chill as States may fail to adopt measures to protect human rights because they fear that such measures might breach trade law.[116]

It is not necessary for the purposes of this book to prove that human rights norms prevail over those in the WTO. If conflicts exist between the two regimes, that circumstance is clearly undesirable and causes damage to the objectives and legitimacy of both regimes. Human rights suffer as the WTO regime is stronger in terms of institutional enforcement, which may lead States to prioritize WTO compliance over human rights compliance if they perceive that a choice must be made. The WTO suffers, as indeed might the entire architecture and legitimacy of global trade and business itself, as resentment by disadvantaged constituencies undermines the WTO's authority, reputation and its ability to further develop its rules.

WTO jurisprudence and human rights

So far, the WTO dispute settlement bodies have not had to directly deal with international human rights law. They have however had to deal with cases of possible conflict between WTO law and other areas of international law, such as

---

[110]   Shelton, above n 95, 294.

[111]   Robert Howse and Ruti Teitel, 'Beyond the Divide: the International Covenant on Economic Social and Cultural Rights and the World Trade Organization' in Sarah Joseph, David Kinley, and Jeff Waincymer (eds), above n 30, 39–40.   [112]   Marceau, above n 95, 797.

[113]   Salomon, above n 54, 155.

[114]   Carlos Manuel Vázquez, 'Trade Sanctions and Human Rights—Past, Present and Future' (2003) 6 *Journal of International Economic Law* 797, 808.

[115]   Pascal Lamy, 'The Place and Role of the WTO (WTO law) in the International Legal Order' (Address before the European Society of International Law, Paris, 19 May 2006). <http://www.wto .org/english/news_e/sppl_e/sppl26_e.htm> accessed 19 September 2010.

[116]   Eg, States might fail to implement pro-poor measures in respect of the provision of certain services for fear of breaching GATS: See Chapter 5, text at notes 46–57.

environmental law, as well as WTO cases on issues of relevance to human rights, such as public health and food safety.

Article 3.2 of the WTO's Understanding on Rules and Procedures Governing the Settlement of Disputes specifies that the WTO Agreements will be interpreted 'in accordance with the customary rules of interpretation', which are enshrined in the Vienna Convention on the Law of Treaties 1969. Article 31(1) of the Vienna Convention states that treaties should be interpreted in accordance with their object and purpose. McBeth argues that the WTO Agreements should therefore be interpreted in light of the preamble to the Marrakesh Agreement, including its references to 'raising standards of living', 'ensuring full employment', and 'sustainable development'.[117] The Panels and Appellate Body have not generally taken such an approach, and relatively few decisions refer to the preamble.[118] It seems that the promotion of free trade per se has more often been viewed as the object and purpose of the agreements.

Article 31(3)(c) of the Vienna Convention states that 'any relevant rules of international law applicable in the relations between the parties' should be taken into account by a body in interpreting a treaty. A WTO panel has confirmed that customary international law is relevant to the application of WTO norms.[119] The Appellate Body and Panels have used customary international law to interpret specific words in the WTO Agreements, as well as issues relating to State responsibility, standing, representation by private counsel, burden of proof, and the treatment of domestic law.[120] Therefore, where possible, the Appellate Body and Panels should construe a WTO provision in conformity with customary international law, including those human rights protected under customary law.[121] Customary law, aside from *jus cogens* norms, will not however displace inconsistent WTO norms.[122]

The Appellate Body in *US—Import Prohibition of Certain Shrimp and Shrimp Products* stated that Panels may take non-WTO treaties into account in interpreting WTO agreements.[123] It took a number of principles from environmental treaties into account in adopting a dynamic (rather than originalist) interpretation of

---

[117]   McBeth, above n 38, 108–9; see also Joe W (Chip) Pitts III, 'Corporate Social Responsibility: Current Status and Future Evolution' (2009) 6 *Rutgers Journal of Law and Public Policy* 334, 355–6, and Joe W (Chip) Pitts III, 'The First U.N. Social Forum: History and Analysis' (2002) 31 *Denver Journal of International Law* 297, 303.

[118]   See however *United States—Import Prohibition of Certain Shrimp and Shrimp Products*, WTO doc. WT/DS58/AB/R, AB-1998–4 (12 October 1998) (Report of the Appellate Body) paras 12, 17, and 129.

[119]   *Korea—Measures Affecting Government Procurement*, WTO doc. WT/DS163/R (19 June 2000) (Report of the Panel) para 7.96.

[120]   Peter Van den Bossche, *The Law and Policy of the World Trade Organization* (Cambridge University Press, Cambridge, 2005) 57.

[121]   McBeth, above n 38, 110–12.

[122]   Eg, in the *EC—Measures concerning Meat and Meat Products ('EC—Hormones')*, WTO doc. WT/DS48/AB/R (16 January 1998) (Report of the Appellate Body), the Appellate body ruled that the environmental 'precautionary principle' would not override the SPS Agreement even if it was a customary norm at paras 120–5. The Appellate Body did not determine that the precautionary principle was in fact a customary norm, as it found that its status was unclear.

[123]   Above n 118, paras 126–34.

Article XX(g) of GATT, even though not all parties in that case were parties to the relevant agreements. However, according to the WTO panel in *EC—Measures Affecting the Approval and Marketing of Biotech Products*, while the panels and the Appellate Body may choose to take a treaty into account in interpreting WTO law, they do not *have to* do so unless all WTO Members are party to the particular treaty.[124] Therefore, the *Biotech* Panel indicates that non-trade rules may be relegated to a minor role, or may even have no role, in the determination of a dispute, regardless of the dispute's non-trade impact.[125]

Joost Pauwelyn has suggested that multilateral treaty obligations, such as those under human rights and environmental treaties, may be used as a defence in WTO proceedings against claims of a breach of the WTO. His reasoning is that WTO obligations are essentially reciprocal, so third parties to a dispute will be unaffected if the reciprocal obligations between a claimant and respondent State in a dispute are modified by multilateral obligations to which both States are bound. Therefore, a State may defend itself against a claim of breach by citing its human rights obligations so long as the claimant State has similar human rights obligations.[126] Pauwelyn's theory is well considered but controversial.[127] It has not yet gained the support of WTO dispute settlement bodies.[128]

Pauwelyn concedes that a WTO panel cannot enforce another treaty obligation: human rights obligations in his view can only be used as a shield rather than a sword. The Appellate Body confirmed in *Mexico—Tax Measures on Soft Drinks and other Beverages* that it is not able to determine rights and duties under other international treaties.[129]

It seems likely that the WTO dispute settlement bodies would adopt one of the following approaches if confronted with a potential conflict between human rights laws and WTO obligations. First, if the human rights treaty was one to which every WTO Member was a party, the dispute settlement body would have to take it into account in interpreting WTO obligations. However, such unanimous membership of another treaty is virtually impossible as the WTO permits the membership of certain non-States, such as Hong Kong, Chinese Taipei, and the EC: non-States are unable to ratify most other treaties.[130] Less strict variations on this first option are for the relevant human rights treaty to bind all State Members of the WTO, or for all State Members to have either ratified or signed the treaty.[131]

---

[124] WTO doc. WT/DS291-293/R (29 September 2006) (Report of the Panel) para 7.68.

[125] See also, generally, Margaret A Young, 'The WTO's use of relevant rules of international law: an analysis of the *Biotech* case' (2007) 56 *ICLQ* 907. *Biotech* was criticized by the International Law Commission, above n 90, at para 471.

[126] Joost Pauwelyn, *Conflict of Norms in Public International Law: how WTO law relates to other norms of International Law* (Cambridge University Press, Cambridge, 2003) eg, 52ff and 491.

[127] Van den Bossche, above n 120, 63.   [128] Harrison, above n 17, 190–1.

[129] *Mexico—Tax Measures on Soft Drinks and Other Beverages*, WTO doc. WT/DS308/AB/R, AB-2005-10 (6 March 2006) (Report of the Appellate Body) para 78. Mexico had argued that a NAFTA tribunal was a more appropriate forum for determination of the dispute.

[130] Harrison, above n 17, 201.

[131] Signature to a treaty of course does not give rise to the same obligations as ratification, but it does give rise, under the Vienna Convention, to an obligation under Article 18(a) not to undermine the object and purpose of the relevant treaty.

An alternative interpretation of Article 31(3)(c) of the Vienna Convention to that in *EC—Biotech* might hold that human rights obligations have to be taken into account if the parties to a dispute are party to that treaty. However, such an interpretation, whilst perhaps preferable to the narrow approach taken in *EC—Biotech*, is not satisfactory from a human rights point of view if dispute settlement bodies consequently ignore human rights norms when those norms do not bind all parties to a dispute. For example, the US is not a party to the ICESCR so that treaty would be irrelevant in (the many) disputes involving that trading giant. The fact of US non-ratification of the ICESCR (or, as another example, Chinese non-ratification of the ICCPR) is not relevant under human rights law in delineating the scope of another State's obligations under the ICESCR (or the ICCPR).[132] This approach would also lead to States having different WTO obligations to different WTO States, in spite of the MFN obligation.[133]

A third option is for the WTO dispute settlement bodies to attempt to interpret WTO law in conformity with and in the light of relevant human rights norms, regardless of whether the parties in a case are party to a treaty protecting those norms. As noted above, the Appellate Body used environmental treaties as interpretive aids in *Shrimp*, even though the parties to the case were not all parties to those treaties, though it did not explicitly base its decision on Article 31(3)(c) of the Vienna Convention. Pauwelyn has suggested that such norms might be relevant under Article 31(3)(c) if they are norms that are at least 'implicitly accepted or tolerated by all WTO members'.[134] Given that all State members of the WTO have endorsed the UDHR when joining the UN, its norms, which are essentially reflected in the two Covenants, may satisfy Pauwelyn's criteria. Furthermore, all State Members are bound by the UN Charter and its human rights provisions, which may incorporate the UDHR.[135] The interpretation of WTO norms in the light of the UDHR and all key global human rights treaties, especially if adopted on a mandatory rather than a discretionary basis by Panels and the Appellate Body, is of course the most preferable of the three approaches from a human rights point of view. This approach is arguably the most preferable from a trade point of view as well, as it removes the possibility of splintered obligations and reinforces the legitimacy of the trade regime by minimizing conflicts with other international law regimes.

In all three scenarios, it seems likely that the dispute settlement bodies would hold that WTO obligations prevailed over human rights obligations in the case of conflicts that could not be resolved by interpretation, except in the rare instance that the human right at issue was found to be a *jus cogens* obligation.[136]

The interpretation of WTO rules by the Panels and the Appellate Body are examined further in Chapter 4.

---

[132] See Harrison, above n 17, 202–3.
[133] It seems likely that that fact influenced the strict approach adopted in *EC—Biotech*, above n 124, see also para 7.71.
[134] Joost Pauwelyn, 'The Role of Public International Law in the WTO: How Far Can We Go?' (2001) 95 *American Journal of International Law* 535, 575–6.   [135] See Chapter 1, text at note 30.
[136] See generally, Marceau, above n 95, 756, 791–5; Harrison, above n 17, 191.

Human rights jurisprudence and the WTO

The human rights bodies have been more bullish than the WTO Panels and Appellate Body in asserting the primacy of their area of law over other areas of law. Given the common assertion by human rights bodies of the primacy of human rights law, it is not surprising that human rights bodies have felt less need to read human rights law as being subject to other areas of international law.

The Committee on Economic Social and Cultural Rights has said that States must take their ICESCR obligations into account when entering into treaties or joining international organizations. For example, the Committee stated that a violation of the right to food would arise if a State failed to take the right into account 'when entering into agreements with other States or with international organizations'.[137] In General Comment 14 on the right to health, the Committee stated:

> In relation to the conclusion of other international agreements, States parties should take steps to ensure that these instruments do not adversely impact upon the right to health. Similarly, States parties have an obligation to ensure that their actions as members of international organizations take due account of the right to health.[138]

Therefore, according to the Committee, a State should take its ICESCR obligations into account when joining the WTO, when negotiating rules in the WTO, when seeking to enforce those rules, and when implementing them at home.[139]

Furthermore, in *Kadi*, the European Court of Justice struck down an EC regulation on the basis that it breached fundamental human rights in EC law, even though the regulation implemented a legal regime imposed by Security Council resolutions.[140] A similar, albeit less conclusive, decision was reached by the HRC in *Sayadi and Vinck v Belgium*.[141] The legal arguments in favour of deference to the Security Council, in light of the apparently superior legal position of Security Council resolutions under Articles 25 and 103 of the UN Charter, are far stronger than any argument in favour of deference to the WTO. Yet the former arguments seem to have been rejected by the ECJ and perhaps the HRC.

The European Court of Human Rights, in *Bosphorus Airways v Ireland*, has also found that it is competent to review the actions of States taken to implement EC regulations which in turn implement Security Council resolutions. It went on to find that there was a presumption that actions taken to implement international obligations as a member of an international organization were compatible with the

---

[137] CESCR, above n 50, para 19.

[138] CESCR 'General Comment 14: The right to the highest attainable standard of health (article 12)', UN doc. E/C.12/2000/4 (11 August 2000) para 39.

[139] See generally, Howse and Teitel, above n 111.

[140] See *Kadi*, above n 96: the relevant regulation enforced the sanctions regime imposed against persons suspected of links with terrorists under various Security Council resolutions.

[141] *Sayadi and Vinck v Belgium* UN doc. CCPR/C/94/D/1472/2006 (2008) (Human Rights Committee). The case again concerned actions taken to implement the Security Council sanctions regime against persons suspected of links to terrorism. The HRC found that it was competent to decide if Belgium had violated the ICCPR in implementing its obligations to the Security Council. In the result, the HRC found that Belgium's impugned actions had not in fact been required under the relevant Security Council resolutions, so its ultimate findings of violation against Belgium did not signal a conflict between the ICCPR and a Security Council resolution.

ECHR if the relevant organization provided equivalent or comparable protection of the rights recognized in the ECHR: no violation was ultimately found.[142] While such a presumption might apply in the context of EC regulations, it is doubtful that it would apply in the context of WTO obligations.[143]

Therefore, under international human rights law it is safe to assume that WTO obligations do not absolve a State from its human rights obligations if the obligations should clash. For example, it is no defence in international human rights law for a State to claim that a breach of the right to health entailed in the introduction of patents on life-saving drugs which price them out of the reach of the poor is justified on the basis that the measure is required under TRIPS.[144]

It may be noted that both the HRC[145] and the European Court[146] have found on the facts presented in particular cases that single States are not responsible for the actions of international organizations themselves. However, a State still violates its human rights obligations when it takes measures to comply with a WTO rule if that implementation breaches human rights (a situation analogous to the case of *Kadi*), and perhaps in regard to its own actions in voting within an international institution for a rights violating rule or in enforcing an international rule that harms human rights against another State. The latter example brings up the issue of a State's human rights responsibility for its extraterritorial actions and the extraterritorial impacts of its actions or omissions. That issue is discussed in Chapter 8.

C. Conclusion

In this chapter, it has been argued that the WTO and human rights have divergent philosophical backgrounds and goals, contrary to the claims of, for example, Pascal Lamy and Professor Ernst-Ulrich Petersmann. The normative relationship between WTO law and human rights law is complex. At least some if not all human rights norms are likely to be hierarchically superior within international law to WTO law. This position is reflected in the case law and statements of numerous human rights bodies as well as the European Court of Justice. On the other hand, while WTO Panels and the Appellate Body have not asserted any normative superiority of WTO law, they have certainly not conceded any inferiority of WTO law.

---

[142] *Bosphorus Hava Yollari Turizm ve Ticaret Anonim Şirketi (Bosphorus Airways) v Ireland* (2006) 42 EHRR 1, para 156. See also *Waite and Kennedy v Germany* (1999) 30 EHRR 261, para 67.

[143] EC regulations operate within the context of the European Union, which played a far larger role in the protection of human rights, even before the advent of the Charter of Fundamental Rights of the European Union, than the WTO.

[144] See Chapter 7 for discussion of the merits of the premise of the example.

[145] *H.v.d.P. v Netherlands* CCPR/C/29/D/217/1986 (8 April 1987).

[146] *Behrami and Behrami v France and Saramati v France, Germany and Norway* (2007) 45 EHRR SE10.

3

Democratic Deficit and the WTO

This chapter will analyse arguments that the WTO suffers from a 'democratic deficit'. Such a deficit would cast doubt on the legitimacy and perhaps the desirability of the WTO's rules.[1] This chapter first outlines the claim that WTO internal processes, such as negotiation and dispute settlement, undermine the capacities of States to act in accordance with the wishes of their populations. A related argument, which is the focus of the opening part of this chapter, is that those same processes act to the disadvantage of particular constituencies, namely developing States and social justice interests. Secondly, the relevance to these issues of international human rights law, particularly the right of political participation in Article 25 of the International Covenant on Civil and Political Rights 1966 (ICCPR), will be explained. Thirdly, many of the alleged democratic deficits of and within the WTO afflict other international regimes. In this regard, a comparison between the WTO regime and the international human rights regime is undertaken in order to identify whether democratic deficiencies within the WTO are of greater concern than the general democratic deficiencies that exist at the international level of governance. Fourthly, I briefly address arguments regarding the effect on democratic practices of the WTO. That section addresses the substantive question of whether the WTO in fact helps to foster democracy in nations, regardless of any lack of internal democratic legitimacy. The fifth section addresses the proposition that the WTO enhances the power of developing States, regardless of internal procedural flaws, due to its multilateral nature. The sixth section concludes the chapter.

A. The Two Components to the WTO/ Democratic Deficit Argument

There are two strands to the 'democratic deficit' arguments. First, there are arguments regarding the substance of WTO rules, the WTO's 'output'.[2] A general contention of critics is that WTO rules unduly restrict the regulatory capacities of

---

[1] See also Sarah Joseph, 'Democratic Deficit, Participation and the WTO' in Sarah Joseph, David Kinley, and Jeff Waincymer (eds), *The World Trade Organization and Human Rights: Interdisciplinary Perspectives* (Edward Elgar, Cheltenham, 2009) 313–43.

[2] I have respectfully borrowed the terminology of 'output' and 'input' (below) from Robert O Keohane and Joseph S Nye Jr, 'The Club Model of Multilateral Cooperation and the World Trade Organization: Problems of Democratic Legitimacy' (Working Paper No 4, John F Kennedy School of Government, undated) <http://www.hks.harvard.edu/visions/publication/keohane_nye.pdf> accessed 24 October 2010.

States, which is problematic if WTO rules undermine the ability of States to enact laws that reflect the democratic will of their people.[3] For example, in *European Communities—Measures Concerning Meat and Meat Products (Hormones)*, the Panel and the Appellate Body decided that the ban on the import of hormone-treated meat by the European Communities was a breach of the Agreement on the Application of Sanitary and Phytosanitary Measures (SPS).[4] The lifting of the ban would be likely to be against the wishes of the majority of European peoples and consumers, who fear that such hormones could be unsafe for their health. Hence, the EC has chosen to maintain the ban and suffer consequent trade sanctions in accordance with WTO rules.[5] A similar issue could arise in the future regarding the EC's restrictions on imports of genetically modified organisms (GMOs).[6]

The second and intrinsically related component to the 'democratic deficit' arguments concerns WTO internal processes,[7] that is its 'input'. If the WTO's input legitimacy is lacking, that circumstance casts doubt on the legitimacy of the substantive rules, that is the output, generated by those processes.[8]

There is commonly little democratic input into a State's decision to join the WTO, even though that decision generates binding WTO obligations which can have a profound impact on people's lives and livelihoods. For example, ratification is often a function of the executive government, rather than the representative legislative arm of a national government. Even if WTO proposals are put before a State's legislature, it is extremely difficult for certain States, especially those that lack economic power, to retreat and back away from a deal in the final stages. This is due to the consensus requirement in the WTO that all must adhere to all of the concluded treaties. It would be extremely difficult for a small State to 'hold out' against all other WTO members.[9]

---

[3] Jeffrey L Dunoff, 'The Death of the Trade Regime' (1999) 10 *European Journal of International Law* 733, 758.

[4] *European Communities—Measures Affecting Meat and Meat Products*, WTO doc. WT/DS26/AB/R, WT/DS48/AB/R, AB-1997-4 (16 January 1998) (Appellate Body Report) ('*EC—Hormones*').

[5] See Grace Skogstad, 'International Institutions and Food Safety Regulation: Values in Conflict' in Ian Holland and Jenny Flemings (eds), *Government Reformed: Values and New Political Institutions* (Ashgate, Dartmouth, 2003) 121. The dispute now seems to be resolved, though the resolution has not involved the lifting of the ban: see, eg, 'For now, an end to the beef hormone dispute', July 2009, at <http://www.thebeefsite.com/articles/2074/for-now-an-end-to-the-beef-hormone-dispute> accessed 26 April 2010.

[6] *European Communities—Measures Affecting the Approval and Marketing of Biotech Products*, WTO docs. WT/DS291/R, WT/DS292/R, WT/DS293/R (29 September 2006) (Report of the Panel) ('*EC—Biotech*') concerned a challenge to a *de facto* moratorium on the approval of GMOs by the EC, as well as bans on GMOs issued by certain individual EC States. The relevant moratorium and bans were found to breach the SPS on the basis that risk assessments on GMOs had not been carried out, or had been unduly delayed. Thus, the substantive issue of whether imports of GMO foods can be restricted or banned was not addressed.

[7] Thomas Cottier, 'Preparing for Structural Reform of the WTO' (2007) 10 *Journal of International Economic Law* 497, 499.

[8] Kal Raustiala, 'Rethinking the sovereignty debate in international economic law' (2003) 6 *Journal of International Economic Law* 841, 862; Daniel C Esty, 'The World Trade Organization's legitimacy crisis' (2002) 1 *World Trade Review* 7, 15–16.

[9] Human Rights Council, 'Report of the Special Rapporteur on the right to food, Olivier De Schutter: Mission to the World Trade Organization', UN doc. A/HRC/10/5/Add.2 (25 June 2008) para 40.

In any case, people have historically not been well informed of the process of negotiating agreements, standards, or accession deals which, historically, have been negotiated by trade technocrats in secret. Negotiating teams have tended to represent a narrow range of interests, and are not necessarily skilled at anticipating or appreciating the 'non-trade' impacts of trade deals, for example in the fields of human rights, environment, and health. Indeed, the branches of government concerned with human rights generally have little input into trade negotiations.[10] There is a need for governments to take a more holistic and 'joined-up' approach to their international obligations, so that their trade experts and human rights experts liaise.[11] Indeed, former World Bank economist Joseph Stiglitz has suggested that trade negotiations are too important to be left to trade ministries.[12] This commercial bias is exacerbated by the fact that the non-State actors directly involved in negotiations normally represent business interests rather than other elements of civil society.[13] For example, the TRIPS agreement was a response to lobbying by a small number of business executives,[14] while the Agreement on Agriculture was reportedly originally drafted by Dan Amstutz, a trade representative who was a former Vice-President of Cargill, one of the major global agribusiness firms.[15] It is arguable that the WTO negotiation process is simply amplifying the lobbying power of actors who already have huge national influence, namely multinational corporations, the major engines of global trade.[16]

'Non-trade' interests

Given the dominant commercial ethos of WTO negotiators, the negotiated rules are naturally dominated by free trade and commercial values. Furthermore, such values are likely prioritized where they conflict with, or diverge from, other values.[17] For example, food safety laws, which have a significant impact on the human rights to adequate standards of health care and food, are analysed in terms

[10] See, eg, Commission on Human Rights, 'Report of the Special Rapporteur on the right to food, Jean Ziegler', UN doc. E/CN.4/2005/47 (24 January 2005) para 40.
[11] Commission on Human Rights, 'The Right of everyone to the enjoyment of the highest attainable standard of physical and mental health: Report of the Special Rapporteur, Paul Hunt: Mission to the World Trade Organization', UN doc. E/CN.4/2004/49/Add.1 (1 March 2004) paras 9–10, and 65.
[12] Joseph Stiglitz, 'Social Justice and Global Trade' (2006) 169 *Far Eastern Economic Review* 18, 22. See also World Bank, *World Development Report 2006: Equity and Development* (World Bank, Washington DC, 2006) 178.
[13] Ilan Kapoor, 'Deliberative democracy and the WTO' (2004) 11 *Review of International Political Economy* 522, 530.
[14] See, generally, Susan K Sell, *Private Power, Public Law: the Globalization of Intellectual Property Rights* (Cambridge University Press, Cambridge, 2003).
[15] Sophia Murphy, *Concentrated Market Power and Agricultural Trade*, August 2006 (Heinrich Boell Stiftung, Berlin, 2006) 30.
[16] See United Nations Conference on Trade and Development (UNCTAD), *World Investment Report 2002, Transnational Corporations and Export Competitiveness*, UN doc. UNCTAD/WIR/2002 (UN, Geneva, 2002) 153, stating that two thirds of world trade in the late 1990s was conducted by MNCs, including trade within MNCs. See also Keohane and Nye, above n 2, 17.
[17] Esty, above n 8, 13.

of their scientific justifiability under the SPS, with a focus on their impact on trade flows rather than human health.[18] Similarly, environmental measures are assessed according to their trade impact, rather than their environmental impact.[19] As many regulations impact on trade (and conversely, trade impacts on many social issues), the foregrounding of trade impacts leads to a backgrounding of so-called non-trade concerns.[20] If 'trade' and 'non-trade' values should clash or diverge from each other, the latter seem to be disadvantaged.

As non-trade interests, such as human rights and environmental lobbies, were not effectively represented in the negotiating phase of the Uruguay Round, it is arguably illegitimate for WTO institutions subsequently to make decisions based on the results of those negotiations that impact on those same non-trade interests.[21] Yet the WTO Panels and the Appellate Bodies have made such decisions in areas regarding the environment and health.[22] A related contention is that the priority given to trade values within the WTO undermines the ability of States to respect international obligations in the non-trade arena. For example, it has been argued that the *Beef Hormone* decision undermined the duty of the States in the European Union (EU) to respect the right to an adequate standard of health in the context of food safety.[23] Indeed, a further advantage to trade interests is that the WTO provides for no process whereby the adverse affects of a trade liberalizing measure can be challenged. If, as a hypothetical example, illnesses and deaths had arisen from hormone-injected beef introduced into the European market pursuant to free trade rules, the WTO would have provided no platform for an affected person to challenge the measures that allowed the beef into the marketplace. Therefore, the WTO does not provide for a true balancing of trade and non-trade interests, as the latter only become relevant when States choose to invoke them as justifications to restrict trade (and thus risk non-compliance with the WTO), rather than when States might threaten non-trade interests by removing barriers to trade in, for example, a harmful product.[24]

---

[18] See David M. Driesen, 'What is Free Trade? The Real Issue Lurking behind the Trade and Environment Debate' (2001) 41 *Virginia Journal of International Law* 279, 295–300. See also Frank Garcia, 'The Global Market and Human Rights: Trading away the Human Rights Principle' (1999) 7 *Brooklyn Journal of International Law* 51, 61.

[19] Driesen, above n 18, 325–7.

[20] See, on this point generally, Andrew TF Lang, 'Reflecting on "Linkage": Cognitive and Institutional Change in the International Trading System' (2007) 70 *Modern Law Review* 523; see also Sara Dillon, 'A Farewell to "Linkage": International Trade Law and Global Sustainability Indicators' (2002) 51 *Rutgers Law Review* 87, 103, 114; Dunoff, above n 3, 746. I will not always precede the words 'non-trade' with the term 'so-called', but the term should be read in throughout this book, because the division between trade and non-trade issues is highly contestible: see generally, Lang.

[21] This is a point commonly made by Driesen, above n 18, eg at 324. See also Esty, above n 8, 13 and Joseph Stiglitz, *Making Globalization Work* (Penguin, London, 2007) 131.

[22] See, eg, *Brazil—Measures Affecting Imports of Retreaded Tyres*, WTO doc. WT/DS332/AB/R (3 December 2007) (Report of the Appellate Body).

[23] Caroline Dommen, 'Raising Human Rights Concerns in the World Trade Organization: Actors, Processes and Possible Strategies' (2002) 24 *Human Rights Quarterly* 1, 17–19. See Chapter 4 below for further discussion of this point.

[24] Anne Orford, 'Beyond Harmonization: Trade, Human Rights and the Economy of Sacrifice' (2005) 18 *Leiden Journal of International Law* 179, 195.

Proposals for the inclusion of social justice and other non-governmental organizations (NGOs) within the negotiating process may be rebuffed on the basis that such organizations themselves lack democratic credentials.[25] Nevertheless, as Steve Charnovitz has argued, input into negotiations by non-trade interest groups, as well as the non-trade areas of government, would ensure that alternative ideas and values are injected into the WTO decision and policy making process, improving its local 'marketplace of ideas'. A broader spectrum of input will improve the legitimacy of the WTO's output.[26]

Relations between the WTO and other organizations, whether intergovernmental or non-governmental, are governed by Article V of the Marrakesh Agreement. Article V provides briefly in paragraph 2 that the 'General Council may make appropriate arrangements for consultation and cooperation with non-governmental organizations concerned with matters related to those of the WTO.' Pursuant to this mandate, the WTO adopted the one-page 'Guidelines for Arrangements with Non-Governmental Organizations' in 1996.[27] These guidelines recognize that NGOs are a 'valuable resource' that have a role 'to increase the awareness of the public in respect of WTO activities'. However, the guidelines also clarified the limits of NGO involvement by confirming that, pursuant to a 'broadly held view' within the WTO, 'it would not be possible for NGOs to be directly involved in the work of the WTO or its meetings'.

To be sure, WTO practices regarding participation and transparency are a great improvement upon those of the GATT. NGOs have run side events at Ministerial conferences since the WTO's first Ministerial in Singapore in 1996, during which there are plenty of opportunities for interaction between State delegations, WTO personnel and NGOs. There are also regular briefings for NGOs by the Secretariat on the work of the various WTO governing bodies.[28] NGO participation in Ministerial meetings has grown exponentially; 159 NGOs were registered to participate in Singapore in 1996 while 1,081 were registered to participate in Hong Kong in 2005.[29]

The WTO has also increased its engagement with non-trade groups, including NGOs and intergovernmental organizations such as the UN Food and Agriculture Organization.[30] However, there remains much scope for enhanced cooperation

---

[25] This point was emphasized in WTO, *The Future of the WTO: Addressing Institutional Challenges in the New Millennium* (Report by the Consultative Board of the Director-General of the WTO to the former Director-General Supachai Panitchpakdi) (WTO, Geneva, 2004) 45–7 (Sutherland Report).

[26] Steve Charnovitz, 'The WTO and Cosmopolitics' (2004) 7 *Journal of International Economic Law* 675, 680.

[27] WTO, 'Guidelines for arrangements on relations with Non-Governmental Organizations', WTO doc. WT/L/162 (Decision adopted by the General Council on 18 July 1996) (23 July 1996).

[28] See World Trade Organization, 'Relations with Non-Governmental Organizations/Civil Society', at <http://www.wto.org/english/forums_e/ngo_e/intro_e.htm> accessed 25 October 2010.

[29] Ciel Grossman, Amy Herrick, and Ting Shao, *From Gas Masks to Chocolate Fountains: The Emerging Influence of NGOs in the WTO and the Implications for Global Trade Governance*, February 2006 (prepared for Charles Leopold Foundation for the Progress of Humankind and the Institute for a New Reflection on Governance) 8.

[30] Charnovitz, above n 26, 676–7; Sutherland Report, above n 25, 41–3.

with such groups.[31] Of particular note is that no human rights organization has observer status at the WTO. Indeed, despite the numerous intersections between trade and health issues,[32] the Special Rapporteur on the Right to Health commented in 2004 that his mission to the WTO at that time was 'one of the first occasions' on which WTO members and observers had discussed the right to health.[33] Four years later, the first (and so far only) mission by the Special Rapporteur on the Right to Food was conducted in 2008, many years after the WTO should have been aware of pervasive concerns regarding the effect of its rules on the right to food.[34]

Much WTO information, including policy documents and plain language explanations of its mandate and purpose, is readily available, particularly via its excellent website. Many nations now publish a substantial proportion, if not all, of their negotiating proposals, allowing time for significant outside input.[35]

Some States have included NGOs and other representatives with social interests beyond trade on their delegations, thus lending them a presence 'at the table',[36] though such people 'do not participate typically in all negotiating activities'.[37] There is no doubt that NGOs, through general lobbying and also through bilateral engagements with separate country delegations,[38] have significantly influenced a number of Doha round developments, such as the WTO's initiatives on access to medicine, and the decision in the Hong Kong Ministerial to address protectionism in the cotton industry (which has devastating effects on the livelihoods of cotton farmers in some of the world's poorest States in Western Africa) as an issue separated out from the broader rubric of agricultural negotiations.[39] However, the impact of these initiatives must not be overstated. After all, the rules concluded after the Uruguay round, which was undoubtedly flawed in terms of participation by social justice bodies, are the same rules which essentially prevail today. The initiatives regarding access to medicines, discussed in detail in Chapter 6, are a rare instance of actual new rules concluded since 1995 (though most of those initiatives probably only clarify existing rules). In contrast, while significant progress on cotton arose before and during the Hong Kong Ministerial of 2005, little progress

---

[31] Dommen, above n 23, 44–5.

[32] See, eg, Article XX(b) of GATT and the SPS.

[33] See Report of the Special Rapporteur on Right of everyone to the enjoyment of the highest attainable standard of physical and mental health, Paul Hunt, Mission to the World Trade Organization, above n 11, para 5.

[34] See Report of the Special Rapporteur on the Right to Food, above n 9.

[35] Commission on Human Rights, 'Mainstreaming the right to development into international trade law and policy at the World Trade Organization (paper prepared by Prof. Robert Howse)', UN doc. E/CN.4/Sub.2/2004/17 (9 June 2004) para 42. Of course, a State's original negotiating position may transform considerably throughout a Ministerial meeting. Also compare Charnovitz, above n 26, 679.

[36] Seem Sapra, 'The WTO System of Trade Governance: The Stale NGO Debate and the Appropriate Role for Non-State Actors' (2009) 11 *Oregon Review of International Law* 71, 90.

[37] Howse, above n 35, para 42. See also Grossman, Herrick, and Shao, above n 29, at 12, and Carin Smaller and Sophia Murphy, *Bridging the Divide: a human rights vision for global food trade* (Institute of Agriculture and Trade Policy, Geneva, 2008) 11.

[38] Sapra, above n 36, 77.

[39] Ibid, 91. See generally, Grossman, Herrick, and Shao, above n 29.

on that issue has been made since, and the rules have not yet been amended to the satisfaction of NGOs and cotton farmers in developing States.[40]

Developing States

Just as there is a bias within the WTO against 'non-trade' interests, there is a bias in WTO processes against developing States (sometimes referred to in this book as 'the South') in favour of industrialized States (sometimes referred to in this book as 'the North'). WTO Members are driven by domestic political agendas to attempt to carve a bargain that is most favourable to their own industries, rather than a fair bargain.[41] A fair deal might still eventuate by default, as negotiators are forced to compromise if everyone has the same cut-throat attitude, but only if negotiating teams possess equal power. However, the strongest Members within the WTO, such as the US and the EC, have clearly exercised greater influence over the negotiations leading up to the WTO and Doha round negotiations than weaker countries, especially small developing countries. Even though the WTO treaties were adopted by consensus, and future negotiating outcomes must be approved by consensus, Professor Thomas Cottier has suggested that the WTO 'in fact operates under a system of de facto preponderance, reflecting political clout and market size'.[42] It is unrealistic to expect small states to hold up the entire WTO membership to seek a more appropriate deal, given the enormous political pressure that would be brought to bear on them.[43]

Furthermore, negotiators and other relevant personnel from developing States may lack the technical expertise to effectively represent their nations' interests.[44] Indeed, huge discrepancies may arise in the size of negotiating delegations. In the Hong Kong Ministerial meeting in 2005, the US had 356 delegates while Burundi had three.[45] Given the intense ongoing nature of WTO negotiations one can surmise that the US delegates were far better informed (and slept!) than those from Burundi. The least developed WTO members are unable to maintain WTO

---

[40] See also Chapter 9, text at notes 50–4.

[41] See, generally, Gregory C Shaffer, *Defending Interests: Public Private Partnerships in WTO Litigation* (Brookings Institution Press, Washington DC, 2003) 137. See also Paul Collier, *The Bottom Billion* (Oxford University Press, New York, 2008) 171; Stiglitz, above n 21, 278.

[42] Cottier, above n 7, 502. See also Bhagirath Lal Das (former Indian Ambassador and Permanent Representative to the GATT), 'Why the WTO decision-making system of "consensus" works against the South' (undated) < http://www.twnside.org.sg/title/bgl3-cn.htm> accessed 19 September 2010.

[43] See also Ha-Joon Chang, *Bad Samaritans: the Myth of Free Trade and the Secret History of Capitalism* (Bloomsbury Press, New York, 2008) 36–7.

[44] See generally, Commission on Human Rights, 'Analytical Study of the High Commissioner for Human Rights on the fundamental principle of participation and its application in the context of globalization: Report of the High Commissioner', UN doc. E/CN.4/2005/41 (23 December 2004) 13 [hereafter, UNHCHR].

[45] See Oxfam, 'What Happened in Hong Kong? Initial Analysis of the WTO Ministerial (Oxfam Briefing Paper 85, December, 2005), 5 <http://www.oxfam.org/en/files/bp85_hongkong> accessed 19 September 2010.

missions in Geneva, so they cannot participate in the numerous interim meetings at WTO headquarters.[46]

The negotiating culture of the GATT served to exclude numerous Members from important aspects of deal-brokering. Policies and treaties were negotiated in notorious 'Green Room' meetings to which only certain Members were invited, and in which discussions were secret. Green Room decisions were then presented to other Members as *faits accomplis*. Of course, this process not only generated substantively unfair outcomes (unsurprisingly, favouring the Green Room participants) but also feelings of marginalization and resentment amongst those excluded.[47]

Under-participation by developing States at various stages in WTO negotiating processes means that the negotiated outcomes of the Uruguay Round are less likely to be in their interests.[48] Indeed, the current Director-General of the WTO, Pascal Lamy, has conceded that current WTO rules favour the rich and economically powerful States over the poor and comparatively powerless States.[49] This imbalance is explored in Chapters 5 and 6.

Other examples of participation difficulties by developing States arise from the SPS and TBT Agreements. These two agreements regulate the use of certain non-tariff barriers, namely sanitary and phytosanitary measures and technical standards. Implementation of these agreements relies heavily on recognized international standards and standard setting bodies.[50] Relevant organizations for the SPS Agreement are the so-called 'three sisters':[51] the International Plant Protection Convention (regarding plant health), the World Organisation for Animal Health (regarding animal health), and the Codex Alimentarius Commission (regarding food safety). Relevant bodies for the TBT include the International Standards Organization (ISO).

Jürgen Kurtz has pointed out the inadequate level of developing country participation in some of these organizations. Codex, for example, often bases its risk assessments on 'data from only 20 of its 170 members'.[52] A Codex standard is often adopted while many developing State members are not present. Kurtz reports that Codex nearly adopted a couscous standard defining it as a wheat product even though couscous is made from non-wheat crops in Sub-Saharan Africa. The definition was changed only at a late stage due to the timely intervention of a single

[46] Kapoor, above n 13, 529. The World Bank reported in 2005 that half of the 38 Sub-Saharan WTO membership had no resident delegate in Geneva: World Development Report 2006, above n 12, 67.

[47] Joseph E Stiglitz and Andrew Charlton, *Fair Trade for All* (Oxford University Press, New York, 2005) 82.

[48] UNHCHR, above n 44, paras 33–4.

[49] Pascal Lamy, 'It's Time for a new "Geneva Consensus" on making trade work for development' (Emile Noel Lecture New York University Law School, New York, 30 October 2006) <http://www.wto.org/english/news_e/sppl_e/sppl45_e.htm> accessed 19 September 2010.

[50] Jürgen Kurtz, 'A Look Behind the Mirror: Standardization, Institutions and the WTO SPS and TBT Agreements' (2007) 30 *University of New South Wales* 504, 517.

[51] AusAID, 'The WTO Sanitary and Phytosanitary (SPS) Agreement' (Department of Agriculture, Fisheries and Forestry, Canberra, undated) 9.

[52] Kurtz, above n 50, 519.

representative from Sub-Saharan Africa.[53] Similar imbalances in participation rates are evident in the ISO.[54]

There have been improvements in WTO processes designed to facilitate greater participation by all Members. The Green Room has been significantly reformed, with more invitees and a more transparent process. The focus in these smaller group discussions is on consensus building rather than on decision making, so Members not involved in the particular discussions are not presented with 'take it or leave it' propositions.[55] The WTO is also attempting to provide greater technical support to improve the negotiating and technical capacities of developing countries through, for example, the *Integrated Framework for Trade-Related Technical Assistance to Least Developed Countries*,[56] which coordinates policy efforts in this regard between the WTO and other international financial and development agencies, and identifies technical assistance needs in relevant States. Since 2001, the WTO has adopted annual Technical Assistance and Training Plans designed to provide training and information to improve the capacities of the poorest States, including their capacities to participate in negotiations.

Furthermore, in the current Doha round of WTO negotiations, developing States have formed stronger coalitions to counterbalance the traditional power of the US and the EC.[57] The negotiating clout of big developing States with huge markets such as India, Brazil, and China cannot be doubted. However, this balancing of power within WTO negotiations has helped to stall the current negotiations, so the unfair 1995 rules largely prevail. Furthermore, while strong developing States such as China, Brazil, and India have accrued greater negotiating muscle, the same cannot be said for the many States with small, vulnerable economies. The Pacific Island WTO members have pressed for the recognition of a new grouping within the WTO of 'Small Vulnerable States'. Such a grouping has not been created, though there is a commitment to integrate such States more fully into the global trading system.[58] Compliance with this vague promise, contained in the Doha Ministerial Declaration of 2001,[59] is difficult to ascertain.

The disadvantages for acceding States in negotiating to join the WTO are worse than those experienced by developing States during the Uruguay Round. Acceding States have been required to accept more onerous undertakings than existing members without reciprocal guarantees.[60] Existing WTO Members have a right of veto to hold as a bargaining chip, while an acceding member, particularly one with a weak economy, has few if any bargaining chips. An acceding State will also have comparatively little negotiating experience in the WTO milieu, and will find itself pitted against experienced trade negotiators from major economic powers, who are largely concerned with extracting the best deal possible for their own country

---

[53] Ibid, 519.   [54] Ibid, 519–23.
[55] Amrita Narlikar, *The World Trade Organization: A Very Short Introduction* (Oxford University Press, New York, 2005) 146.
[56] WTO doc. WT/MIN (96)/14 (7 January 1997).   [57] See Narlikar, above n 55, 112–13.
[58] See Hong Kong Declaration, WT/MIN(05)/W/3/Rev.2, 18 December 2005, para 21.
[59] Doha Ministerial Declaration, WT/MIN(01)/DEC/1, 20 November 2001, para 35.
[60] See Chapter 5, text at notes 89–100.

or with establishing favourable negotiating precedents for the future, rather than with the development needs of the acceding State.[61]

Dispute settlement

The WTO's Dispute Settlement System is probably the most powerful international dispute system in the world.[62] There is a high level of compliance with the findings of adopted Panel and Appellate Body reports,[63] as non-compliance can result in the imposition of economic countermeasures on the recalcitrant Member by the victorious Member. Indeed, the dispute settlement bodies are arguably disproportionately powerful within the WTO.[64] Their decisions can only be overruled by consensus, which is improbable given that a vindicated Member is unlikely to vote against its own victory. The 'law-making' role of the WTO's 'judiciary' is presently more consequential than was possibly ever envisaged, as the legislative process has stalled during the Doha round.[65]

There are criticisms regarding the expertise, accountability and transparency of the WTO's Panels and its Appellate Body. Decisions, especially at first instance, are made by trade experts, who may not be particularly conversant with non-trade issues such as human rights, which can again lead to an undue dominance of trade values over potentially competing values. Hearings are closed to the public unless all parties consent,[66] though final decisions by Panels and Appellate Bodies are publicly available.

Even though the dispute settlement process is only open to States, private commercial interests have been effectively represented in that dispute settlement process.[67] For example, some cases are colloquially known by the names of the private interests behind the litigation, rather than by the States who 'fought' the case: the 'Kodak/Fuji' case is one such example.[68] The dispute between Antigua and

[61] See Oxfam, 'Submission by Oxfam New Zealand to Ministry of Foreign Affairs on the WTO accession negotiations of Samoa' (September 2005) 5–6, noting the disparity of power between the Samoan negotiators and those from New Zealand <http://www.oxfam.org.nz/imgs/whatwedo/mtf/onz%20on%20samoa%20wto%20accession.pdf> accessed 20 September 2010.

[62] This observation was made by Professor John Jackson, a WTO expert, in a public talk at the Lauterpacht Centre for International Law, Cambridge University, on 2 March 2006. See also Carlos Manuel Vázquez, 'Trade Sanctions and Human Rights—Past, Present and Future' (2003) 6 *Journal of International Economic Law* 797, 803 and 807.

[63] Sharyn O'Halloran, 'US Implementation of WTO Decisions' (Address delivered at WTO at Ten: Dispute Settlement and Developing Countries, Columbia University, 6 April 2006).

[64] Jeffery Atik, 'Democratizing the WTO' (2000–2001) 33 *George Washington International Law Review* 451, 455.

[65] Joost Pauwelyn, 'The Sutherland Report: A Missed Opportunity for Genuine Debate on Trade, Globalization and Reforming the WTO' (2005) 8 *Journal of International Economic Law* 329, 336.

[66] See, eg, WTO, 'WTO hearings on banana dispute opened to the public' (News item, 29 October 2007) <http://www.wto.org/english/news_e/news07_e/dispu_banana_7nov07_e.htm> accessed 20 September 2010.

[67] See generally, Shaffer, above n 41.

[68] See Jeffrey L Dunoff, 'The misguided debate over NGO participation at the WTO' (1998) 1 *Journal of International Economic Law* 433, 441–8. The official name of the case is *Japan—Measures Affecting Consumer Photographic Film and Paper*, WTO doc. WT/DS44/R (31 March 1998) (Report of the Panel).

Barbuda and the US concerning the latter's regulation of internet gambling was reported to be driven by a company, World Sports Exchange, incorporated by US citizens in Antigua and Barbuda. Pauwelyn claims that the company director shopped around for a forum to push his trade interests, hence the case concealed the fact that a US investor was in fact suing the US government.[69] In contrast, civil society NGOs have participated on only an indirect basis by submitting amicus briefs. The panels can accept unsolicited briefs, but they do not have to.[70] It is not clear whether such briefs have been significant in the making of any decisions.[71] The unique level of participation by commercial bodies in WTO dispute settlement processes again prioritizes a trade focus to the possible detriment of non-trade interests.

A related bias was manifested in *India-Quantitative Restrictions on Imports of Agricultural, Textile and Industrial Products*.[72] The case concerned the WTO legality of a quota placed by India on the imports of certain products. India claimed that its measures complied with Article XII of GATT, which allows quantitative restrictions in order to safeguard balance of payments, and Article XVIIIB, which allows developing States to adopt quotas to safeguard their external financial positions, and to maintain 'reserves adequate for the implementation of its programme of economic development'. The Appellate Body found that the measures did not fulfil the requirements of Articles XII or XVIIIB, so they breached the prohibition on quantitative restrictions in Article XI of GATT. In order to reach this decision, the Appellate body disagreed with India on the amount necessary to constitute 'adequate' monetary reserves for the purposes of balance of payments, and also disagreed with India that a finding against it would force it to change its development policy, contrary to its rights under Article XVIIIB. In making these decisions, the Appellate Body relied entirely on the opinion of the IMF. While Article XV dictates that the WTO should consult the IMF on such matters, it was possible for it to investigate the opinions of other development agencies in making decisions on India's development policy. Robert Howse has cogently argued that the Appellate Body's approach of relying on the IMF, which adopts a very narrow monetarist approach to the meaning of a 'development policy', blinded the Appellate Body to broader human rights based notions of development, which may have been evident had it consulted other bodies such as the UN Conference on Trade and

---

[69] Joost Pauwelyn, 'WTO Condemnation of US ban on internet gambling pits free trade against moral values' (ASIL insight, November 2004) <http://www.asil.org/insights/2004/11/insight041117.html> accessed 20 September 2010. See also Dunoff, above n 68, 441–8 and generally Shaffer, above n 41.

[70] *United States—Import Prohibition of Certain Shrimp and Shrimp Products*, WTO doc. WT/DS58/AB/R (12 October 1998) (Report of the Appellate Body) ('Shrimp Turtle Case') para 110. See also Adam McBeth, *International Economic Actors and Human Rights* (Routledge, Oxford, 2010) 105–6.

[71] Nathalie Bernasconi-Osterwalder, 'Democratizing international dispute settlement: the case of trade and investment disputes' (Paper presented at the 6th International Conference of New or Restored Democracies, Doha, 29 October–1 November 2006) 3–4. See also Pauwelyn, above n 65, 346.

[72] *India—Quantitative Restrictions on Imports of Agricultural, Textile and Industrial Products*, WTO doc. WT/DS90/AB/R, AB-1999-3 (23 August 1999) (Report of the Appellate Body).

Development (UNCTAD) and the UN Development Program (UNDP).[73] For example, the IMF starkly distinguished between macroeconomic policies and development policies. Howse retorts:

Under a right-to-development approach, it would be obvious that macroeconomic policies, which affect revenues available for government programmes to fulfil social and economic rights, as well as the cost of imported goods and services needed to fulfil such rights and the reserves of currency with which to pay for them, are 'development policies'.[74]

The case may also manifest an inclination within the WTO dispute settlement system to defer to the technocrats of international financial institutions when their judgements are relevant, but to ignore the equally relevant expertise of international institutions concerned with social justice.[75]

Developed states again have the advantage regarding the initiation of challenges and the enforcement of decisions. The initiation of a WTO challenge is an expensive business which requires considerable technical skills.[76] More fundamentally, retaliatory trade sanctions imposed by a rich industrialized nation on a poor nation will be likely to have a much greater impact than countermeasures in the reciprocal situation.[77] When a policy of great domestic political value to a Northern State is successfully challenged, the outcome can be years of further disputes over the correction of those measures. For example, Brazil's successful litigation against US cotton subsidies has dragged on (thus far) for eight years, concluding (perhaps) with the authorization of substantial countermeasures by Brazil against the US in 2009.[78] While Brazil might be able to inflict considerable economic harm on the US, the same probably cannot be said for the 'Cotton-4' (C4) countries of Western Africa (Benin, Burkina Faso, Chad, and Mali), which are suffering grave economic harm from US cotton subsidies.[79]

WTO secretariat

It is often suggested that the WTO secretariat is largely powerless, with the WTO being an organization driven by its Member States.[80] However, the WTO secretariat still has considerable influence in WTO processes. For example, the secretariat often drafts the 'chairman's text' during negotiations, the text that is presented to Members as a starting point for negotiations on a particular topic.[81] While such texts do not necessarily reflect outcomes, they can certainly shape debate.

---

[73] Howse, above n 35, paras 46–9.   [74] Ibid, para 48.
[75] See also Margot Salomon, *Global Responsibility for Human Rights* (Oxford University Press, Oxford, 2007) 152–3.
[76] Shaffer, above n 41, 161–2; Stiglitz and Charlton, above n 47, 83.
[77] World Development Report 2006, above n 12, 213. See also Stiglitz and Charlton, above n 47, 77.
[78] *United States—Subsidies on Upland Cotton—Recourse to Arbitration by the US under Article 22.6 of the DSU and Article 4.11 of the SCM Agreement*, WTO docs WT/DS267/ARB/1 and WT/DS267/ARB/2 (31 August 2009) (Decisions by the Arbitrator).
[79] Note that US cotton subsidies outweigh Burkina Faso's entire GDP.
[80] Xu Yi-Chong and Patrick Weller, *The Governance of World Trade: International Civil Servants and the GATT/WTO* (Edward Elgar, Cheltenham, 2004) 252.
[81] Ibid, 264.

The secretariat also provides technical assistance to developing States to build their capacities for negotiation and implementation of trade policies. Furthermore, the secretariat prepares reports on each member for the Trade Policy Review Mechanism, where the trade policies of each member are assessed in light of their impact on the multilateral system of trade. There is no clear avenue for civil society participation in this review. In 2004, Robert Howse suggested that the reviews have manifested a pro-liberalization bias without any attempt to assess the viability of alternative policy avenues, or the social impact of free trade measures.[82]

Despite their limited powers, WTO personnel should guard against an automatic bias towards neo-liberal policies as the unquestioned recipe for trade policies in the performance of their duties. Yet Yi-Chong and Weller concluded: '[i]f there is a bias, it is . . . towards the objectives of the organization: a multilateral and reciprocal approach leading to a greater liberalization of trade'.[83] On engagement between the secretariat and NGOs, the authors stated:

> Officials in the Secretariat are sceptical about what they regard as a Utopian view that NGOs have of direct democracy. They see the WTO as an arena for the negotiation for trade and *do not know what the NGOs' demands have to do with trade* or what they can bring to the negotiating table.[84]

This conclusion was reached by the authors on the basis of interviews with the secretariat in 2002 and 2003.[85] At that time, it seems the secretariat was operating under the misapprehension that trade issues can be neatly segmented from other issues. On the contrary, as pointed out by Frank Garcia, 'there is no such thing as a pure trade issue'.[86] Writing from the perspective of 2010, it seems likely that the secretariat has a greater understanding of NGO agendas and their relevance to global trade, given that there has been another seven years' experience of engagement with such bodies. However, it seems unlikely that there has been a radical shift within the secretariat towards active support for those agendas if they are seen to conflict with broader free trade objectives.

Conclusion on WTO processes

WTO procedures and processes are currently biased in favour of commercial trade interests and developed States. This systemic bias is likely to generate outcomes that favour such interests and act to the detriment of other interests, such as those of developing States or non-trade (for example, human rights, environmental) interests, if the respective sets of interests should conflict.

It must be noted that the two identified disadvantaged constituencies (non-trade interests and developing States) may be in conflict with each other. Indeed, developing States have traditionally been against the greater involvement of NGOs

---

[82] Howse, above n 35, paras 29 and 40. See also Report of the Special Rapporteur on Right of everyone to the enjoyment of the highest attainable standard of physical and mental health, Paul Hunt, Mission to the World Trade Organization, above n 11, para 64.

[83] Yi-Chong and Weller, above n 80, 266.   [84] Ibid, 274, emphasis added.

[85] Ibid, 279, n 1.   [86] Garcia, above n 18, 65.

in the WTO negotiation or interpretation process, and have generally been suspicious of 'human rights talk' in the WTO.[87] For example, developing States were initially vigorous critics, on both legal and political grounds, of the practice of the Appellate Body and Panels accepting amicus briefs from NGOs.[88] Developing States feared that NGO involvement would exacerbate the dominance of industrialized States within the WTO, as 'Northern' NGOs are more vocal and experienced advocates than their 'Southern' counterparts.[89]

Such concerns assume dissonance between the goals of Northern and Southern NGOs.[90] However, strong NGOs do exist in the South and there are vibrant North/South NGO partnerships.[91] Furthermore, the existence of conflict between Northern and Southern NGOs over trade issues has been exaggerated. For example, there is evidence from a 2002 study that trade unions from both North and South favour explicit linkage of labour and trade in the WTO, contrary to common assertions that Southern trade unions fear protectionist abuse of such a clause to the detriment of their members.[92]

Much of the opposition in the developing world to greater NGO involvement comes from autocratic governments with no democratic credentials, such as those in China and Burma. Such governments are hostile to the overt promotion of social justice interests by non-governmental groups in any forum, whether at the national or international levels. Their opposition is based on ideological opposition to the promotion of human rights beyond those tolerated by the State and to vibrant debate by civil society. Such concerns do not legitimate the continued exclusion of such interests from the WTO.

The misgivings of developing States over the infiltration of human rights arguments and actors into the WTO was prompted by the fact that the dominant human rights/trade discourse in the early years of the WTO concerned the impact of WTO law on the ability of States to impose human rights-based trade sanctions against other States.[93] This issue is discussed in Chapter 4. Trade sanctions are a weapon used far more often and with greater impact by developed States than developing States, so it is hardly surprising that developing States are hostile to any suggestion that the rights of States to impose such sanctions be expanded.[94]

---

[87] Andrew Lang, 'Inter-regime Encounters', in Joseph, Kinley, and Waincymer (eds), above n 1, 177.

[88] C L Lim, 'The *Amicus* Brief Issue at the WTO' (2005) 4 *Chinese Journal of International Law* 85, 87.

[89] Yi-Chong and Weller, above n 80, 273.

[90] See, eg, Jagdish Bhagwati, 'Afterword: the Question of Linkage' (2002) 96 *American Journal of International Law* 126; Kathleen Newland, 'Workers of the World, Now What?' (1999) 114 *Foreign Policy* 52, 56–7.

[91] See also Keohane and Nye, above n 2, 19.

[92] See Gerard Griffin, Chris Nyland, and Anne O'Rourke, 'Trade Unions and the Social Clause: A North South Union Divide?' (Working Paper No 81, National Key Centre in Industrial Relations, Monash University, 2002), <http://www.buseco.monash.edu.au/mgt/research/working-papers/nkcir-working-papers/nkcir-workingpaper-81.pdf> accessed 4 November 2007. See also Chapter 4.

[93] See James Harrison, *The Human Rights Impact of the World Trade Organisation* (Hart, Oxford, 2007) 126 and 176.

[94] See also ibid, 177.

However, as explored in Chapters 5 to 7, there are numerous human rights issues of relevance to the WTO beyond the issue of trade sanctions, including areas where the promotion of human rights and the interests of developing States clearly coincide.[95] Accordingly, there has been significant convergence in the positions of some Northern NGOs and the positions of developing States during the Doha round.[96] For example, some NGOs, such as Oxfam and the Catholic Agency for Overseas Development (CAFOD), have advised developing States on their negotiating positions in the Doha round.[97] Numerous NGOs supported developing States in their attack on the effect of TRIPS on access to medicines, which helped to produce the Doha Declaration on TRIPS and Public Health in 2001 and subsequent related developments.[98] NGOs were also instrumental in assisting West African nations to put cotton on the Hong Kong agenda as a separate item, as discussed above, and to establish cotton negotiations as a litmus test for the success of the Doha round.[99] Brazil defended a ban on the import of retreaded tyres on environmental and health grounds,[100] and its case was supported by numerous amicus briefs from NGOs.[101] In mid-2008, Doha round talks collapsed (again), partly over the extent of demands by India and China for special safeguard measures to protect the livelihoods of poor farmers,[102] a concern echoed by numerous NGOs.

A 2006 empirical study on the role of NGOs in cotton negotiations concluded that there had been a major role reversal within the WTO regarding perceptions of NGOs during the Doha negotiations:

[T]here is a difference between the ways in which Southern countries relate to NGOs (reliance on their expertise for text writing and strategy setting) and how Northern countries relate to them (suspicion, and 'management').[103]

Furthermore:

the extent of [NGO] participation in northern countries decision-making [sic] was definitely seen as less than in developing countries which has [sic] included multiple NGO representatives in their delegations and gave them visible but influential roles.[104]

---

[95] Sapra, above n 36, 92.

[96] See, generally, Oxfam, *Rigged Rules and Double Standards: Trade, Globalisation and the Fight Against Poverty* (Oxfam, London, 2002).

[97] Sutherland Report, above n 25, 44.

[98] Robert Wai, 'Countering, Branding and Dealing: Using Economic and Social Rights in and Around the International Trade Regime' (2003) 14 *European Journal of International Law* 35, 72, 79.

[99] Grossman, Herrick, and Shao, above n 29, 5.

[100] *Brazil—Measures Affecting Imports of Retreaded Tyres*, WTO docs. WT/DS332/R (12 June 2007) (Report of the Panel) and WT/DS332/AB/R, AB-2007-4 (3 December 2007) (Report of the Appellate Body).

[101] See, eg, CIEL and others, 'Amicus Curiae Brief' (Amicus brief submitted by the Center for International Environmental Law (CIEL) (based in the US and Switzerland) and others in *Brazil—Measures Affecting Imports of Retreaded Tyres* (WT/DS332, 3 July 2006) <http://www.ciel.org/Publications/Brazil_Tires_Amicus_3Jul06.pdf> accessed 20 September 2010.

[102] See ICTSD, *Bridges Daily Update*, Issue 10, 30 July 2008 <http://ictsd.net/> accessed 30 July 2008; South Centre, *South Bulletin: Reflections and Foresights*, 16 October 2008, 2.

[103] Grossman, Herrick, and Shao, above, n 29, 10. See also 11–12.   [104] Ibid, 12.

Continued favouring of commercial interests over social justice interests (whether from North or South) will continue to skew WTO outputs in favour of trade and commercial interests to the potential detriment of social justice and other non-trade interests. A continued trade bias within the WTO, while its output continues to impact on non-trade areas, is no more legitimate than a continued bias in favour of developed States.[105] Both biases must be redressed, or else the WTO's legitimacy will continue to be disputed with good cause. In any case, the 'myth that developing countries are opposed to non-state actor participation should be debunked".[106]

B. The Relevance of International Human Rights Law

What human rights are engaged by this issue of democratic deficit in an international organization such as the WTO? The removal of autonomous regulatory power from the State over important issues, such as food safety and intellectual property protection, could breach the right of peoples to self determination, protected under Article 1 of both the ICCPR and the ICESCR. Article 1(1) of each Covenant guarantees the right of peoples to 'freely pursue their economic, social and cultural development'. Furthermore, all States parties to both Covenants have duties under common article 1(3) to respect and promote the right of self determination of others, so they should avoid actions, such as enforcement of WTO rights, if such action might prejudice enjoyment of the right in another State.

The supervision of national regulatory power under international law cannot per se constitute a breach of Article 1 lest nearly all international regimes prejudice that right. The question of breach must therefore depend on the degree and nature of the removal of regulatory power. It is difficult to characterize the WTO regime as constituting a greater interference with State power than other regimes in terms of subject matter. It is not, for example, 'broader' in substantive terms than human rights or environmental treaties. As noted below, however, the intensity of the interference by the WTO in those areas in which it impacts is probably stronger than most other international regimes, and its enforcement mechanisms are stronger. Regarding processes, it has already been noted that 'the peoples' of State members have generally had very little input into the process by which their State becomes bound, and the process by which the relevant obligations are formulated. As noted below, the deficiencies of the WTO are probably worse and more consequential in this regard than other international bodies. Therefore, it is possible that the adoption by States of WTO obligations can be characterized as breaching the right of self determination.

---

[105] See also Dillon, above n 20, 130–5; Robert Howse, 'From Politics to Technocracy—and back again: the Fate of the Multilateral Trading Regime' (2002) 96 *American Journal of International Law* 94, 115.

[106] Sapra, above n 36, 106.

A group must have a long-standing relationship with a territory before they are classified as a 'peoples' entitled to self determination.[107] Many 'peoples' entitled to self determination are effectively represented by the State to which they belong. In such a situation, it is difficult to argue that the right to self determination has been breached, as the State has consented to the measures by joining the WTO in the first place. Therefore, common Article 1 is more relevant in the context of those groups who have a right of self determination but are not effectively represented by their States. Such groups include the indigenous peoples of certain States as well as peoples in occupied territories.[108]

A common misunderstanding is that a right of self determination equates with a right of secession. In fact, there are degrees of the right, ranging from external self determination (where 'peoples have the right to determine freely their political status and their place in the international community'),[109] including a right of secession for those peoples who are wrongly denied statehood, to various forms of internal self determination, which entails the right of a people to choose its political status within an existing State's boundaries or to exercise meaningful political participation.[110] The internal aspect of the right thus overlaps considerably with the right of political participation (Article 25 ICCPR) and minority rights (Article 27 ICCPR). Therefore, it seems likely that any breaches of Article 1 entailed in inadequate participatory mechanisms within the WTO would coincide with breaches of those other rights, which are discussed below.

Article 25 of the ICCPR recognizes an individual right to participate in political processes and public affairs. It states:

Every citizen shall have the right and the opportunity, without [discrimination] and without unreasonable restrictions:
(a) To take part in the conduct of public affairs, directly or through freely chosen representatives;
(b) To vote and to be elected at genuine periodic elections which shall be by universal and equal suffrage and shall be held by secret ballot, guaranteeing the free expression of the will of the electors;
(c) To have access, on general terms of equality, to public service in his country.

Democratic rights are not only about elections and the free choice of government by the majority; they entail individual rights to have a meaningful opportunity to take part in the political process. Of course, no individual has a right of veto, such that his or her political choices must be satisfied, nor do majority preferences always have to be satisfied. Article 25 does not dictate that there be plebiscites on

---

[107] Sarah Joseph, Jenny Schultz, and Melissa Castan, *The International Covenant on Civil and Political Rights: Cases, Materials and Commentary*, 2nd edn (Oxford University Press, Oxford, 2004) 146.

[108] See, eg, UN Declaration on the Rights of Indigenous Peoples (adopted on 2 October 2007, not yet entered into force as at 21 September 2010), UN doc. A/RES/61/295) Article 3.

[109] Committee on the Elimination of Racial Discrimination, 'General Recommendation No. 21: Right to self-determination', UN doc A/51/18 (23 August 1996) para 4.

[110] Joseph, Schultz, and Castan, above n 107, 148. See also Robert McCorquodale, 'Self Determination: a Human Rights Approach' (1994) 43 *International and Comparative Law Quarterly* 857, 864.

all major issues. However, the routine flouting by a State of majority preferences would generally signal inadequate protection of this right. The right has been interpreted broadly by the Human Rights Committee (HRC), the monitoring body established under the ICCPR, to encompass rights to participate in 'all aspects of public administration, and the formulation of policy at the *international*, national, regional and local levels'.[111]

The *Declaration on the Right to Development* describes the right to development in its Article 1 as:

[A]n inalienable human right by virtue of which every human person and all peoples are entitled *to participate in*, contribute to, and enjoy economic, social, cultural and political development, in which all human rights and fundamental freedoms can be fully realized [emphasis added].

It is often argued that WTO rules and policies, which largely promote freer trade, are compatible with the right to development, specifically the economic aspects thereof.[112] It is arguable, however, that the participatory aspects of the right have been neglected by States when acting within and through the WTO. The human right to development entails a process which helps to ensure what the WTO notably does not ensure: equitable and fair distribution of the benefits of development via the opportunity for participation of all individuals concerned.[113] Arjun Sengupta, the (now former) UN Independent Expert on the Right to Development, has emphasized that the right entails more than economic growth per se, and has stated that:

It is not just achieving the objectives of development, but also the way they are achieved that becomes essential to the process. The objective is fulfilling human rights and the process of achieving this is also a human right. That process must possess the features of all human rights, namely respecting the notions of equity and participation...[114]

Participation and inclusivity have been recognized as cross-cutting human rights norms in the sense that they are elements of many substantive human rights.[115] Indeed, participatory rights are now routinely built into interpretations of economic, social, and cultural rights. For example, the Committee on Economic, Social and Cultural Rights has said, regarding the right to health in Article 12 of the ICESCR, that a crucial aspect of that right 'is the participation of the population in all health-related decision-making at the community, national and international levels'.[116]

---

[111] HRC, 'General Comment 25: The right to participate in public affairs, voting rights and the right of equal access to public service (Article 25)', UN doc. CCPR/C/21/Rev.1/Add.7 (12 July 1996) para 5 (emphasis added). See also UNHCHR, above n 44, para 8.

[112] Howse, above n 35, para 50. See also Chapter 5.   [113] Ibid, para 10.

[114] Arjun Sengupta, 'On the Theory and Practice of the Right to Development' (2002) 24 *Human Rights Quarterly* 837, 851, and see more generally 848–52.

[115] See, eg, Office of the High Commissioner for Human Rights, 'Report on Indicators for Promoting and Monitoring the Implementation of Human Rights', UN doc. HRI/MC/2008/3 (6 June 2008) para 10.

[116] CESCR, 'General Comment No 14: The right to the highest attainable standard of health (article 12 of the International Covenant on Economic, Social and Cultural Rights', UN doc. E/C.12/2000/4 (11 August 2000) para 11.

Therefore, from a human rights point of view, the strong European public opinion against the import of hormone-injected beef should have been taken into account in the *Beef-Hormone* case.[117]

As conceded by the United Nations High Commissioner for Human Rights, the exact parameters of participatory rights at the global level are unclear.[118] What is clear is that participatory rights are not confined within national borders, so the inherently limited participation within WTO processes, whether they be negotiation, treaty-making, or dispute resolution, risks classification as a breach of human rights by its Member States, especially given the significant outcomes of those processes.[119]

That said, rights of participation are not absolute. Article 25 of the ICCPR anticipates 'reasonable' restrictions. Most relevantly, the right of *direct* participation in public affairs is possibly limited to the rights outlined in Articles 25(b) (right to vote and stand for elections) and 25(c) (equal access to a State's public service).[120] This issue arose under the ICCPR in *Mikmaq Tribal Society v Canada*,[121] which concerned a complaint by an indigenous tribe regarding Canada's failure to invite it to a constitutional conference on indigenous rights to which other indigenous tribes had been invited. In its decision, the HRC indicated that rights of direct participation in Article 25 are quite narrow. It stated at paragraph 5.4:

Surely, it cannot be the meaning of article 25(a) . . . that every citizen may determine either to take part directly in the conduct of public affairs or to leave it to freely chosen representatives. It is for the legal and constitutional system of the State party to provide for the modalities of such participation.

At paragraph 5.5, it added:

[A]rticle 25(a) of the Covenant cannot be understood as meaning that any directly affected group, large or small, has the unconditional right to choose the modalities of participation in the conduct of public affairs.

In *Beydon v France*,[122] the complainants were members of an NGO, the DIH, which campaigned for France's full participation in and cooperation with the International Criminal Court (ICC). It did not approve of France's decision, upon its ratification of the Statute of the ICC, to make a declaration which limited ICC jurisdiction over war crimes. The complainants alleged a violation of Article 25 entailed in the French government's failure to take into account 'the widespread public opposition expressed both directly and through their elected representatives

---

[117] See, generally, Caroline E Foster, 'Public Opinion and the interpretation of the World Trade Organisation's Agreement on Sanitary and Phytosanitary Measures' in Joseph, Kinley, and Waincymer (eds), above note 1, at 285. See Chapter 4, text at notes 180–187. See also Chapter 9, text at notes 12–15.

[118] UNHCHR, above n 44, para 18.   [119] Ibid, para 18.

[120] Joseph, Schultz, and Castan, above n 107, 657.

[121] UN doc. CCPR/C/43/D/205/1986 (3 December 1991) (HRC).

[122] UN doc. CCPR/C/85/D/1400/2005 (28 November 2005) (HRC).

to the French declaration under Article 124'.[123] The HRC found the complaint inadmissible, and noted at paragraph 4.5:

The Committee has ... noted the [complainants'] claim under article 25 (a), that they were deprived, by the State party, of their right and opportunity to take part in the conduct of public affairs *relating to the negotiations, and subsequent adhesion of France to the ICC Statute* with a declaration ... , the Committee recalls that citizens also take part in the conduct of public affairs by exerting influence through public debate and dialogue with their representatives or through their capacity to organize themselves. In the present case, the [complainants] have participated in the public debate in France on the issue of its adhesion to the ICC and on the issue of [A]rticle 124 declaration; they acted through elected representatives and through their association's actions. In the circumstances, the Committee considers that the [complainants] have failed to substantiate ... that their right to take part in the conduct of public affairs has been violated [emphasis added].

Thus, the limited participation of the complainants in France's decisions regarding negotiation and ratification of the *Rome Statute* did not breach Article 25.

In *Brun v France*,[124] an environmental protester claimed that France had breached Article 25 in allowing the planting of GMO crops on a trial basis without adequate public consultation. The claim was found to be inadmissible, as Brun had participated in that process through his elected representative, and through his activities as an activist in an association opposed to GMOs.

Beydon and *Brun* indicate that citizens, at least those in democratic States, are indirectly participating in the political process through the agency of government representatives, and that such indirect participation satisfies the requirements of Article 25. WTO power is arguably legitimized as the organization is merely exercising the authority delegated to it under treaties negotiated by and assented to by those representatives.

However, the right to political participation in developing States regarding their adherence to WTO treaties is undermined by the way in which the interests of those States were marginalized in the Uruguay round. Moreover, the exclusion of certain groups from WTO processes, either at the national or international level, raises concerns regarding discrimination in conjunction with the right of political participation. The HRC stated in General Comment 25 on Article 25 at paragraph 6:

Where a mode of direct participation by citizens is established, no distinctions should be made between citizens as regards their participation on the grounds mentioned in article 2, paragraph 1,[125] and no unreasonable restrictions should be imposed.

The historic narrowness of interests represented by WTO negotiators, the greater input into WTO processes by business compared to other civic groups, the general

---

[123] Ibid, para 3.1.

[124] UN doc. CCPR/C/88/D/1453/2006 (23 November 2006) (HRC).

[125] The prohibited grounds of discrimination enumerated in Article 2(1) ICCPR are: race, colour, sex, language, religion, political or other opinion, national or social origin, property, birth or other status.

lack of input by historically marginalized groups such as the poor, women[126] and indigenous peoples,[127] all raise legitimate queries regarding the adequacy of the level of participation in WTO negotiations and decision-making. For example, women comprised only 9 per cent of the country representatives at the Doha Ministerial meeting, and top positions within the WTO bureaucracy and in the Appellate body are dominated by men.[128]

Indeed, participatory rights in the context of non-discrimination are also recognized in Articles 7, 8 and 14(2) of CEDAW, as well as Article 5 of CERD. In General Recommendation 23, the CEDAW Committee elaborated on the requirements of CEDAW with regard to participation of women in international bodies and decision-making:

> The globalization of the contemporary world makes the inclusion of women and their participation in international organizations, on equal terms with men, increasingly important. The integration of a gender perspective and women's human rights into the agenda of all international bodies is a government imperative. Many crucial decisions on global issues, such as ... economic restructuring ... are taken with limited participation of women.[129]

Therefore, women must be given equal opportunities to 'represent their governments at the international level and to participate in the work of international organizations', such as the WTO.[130] Such levels of representation have not arisen in most international organizations, and certainly not the WTO.

Furthermore, democratic deficits within WTO procedures may threaten minority rights in Article 27 of the ICCPR and the right of non-discrimination in Article 26 of the ICCPR. Regarding Article 27, the HRC has clearly stated that minority groups have rights of direct participation (for example, consultation with governments) in decisions that impact their interests.[131] Indeed, the HRC recently gave its strongest statement to date on the relevant participatory rights of indigenous peoples in *Poma Poma v Peru*:[132]

> In the Committee's view, the admissibility of measures which substantially compromise or interfere with the culturally significant economic activities of a minority or indigenous community depends on whether the members of the community in question have had the opportunity to participate in the decision-making process in relation to these measures and whether they will continue to benefit from their traditional economy. The Committee considers that participation in the decision-making process must be effective, which requires not mere consultation but the free, prior and informed consent of the members of the

---

[126] See Dillon, above n 20, 146–8, commenting on the general absence of women in the international trade field. See also Shelley Wright, 'Women and the Global Economic Order: a Feminist Perspective' (1995) 10 *American University International Law Review* 861.

[127] UNHCHR, above n 44, 9.

[128] Barnali Choudhury, 'The Façade of Neutrality: Uncovering Gender Silences in International Trade' (2008) 15 *William and Mary Journal of Women and the Law* 113, 129–30.

[129] CEDAW, 'General Recommendation No 23: Women in political and public life (Article 7)', UN doc. A/52/38/Rev.1 (31 January 1997) para 39.

[130] UNHCHR, above n 44, para 35.

[131] See HRC, 'General Comment 23: The rights of minorities (Article 27)', UN doc. CCPR/C/21/Rev.1/Add.5 (8 April 1994) para 7; see also Joseph, Schultz, and Castan, above n 107, 778, 781–2.

[132] *Poma Poma v Peru*, UN doc. CCPR/C/95/D/1457/2006 (24 April 2009) (HRC) para 7.6.

community. In addition, the measures must respect the principle of proportionality so as not to endanger the very survival of the community and its members.

The implementation of WTO commitments has clearly impacted on the traditional lifestyles of minorities, particularly in the agricultural arena.[133] Many of these impacts have been generated by liberalization policies to which indigenous peoples have had very little input.

Writing in 2002, Esty argued:

[T]o limit their participation in global politics to electing national representatives who will designate trade ministry officials to represent the nation in a narrowly confined intergovernmental dialogue produces a terribly thin reed of popular sovereignty on which to build the legitimacy of the WTO.[134]

However, during the Doha round, civil society groups beyond business lobbies have become more aware of the importance and impacts of trade policies. They have therefore made a greater effort to influence domestic policies, which should influence a State's negotiating stance within the WTO. The success of NGOs in mobilizing domestic public opinion on certain issues has undoubtedly forced some States to pay some attention to their views.[135] As noted above, this bilateral engagement (between NGOs and individual States) has occasionally translated into inclusion of NGOs in a State's negotiating team, particularly in some developing States. Nevertheless, while social justice NGOs may be exercising greater influence over the negotiating stances and domestic policies of WTO Member States, the concrete impact of that influence at the international level is extremely difficult to assess, especially as the Doha round has yet to produce many concrete outcomes.[136] It also seems unlikely this greater influence reflects evenly across relevant sectors, for example taking appropriate account of disparate groups such as women and indigenous peoples, or that it remotely matches the influence of traditional players such as business lobbies.

The exercise of greater rights of participation by constituencies not traditionally involved in WTO processes at the national and international levels serves a normative function in helping to ensure against breaches arising from participation deficit, such as breaches of Articles 25 and 27 of the ICCPR and non-discrimination obligations, and perhaps rights of self determination for some groups. They also serve an instrumental function in helping to ensure that the substantive outcomes of negotiations conform to other human rights. For example, attentive consideration by WTO dispute resolution bodies of amicus curiae briefs from a variety of groups would help to ensure that they are aware of the range of non-trade interests that may be impacted by their decision. As another example, the lobbying by civil society at national and international levels, along with developing States, led to the adoption by the WTO of the Doha Declaration on TRIPS and Public Health in 2001 and a subsequent waiver of

---

[133] See also Megan Davis, 'International Trade, the World Trade Organisation, and the Human Rights of Indigenous Peoples' (2006) 8 *Balayi* 5, 18. See also Chapter 6 below.
[134] Esty, above n 8, 15.   [135] Grossman, Herrick, and Shao, above n 29, 11–12.
[136] See also ibid, 29.

certain TRIPS requirements, which brought TRIPS into greater conformity with the right to health in Article 12 of the ICESCR.[137]

C. Democratic Deficit, the WTO, and the International Human Rights Law Regime: A Comparison

WTO membership removes certain policy choices from Member States under international law, as is the case with most international law regimes. Furthermore, other international regimes also allocate power and decision-making 'upwards' to international bodies, which are more remote from people than their own national bodies. Therefore, it is arguable that most if not all international legal regimes impact negatively on the participatory rights of national populations. The United Nations has noted the paradox that the substance of politics has internationalized (for example, in the areas of trade, human rights, and the environment), while political processes and institutions have remained largely national.[138]

Is the democratic deficit within the WTO a 'worse' threat to democratic rights than democratic deficit in other international bodies? Is the allocation of power to the WTO as an international institution more or less appropriate than comparable allocations of power to other international bodies? I will make some observations on this issue by comparing the WTO with international human rights regimes.

Democratic deficit and the international human rights regimes

Like the WTO, international human rights regimes have also been portrayed as threats to the legitimate regulatory power of States and the democratic choices of a State's population. For example, there has been outrage in the UK regarding certain decisions of the European Court of Human Rights, which have found British counterterrorism measures (in the context of Northern Ireland) to breach international human rights standards.[139] In Australia, the government has commonly impugned findings of violation against Australia by the HRC and other human rights bodies on the basis that those decisions lacked legitimacy and undermined policies and laws adopted via Australian democratic processes.[140] Furthermore, the claims by certain States, such as China, Malaysia, and Singapore, that human rights are sovereign domestic matters, are well known and persistent, even if legally incorrect.

---

[137] See UNHCHR, above n 44, 15. See generally, Chapter 7.

[138] UNGA, 'We the Peoples: Civil Society, the United Nations and Global Governance: Report of the Panel of Eminent Persons on United-Nations Civil Society Relations', UN doc. A/58/817 (11 June 2004) 8, paras 7–10. See also Stiglitz, above n 21, 291.

[139] See Kieran McEvoy, 'Law, Struggle, and Political Transformation in Northern Ireland' (2000) 27 *Journal of Law and Society* 542, 557; Sarah Joseph, 'Denouement of the Deaths on the Rock: the Right to Life of Terrorists' (1996) 14 *Netherlands Quarterly of Human Rights* 5, 6, 22.

[140] See, generally, David Kinley and Penny Martin, 'International Human Rights Law at Home: Addressing the Politics of Denial' (2002) 26 *Melbourne University Law Review* 466.

The purpose of international human rights law is in many ways counter-majoritarian. Though all people have human rights, they are probably most important for vulnerable minorities. In democracies, majorities are generally able to take care of themselves.[141] Minorities, however, are in greater need of the support of international human rights regimes to guard against the arbitrary exercise of power by majorities. Majority rule per se is unlikely to cater for the human rights of unpopular minorities such as new refugee arrivals, suspected (and actual) criminals, or vulnerable minorities whose interests do not coincide with those of the majority or whose interests do not attract majority attention.[142] The notion of individual human rights would be considerably undermined if their extent was ultimately determined merely by the exercise of majority choices. Indeed, a key limit to the right of political participation is that majorities cannot compel government policies that breach other human rights. Therefore, there is significant justification for the removal of regulatory power from States under international human rights law (that is, its output) despite claims that such removal undermines majority rights.

In any case, the extent of the interference by international human rights law with State regulatory power is quite weak. The findings of the human rights bodies at the global level are not legally binding, though they have persuasive value. Numerous States have impugned the findings of these bodies on the basis of their non-legal status.[143] Indeed, it is arguable that enforcement under the global human rights treaties has been delegated 'almost exclusively'[144] to the municipal systems of States given the lack of strong international enforcement.

The negotiation of global human rights treaties is an open process, with significant NGO participation in bodies such as the Human Rights Council and its predecessor, the Commission on Human Rights. There is also ongoing civil society involvement in global human rights bodies. NGOs are permitted to participate in debates within the Human Rights Council. NGOs also commonly brief and submit information to the human rights treaty bodies.

Though commercial bodies have generally not been so involved, they have participated in the areas of greatest interest to them. Corporations, for example, have been heavily involved in consultations with the UN's Special Representative on Business and Human Rights since that mandate was created in 2005, and have been generally supportive of his reports. Similarly, the Special Rapporteur on the

---

[141] Of course, human rights are precarious for majorities in non-democracies, governed by dictatorships, such as Burma, or minority rule, such as apartheid South Africa. International human rights law of course also seeks to curb the arbitrary exercises of power of non-democratic governments.

[142] Indigenous peoples in Australia are an example of this latter group. They are not 'unpopular', but their interests (eg land rights, compensation for past wrongs) are sometimes perceived to run counter to those of the majority, or are simply of insufficient importance to the majority to influence the latter's political choices.

[143] See, eg, Australia's response to the adverse finding of the HRC in *A v Australia*, UN doc. CCPR/C/59/D/560/1993 (30 April 1997) (HRC): Darryl Williams MP, Attorney General, 'Australian Government responds to the United Nations Human Rights Committee' (Press Release, 17 December 1997).

[144] Douglas Lee Donoho, 'Relativism versus Universalism in Human Rights: the Search for Meaningful Standards' (1991) 27 *Stanford Journal of International Law* 345, 372–3.

Right to Health consulted extensively with pharmaceutical companies before devising guidelines for such companies with respect to access to medicines.[145]

Despite arguments that human rights are imbued with 'Western' concepts, developing States have played a significant role in drafting human rights treaties.[146] They have more seats on the Human Rights Council than developed States. In any case, no State has to ratify a human rights treaty even if it agrees to the texts thereof, and it can normally enter reservations thereto.

Most UN intergovernmental human rights activity takes place in Geneva during meetings of the Human Rights Council, so the problem regarding the absence of certain permanent State missions, noted above regarding the WTO, is replicated. However, the General Assembly, which sits annually in New York, is able to reopen Council debates. Furthermore, treaties might be drafted by the Council, but are ultimately adopted by the General Assembly. All UN Members have permanent missions in New York.

States have considerable discretionary room for manoeuvre with respect to the implementation and enforcement of most internationally recognized human rights. Economic, social, and cultural rights are inherently flexible, as a State's obligations under the ICESCR are constrained by a State's 'maximum available resources' and by the progressive nature of most aspects of those rights. Most civil and political rights are constrained by concepts such as proportionality and reasonableness.[147] For example, the right to freedom of expression in Article 19 ICCPR may be limited by measures that are 'provided by law and are necessary' to protect national security, public order, public health, public morals, and/or the rights of others. As another example, certain limited impacts on cultural practices entailed in the implementation of economic development programmes are permitted under Article 27 of the ICCPR.[148]

Individuals can access grievance procedures under some human rights treaties, such as the Optional Protocol to the ICCPR. Hearings in regional courts are public, but deliberations over individual complaints at the global level are not. All final decisions are publicly available. A human rights complaint will often already have been litigated at the national level, where there may be an opportunity for interested parties to submit amicus briefs to national courts. Material from those national decisions is made available to the international body. There is considerable deference to national authorities in international human rights decision-making,

---

[145] See General Assembly, 'Report of the Special Rapporteur on the right of everyone to the enjoyment of the highest attainable standard of physical and mental health', UN doc. A/63/263, 11 August 2008.
[146] See, eg, Susan Waltz, 'Universalizing Human Rights: the Role of Small States in the Construction of the Universal Declaration of Human Rights' (2001) 23 *Human Rights Quarterly* 44. See also Chapter 2, pp 44–6.
[147] There are, exceptionally, some absolute rights, which may never be qualified in any circumstance, such as rights to freedom from torture and freedom from slavery.
[148] See Joseph, Schultz, and Castan, above n 107, 772–9. See also, eg, the HRC decisions in *Jouni Länsman, Eino Länsman and the Muotkatunturi Herdsmen's Committee v Finland*, UN doc. CCPR/C/83/D/1023/2001 (15 April 2005), *Jouni Länsman et al v Finland*, UN doc. CCPR/C/58/D/671/1995 (22 November 1996), and *Ilmari Länsman et al v Finland*, UN doc. CCPR/C/52/D/511/1992 (8 November 1994).

with the utilization of doctrines such as the margin of appreciation,[149] the need for complainants to exhaust domestic remedies before seeking international remedies, and the fact that the international bodies will normally defer to local findings of fact and evidence.[150]

It is concluded that it is appropriate to delegate certain decision-making powers 'upwards' to international human rights bodies. A balance is maintained between national decision-making powers and the competence of international bodies. Furthermore, the outputs of human rights bodies are justified by the extent of the inputs. In fact, a common criticism of human rights is that the enforcement powers of international bodies are too weak rather than too strong.

Comparison with the WTO

Let us compare that short overview of human rights systems with the WTO. Trade law does not have the same counter-majoritarian purpose as human rights law.[151] One argument in favour of an international trade organization is to prevent capture of the State by protectionist producer interests that seek to undermine the utilitarian benefits of a liberalized economy for all.[152] Protectionist producer interests are often concentrated and politically mobilized, and are therefore able to manipulate the domestic political process.[153] The WTO is said to help States to reinforce rational majority interests by protecting consumers (a disparate group who often lack a coherent political voice), who benefit from access to cheaper goods, and, according to the theory of comparative advantage, the economic interests of the importing State as a whole as its industries become more competitive and efficient.[154] However, as seen in Chapter 5, the argument that free trade and WTO rules benefit majorities by promoting economic growth is in fact contestable with respect to some developing States.

The WTO also helps to protect the interests of overseas traders from State B who might otherwise be at the mercy of populist decision-making by State A. The WTO enhances the participatory rights of those traders, who are particularly vulnerable to being abused as political pawns as they are excluded from State A's political community.[155] Under international human rights law, only citizens have rights of political participation in a particular State. However, modern global economic interdependence dictates that the right may be permissibly limited in order to prevent undue harm to the interests, including human rights, of non-citizens,

---

[149] The 'margin of appreciation' is a doctrine used by the European Court of Human Rights in interpreting the ECHR. It is akin to a 'benefit of the doubt' given to the State party in implementing certain human rights. If a certain measure is deemed to fall within a State's margin of appreciation, no violation is found.

[150] Joseph, Schultz, and Castan, above n 107, 22–3.

[151] Dunoff, above n 3, 758.

[152] Raustiala, above n 8, 854–5, 864–7.   [153] Narlikar, above n 55, 5; Esty, above n 8, 11.

[154] Narlikar, above n 55, 5; Raustiala, above n 8, 864.

[155] Raustiala, above n 8, 873–4. See also Joel Trachtman, 'Legal Aspects of a Poverty Agenda at the WTO: Trade Law and "Global Apartheid" ' (2003) 6 *Journal of International Economic Law* 3, 18.

such as foreign exporters whose livelihoods might depend on access to State A's markets.[156]

However, there are fears that the WTO itself has been captured by special interests. The domestic power of protectionist interests in the developed world shrunk with each round of GATT talks, with a corresponding increase in the influence and power of their exporter competitors.[157] It is arguable that the WTO serves to reinforce the power of multinational corporations, who are the major direct beneficiaries of world trade.[158] It does not enhance participatory rights if the WTO is effectively promoting the interests of the already powerful. For example, the Special Rapporteur on the Right to Food has reported on a particular power imbalance, which has had consequences for the structure of trade rules regarding agriculture, with knock-on effects for the right to food:

> It is well known that, in developing countries, small-scale farmers form a large but geographically dispersed group, with little or no access to resources for political lobbying, and face prohibitive transaction costs in the organization of collective action. Urban groups, in contrast, find it easier to mobilize through public protests; so do farmers in industrialised economies.[159]

So too, of course, do large agribusiness firms.

The WTO Panels and its Appellate Body do not defer to national regimes in the way that international human rights institutions do. For example, there is no requirement to exhaust domestic remedies or explicit use of any doctrine of a margin of appreciation. Furthermore, WTO norms are less flexible than most human rights norms. Most human rights norms can be limited in proportionate or reasonable circumstances to achieve a number of broad objectives, including protection of 'the rights of others'. In contrast, WTO exceptions, such as those listed in Article XX of the GATT, seem to cover a narrower range of objectives. The Panels and the Appellate Body have arguably been stricter in interpreting and applying limitations to WTO norms than have human rights bodies in interpreting and applying limitations to human rights norms. As discussed in Chapter 4, an exception must overcome two hurdles before it will be acceptable under WTO law: it must satisfy a test of 'necessity' in achieving the desired objective and it must satisfy a second strict test of non-discrimination imposed under the chapeau of Article XX. The single hurdle human rights test of 'proportionality' is a less onerous barrier for the

---

[156] See also Chapter 4, p. 119 and generally, Chapter 8.

[157] Keohane and Nye, above n 2, 6.

[158] Atik, above n 64, 459; Esty, above n 8, 11. See also E-U Petersmann, 'The Human Rights Approach Advocated by the United Nations High Commissioner for Human Rights and by the International Labour Organisation: is it relevant for WTO law and Policy?' (2004) 7 *Journal of International Economic Law* 605, 611. Of course, the interests of multinational corporations and those of consumers can coincide. Eg, the entry of corporations into a market can give consumers access to cheaper goods. However, their interests can diverge, eg, over measures designed to ensure product quality, and arguably over intellectual property laws (see Chapter 7 for discussion of intellectual property).

[159] Human Rights Council, 'Report of the Special Rapporteur on the right to food, Olivier De Schutter: Building resilience: a human rights framework for world food and nutrition security', UN doc. A/HRC/9/23 (8 September 2008) para 17. See also Chapter 6 below.

application of exceptions or qualifications than the double-barrelled test applied by the Appellate Body and Panels.[160]

The process of negotiating WTO treaties and human rights treaties is not comparable. WTO negotiations are conducted in secret. A State's negotiating stance can change markedly in the closed environs of the negotiating rooms. Trade negotiations are characterized by trade-offs of interests: one WTO member might for example trade off its domestic sugar interests in order to gain advantages for its domestic cotton interests. WTO Members do not wish to visibly 'sell out' a domestic industry.[161] In contrast, human rights treaties are negotiated in open meetings, often with NGO participation.[162] There is no comparable 'give and take': a State does not for example trade children's rights for the rights of political prisoners. Furthermore, less is at stake when negotiating a human rights treaty. A State can vote to adopt a treaty yet never ratify it, or, in most cases, ratify it with reservations. In the WTO, negotiations yield 'all or nothing' propositions. States negotiate treaties and then must sign up to the 'single undertaking', that is the entire package deal, generally without reservation.[163]

Finally, the WTO is a stronger regime than most international human rights regimes in terms of enforcement. Breach of WTO obligations can expose a State to economic countermeasures from an aggrieved State. In contrast, if a State is found in violation of a UN human rights treaty and fails to take remedial action, it will rarely suffer consequences beyond condemnation and shame, if that. Such consequences simply do not compare to the effects of punishment within the WTO system.

It must be noted that the decisions of regional human rights courts are binding. Europe, through the mechanisms developed under the ECHR, has the most developed regional system. Execution of judgments is supervised by the Committee of Ministers within the Council of Europe, which can exert heavy political pressure in the case of non-compliance. In general, the Committee has been able to secure execution of judgments through 'constructive and cooperative dialogue' with States.[164] In this regard, one may note that the European human rights system stands alongside a very strong regional free trade system, the EU, which also incorporates some coordination and harmonization on economic and social rights.[165] Human rights agendas have not been marginalized during the process of European economic integration. Indeed, EU members are

---

[160] See United Nations Office of the High Commissioner for Human Rights, *Human Rights and World Trade Agreements: Using General Exception Clauses to Protect Human Rights* (Office of the High Commissioner for Human Rights, New York and Geneva, 2005) 15 <http://www.fao.org/righttofood/kc/downloads/vl/docs/AH311.pdf> accessed 20 September 2010.

[161] See Sutherland Report, above n 25, 45; Keohane and Nye, above n 2, 19.

[162] See Robert McCorquodale, 'An Inclusive International Legal System' (2004) 17 *Leiden Journal of International Law* 477, 493–4.

[163] Narlikar, above n 55, 31–2.

[164] Council of Europe, 'Human Rights and Legal Affairs: Frequently Asked Questions', <http://www.coe.int/t/e/human_rights/execution/01_Introduction/02_FAQ.asp> accessed 14 August 2008.

[165] In respect of the latter, see Bob Hepple, *Labour Laws and Global Trade* (Hart, Oxford, 2005) Chapters 8–9. See also Dillon, above n 20, 123 (fn 140).

now bound by a new Charter of Fundamental Rights of the European Union and the EU is, at the time of writing, on the verge of becoming a party to the ECHR.[166] In comparison, the WTO is not counterbalanced by a comparably strong global human rights body. The coordinated progress of free trade and human rights commitments in Europe contrasts starkly with the uncoordinated progress at the global level.[167]

Conclusion

Democratic deficit is a criticism that can probably be levelled at all international bodies, as there is little popular grassroots input into their processes compared to national political processes. However, democratic deficit in the context of the WTO deservedly generates a greater level of concern than democratic deficit in many other contexts, due to a number of characteristics of that system that are highlighted in the above comparison between the WTO and international human rights regimes.

D. Does the WTO Promote Democracy?

Thus far, this chapter has discussed democratic deficit in the processes of the WTO, which casts doubt on the legitimacy of its exercise of substantive power. This section briefly addresses a related but different issue: do the WTO and the free trade agenda promote democratic governance at national levels? That is, do WTO rules help create the conditions for democracy?

WTO Director-General Pascal Lamy has stated that global trade rules, along with international human rights law, are 'a rampart against totalitarianism'.[168] Indeed, it is commonly argued that economic openness promotes political openness[169] in the following ways. Economic openness promotes economic growth,[170] which helps to create new economic elites, who can challenge the authority of dictatorial government power, creating further space for civil society. It leads to the creation of a middle class, which is more educated and which eventually demands

[166] Such ratification is required under Article 6 of the Lisbon Treaty. See Press Release, 'European Commission and Council of Europe kick off joint talks on EU's Accession to the Convention on Human Rights', 7 July 2010, at <http://europa.eu/rapid/pressReleasesAction.do?reference=IP/10/906&type=HTML> accessed 9 October 2010.
[167] See, eg, World Commission on the Social Dimension of Globalisation, *A Fair Globalization: Promoting Opportunities for all* (ILO, Geneva, 2004).
[168] Pascal Lamy, 'Towards shared responsibility and greater coherence: human rights, trade and macroeconomic policy'(Speech at the Colloquium on Human Rights in the Global Economy, Co-organized by the International Council on Human Rights and Realizing Rights, Geneva, 13 January 2010) <http://www.wto.org/english/news_e/sppl_e/sppl146_e.htm> accessed 20 September 2010.
[169] See Joel R Paul, 'Do International Trade Institutions Contribute to Economic Growth and Development?' (2003) 44 *Virginia Journal of International Law* 285, 337–8.
[170] The orthodox view is that economic openness promotes economic growth. However, there are challenges to that view: see Chapter 5, Parts D and E.

greater political and social freedom.[171] Finally, foreign investors demand adherence to the rule of law, as arbitrary decision-making intolerably threatens their investments.[172] These theories are backed up by evidence: democracy, and civil and political freedoms tend to flourish in richer developed States, which generally have more liberal trade regimes, than poorer developing countries, which generally have more restrictive regimes.[173]

Martin Wolf has posited that economic freedoms and the promotion of a flourishing private sector help to ensure the separation of wealth and power. If the public political sector dominates economic decisions, they dominate economic power. 'Power becomes the only route to wealth.'[174] Furthermore, political elites are inevitably tempted to utilize oppressive means to maintain their power as 'loss of power threatens a loss of livelihood'.[175] Growing economies are also important for the maintenance of democracy and human rights. Not only do they provide governments with the resources to provide for positive rights, but it prevents 'zero sum' societies, where one person's gain necessarily results in another person's loss, which can help to foster authoritarian governments.[176]

However, the above arguments are contestable. As discussed in Chapter 5, some developing States have experienced de-industrialization and poor economic performance rather than growth. The link between free trade and economic growth is not clear-cut. In any case, WTO policies do not dictate domestic wealth distribution, so few may benefit from resultant economic growth. The benefits of economic growth might flow only to a small elite, and there may be corrupt connivance between these elites and the government. Furthermore, foreign investment is attracted to the 'rule of law' in certain areas such as security of contract and property rights; it is generally indifferent to the rule of law in the area of civil, political or social freedoms, such as rights of free expression or freedom to join trade unions. Singapore has long had an open economy, yet has a poor record on civil and political freedoms. Similarly, economic reforms in China have not been matched by significant political and social reform.[177]

In this respect, it may be noted that the spread of marketization across the world has accompanied greater global inequality.[178] When gaps between the elites and the poor grow, there is a more pronounced divergence in their interests, leading

---

[171] Garcia, above n 18, 59. See also Jagdish Bhagwati, *Free Trade Today* (Princeton University Press, Princeton, NJ, 2002) 43–4.

[172] See, eg, World Bank, *World Development Report 2002: Building Institutions for Markets* (World Bank, Washington DC, 2002) via <http://www.worldbank.org/wdr/2001/fulltext/fulltext2002 .htm> accessed 20 September 2010.

[173] See Daniel T Griswold, 'Trading Tyranny for Freedom: How Open Markets till the soil for Democracy' (2004) *Trade Policy Analysis no 26*, 4–12 <http://www.freetrade.org/node/37> accessed 20 September 2010.

[174] Martin Wolf, *Why Globalisation Works* (Yale Nota Bene, London, 2005) 30.

[175] Ibid, 30.   [176] Ibid, 30.

[177] Daniel J Gervais, 'Trips 3.0: Policy Calibration and Innovation Displacement' in Chantal Thomas and Joel P Trachtman (eds), *Developing Countries in the WTO Legal System* (Oxford University Press, New York, 2009) 363, 393.

[178] See Chapter 5, text at notes 151–79.

to the likely generation of rules and institutions which favour the latter over the former.[179] Greater inequality may lead to greater marginalization and intolerance of the poor.

Professor Amy Chua has questioned the assumption that the twin trajectories of free trade and democracy in the developed world recur in the developing world. First, she notes that the development of democracy and free trade regimes in industrialized States was a slow process; universal suffrage and economic liberalization evolved over centuries. In contrast, the comparable transitions in many developing States have been remarkably swift, and have not allowed time for the development of appropriate economic safety nets for losers from economic liberalization, constitutional guarantees or other domestic laws that protect minorities, or the development of aspirational pro-market ideologies amongst a population, including those not currently benefiting from free markets.[180] In such circumstances, the impoverished majority may be very hostile to the inequalities created by free markets, at least until a substantial middle class emerges, so democratization and marketization may pull in different directions unless redistribution measures are put in place.

More disturbingly, Chua notes that many developing States have market-dominant ethnic minorities, who seem to have benefited disproportionately from economic globalization, which in turn has generated hostility and conflict. Examples of this phenomenon include Chinese minorities in South East Asia, Indians in Fiji and Africa, whites in South Africa and Zimbabwe, and foreign investors all over the world. Marketization in such circumstances can generate a majoritarian backlash against the relevant minority (as in Zimbabwe with land seizures from white farmers, anti-Chinese riots in Indonesia in 1998, and measures to penalize foreign investors in Bolivia), a backlash against democracy by a government elite in cahoots with the economic elite (such as the pro-Chinese dictatorship of Suharto in Indonesia or pro-Indian government of Moi in Kenya), or, worst of all, majoritarian ethnic violence, including genocide, against the relevant minority (for example, Hutu against Tutsi in Rwanda, Serbs against Croats in the former Yugoslavia).[181] Chua concedes that ethnic conflict is caused by many factors, but posits that the tension caused by the coincidence of racial divides with economic divides is a dangerous brew.[182]

In order to stave off internal hostility in such situations, States must ensure that domestic inequality is contained and that appropriate redistributive measures are

---

[179] Thomas Pogge, 'Growth and Inequality: Understanding Recent Trends and Political Choices' (Winter 2008) *Dissent*, 6, <http://www.dissentmagazine.org/article/?article=990> accessed 20 September 2010.

[180] See generally Amy Chua, 'The Paradox of Free Market Democracy: Rethinking Development Policy' (2000) 41 *Harvard International Law Journal* 287.

[181] See, generally, Amy Chua, *World on Fire: How Exporting Free Market Democracy Breeds Ethnic Hatred and Global Instability* (Doubleday, New York, 2002). See also Anne Orford, 'Locating the International: Military and Monetary Interventions after the Cold War' (1997) 38 *Harvard International Law Journal* 443, 455–9, detailing the role played by IMF and World Bank policies prior to the eruption of genocidal conflict in the former Yugoslavia.

[182] Chua, above n 181, 16.

in place.[183] Therefore, Chua's contentions do not indicate that States should eschew marketization and free trade. They indicate that the process should be managed and properly sequenced, as is argued in Chapter 5.

E. The Paradox of Power Politics and Participation Rights in the WTO

This chapter has largely focused on institutional problems within the WTO which work to the disadvantage of certain constituencies, including developing States. Essentially, these points relate to discrepancies in the amount of influence and power exercised by certain actors compared to other actors within the WTO. However, an inherent paradox arises in this assertion. That is, despite the flaws and biases in its processes, perhaps it is arguable that the WTO *enhances* the power of developing States.

Developed States are clearly more powerful than developing States in the context of shaping international economic law and policy. Nevertheless, the WTO helps to regulate and control the behaviour of developed States, which would otherwise be legally unconstrained. For example, while the rules regarding agriculture do not go far enough in abolishing Northern protectionism, at least they impose some constraints on those unfair practices, which did not exist prior to the advent of the WTO.[184] Even if the rules generated under the WTO are ultimately unfavourable to developing States, political scientist Dr Ken Shadlen has explained:

under conditions of marked power asymmetries no rules *are* bad rules—they are simply less predictable, changing with the whims of the more powerful actors, and they do not promise reciprocal constraints.[185]

Shadlen goes on to outline how developing States have in fact exercised greater power within the WTO than might be expected, given the power differential between them and the developed States. For example, in the Doha round developed States have managed to stave off the imposition of a tougher intellectual property regime via the WTO and stronger investment measures: neither outcome is likely to eventuate from a concluded Doha deal.[186] However, that power must not be overstated. While developing States have managed to block certain developed country initiatives, they have not generally succeeded in promoting their own agendas.

The deadlock in the WTO has probably contributed to the proliferation of bilateral and regional free trade deals in the last decade.[187] Such agreements are allowed under WTO rules so long as they comply with the requirements of Article XXIV of GATT. This development is not good news for developing States. The

---

[183] Wolf, above n 174, 29.   [184] See Chapter 6, Part B.
[185] Ken Shadlen, 'Resources, Rules and international political economy: the politics of development in the WTO' in Joseph, Kinley, and Waincymer (eds), above n 1, 115.
[186] See generally, ibid.   [187] Ibid, 131.

power differential in some bilateral contexts is much worse than in the WTO, in which the power of developing States is enhanced by the consensus rule.[188] For example, the US clearly had the upper hand in concluding deals with Morocco, Jordan and even Australia. The EU has superior power in its current negotiations over European Partnership Agreements with countries in Asia and the Pacific.[189] It is therefore not surprising that bilateral agreements tend to impose more onerous requirements compared to WTO obligations, which favour the interests of developed States, such as so-called 'TRIPS plus' provisions regarding intellectual property.[190]

The above observations do not mean that developed States should simply accept bad rules and not seek better rules within the WTO. Developing States (and civil society organizations) should seek to amend imperfect world trade laws in the face of the realities of power imbalances. The 'realist' nature of power politics cannot preclude the validity of identifying flaws in the political and other processes of an international organization. It is not acceptable to simply throw up one's hands and lament that such flaws are inevitable and better than some worse alternative.

F. Conclusion

Democratic deficit probably characterizes most international organizations, including the WTO. However, the unusual power of WTO rules, as well as particular characteristics of its internal processes (for example, secrecy within negotiations, the single compulsory undertaking), generate more acute anxieties about its democratic deficit. The WTO's internal processes and its inputs do not justify its output. Therefore, one strategy is to reform the WTO's internal processes. Indeed, it is fair to point out that the constituencies identified as disadvantaged during the Uruguay round of negotiations, social justice interests and developing States, have exercised far more influence in the Doha round. Nevertheless, enormous challenges are entailed in reforming internal processes to allow for the proper consideration of the perspectives of these constituencies. For example, richer States will always have greater economic power than poorer States and will always be tempted to abuse their superior bargaining positions (though the identity of richer States may change). It may be impossible to accommodate all of the various agendas of trade and non-trade NGOs, not to mention the agendas of the various States, within the WTO negotiating framework.[191] The stalling of the Doha round indicates that the increased negotiating clout of developing States and the increased participation and vigilance of NGOs have reduced the possibility of consensus agreement.

Nevertheless, given that the stakeholders in the WTO process extend far beyond the traditional GATT/WTO trade negotiators, continued exclusion or relegation

---

[188] See also World Development Report 2006, above n 12, 215–16.
[189] See Chapter 9, text at notes 72–89.   [190] See Chapter 7, Part F.
[191] UNHCHR, above n 44, para 45; Sutherland Report, above n 25, 44–5; Keohane and Nye, above n 2, 8; Howse, above n 105, 112.

of non-trade interests from and continued negotiation disadvantage for poorer States within WTO internal processes is not justifiable. It may also be impossible to proceed with WTO negotiations without a significantly improved democratic pedigree.[192] An increase in input legitimacy may be needed in order to justify the WTO's output legitimacy. Paradoxically, more inclusive 'input' may inevitably reduce the strength of the WTO's output.[193] The stakes of the WTO's output, in terms for example of a single undertaking and strong legal enforcement of obligations, may have to be lowered, allowing for example for more plurilateral agreements or 'exit options' for States.[194] An easing of the 'legal' side of the WTO to accommodate its political side may be necessary.[195] This may sound like a weak option, especially given that the strong judicialization of trade law has often been regarded as the jewel in the WTO's crown. On the other hand, a better democratic pedigree would render the resultant agreements more legitimate and acceptable to the populations of Member States.[196]

Current WTO output probably exceeds its current input legitimacy, which justifies a dilution of its powers. In any case, increased input would be likely to lead to a dilution of WTO outputs. Deceleration in the global free trade project will be viewed by many as an unfortunate compromise that is a 'second best' option. That said, it may be the only option that is politically feasible in the short term. Specific proposals in this regard are discussed in Chapter 9.

Furthermore, it must be remembered that the supposed 'depoliticization' of free trade by the WTO, by removing domestic political choices in regard to trade liberalization, presumes that that particular demarcation between economics and politics is appropriate and even natural, given that free trade is presumed to be *the* way to achieve economic growth.[197] As will be discussed in Chapter 5, this neoliberal presumption is challengeable.

An alternative strategy, discussed further in Chapter 10, is to boost the strength of non-economic areas of international governance in order to provide for a greater balance of interests and agendas at the international level. Such an option does not seem politically achievable in the short term, but must be a long term goal of the international community.[198]

The vacuum in global trade negotiations is currently being filled by proliferating bilateral and regional free trade agreements. This is an unfortunate development

[192] Howse comments on the potential veto power of 'outsiders' generated by their ability to expose 'fault lines' in proposed deals, which must become public at some stage prior to ratification: Howse, above n 105,116.
[193] See Pauwelyn, above n 65, 337–46.
[194] Pauwelyn, above n 65, 340, 343. See also Wolf, above n 174, 211, and Stiglitz and Charlton, above n 47, 104, questioning the notion of the single undertaking.
[195] See also Joost Pauwelyn, 'The Transformation of World Trade' (2005–2006) 104 *Michigan Law Review* 1.
[196] See also Keohane and Nye, above n 2, 27; Raustiala, above n 8, 862. See also Deborah Z Cass, *The Constitutionalization of the World Trade Organization. Legitimacy, Democracy, and Community in the International Trading System* (Oxford University Press, Oxford, 2005) 221–3.
[197] Chang, above n 43, 175–6.
[198] See also Pascal Lamy, 'The Place and Role of the WTO (WTO law) in the International Legal Order', *Address to the European Society of International Law*, 19 May 2006.

in terms of redressing democratic deficits in trade negotiations and outcomes. Nevertheless, this development does not mean that disadvantaged constituencies should simply accept whatever unsatisfactory deal might be on the table in the Doha negotiations.

Finally, it is often postulated that free trade rules help to promote political openness in conjunction with economic openness. There are however legitimate arguments, including the thesis of Amy Chua, to indicate that a happy marriage between democracy and free markets cannot be presumed in the developing world.

4

'Human Rights' Restrictions On Trade

The WTO is generally designed to facilitate free trade between States. In this chapter, the WTO compatibility of restrictions on trade that States may wish to impose for 'human rights' reasons is examined.

A differentiating feature of the trade restrictions discussed in this chapter, compared to those proposed in following chapters, is that they largely concern restrictions which developed States ('the North') wish to impose on developing States ('the South'). These human rights restrictions are at the cutting edge of the alleged schism between activists in the North and governments in the South, which was discussed in Chapter 3.[1] Indeed, a UN Report from 2000 reveals the deep distrust of the South over trade and human rights linkages:

> The tying of trade to human rights in the fashion in which it has so far been done is problematic for a number of reasons. In the first instance, it too easily succumbs to the charge by developing countries of neo-colonialism. Secondly, the commitment of Northern countries to a genuinely democratic and human rights-sensitive international regime is rendered suspect both by an extremely superficial rendering of the meaning of human rights, and by the numerous double standards that are daily observed in the relations between countries of the North and those of the South.[2]

However, one cannot blithely dismiss the occasional desirability of the imposition of trade measures for human rights reasons. After all, many of the States in the South that object to such measures are in fact terrible abusers of human rights. It might be appropriate to apply such measures as a response to the appalling human rights record of another State, or to restrict or otherwise regulate the import of a product that has been produced in a way that breaches human rights. Furthermore, States in the North (and indeed all States) have a duty under human rights law to take measures to prevent or regulate the entry of products or services into their jurisdictions which might harm the human rights of their own populations.

This chapter first examines the notion of human rights trade sanctions, both on a general and a product basis. The relevant scope of GATT and GATS obligations is then examined, including the prohibitions on discrimination as well as relevant exceptions in Article XX of GATT and Article XIV of GATS. This law is examined with regard to its effect on human rights trade measures. The same

---

[1] See Chapter 3, text at notes 90–4.

[2] J Oloka-Onyango and Deepika Udagama, 'The Realization of Economic, Social and Cultural Rights: Globalization and its impact on the full enjoyment of Human Rights', UN doc. E/Cn.4/Sub.2/2000/13 (15 June 2000) 17 (footnotes omitted).

analysis is then undertaken with regard to the SPS and TBT agreements. The most commonly proposed human rights trade measures relate to labour rights, so the possibility of a new labour rights or 'social' clause in the WTO is examined. The role of waivers in bringing WTO rules into compliance with human rights is then discussed. Finally, the potential for WTO rules to open up States to trade which improves human rights will be examined, by inquiring into whether WTO rules might be used to challenge laws mandating extensive internet censorship.

A. Human Rights Trade Measures

General human rights sanctions

General human rights sanctions arise where a State imposes economic sanctions against a State to protest against the latter State's human rights record, and/or to impose pressure on the latter State to change its ways. Examples are the comprehensive economic sanctions imposed against the military government in Burma by the US and Canada.[3] Burma is a WTO member, so bans on its imports prima facie breach WTO obligations regarding quotas (with a zero quota being imposed on such goods) and MFN. Are such sanctions permissible under the WTO?

Article XXI permits 'national security' exceptions, none of which have been interpreted in the WTO dispute settlement system. The equivalent exception provision in GATS is Article XIV bis. Article XXI(a) only permits the withholding of certain information and is therefore not applicable. Article XXI(b)(i) and (ii) only apply to prevent trade in fissionable material and armaments. Article XXI(c) permits trade restrictions which are mandated under the UN Charter 'for the maintenance of international peace and security'. Article XXI(c) essentially permits States to comply with Security Council sanctions imposed under Chapter VII of the UN Charter: the Security Council may impose mandatory economic sanctions on a State under Article 41 of the Charter if it deems (under Article 39) that the relevant State is threatening international peace and security. Under Article 25, States must comply with these sanctions, so Article XXI(c) ensures that the WTO Agreement does not conflict with the UN Charter. For example, the Security Council imposed extensive sanctions on Iraq throughout the 1990s due to its failure to comply with UN weapons inspections. No question of WTO legality arose as Iraq was and is not a WTO member. Nevertheless, such sanctions would have been legal under Article XXI(c) if Iraq had been a member of the WTO. However, it is doubtful that Article XXI(c) applies to sanctions imposed by the General Assembly (GA), the plenary body within the UN. The recommendation of sanctions by the GA is more common than their imposition by the Security Council, but GA resolutions are not legally binding. Therefore, sanctions that are recommended by the GA, such as those against

---

[3] See Burmese Freedom and Democracy Act 2003 (US) and Special Economic Measures (Burma) Regulations (SOR/2007-85) (Canada), 13 December 2007.

South Africa in the 1970s and 1980s,[4] are not necessarily 'saved' from WTO illegality under Article XXI(c).

Article XXI(b)(iii) permits WTO Members to take actions which '*it considers necessary* for the protection of its essential security interests...taken in time of war *or other emergency in international relations*' (emphasis added). This provision seems to permit trade restrictions between belligerents in a military conflict, and in conflicts which fall short of war but are nevertheless an international relations 'emergency'. The perpetration of egregious human rights abuses by a State such as Burma, coupled with the extreme disapproval of those abuses by another State, might count as such an emergency. On the other hand, it might be difficult to maintain that human rights abuses in a far-off State, even of the most severe kind, threaten a State's security interests.[5]

In any case, States seem to have much discretion under Article XXI(b)(iii). The measures do not actually have to be 'necessary': the inquiry instead seems to focus on whether the State imposing the measures 'considers' that they were necessary. Given a relevant State will inevitably assert that it did consider the measures to be necessary, it would seem difficult for a WTO dispute settlement body to find otherwise. Indeed, given its language, it is questionable whether Article XXI(b)(iii) is even justiciable.[6]

Article XX of GATT and Article XIV of GATS permit restrictions on trade for 'non-trade' reasons beyond national security. These exceptions are discussed in detail below. It is unlikely that any of those provisions would permit such blanket unilateral sanctions.[7]

Is it desirable for general human rights sanctions to be allowed? It is well known that the enforcement system of international human rights law is its Achilles heel. The most common form of sanction against a human rights abusing State is unilateral or multilateral condemnation, that is 'naming and shaming'. While all States attempt to stave off such shaming, the sanction 'has been conspicuously unsuccessful in motivating prompt changes in behaviour by delinquent States',[8] especially the most incorrigible violators who are often immune from domestic pressure due to their extensive suppression of opposition voices and the media.

---

[4] South Africa had been a GATT member since 1948. The Security Council only ever mandated an arms embargo on South Africa, rather than comprehensive sanctions. SC Resolution 418 (4 November 1977) mandated an arms embargo under Chapter VII of the UN Charter. While Resolution 569 (26 July 1985) urged States to adopt further measures against South Africa, that Resolution was not adopted under Chapter VII so those recommendations were not mandatory.

[5] Carlos Manuel Vázquez, 'Trade sanctions and human rights—past, present, and future' (2003) 6 *Journal of International Economic Law* 797, 825.

[6] See Anthony E Cassimatis, *Human Rights Related Trade Measures under International Law* (Martinus Nijhoff, Leiden, 2007) 330; Peter Van den Bossche, *The Law and Policy of the World Trade Organization* (Cambridge University Press, Cambridge, 2005) 629–31; Vázquez, above n 5, 824; Michael Ewing-Chow, 'First do no harm: Trade sanctions and human rights' (2007) 5 *Northwestern Journal of International Human Rights* 153, 168.

[7] See also Vázquez, above n 5.

[8] Sarah Joseph and Joanna Kyriakakis, 'United Nations and Human Rights' in Sarah Joseph and Adam McBeth (eds), *Research Handbook on International Human Rights Law* (Edward Elgar, Cheltenham, 2010) 27.

At the other end of the scale, the use of military force to stop a State from violating human rights is illegal in international law unless authorized by the Security Council.[9] Economic sanctions are therefore the strongest legal measure available in general international law to punish a State for its continuation of human rights abusive behaviour.[10] Therefore, WTO law may be curtailing an important means of enforcing human rights law if it prohibits such sanctions. For example, economic sanctions probably played a large role in the eventual conformity of South Africa and Serbia-Montenegro with international demands regarding human rights.[11]

However, unilateral economic sanctions may often have little effect beyond the symbolic, as the target State may recoup some or even all resultant trade losses with new trading partners. Furthermore, the sanctioning State will lose influence in the target State.[12] Clearly the strongest unilateral sanctions are those imposed by trading giants such as the US and EU, especially in situations where the sanctioning State/s comprise a large percentage of pre-existing trade with a country. Unilateral sanctions can also set off a domino effect, prompting copycat sanctions by other States or action by international institutions.[13] Economic sanctions imposed by the Security Council are of course the most effective sanctions, as they deprive the target State of alternative trading partners. However, Security Council sanctions are rare, and are normally limited rather than comprehensive.[14] Furthermore, comprehensive trade sanctions can have the effect of provoking nationalistic backlashes and entrenching regimes, rather than their presumed desired effect of prompting a disgruntled population to force a regime to change its ways.[15]

Economic sanctions are often deeply problematic from a human rights point of view. Vázquez eloquently notes that sanctions 'treat human beings as pawns in a geo-political game', contrary to the bottom line of human rights which treats human beings as ends rather than means.[16] Unfortunately, sanctions often lead to grave suffering on the part of innocent target populations if a recalcitrant

---

[9] See UN Charter, Articles 2(4) and 2(7). Arguments over the legality or illegality of 'humanitarian intervention' have animated lawyers and scholars for many years, especially since the NATO bombings of Serbia to stop ethnic cleansing in Kosovo. This author believes that the majority of international lawyers consider unilateral humanitarian intervention to be illegal under international law.

[10] See generally on the legality of economic sanctions under general international law, Cassimatis, above n 6, at 259–66, and 433; James Harrison, *The Human Rights Impact of the World Trade Organisation* (Hart, Oxford, 2007) 98–9; Vázquez, above n 5, 799–800.

[11] On South Africa, see Ewing-Chow, above n 6, 174–6. On Serbia, see Charles J Kacsur, 'Economic Sanctions Targeting Yugoslavia: An Effective National Security Strategy Component' (2003) *Storming Media*.

[12] Perhaps such effects are occurring in Sudan and Zimbabwe, which are both the subject of sanctions from Northern countries, and both now engage in extensive trade with China, which never imposes human rights sanctions. Sudan is not a member of the WTO, though it is engaged in accession negotiations. Zimbabwe has been a member since March 1995.

[13] Harrison, above n 10, 105, commenting on the history of sanctions against South Africa.

[14] Political problems, such as the veto power of the five permanent members of the Security Council (namely, China, France, Russia, UK, and the US), hamper the decision-making powers of the Security Council; the only States that are likely to be the subject of Chapter VII sanctions are those States that lack an ally amongst the Permanent 5.

[15] Ewing-Chow, above n 6, 153.   [16] Vázquez, above n 5, 837.

government refuses to cave in to the demands of the sanctioning States.[17] The Iraqi sanctions are illustrative of the devastating effects that sanctions can have. The sanctions severely impacted the economy and many aspects of daily life, affecting the drinking water supply, agriculture, electricity, and the telecommunications and transport systems. This led to significant human rights problems including an increase in infant and maternal mortality rates, malnutrition, illiteracy and even deaths. The most vulnerable groups, such as children, the elderly and nursing mothers, were particularly affected.[18] Similarly, Ewing-Chow reports that US sanctions have caused few problems for Burma's military junta, but have hit the civilian population hard.[19] Concerns regarding effects on innocent parties have led to 'smart sanctions', which are more tailored to harm culpable leaders rather than innocent populations in the form of asset freezes, travel bans, and bans on strategic commodities such as arms. Many smart sanctions regimes do not raise WTO issues as they do not affect the movement of goods and services.

In 1997, the Committee on Economic, Social and Cultural Rights issued General Comment 8 on 'The relationship between economic sanctions and respect for economic, social and cultural rights'. The Committee stated at paragraph 3:

> While the impact of sanctions varies from one case to another, the Committee is aware that they almost always have a dramatic impact on the rights recognized in the Covenant. Thus, for example, they often cause significant disruption in the distribution of food, pharmaceuticals and sanitation supplies, jeopardize the quality of food and the availability of clean drinking water, severely interfere with the functioning of basic health and education systems, and undermine the right to work. In addition, their unintended consequences can include reinforcement of the power of oppressive élites, the emergence, almost invariably, of a black market and the generation of huge windfall profits for the privileged élites which manage it, enhancement of the control of the governing élites over the population at large, and restriction of opportunities to seek asylum or to manifest political opposition. While the phenomena mentioned in the preceding sentence are essentially political in nature, they also have a major additional impact on the enjoyment of economic, social and cultural rights.[20]

Hence, the Committee urged States to consider the likely impacts on the enjoyment of economic, social, and cultural rights in designing and imposing sanctions regimes, and to monitor those impacts while sanctions are imposed.[21] Sanctioning States must take alleviating measures if those impacts breach ICESCR rights,

---

[17] See John Mueller and Karl Mueller, 'Sanctions of Mass Destruction' (1999) 78 *Foreign Affairs* 43.

[18] Office of the High Commissioner for Human Rights (OHCHR), 'The Human Rights Impact of Economic Sanctions on Iraq' (Background paper prepared by the Office of the High Commissioner for Human Rights for the meeting of the Executive Committee on Humanitarian Affairs) (5 September 2000) <http://www.casi.org.uk/info/undocs/sanct31.pdf> accessed 22 September 2010.

[19] Ewing-Chow, above n 6, 174.

[20] See also *Report of the Secretary-General on the Work of the Organization*, UN GAOR 53rd Sess., Supp. No. 1, UN doc. A/53/1 (1998) para 64.

[21] CESCR, 'General Comment 8: The relationship between economic sanctions and respect for economic, social and cultural rights', UN doc. E/C.12/1997/8, 12 December 1997, paras 11–13.

especially if the sanctions cause 'disproportionate suffering [to] vulnerable groups within the targeted country'.[22]

The UN General Assembly adopted a resolution in 2009 which unambiguously condemned the use of unilateral economic sanctions, largely on the basis of their detrimental human rights impacts.[23] The voting pattern confirmed that economic sanctions are an area of North/South dispute, with 132 voting in favour and 54 (largely developed) States voting against.

International human rights law never *requires* the imposition of general sanctions. Rather, human rights law imposes conditions on sanctions regimes if they should be adopted. Therefore, a prohibition on 'human rights trade sanctions' under WTO law would not directly conflict with human rights law, as human rights law does not ever demand that a State enforce its norms by imposing general economic sanctions on a delinquent State.[24]

Product-based trade measures based on human rights

A State may wish to restrict the import of a particular product due to concerns over human rights abuses associated with that product. The concerns may relate to harms the product could cause to the State's own population ('inward measures'), such as the damage caused by asbestos or tobacco products which prejudice rights to health and life. Another relevant measure might be the regulation of water providers in ways that breach GATS but which ensure that low-cost water is available to poor people. A State undoubtedly has obligations to protect the rights of its populous so it is obliged under international human rights law to implement some inward measures. If WTO law prohibits such inward measures, a conflict arises with international human rights law.

Alternatively, the human rights concern might relate to human rights abuses associated with a product from an exporting State ('outward measures'): for example, the targeted products might be those manufactured in conditions of forced labour.[25] Another example would be measures aimed at preventing the trade in certain goods, such as 'conflict diamonds' in Western Africa, which have fuelled conflicts and associated gross human rights violations.[26] The human rights analysis of outward measures is more complex, as the relevant human rights are those of members of the exporting State's population, rather than people in

---

[22] Ibid, para 14. Note that the Committee is confirming a type of extraterritorial obligation for States: see generally, Chapter 8 below. The Committee also confirmed that sanctions do not remove ICESCR obligations from the target State: para 10.

[23] UNGA, 'Human Rights and Unilateral Coercive Measures', UN doc. A/RES/63/179 (18 December 2008).

[24] See also Vázquez, above n 5, 802 and 821; Harrison, above n 10, 100–1.

[25] See also the typology developed by Harrison, above n 10, at 61–7.

[26] For an overview of the issues involved in conflict diamonds, see: Global Witness, 'Conflict Diamonds. Possibilities for the Identification, Certification and Control of Diamonds' (2000) (London, Global Witness) <http://www.globalwitness.org/media_library_detail.php/86/en/conflict_diamonds> accessed 24 April 2010.

the territory of the State imposing the measures. It is argued in Chapter 8 that States have extraterritorial obligations to the people of other States. However, it is doubtful that such extraterritorial duties would generally require a State to restrict the trade in goods from other States that were manufactured in a way that harmed human rights.[27] Rather, extraterritorial obligations are more likely to entail cooperative rather than coercive measures.[28] Outward measures are unlikely to be mandated save in exceptional circumstances, such as perhaps the 'conflict diamonds' situation.[29] Such a duty might arise if an importing State knows or should know that its market for the relevant product is so important that the abuse would stop or significantly decrease if it closed off that market. For example, suppose State A imposes a ban on the import of clothing from State B because that clothing is manufactured by children in exploitative conditions, and suppose that State A's market constitutes 80 per cent of State B's clothing exports. The ban might prompt State B to take measures against child labour so as to re-open its market access to State A. Alternatively, State B might find new markets. In that situation, at least State A has absolved itself of any allegation of complicity in the child labour. Unfortunately, the consequence of such measures in some situations might be to worsen the situation for the relevant children. Perhaps the clothing industry in State B will collapse, and the children forced into worse industries, such as mining or prostitution. Therefore, in the scenario given, it seems unlikely that State A is compelled under international human rights law to ban imports of clothing from State B.[30]

The WTO compatibility of product-based human rights measures, whether inward or outward, is discussed below.

B. Do Human Rights Trade Measures Prima Facie Breach GATT/GATS?

A threshold question in determining whether a human rights measure breaches WTO provisions is whether there is a prima facie breach. The lesser the scope of the WTO provisions, the greater a State's discretion to implement human rights trade measures. In this section, key provisions regarding the scope of GATT and

[27] See also UNHCHR, *Human Rights and World Trade Agreements: Using General Exception Clauses to Protect Human Rights* (Office of the High Commissioner for Human Rights, New York and Geneva, 2005) 8 <http://www.ohchr.org/Documents/Publications/WTOen.pdf> accessed 20 September 2010); see also Adam McBeth, *International Economic Actors and Human Rights* (Routledge, Oxford, 2010) 129; Vázquez, above n 5, 821.

[28] Eg, Article 2(1) of the ICESCR talks of international cooperation, which does not seem to include hostile measures such as targeted trade embargoes.

[29] See also Chapter 6, text at and before notes 158–161 on trade in 'biofuels'.

[30] Note that Harrison, above n 10, at 80 cites *The Economist* from 13 July 1999 in stating that only 5% of working children are employed in export industries. Ewing-Chow, above n 6, reports that thousands of children were laid off in Bangladesh due to the threat of US trade sanctions, with some moving into 'more hazardous activities such as prostitution', at 173.

GATS obligations will be analysed. Issues regarding the SPS and TBT agreements are considered below. TRIPS and the AoA are considered in separate chapters, while the other WTO agreements are examined in less detail in this book.

'Like' goods and services

The discrimination provisions of GATT and GATS, namely MFN and national treatment provisions, are enlivened when 'like' goods or services are treated differently. How has the word 'like' been interpreted? The broader the concept of 'like' goods and services, the broader the scope of the non-discrimination provisions.

A key issue from a human rights point of view is whether goods can be differentiated on the basis of its production or process methods (PPMs). For example, are shoes manufactured by child labourers 'like' shoes when compared to those manufactured by adults? Is salmon that is harvested in a way that harms sustainable rights to food 'like' salmon that is harvested in a sustainable way?

In the GATT *Tuna* cases,[31] the impugned US measures prohibited the import of tuna from a State unless that State satisfied US standards on dolphin safe fishing practices. Both panels decided that tuna caught in a dolphin-safe way could not be distinguished for the purposes of GATT obligations from other tuna. In *US—Shrimp*, measures which distinguished between shrimp caught with a 'turtle excluder device' (TED) and shrimp caught without a TED, so as to protect sea turtles, were also deemed to distinguish between 'like' shrimp products.[32] WTO and GATT jurisprudence therefore suggests that 'PPMs that are not physically evident in the final product cannot be used to distinguish between otherwise "like products"'.[33]

In *European Communities—Measures Affecting Asbestos and Products Containing Asbestos* (*EC—Asbestos*)[34] the impugned provisions concerned an EC ban on building products made with chrysolite asbestos fibres. Canada argued that such products were 'like' other building products used for the same purposes, such as 'PCG' fibres.[35] Were they 'like' products for the purposes of Article III of GATT, which prescribes that imported goods receive the same treatment as local goods? The Appellate Body reasoned that the determination of 'likeness' depended on the degree of competitiveness and substitutability between the two products (asbestos and PCG products).[36] In determining such matters, the Appellate Body paid regard to 'the properties, nature and quality of the products', 'the end use of the products', 'consumers' tastes and habits' (or perceptions and behaviour), and 'the

---

[31] *United States—Restrictions on Imports of Tuna*, GATT doc. DS21/R (Report of the Panel produced 3 September 1991, never adopted) ('Tuna I') and *United States—Restrictions on Imports of Tuna* GATT doc. DS29/R (Report by Panel, adopted 16 June 1994) ('Tuna II').

[32] *United States—Import Prohibition of Certain Shrimp and Shrimp Products*, WTO doc. WT/DS58/R (15 May 1998) (Report of the Panel) ('*US—Shrimp I*').

[33] See also *United States—Taxes on Automobiles*, GATT doc. DS31/R (Report of the Panel) (11 October 1994) para 5.54.

[34] *European Communities—Measures Affecting Asbestos and Products Containing Asbestos*, WTO doc. WT/DS135/AB/R, AB-2000-11 (12 March 2001) (Report of the Appellate Body) ('*EC—Asbestos*').

[35] Polyvinyl alcohol fibres (PVA), cellulose, and glass fibres are collectively referred to as PCG fibres by the Appellate Body. See ibid, para 84.

[36] Ibid, para 98.

tariff classification of the products'.[37] The Appellate Body found that the carcinogenic and toxic nature of asbestos fibres compared to PCG fibres had to be taken into account in assessing the 'competitive relationship' between the products.[38] Ultimately, the different products were found not to be 'like', due to differing physical characteristics and, interestingly, differing consumer perceptions. This decision, while still focusing on physical attributes, might open the way for more nuanced approaches to the notion of 'like' products, potentially for human rights or other social purposes.[39] Furthermore, one may note a comment from the Panel in *EC—Measures Affecting the Approval and Marketing of Biotech Products*,[40] concerning differences in treatment between biotech products and non-biotech products:

it is not self-evident that the alleged less favourable treatment of imported biotech products is explained by the foreign origin of these products rather than, for instance, *perceived* differences between biotech products and non-biotech products in terms of their safety... [41]

The *Biotech* case concerned the SPS agreement, discussed below, rather than the non-discrimination provisions of GATT. However, the comment implies that 'a perceived difference in terms of safety', even if that difference is unproven (distinguishing the circumstances from those in *Asbestos*), may justify a finding that the goods are not 'like'.[42]

Furthermore, it may be noted that one Appellate Body member in *Asbestos*, in a concurring opinion, suggested that the determination of 'like' products should take into account issues beyond economic considerations.[43] This opinion seems to open the door to the possibility that products can be differentiated by reference to non-economic considerations, such as their impact on human rights.

Dr James Harrison has raised the issue of whether goods might be distinguished on the basis of the nature of a producer. For example, could preferential regulations be applied to fruit produced by impoverished small farmers compared to fruit produced by a multinational corporation on the basis that the fruit are not 'like'? A State may wish to apply such regulations in order to boost the incomes and livelihoods of struggling farmers, an aim which would conform with international human rights law. Harrison doubts that the *Asbestos* test of 'likeness' could be stretched so as to permit differential treatment in such an instance.[44] Indeed, the relevance of producer characteristics to a determination of likeness has been rejected by WTO panels.[45]

A test of likeness which focused on the aims and effects of an impugned regulation, as was applied by a GATT panel in *US—Malt Beverages*,[46] might permit

---

[37] Ibid, para 101.   [38] Ibid, para 115.   [39] McBeth, above n 27, 128.

[40] *European Communities—Measures Affecting the Approval and Marketing of Biotech Products*, WTO docs. WT/DS291/R, WT/DS292/R and WT/DS293/R (29 September 2006) (Reports of the Panel). The case concerned a challenge to a *de facto* moratorium on the approval of genetically modified organisms (GMOs) by the EC as well as bans on GMOs issued by certain individual EC States.

[41] Ibid, para 7.2514, emphasis added.   [42] McBeth, above n 27, 135.

[43] *EC—Asbestos* (Appellate Body), above n 34, para 154.   [44] Harrison, above n 10, 195.

[45] *United States—Standards for Reformulated and Conventional Gasoline*, WTO doc. WT/DS2/R (29 January 1996) (Report of the Panel) ('*US—Reformulated Gasoline*') para 6.11.

[46] *United States—Measures Affecting Alcoholic and Malt Beverages*, GATT doc. DS23/R (Report of the Panel, adopted 19 June 1992) paras 5.25 and 5.71ff.

greater regulatory autonomy for States.[47] Such a test might permit more regulations, including those which promote human rights and are adopted for non-protectionist purposes, and which do not have a disproportionate effect on foreign trade. Such an approach would more closely resemble the tests of discrimination adopted under human rights law. For example, the HRC has stated, with regard to the guarantees of non-discrimination in the ICCPR, that:

> not every differentiation of treatment will constitute discrimination, if the criteria for such differentiation are reasonable and objective and if the aim is to achieve a purpose which is legitimate under the Covenant.[48]

However, a test of aims and effects has been rejected under WTO law, for example by the Panel and Appellate Body in *Japan-Alcoholic Beverages II*.[49] The non-trade purpose of a law is generally relevant to the application of GATT exceptions in Article XX, rather than an assessment of whether like goods have been treated differently under Articles I or III. The use of Article XX, an exceptions clause, is a more difficult avenue for justifying regulations adopted for non-trade purposes (including human rights purposes), as the regulating State bears the burden of proof in establishing the application of an exception, whereas the complainant State bears the burden of proof in establishing that discrimination between like goods has arisen.[50]

Regarding GATS, the issue of 'like' services is likely to depend on issues such as the characteristics of the service, the classification and description of the service in the UN Central Product Classification (CPC) system, and 'consumer habits and preferences' regarding the relevant service or service provider.[51] A particular concern regarding GATS is that it may prohibit the regulation of essential services, such as the provision of utilities or education, which are designed to ensure that such services are accessible to the poor. In this regard, it seems unlikely that the interpretation of 'like' services will take into account differences between private utility providers or private education providers in rich areas compared to providers, including government providers, in poorer areas. As noted by Dr Andrew Lang:

> it would be hard to argue that two identical services were not like simply because of the socio-economic status of the consumers of that service. Such a distinction would be unthinkable in the goods context.[52]

---

[47] Harrison, above n 10, 193–4.
[48] HRC, 'General Comment No. 18: Non-discrimination', UN doc. HRI/GEN/1/Rev.1 (10 November 1989) para 13.
[49] See WTO docs. WT/DS8/AB/R, WT/DS10/AB/R, WT/DS11/AB/R (4 October 1996) (Report of the Appellate Body), para 18: see also WTO doc. WT/DS8/R (11 July 1996) (Report of the Panel).
[50] See also Rüdiger Wolfrun, Peter-Tobias Stoll, and Anja Seibert-Fohr, *WTO: Technical Barriers and SPS Measures* (Martinus Nijhoff, Leiden, 2007) para 34. See also Harrison, above n 10, 215.
[51] Van den Bossche, above n 6, 323–4.
[52] Andrew Lang, 'The GATS and Regulatory Autonomy: a Case Study of Social Regulation of the Water Industry' (2004) 7 *Journal of International Economic Law* 801, 830, see generally, 828–30. See also Chapter 5.

Discrimination against 'like' goods

Under both national treatment and MFN obligations, States may not discriminate between like goods. The Appellate Body and Panels have consistently found that both formal (de jure) discrimination and factual (de facto) discrimination are prohibited.[53] Furthermore, discrimination must cause disadvantage to the relevant imported products: there is no problem, for example, if imports are treated more favorably than local goods, or if the application of different rules results in substantively equal conditions of competition.[54] The GATT Panel in *Thailand—Cigarettes* in 1990 gave an interesting example of an apparently neutral law that might nevertheless cause disadvantage to imported goods. A general ban on cigarette advertising would, it was suggested, have favoured local cigarettes because, at that time, Thai brands were better known than imported brands.[55]

The inclusion of de facto discrimination is justified on the basis that the non-discrimination obligations could be circumvented by cleverly drafted laws. The result is that the prohibitions on discrimination have a very broad scope. For example, the adoption by a State of unusually high regulatory standards with regard to a particular product might seem non-discriminatory, as it applies to local goods (so there is no apparent breach of national treatment standards) as well as all overseas goods (so there is no breach of MFN). However, unusually high standards might require foreign producers of the particular product to set up separate production lines to continue exports to the relevant State, so discrimination in effect might almost always arise.[56]

More recently, the Appellate Body appeared to significantly narrow the test of discrimination in *Dominican Republic—Measures affecting the importation and internal sale of cigarettes.*

[T]he existence of a detrimental effect on a given imported product resulting from a measure does not necessarily imply that this measure accords less favourable treatment to imports *if the detrimental effect is explained by factors or circumstances unrelated to the foreign origin of the product...*[57]

The quote seems to indicate that a measure which has a legitimate regulatory purpose, but which impacts disproportionately on imported goods, is not relevantly discriminatory, as the 'detrimental effect is explained' by non-trade factors. If so, the quote would signal a significant rollback of the test of factual discrimination.

---

[53] See, eg, *Canada—Certain Measures Affecting the Automotive Industry,* WTO docs. WT/DS139/AB/R and WT/DS142/AB/R, AB-2000-2 (31 May 2000) (Report of the Appellate Body) para 78.

[54] *United States—Section 337 of the Tariff Act of 1930,* GATT Doc L/6439 (7 November 1989) (Report of the Panel) para 5.11; *Korea—Measures affecting imports of fresh, chilled and frozen beef,* WTO docs. WT/DS161/AB/R and WT/DS169/AB/R, AB-2000-8 (11 December 2000) (Report of the Appellate Body) para 137.

[55] *Thailand—Restrictions on Importation of and Internal Taxes on Cigarettes,* GATT doc. DS10/R (7 November 1990) (Report of the Panel) para 78. Such a measure was not at issue in the case. The Panel also suggested that such a ban would be allowed under Article XX(b).

[56] Robert Hudec, ' "Circumventing" Democracy: the Political Morality of Trade Negotiations' (1993) 25 *NYU Journal of International Law and Politics* 311, 318.

[57] WTO doc. WT/DS302/AB/R (25 April 2005) (Report of the Appellate Body) para 96 (emphasis added).

It arguably reintroduces the 'aims and effects' test as being relevant to the issue of whether discrimination has arisen between like goods, rather than being relevant to the question of whether the relevant goods are actually 'like'. Dr Lorand Bartels has suggested that *Dominican Republic—Cigarettes* indicates that a measure which disproportionately impacts on foreign goods will not be deemed discriminatory under GATT if the importer is 'reasonably able to meet the conditions for more favourable treatment'.[58] It is premature however to confirm such a major reversal of prior GATT/WTO law.

If a State's law is found to discriminate against like goods contrary to its GATT obligations regarding national treatment or MFN, it may attempt to justify the measure under one of the general exceptions recognized in Article XX. Part of the test for compliance with Article XX involves another test for non-discrimination stemming from its introductory clause (or 'chapeau'), which is discussed below.

In any case, the WTO's mandate now clearly extends beyond discriminatory measures under the SPS and TBT agreements. Under those agreements, a measure will be in breach if it fails to satisfy certain minimum requirements, even if it is not discriminatory. Furthermore, as discussed directly below, the prevailing interpretation of 'quantitative restrictions' in Article XI of GATT and Article XVI of GATS lessens the need for a successful WTO complainant to establish that a measure is actually discriminatory.

Quantitative restrictions

Article XI prohibits quantitative restrictions on goods. A narrow interpretation of Article XI would simply prohibit de jure or de facto import quotas.[59] In the *Tuna* cases, the measures were found to impose a zero quota on tuna from certain countries because their tuna catches failed to comply with dolphin conservation standards, so the measures were in prima facie breach of Article XI. A similar decision arose from the Panel in *Shrimp*,[60] and was not questioned before the Appellate Body. Regarding GATS, the US ban on internet gambling services from Antigua was found to breach Article XVI of GATS, as it amounted to the imposition of a zero quota on those services.[61]

David Driesen has convincingly criticized the prevailing interpretation of Article XI. Commenting on the *Tuna* cases, he states that '*Tuna/Dolphin* does not explain why a measure, which allows any country to choose to export unlimited quantities of tuna (by choosing to comply with conservation standards), should be considered a quantitative restriction on trade.'[62] If a State can export without hindrance by

---

[58] See Lorand Bartels, 'Trade and Human Rights' in D Bethlehem, D McRae, R Neufeld, and I Van Damme (eds), *Oxford Handbook of International Trade* (Oxford University Press, Oxford, 2009) 587.
[59] David M Driesen, 'What is Free Trade? The Real Issue Lurking behind the Trade and Environment Debate' (2001) 41 *Virginia Journal of International Law* 279, 293.
[60] *US Shrimp I* (Panel), above n 32, paras 7.17 and 8.1.
[61] Tim Wu, 'The World Trade Law of Censorship and Internet Filtering' (3 May 2006) 10 <http://papers.ssrn.com/sol3/papers.cfm?abstract_id=882459> accessed 22 September 2010.
[62] Driesen, above n 59, 338–9.

complying with a regulation, that circumstance is indicative of a qualitative rather than a quantitative restriction. This interpretation of GATT significantly undermines the ability of States to enforce regulations at its borders.[63] And it might be impossible or impractical to enforce some regulations once the offending goods have passed border control.

Article III of GATT, prescribing national treatment, states in an ad note that 'any regulation' which is enforced on an 'imported product' at the border is nevertheless an internal regulation subject to Article III. In such cases, Article XI should not apply.[64] However, the GATT *Tuna* panels held that the measures regulated a process rather than a product so Article III did not apply. The significance of this outcome is that Article XI, in prima facie prohibiting 'zero quotas', seems to apply to any neutral regulation of goods (which does not distinguish between local and foreign goods) which prohibits non-complying imports.[65]

Tuna/Dolphin's narrow construction of the Ad Note to Article III made the [impugned measure] illegal only because of broad construction of Article XI. This broad construction of Article XI goes beyond the anti-mercantilist limit on quotas necessary to sustain the non-discrimination principle and embraces a laissez-faire rule limited only by applicable defenses. Hence, narrow construction of the ad note implies greater movement toward laissez-faire trade.[66]

Laissez-faire principles, which dictate broad-based 'freedom' for traders to trade without hindrance, pose a greater threat to a State's regulatory capacities than a mercantilist approach, which challenges only discriminatory regulations.

The *Tuna* interpretation of Article XI was essentially followed by the Panel in *Shrimp*, and was not questioned before the Appellate Body. Driesen's insightful analysis of *Tuna* applies equally to *Shrimp*. While there was a zero quota on shrimp caught without a TED, unlimited amounts of shrimp harvested with a TED could be imported: the impugned requirement was again qualitative not quantitative.

A similar approach to quantitative restrictions was taken in *US—Gambling* under GATS. The WTO Appellate body found that the US had opened up its market to gambling and recreational services without specifying any quantitative restrictions.[67] US regulations banned online gambling. The Panel found the ban imposed a 'zero quota' on online gambling services from Antigua, thus prima facie breaching the market access provisions of Article XVI of GATS. On appeal, the US argued that other requirements, such as that of national treatment in Article XVII, should apply in the context of prohibitions on the entry of certain services, and that the Panel's expanded interpretation of Article XVI had disturbed 'the balance between liberalization and the right to regulate'.[68] The Appellate Body upheld the Panel's decision.

---

[63] Ibid, 339–40.   [64] Van den Bossche, above n 6, 329.   [65] Driesen, above n 59, 339.
[66] Ibid, 340.
[67] Market access and national treatment obligations under GATS only apply to the services that a State nominates in its 'schedule of commitments'; qualifications may be included in that schedule (including quantitative restrictions). See Chapter 5.
[68] *United States—Measures Affecting the Cross-Border Supply of Gambling and Betting Services*, WTO doc. WT/DS285/AB/R, AB-2005-1 (7 April 2005) (Report of the Appellate Body) para 224, see also para 222.

It is arguable that a 'quantitative restriction' in relation to online gambling should relate to measures such as limits on the times that US consumers could access the service, or limits on the amounts of money that might be gambled in this way. A total ban seems less concerned with regulating the 'quantity' of a service (or a good), and more designed to protect consumers from the malevolent aspects of a particular service (or a good). The national treatment provisions in GATT and GATS should suffice to prevent the protectionist use of such total bans, so it is submitted that Article XI GATT and Article XVI GATS should not apply in such circumstances. Therefore, this author disagrees with the prevailing interpretations of those provisions.

C. Articles XX GATT and XIV GATS

Article XX GATT and Article XIV GATS are the 'general exception' provisions which allow States to depart from their GATT/GATS obligations to pursue non-trade objectives. While none of the exceptions expressly relate to 'human rights' per se, some of the exceptions might save human rights trade measures from WTO illegality.

Article XX of GATT reads, in part:[69]

Subject to the requirement that such measures are not applied in a manner which would constitute a means of arbitrary or unjustifiable discrimination between countries where the same conditions prevail, or a disguised restriction on international trade, nothing in this Agreement shall be construed to prevent the adoption or enforcement by any contracting party of measures:

(a) necessary to protect public morals;
(b) necessary to protect human, animal or plant life or health;...
(d) necessary to secure compliance with laws or regulations which are not inconsistent with the provisions of this Agreement...;
(e) relating to the products of prison labour;
(f) imposed for the protection of national treasures of artistic, historic or archaeological value;
(g) relating to the conservation of exhaustible natural resources if such measures are made effective in conjunction with restrictions on domestic production or consumption;...

The commentary below will focus on paragraphs (a), (b) and (g), with some reference to analogous jurisprudence under paragraph (d).

Paragraph (e) is the only explicit WTO provision which deals with labour. It is not however a human rights provision as prison labour is not per se prohibited under human rights law.[70] Rather, paragraph (e) is an economic provision which is designed to prevent States from gaining unfair advantages by exporting goods which are artificially cheap due to the availability of inexpensive prison labour.[71]

---

[69] I have omitted clauses that are irrelevant to the purposes of this book.
[70] Eg, Article 8(3)(b) of the ICCPR states that the prohibition on forced labour does not apply to prevent 'hard labour' as a punishment for a crime.
[71] McBeth, above n 27, 119.

Paragraph (f) relates to the human right to enjoy one's culture under Article 15(1)(a) of the ICESCR. Examples of a relevant measure might be a restriction on the export of national treasures.[72] It has not yet been interpreted by the GATT and WTO dispute settlement bodies. However, the exception seems to relate only to trade restrictions on tangible cultural property, rather than trade measures which protect culture generally.[73] It seems unlikely that Article XX(f) is broad enough to safeguard all of the rights in Article 15(1)(a).

Regarding culture, Article IV GATT permits States to impose quotas on the screenings of foreign films. Cultural protection has been an area of dispute within GATT and WTO negotiations, with the EC and particularly France arguing for extensive protection and the US arguing that products of cultural value beyond films are caught within GATT disciplines.[74] An early WTO decision in *Canada—Certain measures concerning periodicals*[75] gives rise to legitimate concern that the dispute settlement bodies may not be sufficiently sensitive to cultural issues. The dispute was triggered by the marketing in Canada of a 'split-run' version of the US magazine, *Sports Illustrated*, whereby a separate 'Canadian' version of the magazine was sold in Canada with some special Canadian sports content. Canada enacted measures to protect Canadian periodicals, with their uniquely Canadian perspective and content, from being squeezed out by US split run periodicals. *Sports Illustrated Canada* shut down within a month of the introduction of the impugned measures, which included a large discriminatory excise.[76] Despite the clear relevance of media products to a State's cultural milieu, as well as the particular risk to Canada of being swamped by US cultural material given its proximity,[77] the Panel stated that 'cultural identity was not an issue' in the case.[78] My concern here is not necessarily with the outcome of the case, in which the Canadian measures were found to breach Canada's WTO obligations. My concern is with the apparent inability by the WTO Panel to recognize the obvious cultural issues at play in this case. On the other hand, as discussed below, WTO dispute settlement bodies were prepared to identify the cultural element in Chinese restrictions on the imports of publications and audio-visual entertainment products in *China—Measures affecting trading rights and distribution services for certain publication and audiovisual entertainment products.*[79]

---

[72] Export limitations are prima facie prohibited under Article XI GATT.

[73] See Chi Carmody, 'When "Cultural Identity was not at Issue": Thinking about Canada-Certain Measures concerning Periodicals' (1999) 30 *Law and Policy in International Business* 231, 256.

[74] Ibid, 259–60.

[75] WTO docs. WT/DS31/R (14 March 1997) (Report of the Panel) and WT/DS31/AB/R, AB-1997-2 (30 June 1997) (Report of the Appellate Body).

[76] Carmody, above n 73, 283–7.   [77] Ibid, 279.

[78] *Canada—Certain Measures Concerning Periodicals*, WTO doc. WT/DS31/R (14 March 1997) (Report of the Panel) para 5.45.

[79] *China—Measures affecting trading rights and distribution services for certain publication and audiovisual entertainment products*, WTO docs. WT/DS363/R (12 August 2009) (Report of the Panel) and WT/DS363/AB/R, AB-2009-3 (21 December 2009) (Report of the Appellate Body) ('*China Entertainment Products*').

Article XIV is the equivalent exceptions provision in GATS. It reads, in part:

Subject to the requirement that such measures are not applied in a manner which would constitute a means of arbitrary or unjustifiable discrimination between countries where like conditions prevail, or a disguised restriction on trade in services, nothing in this Agreement shall be construed to prevent the adoption or enforcement by any Member of measures:
  (a) necessary to protect public morals or to maintain public order;
  (b) necessary to protect human, animal or plant life or health;
  (c) necessary to secure compliance with laws or regulations which are not inconsistent with the provisions of this Agreement including those relating to...
      (ii)   the protection of the privacy of individuals in relation to the processing and dissemination of personal data and the protection of confidentiality of individual records and accounts;
      (iii) safety...

Paragraph (a) is the only provision that has been subject to interpretation by the DSBs, and is discussed below. It differs from its GATT counterpart in that it refers to the maintenance of public order as well as the protection of public morals. Paragraph (b) seems identical to the equivalent paragraph (b) in Article XX GATT. Finally, paragraph (c) has no counterpart in GATT, and provides extra protection for the human right to privacy, and perhaps human rights associated with security of the person and 'safety', such as the right to life.

Before embarking on a detailed examination of the jurisprudence under these exception provisions, some general matters must be addressed, namely extraterritorial application and the process of interpretation.

Extraterritorial application of Article XX exceptions

In the GATT *Tuna* disputes, US measures regarding tuna imports were found to breach GATT in both cases. In *Tuna I*, the Panel suggested that the US was prohibited from adopting measures designed to enforce its environmental standards extraterritorially.[80] *Tuna II* softened that line, indicating that the US could impose extraterritorial measures so long as they were not intended to coerce changes in policies in other States.[81] Of course, outward measures are coercive and would not therefore be allowed according to the *Tuna* panels.

However, in *Shrimp-Turtle*, the WTO Appellate Body explicitly did *not* decide 'whether there [was] an implied jurisdictional limitation in Article XX(g) [and presumably the rest of Article XX], and if so, the nature or extent of that limitation'.[82] A jurisdictional nexus between the US and the sea turtles protected by its impugned measures was found, as some of the migratory turtles passed through US waters, so the question of extraterritoriality did not have to be

---

[80] *Tuna I*, above n 31, paras 5.27 and 5.33.   [81] *Tuna II*, above n 31, para 5.15.
[82] *United States—Import Prohibition of Certain Shrimp and Shrimp Products* ('*US—Shrimp I*'), WTO doc. WT/DS58/AB/R, AB-1998-4 (12 October 1998) (Report of the Appellate Body) para 133.

answered. Therefore, it remains possible for outward measures to be valid under WTO law.[83]

In any case, the *Tuna* jurisprudence on extraterritoriality is arguably incoherent. Any trade measure, whether inward or outward, can have detrimental extraterritorial impacts and therefore be deemed to be coercive. For example, a ban on hormone-injected beef by the EC, a measure challenged in *European Communities—Measures concerning meat and meat products (hormones)* (discussed below), was an inward measure allegedly designed to protect the health of Europeans. However, the ban could have 'coerced' overseas farmers to refrain from using those hormones in order to avoid jeopardizing their European markets.[84]

Process of interpreting Article XX and Article XIV exceptions

Exceptions to treaty provisions are normally interpreted narrowly. For example, human rights bodies openly claim to interpret qualifications to rights strictly.[85] However, the Appellate Body has not explicitly taken this approach to the general exceptions provisions. Rather, it claims to take a 'balancing' approach, whereby it balances in each individual case the interests of trade liberalization against the relevant non-trade value.[86] However, as argued below, that approach has not been borne out in practice. Rather, it is submitted that the dispute settlement bodies have tended to prioritize the trade side of the equation.

In order to rely on Article XX GATT or Article XIV GATS, a State must pass a three-step test before a measure will be saved from WTO illegality.[87] The following rules are gleaned from Article XX jurisprudence and are likely to be the same for Article XIV. First, the impugned measure must 'fall within the range of policies' designed to pursue the relevant end.[88] Second, the impugned measure must be 'necessary' to achieve the desired goal, or, for Article XX(g), it must 'relate to' that goal.[89] The third step is that the impugned measure must satisfy the requirements of the 'chapeau', that is the opening clause, of Article XX.

---

[83] See also Cassimatis, above n 6, 348.

[84] Sarah Joseph, 'Democratic Deficit, Participation and the WTO' in Sarah Joseph, David Kinley, and Jeff Waincymer (eds), *The World Trade Organization and Human Rights: Interdisciplinary Perspectives* (Edward Elgar, Cheltenham, 2009) 338–9.

[85] See, eg, *Belyatsky et al v Belarus*, UN doc. CCPR/C/90/D/1296/2004 (24 July 2007) and *Lee v Republic of Korea*, UN doc. CCPR/C/84/D/1119/2002 (both HRC); see also HRC, 'General Comment No 27: Freedom of Movement (Art. 12)', UN doc. CCPR/C/21/Rev.1/Add.9 (2 November 1999) paras 11–18.

[86] *United States—Standards for Reformulated and Conventional Gasoline*, WTO doc. WT/DS2/AB/R, AB-1996-1 (29 April 1996) (Report of the Appellate Body) para 18. See also Van den Bossche, above n 6, 599–600, and Harrison, above n 10, 206–7.

[87] Lang, above n 52, 832.   [88] *US—Reformulated Gasoline* (Panel), above n 45, para 6.20.

[89] The exact framing of this second step depends on the actual words of the clause of Article XX which is at issue.

Protection of public morals and public order

Article XIV(a) GATS has an ad note, stating that the exception can only be invoked 'where a genuine and sufficiently serious threat is posed to one of the fundamental interests of society'. Article XX(a), drafted in 1947 along with the original GATT, contains no such ad note.

The exceptions regarding public morals are potentially very broad, and there is little indication from the preparatory documents to the treaties to shed light on their meaning. Harrison quotes Charnovitz in saying that morality measures include, 'at least', measures concerning 'slavery, weapons, narcotics, liquor, pornography, religion, compulsory labour and animal welfare'.[90]

US—Measures affecting the Cross-Border Supply of Gambling and Betting Services[91] concerned a challenge by Antigua and Barbuda to a number of US laws which prohibited internet gambling in the US. The US defended the measures under Article XIV GATS on the basis that they were necessary to protect public morals and public order. In particular, the prohibition was said to be necessary to combat 'money laundering, organized crime, fraud, underage gambling and pathological gambling'.[92]

The Panel interpreted the term 'public morals' as denoting 'standards of right and wrong conduct maintained by or on behalf of a community or nation',[93] and 'public order' as pertaining to 'the preservation of the fundamental interests of a society, as reflected in public policy and law'.[94] The Appellate Body agreed that the US measures passed the first step of the Article XIV test, as they were measures that were conceivably necessary to protect morals.[95] The Panel had added that public morals vary according to 'prevailing social, cultural, ethical and religious values', and that Members had some discretion in defining the concepts for themselves 'according to their own systems and scales of values'.[96] This aspect of the Panel's decision was not mentioned on appeal.

Those definitions certainly indicate that a measure imposed for the purposes of protecting human rights, whether inward or outward, could fall within the public morals/order exceptions. Professor Robert Howse has stated:

In the modern world, the very idea of public morality has become inseparable from the concept of human personhood, dignity and capacity reflected in fundamental rights. A conception of public morals or morality that excluded notions of fundamental rights would simply be contrary to the ordinary contemporary meaning of the concept.[97]

---

[90] Harrison, above n 10, 209, citing Steve Charnovitz, 'The Moral Exception in Trade Policy' in Steve Charnovitz (ed), *Trade Law and Global Governance* (Cameron May, London, 2002) 361.
[91] *United States—Measures Affecting the Cross-Border Supply of Gambling and Betting Services*, WTO docs. WT/DS285/R (10 November 2004) (Report of the Panel) and WT/DS285/AB/R, AB-2005-1 (7 April 2005) (Report of the Appellate Body).
[92] *US Gambling* (Panel), above n 91, paras 6.465, 6.486.   [93] Ibid, see also para 6.461.
[94] Ibid, para 6.467.   [95] *US—Gambling* (Appellate Body), above n 91, paras 296–9.
[96] *US—Gambling* (Panel), above n 91, para 6.461.
[97] Robert Howse, 'Back to Court After Shrimp/Turtle? Almost but not quite yet: India's short-lived challenge to labour and environmental exceptions in the European's Union's generalized system of preferences' (2003) 18 *American University International Law Review* 1333, 1368.

Howse adds a further justification for the use of international human rights law as a touchstone for the interpretation of the public morals clauses, in stating that the exceptions could be 'almost limitless if the content of public morals does not have a universal element'.[98] McBeth supports this idea of 'ensuring a degree of universality', given the common fear that Article XX exceptions might be abused to disguise protectionist measures.[99]

The Appellate Body has not confirmed the Howse thesis. If it adopted the evolutionary approach to interpretation that it took in *Shrimp* with regard to Article XX(g) (discussed below), it could use modern human rights treaties to interpret the public morals exceptions.[100] If it was to do so, the full range of human rights based trade measures might plausibly be allowed under the public morals exceptions. An inward measure could be justified on the basis that it fulfilled a State's human rights obligations. A ban on goods manufactured by children, a product-based outward measure, could be said to promote the global moral purpose of combating child labour and thus protecting human rights. General sanctions could be justified as promoting the global moral purpose of combating an egregious regime that violates human rights. Alternatively, the use of public morals may transform outward measures into inward measures. That is, the morals being protected are those of the State's own population, who may not wish to be exposed to goods tainted by human rights abuses. Just as inward measures have an outward effect, outward measures arguably have an inward effect in terms of protecting the 'public morals' of consumers.[101] Therefore, the exceptions regarding public morals and public order (the latter only in GATS) may provide an opportunity for States to justify trade restrictive human rights measures, such as those based on labour rights, which do not otherwise come under another clause in Articles XX or XIV.

In *China—Measures affecting trading rights and distribution services for certain publication and audiovisual entertainment products*,[102] the US challenged Chinese measures which required that foreign books, movies, and music be imported through government-approved agents. China justified the measures as necessary to protect public morals, as the laws ensured that the content of the imports complied with Chinese censorship laws. Both the Panel and the Appellate Body found that the mandated use of government-approved agents to import cultural goods was not necessary to protect public morals. Therefore, both bodies were able to sidestep the issue of whether China's censorship laws were per se justifiable as measures to protect public morals.[103] Indeed, the point was essentially conceded by the US:

China notes that the United States does not appear to dispute that China has a sovereign right to put in place a system designed to review and control the content of cultural goods

---

[98] Robert Howse, 'The World Trade Organization and the Protection of Workers' Rights' (1999) 3 *Journal of Small and Emerging Small Business Law* 131, 143.
[99] McBeth, above n 27, 117; see also Harrison, above n 10, 209.
[100] Harrison, above n 10, 212; Cassimatis, above n 6, 360.
[101] See also Harrison, above n 10, 66. See also text above at n 84.
[102] *China Entertainment Products* (Panel and Appellate Body), above, n 79.
[103] See *Bridges Weekly Trade News Digest*, 'WTO rules against Chinese restrictions on foreign books, movies, music, 9 September 2009. See also below, Part G.

that enter its territory. The United States also does not appear to dispute that China is entitled to decide the level of protection that it requires.[104]

However, the Panel then added:

China has decided that the control of cultural content is a matter of fundamental importance, and that it requires a complete exclusion from its territory of materials which could
have a negative impact on public morals. The right to set such standard of enforcement and
to put in place a system that will maintain such standard is unquestionable and recognized
also by the Appellate Body jurisprudence.[105]

Therefore, the public morals exception may be so broad as to permit a State to
adopt extensive censorship measures. While some censorship is certainly justified
for the purposes of protecting public morals and public order, such as censorship
of child pornography or genuine national security information, China's censorship
laws are excessive from a human rights point of view. This issue is discussed further
below.[106]

Protection of health

Article XX(b) GATT and Article XIV(b) GATS allow for measures that protect public health. Such measures are clearly of relevance to the human right
to an adequate standard of health (Article 12 ICESCR) and the right to life
(Article 6 ICCPR). The HRC has confirmed that the right to life has a broad
interpretation, such that States must take 'positive measures' to protect the
right, including 'positive measures to reduce infant mortality and to increase
life expectancy, especially in adopting measures to eliminate malnutrition
and epidemics'.[107] Trade measures regarding protection of the rights to food
and water, both essential for health and life, should also come within Article
XX(b). A broad interpretation of Article XX(b) might permit measures which
promote all human rights that protect physical and mental security, such as
the right to be free from torture and certain prohibitions on labour rights
abuses.

The following are examples of cases where the impugned measures have been
found to constitute policies aimed at protecting health within the meaning of
Article XX(b) GATT: US measures which specified standards of cleanliness
for gasoline sold in the US in *US—Standards for reformulated and conventional
gasoline*,[108] the ban in *Asbestos* on chrysolite asbestos products,[109] and a ban in

---

[104] *China Entertainment Products* (Panel), above n 79, para 4.573.
[105] Ibid, para 4.574.   [106] See also below, Part G.
[107] HRC, 'General Comment No 6: The right to life (art. 6)', Sixteenth Session, 1982, 30 April
1982, para 5.
[108] WTO docs. WT/DS2/R (29 January 1996) (Report of the Panel) and WT/DS2/AB/R,
AB-1996-1 (29 April 1996) (Report of the Appellate Body).
[109] The Appellate Body considered the Article XX issue in *EC Asbestos* (Appellate Body), above
n 34, even though Article XX was not strictly engaged, as the measures had not breached the national
treatment provisions of GATT.

Brazil—Measures affecting imports of retreaded tyres[110] on the import of retreaded tyres, as discarded tyres were breeding grounds for mosquitoes which increased the incidence of mosquito-borne diseases.

The test of 'necessity'

The public morals and health exceptions are only permissible if they are deemed to be 'necessary' to achieve their respective goals. In *Thailand—Cigarettes*,[111] a GATT panel found that the test of necessity required that there be no available alternative measures that were GATT consistent or less GATT inconsistent which could reasonably be used to achieve the desired ends. The ban on the import of foreign cigarettes in *Thailand—Cigarettes*, which prima facie breached Article XI, was imposed due to harmful additives in imported cigarettes and a desire to reduce tobacco consumption for health reasons. The GATT Panel suggested that the following measures, which did not distort trade as much as the impugned measure, might have sufficed: labelling requirements, ingredient disclosure regulations, and a ban on tobacco advertisements.[112] It is doubtful that such measures were as effective as the impugned measures in achieving Thailand's health aims. The early test of 'necessity' was criticized for being too strict, and arguably 'impossible to satisfy'.[113] Despite criticism of the test, the *Gasoline* Panel adopted the *Thailand—Cigarettes* test and found that the impugned US 'clean air' measures were not necessary in order to promote health as less trade restrictive measures were available.[114]

In *Korea—Various Measures on Beef*,[115] the Appellate Body, in a case on Article XX(d), stated that a measure did not have to be 'indispensable' in order to be 'necessary'. A determination of 'necessity' involved a 'weighing and balancing' process. *Korea—Beef* therefore modified the strict 'least trade restrictive' test. The Appellate Body has followed this modified test in *Asbestos*, *Gambling*, and *Dominican Republic—Measures affecting the importation and internal sale of cigarettes*. The Appellate Body in the latter case summed up the law on 'necessity' as follows:

> The Appellate Body Reports in *Korea—Various Measures on Beef*, *EC—Asbestos* and *US—Gambling* indicate that, in the assessment of whether a proposed alternative to the impugned measure is reasonably available, factors such as the trade impact of the measure, the importance of the interests protected by the measure, or the contribution of the measure to the realization of the end pursued, should be taken into account in the analysis. The weighing and balancing process of these three factors also informs the determination whether a WTO-consistent alternative measure which the Member concerned could

[110] WTO Docs WT/DS332/R (12 June 2007) (Report of the Panel) and WT/DS332/AB/R, AB-2007-4 (3 December 2007) (Report of the Appellate Body).
[111] *Thailand—Restrictions on Importation of and Internal Taxes on Cigarettes*, GATT Doc DS10/R (7 November 1990) (Report of the Panel).
[112] Ibid, paras 77–8.   [113] Lang, above n 52, 833.
[114] The measures were discriminatory, as discussed below in text before n 138, so less discriminatory options were available. *US—Reformulated Gasoline* (Panel), above n 45, para 6.22.
[115] *Korea—Measures affecting imports of fresh, chilled and frozen beef*, above n 54.

reasonably be expected to employ is available, or whether a less WTO-inconsistent measure is reasonably available.[116]

The Appellate Body in *Dominican Republic—Cigarettes* went on to approve a quote from *US—Gambling*, stating that an alternative measure was not available if it was 'merely theoretical in nature' or where it imposed 'an undue burden on that Member'.[117] These clarifications indicate that the Appellate Body will be sensitive to a State's technical and financial capacities to implement alternative measures.[118] Finally, the alternative measure has to 'preserve for the responding Member its right to achieve its desired level of protection with respect to the objective pursued'.[119]

In *Asbestos*, the Appellate Body confirmed that 'necessity' does not relate to the goal of a measure, but rather the necessity of the means to that end.[120] This decision implies that a State may seek to attain any level of health protection that it desires, or, by analogy, any level of protection of public morals (or public order under GATS). However, one outcome of the new balancing test of 'necessity' is that, while the Appellate Body will not question the validity of an end once it is deemed to fall within a paragraph of Article XX, the perceived importance of that end ultimately makes a difference in deciding whether the measure utilized is necessary. The Appellate Body in *Asbestos*, in finding that the measures were in fact necessary, was influenced by the fact that the goal pursued, the protection of human health from well-known and life-threatening health risks, was 'both vital and important in the highest degree'.[121]

In *Brazil—Retreaded Tyres*, the Panel stated that 'few interests are more "vital" and "important" than protecting human beings from health risks'.[122] Brazil explained that it had banned imports of retreaded tyres in order to reduce the health risks posed by waste tyres, which became mosquito breeding grounds and also generated toxic tyre fires. The ban on imports meant that those imports were replaced by domestic retreads, which meant fewer local tyres became waste tyres. The Appellate Body noted that the ban could be justified even though it was as trade restrictive as was possible.[123] However, it disagreed with Brazil's contention

---

[116] *Dominican Republic—Measures Affecting the Importation and Internal Sale of Cigarettes*, WTO doc. WT/DS302/AB/R, AB-2005-3 (25 April 2005) (Report of the Appellate Body) 70. See also *United States—Certain measures relating to shrimp from Thailand*, WTO doc. WT/DS343/AB/R (Report of the Appellate Body) and *United States—Customs Bond Directive for merchandise subject to anti-dumping/countervailing duties*, WTO doc. WT/DS345/AB/R (Report of the Appellate Body) para 316.

[117] *US—Gambling* (Appellate Body), above n 91, para 308, quoted at *Dominican Republic Cigarettes* (Appellate Body), above n 116, para 70.

[118] Lang, above n 52, 834.

[119] *US—Gambling* (Appellate Body), above n 93, para 308, quoted at *Dominican Republic Cigarettes* (Appellate Body), above n 116, para 70.

[120] The Appellate Body examined Article XX on appeal even though the measures did not need to be justified under Article XX as there was no discrimination between like goods. See also *US—Reformulated Gasoline* (Panel), above n 45, para 6.22.

[121] *EC—Asbestos* (Appellate Body), above n 34, para 172.

[122] *Brazil—Measures affecting imports of retreaded tyres*, WTO doc. WT/DS332/R (12 June 2007) (Report of the Panel) para 7.108, cited with approval by the Appellate Body in WTO doc WT/DS332/AB/R, AB-2007-4 (3 December 2007) (Report of the Appellate Body) paras 144 and 179.

[123] *Brazil—Retreaded Tyres* (Appellate Body), above n 122, para 150.

that such a ban would be necessary if it had only a 'marginal or insignificant' effect because it aimed 'to reduce risk exposure to the maximum extent possible'.[124] Thus, the impugned measure must be reasonably effective in order to be deemed 'necessary'.

In its decision in *Brazil—Tyres*, the Appellate Body found that the ban was necessary. Its trade impacts were outweighed by the importance of the ban in reducing health risks caused by waste tyres. It supported the Panel's finding that alternative measures proposed by the appellant, the EC, including the use of tyres in landfill, recycling, incineration, and stockpiling, were not reasonably available to Brazil or were not appropriate alternative policies (for example, they carried their own risks).

Extrapolating from *Asbestos* and *Brazil—Retreaded Tyres*, the Appellate Body has signalled a great willingness to concede the necessity of impugned measures when public health issues are at stake.[125] The promotion of human rights is also of the highest importance.[126] These cases also indicate that a less strict test of necessity, compared to the test from *Thailand—Cigarettes*, has been adopted, which increases the capacities of States to enact human rights measures that restrict trade.

In *US—Gambling*, the Appellate Body overturned the Panel's decision and found that the US's measures were necessary to protect public morals and public order. The Panel had stated that the US should have negotiated with Antigua before banning internet gambling. In the view of the Appellate Body, consultations were 'not an appropriate alternative... because consultations are by definition a process, the results of which are uncertain and therefore not capable of comparison with the measures at issue in this case'.[127] As no other alternative measure had been raised, the Appellate Body found that the measure was necessary to protect the US's chosen level of protection for public morality and public order.

In *China—Audiovisual entertainment products*, the Appellate Body found that the impugned measures were not necessary in order to protect public morals because less trade restrictive measures were reasonably available to achieve the same level of protection of morality, so the measure was not particularly important in achieving China's ends. For example, China could simply apply its national censorship laws to the imported products in the same way as it applied those laws to the like domestic products.[128] There was no need to restrict the entities that could physically import the relevant goods in order to ensure compliance with its censorship regime.

Inward measures, especially those designed to protect health, seem likely to pass the necessity test so long as they are reasonably effective in achieving a goal within Article XX. Outward measures seem to be less likely to satisfy the necessity criterion. Indeed, outward measures would rarely satisfy the test given that unilateral economic sanctions are often ineffective (or even counterproductive)[129]

---

[124] Ibid.   [125] McBeth, above n 27, 125.   [126] Ibid, 123.

[127] *US—Gambling* (Appellate Body), above n 91, para 317.

[128] See *Bridges Weekly Trade News Digest*, above n 103.

[129] Jenny Schultz and Rachel Ball, 'Trade as a weapon? The WTO and human rights-based trade measures' (2007) 12 *Deakin Law Review* 41, 64.

in promoting human rights compliance in the target State. Furthermore, less trade restrictive means of registering a protest against a State's human rights abuses would often be reasonably available.[130] Of course, the effectiveness of sanctions increases according to the power of a State. It would seem unsatisfactory if human rights sanctions were only available to powerful States under WTO law.[131] However, an outward measure designed to protest against a State's human rights abuses, whether general or product-based sanctions, might pass muster under the necessity test if the relevant desired impact was not the effect on the target State's behaviour, but the assuaging of the conscience and satisfaction of the moral code of consumers in the sanctioning State.

Protection of environment

Article XX(g) is not directly relevant to human rights measures. Rather, it concerns measures that protect environmental ends. Nevertheless, Article XX(g) cases are relevant because environmental measures can be necessary to protect human health as well as rights to food and water.[132] Article XX(g) cases also act as signposts to the potential outcomes in future cases concerning human rights.

As noted in Chapter 2, the Appellate Body in *US—Shrimp* utilized a number of modern environmental treaties to interpret the scope of Article XX(g).[133] For example, it rejected an argument that the reference therein to 'exhaustible natural resources' referred only to mineral or 'non-living' resources: the Appellate Body found that living resources were 'susceptible of depletion, exhaustion and extinction'.[134] The Appellate Body went on to note that while Article XX(g) had been drafted over 50 years earlier (under the original GATT treaty), modern and 'evolutionary' notions of environmental protection could inform its interpretation of the provision in 1998.[135] Therefore, a measure designed to protect the endangered sea turtle was a measure 'related to' Article XX(g) purposes.

Unlike Articles XX(a) and XX(b), a measure under Article XX(g) does not have to be 'necessary': it must simply 'relate to' environmental ends. In *US—Gasoline*, the Appellate Body confirmed that this test was not as strict as that of 'necessity' under Articles XX(a) and (b). Indeed, the impugned measures in *US—Gasoline* were not found to be 'necessary' for the purposes of Article XX(b), but they were found to 'relate to' ends that came within Article XX(g). Therefore, the impugned measures 'passed' the second stage of the test for Article XX(g) but not Article XX(b).[136] A measure passes the 'related to' test so long as it was 'primarily aimed at'

---

[130] See also Vázquez, above n 5, 819.
[131] Ibid, 834–5; Schultz and Ball, above n 129, 75–6.
[132] See CESCR, 'General Comment No 14: The right to the highest attainable standard of health', UN doc. E/C.12/2000/4 (11 August 2000) para 15.
[133] See Chapter 2, text at n 123.   [134] *US—Shrimp I* (Appellate Body), above n 82, para 128.
[135] Ibid, paras 129–30.
[136] On *US—Gasoline*, see Jennifer Schultz, 'The demise of "green" protectionism: the WTO decision on the US Gasoline rule' (1996) 25 *Denver Journal of International Law and Policy* 1.

ends within Article XX(g), or is 'reasonably related to' those ends. The less onerous test for Article XX(g) may supply an alternative justification for health measures related to the environment if a justification under Article XX(b) should be found not to be 'necessary'.[137]

The chapeau

The chapeaus in both Articles XX and XIV state that measures passed under one of the relevant sub-paragraphs are not allowed if they amount to 'arbitrary or unjustifiable discrimination between countries where the same conditions prevail, or a disguised restriction on international trade'. The chapeau has been interpreted as a safeguard against abuse of Article XX rights by States. The 'chapeau' test has been the downfall of most measures that a WTO Member has sought to justify under Article XX. Almost all such measures have ultimately been found to be discriminatory in a way that breaches the chapeau.

In *US—Gasoline*, the impugned 'clean gas' measures were not justified under Article XX(g) (having failed to reach even the third stage of the Article XX test under Article XX(b)) as different administrative regulations for measuring pollutants applied, respectively, to US producers of gasoline and to those in the complainant States, Venezuela and Brazil. The measures failed the chapeau test as they were clearly discriminatory. In *US—Gambling*, the US ultimately lost because the federal Interstate Horseracing Act permitted remote gambling on horse races by some US providers. This discrimination in favour of certain US companies suggested that the measures were in fact 'disguised restrictions on trade' rather than measures designed to protect public morals. The discrimination in these two cases was fairly blatant.[138]

In *US—Shrimp*, the measures failed the chapeau test, partly because the US had dealt with different countries in different ways without justification. For example, while it had negotiated a treaty on the issue of saving the sea turtle with Latin American States, it had unilaterally embargoed shrimp from other States without consultation and without sufficient consideration of whether those countries might have adopted equivalent measures which avoided the incidental killing of sea turtles while harvesting shrimp. The US amended its laws in the wake of *Shrimp*; those modifications were challenged by Malaysia in *US—Shrimp (Article 21.5—Malaysia)* ('*Shrimp 2*').[139] The Appellate Body found that the new measures, which allowed shrimp imports from States where there were programmes in place that were comparably effective in saving the turtle, were WTO legal. The *Shrimp* litigation indicated a preference by the WTO for cooperative rather than coercive solutions: States should at least attempt to resolve grievances before imposing trade

---

[137] See Harrison, above n 10, 217.

[138] Note however that the US disputes the interpretation of the relevant horse racing statute by the Panel and Appellate Body in *US—Gambling*.

[139] *United States—Shrimp Import Prohibition of Certain Shrimp and Shrimp Products—Recourse to Article 21.5 by Malaysia*, WTO docs. WT/DS58/RW (15 June 2001) (Report of the Panel) and WT/DS58/AB/RW, AB-2001-4 (22 October 2001) (Report of the Appellate Body).

restrictions. The *Shrimp* precedent indicated that outward product-based measures might need to be preceded by negotiations with the relevant States before their unilateral imposition is permitted under WTO law. However, the imposition of a requirement of negotiations by a Panel was overturned by the Appellate Body in the later decision in *US—Gambling*.[140]

Driesen has queried one of the discrimination findings in *Shrimp*. To recap, both US and foreign shrimp fleets were required to use TEDs. The measure was found to be discriminatory and contrary to the chapeau of Article XX GATT, as the regulation did not take into account the 'different conditions' that might arise in foreign States.[141] However, the decision did not identify why or even whether those 'different conditions' rendered it difficult for other States to install TEDs. The US arguably failed to discriminate *in favour of* the foreign fleets by exempting them from the TED requirement.[142] *Shrimp* arguably indicates that any neutral measure that somehow obstructs international trade, even if applied equally to domestic trade, might nevertheless be construed as discriminatory.[143]

In *Brazil—Retreaded Tyres*, the measures failed the test in the chapeau for two reasons. First, the Appellate Body noted that Brazil's goals were blatantly undermined by the fact that non-retreaded used tyres could still be imported. Secondly, Brazil was a member of the MERCOSUR regional trade grouping, and had exempted its MERCOSUR partners from the retreaded tyres ban. Brazil had lost a challenge to its import ban before a MERCOSUR tribunal, despite the existence of a regional exemption akin to Article XX(b). The Appellate Body found that the MERCOSUR exemption cut against the health promotion goals of the measure, and therefore manifested a breach of the chapeau. As Brazil had not cited health reasons for the ban before the MERCOSUR tribunal, the Appellate Body suggested that its decision did not necessarily 'result from a conflict between provisions under MERCOSUR and the GATT 1994'.[144] However, this circumstance does not seem to have been decisive in the Appellate Body's reasoning: it seems that it was quite prepared to find 'arbitrary and unjustifiable' discrimination, and that the measure was a 'disguised restriction on trade', even if such discrimination arose from a clash between MERCOSUR and GATT obligations. The result in *Brazil—Tyres* is that Brazil can maintain its ban if it extends it appropriately.[145] However, it might not be so easy for Brazil to extend the ban to MERCOSUR countries, due to its apparent obligations (according to a MERCOSUR tribunal) to allow the import of tyres under MERCOSUR.[146]

General human rights sanctions against a State could well fail the chapeau test unless a State imposed like sanctions on all States with a similarly bad human rights record. Such even-handedness is not typical of general human rights sanctions.

[140] See above, text at note 127.
[141] *US—Shrimp I* (Appellate Body), above n 82, para 164.   [142] Driesen, above n 59, 333.
[143] Joseph, above n 84, 337.
[144] *Brazil—Retreaded Tyres* (Appellate Body), above n 122, para 234.
[145] See Hannes Schloemann, 'Brazil Tyres: Policy Space confirmed under GATT Article XX', *Bridges Monthly*, Year 12 No 1, February 2008, via <http://www.ictsd.org>.
[146] See also *Brazil—Measures affecting imports of retreaded tyres*—ARB-2008-2/23—Arbitration under Article 21.3(c)—Award of the Arbitrator, WT/DS332/16 (29 August 2008) ('*Brazil—Retreaded Tyres—Arbitration*').

For example, as noted above, Canada and the US have imposed extensive trade sanctions on Burma. While Burma undoubtedly commits horrendous human rights abuses, other WTO members arguably have similarly bad records, such as the Central African Republic or the Democratic Republic of the Congo.[147] While such measures are unlikely to be imposed for protectionist purposes, they could amount to 'arbitrary or unjustifiable discrimination between countries where the same conditions prevail'.[148]

Conclusion on GATT/GATS jurisprudence

The above survey of WTO cases signals three trends. First, the Appellate Body and the Panels engage in a high level of scrutiny in examining a State's impugned measures under WTO law. There is little sign of a margin of discretion being accorded to States. Notwithstanding the landmark *Asbestos* decision, the goal of a law is normally irrelevant in determining if products are 'like' for the purposes of GATT, and it seems likely the same approach will be adopted under GATS.

Secondly, a wide interpretation has been given to 'discrimination' for the purposes of MFN and national treatment obligations. While the definition may have been rolled back in *Dominican Republic—Cigarettes*, a very broad interpretation has been given to the prohibition of quantitative restrictions. Altogether, these interpretations give GATT and GATS obligations a broad scope. The broader their scope, the greater their impact on a State's regulatory capacities.

Thirdly, the interpretation of the Article XX (and Article XIV) exceptions has arguably been quite narrow. Certainly, the interpretation of the values which are promoted within the various sub-paragraphs has been quite broad. The Appellate Body and Panels will refrain from questioning the validity of the social ends that a State wishes to pursue if those ends feasibly fall within Article XX GATT or XIV GATS. However, their perception of the importance of the ends pursued is clearly important in deciding whether a measure is 'necessary' under Article XX or Article XIV. The Appellate Body in *Shrimp I* confirmed that Article XX(g) and presumably the other sub-paragraphs will be interpreted dynamically in the light of contemporary values. The public morals exceptions appear to be the only provisions which might permit human rights trade measures in general. However, a broad interpretation of Article XX(b) (or Article XIV(b) GATS) could allow a State to defend measures which protect a number of human rights related to human security.

For a time, the utility of these exceptions was undermined by a very strict test of 'necessity' that was manifested in *Thailand—Cigarettes* and *US—Reformulated Gasoline*. This second step in the Article XX test has however become less strict, with the 'least trade restrictive' test being replaced by a 'weighing and balancing' test which gives greater weight to non-trade values. And indeed, the impugned measures in a number of cases have 'passed' this test of necessity, as seen in *Asbestos*, *Gambling*, and *Retreaded Tyres*. The test was not passed in *China—Audiovisual*

---

[147] See also Vázquez, above n 5, 823.   [148] Ewing Chow, above n 6, 166–7.

Entertainment Products. The less strict 'relating to' test under Article XX(g) was 'passed' in *Gasoline* and *Shrimp*. However, the remaining hurdle of the chapeau has only been surmounted fully in *Shrimp II* (with no chapeau analysis taking place in *Asbestos*).

It is submitted that outward measures are far less likely to be legal under WTO law than inward measures. For example, it will be difficult to establish that an outward measure is necessary. It would seem easier to justify an inward measure by reference to public morals, public order (in GATS), or the need to protect human health. All human rights trade measures will have to be carefully crafted in order to avoid falling foul of the non-discrimination requirement in the chapeau.

The outcomes from the WTO's dispute resolution process regarding social measures have been criticized by social justice campaigners. For example, environmentalists have argued that the WTO unduly 'undermines necessary environmental legislation'.[149] Certainly, most challenges to social measures under WTO law have resulted in the legislation being found to breach WTO provisions in some respect. However, the criticism may not be fair. After all, the cases may simply signal that a State can adopt social regulations but must ensure that they are not relevantly discriminatory. However, given the width of the test of discrimination under the chapeau, as pointed out by Driesen in regard to *Shrimp*, that requirement may be more onerous than it sounds. Furthermore, the removal of discrimination can be potentially difficult, as indicated by Brazil in requesting extra time to negotiate with its MERCOSUR partners over a resolution to the *Tyres* dispute.[150]

The human rights obligations of the State adopting human rights trade measures will rarely be at issue with regard to outward measures because States are rarely if ever obliged to impose such sanctions under international human rights law. However, human rights obligations are clearly at issue for many inward measures. From a human rights point of view, it is troubling that an explicit human rights exception is not included within Articles XX and XIV. Furthermore, it is troubling that a human rights measure, such as the health measure in *Brazil Tyres*, should be subjected to scrutiny according to its impact on trade.[151] Perhaps it is unfortunate that human rights considerations are 'weighed' or 'balanced' against non-human rights concerns at all. After all, 'adherence to free trade obligations' is not a recognized limitation to any human right, and international human rights bodies have never indicated that they accept WTO compliance as an excuse for limiting a human rights obligation.[152]

However, there is perhaps nothing wrong, from a human rights point of view, with the Panels and Appellate Body insisting that a less trade restrictive option be taken if it is reasonably available, given that the determination of such reasonable availability pays due deference to a State's desired level of protection of an Article XX (or Article XIV) value, as well as a State's capacities to implement an alternative measure. In this regard, it is interesting to speculate on the outcome of a human

---

[149] Van den Bossche, above n 6, 623 (noting such arguments).
[150] See *Brazil—Retreaded Tyres—Arbitration*, above n 146.
[151] See also McBeth, above n 27, 124.   [152] See also Harrison, above n 10, 218–19.

rights assessment of the *Brazil Tyres* measure. The measure would have been found to conform to the right to health, but the exceptions regarding used tyres and MERCOSUR countries would have been found to undermine that conformity. That is, human rights bodies would possibly have condemned the same flaws in the scheme as the Appellate Body. However, under human rights law, the abolition of the import ban would not be an acceptable solution, whereas trade law dictates the lifting of the import ban if those flaws cannot be fixed.[153]

A social measure which restricts free trade can also impact badly on the enjoyment of human rights. If one accepts that free trade increases wealth, trade restrictions diminish that wealth, and consequently can impact on the enjoyment of economic, social, and cultural rights. However, the 'diminution of aggregate wealth' could not constitute a legitimate limit to human rights, particularly in respect of a measure that simultaneously and directly promotes human rights. On the other hand, severely detrimental impacts on the livelihoods of people, such as those in an offshore export industry who are put out of work by a major trading partner's import ban, could potentially be classified as harms to the right to work (Article 6 ICESCR) and the right to an adequate standard of living (Article 11 ICESCR). Such violations might arise if those offshore workers are vulnerable people in a poor State that lacks the capacity to compensate for their losses or cope with sudden economic adjustments.[154] This issue is discussed in greater detail in Chapters 5, 6, and 8, and below in regard to SPS measures.

Free trade restrictions do not, of course, always have such serious human rights impacts: resultant market losses may only rarely harm the livelihoods of affected offshore traders to such an extent as to harm their human rights. Yet the potential generation of human rights abuses by protectionist measures indicates that, in principle, some limitation on the regulatory power of the State to restrict free trade is welcome from a human rights point of view. However, the WTO dispute resolution bodies do not take into account the 'effect on human rights caused by trade restrictions' in deciding whether protectionist measures are or are not permissible; they explicitly focus on the trade impact per se (which may or may not impact on human rights).

So far, States have not specifically relied on human rights obligations to defend social legislation in WTO litigation. For example, Brazil did not refer to the right to health in *Brazil—Tyres*. It is a matter of speculation as to why States are not using explicit human rights claims to bolster their arguments before the WTO.

---

[153] Indeed, Article 3.7 of the Understanding on Rules and Procedures Governing the Settlement of Disputes states, in part:

> In the absence of a mutually agreed solution, the first objective of the dispute settlement mechanism is usually to secure the withdrawal of the measures concerned if these are found to be inconsistent with the provisions of any of the covered agreements.

Thus, Article 3.7 dictates a preference for withdrawal of the impugned measures if a mutual agreement to a solution does not arise.

[154] See Ha-Joon Chang, *Bad Samaritans: the Myth of Free Trade and the Secret History of Capitalism* (Bloomsbury Press, New York, 2008) 73, commenting that loss of livelihood in the developing world can be a matter of 'life and death'. See also below, note 156, for an example of such arguments being made in the context of indigenous peoples in a developed State.

One reason may be that the bureaucrats that prepare arguments for WTO litigation are not human rights experts.[155]

As noted, very few social measures have survived challenge before WTO panels
or the Appellate Body. This circumstance may have a chilling impact on social
legislation where that regulation has an impact on foreign trade. However, the
case statistics reflect the outcomes of very few cases. A new case on the horizon,
concerning complaints by Canada and Norway against EC bans on seal products,
might reveal more about the approach of the Panels, and perhaps the Appellate
Body, in this respect.[156]

D. The SPS and TBT Agreements

The SPS Agreement regulates sanitary and phytosanitary standards while the TBT
Agreement regulates the technical standards which a State may apply to products.
Both of these Agreements regulate the extent to which a State can use such stand-
ards when those standards restrict foreign trade. They are discussed in turn below.

The SPS

Sanitary and phytosanitary (SPS) standards are measures aimed at protecting
human animal or plant life from food-borne risks, pests or diseases.[157] Hence, they
are standards that are essentially imposed on agricultural goods, which restrict
the entry of non-compliant goods.[158] The SPS Agreement imposes restrictions on
a State's ability to implement certain inward measures. Given the importance of
agriculture to the livelihoods of most of the world's poorest people, as discussed in
Chapter 6, and the importance of quarantine measures in protecting consumers
and others from health risks or risks to food supplies, SPS measures can set up a
clash of respective human rights interests.

The SPS Agreement imposes the following disciplines on SPS measures. States
should only adopt SPS measures which are necessary to protect the health of
humans, animals, and plants (Article 2.2). Such measures should be based on
scientific evidence and principles (Article 2.2), and must comply with MFN and

---

[155] See Stephen Powell, 'The place of human rights law in World Trade Organization rules' (2004)
16 *Florida Journal of International Law* 219, 220.

[156] *European Communities—Measures prohibiting the importation and marketing of seal products*,
WTO docs. WT/DS400/1 (2 November 2009) (Requests for Consultations by Canada) and WT/
DS401/1 (5 November 2009) (Request for Consultations by Norway). It is notable, from a human
rights point of view, that the Canadian Inuit argue that the ban threatens their livelihoods and their
communities: see, eg, 'Canadian Seal Hunters lose bid to lift EU import ban', *ABC News*, 29 October
2010, at <http://www.abc.net.au/news/stories/2010/10/29/3051380.htm?section=world>.

[157] Van den Bossche, above n 6, 463.

[158] In the *Asbestos* case, Canada had initially claimed that the ban on asbestos products was in
breach of the SPS Agreement as well as the GATT (see WT/DS/135/3, 9 October 1998). Presumably
this claim was based on the reference in the SPS Agreement to 'diseases' (such as, perhaps, asbestos-
related cancer). However, Canada did not pursue the claim before the Panel (see Appellate Body
report, above n 34, fn 4).

national treatment principles (Article 2.3).[159] Finally, Article 2.4 confirms that SPS measures are permissible under WTO law so long as they comply with the SPS agreement: they are not subject to a separate challenge under GATT.

Article 3 of the Agreement expresses a preference for harmonized SPS standards. To that end, States may base their standards on international standards or conform to those standards. If a State does so, its SPS measures are presumed to comply with the SPS Agreement. A State may still choose to impose a higher level of protection of health under its SPS standards than is achieved under a relevant international standard. However, if a State does so, it must justify its SPS standards by reference to a scientific risk assessment.[160]

The concept of risk is crucial under the SPS Agreement. 'Risk assessment' is a scientific process for establishing the risks entailed (for example, in the ingestion of a certain microbe), taking into account likelihood and magnitude of risk. 'Risk management' is a process for determining the level of protection required from a certain risk and choosing SPS measures accordingly. Risk management decisions take into account risk assessment, but also societal values, consumer preferences, industry interests and costs.[161]

Article 5.1 requires that SPS measures be based on a risk assessment, taking into account recognized risk assessment techniques. In *EC—Measures concerning meat and meat products (hormones)*,[162] the Appellate Body clarified that there must be a rational relationship between risk assessment and the measure adopted, and that the assessment must 'reasonably support' the measure.[163]

Article 5.2 specifies some scientific and technical factors that Members should take into account in assessing risks such as the existence of 'pest- or disease-free areas';[164] that list is not exhaustive. Article 5.3 specifies certain economic criteria that should be taken into account in devising SPS standards, such as production losses in the event of the entry of a particular pest or disease into the country.[165]

Article 5.5 requires that Members avoid 'arbitrary or unjustifiable distinctions' in their SPS measures if these distinctions 'result in discrimination or a disguised restriction on international trade'. Article 5.6 requires Members to ensure that their SPS measures are 'not more trade-restrictive than required to achieve their appropriate level of sanitary or phytosanitary protection, taking into account technical and economic feasibility'. That is, a State should adopt a less trade restrictive measure if it is reasonably available and will achieve the same level of desired protection.

Finally, Article 5.7 deals with the situation where there is a dearth of scientific evidence on relevant risks. WTO Members in that situation may adopt provisional

---

[159] Van den Bossche, above n 6, 463.   [160] Ibid, 464.   [161] Ibid.

[162] *European Communities—Measures concerning meat and meat products (hormones)*, WTO docs. WT/DS26/AB/R and WT/DS48/AB/R, Ab-1997-4 (16 January 1998) (Report of the Appellate Body).

[163] Ibid, para 193.

[164] Eg, Australia can justify stronger measures to keep out rabies, given that rabies does not exist in Australia, compared to a country that already has rabies.

[165] See also Van den Bossche, above n 6, 465.

SPS measures. Members should review provisional SPS measures as more evidence becomes available, with a view to modifying them as appropriate.

It is clear that the SPS Agreement is not only concerned with eliminating trade discrimination: it imposes minimum standards on permissible SPS standards to the extent that they affect trade. Those minimum standards relate to the requirements for risk assessments and the need for proportionality to be maintained between those risk assessments and the measures adopted. In *Beef Hormone*, the Appellate Body found that the impugned measures breached the SPS Agreement even though they did not discriminate between EC and foreign products. Driesen argues that the decoupling of the regulation of SPS measures from non-discrimination provisions was a big step by the WTO towards 'trade free of national regulation under a broad laissez-faire conception'.[166]

The cases decided so far under WTO law have essentially concerned the provisions regarding risk assessment.[167] Restrictions on genetically modified organisms (GMOs) were subject to a challenge before a WTO Panel in *EC—Measures affecting the approval and marketing of biotech products*.[168] The case concerned a challenge to a de facto moratorium on the approval of GMOs by the EC as well as bans on GMOs by certain individual EC States. The relevant moratorium and bans were found to breach the SPS on the basis that risk assessments on GMOs had not been carried out and had been unduly delayed. The breaches of the risk assessment requirements were blatant. Thus, the substantive issue of whether imports of GMO foods could be restricted or banned was not addressed.

EC—Beef Hormone concerned an EC ban on all hormone-treated meat, including local products and imports, due to concerns about the health impacts of hormones including possible carcinogenic effects. The EC measures applied a higher sanitary protection measure than that recommended by the Codex Alimentarius, the relevant international standards body. The ban was found to breach the SPS Agreement, as it was found not to be properly based on a risk assessment.

The Appellate Body in *Beef Hormone* confirmed strict requirements for risk assessments.[169] There must be proof of risk, rather than mere theoretical uncertainty.[170] However, an assessment may go beyond 'controlled laboratory conditions' and take into account consequences 'in the real world where people live and work and die'.[171] The assessment must be focused on the particular type of risk at issue rather than on a generalized risk of harm.[172] Risk assessments can focus on qualitative and quantitative assessments of risk. That is, assessments do not have to establish a 'minimum magnitude of risk'; they must simply establish that

---

[166] Driesen, above n 59, 285.
[167] Caroline E Foster, 'Public Opinion and the interpretation of the World Trade Organisation's Agreement on Sanitary and Phytosanitary Measures' in Joseph, Kinley, and Waincymer (eds), above n 84, 288.
[168] WT/DS291-293/R (29 September 2006) (Report of the Panel).
[169] The following summary is taken from Van den Bossche, above n 6, 465.
[170] *EC—Hormones* (Appellate Body), above n 162, para 186.   [171] Ibid, para 187.
[172] Ibid, para 200.

a risk assessment justifies the measure taken.[173] Finally, a Member may rely on risk assessments conducted by other States or by international organizations.[174]

The dispute resolution bodies have used scientific risk assessment as the touchstone for deciding whether an SPS measure is rational, implying that scientific assessments are objective and relatively unimpeachable. The *Beef Hormone* decision was heavily influenced by the relevant Codex standard, which was lower than that of the EC. However, the relevant standard had been adopted by the organization by a margin of 33-29 with seven abstentions,[175] a vote which is hardly indicative of an uncontroversial standard. The marginal nature of this vote was not taken into account by the Panel (or the Appellate Body). While that approach showed more fidelity to the words of the SPS Agreement,[176] it probably unduly undermined the ability of States to depart from Codex standards in the interests of promoting the right to health. In fact, this level of reliance on science raises greater problems 'in terms of cultural autonomy and democratic legitimacy'.[177] Scientific assessments are not value-free or culturally uniform.[178] Science is also often 'incomplete and uncertain'.[179] Nor is it stable, as scientific opinion on a matter constantly evolves.

Dr Caroline Foster has argued that the assessment of risk must involve objective and subjective elements. While risk involves consideration of the likelihood and magnitude of an eventuality, the Panels and Appellate Body have tended to focus on likelihood, which is much easier to measure in objective technical terms (so long as there is sufficient available scientific evidence).[180] Yet an assessment of magnitude clearly entails subjective elements, as questions of magnitude 'will always hinge partly on value judgments by the society that is to be subjected to the risk'.[181] Therefore, in her view, the Panels should take public opinion into account in making decisions under the SPS. Such consideration would result in more transparent decision-making. Presently, Panels and Appellate Body are likely influenced by their own views of the risk at issue but they do not tend to acknowledge those views.[182] A problem with Foster's proposal is that consumer choice might be manipulated for protectionist ends. For example, regarding the GMO issue, it has been argued that European consumers are being brainwashed by a barrage of GMO-propaganda produced by protectionist farmers in an unholy alliance with

---

[173] Ibid, para 186. See also *Australia—Measures affecting importation of salmon*, WTO doc. WT/DS18/AB/R, AB-1998-5 (20 October 1998) (Report of the Appellate Body) para 124.

[174] *EC—Hormones* (Appellate Body), above n 162, para 190.

[175] Jürgen Kurtz, 'A Look behind the Mirror: Standardization, Institutions and the WTO SPS and TBT Agreements' (2007) 30 *University of New South Wales Law Journal* 504, 518.

[176] *European Communities—Measures concerning meat and meat products (hormones)*, WTO doc. WT/DS48/R/CAN (18 August 1997) (Report of the Panel) para 8.69.

[177] David Winickoff and others, 'Adjudicating the GM food wars: Science, Risk, and Democracy in World Trade Law' (2005) 81 *Yale Journal of International Law* 81, 91, 92.

[178] Winickoff and others, ibid, trace the differing social science and regulatory experiences of the EC and the US in the context of 'testing' GMOs at 93–6.

[179] Foster, above n 167, 309.   [180] Ibid, 297–8.   [181] Ibid, 298.

[182] At 299, ibid, Foster notes that the Panel in *Biotech* seemed to believe that the risk entailed in biotech products was not great, 'a view seemingly not shared by Austria, France, Germany, Italy, Greece and Luxembourg'.

influential NGOs.[183] However, Foster argues that evidence of the provision to the public of appropriate information could be sought, including evidence of a process of public consultation and deliberation (including processes which take account of the views of affected offshore exporters).[184] Furthermore, she does not argue that public opinion should be the decisive consideration. Scientific risk assessment would retain an important role in SPS decisions,[185] but the opinions of the people to be affected by the decisions would be another relevant consideration. Consideration of public opinion would accord with democratic principles, including rights of political participation in Article 25 of the ICCPR.[186] Finally, it may lend some much-needed legitimacy to the WTO's dispute resolution processes, given that States have been very reluctant to implement WTO decisions which run counter to domestic public opinion.[187]

The EC in *Beef Hormone* attempted to justify its ban on the basis of the precautionary principle, to the effect that it was entitled to ban hormone-injected beef to ensure protection for European consumers from potentially deadly harm until the safety of such hormones was established. The Appellate Body found that the precautionary principle was partially enshrined in Article 5.7, but that Article 5.7 did not override the risk assessment requirements of Articles 5.1 and 5.2.[188]

It is possible that the interpretation of the SPS decision in *Beef Hormone* overly constrains a Member's ability to adopt inward health measures, particularly in situations where there is insufficient scientific evidence accompanied by a suspicion of serious health risks. Certainly, the EC policy probably would have been applauded by international human rights bodies, though it is perhaps a stretch to claim that the forced entry of hormones into the EC beef market would breach the right to health. On the other hand, Special Rapporteurs on the Right to Health[189] and the Right to Food[190] have endorsed the precautionary principle, with the latter claiming that it was an especially appropriate principle to apply in the context of genetically modified foods.

Despite their positive impact on the right to health, SPS measures are highly problematic for developing States. Most of the poorest people in the world depend on agriculture for their livelihoods and SPS measures can pose onerous trade barriers which threaten those livelihoods, and hamper the abilities of agricultural workers to climb out of poverty. For example, an EU regulation, which requires dairy products made from cow's milk to be produced from cattle milked mechanically, effectively prevents trade with the many small producers who cannot afford

---

[183] Lawrence A Kogan, 'Trade protectionism: Ducking the truth about Europe's GMO policy' *International Herald Tribune* (New York), 27 November 2004.

[184] Foster, above n 167, 303–4.   [185] Ibid, 290 and 306.

[186] Ibid, 306–8. See also Chapter 3, Part B.   [187] Ibid, 287 and 309.

[188] *EC—Hormones* (Appellate Body), above n 162, paras 124–5.

[189] See Human Rights Council, 'Report of the Special Rapporteur on the right of everyone to the enjoyment of the highest attainable standard of physical and mental health; Preliminary note on the mission to Ecuador and Colombia', UN doc. A/HRC/7/11/Add.3 (4 March 2007) 17.

[190] See UN Press Release, 'Statement on Issue of Genetically Modified Food by Special Rapporteur on the Right to Food', 12 November 2002, <http://www.unhchr.ch/huricane/huricane.nsf/view01/40D2D521A7678C13C1256C6F005688C3?opendocument> and <http://www.ohchr.org/EN/NewsEvents/Pages/DisplayNews.aspx?NewsID=2251&LangID=E> accessed 7 May 2010.

mechanization.[191] As another example, a World Bank report in 2001 found that the SPS standards imposed by the EU in respect of aflatoxins, which were set above international standards, would cut African exports of nuts and grains by 64 per cent at a cost of US$640 million.[192] Those trade losses caused significant human rights harms in terms of the right to work and the right to an adequate standard of living, especially given the limited adjustment capacities of African economies. At the same time, it was estimated that the aflotoxin measures reduced health risks by 1.4 deaths per billion per annum.[193]

The aflatoxin case study gives rise to a difficult conundrum from a human rights point of view. Those 1.4 per billion people undoubtedly have a right to life. Should Europe be required to lower its SPS standard and jeopardize the lives of 1.4 people per billion in order to safeguard the livelihoods and the rights of those dependent on the nut and grain export industry?[194] The right to life is not absolute: one may not be 'arbitrarily' deprived of one's life.[195] Is the subjection of a person to such a low risk a breach of the right to life? Certainly, no State has an obligation to reduce all lethal risks to zero. Otherwise, for example, States would be commonly condemned by human rights bodies for permitting people to drive cars at potentially lethal speeds.

The Appellate Body in *Beef Hormone* added in a footnote which noted that if the arguments regarding the dangers of the hormones were true, 371 women in the EU out of a population in 1995 of 371 million were likely to develop breast cancer, perhaps implying that those potentially lethal illnesses were justified by the liberalizing effects of allowing hormone-injected beef into the EU.[196] In contrast, the EC had argued that any risk, even 'a risk of one in a million', was sufficient justification for an SPS measure.[197] From a human rights point of view, it is questionable whether a State is obliged to protect against such slight threats to life and health. On the other hand, trade liberalization per se does not justify a retrogressive measure (such as the removal of the hormone ban if one accepts that the hormones might cause breast cancer for a few women) with regard to the right to health, even one which only raises the risk by a 'one in a million' chance.[198] However, the countervailing human rights of traders, if their rights to work and to a livelihood

---

[191] Kurtz, above n 175, 512.

[192] Tsenuhiro Otsuki, John S Wilson, and Mirvat Sewadeh, 'A Race to the Top? A Case Study of Food Safety Standards and African exports'(World Bank Policy Research Working Paper No 2563) (World Bank, Washington DC, February 2001).

[193] Ibid.

[194] See also Joel P Trachtman, 'Developing Countries, the Doha round, Preferences, and the Right to Regulate' in Chantal Thomas and Joel P Trachtman (eds), *Developing Countries in the WTO Legal System* (Oxford University Press, New York, 2009) 122. See also Chapter 8 below on the notion of extraterritorial obligations.

[195] See Article 6 ICCPR. I will not undertake a comparable analysis regarding a possible limit to rights of political participation in Article 25, which could also be qualified by being balanced against the human rights of offshore traders. See also Chapter 3, text at notes 155–6.

[196] *EC—Hormones* (Appellate Body), above n 162, fn 182; see also Anne Orford, 'Beyond Harmonization: Trade, Human Rights and the Economy of Sacrifice' (2005) 18 *Leiden Journal of International Law* 179, 191.

[197] *EC—Hormones* (Appellate Body), above n 162, para 29.

[198] See also Chapter 1, text at notes 71–2 on retrogressive measures under the ICESCR.

were seriously threatened, might justify such a measure. It is doubtful that such human rights were threatened by the EU's hormone ban, given that the aggrieved traders were located in developed States, so it is unlikely their rights to an adequate standard of living were seriously threatened.[199]

At the least, developed States (which generally impose the strictest SPS standards) must negotiate with and supply technical assistance to developing States (which are the least able to comply with strict SPS standards) to ameliorate the harshest impacts of their SPS measures. Furthermore, efforts must be made to increase developing country participation in relevant standard setting bodies such as Codex.[200] Article 9 of the SPS agreement recommends the provision of technical assistance. Article 9(2) specifies:

Where substantial investments are required in order for an exporting developing country Member to fulfil the sanitary or phytosanitary requirements of an importing Member, the latter *shall consider* providing such technical assistance as will permit the developing country Member to maintain and expand its market access opportunities for the product involved (emphasis added).

Like most provisions concerning the provision of international assistance, Article 9(2) is not mandatory.[201]

Further illumination of the impact of the SPS Agreement on the right to health may be forthcoming if a current trade dispute between South Korea and Canada leads to a Panel decision. The dispute concerns Korean restrictions on bovine meat and meat products from Canada due to the risk of bovine spongiform encephalopathy ('mad cow disease').[202]

The TBT

The TBT agreement regulates 'technical regulations and standards' which might impose barriers to trade. Like the SPS, it imposes requirements of national treatment and MFN, and certain minimum standards.[203] Technical regulations and standards are mandatory measures which prescribe product characteristics for an identifiable product or group of products.[204] Examples of such regulations include labelling and packaging requirements. Onerous requirements can unduly hinder foreign trade.

Under Article 2.2, technical requirements must not be more trade restrictive than necessary. They must be adopted for a legitimate purpose, which imposes a minimum standard requirement rather than a requirement of non-discrimination: a non-discriminatory technical requirement which fails to

---

[199] They also probably had access to alternative markets, including local markets. Furthermore, alternative hormone-free methods of production may have been available to affected producers.

[200] See generally, Kurtz, above n 175. See also Chapter 3, text at notes 52–4.

[201] See also SPS, Article 10. See also Chapter 5, text at notes 31–4.

[202] *Korea— Measures affecting the importation of bovine meat and meat products from Canada*, WTO doc. WT/DS391/1 (15 April 2009) (Request for Consultations by Canada).

[203] TBT, Articles 2.1, 2.2.   [204] Van den Bossche, above n 6, 458.

appropriately serve a legitimate purpose will breach the TBT. Article 2.2 contains a non-exhaustive list of such purposes, such as the protection of human health and the environment. Presumably, the protection of human rights would suffice as a legitimate purpose. Where an international standard for a technical requirement exists, a Member's technical requirement should be based on that standard (Article 2.4).[205] However, a Member may depart from that standard if the standard is not effective in fulfilling the objective pursued, or if there are geographical or climatic factors, or technological problems, that render the international standard inappropriate.

The definition of a technical standard is very broad. In *Asbestos*, the Appellate Body gave some clues as to the measures affected by the TBT agreement. It found that the ban on asbestos fibres (with some limited exceptions) prescribed technical requirements for an identifiable group of products, that is 'all products that might contain asbestos'.[206] Therefore, it overruled the Panel and found that the measures fell within the TBT. However, the Appellate Body did not go on to examine whether the asbestos prohibition breached the TBT. The Panel, having decided that the TBT did not apply, accordingly failed to rule on Canada's claims under the TBT. As the Panel had not dealt with the TBT claims in detail, the Appellate Body found itself unable to do so.[207] The Appellate Body did note that the TBT obligations were '*different* from, and *additional* to' GATT obligations.[208] Therefore, it is possible that the win for the right to health in the *Asbestos* case could possibly be undone by a new claim regarding the TBT compliance of the prohibition.[209]

The Appellate Body perhaps recognized the breadth of the consequences of its finding regarding the TBT Agreement in *Asbestos* in stating:

We note, however—and we emphasize—that this does not mean that *all* internal measures covered by Article III:4 of the GATT 1994 'affecting' the 'sale, offering for sale, purchase, transportation, distribution or use' of a product are, necessarily, 'technical regulations' under the *TBT Agreement*. Rather, we rule only that this particular measure... falls within the definition of a 'technical regulation' given in Annex 1.1 of that Agreement.[210]

Nevertheless, the Appellate Body did not hint at any particular limit to the definition of a 'technical standard' beyond an indication that a total prohibition on a particular product might not be a technical standard in regard to that product.[211] It is therefore very possible that the TBT, especially given its explicit prescription of minimum standards beyond non-discrimination obligations, significantly

---

[205] See, on this requirement, *European Communities—Trade Description of Sardines*, WTO doc. WT/DS231/AB/R, AB-2002-3 (26 September 2002) (Report of the Appellate Body) para 249.
[206] *EC—Asbestos* (Appellate Body), above n 34, para 75.   [207] Ibid, para 83.
[208] Ibid, para 80, emphasis not added.   [209] No such challenge has arisen.
[210] *EC—Asbestos* (Appellate Body), above n 34, para 77.
[211] Ibid, para 71. The Appellate Body suggested that the ban on asbestos fibres prescribed no characteristics for the fibres themselves. Note also that the TBT Agreement does not apply to SPS standards, which are dealt with exclusively under the SPS Agreement (Article 1.5).

constrains the regulatory capacities of States, and may therefore limit their abilities to implement human rights trade measures.

For example, it is fairly certain that the TBT regulates the mandatory imposition of labeling requirements.[212] While spurious and onerous labelling requirements should probably be restricted, human rights considerations demand that the interpretation of the TBT ensures that consumer rights to informed choices regarding the food they consume are not prejudiced by overzealous labeling prohibitions.[213] For instance, labels which identify GMOs should be permitted under the TBT, so as to enable a consumer to avoid such products if he or she wishes. Such a labelling requirement would not be onerous.[214] While such labels might place genetically modified products at a disadvantage in markets where consumers are largely hostile to GMOs, the rights of consumers to such information should prevail over rights of free trade.

We await further interpretation of the TBT by the Panels and the Appellate Body to clarify the extent of its constraints on State regulatory capacities. However, human rights advocates might be skeptical that the right balance will be struck, given the lack of human rights expertise and the predominance of trade expertise on the Panels and the Appellate Body.

However, the breadth of the TBT might open a door for the application of human rights measures. McBeth has suggested that any measure which sought to impose labour rights standards as a condition for the importation of goods might be a technical requirement subject to the TBT.[215] If such measures were imposed by reference to the standards of the International Labour Organization (ILO), they might be deemed to be based on an international standard and therefore 'rebuttably presumed not to create an unnecessary obstacle to trade' under Article 2(5). Such a measure would not be totally immune from WTO challenge under the TBT or the GATT,[216] but would at least benefit from a presumption of WTO compatibility. Indeed, that approach could perhaps be applied to any trade restrictive measure that applied a human rights standard. This argument is stronger in regard to inward measures, where human rights obligations apply, rather than outward measures, where they would rarely if ever apply.

---

[212] The TBT would not constrain voluntary labeling schemes adopted by industry groups: Cassimatis, above n 6, 401.

[213] See CESCR, 'General Comment 12: The Right to Adequate Food', UN doc. E/C.12/1999/5 (12 May 1999) para 11, on the right of consumers to information about the nature of the food they are eating. Similarly, people have a right to make informed choices regarding their own health, including perhaps the right to choose to avoid GMOs which can only be protected if labelling is allowed: see General Comment 14, above n 132, para 37. Article 19(2) ICCPR guarantees the right to freedom of expression, including the right to seek and receive information, though this right may not apply outside the context of government information. See also Schultz and Ball, above n 129, 57–9.

[214] I would include here labels which identify the possibility of some GMOs in the product, given that some manufacturers might be unable to guarantee the total absence of GMOs.

[215] McBeth, above n 27, 131–2.

[216] The GATT also applies to technical measures, though the TBT would prevail in the unlikely event of a clash between the two treaties: Van den Bossche, above n 6, 459.

E. Waivers

Under Article IX of the Marrakesh Agreement, a WTO obligation may be waived
in exceptional circumstances if approved by three quarters of WTO members.
Waivers may be used to allow the departure from WTO rules for human rights
reasons. For example, the General Council adopted a waiver to permit Members
to restrict the diamond trade to diamonds certified under the Kimberley Process
Certification Scheme.[217] The Kimberley Process Certification Scheme is designed
to guard against the trade in diamonds that indirectly fund civil wars in Africa.
In the waiver, initially adopted in May 2003, the General Council explicitly
recognizes:

the extraordinary humanitarian nature of this issue and the devastating impact of conflicts
fuelled by the trade in conflict diamonds on the peace, safety and security of people in
affected countries and the systematic and gross human rights violations that have been
perpetrated in such conflicts...[218]

Susan Aaronsen describes the waiver as an important precedent, which was 'the
first time that the WTO...approved a waiver to protect human rights'.[219] It may
be noted that the US and Canada refused to join the Kimberley Scheme unless the
WTO adopted an explicit waiver to permit that Scheme. That reluctance demonstrates how States can prioritize WTO considerations over human rights considerations, given the clear link between the diamond trade and gross human rights
violations in West Africa.[220]

Another waiver with positive ramifications for human rights was adopted in
August 2003, concerning the 'Implementation of Paragraph 6 of the Doha
Declaration on the TRIPS Agreement and Public Health'.[221] This waiver has
important implications for the right to health and is discussed in Chapter 7 of this
book.

As a 'solution' to any possibility that WTO rules might hinder the adoption
of human rights trade measures, the possibility of waiver is important but limited. Most obviously, waivers can only be adopted if there is a significant degree of
political will in the form of the consent of three quarters of the WTO membership.
Waivers are therefore unlikely to arise in contentious areas. Nor are they likely to
arise if the waiver authorizes trade measures against politically powerful Members,

[217] See WTO, 'Waiver Concerning Kimberley Process Certification Scheme for Rough
Diamonds' (Decision of 15 May 2003), WTO doc. WT/L/518 (27 May 2003). See also <http://
www.kimberleyprocess.com>; Harrison, above n 10, 92–5.
[218] WTO, above n 217, preamble.
[219] Susan Aaronsen, 'Seeping in slowly: how human rights concerns are penetrating the WTO'
(2007) 6 *World Trade Review* 413, 428.
[220] See Harrison, above n 10, 94, and 236. Even though the Kimberley Scheme regulated outward
measures, it is possible that the continued engagement in trade in conflict diamonds by the US and
Canada would breach their human rights obligations, given the close causal relationship between
that trade and the financial base of groups perpetrating egregious human rights abuses.
[221] WTO, 'Implementation of Paragraph 6 of the Doha Declaration on the TRIPS Agreement
and Public Health' (Decision of 30 August 2003), WTO doc. WT/L/540 (2 September 2003).

as those Members will likely mobilize enough political support to prevent the adoption of a waiver. Furthermore, waivers are only meant to be temporary measures, and human rights problems often cannot be 'temporarily' resolved.[222] Having said that, waivers can be extended. For example, the Kimberley waiver initially only lasted until the end of 2006. It has since been extended to the end of 2012.[223]

F. A 'Labour Rights' Clause for the WTO?

Labour rights are recognized in many treaties under the auspices of the ILO. 'Core labour standards' are recognized in the ILO Declaration on Fundamental Rights at Work 1998 as: freedom of association and the right to collective bargaining, freedom from forced labour, freedom from child labour, and the right to non-discrimination in employment. Aspects of labour rights are also recognized in the ICESCR in articles 6 (the right to work), 7 (right to just and equitable conditions of work) and 8 (trade union rights), as well as in articles 8 (freedom from slavery and forced labour) and 22 (freedom of association) of the ICCPR.

The most commonly mooted outward measures in academic and activist literature are those targeted at labour rights violations in other States. Examples are measures which restrict imports of goods that are manufactured by children, under conditions of forced labour, or in States where trade unions are suppressed or banned. Relevant trade measures might be aimed at coercing a State into raising its labour standards.

Labour rights measures may however be conceptualized as inward measures, designed to rectify the distorting effects of unfair trade practices.[224] An exporting State may be attaining an unfair competitive advantage in permitting excessively low wages and exploitative practices, lowering the 'normal' cost of the labour component of goods or services. The effect can be to drive workers out of jobs in the importing State, or to depress their working conditions. This phenomenon (if it exists) is sometimes termed 'social dumping'.[225] Ordinary dumping arises when goods are exported at less than their normal value. Dumping is not prohibited under WTO law, but States are permitted to respond to dumping by taking anti-dumping measures pursuant to Article VI GATT and the Agreement on Implementation of Article VI. Anti-dumping measures are supposed to counteract the unfair nature of dumping. By analogy, social dumping also constitutes unfair trade, which should therefore justify analogous countermeasures.[226] Indeed,

---

[222] Aaronsen, above n 219, 429.

[223] WTO, 'Kimberley Process Certification Scheme for Rough Diamonds' (Decision of 15 December 2006), WTO doc. WT/L/676 (19 December 2006).

[224] Robert Wai, 'Countering, Branding and Dealing: Using Economic and Social Rights in and Around the International Trade Regime' (2003) 14 *European Journal of International Law* 35, 60.

[225] Walter Goode, *Dictionary of Trade Policy Terms*, 5th edn (Cambridge University Press, Cambridge, 2007) 392.

[226] See also Joseph E Stiglitz and Andrew Charlton, *Fair Trade for All* (Oxford University Press, New York, 2005) 153–4.

notions of social dumping probably underpin the exception in Article XX(e) concerning prison labour.

A related concern is that the global trade competition catalysed by WTO rules generates a 'race to the bottom' in that States will compete with each other to offer conditions designed to attract investment, such as low wages and poor labour conditions, or will depress labour conditions to maintain trade competitiveness. If the 'race to the bottom' thesis is true, the progressive realization of labour rights is being undermined, and free trade is acting as a catalyst for human rights abuses. In such a case, it would be appropriate for WTO rules to alleviate that impact by safeguarding labour rights in some way.

Labour is an inherent aspect of trade. The trade/labour link is explicitly recognized in the preamble to the Marrakesh Agreement, with its references to 'economic endeavour' and 'full employment and a large and steadily growing volume of real income'.[227] Proposals for inclusion of a 'social clause' to protect against labour rights violations were part of the proposals for an International Trade Organization in the immediate post-war period.[228] Indeed, social clauses have been included in a number of commodities agreements.[229] It is arguably odd that a topic such as intellectual property is within the WTO tent, which came late to the trade debate, while labour remains outside.[230] Indeed, the inclusion of intellectual property rights in the WTO agreements was ostensibly motivated by similar arguments that arise today with regard to labour: the intellectual property regime needed to be strengthened in order to prevent it from being weakened by the growth of global trade.[231] That is, the enforcement regime that pre-existed TRIPS was weak, as is the case today with the ILO and labour rights.

Labour rights reform became a necessary part of the industrial revolution in developed States to curb abuses.[232] Likewise, stronger global labour rights protection is probably needed to ward off labour abuses in the current globalized economic revolution.[233] Such protection could take the form of a minimum standards clause, performing a similar function to TRIPS regarding intellectual property protection. Alternatively, the protection of labour rights could form an exception to WTO free trade obligations along the lines of the existing Article XX/XIV

---

[227] World Commission on the Social Dimension of Globalisation, *A Fair Globalization: Promoting Opportunities for all* (ILO, Geneva, 2004) para 505.

[228] Steve Charnovitz, 'The (neglected) employment dimension of the World Trade Organization' in Virginia A Leary and Daniel Warner (eds), *Social Issues, Globalisation and International Institutions* (Martinus Nijhoff, Leiden, 2006) 138–9. See Chapter 1, text at n 2.

[229] Eg, social clauses were included in the International Coffee Agreement of 2001 and in the tin and sugar agreements of 1954: Goode, above n 225, 392.

[230] See also Deborah Z Cass, *The Constitutionalization of the World Trade Organization* (Oxford University Press, New York, 2005) 235.

[231] Chantal Thomas, 'The WTO and labor rights: strategies of linkage' in Joseph, Kinley, and Waincymer (eds), above n 84, 276–7.

[232] See Simon Deakin, 'Social Rights in a Globalized Economy' in Philip Alston (ed), *Labour Rights as Human Rights* (Oxford University Press, Oxford, 2005) 38, and, for an account of the evolution of social rights in Great Britain, 26–38.

[233] See also World Commission on the Social Dimension of Globalisation, above n 227, at xiii and paras 426, 501.

exceptions, permitting the unilateral imposition of trade sanctions in response to poor labour rights standards in the sanctioned State. As noted below, there are other potential models for a social clause which may be worth exploring.

The idea of a social clause within the WTO agreements was defeated at the WTO Ministerial Conference in Singapore in 1996.[234] In the Singapore Ministerial Declaration, WTO Members reaffirmed a 'commitment to the observance' of core labour standards, but they rejected 'the use of labour standards for protectionist purposes, and [agreed] that the comparative advantage of countries, particularly low-wage developing countries' must not be 'put into question'.[235] Thus, developing States are generally opposed to a social clause because they fear that it would be abused for protectionist purposes to undercut their comparative advantages in labour costs.[236] Hence, the WTO confirmed that the ILO was 'the competent body to set and deal with [labour] standards', rather than the WTO.[237] Whilst it is laudable that the WTO Members affirmed their support for the ILO's work, the fact remains that the ILO's record in enforcing labour rights is, in the words of Professor Chantal Thomas, 'woeful'.[238] It is therefore submitted that there is merit in reviving the debate over the explicit linkage of trade and labour within the WTO framework.

The existence of a race to the bottom regarding labour standards is disputed.[239] While workers across the industrialized world perceive greater job insecurity due to globalization, those fears are not necessarily well founded.[240] Certainly, any increase in jobs caused by export markets might create demand for labour by providing jobs where there were none, and even drive up wages.[241] For example, reports from China in mid-2010 suggest that this phenomenon may be starting to take place in that country.[242]

There is no evidence that foreign investment is generally being redirected to states with poor labour rights regimes.[243] Many factors drive foreign investment, of which the price of labour is but one, including the adequacy of infrastructure,

---

[234] Thomas, above n 231, 281.

[235] WTO, 'Singapore Ministerial Declaration' (Adopted on 13 December 1996), WTO doc. WT/MIN(96)/DEC (18 December 1996) para 4.

[236] See also Anita Chan and Robert JS Ross, 'Race to the Bottom: international trade without a social clause' (2003) 24 *Third World Quarterly* 1011, 1012; Ilan Kapoor, 'Deliberative democracy and the WTO' (2004) 11 *Review of International Political Economy* 522, 534; World Commission on the Social Dimension of Globalisation, above n 227, para 425. See also Mahathir Mohammed, 'East Asia will find its own roads to democracy' *International Herald Tribune*, 17 May 1994.

[237] Singapore Ministerial Declaration, above n 235, para 4.

[238] Thomas, above n 231, 258.   [239] See also Harrison, above n 10, 77–80.

[240] WTO and ILO, *Trade and Employment: Challenges for Policy Research* (WTO Secretariat, Geneva, 2007) 89.

[241] Department of Foreign Affairs and Trade, *Globalisation: Keeping the Gains* (Commonwealth of Australia, Canberra, 2003) 11; Oxfam, *Rigged Rules and Double Standards* (Oxfam, London, 2002) 51 and 55.

[242] See, eg, David Barboza, 'As China's Wages Rise, Export Prices Could Follow' *New York Times*, 7 June 2010 <http://www.nytimes.com/2010/06/08/business/global/08wages.html> accessed 22 September 2010.

[243] See, eg, Bob Hepple, *Labour Laws and Global Trade* (Hart, Oxford, 2005) 14–15. See also OECD, *Trade, Employment and Labour Standards* (OECD, Paris, 1996) and OECD, *International Trade and Core Labor Standards* (OECD, Paris, 2000).

property rights regimes, availability of and attractiveness to skilled staff, levels of crime and corruption, and security issues. Notwithstanding higher labour rights protection, developed States clearly have huge advantages over developing States in attracting foreign investment. They also have huge advantages in terms of worker productivity.

Indeed, a pattern has emerged in many developing States with some of the worst labour records of de-industrialization (indicating jobs lost in the manufacturing sector)[244] and transformation from food exporting to food importing status (indicating a loss of jobs in the agricultural sector).[245] Low labour costs do not seem to coincide with success in the modern global economy.[246] Furthermore, numerous studies have indicated that conditions in factories in developing States run by foreign investors, even if poor, are better than those run by local entrepreneurs.[247] The same is reportedly true of the much-maligned export processing zones (EPZs),[248] though there is evidence of widespread gender discrimination, poor occupational health and safety (which impacts on rights under Article 7 ICESCR) and occasional mistreatment of workers.[249]

However, the above circumstances do not mean that there is no race to the bottom. In response to claims regarding the 'good' labour rights record of foreign investors in developing States compared to local businesses, it may be noted that foreign investors often do not run factories themselves, but instead source supplies from local contractors. Those contractors may compete with each other to offer attractively cheap labour to those investors.[250] Therefore, unconscionable labour standards may be hidden in a supply chain. Furthermore, there are some instances where labour standards in EPZs are 'explicitly lower' than in the rest of a country.[251]

A relevant indicator in identifying a race to the bottom is whether the advent of global competition has prompted governments to reduce labour entitlements. Indeed, many governments certainly act as if deregulation of the labour force and a diminution of labour rights is needed in order to compete in the global economy.[252] For example, a recent report by the NGO War on Want, based on ILO reports and other authoritative materials, asserts that free trade has caused or at

[244] See also Chapter 5, Part E. See also War on Want, 'Trading away our jobs: How free trade threatens employment around the world' (2009) at <http://www.waronwant.org/attachments/Trading%20Away%20Our%20Jobs.pdf>.
[245] See also Chapter 6, text at notes 75–8.
[246] See also Martin Wolf, *Why Globalisation Works* (Yale Nota Bene, London, 2005) 233.
[247] Ibid, 238–9.
[248] An EPZ is an area where a State permits the duty-free import of primary goods or components for the purposes of further processing and assembly and subsequent export: Goode, above n 225, 182.
[249] Andrew Lang, *Trade Agreements, Business, and Human Rights: the case of export processing zones* (Corporate Responsibility Initiative, Working Paper no 57) (April 2010) 18–20.
[250] See Van den Bossche, above n 6, 15, citing a War on Want report, 'The Global Workplace', from 2004.   [251] Lang, above n 249, 20.
[252] Hepple, above n 243, 10 and 17; Steve Charnovitz, 'Labor in the American Free Trade Area' in Philip Alston (ed), above n 232, 163–5; United Nations Human Settlements Programme, *Global Report on Human Settlements 2006: The Challenge of Slums* (UN Habitat, London, 2006) 53; Harrison, above n 10, 79.

least coincided with widespread job losses and deteriorating job conditions across the world.[253] While some deregulation in some markets might be warranted, a labour rights clause in the WTO might curb measures which ill-advisedly drive standards so low as to breach human rights.

In a 2007 report on trade and employment compiled under the joint auspices of the WTO and the ILO, the authors concluded:

trade policies and labour and social policies do interact and that greater policy coherence between the two domains can help ensure that trade reforms have significantly positive effects on both growth and employment.[254]

The report does not explicitly discuss a labour rights clause. However, it does recognize that trade and labour policies should not develop in isolation from each other, and that benign or beneficial impact on the latter by the former cannot be presumed.

If global economic integration and competition is generating a race to the bottom, there is a human rights imperative to address that circumstance to ensure the maintenance of some form of minimum social floor. If the race to the bottom does not exist, that circumstance would indicate that there is no real comparative advantage in the maintenance of low labour conditions. In that case, a social clause should not disrupt the balance of trade, but it might facilitate a decrease in labour rights violations. While this author believes that respect for labour rights is important in and of itself, I add that an increase in labour rights and conditions can have beneficial economic effects, such as the creation of a more productive and healthier workforce with higher morale.[255] Furthermore, a social clause might incentivize diversification away from low-skilled labour as a basis for a State's comparative advantage. An export economy based on such labour is highly vulnerable, so such diversification is beneficial where possible.[256]

The labour rights debate in the WTO has been an area of North/South dispute. However, international labour rights are designed to protect all workers all over the world. There are demands in developing States for decent jobs just as there are in industrialized nations.[257] Indeed, a labour rights clause is perhaps more likely to protect jobs in developing States from unconscionable competition from other developing States.[258] The demand for labour in a State can easily be undermined by the cheaper availability of labour in another State. For example, War on Want has reported how one in seven 'maquilas' in Mexico (where raw products are processed via assembly lines in sectors such as textiles and electronics) closed within a year of China joining the WTO; the number of closures had nearly doubled a

---

[253] See generally, War on Want, above n 244.

[254] WTO and ILO, above n 240, 10.

[255] At ibid, 66, the WTO and ILO note studies that show that freedom of association and collective bargaining rights 'do not harm the export potential of developing countries and may even stimulate it'. See also Hepple, above n 243, 15–16.   [256] See Chapter 5, text at notes 196–200.

[257] World Commission on the Social Dimension of Globalisation, above n 227, paras 66–9, 92–4.

[258] See, generally, Anita Chan and Robert J S Ross, above n 237. See also World Commission on the Social Dimension of Globalisation, above n 227, para 389.

year later.[259] The same report states that Chinese jobs are now threatened by even cheaper labour in Vietnam.[260]

While the governments of developing States are against a social clause, the same is not necessarily true of their trade unions, many of which are supportive of a social clause.[261] An empirical survey in 2002 of the attitudes of members of two major global union federations (representing members from across the world) in the education and metalwork sectors uncovered 'overwhelming support among union official and delegates' for a social clause.[262]

Labour standards are currently imposed under regional[263] and bilateral trade and investment treaties.[264] Furthermore, the WTO permits States to unilaterally offer preferential trade terms to underdeveloped States under the General System of Preferences (GSP).[265] Both the US and the EU base certain GSP schemes on adherence to labour and human rights standards.[266] In *European Communities— Conditions for the granting of tariff preferences to developing countries*, the Appellate Body indicated that such conditions can be attached to GSP schemes so long as they are offered and applied in a non-discriminatory manner.[267] GSP measures might be characterized as carrots rather than sticks, enticing but not forcing States to adopt appropriate labour standards. However, a trade carrot can rapidly meta-morphose into a stick, as the sudden withdrawal of preferential market access can

---

[259] War on Want, above n 244, 13; see also B Lynn, 'Trading with a Low-Wage Tiger' (2003) 14 *The American Prospect* 10 (available via <http://www.prospect.org/print/V14/2/lynn-ba.html> accesssed 24 January 2006; Oxfam, above n 242, 79 and 139. See also Stiglitz and Charlton, above n 226, 23.

[260] War on Want, above n 244, 32. See, however, text at note 242 above.

[261] See also Robert JS Ross and Anita Chan, 'Reframing the Issue of Globalization and Labor Rights' (Revised from Presentation at the Political Economy of World Systems 2002 Conference, University of California at Riverside) (undated) 10–11 <http://irows.ucr.edu/conferences/pews02/pprross.doc> accessed 22 September 2010.

[262] See, generally, Gerard Griffin, Chris Nyland, and Anne O'Rourke, 'Trade Unions and the Social Clause: A North South Union Divide?' (National Key Centre in Industrial Relations, Monash University, Working Paper No 81, December 2002) <http://www.buseco.monash.edu.au/mgt/research/working-papers/nkcir-working-papers/nkcir-workingpaper-81.pdf> accessed 20 September 2010 (quote from 15).

[263] Eg, the North American Free Trade Agreement (NAFTA) contains a side agreement on labour rights in the North American Agreement on Labor Cooperation. See also the Central American Free Trade Agreement (CAFTA), Chapter 16. The US launched the first ever labour dispute under a free trade agreement against Guatemala in 2010: see ICTSD, 'Targeting Guatemala, US Launches First-Ever Labour Rights Dispute Under an FTA' (2010) 14 *Bridges Weekly Trade News Digest*.

[264] See, eg, the Free Trade Agreements between the US and Jordan, and the US and Morocco. See generally, Hepple, above n 243.   [265] See Chapter 5, text at notes 25–30.

[266] Eg, under the 'GSP +' arrangements of the EU, GSP preferences may be granted to certain states if they ratify and implement certain labour rights treaties (and other human rights treaties), and GSP preferences may be withdrawn due to systemic violations of certain labour rights conventions. GSP preferences have been withdrawn from Burma and Belarus on the basis of labour rights violations. See *Council Regulation (EC) No 552/97 of 24 March 1997 temporarily withdrawing access to generalized tariff preferences from the Union of Myanmar* (1997) Official Journal L 085, 8; *Council Regulation (EC) No 1933/2006 of 21 December 2006 temporarily withdrawing access to the generalised tariff preferences from the Republic of Belarus* (2006) Official Journal L 405, 35. On the US GSP scheme, see Lang, above n 249, 31–2, and Harrison, above n 10, 112–13.

[267] See *European Communities—Tariff Preferences*, WTO doc. WT/DS246/AB/R (7 April 2004) (Report of the Appellate Body).

have severe consequences for industries that have depended on that access and have structured their business accordingly.[268]

The existence of regional, bilateral and unilateral imposition of labour standards strengthens the argument for a general WTO labour rights clause. A multilateral approach to labour standards ensures greater consistency, and is less prone to abuse and political arbitrariness than bilateral and unilateral approaches.[269] Of course, a multilateral approach is also preferable from a labour rights perspective.

As noted above, labour rights measures might feasibly be permitted under the 'public morals' exceptions in Articles XX(a) GATT and XIV(a) GATS. From the perspective of developing States, an explicit clause, with its parameters negotiated openly by the plenary WTO membership, is preferable to a clause imposed via interpretation by the judicial branch of the WTO.

If the threshold for minimum labour standards was set at an appropriate level, those standards should not undercut any legitimate comparative advantages of a State. There is, for example, nothing wrong per se from a human rights point of view for State A to have lower wages than State B if State A has a lower cost of living compared to State B. This will normally be the case if State A is a developing State and State B is a developed State. Nor is there anything wrong with an industry moving to take advantage of lower wages in State A, so long as some appropriate provision for the loss of jobs in State B is made.[270] In such a scenario, State B has a greater capacity to provide compensation for the loss of jobs if it is a developed State through, for example, alternative employment, social security benefits, or retraining programmes.

Labour rights protection in the WTO could take many forms. A starting point would be to provide for protection of the core labour rights recognized by the ILO complemented by the extra labour rights in the ICESCR. A labour rights clause could constitute a sword, that is the mandating of minimum standards by the WTO, or a shield, by permitting the unilateral enforcement of labour rights by way of trade sanctions. Just as important as the substantive content of such a clause would be its institutional platform. Labour rights protection could arise within the WTO framework, or be a joint initiative between the WTO and the ILO, or could entail the strengthening of existing ILO mechanisms, coupled with assurances that WTO rules would 'stay out of the way' and not obstruct those mechanisms.[271] For example, persistent and egregious labour rights abuses in Burma have resulted in the exceptional authorization of trade (and other) sanctions by the ILO under article 33 of the ILO Constitution in 2000.[272] The US has accordingly imposed sanctions on Burma in 2003.[273] So far, the US has not been criticized by

[268] Hepple, above n 243, 102–3; UNDP, *Asia Pacific Human Development Report 2006: Trade on Human Terms* (UNDP, Colombo, 2006) 137.
[269] See Chapter 3, Part E.   [270] WTO and ILO, above n 240, 60.
[271] See Robert Howse, Brian Langille, with Julien Burda, 'The World Trade Organization and Labour Rights: Man bites Dog' in Leary and Warner (eds), above n 228, esp at 173–4, 189, 194–8, 223 and 229–31.
[272] Constitution of the International Labour Organization (1919).
[273] It may be noted that the ban affects all goods, rather than only goods likely to have been manufactured under poor labour conditions: see Ewing-Chow, above n 6, 157.

or within the WTO for these measures, perhaps an appropriate example of de facto forbearance regarding an issue that is a serious human rights issue and perhaps only incidentally a trade issue.[274]

An explicit labour rights clause could introduce measures outside the blunt instrument of sanctions, with trade sanctions only being authorized as an explicit last resort.[275] There could for example be a peace clause dictating a moratorium on sanctions for a number of years. Developing States could benefit from longer time-lines for full compliance, as occurred under TRIPS. Such timelines could accord with the ICESCR in light of the principle of progressive realization. Technical assistance could be provided on a mandatory basis to facilitate transition and implementation by the poorest States. Instead of being subjected to sanctions, a delinquent State could first be compulsorily referred to investigation by and/or compulsory consultation with the ILO.[276] An attractive component of this last proposal is that labour matters would be entrusted to a specialist labour rights body, rather than the WTO's dispute settlement bodies, who lack labour rights expertise. Such a proposal would also add flesh to the bones of the decision adopted in the Singapore Declaration of 1996 that labour rights be addressed by the ILO, and that the WTO support it in that endeavour.

This latter model of cooperation, whereby labour rights are strengthened by their inclusion within WTO agreements, but remain 'enforced' by the ILO, could be exported to other areas, such as other human rights or the environment. Indeed, the effective incorporation of certain ILO standards within the WTO framework would not be so revolutionary: it would follow the precedent set under TRIPS whereby the intellectual property standards established by the World Intellectual Property Organization (WIPO) are incorporated within the WTO framework.[277] These themes of inter-institutional cooperation and the strengthening of bodies outside international economic law are further elaborated in Chapter 10, Part D.

G. The Potential Emancipatory Effect of 'Good' Trade

The above commentary focuses on the impact of WTO rules on the ability of States to prohibit trade that is potentially 'bad' for human rights. In this section, I examine the potential for WTO rules to promote trade that is 'good' for human rights. In other words, WTO rules might compel the import of goods or services which in some way promote human rights. A timely example is to ask whether WTO

---

[274] See also Jeffrey L Dunoff, 'The Death of the Trade Regime' (1999) 10 *European Journal of International Law* 733, 757ff.

[275] Sarah Joseph, 'Trade to Live or Live to Trade' in M Baderin and R McCorquodale (eds), *Economic, Social and Cultural Rights in Action* (Oxford University Press, Oxford, 2006) 413–14. See also Griffin, Nyland, and O'Rourke, above n 262, 5.

[276] See also Bryan Schwartz, 'The Doha Round and Investment: Lessons from Chapter 11 of NAFTA' (2003) 3 *Asper Review of International Business and Trade Law* 1, 8; Hepple, above n 243, 274.

[277] See Frederick M Abbott, 'Distributed Governance at the WTO-WIPO: an evolving model for open-architecture integrated governance' (2000) *Journal of International Economic Law* 63, esp at 75ff.

rules might prohibit China's current rules on internet and media censorship, which arguably breach the human right to freedom of expression.

The 'Great Firewall of China' is 'a system of filters and bottlenecks that effectively shutters the country within its own intranet'.[278] The firewall restricts access by Chinese internet users to much information, such as information about the Tianenmen Square protests and crackdown of 1989, and dissidents such as the Dalai Lama, Uigher leader Rebiya Kadeer and the Falun Gong. Censorship is permitted under international human rights law to the extent that it might be necessary to promote legitimate countervailing interests such as public morals or public order.[279] However, the level of censorship practised by China does not conform with the right to freedom of expression. China however is not a party to any treaty which protects that right.[280] It is of course arguable that freedom of expression is protected under customary international law and that China is therefore bound to respect the right in international law. Furthermore, other WTO members which heavily censor the internet, such as Vietnam and Turkey, clearly have international obligations to protect freedom of expression.

In early 2010, the First Amendment Coalition, a California-based NGO, urged the US government to challenge the WTO legality of Chinese internet restrictions. Internet giant Google similarly lobbied the US government in 2007.[281] The First Amendment Coalition claims that the firewall is an illegal barrier to trade. For example, it 'degrades the performance of websites based outside the country',[282] so the argument may be made that it impairs foreign competition via the internet in China's huge market. Indeed, it was reported that Google rapidly lost market share in China after moving its operations outside the firewall to Hong Kong early in 2010.[283]

Professor Tim Wu has surveyed some of the issues that would arise in any relevant WTO challenge to Chinese internet censorship. He notes that physical goods ordered over the internet are goods subject to GATT regulations. Online services which do not involve downloads, such as the use of search engines, are probably services subject to GATS. There is uncertainty over the classification of a third category: downloads that are kept in digital form, such as electronic books.[284] It is possible that the latter category could fall under both GATT and GATS.[285] China's commitments are broader under GATT, as its GATS obligations are largely dependent upon its voluntary commitments in its GATS 'schedule of commitments'. However, China's services commitments are quite extensive, reflective of the extra commitments that are often extracted from acceding States. China

---

[278] Peter Scheer, 'Obama should back Google with more than rhetoric: the US should challenge China's "firewall" before the WTO', 19 January 2010, <http://www.firstamendmentcoalition.org/2010/01/obama-should-back-up-google-with-more-than-rhetoric-the-us-should-challenge-chinas-firewall-before-the-wto/> accessed 7 February 2010.

[279] See Article 19(3) ICCPR.   [280] China has signed but not ratified the ICCPR.

[281] See, eg, Christopher S Rugaber, 'Google fights internet censorship' *Washington Post*, 25 June 2007.

[282] Scheer, above n 278.

[283] See, eg, 'Google losing market share in China' *The Boston Globe*, 23 April 2010.

[284] Wu, above n 61, 7.

[285] In *China—Audiovisual Entertainment Products*, the Appellate Body confirmed that a measure could fall under both sets of provisions: see above n 79, paras 193–4.

has committed to some liberalization of 'online information and database retrieval services' and to 'open' access for the crossborder supply of 'data processing services'. It is possible that such commitments could be interpreted dynamically to entail market access commitments to the provision of search engines.[286] Furthermore, *US—Gambling* indicates that censorship, even of limited websites, amounts to a zero quota in respect of those websites, in potential breach of the market access provisions in Article XVI of GATS.[287]

Other Chinese regulations might also simultaneously breach human rights law and WTO law, such as regulations which limit the wi-fi capabilities and mobile applications of mobile phones and computers in order to preserve the Chinese government's ability to eavesdrop on its population. Such practices breach the human right to privacy, and of course have detrimental effects on political rights as it allows the Chinese government to identify and track political dissidents. These regulations also impact on trade. The Apple I-Phone was released in the Chinese market two years after its global launch without its wi-fi capabilities. New software must be installed in computers before they can be shipped to China.[288] Again, it is plausible that such measures breach WTO rules in the GATT and/or the TBT.[289]

Of course, China would seek to justify its laws under the public morals exceptions of GATT and GATS, and the public order exception in GATS. It would be very interesting to see how a Panel or the Appellate Body would deal with China's extensive political censorship. If the exceptions were interpreted in light of international human rights law, just as Article XX(g) was interpreted in light of international environmental law in *Shrimp I*, it might be concluded that measures which breach human rights cannot be classified as measures which protect public morals or public order. While China might be able to plea that it is not bound by those human rights obligations, it is notable that one of the parties in *Shrimp I*, the US, was not a party to the relevant environmental treaties.[290] Furthermore, under the ad note to Article XIV, China may find it difficult to maintain that its level of censorship counters a 'genuine and sufficiently serious threat...to one of the fundamental interests of society'.[291] On the other hand, the Panel seemed to concede a very broad scope for China's sovereign right to censor cultural products in *China-audiovisual entertainment products*, as noted above.[292] Neither the Panel nor the Appellate Body had reason, however, in that case to extensively discuss the substance of the Chinese censorship regime, as their decisions focused on the means by which China was enforcing that regime.

Even if China could establish that its censorship laws fell within the realm of public morals/public order laws, it would still have to overcome the hurdles of the necessity test and, perhaps most problematically, the chapeau test. Regarding the

---

[286] Wu, above n 61, 24–6.

[287] Brian Hindley and Hosuk Lee-Makiyama, 'Protectionism Online: Internet Censorship and International Trade Law' (2009) *ECIPE Working Paper No 12/2009*, 9.

[288] See Fredrik Erixon and Hosuk Lee-Makiyama, 'Chinese Censorship Equals Protectionism' *Wall Street Journal*, 6 January 2010.   [289] Hindley and Lee-Makiyama, above n 287, 8.

[290] See also Chapter 2, text at notes 123–6.

[291] Hindley and Lee-Makiyama, above n 287, 14.   [292] See above, text at note 105.

necessity test, China might find it difficult to justify the total block placed on certain overseas internet sites by the Great Firewall, compared to more selective filtering mechanisms.[293] For example, Thailand censors certain pages of Amazon, rather than the whole site.[294] China has the technological capacity to adopt selective filtering, given the investment made to set up the Great Firewall, unlike poorer countries.[295] Regarding the chapeau, China's laws impose different standards of censorship, depending on whether a site is located within or outside China. While China-based companies are not in an 'enviable position', given that breach of Chinese censorship law leads to 'crackdowns, expropriations and jail sentences', offshore sites are 'simply censored without official notice or any possibility of taking the matter to domestic courts'.[296] The difference in treatment might amount to arbitrary discrimination and disguised protectionism under the chapeau to Article XX or XIV.

H. Conclusion

The obligations of WTO Members under GATT, GATS, the SPS, and the TBT are very broad. The broader a Member's WTO obligations, the more a State's regulatory capacities are restricted. The extent of the restriction on State capacities to discharge human rights obligations is uncertain, largely due to the dearth of relevant WTO cases. A survey of that case law indicates that States are more likely to be permitted to adopt inward measures rather than outward measures.

Certain exceptions to WTO obligations are permitted. Waivers provide one avenue for preserving the ability of States to implement their human rights duties, though significant political will is needed in order for such waivers to be adopted. The impact of Article XXI GATT and Article XIV bis GATS is uncertain given that there are no cases on those provisions. In contrast, there have been a number of relevant cases on Article XX GATT and Article XIV GATS.

The effect of WTO laws on State human rights regulatory capacities is probably not as profound as had been indicated by earlier GATT cases, such as the *Tuna* cases and *Thailand—Cigarettes*. The most problematic WTO case to date, from a human rights point of view, is probably *Beef—Hormone*, where greater deference to the precautionary principle would have been preferable from a human rights perspective. Other cases, such as *Asbestos*, *US—Gambling* and *Brazil—Tyres*, have indicated that States retain significant regulatory capacities to protect public health, and perhaps a raft of human rights considerations under the public morals exceptions, so long as the relevant measures are necessary and non-discriminatory. The latter requirement has been the downfall of many challenged social measures, and from a human rights point of view, has probably been interpreted more extensively than is desirable.

---

[293] Hindley and Lee-Makiyama, above n 287, report at 5 that 18,000 foreign websites are totally blocked.
[294] Ibid, 6.   [295] Ibid, 14.   [296] Ibid, 15.

The global competition prompted by WTO rules may have prejudiced the global enjoyment of labour rights. It is argued above that the idea of some form of labour rights clause within the WTO should be revisited.

The detrimental human rights impact of certain measures which obstruct free trade, such as consequences for offshore rights to livelihood amongst affected traders, particularly in poor States, must not be forgotten. In that respect, the benefit to human rights of some restrictions on protectionist measures must be acknowledged. This issue arises again in Chapter 6, in regard to the failure of the Agreement on Agriculture to adequately restrain certain protectionist measures. However, it may be noted that no WTO decision has been explicitly influenced by consideration of offshore human rights impacts. It is doubtful that WTO law dictates that the permissibility of a measure with a protectionist effect varies according to its impact on the human rights of persons in the relevant export industry.

Certain trade restrictions may harm the enjoyment of human rights inside the regulating State, such as overly broad restrictions on internet content. The potential emancipatory effect of WTO laws in such situations is examined above. If such a case is ever to be brought to the WTO dispute resolution bodies, the extent of the use of human rights law on the interpretation of relevant WTO rights, duties and exceptions will be particularly instructive.

5

The WTO, Poverty, and Development

Poverty is the major cause of human misery in today's world. World Bank figures indicate that 25 per cent of the world's population live in extreme poverty, defined as US$1.25 a day, calculated according to the dollar's purchasing power in 2005.[1] Ongoing extreme poverty severely undermines their enjoyment of their human rights, and of itself may represent a human rights violation.[2] The imperative of addressing poverty and underdevelopment is consistently stressed by the international community, such as in the Millennium Development Goals[3] and the UN World Summit in September 2005.[4] For example, the first Development Goal is to halve extreme poverty and hunger by 2015.

The WTO promotes market freedoms which, it is argued in orthodox trade theory, increase aggregate wealth, which should enhance the ability of all States to protect economic and social rights and alleviate poverty. Indeed, Oxfam estimated in 2002 that an increase of 5 per cent in the share of world trade by low income states 'would generate more than $350 billion—seven times as much as they receive in aid'. Trade is a more empowering way of climbing out of poverty, and frees the poor from 'exposure to the whims and fads of donors who govern access to aid budgets'.[5]

Evaluation of the human rights impact of the WTO necessarily involves an assessment of its impact on poverty and development. In this chapter, the first section will focus on the links between poverty and human rights violations. The argument that current WTO rules are unfair to poorer developing States compared to richer developed States is then explored. The impact of trade liberalization on poverty and inequality is then discussed. Suggestions for WTO reforms in favour of developing States are then proposed.

---

[1] Shaohua Chen and Martin Ravallion, 'The developing world are poorer than we thought, but no less successful in the fight against poverty' (World Bank Policy Research Working Paper 4703, August 2008) (World Bank Development Research Group).

[2] See A Sengupta, 'On the Theory and Practice of the Right to Development' (2002) 24 *Human Rights Quarterly* 837, 884–6.

[3] See <http://www.un.org/millenniumgoals/index.html> accessed 31 January 2006.

[4] UNGA, 'Resolution adopted by the General Assembly', UN doc. A/Res/60/1 (24 October 2005) (adopting the 2005 World Summit Outcome) paras 17–68.

[5] Oxfam, *Rigged Rules and Double Standards* (Oxfam, London, 2002) 48.

A. Poverty and Human Rights Violations

Some characterize living in a state of poverty as a human rights abuse in itself.[6] At the very least, the poor suffer disproportionately from human rights abuses. The link between poverty and violations of economic, social, and cultural rights is obvious: the poor clearly fare worst in terms of access to food, water, housing, health care, education, social security, and employment. Their opportunities are limited due to a greater lack of influence, literacy, housing standards and nutrition, as well as their subjection to pronounced discrimination and social exclusion. Their life expectancies are shorter, and rates of infant and maternal mortality are higher. Their civil and political rights are clearly compromised, with less physical security, greater exposure to forced labour and modern forms of slavery, lesser access to justice (for example, legal institutions and representation may be practically unavailable due to lack of funds and knowledge), greater levels of discrimination, and less participation in political life. In short, the elimination of poverty and the promotion of human rights are clearly inter-related objectives.[7] The link was recognized by US President Roosevelt in his famous address to Congress on 6 January 1941 which prepared the US for the possibility of entering into the Second World War, where he proclaimed 'freedom from want' as one of four essential human freedoms. The importance of freedom from want is now proclaimed in the preamble to the UDHR and the two Covenants.

The Committee on Economic, Social and Cultural Rights has defined poverty as 'a human condition characterized by sustained or chronic deprivation of the resources, capabilities, choices, security and power necessary for the enjoyment of an adequate standard of living and other civil, cultural, economic, political and social rights'.[8] The need to combat poverty is one of the recurring themes in the ICESCR and one of the major preoccupations of the Committee in conducting dialogues with States.[9]

The main argument in favour of free trade is that it leads to economic growth and development. To the extent that poverty is exacerbated by a State's lack of resources, economic growth and development within that State should help a State alleviate poverty. However, economic growth by itself does not necessarily lead to poverty alleviation due to possible inequities in the distribution of extra wealth. The right to development enshrined in the Declaration on the Right to Development (DRD) recognizes that development is more than an economic process, and entails far more than an increase in GDP figures. Far too often,

---

[6] See, eg, United Nations Development Programme (UNDP), *Poverty Reduction and Human Rights: A Practice Note* (2003) iv; Thomas Pogge, 'Recognized and Violated: the Human Rights of the Global Poor' (2005) 18 *Leiden Journal of International Law* 717.

[7] See generally, UNGA, 'Report of the Independent Expert on the Question of Human Rights and Extreme Poverty', UN doc. A/63/274 (13 August 2008).

[8] Committee on Economic, Social and Cultural Rights, 'Poverty and the International Covenant on Economic Social and Cultural Rights', UN doc. E/C.12/2001/10 (10 May 2001) para 8.

[9] Ibid, para 1.

development projects take place in disregard of the rights of local people, particularly the poor, who might for example be arbitrarily evicted without compensation to make way for an infrastructure or investment project. In contrast, the human right to development prescribes the realization of all human rights (civil, political, economic, social, and cultural) through an equitable process, entailing 'the free, effective and full participation of all individuals concerned and that individuals must have equal opportunity of access to the resources of development and receive fair distribution of the benefits of development and income'.[10] Such a process takes account of and includes the poor.

B. Current WTO Rules and Developing States

In order to assess the effect of WTO rules on poverty and the development process, it is necessary to assess its impact on developing States, the home of the vast majority of the world's poor. That is not to deny the existence of poverty in developed States; it is to recognize that developed States have greater capacities to combat poverty within their own borders if they have the political will to do so. Developing States have lesser capacities and far greater numbers of poor people, and are therefore more vulnerable if dislocations and adjustments are forced on them by international trade rules and policies.

Of course, States themselves do not have human rights, so any 'unfairness' or 'inappropriateness' within WTO rules with respect to developing States does not directly raise human rights issues. However, the impact of WTO rules on particular types of States bears an instrumental relationship with the facilitation of those States' capacities to fulfil their human rights obligations. In particular, increased growth should increase available resources, which should in turn facilitate development and poverty alleviation and a concomitant increase in the level of enjoyment of human rights. However, growth and development may not necessarily lead to such outcomes. Thus, this issue bears an instrumental and indirect relationship with human rights rather than a direct relationship. Nevertheless, this issue is of crucial importance to the subject matter of this book.

A rights consistent trade policy with respect to poverty and development will have the following elements. First, a State's trade policy should actually contribute to economic development and growth so as to enhance opportunities for climbing out of poverty. Secondly, the State must ensure that it retains and improves its capacities to fulfil its human rights obligations, including its obligations to provide for the rights of those who need assistance. It must also of course exercise those capacities in good faith. Thirdly, the State should implement strategies to ensure that the gains from economic growth and development are equitably distributed. Finally, the trade policy should be rooted in core human rights principles such

---

[10] Commission on Human Rights, 'Mainstreaming the right to development in international trade law and policy at the World Trade Organization (paper prepared by Robert Howse)', UN doc. E/CN.4/Sub.2/2004/17 (9 June 2004) para 10.

as non-discrimination, participation, empowerment, and accountability.[11] While these factors are intrinsically linked, it is the first factor which is the main focus of this chapter.

At this point, it is worth noting that developing States are differentiated within the WTO between developing States and least developed countries (LDCs). LDCs have a GNI per capita of around $US750 per person and graduate from LDC status when they reach $US900 GNI per capita.[12] Hence a State is not an LDC if it has a per capita income of $US2.50 per day. A further unofficial category of developing States is that of small and vulnerable economies (SVEs), which are characterized by certain vulnerabilities, such as 'physical isolation, geographical dispersal and distance from the main markets', as well as inadequate infrastructure and markets.[13] While SVEs may be richer than LDCs, they are still very poor countries.

Bias against developing States within the WTO

In Chapter 3, the disadvantages for developing States within WTO processes were discussed. Current substantive WTO rules, as reflected in the Marrakesh Agreement, are also biased in favour of developed States against developing States,[14] as has been conceded by the Director-General of the WTO, Pascal Lamy. He stated, in his famous call for a 'Geneva consensus' in a speech in New York in 2006:

The impression has also arisen that in the case of the multilateral trading system, [flaws in the system] have tended to work to the disadvantage of a certain part of the WTO Membership, that comprising the developing countries. This bias will in the long run not be sustainable and it is therefore necessary to correct it if we want the multilateral trading system to thrive. . . .

In sum, while the political decolonization took place more than 50 years ago, we have not yet completed the economic decolonization. It is therefore one of the purposes of the current multilateral negotiations to continue the rebalancing of our rules in favour of developing countries.[15]

---

[11] See, eg, Office of the High Commissioner for Human Rights, 'Report on Indicators for Promoting and Monitoring the Implementation of Human Rights', UN doc. HRI/MC/2008/3 (6 June 2008) para 10.

[12] The income criteria for LDCs varies from year to year. These income estimates reflect the World Bank's 2006 triennial review of LDCs. There are also other criteria, relating to low levels of human resource development and high degrees of economic vulnerability. See, generally, <http://www.un.org/esa/policy/devplan/profile/criteria.html> accessed 20 September 2010.

[13] See WTO doc. WT/COMTD/SE/W/20, 9 February 2006 and Rashid S Kaukob, 'Development Effects of the Doha Round on Small and Vulnerable Economies [SVEs]' (CUTS CITEE Working Paper 1/2009) <http://www.cuts-citee.org/pdf/WP09-01.pdf> accessed 20 September 2010.

[14] Sarah Joseph, 'Trade to Live or Live to Trade' in Mashood Baderin and Robert McCorquodale (eds), *Economic, Social and Cultural Rights in Action* (Oxford University Press, Oxford, 2006) 393– 400. See also Ilan Kapoor, 'Deliberative democracy and the WTO' (2004) 11 *Review of International Political Economy* 522, 527.

[15] Pascal Lamy, 'It's Time for a new "Geneva Consensus" on making trade work for development' (Emile Noel Lecture New York University Law School, New York, 30 October 2006) esp at 3–4 <http://www.wto.org/english/news_e/sppl_e/sppl45_e.htm> accessed 19 September 2010.

Much permissible protectionism under WTO rules affects goods in which some developing States have a comparative advantage, particularly agricultural goods, which deprives developing States of external markets. At the same time their underdeveloped industries have been exposed to competition from the developed world. The asymmetrical impact of international economic law is exacerbated by the policies of the International Monetary Fund (IMF) and the World Bank, which are largely dictated by developed States, but which only bind their client borrowers, largely developing States.[16] The political philosopher Professor Thomas Pogge has suggested, bluntly, that:

the design of the global institutional order reflects the shared interests of the governments, corporations, and citizens of the affluent countries more than the interest in global poverty avoidance, insofar as these interests conflict.[17]

The implementation of WTO rules is not currently achieving optimal outcomes regarding promotion of the right to development and the alleviation of poverty because current rules are biased against the poorest States. At worst, unbalanced WTO rules could exacerbate underdevelopment and poverty in those States, and therefore prejudice the right to development as well as economic, social, and cultural rights in the poorest States. In this respect, the economists Joseph Stiglitz and Andrew Charlton report that, by some estimates, 48 LDCs have suffered economic losses of around US$600 million per year as a result of the Uruguay Round.[18]

The unfairness in the current rules as well as Doha Round proposals is explained below.

Special and differential treatment

The development needs of the developing States ('the South') are blatantly more pressing than those of developed States ('the North'). These special needs are recognized in the WTO and are served by numerous provisions allowing for 'special and differential treatment' (SDT). The need for SDT is referenced in the preamble to the Marrakesh Agreement which states:

Recognizes...that there is a need for positive efforts designed to ensure that developing countries, and especially the least developed among them, secure a share in the growth of international trade commensurate with the needs of their economic development.

---

[16] In late 2008, the IMF lent money to Iceland after the collapse of its banking system in the wake of the Great Financial Crisis, a rare instance of a developed State being subjected to IMF disciplines. 'IMF approves $2.1bn Iceland loan', *BBC News* (online at <http://news.bbc.co.uk/1/hi/7738874.stm>), 20 November 2008. Greece received a loan in 2010. Helena Smith, 'Greece activates €45bn EU/IMF loans' *The Guardian*, 23 April 2010 <http://www.guardian.co.uk/business/2010/apr/23/greece-activates-eu-imf-loans> accessed 22 September 2010.
[17] Pogge, above n 6, 725.
[18] Joseph E Stiglitz and Andrew Charlton, *Fair Trade for All* (Oxford University Press, New York, 2005) 47.

Most SDT provisions in WTO agreements permit longer timelines for compliance for developing nations.[19] Furthermore, developing States have relatively high tariff bindings,[20] so their WTO obligations in respect of granting market access to goods are not generally as onerous as those of developed States.

'Trade aid', that is aid designed to alleviate the burdens of trade liberalization, is recognized as essential, and was formalized after the Singapore Ministerial meeting in 1996. The Singapore Plan of Action provided for the creation of the 'Integrated Framework for Trade-Related Technical Assistance to Least Developed Countries',[21] which coordinates policy efforts in this regard between the WTO and other international financial and development agencies,[22] and identifies technical assistance needs in relevant States. Since 2000, the Integrated Framework has presided over a trust fund to finance trade reform in LDCs.[23] However, there are concerns that trade aid has not added to the aid budgets of donor States: rather aid money is being redirected into trade aid leaving recipient States no better off in terms of total aid receipts.[24]

SDT measures were authorized in the GATT after the Tokyo Round (1973–1979) with the introduction of the 'Enabling Clause', which permits preferential market access for developing States and limits the expectations of reciprocity in negotiating rounds to levels 'consistent with development needs'.[25] Thus, States (especially developed States) may offer preferential market access to developing States under the 'General System of Preferences' (GSP) without breaching the MFN principle. An example of a current GSP measure is the European Union's 'Everything but Arms' (EBA) initiative, under which the EU imposes no duties or quotas on imports from LDCs apart from arms and armaments.[26] The EBA is a welcome departure from the normal practice of States excluding goods of the greatest interest to developing States from GSP schemes, which seriously undermines their utility for GSP beneficiaries. However, the effectiveness of the EBA

[19] Bernard Hoekman, 'Operationalizing the Concept of Policy Space in the WTO: Beyond Special and Differential Treatment' (2005) 8 *Journal of International Economic Law* 405, 406; J Hunter, 'Broken Promises: Agriculture and Development in the WTO' (2003) 4 *Melbourne International Law Journal* 299, 315.

[20] Each WTO Member commits to a schedule of 'tariff bindings' regarding named goods. A Member may not impose tariffs above those bound rates.

[21] WTO, 'Singapore Ministerial Declaration' (Adopted on 13 December 1996), WTO doc. WT/MIN(96)/14 (18 December 1996).

[22] Those other agencies are the IMF, the International Trade Centre, UNCTAD, the UNDP, and the World Bank.

[23] Hunter, above n 19, 317.

[24] See Human Rights Council, 'The Cotonou Partnership Agreement between the European Union (EU) and the African, Caribbean and Pacific Countries (ACP countries) (Report by Dr Maria van Reisen, High Level Task Force on the Right to Development), UN doc. A/HRC/12/Wg.2/TF/CRP.3/Rev.1 (5 May 2009), para 59, commenting on the EU's aid budget.

[25] Hoekman, above n 19, 405–6. The full name of the Enabling Clause is 'Differential and More Favourable Treatment, Reciprocity and Fuller Participation of Developing Countries', L/4903, GATT BISD 26S/203, 28 November 1979.

[26] See European Commission, 'Everything but Arms' (undated) <http://ec.europa.eu/trade/wider-agenda/development/generalised-system-of-preferences/everything-but-arms/> accessed 20 September 2010. Full trade liberalization under the EBA (outside the arms field) has only recently been completed, as liberalization for bananas, rice, and sugar was phased in over a decade.

(and other GSP schemes) is undermined by complex requirements regarding rules of origin, whereby all production must be verified as taking place in an LDC, creating administrative and compliance costs for LDCs.[27] While richer States are not required to implement the Enabling Clause by offering preferential terms to poorer States, conditions apply if they do, such as the requirement of non-discriminatory implementation: preferences must be offered on similar terms to similarly situated States and be based on objective criteria.[28]

One problem with GSPs is that they are dependent upon the largesse of the importing State: their withdrawal can have sudden and dramatic impacts on the exporting State if it has become dependent on the maintenance of the GSP. This situation can easily arise in developing economies with little diversification. Therefore, GSP schemes can be manipulated to secure desirable outcomes for the importer rather than the intended beneficiary, the exporter. For example, the US has threatened withdrawal of GSP preferences from States which do not respect higher standards of intellectual property protection than those mandated under TRIPS.[29] The vagaries of GSPs mean that they do not necessarily promote sustainable economic policies. GSPs leave developed States as the drivers of trade policies in developing States, rather than developing States driving their own policies.[30]

The most important SDT provisions are not compulsory: developed States do not have to offer trade aid nor do they have to offer preferential market access to developing States.[31] Hortatory provisions which call for special treatment are far more common in WTO rules than the granting of enforceable advantages to developing States.[32] Furthermore, most of the longer timelines granted under WTO agreements have expired, yet massive economic inequalities remain. The timelines have proven to be arbitrary: a better trigger for the end of SDT is the attainment of some level of development rather than the expiry of a particular month of December.[33] SDT provisions have not apparently accommodated the 'real needs' of developing States.[34]

---

[27] See Olivier Cadot and Jaime de Melo, 'Why OECD Countries should reform Rules of Origin' [2008] 23 *World Bank Research Observer* 77. See also Paul Collier, *The Bottom Billion* (Oxford University Press, New York, 2008) 169; Stiglitz and Charlton, above n 18, 181.

[28] See *European Communities—Tariff Preferences*, WTO doc. WT/DS246/AB/R (7 April 2004) (Report of the Appellate Body), and discussion in J Harrison, 'Incentives for Development: the EC's Generalized System of Preferences, India's WTO Challenge and Reform' (2005) 42 *Common Market Law Review* 1663.

[29] Ken Shadlen, 'Resources, Rules and international political economy: the politics of development in the WTO' in Sarah Joseph, David Kinley, and Jeff Waincymer (eds), *The World Trade Organization and Human Rights: Interdisciplinary Approaches* (Edward Elgar, Cheltenham, 2009) 119, n 22.

[30] See also Stiglitz and Charlton, above n 18, 100.

[31] J Michael Finger and Philip Schuler, 'Implementation of Uruguay Round Commitments: the Development Challenge' (World Bank policy research working paper no. 2215, September 1999) 5.

[32] Anthony E Cassimatis, *Human Rights Related Trade Measures under International Law* (Martinus Nijhoff, Leiden, 2007) 405.

[33] See also Yong-Shik Lee, *Reclaiming Development in the World Trading System* (Cambridge University Press, Cambridge, 2006) 157.

[34] Thomas Cottier, 'From Progressive Liberalization to Progressive Regulation' (2006) 9 *Journal of International Economic Law* 779, 788. See also Joel Trachtman, 'Legal Aspects of a Poverty Agenda

It is also worth noting that significant pressure on developing States regarding trade liberalization has been generated outside the WTO. For example, many developing States have been forced by bodies such as the IMF and the World Bank, as part of loan conditions, to impose much lower tariffs than those to which they are bound under the WTO.[35] These external pressures from international financial institutions pertain largely to developing States as they are by far the major clients of such institutions. The existence of such 'arm-twisting', even though the WTO is not responsible for it, undermines the efficacy of the WTO's SDT provisions and is probably not taken into sufficient account in WTO negotiations.

C. The Uruguay Round Bargain

It is simplistic to analyse the Uruguay Round bargain as a deal between the North and the South. Of course, the trading interests of States within these two blocs are not uniform.[36] Nevertheless, the following analysis will demonstrate significant iniquities between North and South in current WTO rules.[37]

Developing States undertook proportionately more obligations to open up market access to foreign goods than developed States in the Uruguay Round: their tariff cuts were deeper.[38] Admittedly, their tariff bindings were higher thus allowing greater room for significant cuts. However, as noted above, many developing States have been forced to maintain tariff levels lower than those to which they are committed under the WTO due to loan conditions imposed by international financial institutions.

Developing States reluctantly agreed to the extension of the old GATT regime into areas such as services and intellectual property, which operate to the advantage of the North.[39] Furthermore, provisions regarding investment measures, accession and non-tariff barriers also work to the disadvantage of developing States. These disadvantages are now explained.

---

at the WTO: Trade Law and "Global Apartheid"' (2003) 6 *Journal of International Economic Law* 3, 10–11.

[35] Joel R Paul, 'Do International Trade Institutions Contribute to Economic Growth and Development?' (2003) 44 *Virginia Journal of International Law* 285, 319; Oxfam, above n 5, 126–8.

[36] Eg, EU preferences for certain African and Caribbean and Pacific States (ACP States) were challenged successfully by Latin American developing States in *European Communities—Regime for the Importation, Sale and Distribution of Bananas*, WTO docs. WT/DS27/R/ECU, WT/DS27/R/GTM, WT/DS27/R/HND, WT/DS27/R/MEX (all 22 May 1997) (Reports of the Panel), WTO doc. WT/DS27/AB/R, AB-1997-3 (9 September 1997) (Report of the Appellate Body): the *Bananas* litigation essentially pitted the interests of banana producers in Latin America against those in ACP States.

[37] See also Shadlen, above n 29, 111.   [38] Finger and Schuler, above n 31, 6.

[39] Caroline Dommen, 'Raising Human Rights Concerns in the World Trade Organization: Actors, Processes and Possible Strategies' (2002) 24 *Human Rights Quarterly* 1, 12; Amrita Narlikar, *The World Trade Organization: A Very Short Introduction* (Oxford University Press, New York, 2005), 74; Shadlen, above n 29, 109.

GATS

The Marrakesh Agreement introduced the General Agreement on Trade in Services (GATS). MFN obligations under Article II apply to all services, so a State must ensure non-discriminatory treatment with regard to all foreign service providers viz each other.[40] Market access and National Treatment obligations under Articles XVI and XVII only apply to the services that a State nominates. Once a service has been so nominated in a State's 'schedule of commitments', a State is required not to discriminate against foreign commercial providers in favour of local providers, subject to any qualifications it has made in its schedule.[41] Under Article XXI, a State can only withdraw a service liberalization commitment if it compensates affected WTO Members, a considerable disincentive against such withdrawal.[42] In *US—Measures affecting the Cross-Border Supply of Gambling and Betting Services*,[43] the WTO's Appellate Body confirmed that it takes a dynamic approach to interpretation of a State's schedule. As the US had nominated 'recreational services' in its Schedule, the Appellate Body concluded that those services included online betting services, even though online gambling did not exist at the time the US drafted the relevant part of its Schedule.[44]

Of course, foreign service providers can play a very positive role in improving service infrastructure, and providing more efficient services at a higher quality than governments or local providers. However, GATS constrains the capacities of States to regulate such foreign providers: the extent of these regulatory constraints is uncertain given the dearth of cases on GATS. A concern in this regard is that many services, such as the provision of water, health services or education, directly impact on the enjoyment of economic, social, and cultural rights. GATS disciplines might undermine access by the poor to such services as commercial providers of servicers focus on profit rather than the satisfaction of human rights.[45] For example, the prohibitions on discrimination might render it difficult for a State to impose differing regulations, such as pricing regulations, across its territory according to regional or social needs.[46] This problem

---

[40] States were able to list MFN exemptions under Annex II GATS prior to its adoption on 1 January 1995. In principle, these exemptions should have been withdrawn by 2005 (Annex II, para 6), and must at least be reviewed and be the subject of current negotiations.

[41] Eg, typical conditions include nationality or residence requirements for executives, the holding of a certain amount of assets in local currency, and conferral of tax privileges on local suppliers. See Peter Van den Bossche, *The Law and Policy of the World Trade Organization* (Cambridge University Press, Cambridge, 2005) 365.

[42] Adam McBeth, *International Economic Actors and Human Rights* (Routledge, Oxford, 2009) 157.

[43] WTO doc. WT/DS285/AB/R, AB-2005-1 (7 April 2005) (Report of the Appellate Body).

[44] See also *China—Measures Affecting Trading Rights and Distribution Services for Certain Publication and Audiovisual Entertainment Products*, WTO doc. WT/DS363/AB/R, AB-2009-3 (21 December 2009) (Report of the Appellate Body) paras 338–411, where the Appellate Body agreed with the Panel's finding that China's GATS commitments regarding 'sound recording distribution services' included distribution via internet and other electronic means. See also Tim Wu, 'The World Trade Law of Censorship and Internet Filtering', 3 May 2006, available via <http://papers.ssrn.com/sol3/papers.cfm?abstract_id=882459> accessed 7 February 2010, 13, 19.

[45] Oxfam, above n 5, 227 and 229.   [46] McBeth, above n 42, 155.

is of most concern in developing States, which lack adequate social safety nets to assist the poor if they should be deprived of access to essential services.[47] A number of States, including developing States, have made commitments to open up services in the arenas of primary and secondary education (for example, Tonga, Mexico) and health related and social services (for example, Cambodia, Sierra Leone).

Under Article I(3) GATS, the treaty does not apply to services 'supplied in the exercise of governmental authority', which is defined in sub-paragraph (c) as 'any service which is supplied neither on a commercial basis nor in competition with one or more service suppliers'. This exception could ensure that many social measures adopted by governments in providing services are unaffected by GATS.[48] However, its scope is unclear. A plain language reading indicates that it only applies to those (increasingly rare) instances of not-for-profit government monopolies.[49] Its language seems to not apply, for example, in the context of education if any private schools exist in a State. Even a government run service that charges a nominal fee might be excluded.[50] Furthermore, the opportunity for developing States to utilize this exception has been undercut by past World Bank and IMF loan conditionalities, which have dictated the privatization of many services.[51]

One of the most prominent areas of contention over GATS concerns its potential impact in the arena of the provision of water services. This author knows of no specific commitments in the area of water provision as yet,[52] though such commitments may be made in the future. GATS, after all, promotes 'progressively greater liberalisation from initially modest levels'.[53] In any case, it is wrong to say that no water commitments have been made, as provision of water may be ancillary to the provision of other services which have been scheduled, such as sewage services (where numerous commitments have been scheduled by WTO members).[54]

Dr Andrew Lang has investigated the claims that GATS unduly restricts social regulations designed to help the poor in respect of access to water, and concluded that GATS might threaten such regulations. He notes that the differential treatment of two private operators, if one operates in an impoverished area and another in a rich area, might breach GATS.[55] Furthermore, some preferential treatment

---

[47] See generally, Commission on Human Rights, 'Liberalization of Trade in Services and Human Rights: Report of the High Commissioner on Human Rights to the Economic and Social Council', UN doc. E/CN.4/Sub.2/2002/9 (25 June 2002), especially at paras 51–67.

[48] Another exception in Article XIII(1) concerning government procurement is also unclear, but is likely to be narrower than the Article I(3) exception: see Andrew Lang, 'The GATS and Regulatory Autonomy: a Case Study of Social Regulation of the Water Industry' (2004) 7 *Journal of International Economic Law* 801, 821–2.

[49] McBeth, above n 42, 155.   [50] Ibid, 155.

[51] Martin Khor, 'Implications of some WTO rules on the Realisation of the MDGs', *Third World Network Trade & Development Series 26* (TWN, Malaysia, 2005) 23.

[52] WTO, 'Misunderstandings and scare stories: the WTO is not after your water' <http://www .wto.org/english/tratop_e/serv_e/gats_factfiction8_e.htm> accessed 20 September 2010.

[53] Lang, above, n 48, 814.   [54] Ibid, 815–6.   [55] Ibid, 811–12.

might often be conferred on a government water provider in order to ensure it can continue operations and provide low cost water. According to Lang:

non-discrimination obligations may make such treatment practically impossible, by requiring that any preferential treatment is offered on an objective basis to all service providers, whether public or private.[56]

There is also a danger of 'regulatory chill', in that States may refrain from adopting measures such as cross-subsidies from richer water consumers to poorer water consumers for fear of breaching GATS.[57]

Article XIV GATS allows general exceptions to the treaty's application for the purpose of promoting certain non-trade ends, such as the protection of 'public morals' and 'public order' in Article XIV(a). One cannot state with confidence that these exceptions ensure that a State can regulate foreign service providers in order to ensure human rights protection. These exceptions are discussed in light of WTO case law in Chapter 4.

Finally, services liberalization has arisen in areas where developed States have a comparative advantage, such as in financial and telecommunications services. Comparatively little progress has arisen with regard to the cross-border provision of a temporary unskilled labour force, where developing States have a comparative advantage.[58]

TRIPS

The TRIPS Agreement has probably generated the greatest concern over its effect on developing nations and human rights. Developed nations had to comply fully by 1 January 1996, while developing nations had until 2000 and the LDCs had to comply by 2006. The timeline for the latter has now been extended to 2013, but LDCs are not allowed to wind back their level of implementation.[59] Worryingly, Amrita Narlikar has stated:

at least some developing countries have revealed in subsequent interviews that the technicalities of TRIPS had evaded them at the time when the agreement was being negotiated. Rather, they had believed that the TRIPS agreement would be limited to counterfeit goods.[60]

Intellectual property (IP) rights grant innovators and inventors monopoly rights over the sale of their creations for a certain period of time. This facility encourages

---

[56] Ibid, 823: see also 812.   [57] Ibid, 812.

[58] Stiglitz and Charlton, above n 18, 116–17. See generally, Dipankar Dey, 'Movement of Natural Persons (Mode 4) under GATS: Advantage Developing Countries' (2006) *Social Science Research Network* <http://papers.ssrn.com/sol3/papers.cfm?abstract_id=949435> accessed 19 September 2010. See also generally Joel P Trachtman, 'The Role of International Law in Economic Migration' (2008) (Society of International Economic Law Inaugural Conference 2008 Paper) <http://papers.ssrn.com/sol3/papers.cfm?abstract_id=1153499> accessed 19 September 2010; World Bank, *World Development Report 2006: Equity and Development* (World Bank, Washington DC, 2006) 208–9.

[59] See WTO, 'Poorest countries given more time to apply intellectual property rules' (WTO 2005 Press Releases, 29 November 2005), WTO doc. IP/C/40.

[60] Narlikar, above n 39, 82.

people to market their creations, thus making them publicly available, and also encourages research and creative endeavour, which might be stymied if copycats could immediately compete with creators and inventors. A rationale for the global extension of IP rights under TRIPS is to encourage greater foreign investment and local innovation in the South.[61] Indeed, the right to enjoy the fruits of one's creations is recognized by Article 15(1)(c) of the ICESCR.

Of course, the prices of IP-protected goods are inflated by the lack of competition. Therefore, under international human rights law, IP rights must be balanced for example against the rights of the general community to enjoy the benefits of new technological developments. The latter rights are recognized in the ICESCR at Article 15(1)(b). Further, 'there is substantial evidence that the existing rules for patents and copyrights are overly protective, providing a larger reward than is necessary and stifling competitive forces'[62] and further innovation. Jagdish Bhagwati has stated that 'few believe that the optimum [patent] extends as high as the 20-year patent rule that was forced into the World Trade Organization by the business lobbies'.[63]

TRIPS presently mandates the regressive transfer of wealth from the South to the North because most patents are owned by people, particularly companies, from the North.[64] Populations in the South, where patent rights were not generally respected prior to TRIPS, must now pay more for patented goods. The biggest losers are the poor in developing countries, who cannot afford the price increases. This situation is particularly problematic when the goods are essential for the enjoyment of human rights, such as foods and essential medicines, as is discussed in Chapters 6 and 7.

Even prominent free trade advocates are wary of TRIPS. Contrary to the thrust of the other WTO agreements, TRIPS restricts trade as it bans trade by non-IP holders in IP-protected goods. Bhagwati has stated that the TRIPS agreement 'does not belong' and 'retards the process of trade liberalisation'.[65]

The United Nations Development Program (UNDP) has proposed that a moratorium on TRIPS enforcement with respect to patents of essential items should be imposed, during which the WTO should thoroughly review its impact on the

---

[61] See Shanker A Singham, 'Competition Policy and the Stimulation of Innovation: TRIPS and the interface between Competition and Patent Protection in the Pharmaceutical Industry' (2000) 26 *Brooklyn Journal of International Law* 363, 375–85.

[62] Paul, above n 35, 329. See also, eg, Tom G Palmer, 'Are Patents and Copyrights Morally Justified? The Philosophy of Property Rights and Ideal Objects' (1990) 13 *Harvard Journal of Law and Public Policy* 911, 914; Peter Drahos, 'The Rights to Food and Health and Intellectual Property in the Era of 'Biogopolies' in Stephen Bottomley and David Kinley (eds), *Commercial Law and Human Rights* (Ashgate, Dartmouth, 2002) 227.

[63] J Bhagwati, 'Economic Freedom: Prosperity and Social Progress' (Keynote Speech at the Conference on Economic Freedom and Development in Tokyo, 17–18 June 1999), 7 <http://time .dufe.edu.cn/wencong/bhagwati/freedom_tokyo.pdf> accessed 20 September 2010.

[64] United Nations Development Programme (UNDP), Human Development Report 2005: International Cooperation at a Crossroads: Aid, Trade and Security in an Unequal World (UNDP, New York, 2005) 135.

[65] Jagdish Bhagwati, 'Afterword: The Question of Linkage' (2002) 96 *American Journal of International Law* 126, 128.

poor.[66] However, that is not the trend of world trade negotiations. Numerous 'TRIPS plus' agreements, that is agreements which provide even greater IP protection than that imposed under TRIPS, have been concluded on a regional and bilateral basis throughout the world. As noted by Oxfam, 'TRIPS has now become a bottom line rather than a top line'.[67] TRIPS is discussed in greater detail in Chapters 6 and 7.

TRIMS

The Agreement on Trade Related Investment Measures (TRIMS) prohibits the use of certain regulatory measures by a State against foreign investors who manufacture goods in its territory. Prohibited measures include conditions relating to local content (that is, a requirement that certain supplies, or a quota of supplies, be sourced locally by the investor), which have historically been used by States to promote domestic industrial development.[68] Developing States were given more time to comply with TRIMS: only LDCs are still permitted to depart from TRIMS and only under strict conditions.[69]

TRIMS is arguably not a particularly consequential agreement. It probably does not, for example, prohibit measures such as regulation of the hiring practices of foreign investors, or technology transfer or joint venture requirements, all 'time-honoured...instruments of industrial promotion'.[70] However, local content requirements are also important development instruments, as they aim to 'generate backwards linkages from foreign investors to local manufacturers'.[71] Nevertheless, local content measures are probably inconsistent with Articles III (National Treatment) and XI (prohibition on quotas) GATT, so TRIMS may simply confirm an interpretation of Articles III and XI which would otherwise have been reached by the dispute settlement bodies.[72] Such an interpretation was signalled in 1984 in a successful GATT challenge by the US against Canadian local content laws in its automotive industry.[73] Nevertheless, it is possible that TRIMS represents an undesirable *fait accompli* in terms of the definitions of those GATT provisions, and an unjustified constraint on development policies.[74]

---

[66] UNDP, above n 64, 148. See also Frederick M Abbott and Jerome H Reichmann, 'The Doha Round's Public Health Legacy: Strategies for the Production and Diffusion of Patented Medicines under the Amended TRIPS Provisions' (2007) 10 *Journal of International Economic Law* 921, 987.

[67] Oxfam, above n 5, 221; see also UNDP, above n 64, 136.

[68] Khor, above n 51, 35. See also below, text at notes 225–34.

[69] The Hong Kong Declaration permits LDCs to phase out all such investment measures by 2020, subject to various conditions; see Hong Kong Declaration, Annex F: Special and Differential Treatment.

[70] Shadlen, above n 29, 125.   [71] Ibid, 126.

[72] See TRIMS, Article 2.

[73] *Canada—Administration of the Foreign Investment Review Act*, BISD 30S/140 (1984) (GATT). See also *Indonesia—Certain Measures Affecting the Automobile Industry*, WTO docs. WT/DS54/R, WT/DS55/R, WT/DS59/R, WTDS64/R (2 July 1998) (Report of the Panel).

[74] See Robert Wade, 'What Strategies are Viable for Developing Countries Today? The World Trade Organization and the Shrinking of Policy Space' (2003) 10 *Review of International Political Economy* 621, 627–8. See also *Canada—Administration of the Foreign Investment Review Act*, above

Non-tariff barriers

Certain non-tariff barriers are regulated for the first time under the WTO, namely technical barriers to trade under the TBT agreement and sanitary and phytosanitary measures under the SPS agreement. In a sense, their adoption was a win for developing States, as such measures are sometimes imposed arbitrarily by developed States. Hence, their regulation at least restricted the use of such barriers.[75]

However, these rules regarding non-tariff barriers largely reflect the standards of developed States. For example, developing State participation in some of the organizations which develop universal standards for the purposes of the SPS agreement, such as the Codex Alimentarius regarding food safety standards, is inadequate.[76] Developing States have also incurred disproportionate implementation costs regarding those new standards.[77] Harvard economist Dani Rodrik states that it:

has been estimated that it costs a typical developing country $150 million to implement requirements under just three of the WTO agreements; [those regarding] customs evaluation, sanitary and phytosanitary measures, and intellectual property.... [T]his is a sum equal to a year's development budget for many of the least developed countries.[78]

The costs include the development of the institutions needed to comply with developed country standards, monitoring and testing programmes, and 'non-recurring commitments such as the development of laboratory infrastructure and processing facilities'.[79] Given other government imperatives, such as providing for education and shelter, this may not be 'money well spent'.[80]

The rules regarding subsidies under the Agreement on Subsidies and Countervailing Measures (SCM) do not favour developing States. Subsidies consist of government supports for industry. They obstruct trade if they favour local traders over foreign traders. Certain subsidies, such as export subsidies and import substitution subsidies, which have historically been used by successful industrializers to kickstart industries, are now forbidden.[81] Other subsidies, also used in the past to promote industrialization by now-developed States, may be challenged and subjected to countervailing measures (which are designed to offset the effect

n 73, para 5.2, where the Panel implies that the same interpretation of GATT might not apply to developing States.

[75] See Caroline E Foster, 'Public Opinion and the interpretation of the World Trade Organisation's Agreement on Sanitary and Phytosanitary Measures' in Joseph, Kinley, and Waincymer (eds), above n 29, 285 at 286; Joel P Trachtman, 'Developing Countries, the Doha round, Preferences, and the Right to Regulate' in Chantal Thomas and Joel P Trachtman (eds), *Developing Countries in the WTO Legal System* (Oxford University Press, New York, 2009) 122.

[76] See Jürgen Kurtz, 'A Look behind the Mirror: Standardization, Institutions and the WTO SPS and TBT Agreements' (2007) 30 *University of New South Wales* 504, 517–19. See also Chapter 3, text at notes 52–54.

[77] Narlikar, above n 39, 71; Hoekman, above n 19, 410.

[78] Dani Rodrik, *The Global Governance of Trade: As if Development Really Mattered* (UNDP, New York, 2001) 26.

[79] Kurtz, above n 76, 514.   [80] Ibid, 514.

[81] Note that developing States are permitted to use export subsidies under Article 27(2) of the SCM until they reach an average annual income of $1000USD per person.

of subsidies and therefore to punish the State utilizing those subsidies). These bans and restrictions on subsidies hinder the ability of developing States to 'catch up', as discussed below.[82] Indeed, most countervailing measures have targeted policies in developing States.[83] In contrast, certain agricultural subsidies are permitted, and have been used by developed States to severely harm agricultural industries in the South, as described below and in Chapter 6. Finally, certain subsidizing activities, which are effectively only available to rich States, are allowed.[84] For example, the extensive investments into research in the US defence industry, which have historically had beneficial spill-over benefits for civilian industries such as information technology and aviation, are permitted.[85] It is fair to suggest that WTO rules forbid the types of subsidies which developing States might realistically aim to use, but permit those effectively only available to developed States.[86]

Anti-dumping measures are permitted under Article VI GATT and the Agreement on Implementation of Article VI of the General Agreement on Tariffs and Trade to counteract the practice of dumping in order to combat unfair competition from goods imported at less than their normal value. Thus, anti-dumping measures are another non-tariff barrier. The WTO's dumping rules are extremely complex, which favours developed States given their wealth of technical expertise. Furthermore, certain developed States are hypocritical in their imposition of dumping measures. The US standards used to determine if another State is engaged in dumping are different to its comparable domestic standards regarding anti-competitive practices. Stiglitz has suggested that few US companies could satisfy the international standard, while most international traders could satisfy the domestic standard. Thus, US dumping law is abused to target international competition rather than to target unfair competition.[87]

As with dumping measures, developed States have also abused the leeway offered under WTO laws regarding safeguards under Article XIX GATT and the Agreement on Safeguards.[88] Agricultural safeguards are governed by different rules, and are discussed in Chapter 6.

Accession

WTO rules and practices are particularly unfair to States that choose to accede to the WTO. An acceding State essentially has to satisfy the demands of each WTO member that chooses to join the Working Party established for its accession:

[82] See also Lee, above n 33, 74–6.   [83] Ibid, 76.
[84] Ha-Joon Chang, *Bad Samaritans: the Myth of Free Trade and the Secret History of Capitalism* (Bloomsbury Press, New York, 2008) 77.
[85] Stiglitz and Charlton, above n 18, 131; see also Ha-Joon Chang, *Kicking Away the Ladder* (Anthem Press, London, 2003) 31.
[86] See Mehdi Shafaeddin, 'Is Industrial Policy Relevant in the 21st Century?' *Third World Network Trade & Development Series 36* (TWN, Malaysia, 2008) 19.
[87] Joseph Stiglitz, *Making Globalization Work* (Penguin, London, 2007) 93.
[88] Stiglitz and Charlton, above n 18, 128–9.

any WTO Member can join such a Working Party.[89] Incumbent Members have exploited accession processes to impose onerous conditions on acceding Members which they do not need to reciprocate.[90] These conditions can set precedents for future Members, who may face even more onerous requirements. For example, Oxfam has suggested that the proposed conditions for Samoa, which had not yet joined the WTO at the time of writing, are more onerous than the 'bad deal' received by Cambodia, which acceded in 2004.[91] The precedent value of accession deals explains why harsh requirements are extracted from SVEs and LDCs by States that hardly trade with them: those precedents are perceived as valuable for future negotiations with States with significant economies such as Russia.[92]

Conditions for new members often include additional obligations, not imposed under existing WTO rules ('WTO plus' conditions), as well as a loss of concessions that a State would normally be entitled to under WTO rules ('WTO minus' conditions).[93] For instance, the Commonwealth secretariat has determined that acceding States typically commit to greater liberalization in the trade in services than incumbents.[94] As an example of a 'WTO plus' requirement, Tonga, which acceded to the WTO in 2007, had to commit to liberalizing a large number of services, even though GATS generally permits States to choose which services they will open up to foreign competition.[95] Tonga has an average tariff binding of 35 per cent, which is much lower than most comparable developing States.[96] Regarding 'WTO minus' conditions, Tonga became fully bound by TRIPS as of 1 January 2008, so there was virtually no delay in full implementation, even though all incumbent developing States had benefited from longer timelines to facilitate implementation in the original Marrakesh Agreement.

Most acceding States, and most of those yet to accede, are developing States. Of course, a State can choose not to accede, at the risk of being shut out of the world economy. Nevertheless, it is difficult to justify such lopsided 'bargains', concluded without recognizable reciprocity in either negotiating power or outcomes.[97] The General Council of the WTO has urged Members to exercise restraint in

[89] Jane Kelsey, 'World Trade and Small Nations in the South Pacific Region' (2004–05) 14 *Kansas Journal of Law and Public Policy* 248, 265.
[90] UNDP, *Asia Pacific Human Development Report 2006: Trade on Human Terms* (UNDP, Colombo, 2006) 131.
[91] See Oxfam, 'Submission by Oxfam New Zealand to Ministry of Foreign Affairs on the WTO accession negotiations of Samoa' (September 2005) 5–6, 10, <http://www.oxfam.org.nz/imgs/whatwedo/mtf/onz%20on%20samoa%20wto%20accession.pdf> accessed 20 September 2010.
[92] Kelsey, above n 89, 274; Stiglitz and Charlton, above n 18, 161.
[93] UNDP, above n 90, 131.
[94] R Grynberg and others, *Paying the Price for Joining the WTO* (Commonwealth Secretariat, London, 2002) 39, quoted in Commission on Human Rights, 'The right of everyone to the enjoyment of the highest attainable standard of physical and mental health: Report of the Special Rapporteur, Paul Hunt: Mission to the World Trade Organization', UN doc. E/CN.4/2004/49/Add.1 (1 March 2004) para 68.
[95] Kelsey, above n 89, 271: see also Oxfam, 'Proposed WTO Accession: Key Issues for Tonga' (Oxfam New Zealand Discussion Paper, Auckland, 2005) 8–11 <http://www.oxfam.org.nz/imgs/pdf/wto%20key%20issues%20for%20tonga.pdf> accessed 20 September 2010.
[96] Oxfam New Zealand Discussion Paper, above n 95, 13.
[97] Kelsey, above n 89, 266 (fn 132).

negotiating deals with LDCs in a Decision on 'Accession of Least Developed Countries' from 20 January 2003.[98] Unfortunately, Samoa, an LDC which is still negotiating its accession protocol at the time of writing, reported that the Decision changed nothing.[99]

The rules regarding accession must be amended as they cannot be described as remotely fair. Objective rules should be prescribed and applied to States according to their levels of economic development.[100]

The Northern side of the bargain

The developed States' side of the bargain was to agree to some liberalization regarding agriculture and textiles, products which had been omitted from prior GATT negotiations, under the Agreement on Agriculture (AoA) and the Agreement on Textiles and Clothing (ATC).[101] Agricultural goods and textiles are products where many developing states have a comparative advantage. However, the AoA and the ATC 'left vast scope for continued protectionism'.[102]

Indeed, despite the fact that average tariffs in developed States are quite low, goods of interest to developing States are disproportionately targeted by tariff peaks, that is those tariff bindings that are considerably higher than those averages.[103] In 2005, the UNDP stated:

On average, low-income developing countries exporting to high-income countries face tariffs three to four times higher than the barriers applied in trade between high-income countries.... Developing countries count for less than one-third of developing country imports but for two-thirds of tariff revenues collected.[104]

As a concrete example, Valentine Sendanyoye-Rugwabiza, a Deputy Director General of the WTO, reported in 2006 that the US collected more tariffs from imports from Cambodia than from French imports, even though the amount of the former imports equated with one tenth of the latter.[105]

Prior to the WTO, trade in textiles was regulated by the Multi Fibre Agreement, under which several States imposed quotas on textiles from developing States.[106] Under the ATC, the EC, the US, Canada and Norway (ATC States) were permitted to maintain quotas but had to progressively increase

[98] WTO, 'Accession of Least-Developed Countries' (Decision of 10 December 2002), WTO doc. WT/L/508.
[99] Kelsey, above n 89, 266 (fn 132).   [100] Stiglitz and Charlton, above n 18, 163.
[101] This Agreement was a transitional arrangement which terminated on 1 January 2005, so trade in textiles and clothing is now subject to normal GATT rules.
[102] Narlikar, above n 39, 26. See generally, Hunter, above n 19, and Christine Breining-Kaufman, 'The Right to Food and Trade in Agriculture' in Thomas Cottier, Joost Pauwelyn, and Elizabeth Bürgi (eds), *Human Rights and International Trade* (Oxford University Press, Oxford, 2005) 341–81.
[103] Lee, above n 33, 35; Stiglitz and Charlton, above n 18, 51 and 125.
[104] UNDP, above n 64, 127. See also Stiglitz and Charlton, above n 18, 47–8.
[105] Valentine Sendanyoye-Rugwabiza, 'Is the DDA a Development Round' (Address at the London School of Economics, 31 March 2006) 3 <http://www2.lse.ac.uk/PublicEvents/pdf/20060331-WTO.pdf> accessed 20 September 2010.
[106] Stiglitz and Charlton, above n 18, 44.

them through three stages until 2005, when all quotas had to be abolished and textiles integrated into normal GATT disciplines. As it happened, ATC States backloaded their quota reduction commitments and utilized permissible safeguards as much as possible to delay commercial benefits to developing countries until the expiry of the ATC,[107] in accordance with the letter but not the spirit of the ATC.[108] In effect, some of the richest States took full advantage of their own SDT provisions! This backloading also gave the beneficiaries of those quotas, often LDCs like Bangladesh, less time to adjust to the loss of those quotas and subsequent exposure to greater competition from non-beneficiaries like China and India. Furthermore, developed States dominated exports in the textiles sector, and the ATC States increased their export shares between 1995 and 2002, 'indicating that the case for continued protection [was] weak'.[109] Since expiry of the ATC, developed States, even non-ATC States such as Australia and New Zealand, have maintained above-average tariff rates on textiles and especially clothing.[110]

Agricultural produce in the US and the EU remains heavily subsidized, so developing States have found it difficult to penetrate those lucrative markets.[111] Indeed, subsidized agricultural exports have made their way to developing states, undercutting local farmers and driving them out of business.[112] Furthermore, while the AoA mandated the binding of all agricultural tariff lines, developed States only committed to prohibitively high tariffs. The World Bank, in its World Development Report of 2008, estimated that the removal of protectionist measures by developed States 'would induce annual welfare gains for developing countries estimated to be five times the current annual flow of aid to agriculture'.[113]

Cotton subsidies have been particularly controversial, and have been described as an 'iconic issue' in the lead-up to the ill-tempered Cancún Ministerial.[114] Indeed, certain aspects of the US's subsidies programme were found to contravene WTO laws in *United States—Subsidies on Upland Cotton* in 2002 by a WTO Panel, affirmed by the Appellate body in 2005.[115] By 2009, the US had still not complied with the decision, so an arbitrator authorized $US295 million worth of

---

[107] Khor, above n 51, 9.

[108] Hildegunn Kyvik Nordås, 'The Global Textile and Clothing Industry post the Agreement on Textiles and Clothing' (Discussion Paper No 5) (WTO, Switzerland, 2004) 14–16.

[109] Ibid, 16.

[110] See Indicator 39 for the Millennium Development Goals, 'Average Tariffs imposed by Developed Countries on Agricultural Products and Textiles and Clothing from Developed Countries' <http://www.statistics.gov.lk/MDG/Indicators%20New/Poverty%20Indicators%2039 .pdf> accessed 15 May 2010.

[111] Paul, above n 35, 325–6; Breining-Kaufman, above n 102, 368.

[112] Breining-Kaufman, above n 102, 368; Oxfam, above n 5, 93 and 116.

[113] *World Bank, World Development Report 2008: Agriculture for Development* (World Bank, Washington DC, 2008) 11.

[114] Trachtman, above n 75, 124.

[115] *United States—Subsidies on Upland Cotton*, WTO doc. WT/DS297/R (8 September 2004) (Report of the Panel); *United States—Subsidies on Upland Cotton*, WTO doc. WT/DS267/AB/R (3 March 2005) (Report of the Appellate Body).

retaliatory measures by Brazil.[116] The impact of the cotton subsidies is particularly acute in the 'C4' countries of West Africa: Benin, Burkina Faso, Chad, and Mali. These States produce cotton at half the cost compared to the US, yet the the US is the world's largest cotton exporter. In 2003, the C4 reported in the WTO that US cotton subsidies in 2001 amounted to 60 per cent more than Burkina Faso's entire GDP: the subsidies benefited a few thousand American farmers and penalize about a million farmers in Africa. The C4 States, some of the poorest in the world, estimated that their consequent direct and indirect losses amounted to $1 billion a year.[117]

Subsidies also artificially lower commodity prices on the world market. If growers from developing States were not forced to compete by offering their produce at low prices, the higher prices would assist to alleviate poverty in grower communities. For example, the World Bank has reported that US and European cotton subsidies depressed world cotton prices by 71 per cent in 2001–2002, again with devastating effects on the incomes of cotton growers in Africa and central Asia.[118]

The unfairness and perverse consequences of the current WTO arrangements for agriculture are further discussed in Chapter 6.

Conclusion on current WTO rules

Current trade rules, such as those allowing for the maintenance of trade barriers regarding agriculture and the mandating of trade barriers in the form of intellectual property rights, are biased against developing states. This circumstance undermines the WTO's stated goal of improving living standards across the world, and its potential for promoting development and alleviating poverty, as the populations in greatest need are disadvantaged.

D. Free Trade, Economic Growth, and Poverty

Clearly, the introduction of balance and fairness into WTO rules is desirable from the perspective of developing States. A different question arises as to whether liberalization per se is a prudent strategy from a human rights point of view. The justification for trade liberalization is that it will improve global and national economic efficiency, and lead to economic growth and development. This is said to be so even on a unilateral basis, as liberalization will improve the efficiency of a State's industries and allow its consumers access to cheaper goods.

---

[116] See *United States—Subsidies on Upland Cotton—Recourse to Arbitration by the United States under Article 22.6 of the DSU and Article 4.11 of the SCM Agreement*, WTO docs. WT/DS267/ARB/1 and WT/DS267/ARB/2 (31 August 2009) (Decision by the Arbitrator).

[117] See WTO, 'Poverty Reduction: Sectoral Initiative in Favour of Cotton' (WTO Committee on Agriculture), WTO doc. TN/AG/Gen.4 (16 May 2003).

[118] World Development Report 2006, above n 58, 212.

From a human rights point of view, the important issue is whether liberalization is likely to lead to poverty alleviation and better economic outcomes on a distributive basis rather than better economic performance on a national or global basis. Nevertheless, it is relevant to human rights to assess whether liberalization promotes economic growth, as that outcome should increase a State's capacities to fulfil its human rights obligations. Conversely, economic regression decreases those abilities. Furthermore, the short term detrimental impacts of free trade, which are undeniable for those in inefficient industries, cannot be justified if the long term benefits are not in fact likely to eventuate.[119] Of course, if free trade is promoting economic growth, such growth per se does not alleviate poverty due to possible distributional discrepancies. The impact of trade liberalization on economic growth, poverty, inequality and development is therefore examined further below.

Comparative advantage: theory and practice

In 1776, the economist Adam Smith challenged the protectionist orthodoxies of the time by proposing the theory of 'absolute advantage'—that State A should produce goods for which it has an advantage over State B, and should export those goods to B, while importing from B goods for which B has an advantage with regard to State A. Advantages derive from country conditions, such as climate, natural resources, size of population, and levels of urbanization. So long as trade between the States is not obstructed by trade barriers, both countries benefit from cheaper goods and have more efficient industries which concentrate on the most suitable production outputs, rather than wasting resources on inefficient industries. David Ricardo advanced Smith's theory in 1817 by promulgating the theory of 'comparative advantage', which applied to all countries regardless of whether they had an 'absolute advantage' in the production of any product. State A, according to Ricardo, should concentrate on producing and exporting those goods which it is best suited to produce while importing from State B those goods that B is best at producing. The theory applies even if State A has an absolute advantage over State B with regard to the production of all goods. Suppose A is better at producing both wheat and grapes than B, and that A is better at producing wheat than grapes. B is better at producing grapes than wheat. Under Ricardo's theory, A should concentrate on producing and exporting wheat to B, while importing grapes from B, as A suffers an opportunity cost in diverting resources from wheat to grapes. B should concentrate on its grape production. Under this theory of comparative advantage, numerous advantages accrue to all States if they trade freely without trade barriers. The production processes brought about by specialization become more efficient and sustainable in each State, while consumers in all States enjoy access to lower priced goods of the best

---

[119] The converse proposition however is not necessarily true. That is, short term consequences are not necessarily justified under international human rights law, even if the long term benefits do arise.

quality. Furthermore, increased competition from free trade provides incentives to increase efficiency and to innovate.[120]

Of course, numerous economic theories have built on or departed from this 200-year-old theory. Many modern economists recognize qualifications and nuances to this pure trade theory.[121] However, most free trade advocates still see comparative advantage as 'offering the best description of how international trade creates wealth'.[122] The WTO's website proclaims the theory of comparative advantage as 'arguably the single most powerful insight into economics'.[123]

Ricardo's theory is based on a perfect market.[124] Professor Joel R Paul has listed four requirements for a perfect market where prices reflect the true costs of production: an absence of trade barriers, homogeneous goods (where a product from State A may substitute for a product from State B), perfect consumer knowledge of the relevant market so that consumers buy goods at the most competitive price, and an adequate pool of buyers and sellers to stave off market manipulation by monopolistic practices.[125]

The most obvious trade distortions arise from barriers to free trade. Despite the efforts of the GATT and the WTO, numerous trade barriers still exist. Indeed, certain trade barriers are mandated, namely IP rights under TRIPS. Linked to IP protection are distortions which arise from marketing, whereby consumers are convinced that certain branded products (where trademarks are protected IP) are better than others, which allows those products to be sold for a higher price.

Markets are also distorted by monopolies and anti-competitive practices, which currently remain outside the mandate of the WTO. Multinational corporations (MNCs) dominate world trade and have enormous exploitable advantages against new competitors. Much international trade today is in fact conducted within MNCs: an MNC will often import components from its offshore subsidiaries even if lower priced components are available elsewhere.[126] The severe impact of monopolies in agricultural markets is discussed in Chapter 6.

The application of the theory of comparative advantage in the context of a free flow of capital resources across borders, such that the trade advantages within a

---

[120] Paul, above n 35, 290–2.

[121] Van den Bossche, above n 41, 19–20.

[122] G Richard Shell, 'Trade Legalism and International Relations Theory: An Analysis of the World Trade Organization' (1995) 44 *Duke Law Journal* 829, 858. See also Jagdish N Bhagwati, 'Challenges to the Doctrine of Free Trade' (1993) 25 *New York University Journal of International Law and Politics* 219 (1993); Michael H Davis and Dana Neascu, 'Legitimacy, Globally: The Incoherence of Free Trade Practice, Global Economics, and the Governing Principles of Political Economy' (2001) 69 *University of Missouri Kansas City Law Review* 733.

[123] WTO, 'Understanding the WTO: The Case for Open Trade' (undated) <http://www.wto .org/english/thewto_e/whatis_e/tif_e/fact3_e.htm> accessed 18 September 2010. Martin Wolf, in *Why Globalisation Works* (Yale Nota Bene, London, 2005), describes the idea of comparative advantage as 'perhaps the cleverest in economics' at 80.

[124] See also Stiglitz and Charlton, above n 18, 115.

[125] Paul, above n 35, 292. See also 292–6.

[126] Ibid, 295. Van den Bossche, above n 41, states that 'two thirds of all trade takes place within companies' at 9. However, he states that the amount is 'one third' at 703.

State can be appropriated by offshore traders, is dubious.[127] In this respect, one may note the difference between measuring economic performance by Gross Domestic Product (GDP), the market value of all goods and services produced within a State, and Gross National Income (GNI), which differentiates according to the ownership of income, thus taking account of the income which stays in a country, or which is imported into a country by its nationals (such as those MNCs headquartered in a country), and excluding income exported out of the country (such as by foreign MNCs).[128] If production (of goods or services) in a State is dominated by foreign MNCs with little trickle-down to local businesses, and the State is home to few investors with offshore activities, its GNI will lag significantly behind its GDP. In such a situation, GDP is an over-optimistic indicator of the State's economic performance.[129] This is not to say that foreign investment is bad for an economy: such investment can of course provide jobs, technological transfer, and business for local industries. It is simply to suggest that outflows of capital ultimately benefit or 'confer advantage' on the receiving rather than the sending State.[130]

Finally, comparative advantage theory dictates that efficiency gains will ensue from the transfer of the means of production, such as labour and capital, from inefficient industries to efficient industries.[131] However, the freed-up capital may in some cases move offshore. Furthermore, Stiglitz and Charlton have noted that developing States in fact have vast labour reserves. Therefore, 'trade liberalization is not required to "free up" these resources for use in new industries'.[132] Removal of protection for existing industries therefore may mean that underemployed people in inefficient industries move to 'zero-productivity unemployment'.[133]

Therefore, the relevance of Ricardo's theory to the realities of the present day is questionable.[134] Paul has estimated the amount of goods traded in a 'perfect market' to be 25 per cent of the world's exports 'and probably significantly less'.[135] In any case, assertions of the benefits of a truly free trade regime may never move beyond the theoretical. Free markets are currently impeded by the significant level of protectionism which is permitted under WTO rules as well as globally mandated IP rights. Political realities render it unlikely that world barriers will ever

---

[127] See also Wolf, above n 123, 83 (quoting Ronald Jones, *Globalization and the Theory of Input Trade* (MIT Press, Cambridge, Massachusetts, 2000) 135–6), though Wolf argues that 'this qualification to the theory seems far less important than one might expect' due to the general lack of foreign direct investment in many developing States.

[128] See OECD, 'Glossary of Statistical Terms' <http://stats.oecd.org/glossary/detail.asp?ID=1176> accessed 20 September 2010.

[129] See 'GDP and GNI', *OECD Observer No 246–247*, December 2004–January 2005 <http://www.oecdobserver.org/news/fullstory.php/aid/1507/GDP_and_GNI.html> accessed 22 September 2010.

[130] Of course, outflows may be matched by inflows, in which case GDP and GNI are equivalent. And in some States, GNI outpaces GDP, as in Japan in 2004.

[131] Wolf, above n 123, 81.   [132] Stiglitz and Charlton, above n 18, 6.

[133] Ibid, 26; see also 194.   [134] Oxfam, above n 5, 57–60.

[135] Paul, above n 35, 298.

allow for the truly free movement of labour, so a truly free trade regime will never materialize.[136]

Freer trade and economic growth

Nevertheless, trade barriers across the world have dropped under the auspices of the GATT and the WTO,[137] so orthodox economic theory holds that there should have been significant increases in wealth across the world, even if those increases are not as much as could be expected in a perfectly free market. And indeed, global economic output has soared in the last 20 years.[138] However, this does not mean that trade liberalization in a State will automatically lead to decreases in poverty in that State.

The positive effect of free trade on economic growth is often presumed.[139] However, world economic patterns have not conformed to orthodox theoretical expectations.[140] While certain influential studies have purported to compare groups of 'globalizing' countries with 'non-globalizers', reporting that the former group has recorded greater rates of economic growth,[141] those studies reveal nothing about the trade policies of the respective States.[142] States that engage in significant international trade may nevertheless maintain highly trade restrictive policies. China (which only joined the WTO in 2001), India, South Korea, and Taiwan have all experienced outstanding rates of growth, but those growth spurts began long before those States undertook liberalizing reforms.[143] Vietnam, which only joined the WTO in 2007, is another apparent economic success story, where growth and poverty reduction have occurred under a protectionist regime.[144] On the other hand, the results in the open economies of El Salvador and Mexico have

---

[136] Dani Rodrik, 'How to Save Globalisation from its Cheerleaders' (2007) 1 *The Journal of International Trade and Diplomacy* 1, 10–11. <http://dev.wcfia.harvard.edu/sites/default/files/Rodrick_HowToSave.pdf> accessed 20 September 2010; World Development Report 2006, above n 58, 210. See also Wolf, above n 123, 89.

[137] Furthermore, liberalization outside the GATT/WTO framework has been induced in developing countries by international financial institutions as conditions for loans.

[138] See the statistics cited in David Kinley, *Civilising Globalisation* (Cambridge University Press, Cambridge, 2009) 14.

[139] See, eg, Robert Howse, above n 10, paras 15 and 29 (criticizing this 'neo-liberal article of faith').

[140] World Bank, *Economic Growth in the 1990s: Learning from a Decade of Reform* (World Bank, Washington DC, 2005) <http://www1.worldbank.org/prem/lessons1990s/> accessed 19 September 2010; Rodrik, above n 136.

[141] See, eg, David Dollar and Aart Kraay, 'Trade, Growth and Poverty' (World Bank Policy Research Working Paper No 2615) (World Bank, Washington DC, June 2001) <http://wdsbeta.worldbank.org/external/default/WDSContentServer/IW3P/IB/2002/08/23/000094946_02082304142939/Rendered/PDF/multi0page.pdf> accessed 22 September 2010 and David Dollar and Aart Kraay, 'Growth is Good for the Poor' (World Bank Policy Research Working Paper No 2587) (World Bank, Washington DC, April 2001) <http://wdsbeta.worldbank.org/external/default/WDSContentServer/IW3P/IB/2001/05/11/000094946_01042806383524/Rendered/PDF/multi0page.pdf> accessed 22 September 2010.

[142] Oxfam, above n 5, 130–1.

[143] Rodrik, above n 78, 18 and 24; Paul, above n 35, 312–13.   [144] Rodrik, above n 78, 21.

been 'underwhelming' in terms of growth, employment, poverty reduction, and real wages.[145]

Furthermore, the economist Ha-Joon Chang states that growth rates across the world and particularly in developing States from 1960 to 1980 were higher than those between 1980 and 2000, even though economic policies were far more liberal in the later period. He states:

So we have an apparent 'paradox' here—at least if you are a Neo-liberal economist. All countries, but especially developing countries, grew much faster when they used 'bad' policies during the 1960–1980 period than when they used 'good' ones in the following two decades.[146]

The studies essentially demonstrate that countries reduce trade barriers as they have become richer,[147] but some countries may have reduced trade barriers prematurely. The studies do not demonstrate that trade liberalization per se is a guarantor of or a prerequisite to growth,[148] though it often boosts pre-existing growth.[149] A 2005 World Bank report concedes that the correlation between trade liberalization and economic growth is inconclusive.[150]

Freer trade, poverty, and inequality

Even if economic liberalization promotes economic growth, that circumstance may not translate into benefits for the poor. Growth per se does not necessarily mean that the increases in wealth are fairly distributed. The Committee on Economic, Social and Cultural Rights recently stated:

Economic growth has not, in itself, led to sustainable development and individuals and groups of individuals continue to face socio-economic inequality, often because of entrenched historical and contemporary forms of discrimination.[151]

Let us turn to examine statistics regarding the incidence of poverty in this age of global economic integration, which has undoubtedly been facilitated by the WTO and its predecessor GATT. A word of caution must however be noted: global statistics regarding poverty are the subject of enormous dispute.[152] It is

---

[145] Rodrik, above n 136, 14–15. See also Oxfam, above n 5, 127; Chantal Thomas, 'Poverty Reduction, Trade, and Rights' (2003) 18 *American University International Law Review* 1399, 1406.

[146] Chang, above n 85, 128–9. See also Chang, above n 84, 27–8.

[147] Rodrik, above n 78, 22.

[148] UNDP, above n 64, 119; Dan Ben-David, Håkan Nordström, and Alan Winters, 'Trade, Income Disparity, and Poverty' (WTO Special Studies 5) (WTO, Geneva, 1999), 59.

[149] UNDP, above n 64, 119.

[150] World Bank, above n 140; see also UNDP, above n 64, 119.

[151] Committee on Economic, Social and Cultural Rights, 'General Comment No 20: Non-Discrimination in Economic, Social and Cultural Rights (art 2, para 2)', UN doc. E/C.12/GC/20 (2 July 2009) para 1.

[152] See, for a discussion on the difficulty of estimating poverty, Sanjay G Reddy and Thomas W Pogge, 'How *not* to count the poor' (Columbia University paper, version 6.2) (2005) <http://www.columbia.edu/~sr793/count.pdf> accessed 22 September 2010. See also World Development Report 2006, above n 58, 44. Wolf, above n 123, describes 'all poverty estimates' as 'inherently arbitrary' at 163.

therefore not possible to present unimpeachable statistics regarding poverty and inequality.[153]

There is general agreement that there has been improvement in the absolute and proportionate number of poor people since 1980, if living in a state of poverty is defined as living on the World Bank standard of $US1.25 or less a day (with the US dollar calculated as having the same purchasing power as in 2005).[154] For example, World Bank economists Shaohua Chen and Martin Ravallion estimated that there were 1.9 billion poor people in 1980, about half the world's population, compared to 1.4 billion, or a quarter of the world's population, in 2005.[155] However, patterns in this respect differ across the world. In 2005, the UNDP reported a decrease in poverty from 1990 in Asia, calculated at the old World Bank rate of $US1 a day at 1993 rates, a slight increase in Africa, static poverty lines in Latin America, and an increase in poverty in Central and Eastern Europe and the former Soviet bloc.[156] Furthermore, the reduction in absolute poverty is not so clear-cut if China is taken out of the equation.[157]

In any case, the number of people living in poverty remains enormous. To recap, Chen and Ravallion found that a quarter of the world's people lived in extreme poverty in 2005. Furthermore, a simple thought experiment serves to indicate that the $US1.25 a day marker is very low indeed:[158] it is intuitively difficult to conceive of a person living on $US2 a day as not being 'poor'. The following figures may be gleaned from statistics gathered by the World Bank on poverty levels in 2005: 40 per cent of people in the world live on $US2 or less a day and 95 per cent of the developing world live on less than $US10 a day.[159]

Has the gap between rich and poor expanded in the last few decades? Measurement of inequality is complicated by the existence of different measures of inequality: inter-State inequality (comparing median incomes between

---

[153] Eg, while it is contended below that inequality has increased in the last two decades, Wolf contends otherwise in Wolf, above n 123, Chapter 9.

[154] See also Pranab Bardhan, 'Globalisation and human rights: an economist's perspective' in Joseph, Kinley, and Waincymer (eds), above n 29, 92–3; Kinley, above n 138, 15.

[155] Shaohua Chen and Martin Ravallion, 'The developing world are poorer than we thought, but no less successful in the fight against poverty' (World Bank Policy Research Working Paper No 4703) (World Bank, Washington DC, August 2008) <http://siteresources.worldbank.org/JAPANINJAPANESEEXT/Resources/515497-1201490097949/080827_The_Developing_World_is_Poorer_than_we_Thought.pdf> accessed 22 September 2010.

[156] Oxfam, above n 5, 66. See also United Nations Development Programme (UNDP), *Human Development Report 2004: Cultural Liberty in Today's Diverse World* (UNDP, New York, 2004) 130.

[157] UN Commission on the Private Sector and Development (CPSD), *Unleashing Entrepreneurship: Making Business work for the Poor* (UNDP, New York, 2004) 6, via <http://www.undp.org/cpsd/report/index.html> accessed 22 September 2010.

[158] Reddy and Pogge, above n 152, disputed the validity of the $US1 a day marker: the same arguments would apply to the new poverty marker of $US1.25 a day.

[159] These figures are gleaned from graphs available from the World Bank's site on 'Poverty Reduction and Equity' (see <http://siteresources.worldbank.org/INTPOVERTY/Images/PovTrends_large1.gif> accessed 22 September 2010) for the $US2 a day figure and Martin Ravallion, Shaohua Chen, and Prem Sangraula, 'Dollar a Day Revisited' (World Bank Policy Research Working Paper No 4620) (World Bank, Washington DC, May 2008) fn 5 (for the $US10 a day figure)). See also <http://www.globalissues.org/article/26/poverty-facts-and-stats> accessed 22 September 2010, which reports that 80% of the world live on less than $US10 a day, and 50% on less than $US2.50.

States), population-weighted State inequality (comparing median incomes between States, taking into account the population of each State), and global inequality (comparing income inequality between all human beings in the world).[160] Inequality has worsened on all measures bar the population weighted comparison of States,[161] where inequality has decreased largely due to significant economic growth in China and India, which account for nearly 40 per cent of the world's population.[162] However, both countries seem to be experiencing increased intra-State inequality.[163] On intra-country inequality generally, the data indicate an ambiguous picture that is difficult to interpret:[164] it 'is increasing in some countries but is decreasing or ambiguous in other countries'.[165]

As with absolute poverty, the statistics regarding inequality in the world are staggering. In 2007, the UNDP reported that the richest 20 per cent of people accounted for 75 per cent of world income, while the bottom 40 per cent accounted for 5 per cent, and that 80 per cent live in States where 'income differentials are widening'.[166] World Bank figures indicate that the top 10 per cent are responsible for 59 per cent of world consumption, the top 20 per cent for 76.6 per cent, the bottom 50 per cent just 7.2 per cent, and the bottom 20 per cent for 1.5 per cent.[167]

Perhaps it is arguable that increasing inequality is not objectionable if the plight of the poor nevertheless improves: it is perhaps acceptable for economic globalization to improve the welfare of the poor at a lesser rate than that enjoyed by the rich.[168] However, a situation of extreme inequality, termed 'global apartheid' by South African President Thabo Mbeki in 2002,[169] is inherently undesirable. Amartya Sen has stated that '[r]elative deprivation in the space of incomes can yield absolute deprivation in the space of capabilities'.[170] Sen's 'capabilities' refer to a person's ability to function in society. While there is clearly a difference between the absolute and relative poor in terms of some capabilities, such as

---

[160] World Development Report 2006, above n 58, 57. See also Kinley, above n 138, 27–8.

[161] World Development Report 2006, above n 58, 63–5. See also Anthony B Atkinson and Andrea Brandolini, 'Global World Inequality: Absolute, Relative or Intermediate?' (2004) <http://www-1.unipv.it/deontica/ca2004/papers/atkinson%20brandolini.pdf> accessed 22 September 2010. See also Thomas Pogge, 'Growth and Inequality: Understanding Recent Trends and Political Choices' (2008) *Dissent* <http://www.dissentmagazine.org/article/?article=990> accessed 20 September 2010.

[162] See also World Development Report 2006, above n 58, 68.

[163] See ibid, 45. See Save the Children, *Freedom from Hunger for Children under Six* (Save the Children, India, 2009), for a recent disturbing report on the continuing severity of child malnutrition in India despite the fast growth in its economy. On inequality in China, see Pogge, above n 161, 6–7.

[164] World Development Report, above n 58, 45–6.   [165] Bardhan, above n 154, 92.

[166] UNDP, *Human Development Report 2007/2008. Fighting climate change: Human solidarity in a divided world* (Palgrave Macmillan, Hampshire/New York, 2007) 25.

[167] World Bank, *World Development Indicators database* (2008) 4 <http://databank.worldbank.org/ddp/home.do> accessed 22 September 2010.

[168] Thomas, above n 145, 1403; Wolf, above n 123, 140.

[169] Mbeki is quoted by Trachtman, above n 34, 3. See also Oxfam, above n 5, 23.

[170] Amartya Sen, *Inequality Re-Examined* (Oxford University Press, Oxford, 1995) 115.

freedom from hunger, there may be little difference between the absolute and relative poor regarding other capabilities, such as the 'capability to live without shame' or to have self respect.[171] Furthermore, inequality can generate social instability and conflict: '[a]n island of affluence surrounded by an ocean of poverty feels no security in a rising tide'.[172] Finally, the further removed the rich are from the poor, the greater the divergences in their interests, and the greater the likelihood that rules (over which the rich have greater control and influence) will be generated which benefit the former at the expense of the latter.[173]

International human rights law does not demand that there be no inequality. It is not a breach of human rights for there to be rich people and poor people in a society. But there should be reasonable equality of opportunity in terms of, for example, access to education and participation in the political process. As with poverty, extreme inequality often accompanies human rights abuses or is generated by human rights abuse. Most obviously, inequality is generated by discrimination, long prohibited in international human rights law. For example, discrimination on various grounds, including discrimination on 'any...status', is prohibited under Articles 2(1) and 26 of the ICCPR and Article 2(2) of the ICESCR. The Committee on Economic, Social and Cultural Rights remarked, regarding discrimination on the basis of one's socio-economic situation:

Individuals and groups of individuals must not be arbitrarily treated on account of belonging to a certain economic or social group or strata within society. A person's social and economic situation when living in poverty or being homeless may result in pervasive discrimination, stigmatisation and negative stereotyping which lead to the refusal of or unequal access to the same quality of education and health care as others, as well as the denial of or unequal access to public places.[174]

It is difficult to determine the causes of persistent grave poverty and increased inequality.[175] Globalization, including the economic interactions mandated under the WTO, such as decreased trade barriers and increased IP protection, is one potential cause: other likely factors include technological change, which tends to benefit the rich more than the poor,[176] and local instability in poor countries.[177] The World Bank reported in 2006 that the relationship between trade openness

---

[171] See also Amartya Sen, 'Poor, Relatively Speaking' (1983) 35 *Oxford Economic Papers* 153, 159–63.

[172] Paul, above n 35, 320.

[173] Pogge, above n 161, 6. See also Margot Salomon, 'Global Economic Policy and Human Rights: Three Sites of Disconnection' (2010) *Carnegie Ethics Online* <http://www.cceia.org/resources/ethics_online/0043.html> accessed 22 September 2010.

[174] General Comment No 20, above n 151, para 35.

[175] Bardhan, above n 154, 92–3. Wolf, above n 123, 140 and 170.

[176] The mobile phone is a rare instance of a recent technological change that has radically changed the lives of poor people. In contrast, few poor people have access to a television set or a computer. See, eg, Matthew Bishop, 'Mobile Phone Revolution', *Developments* (undated) <http://www.developments.org.uk/articles/loose-talk-saves-lives-1/> accessed 14 May 2010.

[177] Bardhan, above n 154, 92–3.

and inequality was ambiguous and diverse across states and within different state sectors (for example, urban and rural populations).[178]

In light of the statistics, it seems fair to surmise that the modern era of globalization has served the interests of the richer 'few' far more than the poor 'many', and that it has sustained if not created a system of astonishing global inequity. At the least, it seems that the design of the global economy, including the mechanisms for free trade, should be adjusted to make a greater effort to combat poverty and inequality. As the World Bank has stated:

In sum, global actions can play a key role in redressing inequitable rules and helping equalize endowments. The rules that govern markets for labour, goods, ideas, capital, and the use of natural resources need to become more equitable.[179]

E. Liberalization and Development: The Way Forward for Developing States

All developing States wish to catch up in economic terms to industrialized countries in the North. Success in doing so should lead to massive decreases in world poverty. What strategies, in terms of trade liberalization, should be followed by developing States? What should the States of the South be aiming for in terms of their own WTO obligations in order to appropriately develop their economies?

Orthodox economic thinking, particularly since the 1980s, favours trade liberalization as a path to industrialization and development. However, as noted above, the linkage between liberalization of trade and greater growth cannot be taken for granted. As stated by the UNDP:

The evidence to support the proposition that import liberalization is automatically good for growth is weak—almost as weak as the opposite proposition that protectionism is good for growth.[180]

As conceded by the UNDP, ongoing static protectionism is not a long term prescription for economic success.[181] Once an industry has been appropriately fostered by relevant domestic policies, only export markets can assist those industries to grow. Participation in world markets has certainly assisted many economies in the North and the South to grow and to gain access to imported technologies.[182]

Liberalization in most industrial sectors should probably occur at some stage in a State's development, so the question is one of 'when' and at what rate liberalization should occur, rather than 'if' it should ever occur. Implicit in such propositions is that liberalization can be premature and counterproductive. The following concerns arise with regard to premature liberalization in developing states.

---

[178] World Development Report 2006, above n 58, 194–5.   [179] Ibid, 223.
[180] UNDP, above n 64, 119.   [181] Rodrik, above n 78, 24; Oxfam, above n 5, 24 and 61–2.
[182] Department of Foreign Affairs and Trade, *Globalisation: Keeping the Gains* (Commonwealth of Australia, Canberra, 2003) 5.

Loss of tariff revenue

The reduction of tariffs in developing States is problematic, as tariffs are an effective source of government revenue which is necessary for the provision of government services and programmes crucial to the enjoyment of economic, social, and cultural rights by the poor, as well as other government initiatives.[183] Stiglitz and Charlton report that tariff revenues comprise one third of the budgets of LDCs.[184] Tariffs are relatively simple to administer and collect compared to other taxes, such as goods and services taxes or income taxes.[185] Many developing States lack the infrastructure to properly police collection of the latter types of taxes, especially given the prevalence in developing States of informal workforces and black markets.[186] The IMF has estimated that, in the 25 years to 2005, less than 30 per cent of lost tariff revenue was recovered by developing States through other means.[187]

Institutional reforms and social safety nets

There is no doubt that local and international factors outside the remit of the WTO will impact on a State's ability to maximize the benefits and minimize the detriments of free trade. A State's levels of political stability, corruption, infrastructure and welfare support, indebtedness, and social services such as education and health, are all highly determinative of a State's ability to benefit from WTO rules.[188] Reform in these areas will provide a greater fillip to a State's development prospects than rapid liberalization.[189] States must develop infrastructure to cope with the inevitable social consequences of liberalization. For example, social safety nets should exist to compensate the inevitable losers from liberalized trade.[190] States should also build up the capacity of their social services such as education and health to facilitate the creation of a higher skilled, more productive workforce.[191] Of course, such capacity-building also facilitates the enjoyment of economic, social, and cultural rights. In this respect, the World Bank stated in its World Development Report of 2006:

The ideal balance is a combination of gradual but committed liberalisation with extensive engagement in complementary measures that broaden opportunities for all: education, infrastructure, competition, and safety nets.[192]

---

[183] Mehdi Shafaeddin, 'Does Trade Openness Favour or Hinder Industrialization and Development?' *Third World Network Trade & Development Series No. 31* (TWN, Malaysia, 2006) 6.
[184] Stiglitz and Charlton, above n 18, 188.   [185] Van den Bossche, above n 41, 379.
[186] See also Lorand Bartels, 'Trade and Human Rights' in Daniel Bethlehem, Donald McRae, Rodney Neufeld, and Isabelle Van Damme (eds), *Oxford Handbook of International Trade* (Oxford University Press, Oxford, 2009) 579, and International Assessment of Agricultural Knowledge, Science and Technology for Development (IAAKSTD), Agriculture at the Crossroads (IAAKSTD, Washington DC, 2009), 456. See also Stiglitz and Charlton, above n 18, 28.
[187] Thomas Baunsgaard and Michael Keen, 'Trade Revenue and (or?) Trade Liberalisation' (2005) *IMF Working Paper No. 05/112*. See also Carin Smaller and Sophia Murphy, *Bridging the Divide: a human rights vision for global food trade* (Institute of Agriculture and Trade Policy, Geneva, 2008) 13.
[188] Thomas, above n 145, 1408.   [189] Trachtman, above n 34, 18.
[190] Paul, above n 35, 300; see also Oxfam, above n 5, 91. See also Lamy, above n 15, 5.
[191] Thomas, above n 145, 1408; Trachtman, above n 34, 18; see also World Commission on the Social Dimension of Globalisation, *A Fair Globalization: Promoting Opportunities for all* (ILO, Geneva, 2004) para 73; Chang, above n 85, 102.
[192] World Development Report 2006, above n 58, 198.

Ironically, given this statement by the World Bank, the capacities for developing States to provide such 'complementary measures' have been undermined by loan conditions imposed by the international financial institutions which have dictated the slashing of public spending.

Arguably, the building up of such capacities constitutes a 'development policy'. Developing States have a limited amount of leeway under Article XVIIIB GATT to take certain measures to implement a programme of economic development. A narrow meaning was given to 'economic development' programmes in *India-Quantitative Restrictions on Imports of Agricultural, Textile and Industrial Products*,[193] indicating that little policy space is in fact available under this provision.[194]

Static and dynamic comparative advantage

Premature liberalization may trap a developing State in sectors in which it has a comparative advantage, namely primary production and low cost unskilled manufacturing, which is not in the longer term interests of that State.[195] In this respect, the problems associated with liberalization in agriculture are discussed in Chapter 6.

Specialization in low skilled manufacturing can generate mass migration to urban areas, leading to overcrowding and social stresses as many of the affected cities lack adequate infrastructure to cope with this influx of people many of whom, whilst employed, remain poor.[196] As noted in Chapter 4, a comparative advantage based on low labour costs can be swiftly undermined by the availability of lower cost labour from other States:[197] such job creation is 'unstable and dependent on low labour standards'.[198] Foreign capital is highly mobile so it can easily relocate to cheaper countries quickly.[199] Technological changes can also render low-skilled workforces redundant. Resultant job losses cause severe economic dislocation and hardship, as low skilled labourers may find it very difficult to migrate to other sectors[200] and developing States are rarely able to provide adequate social security.

---

[193] WTO docs. WT/DS90/R (6 April 1999) (Report of the Panel) and WT/DS90/AB/R, AB-1999-3 (23 August 1999) (Report of the Appellate Body).

[194] See Chapter 3, text at notes 72–75.   [195] Shafaeddin, above n 183, 12.

[196] In this respect, see United Nations Human Settlements Programme, *Global Report on Human Settlements 2006: The Challenge of Slums* (UN Habitat, London, 2006) xxv, reporting that in 2001, 924 million people, or nearly one third of the global urban population, lived in slums. Slums dominated urban centres in Sub-Saharan Africa (71.9 % of residents), with high rates in other developing countries (58% in South-Central Asia, 36.4% in Eastern Asia, 33.1% in Western Asia, 31.9% in Latin America and the Caribbean, 28.2% in Northern Africa, and 28% in South East Asia). Slum populations soared during the 1990s, and the same is likely to have happened in the 2000s.

[197] See Chapter 4, text at notes 257–260.

[198] War on Want, 'Trading away our jobs: How free trade threatens employment around the world' (2009) 22.

[199] Oxfam, above n 5, 40 and 82–3.

[200] Paul, above n 35, 315; Robert Wai, 'Countering, Branding and Dealing: Using Economic and Social Rights in and Around the International Trade Regime' (2003) 14 *European Journal of International Law* 35, 50; Oxfam, above n 5, 40 and 82–3; Bob Hepple, *Labour Laws and Global Trade* (Hart, Oxford, 2005) 17.

Finally, developing economies based on mineral or energy resources seem to have been afflicted by the so-called 'resource curse', whereby such States have suffered from conflict (as groups fight for control of the territory containing the resources), corrupt politics[201] (partially fed by MNCs bargaining for control over the resources),[202] disconnection from other parts of the economy leading to uneven development and inequality,[203] overinflated currencies which harm other exports,[204] and volatile prices.[205]

A developing State will be a very vulnerable player in the global economy if its comparative advantages lie solely in primary commodities and low-skilled manufacturing, which is the situation of most developing States.[206] Their prospects for sustained economic growth are not high without a path to significant diversification.

As noted by Mehdi Shafaeddin, a former economist for the United Nations Conference on Trade and Development (UNCTAD), the theory of comparative advantage, which underlies the promotion of swift liberalization, does not explain how underdeveloped States, or 'latecomers', can upgrade their economies so as to properly 'catch up'.[207] The economist Yong-Shik Lee adds:

Despite the brilliance of the market economic theory developed by Adam Smith and accepted and elaborated by subsequent economists, it is intrinsically difficult to understand *how* economies in the relatively primitive stages, depending heavily on the production of primary products, can build industries that would yield higher income without some deliberative effort on the part of the government, particularly when the private sectors lack both resources and information to do so.[208]

Ha-Joon Chang adds that Ricardo's theory is 'absolutely right' for States that are willing to accept their 'current levels of technology as given', but that the theory fails where States wish to 'acquire more advanced technologies' and develop their economies.[209]

Free trade theory focuses on static comparative advantages, which are of low quality in many developing States, rather than dynamic comparative advantages, those that are created by targeted economic policies, and provides no means for a State to graduate from the former to the latter and broaden its industrial base.[210] Underdeveloped industries are not able to compete in a free market with developed industries from overseas, and are not able to develop in the absence of protection.

---

[201] See Collier, above n 27, 44–50.   [202] Stiglitz, above n 87, 138–44.
[203] Collier, above n 27, 81.
[204] See ibid, 39–40, explaining this aspect of the resource curse, known as the 'Dutch disease' after the effect of North Sea gas on the Dutch economy in the 1960s: resource exports caused the local currency to rise against foreign currencies, rendering other exports less competitive. See also Stiglitz, above n 87, 147–9.   [205] Wolf, above n 123, 147; Collier, above n 27, 40–1.
[206] UNDP, above n 64, 118–19; Oxfam, above n 5, 62, 71–3, 75, and 77.
[207] Shafaeddin, above n 183, 12; see also Chang, above n 85, 126.
[208] Lee, above n 33, 54.   [209] Chang, above n 84, 47.
[210] SM Shafaeddin, 'Towards an Alternative Perspective on Trade and Industrial Policies' (2005) 36 *Development and Change* 1143, 1145–6.

Infant industry protection

An alternative path to swift trade liberalization is that of infant industry protection. This strategy involves the temporary protection and development of select industries by government policies (for example, regarding tariffs and subsidies). Those industries are gradually exposed to greater competition until they near maturity, when liberalization is feasible and even necessary to ensure competitive and innovative practices.[211] Indeed, the economist Ha-Joon Chang reports how Adam Smith himself advised the newly independent US to focus on agriculture rather than protect its nascent manufacturers from European competition. Smith's advice was not followed. Instead, high tariff barriers were erected to protect US manufacturing.[212] The US is of course now the world's major industrialized nation. Chang confidently asserts that 'the US economy would not have got where it is today without strong tariff protection at least in some key infant industries'.[213]

Infant industry protection ideally takes place in stages, with the first stage industries leading to diversification into second stage industries, which again need to benefit from a period of protection, and so on. For example, a State might choose to protect the production of textiles, and then diversify into the higher value and higher skilled arena of textile machinery.[214] An example of successful infant industry protection, which led to the creation of significant industrial capacity and comparative advantage in a cutting edge industry, is that of Brazil's aerospace industry.[215] Oxfam cites Mauritius as another State which has successfully and recently adopted infant industry policies.[216]

Indeed, all successful industrializers went through a phase of protecting infant industries, with the exceptions of the city territory of Hong Kong,[217] Chile,[218] and perhaps, in the nineteenth century, Switzerland and the Netherlands.[219] In contrast, premature liberalization has generated de-industrialization and disappointing economic outcomes. The US for example reverted to protectionism to protect its industries from the UK after a period of ill-considered liberalization between 1847 and 1861.[220] The free trade mantra that is being foisted upon developing States through the WTO and other institutions is a clear case of: 'do as we say, not as we did'.[221]

Colonies, which had liberal economies forced upon them by colonizers, experienced sluggish economies and de-industrialization. The economic situation was exacerbated by colonial policies which discouraged competition with the colonizer and the upgrading of industrial capacities beyond primary production.[222] The

---

[211] Shafaeddin, above n 183, 63.   [212] Chang, above n 85, 5.   [213] Ibid, 61.

[214] Shafaeddin, above n 210, outlines the process of infant industry protection at 1152–4.

[215] Shafaeddin, above n 183, Chapter 8. See, eg, the website for Embraer-Empresa Brasilia de Aeronáutica S.A. <http://www.embraer.com/english/content/home/> accessed 22 September 2010.

[216] Oxfam, 'Partnership or Power Play? How Europe should bring Development into its trade deals with African, Caribbean, and Pacific countries' (Oxfam Briefing Paper 110, 21 April 2008) 12.

[217] Shafaeddin, above n 183, 20.   [218] Chang, above n 84, 28.

[219] See, generally, Chang, above n 85, esp at 18, 60, 64 and 127.

[220] Shafaeddin, above n 183, 21. See also Chang, above n 85, 27 and 30.

[221] Chang, above n 84, 16.   [222] Shafaeddin, above n 183, 22; Chang, above n 85, 51–3.

trend of negative growth in the colonies was only reversed after 1880, when they regained some policy autonomy and introduced protectionist measures.[223] It has been estimated that this period of tight colonial control retarded the growth of the manufacturing sector in the developing world by 85 to 95 per cent.[224]

States should therefore target and nurture niche industries to facilitate the development of dynamic and sustainable comparative advantages.[225] As noted, all developed States built their industries and developed their comparative advantages on the back of protectionist policies prior to their current states of liberalization.[226] The same is true of the 'tiger economies' of South East Asia.[227] For example, had South Korea freed up its economy 35 years ago, it would probably be a poor country specializing in the production of rice.[228] Instead it protected its steel and automobile industries from competition until they were able to withstand it. It is now an acknowledged success story of globalization.[229] Similarly, Rodrik notes:

[T]he Republic of Korea and Taiwan freely resorted to unorthodox strategies: they protected the home markets to raise profits, implemented generous export subsidies, encouraged their firms to reverse engineer foreign patented products and imposed performance requirements such as export-import balance requirements and domestic content requirements on foreign investors (when foreign companies were allowed in).[230]

In contrast, Mexico has failed to significantly upgrade or diversify its industrial capacities after over two decades of liberalization.[231]

It is therefore legitimate for developing States, in their own self interest, to resist pressure towards rapid liberalization. However, many of the strategies used to build successful industries, which have catalysed high quality growth in certain East Asian economies, are now restricted or banned under WTO rules.[232] For example, targeted protectionism via tariffs is illegal under GATT while subsidies are prohibited or actionable under the Agreement on Subsidies and Countervailing Measures (SCM).[233] Reverse engineering is illegal under TRIPS and domestic content requirements for foreign investors are outlawed under TRIMS and probably GATT.[234] Rodrik has summarized the situation by stating that '[t]he exchange

---

[223] Shafaeddin, above n 183, 22.

[224] Ibid, 23–4, citing P Bairoch, *Economic and World History* (Brighton, Wheatsheaf, 1993) 88.

[225] Rodrik, above n 78; Oxfam, above n 5, 233. World Commission on the Social Dimension of Globalisation, above n 191, xiii.

[226] Oxfam, above n 5, 26; World Commission on the Social Dimension of Globalisation, above n 191, para 362.

[227] Thomas, above n 145, 1406; Oxfam, above n 5, 147. See also UNDP, above n 90, 146.

[228] Joseph Stiglitz, 'Social Justice and Global Trade' (2006) 169 *Far Eastern Economic Review* 18, 19. See also Lee, above n 33, 7–8.

[229] World Commission on the Social Dimension of Globalisation, above n 191, paras 364–5.

[230] Rodrik, above n 78; Oxfam, above n 5, 147 and 233; Thomas, above n 145, 1406.

[231] Shafaeddin, above n 183, Chapter 7, esp at 58. See also Stiglitz and Charlton, above n 18, 24; Chang, above n 84, 68.

[232] Rodrik, above n 78, 19; Oxfam, above n 5, 233.   [233] Shafaeddin, above n 86, 12–13.

[234] See also Michael H Davis and Dana Neacsu, 'Legitimacy, Globally: The Incoherence of Free Trade Practice, Global Economics, and the Governing Principles of Political Economy' (2001) 69 *University of Missouri Kansas City Law Review* 733, 777–8.

of reduced policy autonomy in the South for improved market access in the North is a bad bargain where development is concerned'.[235]

Finally, as wryly noted by Shafaeddin:

[a] long period (20 years) of infant-industry protection of new technologies and new products is allowed under the TRIPS Agreement, but temporary infant-industry protection of new industries, or new export activities, in developing countries is not allowed.[236]

Shafaeddin's contention reveals pertinent hypocrisy in the current WTO regime. IP rights provide infant industry protection to innovative products, where the North has a comparative advantage. Beneficiaries receive this protection regardless of whether they are vulnerable entities in actual need of protection in order to thrive in the global marketplace. As noted in Chapter 7, the pharmaceutical industry is a major beneficiary of IP rights even though it was extraordinarily profitable before and certainly after the advent of TRIPS. The same type of protection is not available in the South to the infant industries they might wish to protect, such as promising yet underdeveloped domestic industries, which are far more likely to be entities that will die without protection.

Article XVIII:7 GATT permits developing States to modify their tariff schedules 'in order to promote the establishment of a particular industry', thus providing for a limited infant industry exception. The modification of tariffs however does not address some of the other policy restrictions outlined above. Furthermore, a State must negotiate with affected Members and provide compensation to them in order to utilize this exception. Negotiation can take considerable time, entailing significant delays, while the provision of compensation is burdensome and therefore a disincentive for developing States.[237] No State has made use of this exception, indicating that it is not an adequate proviso regarding infant industries.[238]

Conclusion

A gradual sequenced approach to liberalization in underdeveloped States, incorporating the development of appropriate institutional capacities and dynamic niche markets, is preferable to the reduced policy space entailed in rapid and potentially premature liberalization.[239] A gradual approach allows a State to prepare for and absorb the inevitable adjustments of trade liberalization.[240] The UNDP has stated:

The starting point should be the recognition that the purpose of multilateralism is not to impose common rules or a free market blueprint on all countries with different

---

[235] Rodrik, above n 78, 27.
[236] Shafaeddin, above n 86, 19   [237] Lee, above n 33, 31.
[238] Van den Bossche, above n 41, 678.
[239] UNDP, above n 64, 135; Dani Rodrik, 'Trading in Illusions' (March/April 2005) *Foreign Policy* 55. See also Rodrik, above n 136, and Robert Driskill, 'Deconstructing the arguments for free trade' (February 2007) 15–16 <http://www.vanderbilt.edu/econ/faculty/Driskill/DeconstructingfreetradeAug27a2007.pdf> accessed 22 September 2010.
[240] Rodrik, above n 78, 24; Oxfam, above n 5, 139, 145, 241 and 246; Ben-David and others, above n 49, 61–2. See also World Development Report 2006, above n 58, 179.

approaches and different levels of development, but to accept the case for diverse public policies.[241]

Hence, developing States should be granted significant policy autonomy to be able to develop their economies.

Stiglitz and Charlton have suggested that all States, including developing States, should be required to open up to developing States which are 'poorer and smaller than themselves'.[242] Adoption of this proposal would depart from a core tenet of the WTO, the principle of MFN. It would accord with the human rights version of the principle of non-discrimination (as opposed to the trade version), which dictates that unequals need not (and sometimes must not) be treated equally. In any case, MFN is already considerably undermined by the spider's web of bilateral and regional free trade agreements and by the GSP. The Stiglitz/Charlton proposal would avoid some of the problems of free trade agreements, discussed in Chapter 9, and the arbitrariness of the GSP, under which development policy is driven too much by developed States.

The Stiglitz/Charlton proposal would help to increase burgeoning South/South trade. Indeed, lesser policy autonomy is needed for emerging economies, such as China and India, but such States cannot be treated as if they are already developed: both States contain massive populations of poor people, and remain far poorer than the States of the North. They should be entitled, like their Northern competitors in previous decades and centuries, to continue to adopt 'catch up' policies.[243] However, the required policy space for developing States is not currently permitted under WTO rules or envisaged under current Doha proposals.[244]

There are of course economic arguments against such proposals. Greater policy space for developing States could undermine their resolve to innovate and create competitive industries.[245] Infant industry protection may result in costly failure as governments might choose the wrong industries to protect, or be convinced by local vested interests to simply protect all industries with across-the-board policies of import substitution. States might find it politically difficult to wind down protection when it is no longer needed,[246] leading to 'complacency and sloth'.[247] In short, governments may well be too inept and corrupt to manage the infant industry process.[248]

---

[241] UNDP, above n 64, 135.

[242] Stiglitz and Charlton, above n 18, 94; see also 95–103.   [243] Wade, above n 74, 631.

[244] Wolf, above n 123, concedes that current WTO rules may place 'unreasonable constraints' on the 'policy discretion' of developing States at 204. At 211–12, he states that infant industry arguments should be re-examined in the context of WTO obligations.

[245] Cottier, above n 34, 788; Fernando R Tesón and Jonathan Klick, 'Global Justice and Trade: a Puzzling Omission' (2007) *FSU College of Law, Public Law Research Paper No. 285, FSU College of Law, Law and Economics Paper No. 07-24*, 28 <http://papers.ssrn.com/sol3/papers.cfm?abstract_id=1022996> accessed 22 September 2010.

[246] See Van den Bossche, above n 41, 26.   [247] Chang, above n 84, 66.

[248] Daniel J Gifford and Robert J Kudrle, 'Trade and Competition Policy in the Developing World' in Thomas and Trachtman (eds), above n 75, 395 at 411. See also David M Trubek and M Patrick Cottrell, 'Robert Hudec and the Theory of International Economic Law' in Thomas and Trachtman (eds), above n 75, 129 at 145.

Many economists believe that the widespread use of protectionist policies by developing States, particularly in Latin America, in the 1950s and 1960s, have discredited the infant industry argument. Those policies led to false dawns in terms of economic growth until the early 1970s, but those economies flat-lined in the 1970s and crashed in the 1980s.[249] However, there were possible alternative causes for the 1980s crises, such as 'exogenous factors independent of domestic politics', debt policies or capital market policies.[250] In this respect, Stiglitz and Charlton point out that all Latin American economies failed in the 1980s, even those that had not pursued infant industry policies.[251] Furthermore, just as the crises of the 1980s prompted the discrediting of infant industry protection and the global promotion of neo-liberal policies, perhaps the Great Financial Crisis of 2008–2009 has discredited those latter policies, especially given the massive levels of government intervention, generally anathema to neoliberal policies, which ensued to steady the economic ship.[252] The fact is that the automatic discrediting of policies due to large scale economic crises is simplistic as numerous causes have probably contributed to the crises of the 1980s and the late 2000s.

Government failure in the management of the infant industry process is of course possible. Indeed, an absence of failures would probably indicate that infant industry policies are overly timid.[253] More concerning perhaps is the possibility of corruption or weak political will in removing industry protections. In this regard, Rodrik has suggested that the dangers of government abuse of policy space could be tempered by the placement of procedural conditions on States. In particular, protectionist policies should be targeted, maintained and reduced by an open and transparent process within a State, to help to ensure against undue influence by influential sectors at the expense of society at large.[254] Furthermore the capacities of many of today's underdeveloped States are no worse than those of war-torn South Korea in the 1950s, so replication of that country's success is possible,[255] at least in the absence of certain WTO rules. Ironically, proponents of free trade do not tend to cite government ineptitude as a reason to delay trade liberalization, even though such ineptitude undermines a State's ability to benefit from liberalization, and certainly undermines its ability to safeguard the rights of those displaced from their livelihoods by such liberalization. As noted in Chapter 8, corruption can arise during the process of opening up markets as well as in the process of regulating markets.[256]

The varying scenarios for underdeveloped States arising from the restoration of policy space to facilitate potential protectionism contrast with the extreme

---

[249] Wolf, above n 123, 130–1; Stiglitz and Charlton, above n 18, 19–20.

[250] Stiglitz and Charlton, above n 18, 21.   [251] Ibid, 22.

[252] See also Joseph Stiglitz, *Freefall: Free Markets and the Sinking of the Global Economy* (Allen Lane, London, 2010) 222.

[253] Stiglitz and Charlton, above n 18, 37; see also 90.

[254] Dani Rodrik, *One Economics, Many Recipes: Globalization, Institutions, and Economic Growth* (Princeton, Princeton University Press, 2008) 231. See also Trubek and Cottrell, above n 248, 145–6; Stiglitz and Charlton, above n 18, 38.

[255] Shafaeddin, above n 86, 44.   [256] See also Chapter 8, text at notes 76–84.

likelihood that premature liberalization will destroy underdeveloped yet promising industries 'without necessarily leading to the emergence of new ones'.[257] Rapid liberalization forces developing States to continue specializing in low growth primary production and unskilled labour at the bottom of the development ladder while industrialized States specialize in high value manufactured and technological commodities and services. The most vulnerable developing States may specialize in 'losing' while developed States specialize in 'winning'.[258] It also denies developing States the policy space, and the room to dictate industrial policy and even to make mistakes, which was enjoyed by now-developed States during their own path to development.[259]

At the same time, the general benefits of market access for the South to the North are clear. An optimal outcome for the South from future WTO negotiations is therefore true asymmetry, arguably reflecting the intended spirit of the Enabling Clause of 1979, as well as certain sentiments in the preamble to the Marrakesh Agreement.[260] Implementation of the current SDT provisions are however premised on the South continuing to 'move forward' on liberalization, when a pause or even a reversal in that regard would be more beneficial for many States.[261] As noted by Shafaeddin, SDT should be a rule rather than an exception within the WTO, at least at this point in time given the huge inequalities in economic capacities among States.[262]

F. Developing States, the WTO, and Human Rights

Current WTO rules undoubtedly favour the interests of the North over the South, which undermines the WTO's capacity to alleviate poverty, as its rules favour the richest nations on earth. Even worse, adherence to current WTO rules is counterproductive in some situations for the development of the economy of developing States. Indeed, the Uruguay round reportedly delivered 70 per cent of its benefits to developed States,[263] while some of the poorest States in the world were net losers.[264] In such circumstances, it might be argued that WTO rules are preventing those States from fulfilling their human rights obligations, thus generating or at least contributing to human rights violations by those States. WTO rules may be removing or weakening essential policy levers needed to pursue development

---

[257] Shafaeddin, above n 183, 66.
[258] See Olivier De Schutter, *International Trade in Agriculture and the Right to Food* (Dialogue on Globalization Occasional Paper No 46) (Friedrich Ebert Stiftung, Geneva, 2009) 22, citing Eduardo Galeano, *Las venas abiertas de América Latina*, xxi Siglo Veintuno de Espana, 1971.
[259] See also Lee, above n 33, 159; Stiglitz and Charlton, above n 18, 89.
[260] Collier, above n 27, 171 recommends 'an *unreciprocated* reduction in trade barriers against the bottom billion' (emphasis in the original).
[261] See Breining-Kaufman, above n 102, 373–6, on the need for 'affirmative action' or 'positive discrimination' within the WTO. See also Thomas Pogge, 'Priorities of Global Justice' (2001) 32 *Metaphilosophy* 6, 13.
[262] Shafaeddin, above n 210, 1159.   [263] Stiglitz, above n 87, 78.
[264] Stiglitz and Charlton, above n 18, 47.

goals, in order to fulfil the right to development and economic social and cultural rights.[265]

For example, the generation of further unemployment in some developing States, through de-industrialization brought about premature trade liberalization represents a retrogressive step with regard to the right to work in Article 6 of the ICESCR. The right to work does not equate with an unconditional right to be employed,[266] especially given that it is a progressive right. Instead, States should adopt, 'as quickly as possible, measures aiming at achieving full employment'.[267] As with all ICESCR rights, retrogressive measures, such as those which increase unemployment, are a presumptive breach of Article 6.[268] The introduction of liberalizing measures which squeeze out local industries by opening up economies to well-financed offshore competitors, leading to unemployment in many underdeveloped States because there are few alternative industries for workers to migrate to, is such a regressive measure. A classical economic response to this argument would be to say that further jobs will be created in the long term through liberalization. However, further jobs could perhaps be saved in the short term without sacrificing long term societal employment prospects by adopting policies of gradual liberalization along with well-targeted protectionism. The Committee on Economic, Social and Cultural Rights has stated, regarding Article 6:

The failure of States parties to take into account their legal obligations regarding the right to work when entering into bilateral or multilateral agreements with other States... constitutes a violation of their obligation to respect the right to work.[269]

Further detrimental human rights outcomes prompted by WTO rules, it will be argued, arise in the case of the right to food (Chapter 6) and the right to health (Chapter 7).

The previous paragraphs focus on the impact of WTO rules on the capacity of a State to fulfil its human rights obligations to persons within its territory.[270] An issue arises as to whether the North has any obligations to the South under human rights law to facilitate the creation of fairer WTO rules. This issue is discussed in Chapter 8.

---

[265] Robert E Robertson, 'Measuring State Compliance with the Obligation to Devote the "Maximum Available Resources" to Realizing Economic, Social, and Cultural Rights' (1994) 16 *Human Rights Quarterly* 693, 694. See also Olivier De Schutter, 'A Human Rights Approach to Trade and Investment Policies' in *The Global Food Challenge: Towards a Human Rights Approach to Trade and Investment Policies* (FIAN and others, 2009) 22.

[266] Committee on Economic Social and Cultural Rights, 'General Comment 18: The right to work (art. 6)', UN doc. E/C.12/GC/18 (6 February 2006) para 6.

[267] Ibid, para 19.   [268] See Chapter 1, text at notes 71–2.

[269] General Comment 18, above n 266, para 33.

[270] Note that human rights obligations are generally owed to all persons within territory and jurisdiction (see below, regarding jurisdiction), regardless of their nationality. That is, human rights are not confined to a State's citizens.

G. Conclusion

Current WTO rules are unfair to developing States. This unfairness is undermining the ability of the WTO to fulfil its mandate, mentioned in the WTO preamble, to improve living standards across the world. This statement is not controversial: the WTO Director-General, Pascal Lamy, has conceded as much. A more controversial proposition is that further liberalization across all States is not a panacea for alleviating ongoing poverty in developing States, as it could lead to premature liberalization. A preferable policy trajectory within the WTO is for policy space to be preserved and indeed restored to poorer States within the WTO, while markets for developing States within developed States are opened. Alas, as will be seen in Chapter 9, such proposals are not reflected in current Doha proposals.

6

The WTO and the Right to Food

In this chapter, the effect of WTO rules on the enjoyment of the right to food is examined. The human right to food will first be described, followed by an overview of current statistics regarding world hunger. The biased impact of current international trade rules on agricultural trade between developed and developing States, which was raised in Chapter 5, will be analysed in fuller detail. Problems regarding free trade and agriculture are then examined, such as the detrimental effects of volatile markets, cartels and specialization, and the alternative path of empowering small farmers is explored. The impact of TRIPS on the right to food is then analysed, before moving to the chapter's conclusions with recommendations for relevant WTO reforms.

Much of the analysis in this chapter focuses on whether WTO rules and free trade policies generally are producing or are likely to produce an environment in which States, particularly developing States, can discharge their obligations with regard to the right to food. Thus, the analysis largely concerns the instrumental relationship between WTO rules and free trade to human rights protection, rather than direct implementation of the right to food.

A. The Right to Food

The right to food is recognized in Article 11 of the ICESCR. Article 11(1) generally guarantees the right to an adequate standard of living for a person and his/her family, including 'adequate food'. States must take appropriate steps to realize the right, 'recognizing to this effect the essential importance of international cooperation based on free consent'. Article 11(2) specifically concerns the right to food and reads:

2. The States Parties to the present Covenant, recognizing the fundamental right of everyone to be free from hunger, shall take, individually and through international cooperation, the measures, including specific programmes, which are needed:
   (a) To improve methods of production, conservation and distribution of food by making full use of technical and scientific knowledge, by disseminating knowledge of the principles of nutrition and by developing or reforming agrarian systems in such a way as to achieve the most efficient development and utilization of natural resources;
   (b) Taking into account the problems of both food-importing and food-exporting countries, to ensure an equitable distribution of world food supplies in relation to need.

In General Comment 12, the Committee on Economic, Social and Cultural Rights confirmed that the right to food entails, for all, 'physical and economic access at all times to adequate food or means for its procurement'.[1] Food must be available in a quantity and of a quality 'sufficient to satisfy the dietary needs of individuals, free from adverse substances, and acceptable within a given culture'.[2] Availability means that food must be accessible 'either for feeding oneself directly from productive land or other natural resources, or for well functioning distribution, processing and market systems' which can ensure that food reaches those who need it, rather than only those who can afford it.[3]

As with all human rights, States must respect, protect, and fulfil the right to food. As with all economic, social, and cultural rights, there is a minimum core content to the right to food:[4] its core content essentially consists of ensuring that people within jurisdiction are 'free from hunger'.[5] If a State lacks the resources to guarantee this minimum standard, it must demonstrate that it has sought international assistance to 'ensure the availability and accessibility of the necessary food'.[6]

Of particular relevance to States as Members of the WTO, General Comment 12 states at paragraph 36:

States should recognize the essential role of international cooperation and comply with their commitment to take joint and separate action to achieve the full realization of the right to food. In implementing this commitment, States parties should take steps to respect the enjoyment of the right to food in other countries, to protect that right, to facilitate access to food and to provide the necessary aid when required. States parties should, in international agreements when relevant, ensure that the right to adequate food is given due attention and consider the development of further international legal instruments to that end.

General Comment 12 thus endorses the notion of extraterritorial obligations owed by a State to the people of another State. This notion is discussed in Chapter 8. Indeed, an obligation regarding international cooperation is stressed within Article 11 itself.

Related to the right to food is the concept of 'food security', which is defined by the FAO as follows:

Food security exists when all people, at all times, have physical, social and economic access to sufficient, safe and nutritious food to meet their dietary needs and food preferences for an active and healthy life.[7]

Enjoyment of food security is a key component of the right to food, to which the Committee has added a requirement that food be accessible for both present and future generations, is a key component of the right to food.[8]

---

[1] Committee on Economic, Social and Cultural Rights, 'General Comment 12: The right to adequate food (Art. 11)', UN doc. E/C.12/1999/5 (12 May 1999) para 6.
[2] Ibid, para 8.   [3] Ibid, para 12.   [4] See Chapter 1, text after note 81.
[5] General Comment 12, above n 1, para 17.   [6] Ibid.
[7] Rome Declaration on World Food Security and World Food Summit Plan of Action, 17 November 1996 (Rome, Italy).
[8] General Comment 12, above n 1, para 7.

Finally, national strategies regarding the right to food should be implemented in accordance with core human rights principles: 'accountability, transparency, people's participation, decentralization, legislative capacity and the independence of the judiciary'.[9] Thus, food policies should not be dictated or overly influenced by remote international bodies, or foreign countries, to which a State's people have little input.

General Comment 12 was essentially endorsed by the intergovernmental Council of the Food and Agricultural Organization (FAO) when it adopted the Voluntary Guidelines on the Right to Food.[10] Given its endorsement by governments, these Guidelines are vested with significant authoritative status.

World hunger statistics

As of 2009, the figures regarding world hunger are truly distressing. The *Millennium Development Goals Report* of 2009 stated that 17 per cent of the population in developing countries were undernourished (including 29 per cent of those in sub-Saharan Africa), while 26 per cent of children in the developing world are underweight.[11] Indeed, 'one third of child deaths worldwide are attributable to under-nutrition'.[12] Overall, more than a billion people live in hunger.[13]

This desperate picture was exacerbated by the advent of a World Food Crisis of 2007–2008. During this period world food prices soared due to a variety of factors. Oil price hikes caused rises in the prices of transportation, as well as agricultural inputs such as pesticides and fertilizers.[14] Commodities speculation caused price rises unrelated to the supply and demand of the agricultural commodities in question.[15] Increased production of biofuels, discussed below, led to diversion of food crops and therefore higher prices brought about by greater scarcity. Weather-related events, such as ongoing drought in Australia, a key grain producer, generated smaller grain harvests, again leading to higher prices.

The higher prices, ironically, could have assisted the poor as poor farmers might have been able to take advantage of the high selling prices. Indeed, large gains in food trade balances were experienced by Russia, Kazakhstan and Argentina, as well as some other developing States, particularly in South America and South-East Asia. However, large food trade imbalances arose in Africa and Southern Asia.[16] Most poor farmers were not in a position to take advantage of the opportunities

---

[9] Ibid, para 23.
[10] FAO, *Voluntary Guidelines to support the progressive realization of the right to adequate food in the context of national food security* (FAO, Rome, 2005) 5–7.
[11] UN, *The Millennium Development Goals Report 2009* (DESA, New York, 2009) 4, 11–12.
[12] Ibid, 12.
[13] See Olivier De Schutter, *International Trade in Agriculture and the Right to Food* (Dialogue on Globalization Occasional Paper No. 46) (Friedrich Ebert Stiftung, Geneva, 2009) 11.
[14] See Human Rights Council, 'Report of the Special Rapporteur on the right to food, Olivier De Schutter: Building resilience: a human rights framework for world food and nutrition security', UN doc. A/HRC/9/23 (8 September 2008) Annex 1, para 2.
[15] Peter Wahl, 'The Role of Speculation in the 2008 Food Price Bubble' in FIAN and others (eds), *The Global Food Challenge: Towards a Human Rights Approach to Trade and Investment Policies* (FIAN, Germany, 2009) 68–75.   [16] Report of the Special Rapporteur on the right to food, above n 14, 31.

afforded by higher produce prices due to an inability to afford necessary inputs, such as fertilizer and oil, and the suddenness of, and their consequent unpreparedness for, the price rises.[17] Rather, many farmers suffered in their capacity as consumers of food.

A real tragedy regarding hunger is that there is, presently, enough arable land to provide for food for everybody. In 2005, the then Special Rapporteur on the Right to Food, Jean Ziegler, stated:

According to the FAO, the planet could already produce enough food to provide 2,100 kcals per person per day to 12 billion people (double the existing world population).[18]

The pervasive nature of hunger and its spike during the World Food Crisis is and was not caused by a lack of food supply.[19] Certainly, serious threats to food supply, particularly in the form of climate change, loom large on the horizon.[20] Nevertheless, it is scandalous that vast numbers suffer and die of malnutrition while huge amounts of food are wasted. Large percentages of post-harvest crops spoil in developing States due to a lack of storage facilities and poor means of transport.[21] This anomaly regarding supply existing alongside hunger arises on an international and a national basis: India for example has a trade surplus in food and yet is home to 231 million starving people.[22] Given that the problem currently lies with distribution rather than supply, it is arguable that the MDGs, in aiming only to halve hunger by 2015, are outrageously under-ambitious.[23] The problem is that the hungry are generally unable to afford food at prevailing prices, and are therefore often bypassed in the food distribution chain. The solution is to find a way to deliver food to the hungry who cannot presently afford it, even if it is physically available.

However, this 'solution' is not as simple as it may appear, given that half of the undernourished are in fact smallholder farmers,[24] who have become or have remained poor due to poor prices for their produce and an inability to take

---

[17] Ibid, para 28.
[18] Commission on Human Rights, 'Report of the Special Rapporteur on the right to food, Jean Ziegler', UN doc. E/CN.4/2005/47 (24 January 2005) para 5.
[19] FIAN and others, above n 15, Introduction, 3.
[20] See International Assessment of Agricultural Knowledge, Science and Technology for Development (IAAKSTD), *Agriculture at the Crossroads* (IAAKSTD, Washington DC, 2009) 35–43.
[21] See Peggy Oti-Boateng, *Losses and Wastes in the Food Chain* (FAO, Rome, 2001). A study from the University of Arizona from 2004 indicates that 40–50% of food which is ready for harvest in the US is wasted, as is 14% of household food purchases. See Jeff Harrison, 'Study: Nation Wastes Nearly Half its Food', *UA News*, 18 November 2004 <http://uanews.org/node/10448> accessed 22 September 2010. See also Carin Smaller and Sophia Murphy, *Bridging the Divide: a human rights vision for global food trade* (Institute of Agriculture and Trade Policy, Geneva, 2008) 5.
[22] WTO, 'Trade liberalization and the right to food' (Forum debate) transcript available via <http://www.wto.org/english/forums_e/debates_e/debate14_e.htm> accessed 22 September 2010.
[23] See Thomas Pogge, 'Growth and Inequality: Understanding Recent Trends and Political Choices' (2008) *Dissent* <http://www.dissentmagazine.org/article/?article=990> accessed 20 September 2010.
[24] Special Rapporteur on the Right to Food, above n 14, n 8, citing UN Millennium Project, *Halving Hunger: It can be done, summary version of the report of the task force on hunger* (The Earth

advantage of sporadic higher prices (such as those available in 2007–2008). The current Special Rapporteur on the Right to Food, Olivier De Schutter, recently described smallholders as 'the single most important group of those who are food insecure in the world today'.[25] In order to preserve the interests and rights of those farmers, any delivery of food in the form, for example, of food aid or unduly cheap exports must not be done in such a way as to deprive such farmers of viable markets in which to earn their livelihoods.

B. Trade and Food

In order to examine the effect of international trade rules on the right to food, it is necessary to first analyse its effect in the agricultural arena, the source of food.

WTO agricultural rules

As noted in Chapter 5, WTO rules presently permit developed States to protect their agricultural markets to the detriment of those in developing States by way of high tariffs and continued subsidies. These issues are further discussed below. These issues are instrumentally related to human rights protection, as they impact on the capacity of States to fulfil their obligations regarding the right to food.

Agriculture was excluded from GATT until the adoption of the Agreement on Agriculture (AoA) in 1995 as part of the WTO package. For several decades prior to 1995, the EU and US in particular had extensively subsidized their agricultural industries, largely in competition with each other.[26] Developing States used different mechanisms to intervene and support their own agricultural sectors. However, these programmes were forcibly dismantled from the 1980s onwards due to loan conditionalities imposed by the IMF and World Bank, the international financial institutions (IFIs). During the Uruguay round negotiations, the EC and US were largely concerned with and influenced by each other: the interests of the developing world were a back seat concern.

All this meant that the WTO's AoA was primarily designed to accommodate the agricultural trade interests of the major industrialized countries. It hardly addressed the specific needs of developing countries with food security problems, including the need to support and promote agriculture.[27]

Institute, Columbia University, 2005) 6. Those figures state that 50% of the hungry are smallholders, 20% are landless, 10% are pastoralists, fisherfolk and forest users, and 20% live in urban areas.

[25] See Human Rights Council, 'Report of the Special Rapporteur on the Right to Food, Olivier De Schutter: Agribusiness and the Right to Food', UN doc. A/HRC/13/33 (22 December 2009) para 28.

[26] Tobias Reichert, 'Agricultural Trade Liberalization in Multilateral and Bilateral Trade Negotiations' in FIAN and others, above n 15, 31.

[27] Ibid, 31. See also Martin Wolf, *Why Globalisation Works* (Yale Nota Bene, London, 2005) 216.

The AoA contains the following provisions regarding the troublesome issue of subsidies. Developed states are permitted to provide support for 5 per cent of the total value of agricultural goods per annum, while developing States are permitted to provide support for 10 per cent of such product. Few developing States can afford to reach their minimum threshold, while all developed States can.[28] Beyond those minimum thresholds, members are obliged to reduce levels of support for domestic agriculture, known as Aggregate Measures of Support (AMS) or 'amber box' measures. Developed States had to reduce domestic support by 20 per cent, and developing States had to reduce such subsidies by 13.3 per cent, from the levels of support provided in 1986–1988. No WTO member can introduce new types of domestic support. These rules in fact benefit developed States, which had much greater levels of domestic support during that base period.[29] Export subsidies must be reduced, and new export subsidies cannot be introduced if they did not exist in a base period of 1986–1990. As developing States did not have export subsidies in this period, they are precluded from introducing such subsidies yet they must tolerate competition from subsidized agricultural exports from developed countries.[30]

Some types of support, known as 'blue box' or 'green box' subsidies, are exempt from AoA rules so there are no obligations to reduce them. Blue box subsidies are amber box subsidies coupled with a condition that recipient farmers limit their production, so they should discourage overproduction which distorts world trade. Developing States cannot generally afford such subsidies, and there is no restriction on exporting blue box products.[31] Green box subsidies are deemed to be non-trade distorting or minimally trade distorting, and must comply with conditions in Annex 2 of the AoA. Such subsidies may for example be designed to promote agricultural research, food security, environmental protection, and rural infrastructure. They may also involve 'decoupled' direct payments to and income support for farmers, that is payments that are not linked to production rates. The blue and green boxes have proven controversial as it is argued that these subsidies in fact have significant protectionist effects,[32] and that the EU and the US in particular have manipulated the box designations to maintain current spending levels.[33] Indeed, while AMS measures have reduced significantly since the advent of the AoA, no significant reduction is evident when using the alternative OECD measurement of protectionist support measures, the production support estimate (PSE).[34]

---

[28] Human Rights Council, 'Report of the Special Rapporteur on the right to food, Olivier De Schutter: Mission to the World Trade Organization', UN doc. A/HRC/10/5/Add.2 (25 June 2008) para 11; FAO, *The State of Food and Agriculture: Agricultural Trade and Poverty—Can Trade Work for the Poor?* (FAO, Rome, 2005) 31–2.

[29] Caroline Dommen, 'Raising Human Rights Concerns in the World Trade Organization: Actors, Processes and Possible Strategies' (2002) 24 *Human Rights Quarterly* 1, 35; Report of the Special Rapporteur on the right to food, above n 28, para 11.

[30] Report of the Special Rapporteur on the right to food, above n 28, para 13.

[31] De Schutter, above n 13, 14.   [32] FAO, above n 28, 8 and 32.

[33] See, generally, Ricardo Meléndez-Ortiz, Christophe Bellmann, and Jonathan Hepburn (eds), *Agricultural Subsidies in the Green Box* (Cambridge University Press, Cambridge, 2009).

[34] FAO, above n 28, 30–1. See also Wolf, above n 27, 216; Joseph E Stiglitz and Andrew Charlton, *Fair Trade for All* (Oxford University Press, New York, 2005) 50.

Amber box measures will be likely to be significantly reduced upon conclusion of the Doha round, and a timetable laid out for elimination of export subsidies. However, trade distortions will remain due to continued use and abuse of the green and blue boxes, as there are no serious indications that those boxes will be disciplined after the Doha round. Doha round proposals are discussed in Chapter 8.

The AoA does not combat 'tariff escalation'.[35] Processed agricultural commodities are subjected to higher 'escalating' tariffs than raw or primary goods. The UNDP in 2005 reported:

In Japan tariffs on processed food products are 7 times higher than on first-stage products; in Canada they are 12 times higher.[36]

Tariff escalation encourages developing States to concentrate on primary agrarian production, while further refinement and processing of products takes place elsewhere. A large component of the price of commodities such as coffee and cocoa reflects post-harvest processing such as roasting of coffee beans or grinding of cocoa, which largely occurs in richer countries.[37] This perverse tariff structure discourages nations from developing secondary agricultural industries and higher level industrial capacities.[38] Essentially, tariff escalation helps to prevent, and is arguably designed to prevent, developing States from climbing the ladder of development.[39]

The AoA rules permit the North to protect its agricultural markets from competitive growers in the South through the use of high tariffs and subsidies. Worse still, Northern protectionism deprives Southern agriculture of other markets, and even competes, unfairly, with local farmers in their own markets. For example, Wouter Vandenhole has written a compelling case for the harm caused in developing States by EU sugar subsidies which have not only blocked imports from developing States, but have also caused overproduction, so sugar is exported to developing States, destroying local markets.[40]

Overproduced subsidized Northern produce are one of the main causes of import surges, which hurt local producers as they reduce demand and lower prices.[41] A study by the South Centre of import surges in 56 developing States found that 16 per cent of agricultural imports were imported under a surge. The

---

[35] J Hunter, 'Broken Promises: Agriculture and Development in the WTO' (2003) 4 *Melbourne International Law Journal* 299, 311.

[36] United Nations Development Programme (UNDP), *Human Development Report 2005: International Cooperation at a Crossroads: Aid, Trade and Security in an Unequal World* (UNDP, New York, 2005) 127.

[37] IAAKSTD, above n 20, 459; Oxfam, *Rigged Rules and Double Standards* (Oxfam, London, 2002) 161.

[38] Hunter, above n 35, 312. See also Oxfam, above n 37, 102–3.

[39] De Schutter, above n 13, 13. See also Wolf, above n 27, 213–14; Stiglitz and Charlton, above n 34, 125.

[40] Wouter Vandenhole, 'Third states obligations under the ICESCR: a case study of EU sugar policy' (2007) 76 *Nordic Journal of International Law* 73. See also Report of the Special Rapporteur on the right to food, Jean Ziegler, above n 18, para 51.

[41] Martin Khor, 'Implications of some WTO rules on the Realisation of the MDGs' *Third World Network Trade & Development Series 26* (TWN, Malaysia, 2005) 17–18.

surges disproportionately affected the poorest States: surges affected 23 per cent of agricultural imports in LDCs and 21 per cent of imports in Small and Vulnerable Economies.[42] The frequency of surges is also confirmed in the Import Surge Briefs of the FAO.[43]

The AoA is probably not the main reason why developing States are unable to combat import surges. The tariff bindings for agricultural products in developing States are generally in the very high band of 50 to 100 per cent,[44] though the bound rates for acceding States are far lower.[45] Since the 1980s, IFI conditionality has forced many developing States to maintain far lower applied rates to their Uruguay round bound rates. Since the 1990s, regional and bilateral trade treaties have also imposed stronger constraints on developing States.[46] Indeed, the IMF has intervened to prevent the defensive raising of tariffs to combat these surges.[47] Current Doha proposals would effectively remove flexibility from many developing States.[48]

Unfair trade measures which harm local markets under the WTO may be challenged under the provisions regarding dumping (Article VI GATT and the Agreement on Implementation of Article VI of the General Agreement on Tariffs and Trade 1994). 'Dumping' arises where goods are exported at a lower price than their normal value, causing injury to the competing local industries. However, the export and local prices of a product may well be the same if all of its production is subsidized. In any case, dumping rules have proven to be too cumbersome and complicated to provide an appropriate remedy for developing States against import surges.[49] The complexity of dumping rules plays into the hands of developed States, who have the expertise and facilities to comply with the requirements for anti-dumping measures.[50]

A more promising defensive route for developing States, perhaps, is to use the Agreement on Subsidies and Countervailing Measures (SCM) to combat subsidies.[51] The SCM prohibits certain subsidies and renders other subsidies 'actionable' if they cause injury to local industry. Under Article 13 of the AoA, subsidies

[42] South Centre, *The Extent of Agricultural Import Surges in Developing Countries: What are the Trends?* (November 2009, Geneva).

[43] These papers are available via <http://www.fao.org/corp/google_result/en/?cx=01817062 0143 701104933%3Aqq82jsfba7w&q=import+surges&cof=FORID%3A9#1075> accessed 22 September 2010.

[44] Reichert, above n 26, 32.   [45] Ibid, 32.

[46] Ibid, 33. See also Chapter 9, text at note 72–90.

[47] Armin Paasch, 'World Agricultural Trade and Human Rights: Case Studies on Violations of the Right to Food of Small Farmers' in FIAN and others, above n 15, 39, cites at 43–4 the example of Ghana in 2003, which was apparently convinced by the IMF not to raise its rice tariff from 20% to 25% to combat an import surge, even though the higher rate was well under its WTO tariff binding.

[48] Reichert, above n 26, 36. See Chapter 9, Part B.

[49] Smaller and Murphy, above n 21, 18.

[50] In fact, there are many examples of anti-dumping measures by developed States breaching WTO law—see, *United States—Laws, Regulations and Methodology for Calculating Dumping Margins (zeroing)*, WTO docs. WT/DS294/R (31 October 2005) (Report of the Panel) and WT/DS294/AB/R, Ab-2006-2 (18 April 2006) (Report of the Appellate Body). It must be noted, however, that China and especially India have become more avid users of anti-dumping measures in the manufacturing context: Peter Van den Bossche, *The Law and Policy of the World Trade Organization* (Cambridge University Press, Cambridge, 2005) 513–14.

[51] See also Article XVI GATT.

which complied with AoA requirements were not subject to challenge under the SCM until 1 January 2004. That 'peace clause' has expired so agricultural subsidies are now challengeable under the SCM.

In 2006, a report was prepared for the US congress on the threat to US farm subsidies posed by the expiration of the peace clause. The report concluded that many of the subsidies were vulnerable, but added:

some trade specialists argue that numerous new WTO challenges of U.S. farm support are unlikely. They contend that challenges require intense effort, the financial costs are high, and the broader geopolitical consequences may far outweigh any potential trade gains. Few developing countries have the needed resources for a challenge. In addition, there is the inherent risk that, if the challenge fails, the effort could legitimize those very programs targeted for discipline.[52]

This author is not aware of any WTO case where agricultural subsidies have been found in breach of the SCM but not the AoA, so the expiration of the peace clause has not yet yielded substantive legal consequences. Therefore, the relationship between the complex requirements of a challenge under the SCM and the subsidies permitted under the AoA remains unclear. However, ongoing litigation by Canada in respect of US corn subsidies could yield some answers.[53] Furthermore, there are signs that some Northern countries are seeking a new peace clause in the Doha round in return for further reductions of amber box subsidies.[54]

In 2002, prior to expiry of the peace clause, Brazil successfully challenged certain US cotton subsidies in *United States—Subsidies on Upland Cotton*.[55] The relevant subsidies were found not to comply with AoA requirements and thus were not protected by the peace clause: they were consequently prohibited or actionable under the SCM. Similarly, EU sugar export subsidies were found in 2002 to breach AoA requirements in *EU—Export Subsidies on Sugar*.[56] However, in both cases, the relevant subsidy schemes were recast in attempts to technically comply with AoA and SCM requirements, causing continuing harm to foreign markets. Indeed, the US's 'corrective' measures have been found not to satisfy its obligations, so massive countermeasures by Brazil were authorized by an arbitrator in 2009,[57] many years after the launch of the litigation. The EU's sugar policies continue to harm

---

[52] Randy Schnepf and Jasper Womach, 'Potential Challenges to US Farm Subsidies in the WTO: a Brief Overview', *CRS Report for Congress* (25 October 2006) 2.

[53] *United States—Subsidies and other Domestic Support for Corn and other Agricultural Products*, WTO doc. WT/DS357/1 (8 January 2007) (Request for Consultations by Canada).

[54] See Chakravarthi Raghavan, 'Did Schwab mean the US to have a Peace Clause Plus?' *TWN Info Service on WTO and Trade Issues*, 24 July 2008.

[55] *United States—Subsidies on Upland Cotton*, WTO docs. WT/DS297/R (8 September 2004) (Report of the Panel) andWT/DS267/AB/R (3 March 2005) (Report of the Appellate Body).

[56] *European Communities—Export Subsidies on Sugar*, WTO docs. WT/DS265/AB/R, WT/DS266/AB/R and WT/DS283/AB/R, AB-2005-2 (28 April 2005) (Report of the Appellate Body). See Vandenhole, above n 40, 81.

[57] *United States—Subsidies on Upland Cotton—Recourse to Arbitration by the United States under Article 22.6 of the DSU and Article 4.11 of the SCM Agreement*, WTO doc. WT/DS267/ARB/1 and WT/DS267/ARB/2 (31 August 2009) (Decision by the Arbitrator). See also Chapter 3, text at n 78.

the livelihoods of cane farmers in the developing world.[58] The outcomes of these successful instances of litigation against Northern subsidies are not encouraging for developing States, especially the poorest who are incapable of retaliating with consequential countermeasures.[59]

Another protective measure that could perhaps be used against import surges is the use of safeguards under Article XIX GATT and the Agreement on Safeguards. Safeguards permit temporary restrictions on imports in order to give a competing local industry some time to adjust.[60] For a variety of reasons, these provisions have been of little use to protect developing States from subsidized imports. A State seeking to use a safeguard must prove that an unexpected surge of imports has caused serious harm to its like industry. In proving causation, that State must separate out harms caused by other factors, and explain why those other factors have not caused the harm sought to be remedied by the safeguard. These proof requirements are very onerous.[61] Furthermore, given the frequency of surges, it is difficult to maintain that they are unforeseen or unexpected. Finally, safeguards can only be imposed if trade compensation is given to affected States, which clearly restricts the capacities of poorer States to impose safeguards.

A special safeguards mechanism is contained in Article 5 of the AoA, whereby safeguards can be implemented without having to prove serious injury to local industry. However, it only applies to products that had been 'tariffied' (that is, subject to tariffs) prior to the AoA. As most developing States had used other protectionist mechanisms such as quotas, the safeguard is not available to them.[62] Only 39 WTO members, including 22 developing States, have reserved the right to use such safeguards.[63] They have rarely been used by developing States, possibly due to their rigid and overly complex nature.[64] In contrast, EU states have commonly used this safeguard mechanism.[65]

Doha negotiations stalled in July 2008 over proposals, particularly from India, regarding a new special safeguard mechanism (SSM) to protect food security and smallholder livelihoods in developing countries.[66] The main points of contention were the conditions that trigger the SSM, and the rate of protective tariffs that can be imposed under the SSM. The Hong Kong Ministerial Declaration

---

[58] See, generally, Vandenhole, above n 40.   [59] See Chapter 5, text at notes 116–17.

[60] Van den Bossche, above n 50, 633–4.

[61] Robert Howse and Ruti Teitel, 'Beyond the Divide: The Covenant on Economic, Social and Cultural Rights and the World Trade Organization' in Sarah Joseph, David Kinley, and Jeff Waincymer, *The World Trade Organization and Human Rights: Interdisciplinary Perspectives* (Edward Elgar, Cheltenham, 2009) 54–5; Aileen Kwa, 'African Countries and EPAs: do Agricultural Safeguards afford Adequate Protection?' (2008) 25 *South Centre Bulletin: Reflections and Foresights*.

[62] Dommen, above n 29, 36; Report of the Special Rapporteur, above n 28, para 23.

[63] WTO, 'Market Access: special agricultural safeguards (SSGs)' <http://www.wto.org/english/tratop_E/agric_e/negs_bkgrnd11_ssg_e.htm> accessed 22 September 2010.

[64] FAO, 'A Special Safeguard Mechanism for developing countries' (undated) (Trade Policy Briefs on issues related to WTO negotiations on agriculture, No 9) 2.

[65] South Centre, above n 42, 2.

[66] See *Bridges Daily Update,* Issue 10, 30 July 2008 <http://ictsd.net/> accessed 30 July 2008.

indicated that the trigger could relate to a surge of imports in terms of volume, which would affect demand, *or* a significant drop in the price of an agricultural import.[67] In July 2008, however, a draft put forward by WTO Director-General, Pascal Lamy seemed to link the two requirements, meaning that the SSM would rarely be applicable unless both conditions were present. Regarding the rate of protective tariffs which can be imposed under the SSM, the July draft introduced new and severe limits on the circumstances in which a tariff could rise above pre-Doha levels (that is, above the current tariff ceilings imposed after the Uruguay round).[68] There are no like requirements for use of the normal safeguard under the Safeguards Agreement. Indeed, many proposed constraints on the SSM, such as the proposal to limit it to no more than 2.5 per cent of tariff lines in a 12-month period, impose conditions above and beyond those applicable to normal safeguards.[69]

A final issue under WTO agricultural rules concerns the extent to which States can impose non-tariff barriers to trade under the TBT and especially the SPS Agreements. Smallholders are finding it increasingly difficult to comply with the SPS standards imposed by developed States.[70] At the same time, SPS standards are important in protecting the right to health of consumers. SPS standards should be negotiated fairly between North and South, and should not impose unduly rigorous standards.[71] This issue was discussed in Chapter 4.

Developed country subsidies predate the AoA. However, the AoA has not done enough to control those subsidies, representing a failure in the Uruguay bargain, given it was (along with the Agreement on Textiles and Clothing) the effective *quid pro quo* for the North in return for agreement by the South on GATS and TRIPS.[72] The AoA has reduced Northern subsidies, but they remain at very high levels, and current Doha round proposals suggest that subsidies will simply shift boxes rather than be effectively reduced. The structure of the AoA is on occasion blatantly unfair, for example in the use of arbitrary base periods for calculation periods which benefit the North. While tariffication of agricultural goods has not removed significant policy space for developing States, that policy space is constrained by IFI conditionality or other (bilateral and regional) arrangements: remaining

---

[67] WTO, 'Ministerial Declaration' (Adopted on 18 December 2005, Hong Kong), WTO doc. WT/MIN(05)/DEC (22 December 2005) para 7.

[68] Martin Khor, 'Analysis of the new WTO Agricultural and NAMA texts of 6 December 2008' *Third World Network Trade & Development Series 37* (TWN, Malaysia, 2009) para 14. See also Reichert, above n 26, 36.

[69] Khor, above n 68, paras 15–16.

[70] UNGA, 'Report of the Special Rapporteur on the Right to Food, Olivier De Schutter', UN doc. A/63/278 (21 October 2008) para 22; Joachin von Braun, 'Small-Scale Farmers in Liberalised Trade Environment' in Tiina Huvio, Jukka Kola, and Tor Lundström (eds), *Small Scale Farmers in Liberalised Trade Environment: Proceedings of the Seminar on October 2004 in Haikko Finland* (University of Helsinki, Helsinki, 2005) 40–1; Rosebud V Kurwijila, 'Small-scale farmers' role and challenges in developing Africa's agriculture sector' in Tiina Huvio, Jukka Kola, and Tor Lundström, ibid, 82–3.

[71] See, eg, World Commission on the Social Dimension of Globalization, *A Fair Globalization: Creating Opportunities for all* (ILO, Geneva, 2004) para 380.

[72] See Chapter 5, Part C.

flexibilities under WTO law will be significantly reduced under current Doha proposals. Finally, 'defence' mechanisms such as anti-dumping laws, countervailing measures against subsidies, and safeguards are currently inadequate shields for developing States against subsidized Northern imports.

C. Food and Trade: An Uneasy Combination

Given the present inadequacy in WTO rules regarding agriculture, further and fairer agricultural liberalization is unsurprisingly one of the main demands of developing countries in the Doha round. Certainly, agricultural liberalization would benefit the agricultural industries in Russia, Brazil and Argentina, as well as States in the Cairns group,[73] which contain many of the world's food insecure people.[74] However, many developing countries do not have a comparative advantage in agriculture. Agricultural liberalization could be counterproductive or even disastrous for some of the poor in developing countries, and could have detrimental effects on enjoyment of the right to food.

Inequities in trade and lack of investment in agriculture have transformed former exporting countries into importing countries. Whereas developing States had an agricultural trade surplus of US$7 billion per annum in the 1960s, they had a food trade deficit of US$11 billion by 2001.[75] Many African States have become net food importers after being net food exporters up until the 1970s.[76] To be sure, this process of poor countries evolving into net food importers began before the advent of the WTO. Trade liberalization in the 1980s was forced upon many developing States by loan conditions imposed by the IFIs along with reductions in government support for farmers: the combined effect wiped out local agricultural industries which could not compete with subsidized imports from the North.[77]

A reversal of the status of food importer to self-sustainability or even food exporter cannot be expected to happen even if trade rules are now 'fixed' to reduce global agricultural protectionism. Even if Northern subsidies were abolished, the huge differences in productivity between the mechanized long-protected farms of the North and the more rudimentary long-neglected agricultural operations in many parts of the South would hardly create a level playing field: UNCTAD

---

[73] The Cairns group consists of a mixture of developed and developing States with strong agricultural sectors: Argentina, Australia, Bolivia, Brazil, Canada, Chile, Colombia, Costa Rica, Guatemala, Indonesia, Malaysia, New Zealand, Pakistan, Paraguay, Peru, the Philippines, South Africa, Thailand, and Uruguay.

[74] Report of the Special Rapporteur on the Right to Food, above n 14, para 5; WTO, 'Trade liberalization and the right to food', above n 22. See also Ha-Joon Chang, *Bad Samaritans: the Myth of Free Trade and the Secret History of Capitalism* (Bloomsbury Press, New York, 2008) 79.

[75] Special Rapporteur on the Right to Food, above n 14, Annex 1, n 56, citing the FAO; see also IAAKSTD, above n 20, 455.

[76] Special Rapporteur on the Right to Food, above n 28, para 21. See also South Centre, above n 42, 1; FAO, above n 28, 17.

[77] Reichert, above n 26, 31; De Schutter, above n 13, 17.

reported in 2006 that the productivity of farmers in LDCs was less than one per cent of those in the North.[78]

For rich States that are net food importers, such as Saudi Arabia and Qatar, continued dependence on food imports is sustainable due to their purchasing power: they are attractive markets for food sellers.[79] However, dependence on food imports is not sustainable for poor countries. As noted below, agricultural markets are extremely volatile, so such countries suffer when prices rise, as occurred during the recent food crisis. They are also vulnerable to export embargoes. For example, certain rice exporting States, such as China and Vietnam, reduced exports in order to ensure their own food security during the World Food Crisis, gravely affecting food supplies in poorer rice importing States. The incentive to sell to poor countries did not outweigh those States' understandable concern to feed their own people. The development of self-sustaining food supplies by poor States is therefore highly desirable, in order to ensure the enjoyment of the right to food by their populations.[80] Yet such a strategy, which would necessarily involve increased protectionism on the part of the States with the most vulnerable food sectors, cuts against the grain of WTO disciplines and negotiations.

Subsidized imports and food aid

Some developing countries are dependent on imports for food and have limited resources to purchase food.[81] Many such States have therefore relied for food supply on cheap subsidized Northern imports. Of course, these imports harm the competitiveness of Southern farmers. Nevertheless, the removal of subsidized imports by way of further liberalization is of considerable concern to net food-importing developing countries.[82] These potential negative effects of the AoA were acknowledged in the 1993 *Ministerial Decision on Measures Concerning the Possible Negative Effects of the Reform Program on Least Developed and Net Food-Importing Developing Countries.*[83] However, while that document is characterized by sympathy and recommendations, it introduces no binding obligations.[84] 'There is no mechanism

---

[78] See UNCTAD, *The Least Developed Countries Report 2006: Developing Productive Capacities* (UN, New York and Geneva, 2006) 137.
[79] De Schutter, above n 13, 10. Even so, such States are taking measures to preserve their own food security by buying up land in poorer States, particularly in Africa, to grow food for their own peoples, perhaps at the expense of consumers in the latter countries. See, eg, John Vidal, 'How food and water are driving a 21st century African land grab' *The Guardian* (London), 7 March 2010.
[80] HE Mamadou Sanou, Minister for Trade of Burkina Faso, stated that self-sustainability was probably the only way of ensuring food security for poor nations such as his own during an NGO side event at the Geneva Ministerial, 2 December 2009. See also De Schutter, above n 13, 18.
[81] See also 'WTO List of Net Food Importing Developing Countries', G/AG/5/Rev.6, 10 April 2003.
[82] Hunter, above n 35, 307, fn 56; Christine Breining-Kaufman, 'The Right to Food and Trade in Agriculture' in Thomas Cottier, Joost Pauwelyn, and Elizabeth Bürgi (eds), *Human Rights and International Trade* (Oxford University Press, Oxford, 2005) 343.
[83] GATT doc. LT/UR/D-1/2 (1993).
[84] Hunter, above n 35, 312–4; Dommen, above n 29, 33; Breining-Kaufman, above n 82, 368.

within the WTO to monitor systematically the impact of the AoA reform process on the' Net Food Importing Developing Countries.[85]

Similar concerns may be raised regarding food aid. Food aid should be designed to fulfil the nutritional needs of deprived States. However, food aid can be abused to serve commercial interests rather than the interests of the hungry. At the Hong Kong Ministerial, WTO Members reiterated the need to eliminate the abuse of food aid whilst guaranteeing the maintenance of genuine emergency food aid, but the details must still be worked on.[86]

Guideline 15 of FAO's Voluntary Guidelines outlines the balance that should be achieved in food aid programmes thus:

15.1 Donor States should ensure that their food aid policies support national efforts by recipient States to achieve food security, and base their food aid provisions on sound needs assessment, targeting especially food insecure and vulnerable groups. In this context, donor States should provide assistance in a manner that takes into account food safety, the importance of not disrupting local food production and the nutritional and dietary needs and cultures of recipient populations. Food aid should be provided with a clear exit strategy and avoid the creation of dependency. *Donors should promote increased use of local and regional commercial markets to meet food needs in famine-prone countries and reduce dependence on food aid* [emphasis added].

15.4 The provision of international food aid in emergency situations should take particular account of longer-term rehabilitation and development objectives in the recipient countries, and should respect universally recognized humanitarian principles.

It is preferable if donors procure food from local or regional markets,[87] rather than send food from their own countries. Such procurement will assist local and regional producers, and is more likely to be culturally appropriate. The food can be delivered faster with lower transport costs.[88] However, US legislation requires that 75 per cent of its food aid be procured from US markets, be packed and processed in the US, and transported by US ships.[89] The food is also delivered by contracted US-based NGOs. Food aid programmes should be designed to alleviate a food crisis and facilitate sustainable food security in the target State, rather than to promote commercial interests in the donating or exporting country by removing unwanted surpluses.[90]

Trade efficiency and food

There are a number of reasons why the 'efficiency' gains driven by trade liberalization are not appropriate in the area of food. Trade efficiency denotes that solvent

---

[85] Report of the Special Rapporteur on the right to food, above n 28, para 15.

[86] Hong Kong Declaration, above n 67, para 6. See also Howse and Teitel, above n 61, 65–7.

[87] Report of the Special Rapporteur, above n 70, para 15; M Mazoyer, 'Protecting Small Farmers and the Rural Poor in the Context of Globalisation' (FAO, Rome, 2001) section 5.

[88] See Katarina Wahlberg, 'Food Aid for the Hungry?' (2008) *Global Policy Forum*, 2 <http://www.globalpolicy.org/component/content/article/217-hunger/46251-food-aid-for-the-hungry.html> accessed 22 September 2010.

[89] Ibid, 2.   [90] Ibid, 1.

consumers purchase products (or services) at an optimum price from sellers, who make profits to sustain and grow their business. Trade literature emphasizes that markets will divert to those who sell for less.[91] At the same time however, markets also divert to those willing to pay more.[92] For example, land will be used to cultivate and feed livestock for meat to satisfy the more expensive tastes of a growing South East Asian middle class, rather than to grow staple foods for the poor and the hungry.[93] There is a finite amount of arable land, particularly given the environmental consequences of clearing more land for farming, so production of 'expensive' agricultural products, including the rearing of livestock which is much more resource intensive than the growing of vegetables, leads to the lesser production of cheaper staples.[94] Yet food is a necessity of life, unlike most products and services.[95] From a human rights point of view, those who are too poor to purchase food cannot be excluded from the food market in the same way that they can be excluded from the markets for cars or television sets. In the wake of the World Food Crisis, former US President Bill Clinton, who presided over the US's final negotiation of and ratification of the WTO Agreements, admitted in 2008 that the world, including his administration, 'blew it' by treating food as if it was an ordinary commodity.[96]

Agricultural activities are commercial activities, but they are also truly multifunctional, serving purposes beyond the production of commodities such as the promotion of human welfare (nutrition, livelihoods, sustaining rural communities), traditional cultural practices (for example, hunting, gathering, food rituals), and provision of environmental and ecological services, such as the management of forests.[97] Agricultural management systems must be devised so as to serve these multifunctional purposes, rather than be based only on economic criteria.[98] While the AoA acknowledges 'non-trade' concerns in some of its provisions, such as food security and environmental protection, overall it 'clearly fits into a programme of trade liberalization in agricultural products', with food security and other non-trade aims to be achieved by support rather than by any retreat from liberalizing measures.[99]

[91] See also United Nations Human Settlements Programme, *Global Report on Human Settlements 2006: The Challenge of Slums* (UN Habitat, London, 2006) 52.
[92] De Schutter, above n 13, 10–11.
[93] Sophia Murphy, *Concentrated Market Power and Agricultural Trade*, August 2006 (Heinrich Boell Stiftung, Berlin, 2006) 27.
[94] Similarly, food production competes with other uses of land, such as golf courses, hotels, and urbanization in general. See James A Paul and Katarina Wahlberg, *A new era of world hunger?— the Global Food Crisis Analyzed* (Friedrich Ebert Stiftung, New York, August 2008) 3.
[95] The market ethic promoted by WTO rules also poses problems with regard to other essential goods or services, such as life-saving medicines (see Chapter 7) and provision of water (see Chapter 5).
[96] Bill Clinton: '"We Blew It" on Global Food: Ex-President tells UN World erred in treating food as a commodity instead of a vital right', *CBS News*, 23 October 2008 <http://www.cbsnews.com/stories/2008/10/23/world/main4542268.shtml> accessed 22 September 2010.
[97] IAAKSTD, above n 20, Executive Summary, 6; World Bank, *World Development Report 2008: Agriculture for Development* (World Bank, Washington DC, 2008), 2; Von Braun, above n 70, 22.
[98] IAAKSTD, above n 20, 50.
[99] Special Rapporteur on the Right to Food, above n 28, para 14.

Only a small percentage of food, estimated at 15 per cent of food grown, is actually traded across borders.[100] Yet 'international trade and investment requirements dictate food and agricultural policies'.[101] However, international agricultural markets suffer from a number of flaws apart from the anomalies in current trade liberalization arrangements discussed above. These flaws include: volatile markets with predominantly low prices for primary goods, concentration of market power, problems caused by the focus on export crops compared to food staples, and problems caused by specialization and intensive mono-cropping. These issues are now discussed in turn.

Volatile markets

Agricultural commodities markets have generally delivered poor and erratic returns to producers over the last three decades,[102] partly due to chronic overproduction.[103] These markets suffer from a number of factors which defy the application of orthodox economic theories regarding supply and demand.[104] It is difficult to tailor supply to demand due to the vagaries of climatic conditions, and the fact that it is not easy to simply 'move land in and out of production'[105] to suit market conditions. It is also expensive to store food, especially for poorer farmers, who cannot therefore stockpile produce until market conditions are more advantageous.[106]

The so-called 'cobweb effect' may explain some of the structural reasons for inherent agricultural volatility. Producers choose which crops to grow during the planting season, four to six months prior to harvest. They will often plant large amounts of high priced crops, and less of low priced crops. If all producers adopt that strategy, there will be an overabundance of the high priced crops come harvest time, so their price will drop, and a shortage of the low-priced crop, so its price will rise. This problem is exacerbated when markets are global.[107]

Low prices mean that farmers cannot make a decent living. Price hikes are too unpredictable for those farmers to take advantage of, so they suffer again as consumers with sudden rises in food prices. As noted above, poor States which are net food importers cannot afford sudden price rises. At the Hong Kong Ministerial, the problems caused by unstable commodities markets were acknowledged, yet no solid commitments in that regard were made.[108]

---

[100]   De Schutter, above n 13, 43.

[101]   Smaller and Murphy, above n 21, 8; IAAKSTD, above n 20, 454.

[102]   See generally IAAKSTD, above n 20, 454, 458; Report of the Special Rapporteur on the Right to Food, above n 70, para 18; Kurwijila, above n 70, 82.

[103]   Von Braun, above n 70, 30–1; Mazoyer, above n 87, Section 2.3.

[104]   See also Report of the Special Rapporteur on the Right to Food, above n 28, para 21; Wolf, above n 27, 206.

[105]   Sophia Murphy, 'WTO Agreement on Agriculture: Suitable Model for a Global Food System?' (2002) 7 *Foreign Policy in Focus* 3.

[106]   Murphy, above n 93, 5.

[107]   De Schutter, above n 13, 24–5.

[108]   See Hong Kong Declaration, above n 67, para 55.

In general, price stability and managed production, along with sustainable methods of production, must be promoted to combat excessive market volatility.[109] The WTO cannot shut its eyes to such widespread market failures with human consequences. In order to do so, certain barriers to trade and the free market will have to be promoted. For example, state trading enterprises may have a significant role to play in stabilizing markets,[110] lending market muscle to farmers, and in fact providing robust competition to dominant agribusiness conglomerates,[111] whose market power is discussed directly below. Such state-run marketing boards would, however, have to avoid the inefficiency and corruption that has beset such institutions in the past, particularly in developing countries.[112]

It is difficult to reconcile such methods of price stabilization with free markets. International commodities agreements, which seek to stabilize prices and supply of particular commodities, and which clearly restrict free trade, are permitted under Article XX(h) GATT.[113] However, such agreements probably need to be mandatory rather than merely permitted in order to avoid the undermining of the agreements by non-participants.[114] Furthermore, the parameters of the WTO rules regarding commodities agreements, which cut against the grain of the free trade ethos of WTO rules, are not clear. Hence, the African Group in the WTO suggested in 2006 that the rules regarding commodities agreements be clarified as part of the Doha negotiations.[115]

Cartelization

Agricultural trade is dominated by large-scale single-crop farms owned by multinational agribusiness companies.[116] Indeed, many commodities markets are dominated by only a few multinational corporations (MNCs). In its World Development Report of 2008, the World Bank stated that when the percentage of business held within an industry by its top four companies (CR4 rating) is over 40 per cent, 'market competitiveness begins to decline'.[117] It reported that coffee had a CR4 rating of 40 per cent while the rating for coffee roasting was 45 per cent. There was a CR4 rating of 40 per cent for international traders of cocoa, 51 per cent for coffee grinders, and 50 per cent for confectionary manufacturers. Three companies controlled 80 per cent of the tea market.[118]

---

[109] Murphy, above n 93, 29.
[110] FAO, above n 28, 35–6; Wolf, above n 27, 206.
[111] See Murphy, above n 93, 38.
[112] See Report of the Special Rapporteur on the Right to Food, above n 25, para 32.
[113] See also Article XI(2)(b) and XXXVI(4).
[114] Mehmet Arda, 'Global Mechanisms Relevant to Small-Scale Farmers in Liberalised Trade Environment' in Tiina Huvio, Jukka Kola, and Tor Lundström (eds), above n 70, 189–92; Reichert, above n 26, 30.
[115] WTO, 'Modalities for Negotiations on Agricultural Commodity Issues—Proposal Submitted by the African Group to the Special Session of the Committee of Agriculture', WTO doc. TN/AG/GEN/18 (7 June 2006).
[116] Breining-Kaufman, above n 82, 368; Wolf, above n 27, 206.
[117] World Development Report 2008, above n 97, 135–6.   [118] Ibid, 136.

The growth of global supply chains benefits smaller farmers by connecting them to global markets.[119] However, cartelization within these supply chains has led to severe power imbalances between producers and buyers, allowing the latter to exercise effective monopsony power to drive down prices paid to producers.[120] The price received by farmers for their produce now accounts for a tiny proportion of the value of the final product for consumers, which instead increasingly reflect inputs by and the profits of others further up the chain, such as wholesalers, processers, retailers,[121] and other add-ons, such as the costs of a lease on a retailer's premises.[122] The Special Rapporteur on the Right to Food, Olivier De Schutter, stated in 2008:

> The World Bank has noted…that…the share of the retail price retained by coffee-producing countries Brazil, Colombia, Indonesia and Viet Nam accounting for 64 per cent of global production declined from a third in the early 1990s to 10 per cent in 2002, while the value of retail sales doubled. It also calculated that the developing countries' claim on value added in agricultural commodities declined from around 60 per cent in 1970–1972 to around 28 per cent in 1998–2000.[123]

Other powerful players also now play a role in agricultural markets, further shifting profits and influence away from producers.[124] Farmers are dependent on certain inputs such as fertilizers and machinery in order to harvest a decent crop. These markets are also overly concentrated, with the World Bank reporting a CR4 ratio of 60 per cent in the agrochemicals business in 2004.[125] Furthermore, farmers buy these inputs at retail prices yet sell their produce at wholesale prices to commodity buyers.[126]

Commercial farming now relies on genetically modified seeds, which are owned by companies, and cannot legally be replanted without their permission. Some of these seeds decline in their productivity, so farmers must eventually purchase new seeds rather than save seeds for replanting. Alternatively, farmers may become tied to certain seed companies by contracts, which may be concluded without meaningful equality of bargaining power.[127] As an indicator of unfortunate market dominance, Monsanto reportedly controls 41 per cent of the commercial maize market and 25 per cent of soybean seeds globally.[128]

---

[119] De Schutter, above n 13, 30.

[120] UNDP, above n 36, 142–3; Department of Foreign Affairs and Trade (DFAT)], *Globalisation: Keeping the Gains* (Commonwealth of Australia, Canberra, 2003) 47, 50.

[121] The Special Rapporteur on the Right to Food reported in 2008 that 10 retailers shared 24% of the global market: above n 14, para 36.   [122] Ibid, para 36; Oxfam, above n 37, 161.

[123] Report of the Special Rapporteur on the Right to Food, above n 14, para 37, quoting World Development Report 2008, at 136; Gary Howe and others, 'Trade, Trade Liberalisation and Small-Scale Farmer in Developing Countries: Beyond the Doha Round' in Tiina Huvio, Jukka Kola, and Tor Lundström (eds), above n 70, 123 at 135–6.

[124] IAAKSTP, above n 20, 465–6; Arda above n 114, 177 at 182.

[125] World Development Report 2008, above n 97, 135.

[126] Report of the Special Rapporteur on the Right to Food, above n 14, para 36.

[127] Arda, above n 114, 198; UNGA, 'Report of the Special Rapporteur on the Right to Food, Olivier de Schutter: Seed policies and the right to food: enhancing agrobiodiversity and encouraging innovation', UN doc. A/64/170 (23 July 2009) para 12.

[128] Murphy, above n 93, 6.

Supermarkets are also 'consolidating distribution and retail markets on every continent', and now dominate final retail sales of agricultural products.[129] The quality demands of supermarkets are very difficult for smallholders to comply with, regarding, for example, uniformity of produce and volume.[130] While quality control of food products is of course important, some of these standards relate to less important marketing issues such as 'the look' of a product. Furthermore, the standards are imposed at the whim of the supermarket with little consultation with farmers.[131] The private source of these standards indicates that governments have not seen such standards as necessary to protect consumers. However, the private source also means that the standards are not challengeable under the SPS Agreement.[132] Finally, these retail industries are characterized by a high degree of concentration and consequent market power.[133]

As the gap between prices paid to producers and profits reaped by agribusiness and other players, such as retailers and processors, grows, small farmers simply cannot compete. For example, the increased demand by agribusiness and big farmers for land in order to cultivate export crops threatens the security of tenure of smaller farmers, and there have been instances of forced eviction and expropriation with inadequate (or no) compensation.[134] There is also a vast gap in terms of the respective access to relevant business information of the two groups.[135] In the result, smallholders are either driven out of business and deprived of their livelihoods, or they struggle on, adding to the ranks of the world's hungry.

Problems regarding private monopolies are 'conspicuously absent' from binding ameliorating WTO initiatives.[136] Trade is hardly free in the absence of free competition. At the least, the permitting of monopolies undermines one strong rationale for free trade: lower prices for consumers.[137] Indeed, 'analyses that have been used to bolster the case for further trade liberalisation . . . assume that markets function competitively (ignoring vertical integration within value chains that can limit competition)'.[138] Instead, there is a danger that agricultural liberalization without the opening up of competition in the sector simply replaces 'border protections with cartels'.[139] Domestic competition policy in developed States is largely concerned with protecting consumers from monopoly producers, rather than protecting offshore consumers or producers from the monopoly or monopsony power of MNCs based in their territory.[140]

[129] Ibid, 6.   [130] Kurwijila, above n 70, 85; Arda, above n 114, 180.
[131] Murphy, above n 93, 14.   [132] Arda, above n 114, 184 and 195. See also Chapter 4, Part D.
[133] Murphy, above n 93, 11–12. See also Thomas Reardon and others, 'The Rise of Supermarkets in Africa, Asia and Latin America' (2003) 5 *American Journal of Agricultural Economics* 1140–6. Alexandra Spieldoch, *A Row to Hoe: the Gender Impact of Trade Liberalization on our Food System, Agricultural Markets and Women's Human Rights* (Friedrich Ebert Stiftung, Geneva, 2007) reports that 30 supermarket chains control one third of global food sales at 14, quoting an Oxfam report from 2004.
[134] Report of the Special Rapporteur on the Right to Food, above n 70, para 34.
[135] Von Braun, above n 70, 22.   [136] UNDP, above n 36, 139.
[137] See Paasch, above n 47, 44.   [138] IAAKSTD, above n 20, 455.
[139] Murphy, above n 93, 29.
[140] See Report of the Special Rapporteur on the Right to Food, above n 25, para 35; Murphy, above n 93, 32; Smaller and Murphy, above n 21, 14. See also Daniel J Gifford and Robert J Kudrle,

Attempts to introduce competition policy into the WTO failed at the Singapore Ministerial of 1996. The focus of those discussions had been on promoting foreign competition against local firms in domestic markets, rather than on curbing the power of certain MNCs in global markets.[141] Instead, mechanisms must be introduced to guard against abuse of market power by the agribusiness sector, the providers of inputs such as seeds, and supermarkets.[142] Otherwise trade liberalization will disproportionately favour such entities, which are already in the best position to take advantage of the dismantling of global barriers, and widen the gap to their impoverished competitors.[143] At the least, relevant WTO committees should seek information on the extent of market power exerted by certain firms, just as they routinely seek such information on the practices of State trading enterprises.[144] Indeed, the fact that the latter information is sought, while the former is not, reflects the WTO's inherent suspicion of the public sector, compared to its inherent and ocasionally misplaced faith in the private sector.

Export orientation

Export orientation in agriculture has prompted switches from subsistence products to non-food cash crops, such as coffee, cocoa, and tobacco: conversion to cash crops has in many cases weakened local food security.[145] Agribusiness corporations, which dominate the market, are more likely to be 'concerned with profitable trade than with local-level food security'.[146] The diversion of resources from food can transform a country into a net food importing country,[147] with all of the vulnerabilities associated with that status.

Furthermore, an export emphasis promotes investment in areas which are linked to facilities which are necessary for the transportation of goods, such as ports and airports. There has however been a concomitant lack of investment and provision of infrastructure for more remote areas that are capable, if such investment took place, of providing local and regional markets.[148]

The cash crop focus has resulted from an undue focus on export markets. Food products are probably more in demand amongst regional and local markets in

'Trade and Competition Policy in the Developing World' in Chantal Thomas and Joel P Trachtmann (eds), *Developing Countries in the WTO Legal System* (Oxford University Press, Oxford, 2009) 395, esp at 427–8.

[141] Stiglitz and Charlton, above n 34, 85; Murphy, above n 93, 33; Khor, above n 41, 37–8.
[142] Report of the Special Rapporteur on the Right to Food, above n 14, para 38.
[143] See also IAAKSTD, above n 20, 7.
[144] Murphy, above n 93, 36; Arda, above n 114, 195–6.
[145] United Nations Human Settlements Programme, above n 91, 41.
[146] Dommen, above n 29, 34.
[147] See Dan Ben-David, Håkan Nordström and Alan Winters, 'Trade, Income Disparity, and Poverty' (WTO Special Studies 5) (WTO, Geneva, 1999) 57, on the example of Zambia, where the switch to cash crops 'apparently eliminated the knowledge and seed supplies required for subsistence varieties, preventing farmers from reverting to traditional methods when the cash crop market disappeared'.
[148] IAAKSTD, above n 20, 459.

developing States; they are important yet neglected outlets for agricultural traders in many regions.[149]

Of particular concern to the enjoyment of the right to food in recent years has been the shifting of agricultural resources to the production of 'biofuels', fuels derived from plant materials.[150] The trend towards biofuels is driven by a need to find alternatives to fossil fuels and a desire for energy security. However, biofuel production has diverted many crops which traditionally feed the poor, such as maize, sugarcane, cassava, palm oil, and sorghum,[151] into products which are used by the rich to drive their cars.[152] Most biofuel is currently produced in developed States. However, that situation is expected to change, given the availability of agricultural land and appropriate climatic conditions in many developing States, which are increasing production of primary commodities (for example, palm oil) for biofuel conversion.[153] Significant production already takes place, largely for export, in Brazil, Indonesia, and Malaysia.[154]

The result has been to drive up land prices[155] and food prices, due to the lesser availability of such products as edible commodities. The IMF has calculated that biofuel production raised the price of maize by 70 per cent and soybeans by 40 per cent.[156] Yet the positive environmental impacts of biofuels are questionable, due to the unsustainable practices used to produce them, such as extensive forest clearance and energy usage to convert plants into fuel. It seems very unlikely that biofuels will make a significant dent, at least in the short term, in demand for fossil fuels, when one compares the massive volume of grain and land used to produce biofuel with the tiny portion of the fuel market occupied by biofuels.[157]

The present Special Rapporteur on the Right to Food, Olivier De Schutter, has gone so far as to say that the promotion of biofuel production and trade is so detrimental that it represents 'a deliberately retrogressive measure' in respect of the right to food. In such a situation, relevant States (whether producing or importing) have to demonstrate that biofuel production and trade is justified according to the

---

[149] Ibid, 453.
[150] UNGA, 'Report of the Special Rapporteur on the right to food, Jean Ziegler', UN doc. A/62/289 (22 August 2007) paras 19–44.
[151] Report of the Special Rapporteur on the right to food, above n 14, para 28.
[152] Report of the Special Rapporteur on the right to food to the General Assembly, Jean Ziegler, above n 150, para 23; Annex 2, para 10.
[153] See Report of the Special Rapporteur on the Right to Food, above n 14, Annex 2, para 10.
[154] Nicola Colbran and Asbjørn Eide, 'Biofuel, the Environment, and Food Security' (Fall, 2008) *Sustainable Development Law & Policy* 4.
[155] The increased competition for land has also led to forced evictions for vulnerable peoples who lacked secure tenure, particularly indigenous peoples. Report of the Special Rapporteur on the right to food to the General Assembly, Jean Ziegler, above n 150, paras 38–9.
[156] Report of the Special Rapporteur on the Right to Food, above n 14, Annex 2, para 3, n 66, citing John Lipsky, Managing Director, IMF, *Commodity Prices and Global Inflation: Remarks at the Council on Foreign Relations*, New York City, 8 May 2008.
[157] Report of the Special Rapporteur on the Right to Food, above n 14, Annex 2, quoting US National Academics of Sciences. IAAKSTD, above n 20, 464 cites a study which indicates that only 15% of US transportation needs would be satisfied if all of its corn was converted into biofuel.

totality of the rights in the ICESCR.[158] He doubts that that burden can be met, especially when the environmental benefits of biofuels are highly suspect.[159]

De Schutter's statements may indicate that the import of biofuels constitutes an extraterritorial breach by a State of the right to food. If so, this could be a rare example of international human rights law compelling the adoption by a State of trade bans (that is, 'outward measures') on a product.[160] However, De Schutter may not be going so far. He seems to be saying that States should not *encourage* biofuel production (whether at home or overseas) through, for example, offerings of subsidies and tax breaks. Removal of subsidies and other incentives would probably bring biofuel production to a halt, as biofuel use is not currently economically viable without them.[161]

In any case, the clear link between some biofuel production and detrimental impacts on the right to food indicate that measures which deter such production are welcome from a human rights point of view. Yet a managed phase-out of the trade of biofuels, or a phased-in policy of only importing biofuels produced in a manner which preserves rights to food, could possibly be illegal under WTO rules.[162]

In this respect, I note that the European Union has adopted ambitious targets to promote the use within the EU of non-fossil fuels, which will 'trigger a large increase in the consumption of biofuel in the EU'.[163] Its Renewable Energy Directive[164] sets out support schemes to facilitate the production and import of biofuels which meet certain 'sustainability criteria'. These criteria are arguably designed to ensure that eligible biofuels have a minimal carbon footprint. The criteria are not however aimed at mitigating effects on the right to food, and their suitability for minimizing detrimental environmental impacts is debatable.[165] The sustainability criteria may also breach WTO law. Unfortunately, more robust criteria, which could be designed to protect the right to food and to redress criticisms of the environmental impact of the current criteria, could be even more vulnerable to being found in violation of international trade rules.[166]

Specialization

The theory of comparative advantage encourages specialization rather than diversity in agricultural outputs. This emphasis on specialization, along with the

---

[158] See Chapter 1, text at notes 71–2.

[159] Report of the Special Rapporteur on the Right to Food, above n 14, Annex 2, paras 5–6.

[160] See Chapter 4, text at notes 17–30.

[161] Actionaid, 'Meals per Gallon: The Impact of Industrial Biofuels on People and Global Hunger' (Actionaid, London, 2010) <http://www.actionaid.org/micrositeAssets/eu/assets/aa_biofuelsreportweb100210.pdf > accessed 29 October 2010, 10. The existence of extraterritorial obligations does not exonerate the territorial State from its own obligations in respect of its own territory. See also Chapter 8, text between notes 91 and 92.

[162] Report of the Special Rapporteur on the Right to Food, above n 14, para 32. The impact of WTO rules on the trade in 'bad' products is discussed in Chapter 4.

[163] Andreas Lendle and Malorie Schaus, 'Sustainability Criteria in the EU Renewable Energy Directive: Consistent with WTO Rules?' ICTSD Information Note No 2, September 2010, 1.

[164] Directive 2009/28/EC, 5 June 2009.

[165] See generally, Actionaid, above n 161, and Lendle and Schaus, above n 163.

[166] See Lendle and Schaus, above n 163, esp at 15.

commercial benefits of relevant intellectual property protection,[167] encourages 'vast monocultures being planted with genetically identical seed'.[168] However, specialization can magnify losses if a crop should fail or plummet in price,[169] and leads to a loss of biological diversity and ecological resilience.[170]

Environmental damage

Global production of food in many developing States in the developing world, such as Mexico and India, was fired from the 1950s by the Green Revolution, a process involving intensive use of fertilizers, pesticides, irrigation, and better plant varieties.[171] The Green Revolution is a classic example of the economic focus of agricultural policy with an emphasis on boosting yields. The benefits of the Green Revolution cannot be denied, with those extra yields feeding previously hungry people. Furthermore, the Green Revolution permitted increases in production without the need to significantly expand areas of cultivation, which led to the preservation of forests, wetlands and greater biodiversity.

However, the extensive use of chemical fertilizers and pesticides has also caused water pollution, soil degradation, and health problems. Cancer rates have reportedly soared in the Punjab, one of the major sites of the Green Revolution in India.[172] Intensive agricultural operations also place 'enormous stress' on ecological resources, including water[173] and soil,[174] and have even given rise to new diseases, such as BSE (mad cow disease)[175] and, possibly, avian flu and swine flu.[176] Furthermore, globalization has caused environmental damage by facilitating the 'introduction of alien species' to fragile ecosystems.[177] Finally, current agricultural activity is calculated to be the second biggest generator of global greenhouse gas emission.[178] A second era of like green revolution policies is not sustainable.

---

[167] Problems regarding intellectual property protection and loss of biodiversity are further discussed below.

[168] Dommen, above n 29, 40.

[169] Ibid, 40. See also Nicola Colbran, 'Indigenous Peoples in Indonesia: at risk of disappearing as distinct peoples in the rush for biofuel?' (2010) *International Journal for Minority and Group Rights*, forthcoming, paper on file with the author, 16.

[170] IAAKSTD, above n 20, 10. [171] Ibid, 20.

[172] See Mira Kamdar, 'The threat to global food shortages', *Business Standard*, 10 May 2008; Mark Doyle, 'The limits of a Green Revolution?' *BBC News* (United Kingdom), 29 March 2007; Daniel Zwerdling, 'In Punjab, crowding onto the cancer train', *NPR*, 11 May 2009 <http://www .npr.org/templates/story/story.php?storyId=103569390)> accessed 22 September 2010.

[173] IAAKSTD, above n 20, 20–1.

[174] Murphy, above n 105, 4. Oxfam uses the Bangladeshi prawn industry as an example of a commodities market that has impacted detrimentally on the environment, through massively increased soil salinity, which has not benefited the poor due to 'the high capital costs involved' (above n 37, 92–3).

[175] Wolf, above n 27, 191.

[176] IAAKSTD, above n 20, 72 (the report does not mention swine flu; it predated that pandemic).

[177] Ibid, 40.

[178] Smaller and Murphy, above n 21, 2. See also IAAKSTD, above n 20, 30, reporting that 30% of emissions which generate climate change are attributable to agricultural activities: 3 and 11.

Conclusion

There is a need to break from the purely economic focus in agriculture to promote more sustainable modes of agriculture.[179] A shift in global agricultural policy from current modes, which are focused largely on improving productivity, to a multi-faceted approach aimed at empowering smallholders and designed to boost development and sustainability, including food security, was recently advocated in the Synthesis Report of the International Assessment of Agricultural Knowledge, Science and Technology for Development (IAAKSTD). The IAAKSTD is an intergovernmental entity created by the World Bank and the FAO. The report was compiled over three years by 400 experts, including a wide range of scientists and development specialists. Fifty-eight governments unreservedly accepted the report in April 2008, which endorsed the report's findings, while three governments expressed reservations.[180] The report's main conclusion was that '[b]usiness as usual is no longer an option'.[181]

D. Empowering Smallholder Farmers

As noted above, half of the world's underfed are smallholder farmers. Furthermore, nearly 90 per cent of farms are smallholder operations.[182] Around 40 per cent of the world's population are employed in agriculture, with the large majority of those in small-scale farms.[183] Three quarters of the world's poor are located in rural areas,[184] and more than half of extremely poor people make their livelihoods from agriculture.[185] Given those figures, it is hardly surprising that smallholders constitute 'the largest employment and small business group among the world's poor'.[186] Yet a vastly disproportionate share of farm income, including subsidies, goes to the 0.5 per cent of farms which are over 100 hectares in size,[187] leading to great bifurcation in world agricultural markets. Global agricultural policy is largely driven by the interests of those bigger farms, rather than the vast number of smaller farmers.

In alignment with the IAAKSTD conclusions, an appropriate strategy from the perspective of the right to food, and poverty reduction generally, is to empower small farmers so that they can sell their stock at prices which enable them to become food secure and to maintain their livelihoods.[188]

---

[179] IAAKSTD, above n 20, 44; World Development Report 2008, above n 97, 1.

[180] Australia, Canada, and the US submitted some reservations. The 58 approving governments included a range of developing nations, along with Finland, France, Ireland, Sweden, Switzerland, and the UK. See IAAKSTD, above n 20, vii.

[181] IAAKSTD, above n 20, Executive Summary, 4.   [182] Von Braun, above n 70, 25.

[183] IAAKSTD, above n 20, 8.   [184] World Development Report 2008, above n 97, 1.

[185] IAAKSTD, above n 20, 14.   [186] Von Braun, above n 70, 21.

[187] Marc Cohen and others, *Impact of Climate Change and Bioenergy on Nutrition* (FAO and IFPRI, Rome, 2008), 3 and 31 <http://www.fao.org/docrep/010/ai799e/ai799e00.HTM> accessed 22 September 2010.

[188] IAAKSTD above n 20, 7–8, 15, 45, 454; World Development Report 2008, above n 97, 2, 8, 10; FAO, above n 28, 100; Howe, above n 123, 137–8.

Women are the main producers of stable crops, 'providing up to 90 per cent of the rural poor's food intake'.[189] The empowerment of smallholders will necessarily involve the empowerment of women in countries where they continue to suffer from entrenched discrimination, for example in terms of security of title to land.[190]

Perhaps it could be argued that smallholders would be better off selling their farms and moving into more appropriate efficient sectors.[191] For example, they could be employed by the export firms or large entrepreneurial holdings which will probably buy them out if they sell.[192] Certainly, some diversification of livelihoods away from agriculture is probably desirable.[193] However, where are the smallholders to go? Agricultural workers, whether landed or not, dominate the populations of poorer countries, so labour is hardly scarce. Indeed, agricultural labour is one of the worst sectors in terms of labour rights abuses: child labour, informal, forced and bonded labour are prevalent,[194] as are occupational work hazards.[195] Furthermore, many rural households are headed by women: it is extremely difficult in practice in many countries for women to leave their rural communities and seek new opportunities elsewhere. In any case, agribusiness and the larger farms are unlikely to be able to gainfully employ all smallholders who lose livelihoods, especially given greater mechanization and the truly vast number of people to absorb.[196] The Dutch NGO, Milieudefensie (Friends of the Earth), reported the following employment statistics in agriculture in Sambas in West Kalimantan in Indonesia from 2006: 80,000 hectares provided subsistence and employment for 207,350 small farmers, while 199,200 hectares run by 15 plantation companies employed only 1,944 people.[197] For those who cannot be employed in the agricultural industry, prospects are grim due to a lack of alternative skills. The choice may then be between staying on small plots or joining the 'rapidly expanding slums' in overburdened cities.[198]

Moreover, extensive reduction in smallholders will only exacerbate the problems, discussed above, regarding the lack of competition in food and agricultural

---

[189] Spieldoch, above n 133, quoting an FAO fact sheet from 2006 at 16.   [190] Ibid, 19.
[191] See Howe, above n 123, 140–1.   [192] IAAKSTD, above n 20, 7.   [193] Ibid, 27.
[194] See generally, ILO and FAO, 'Food, Agriculture and Decent Work: Decent Employment for the Rural Poor' (undated) <http://www.fao-ilo.org/ilo-dec-employ/en/?no_cache=1> accessed 22 September 2010; see also IAAKSTD, above n 20, 35; World Development Report 2008, above n 97, 6 and 17; Murphy, above n 93, 24–5. Some of these abuses arise on smallholder farms but many arise on large farms where the labourers have no ultimate stake in the output beyond their low wages: Paul and Wahlberg, above n 94, 8.
[195] Agricultural work accounts for 170,000 occupational deaths per year, half of all workplace accidents: IAAKSTD, above n 20, Executive Summary, 17.
[196] IAAKSTD, above n 20, 44 and 457 (containing graphs indicating that further liberalization along the lines of Doha proposals will boost land-intensive agriculture and processed agriculture, but lead to a reduction in export markets for labour-intensive agriculture). Murphy, above n 93, 7 and 21; FAO, above n 28, 63.
[197] Milieudefensie (Friends of the Earth Netherlands), Lembaga Gemawan, and KONTAK Rakyat Borneo, *Policy, Practice, Pride and Prejudice: Review of Legal, Environmental and Social Practices of Oil Palm Plantation Companies of the Wilmar Group in Sambas District, West Kalimantan (Indonesia)*, July 2007, 20–1, as reported in Colbran, above n 169, 22.
[198] Report of the Special Rapporteur on the Right to Food, above n 14, para 5; IAAKSTD, above n 20, 43.

markets, over-attention to cash crops, specialization and environmental degradation. Von Braun adds that inequality is worse in those developing States, mainly
in Latin America and the Caribbean, where the average farm size is larger.[199]
Furthermore, while '[i]n some contexts small farm size may be a barrier to investment', small farms are nevertheless 'often among the most productive in terms of
output per unit of land and energy'.[200] While smallholder farms cannot compete
easily with large plantations, they can nevertheless be just as if not more efficient.
After all, efficient food production is not the same thing as globally competitive mass food production. In any case, the idea of shifting small farmers into
larger operations is not realistic according to current trends, which suggest that
'small-scale farms will continue to dominate the agricultural landscape in the
developing world, especially Asia and Africa, at least for the coming two or three
decades'.[201]

Of course, the assertion that smallholders should give up their land and
independence to work for larger competitors is to treat those smallholders as
economic units rather than human beings, that is means rather than ends.
Indeed, other human rights issues beyond the right to food are at stake in the
notion of letting smallholders and their communities wither and be replaced by
larger plantations focused on monocultures and exports. Local farming practices and associated communities may be essential to the maintenance of certain cultural practices, which are simply not within the concerns of modern
agribusiness.[202] In particular, indigenous peoples continue to engage, where
unmolested, in traditional hunting and gathering, fishing, and/or other agricultural practices. As noted by Sophia Murphy, 'food . . . is tied into some of
people's oldest and most important rituals, religious beliefs and cultural practices'.[203] Relevant human rights include many recognized in the Declaration on
the Rights of Indigenous Peoples, and Article 27 of the ICCPR, which protects
the rights of minority groups.[204]

As noted by the current Special Rapporteur on the Right to Food, the 'search for
sustainable solutions' to world hunger may not be particularly attractive to private
interests.[205] In particular, regarding the need to protect smallholders:

Governments should have the policy flexibility both to protect their agricultural producers
whose livelihoods may be threatened by import surges or repressed prices and to allow for
a sufficient degree of diversity in various types of production. Second, smallhold farmers
from developing countries . . . must not be marginalized as a result of the development of
global supply chains, and they must be either better integrated in those chains (provided
the means to reap the gains from the lowering of trade barriers) or allowed to prosper by

---

[199] Von Braun, above n 70, 26.
[200] IAAKSTD, above n 20, 9; see also Von Braun, above n 70, 24. See also Camilla Toulmin and
Bara Guèye, 'Is there a future for family farming in West Africa?' in Tiina Huvio, Jukka Kola, and
Tor Lundström (eds), above n 70, 53–73. [201] IAAKSTD, above n 20, 9.
[202] Dommen, above n 29, 46.   [203] Murphy, above n 93, 20.
[204] See the Article 27 cases discussed in Sarah Joseph, Jenny Schultz, and Melissa Castan, *The
International Covenant on Civil and Political Rights: Cases, Materials and Commentary*, 2nd edn
(Oxford University Press, Oxford, 2004) paras 24.22–24.44.
[205] Report of the Special Rapporteur on the Right to Food, above n 14, para 10.

relying on local and regional markets, which must be insulated from the damaging effects of global trade liberalization.[206]

Significant investment, whether from national governments or international donors, in better education,[207] research, facilities for credit (including microcredit) and risk management, infrastructure, security of land tenure, safety nets for losers from trade reform, and support for producer collectives is needed to empower small-scale farming. If such reform does not precede greater liberalization, small-holders in the poorest countries are likely to lose from the liberalization process.[208] Rather, trade liberalization is likely to favour large agribusiness firms and exacerbate the gap and dichotomization between smallholders and agribusiness.[209] One size does not fit all: instead, '[f]lexibility and differentiation in trade policy frameworks' is needed to ensure that the poorest can also benefit from agricultural liberalization.[210]

Doha round negotiations in the WTO in July 2008 broke down, ostensibly over the issue of safeguards for farmers in the developing world. The issue is however of crucial importance if the Doha round is to conclude in a manner that promotes or at least does not harm enjoyment of the right to food.

E. Food and Intellectual Property

Article 27(3)(b) of TRIPS requires States to provide for either patent or *sui generis* intellectual property (IP) rights in 'plant varieties', including 'seeds, plant cells or DNA sequences'.[211] As noted above, commercial farming is reliant on genetically modified seeds, which are only likely to become more prevalent on present policy trajectories. There are benefits in developing new seed varieties which might, for example, be more resistant to diseases, pests or drought, or have higher nutritional value.[212] However, the trend towards commercialization and privatization of food products is not good news for the poor. Article 27(3)(b) mandates the private commercialization of certain food sources which will inevitably lead to rising prices which again threatens enjoyment of the right to food for the poor.[213] This is especially so, given the concentration of market power in companies that own the relevant rights.

It is therefore important that the traditional and informal seed systems of farmers be preserved within global agricultural policy. Sometimes farmers have little practical choice but to purchase commercial seeds. Usage of commercial seed

---

[206] Report of the Special Rapporteur on the Right to Food, above n 70, para 21.
[207] The World Development Report 2008, above n 97, describes education as 'often the most valuable asset for rural people to pursue opportunities', yet 'education levels in rural areas are dismally low worldwide', 9.
[208] IAAKSTD, above n 20, 452–3; see also FAO, above n 28, 6–7, 106.
[209] IAAKSTD, above n 20, 44.   [210] Ibid, 452.
[211] Report of the Special Rapporteur on the Right to Food, above n 127, para 12.
[212] Ibid, para 9.   [213] Breining-Kaufman, above n 82, 355.

packages may be a condition of receipt of certain subsidies or credit schemes,[214] or a condition for smallholders to sell their produce to a nucleus estate.

TRIPS standards of intellectual property, which are discussed in greater detail in Chapter 7, are inherently biased towards Northern notions of invention and innovation compared to ancient and local indigenous knowledge systems. Indeed, the latter have long been neglected in agricultural policy debates.[215] Yet such knowledge is invaluable in dealing with environmental crises given that traditional farming communities have been masters at adapting to environment change for generations.[216] However, 'indigenous' or 'traditional' knowledge is generally not patentable. For example, indigenous knowledge lacks an identifiable author as it has often been passed down communally from generation to generation. Its long term evolutionary nature may also lack the requisite 'originality'.[217] In any case, Northern notions of commodification and property rights over knowledge and innovation are not culturally consistent with indigenous notions of community rights and individual responsibilities over indigenous knowledge.[218]

On the other hand, minor industrial modifications of indigenous discoveries are patentable. In such situations of 'bio-piracy', the patent-holder (often a Northern company) reaps the commercial benefits without any requirement under TRIPS to compensate the relevant indigenous communities who are largely responsible for the relevant idea and concept. Instead, the 'people who originally developed [the plant or seed varieties] must buy them back at exorbitant rates'.[219] Megan Davis has commented that the past two decades has seen 'aggressive commercial exploitation of Indigenous knowledge' which is worth billions to corporations and States, with little economic benefit for indigenous peoples.[220]

Hence, TRIPS prescribes a discriminatory IP regime. Northern commercial interests and notions of invention are protected, while biopiracy is permitted to undermine the enjoyment of cultural rights by communities, particularly indigenous communities.[221] Examples of attempted biopiracy include the granting of a patent (later overturned) in the US with regard to medical uses for tumeric,[222] the attempt by US company Rice-Tec to patent strains of basmati rice[223] and US company Thermo Trilogy's attempt to patent a medicinal product derived from the

---

[214] Report of the Special Rapporteur on the Right to Food, above n 127, para 36.
[215] IAAKSTD, above n 20, 17–18, 51.
[216] Ibid, 41; Report of the Special Rapporteur on the Right to Food, above n 127, para 8.
[217] See Breining-Kaufman, above n 82, 356.
[218] Megan Davis, 'International Trade, the World Trade Organisation, and the Human Rights of Indigenous Peoples' (2006) 8 *Balayi* 5, 20.
[219] Marjorie Cohn, 'The World Trade Organization: Elevating Property Interests above Human Rights' (2001) 29 *Georgia Journal of International and Comparative Law* 427, 435. See also generally, Dr John Mugabe, 'Intellectual Property Protection and Traditional Knowledge' (WIPO Discussion on Intellectual Property and Human Rights, Geneva, 9 November 1998) via <http://www.wipo.int> accessed 25 November 2005; Joseph Stiglitz, *Making Globalization Work* (Penguin, London, 2007) 125.
[220] Davis, above n 218, 19: the same point may be made about the commercialization of indigenous works of art, including paintings and performances.   [221] Dommen, above n 29, 9.
[222] Stiglitz, above n 219, 126.
[223] See, eg, Luke Harding, 'India outraged as US company wins patents on rice' *The Guardian*, 23 August 2001.

Indian neem tree.[224] Demonstrating the extent of this problem, the Traditional Knowledge Digital Library was compiled over a period of eight years in India as a tool for the prevention of misappropriations of traditional knowledge by so-called bio-prospectors, following the finding of at least 2,000 patents worldwide for 'medical plants and traditional systems' that related to natural remedies and traditional treatments that had long been part of Indian systems of medicine.[225]

IP rewards homogeneity and standardization rather than agrobiodiversity.[226] Commercial efforts have been concentrated, so that only around 150 species are cultivated now, and most of the world lives off only 12 species of plants.[227] The Special Rapporteur on the Right to Food reported in 2009 that 75 per cent 'of plant diversity has been essentially lost from the agricultural cycle because farmers have foregone local varieties in favour of genetically uniform varieties'.[228] Furthermore, overly protective IP systems can hinder research by closing off the opportunities for rival researchers to perform public interest research using patented products.[229]

Another potential problem concerns the quest for originality, which encourages genetic modification of plant breeds. Modified foods can pose dangers to unmodified crops through cross-fertilization. Furthermore, the potential risks posed by genetically modified food sources to human health are hotly debated.[230]

Certainly, TRIPS permits the adoption of *sui generis* IP systems rather than strict patent protection for plant varieties. Therefore, IP systems may perhaps be developed which account for the right to food and any other relevant human rights.[231] It is presently uncertain whether TRIPS allows such flexibility, as *sui generis* regimes must, under Article 27(3)(b), be 'effective'.[232] Article 27(3) does not seem to recognize relevant stakeholders beyond breeders, such as farmers, so an effective *sui generis* regime under TRIPS may require greater protection for breeders than is desirable under international human rights law.[233] On the other hand,

---

[224] See Organic Consumers Association, 'EU Patent Office revokes USA "Biopiracy" Patent on Fungicide derived from Neem Tree Seeds' (Press Release of 8 March 2005) <http://www.organicconsumers.org/patent/neemtree030905.cfm> accessed 22 September 2010.

[225] See the Traditional Knowledge Digital Library at <http://www.lexorbis.com/Traditional_Knowledge_Digital_Library.htm> accessed 8 December 2010. Examples of revoked or withdrawn patents, as well as active patents relating to indigenous knowledge (eg, particular uses of Ayahuasca and Kava) can be found at <http://www.tkdl.res.in> accessed 23 May 2010.

[226] Dommen, above n 29, 39; Shelley Edwardson, 'Reconciling TRIPS and the Right to Food' in *Human Rights and International Trade* above n 82, 387; Oxfam, above n 37, 224; Report of the Special Rapporteur on the Right to Food, above n 127, para 38.

[227] Report of the Special Rapporteur on the Right to Food, above n 127, para 38.

[228] Ibid, para 38.   [229] Ibid, paras 28–33.   [230] IAAKSTD, above n 20, 12.

[231] Edwardson, above n 226, 383.

[232] See Report of the Special Rapporteur on the Right to Food, above n 70, para 26, on the uncertainty surrounding the meaning of these provisions.

[233] Dan Leskien and Michael Flinter, *Intellectual Property Rights and Plant Genetic Resources: Options for a Sui Generis System* (Issues in Genetic Resources no 6) (International Plant Genetic Resources Institute, Rome, Italy, 1997), in discussing the minimum requirements of a *sui generis* system for the protection of plant varieties, stated at 26 that an effective *sui generis* system 'has to be an Intellectual Property Right (IPR), i.e. a legally enforceable right either to exclude others from certain acts in relation to the protected plant variety, or to obtain a remuneration in respect of at least certain uses of the plant variety by third parties.'

Article 8 of TRIPS permits Members to take measures to protect 'nutrition' so long as they are consistent with TRIPS: this article may imply that TRIPS permits *sui generis* regimes that are compatible with the protection of the right to food.

Most States that have eschewed patents for plant varieties have opted or been pressured to adopt the IP system developed in Europe by the International Union for the Protection of New Varieties of Plants (UPOV).[234] The European Union is trying to inject UPOV compliance into its European Partnership Agreements, currently being negotiated with numerous developing States.[235] UPOV grants monopoly rights to breeders.[236] Farmers are permitted to reuse seeds but they cannot sell produce from those harvested seeds.[237] It is to be hoped that in the future WTO Members will make use of the more balanced regimes recommended in the UN Convention on Biological Diversity 1992 (CBD) and the International Treaty on Plant Genetic Resources for Food and Agriculture 2001, which both provide greater recognition for the rights of farmers (and indigenous peoples), and that such regimes are recognized as TRIPS compliant.[238] For example, the CBD acknowledges the need for recognition and compensation for the commercialization of indigenous knowledge in Articles 8(j) and 10(c). At the time of writing, consultations were continuing within the WTO on 'the relationship between the TRIPS Agreement and the [CBD]'.[239]

Finally, the flexibilities available in TRIPS might be undermined by bilateral or other free trade deals, as discussed in Chapter 7, or by contractual clauses between farmers and the owners of seed technology.[240]

F. Conclusion

What recommendations, in light of the above, can be made in respect of ongoing Doha negotiations on agriculture? Pascal Lamy has stated that:

> The reduction of trade barriers in agriculture, enhanced market access for agricultural products and the gradual decrease in subsidies provided by rich countries to their farmers... all contribute to the same objective: the implementation of the right to food for all.[241]

---

[234] Report of the Special Rapporteur on the Right to Food, above n 127, para 16; Edwardson, above n 226, 388.

[235] See also Chapter 9, text at notes 72–90.

[236] See International Convention for the Protection of New Varieties of Plants (of 2 December 1961, revised at Geneva on 10 November 1972 and on 23 October, 1978, entered into force 8 November 1981) 1861 UNTS) (UPOV Convention). See also Report of the Special Rapporteur on the Right to Food, above n 127, para 14; see also Dommen, above n 29, 39; Edwardson, above n 226, 383; Oxfam, above n 37, 221.

[237] UPOV Convention, above n 236, Article 5.

[238] Edwardson, above n 226, 388–90; Breining-Kaufman, above n 82, 357.

[239] See WTO, 'The Relationship between the TRIPS Agreement and the Convention on Biological Diversity (Council for Trade-Related Aspects of Intellectual Property Rights', WTO doc. IP/C/W/368/Rev.1 (8 February 2006). See generally, Laurence R Helfer, 'Regime Shifting: The TRIPS Agreement and the New Dynamics of International Intellectual Property Lawmaking' (2004) 29 *Yale Journal of International Law* 1. See also Chapter 5.

[240] Report of the Special Rapporteur on the Right to Food, above n 127, para 41.

[241] Pascal Lamy, 'Towards shared responsibility and greater coherence: human rights, trade and macroeconomic policy'(Speech at the Colloquium on Human Rights in the Global Economy,

With respect to Lamy, this statement manifests the absolute faith shown by many free trade advocates in the beneficial outcomes of free trade. Yet such faith may be blind.

Developed States must reduce their protectionist barriers to facilitate the development of the agricultural industry in poorer countries, and to cease the harm done to developing States by those measures. But what about the rights of Northern farmers, whose rights might be harmed by the removal of Northern protectionism?[242] Farmers are only a small part of the population in Northern countries.[243] The trend in Northern farming is towards small hobby farms and large agribusiness farms.[244] In fact, 'the main beneficiaries of current [Northern] farm support are the largest farmers and agribusiness companies'.[245] In 2005, the UNDP reported that three quarters of EU agricultural subsidies under its Common Agricultural Policy (CAP) went to 10 per cent of subsidy recipients.[246] Wolf's figures are less extreme but still worrying: he reports that 50 per cent of CAP subsidies went to 17 per cent of farmers.[247] Stiglitz reports that 1 per cent of US farms receive 25 per cent of agricultural support, while 87 per cent goes to the top 20 per cent of farms. He thus argues that US subsidies have in fact 'driven out the small farmers', who have been tempted to sell out to agribusiness due to increased land prices.[248] Thus, a severe reduction in subsidies would not hurt the individual farmer so much as agribusiness profits.[249] Subsidies for poorer farmers could be phased out more slowly to allow for adjustment periods for those farmers. Furthermore, the large differences in productivity between Northern farmers and Southern farmers indicate that Northern farms can expect to maintain a competitive edge if subsidies were significantly reduced or even abolished.[250] Northern States would certainly remain food secure and essentially self-sufficient, despite increased competition from the South.[251]

Some liberalization by and between Southern countries should probably take place. Those States that will benefit from the lowering of barriers by developed States, such as China and Brazil, could also be required to open markets to poorer States. Indeed, inter-South trade already constitutes about one third of agricultural trade, and this trade can be expected to grow.[252] Such States will probably be able

---

Co-organized by the International Council on Human Rights and Realizing Rights, Geneva, 13 January 2010) <http://www.wto.org/english/news_e/sppl_e/sppl146_e.htm> accessed 18 September 2010.

[242] See Chapter 8, Part E.　　[243] IAAKSTD, above n 20, 7; Dommen, above n 29, 34.
[244] Spieldoch, above n 133, 13.　　[245] Oxfam, above n 37, 114.
[246] UNDP, above n 36, 130.　　[247] Wolf, above n 27, 215–16.
[248] Stiglitz, above n 219, 86.
[249] See also J Bhagwati, 'The Poor's Best Hope' *The Economist*, 20 June 2002, 24 and Martin Khor, 'Implications of some WTO rules on the Realisation of the MDGs' *Third World Network Trade & Development Series 26* (TWN, Malaysia, 2005).
[250] De Schutter, above n 13, 18.
[251] Reichert, above n 26, at 30 explains that the CAP originally came into being in order to make the European Community self-sufficient in food: that goal was achieved in the late 1970s.
[252] FAO, above n 28, states at 19–20: 'The proportion of developing country agricultural exports going to other developing countries grew from 31 percent in 1990 to 40 percent in 2002, while on the import side the share of developing country imports originating in other developing countries

to provide institutional support mechanisms for local smallholders, given their likely gains if Northern subsidies are reduced. Therefore, some lowering of barriers by those States to developed States might be justified. However, care must still be taken to ensure that safeguards are available to protect the livelihoods and rights in such States of their large populations of poor farmers, so a well-designed safeguard mechanism must be put in place.

The removal of subsidies will affect the availability of cheap food and food aid, which could harm the right to food in net food importing developing States. In that case, Northern subsidies would have to be phased out gradually to allow for adjustment. Alternatively, adjustment costs could be assisted by the provision of aid through this adjustment period, probably 'at a fraction' of the costs of current subsidies.[253] Food aid should be reformed to ensure that it conforms to the needs of the recipients rather than those of donors and exporters, and does not disrupt smallholder livelihoods in recipient states. Food aid should preferably be procured from local or regional markets, rather than from the donor's market. The outcomes of WTO negotiations should facilitate such reforms of food aid. At present, this issue is being largely ignored within the WTO.

For the majority of developing States, including poor net food importing states, further liberalization of their own markets must be preceded by institutional reforms, such as significant investment in local agricultural capacities designed to ensure food security for the most vulnerable. As noted in Chapter 5, policy space must be preserved to avoid premature liberalization with potentially or even likely disastrous consequences.

A difficult issue arises with regard to the perverse incentives that might arise for some developing States with the opening up of foreign agricultural markets. Such measures might encourage certain developing States to continue to concentrate their agricultural output on cash crops, including biofuel production, when a focus on local food production is a better way of ensuring local food security.[254] If policy space was preserved for the less agriculturally competitive developing States, such a choice (between a focus on cash crops, food production for local markets, or a mix thereof) would at least be their own rather than a policy dictated by external actors.

In order to reduce present problems in cash crop markets, liberalizing measures (for developed and the more agriculturally competitive developing States) within the WTO should be accompanied by measures (either within or outside the WTO) designed to control global volatility in agricultural markets,[255] to unravel existing market concentrations, and to upgrade the agricultural sectors in vulnerable developing States, especially those States where the sector has declined spectacularly during the last four decades.

---

expanded from 36 percent to 45 percent over the same period.' <ftp://ftp.fao.org/docrep/fao/008/a0050e/a0050e_full.pdf> accessed 22 September 2010.

[253] Stiglitz, above n 219, 87.

[254] Olivier De Schutter, 'A Human Rights Approach to Trade and Investment Policies' in FIAN and others, above n 15, 20.

[255] De Schutter, above n 13, 48–9.

Nevertheless, a persistent focus by a State on cash crop exports, if such a focus was to continue to harm food security in that State, would violate that State's obligations with respect to the right to food.[256] However, it is difficult to predict whether a focus on cash crops within a fairer agricultural trade system, with diminished agricultural protection amongst Northern States and other States with powerful agricultural sectors, and preserved policy space for those States with vulnerable agricultural sectors, would be a threat to food security or an avenue out of poverty for hungry people.

The bottom line, from a human rights point of view, is that the enjoyment of the right to food and the eradication of hunger are more important than the efficient functioning of global agricultural markets if those two goals should clash. While the assertion that human rights always prevail over free trade obligations is supported by this author, I recognize that that proposition remains legally controversial.[257] The proposition is surely less controversial when the right at issue (here, the right to food and especially the right to be free from hunger) concerns life and death, or 'human security'.[258] Market efficiency does not ensure that the hungry have access to food. It may well dictate the diversion of finite food resources to wealthier markets, leaving behind those who are too poor to attract markets and too under-resourced to compete even in a 'fair' market in order to climb out of poverty. Therefore, the effects of proposals for WTO agricultural rules on human rights and the right to food in particular should be explicitly considered during negotiations, monitored after the rules come into effect,[259] and be adjusted if the effects should be negative.[260] Indeed, the Office of the High Commissioner for Human Rights recommended human rights impact studies with regard to the right to food and trade liberalization as early as 2002, yet neither the WTO nor its members have seen fit to do so, despite the manifest human rights obligations of the latter.[261] Given the reality of hunger today, and the misery caused by the World Food Crisis, such an approach smacks of sticking one's head in the sand, or a slavish belief in the benefits of free trade, or both.

---

[256] Ibid, 43: 'each State should decide whether or not it is resilient enough to take the risk of increased vulnerability to external shocks, by maintaining or increasing its reliance on international markets to increase food security at home—but it must to do in full awareness of the implication.'
[257] See Chapter 2, Part B. [258] See, generally, Howse and Teitel, above n 61.
[259] Report of the Special Rapporteur on the Right to Food, above n 28, paras 36 and 37.
[260] See, generally, De Schutter, above n 254, 14 at 22–5. See also Smaller and Murphy, above n 21.
[261] Paasch, above n 47, 42.

7

TRIPS and the Right to Health

In Chapter 6, the problematic effects of TRIPS in the area of agriculture and the right to food were discussed. Another debate has arisen with regard to the effect of TRIPS on the right to health, in particular its effect on access to life-saving medicines. This issue is the subject matter of this chapter, along with a more extensive discussion of TRIPS.

A. Intellectual Property Protection: A Human Right?

TRIPS provides for the compulsory protection of intellectual property (IP) rights by Member States of the WTO. It effectively supplanted earlier global IP regimes, which recognized far greater flexibility for States in applying IP regimes to suit their socio-economic needs. For example, under the Paris Convention for the Protection of Industrial Property, States were permitted to exclude entire sectors from patentability and to individually determine the length of IP protection.[1]

IP rights reward the creators of new products. IP rights generally comprise the protection of rights of copyright (for authors of creative works), patents (for inventors of industrial goods), trademarks (recognizable brands which convey information to consumers about the origins and quality of goods) and trade secrets. IP regimes typically involve the conferral of monopoly rights on the owners of the relevant IP rights. For example, Part II of TRIPS requires States to confer patent rights, that is exclusive rights of exploitation, for 20 years in respect of 'new' inventions involving an 'inventive step' and which 'are capable of industrial application'. IP regimes are said to be justified because they encourage research, creative endeavour and innovation. For example, patent-holders enjoy commercial benefits from their inventions before being exposed to competition. A natural outcome from such monopoly rights is that prices for IP-protected products are inflated. This circumstance creates problems in terms of human rights if the product is essential for the enjoyment of human rights yet it becomes inaccessible to poor people. A paradigmatic example of

---

[1] Human Rights Council, 'Report of the Special Rapporteur on the right of everyone to the enjoyment of the highest attainable standard of physical and mental health, Anand Grover', UN doc. A/HRC/11/12 (31 March 2009) para 24.

such a problem concerns the impact of compulsory global patents on the price of life-saving medicines.

Before investigating the specific issue of the impact of TRIPS on access to drugs, one must examine whether IP rights are themselves human rights. Article 15(1)(c) of the ICESCR recognizes the right of everyone 'to benefit from the protection of the moral and material interests resulting from any scientific, literary or artistic production of which he is the author'. The bare words of Article 15(1)(c) seem to indicate that IP rights might be human rights.

Article 15(1)(c) was the subject of General Comment 17 of the Committee on Economic, Social and Cultural Rights. The Committee distinguished Article 15(1)(c) rights from IP rights by noting that the latter were 'of a temporary nature' and could be 'revoked, licenced or assigned to someone else', whereas human rights were 'timeless expressions of the fundamental entitlements of the human person'.[2] The right in Article 15(1)(c) protects 'the personal link between authors and their creations and between peoples, communities, or other groups and their collective cultural heritage, as well as their material interests which are necessary to enable authors to enjoy an adequate standard of living'. In contrast, IP rights 'primarily protect business and corporate interests and investments'.[3] In that respect, the Committee added that Article 15(1)(c) rights vest only in human beings, rather than corporations.[4]

Having distinguished IP rights from those in Article 15(1)(c), the Committee nevertheless outlined a number of characteristics of Article 15(1)(c) rights which resemble those commonly found under IP regimes. For example, a key justification for IP regimes is that they encourage innovation, research and development. Similarly, Article 15(1)(c) encourages 'the active contribution of creators to the arts and sciences and to the progress of society as a whole'.[5] Furthermore, protection of the material interests of authors must be 'effective',[6] and there is a core obligation to 'respect and protect the basic material interests of authors resulting from their scientific, literary or artistic productions, which are necessary to enable those authors to enjoy an adequate standard of living'.[7] The General Comment does not spell out the specific modalities of such effective protection,[8] but does suggest that the material interests of authors might be protected by vesting authors with exclusive rights to exploit their work for a period of time.[9]

However, recognition of such similar characteristics does not mean that the material interests of authors are protected to the same extent as is found in TRIPS.[10] Indeed, divergence from TRIPS is inevitable given the non-recognition of corporate rights and the greater recognition of qualifications to

---

[2] Committee on Economic, Social and Cultural Rights, 'General Comment No. 17: The right of everyone to benefit from the protection of the moral and material interests resulting from any scientific, literary or artistic production of which he or she is the author (art. 15, para. 1(c))', UN doc. E/C.12/GC/17 (12 January 2006) para 2.

[3] Ibid, para 2. [4] Ibid, para 7. [5] Ibid, para 4. [6] Ibid, para 11.

[7] Ibid, para 39(c). [8] Ibid, para 10. [9] Ibid, para 16. [10] Ibid, paras 2, 10.

Article 15(1)(c) due to the need to balance countervailing human rights.[11] In particular:

> The right of authors to benefit from the protection of the moral and material interests resulting from their scientific, literary and artistic productions cannot be isolated from the other rights recognized in the Covenant. States parties are therefore obliged to strike an adequate balance between their obligations under article 15, paragraph 1 (c), on one hand, and under the other provisions of the Covenant, on the other hand, with a view to promoting and protecting the full range of rights guaranteed in the Covenant. In striking this balance, the private interests of authors should not be unduly favoured and the public interest in enjoying broad access to their productions should be given due consideration. States parties should therefore ensure that their legal or other regimes for the protection of the moral and material interests resulting from one's scientific, literary or artistic productions constitute no impediment to their ability to comply with their core obligations in relation to the rights to food [article 11], health [article 12] and education [articles 13 and 14], as well as to take part in cultural life [article 15(1)(a)] and to enjoy the benefits of scientific progress and its applications [article 15(1)(b)], or any other right enshrined in the Covenant. Ultimately, intellectual property is a social product and has a social function. States parties thus have a duty to prevent unreasonably high costs for access to essential medicines, plant seeds or other means of food production, or for schoolbooks and learning materials, from undermining the rights of large segments of the population to health, food and education.[12]

As noted below, exceptions to TRIPS are allowed, though it is uncertain whether the exceptions are flexible enough to cater for the competing human rights of others. It is arguable that they disproportionately favour the commercial interests of IP holders over countervailing public interests, including the human rights of others. Certainly, countervailing rights are only 'protected' as exceptions to the TRIPS regime. They are only relevant as a shield in defending against a failure to fully implement TRIPS, rather than as a sword to challenge the implementation of TRIPS. Therefore, the TRIPS regime undoubtedly elevates IP rights over other potentially conflicting rights.

The Committee also anticipates alternatives to IP-like regimes, such as 'one off payments' to creators.[13] In line with the notion that the right is largely progressive (as with most ICESCR rights), States have some margin of discretion in choosing the protection regime that best suits its needs and circumstances: the Committee also recognizes that relevant national regimes will 'vary significantly'.[14] This is quite different to the 'one size fits all' regime in TRIPS.[15]

The General Comment has distinguished IP rights from those in Article 15(1)(c). It is clear that TRIPS does not protect recognized human rights, especially

---

[11] Higher standards of protection are permitted, but only so long as they do not 'unjustifiably limit the enjoyment by others' of other human rights: ibid, para 11.

[12] Ibid, para 35; see also paras 22 and 39(e).   [13] Ibid, para 16.   [14] Ibid, para 47.

[15] A different regime is now prescribed for LDCs, who do not have to fully comply with TRIPS until 2013, nor do they have to protect pharmaceutical products with patents until 2016. However, it is envisaged that TRIPS will provide the model for IP protection in those States.

given that the vast majority of the rights protected under that treaty belong to corporations.

B. The Right to Health

The most vocal criticisms of TRIPS have concerned its impact on the right to health, particularly the impact of patent rights on the price of medicines. Prices will be artificially inflated for the prescribed 20-year period as patent-holders seek to maximize returns on their investment. For example, the costs of patented drugs which combat the HIV virus are enormous. A month's worth of Atripla, an anti-HIV drug, costs US$1,300 a month.[16] Such prices are only affordable in industrialized countries due to government benefits, which are not available in the developing world. Clearly, it is impossible for most people in the developing world, where most HIV cases arise, to pay such prices. The result is a health divide: HIV remains a death sentence for most sufferers in the developing world whereas it can be managed for many years by sufferers in the developed world who have access to alleviating medication.[17] Similar problems, which have received far less attention than issues regarding access to AIDS drugs, arise with regard to access to drugs and vaccines for other treatable killer diseases. For example, most women in the developing world cannot afford the new vaccine for cervical cancer, which is widely available to women in the North.[18] Numerous factors impact detrimentally on access to medicines, such as irrational use of existing supplies,[19] but high prices brought about by patents are a key factor.[20]

Article 12 of the ICESCR recognizes the right of everyone to the enjoyment of the highest attainable standard of physical and mental health. Given the subject matter of this chapter, the right will not be analysed in *toto*: only the aspects of the right which may be affected by the implementation of TRIPS are highlighted.

Steps to be taken by States in respect of implementing Article 12 explicitly include the 'prevention, treatment and control of epidemic, endemic, occupational and other diseases' (Article 12(2)(c)) and the 'creation of conditions which would assure to all medical service and medical attention in the event of sickness' (Article 12(2)(d)).

---

[16] Daniel Costello, 'HIV treatment becoming profitable' *Los Angeles Times,* 21 February 2008.

[17] Sarah Joseph, 'Trade and the Right to Health' in Andrew Clapham and Mary Robinson (eds), *Realizing the Right to Health* (Swissbook, Geneva, 2009) 362–3.

[18] Kevin Outterson, 'Should access to medicines and TRIPS flexibilities be limited to specific diseases?' (2008) 34 *American Journal of Law and Medicine* 279, 292–3. See also Ellen FM 't Hoen, 'The Global Politics of Pharmaceutical Monopoly Power: Drug patents, access, innovation and the application of the WTO Doha Declaration on TRIPS and Public Health' (AMB Publishers, the Netherlands, 2009) 8 <http://www.msfaccess.org/main/access-patents/the-global-politics-of-pharmaceutical-monopoly-power-by-ellen-t-hoen/> accessed 20 September 2010.

[19] 't Hoen, above n 18, 3.

[20] Frederick M Abbott and Jerome H Reichmann, 'The Doha Round's Public Health Legacy: Strategies for the Production and Diffusion of Patented Medicines under the Amended TRIPS Provisions' (2007) 10 *Journal of International Economic Law* 921, 968.

The Committee's General Comment 14 fleshed out the requirements of Article 12. The right is not a right to be healthy: clearly a variety of factors, such as lifestyle and genetic predispositions, impact on whether a person is in good health or not. Instead, the 'right to health must be understood as a right to the enjoyment of a variety of facilities, goods, services and conditions necessary for the realization of the highest attainable standard of health'.[21] Health facilities, programmes, and resources (goods and services) must be available, accessible, acceptable and of good quality.[22] An element of accessibility is affordability.[23]

The right includes access to 'essential drugs', as defined by the World Health Organisation (WHO),[24] of suitable quality[25] on a non-discriminatory basis.[26] In fact, the right of access to such drugs is described as a core obligation, a presumptively immediate rather than progressive obligation.[27]

General Comment 14 links the identification of essential drugs to the WHO's list of essential medicines, which has been updated from time to time since its initial adoption in 1977. Only about 5 per cent of drugs on the current list are protected by patent.[28] How can this be, when numerous patented medicines are the only treatments available, or are the most effective treatments, for certain deadly diseases? One important criterion for inclusion on the WHO list is cost effectiveness. Given that many States cannot afford patented medicines, they are not 'cost effective' so they are excluded from the list.[29] The exclusion of patented medicines is caused by their high prices rather than any lack of comparable (or superior) effectiveness compared to the cheaper medicines on the list.

General Comment 14 was adopted in 2000. A report by the Special Rapporteur on the Right to Health, Paul Hunt, in 2006 revisited the issue of the 'human right to medicines'.[30] The WHO list was retained as a starting point for identifying the core obligation of a State in respect of providing essential medicines.[31] However, States also have progressive obligations with regard to the provision of all effective drugs, whether on the list or not.[32] As with all progressive obligations, States should not take retrogressive steps[33] with regard to the availability of such drugs, which may preclude the introduction of a patent regime which causes prices to skyrocket.

Another core obligation identified in General Comment 14 is to 'take measures to prevent, treat and control epidemic and endemic diseases'.[34] This obligation is

---

[21] Committee on Economic, Social and Cultural Rights, 'General Comment 14: The right to the highest attainable standard of health (art. 12)', UN doc. E/C.12/2000/4 (11 August 2000) para 9.
[22] Ibid, para 12.   [23] Ibid, para 12(b).   [24] Ibid, para 12(a).
[25] Ibid, para 12(d).   [26] Ibid, para 12(b).
[27] Ibid, para 43(d); see Chapter 1, text after note 81.
[28] See Amir Attaran, 'How Do Patents And Economic Policies Affect Access To Essential Medicines In Developing Countries?' (May/June 2004) *Health Affairs* 155.
[29] See World Health Organization, *The World Medicines Situation* (WHO, 2004) Chapter 7, via <http://apps.who.int/medicinedocs/en/d/Js6160e/9.html> accessed 20 September 2010.
[30] UNGA, 'Report of the Special Rapporteur on the right of everyone to the enjoyment of the highest standard of physical and mental health, Paul Hunt', UN doc. A/61/338 (13 September 2006) para 37.
[31] Ibid, para 57.   [32] Ibid, para 58.
[33] See Chapter 1, text at notes 71–2. See also General Comment 14, above n 21, para 32.
[34] Ibid, para 44(c).

separate to the obligation regarding the provision of essential medicines. Of course, one way of combating epidemics and endemic diseases is to facilitate access to the drugs which counter those illnesses, whether they are on the WHO list or not.

Furthermore, the Committee has included the following as examples of State practices that violate Article 12:

the adoption of laws or policies that interfere with the enjoyment of any of the components of the right to health; and the failure of the State to take into account its legal obligations regarding the right to health when entering into bilateral or multilateral agreements with other States, international organizations and other entities, such as multinational corporations.[35]

Clearly, the Committee believes that a State's acceptance of TRIPS or other WTO obligations breaches its ICESCR obligations if fulfilment of the former obligations jeopardize enjoyment of the right to health.

In an earlier statement about the relationship between IP and other ICESCR rights in 2001, the Committee was more blunt:

any intellectual property regime that makes it more difficult for a State to comply with its core obligations in relation to health, food, education, especially, or any other right set out in the Covenant, is inconsistent with the legally binding obligations of the State party.[36]

As noted in Hunt's 2006 report, States are at the least expected to take advantage of TRIPS flexibilities (discussed below) to make life-saving medicines available to their populations.[37]

Of relevance to States' obligations as members of the WTO is the following statement from General Comment 14:

Depending on the availability of resources, States should facilitate access to essential health facilities, goods and services *in other countries*, wherever possible and provide the necessary aid when required. States parties should ensure that the right to health is given due attention in international agreements and, to that end, should consider the development of further legal instruments. In relation to the conclusion of other international agreements, States parties should take steps to ensure that these instruments do not adversely impact upon the right to health. Similarly, States parties have an obligation to ensure that their actions as members of international organizations take due account of the right to health.[38]

The Committee in General Comment 14 thus endorses the notion of extraterritorial obligations, which is discussed in Chapter 8.

The recognition of a right of access to medicine was endorsed by consensus in the UN Human Rights Council in 2009.[39] The 53 Council members, most of whom

---

[35] Ibid, para 50.
[36] Committee on Economic, Social and Cultural Rights, 'Human Rights and Intellectual Property: Statement by the Committee on Economic Social and Cultural Rights', UN doc. E/C.12/2001/15 (14 December 2001) para 12.
[37] Report of the Special Rapporteur on the right to health, above n 30, para 47.
[38] General Comment 14, above n 21, para 39 (emphasis added).
[39] See Human Rights Council, 'Access to Medicine in the context of the right of everyone to the enjoyment of the highest attainable standard of physical and mental health', UN doc. A/HRC/RES/12/24 (12 October 2009).

are WTO Member States, recognized that access to medicines was a fundamental element of the right to health, and called upon States to ensure that 'the application of international agreements' was 'supportive of public health policies that promote broad access to safe, effective and affordable medicines'.[40] While the Council recognized the importance of IP protection, it also expressed 'concerns about its effect on prices'.[41] Finally, it called on all States to enforce IP rights in a manner which did not restrict the 'legitimate trade in medicines' and which provided 'safeguards against the abuse' of such rights.[42]

It is also worth mentioning the right to life in Article 6 of the ICCPR. The HRC stated in an early General Comment that States should take 'all possible measures to reduce infant mortality and to increase life expectancy, especially in adopting measures to eliminate malnutrition and epidemics'.[43] The General Comment indicates measures that hamper access to life-saving drugs are probably in breach of Article 6.

C. Arguments in Favour of Patents

IP protection restricts trade and competition, so IP clauses are somewhat anomalous in trade agreements, which are normally designed to decrease trade barriers. What is the justification for IP protection?[44] Due to their relevance to this chapter, I will concentrate on arguments in favour of patents.[45] Patents reward people for their inventions, thus encouraging creativity and innovation. Patents operate on the assumption that people are not inherently altruistic, and expect rewards for their endeavours, especially when those endeavours are risky as they may, and often do, result in costly failure.[46] Furthermore, the money raised from patent protection is said to be necessary to fund the considerable costs of research and development (R&D).[47] Therefore, without patents, innovation in the pharmaceutical field (or any industrial field) might grind to a standstill. While it is true that the high prices generated by patent protection may render access to drugs selective,

---

[40] Ibid, para 3.   [41] Ibid, para 5.   [42] Ibid, para 6.

[43] Human Rights Committe, 'General no. 6, The Right to life (art. 6)', Sixteenth session 1982 (30 April 1982), para 5.

[44] The following commentary is adapted from Sarah Joseph, 'Pharmaceutical Corporations and Access to Drugs: the "Fourth Wave" of Corporate Human Rights Scrutiny' (2003) 25 *Human Rights Quarterly* 425, 431–5.

[45] It may be noted that many of the arguments in favour of patents apply analogously to other IP rights such as copyright.

[46] Apparently, 'only one of 4000 new chemical compounds discovered in the laboratory is ever marketed.' See Shanker A Singham, 'Competition Policy and the Stimulation of Innovation: TRIPS and the Interface Between Competition and Patent Protection in the Pharmaceutical Industry' (2000) 26 *Brooklyn Journal of International Law* 363, 373.

[47] Ibid, 372–4; see also James Thou Gathii, 'Construing Intellectual Property Rights and Competition Policy Consistency with Facilitating Access to Affordable AIDS drugs to low-end consumers' (2001) 53 *Florida Law Review* 727, 771–83, commenting on the costs of R&D in the US drug industry caused by the (perhaps overly) high standards of the Food and Drug Authority (FDA).

it is nevertheless better that a drug is available to some rather than non-existent and available to no one.

The global extension of patent law mandated by TRIPS helps to ensure that patents are not undermined by the sale of competing pirated copies. Furthermore, global IP regimes should theoretically encourage greater technology transfer between countries, greater foreign direct investment, and greater local innovation within compliant states.[48] All of these outcomes should accelerate the economic development of poor countries, with positive knock-on effects for human rights.

Thus, perhaps it is arguable that pharmaceutical patents are justifiable under international human rights law, as they promote R&D which is essential for the future enhancement of rights to life and health. Furthermore, to the extent that they are held by natural persons, they are one way of protecting that person's rights under Article 15(1)(c) of the ICESCR.

The issue of justifications for patents is revisited below. Before doing so, it is necessary to outline the effect of the TRIPS regime on pharmaceutical patents.

D. TRIPS Requirements for Pharmaceutical Patents

Article 33 of TRIPS requires Member States of the WTO to provide protection for patent rights for 20 years. Developing States were given a period of time to comply, but these timelines have now run out for all but LDCs. Does TRIPS provide for any exceptions, which permit States to make medicines available at a cheaper price than that prescribed by the patent-holder? If it does not, TRIPS may well prescribe a collision course with Article 12 of the ICESCR, and even the right to life in Article 6 of the ICCPR.

Article 27(2) of TRIPS allows States to prohibit the patentability of products, 'the prevention within their territory of the commercial exploitation of which is necessary to protect... human, animal or plant life or health'. Some have argued that this provision permits States to deny patentability to medical products.[49] However, Dr Adam McBeth's rejection of that argument is persuasive: he argues that the provision is more likely to be aimed at the rejection of patents for harmful products such as inhumane weapons and dangerous narcotics.[50] It seems unlikely that a prohibition of *any* commercial exploitation of medicines could be deemed necessary to protect health.

Article 30 contains another exception to TRIPS obligations regarding patents:

Members may provide limited exceptions to the exclusive rights conferred by a patent, provided that such exceptions do not unreasonably conflict with a normal exploitation of the patent and do not unreasonably prejudice the legitimate interests of the patent owner, taking account of the legitimate interests of third parties.

---

[48] Singham, above n 46, 375–85.

[49] See, eg, Sara Ford, 'Compulsory Licensing Provisions under the TRIPS Agreement: Balancing Pills and Patents' (2000) 15 *American University International Law Review* 941, 965.

[50] Adam McBeth, *International Economic Actors and Human Rights* (Routledge, Oxford, 2009) 140.

The rights of impoverished sick people should be recognized as legitimate third party interests for the purposes of Article 30. However, the setting aside of a patent in order to facilitate their access to drugs might be deemed by WTO panels or its Appellate Body to unreasonably conflict with the rights of the patent owner. Article 30 has rarely been interpreted, so its scope remains unclear. In *Canada— Patent Protection of Pharmaceutical Products*,[51] a WTO panel found that Canadian laws, known as 'Bolar provisions', which permitted the testing of generic drugs prior to the expiry of a patent in order to ensure that they could be marketed as soon as the patent expired, were valid. The stockpiling of generic drugs by generic manufacturers in anticipation of the expiry of a patent was not, however, permitted under Article 30. Testing and stockpiling are incidental measures which are not comparable to a measure which might significantly reduce the price of patented drugs for poor people. It seems unlikely that the wholesale rejection of patent rights for life-saving drugs is envisaged under Article 30. On the other hand, it has been suggested that the shortening of a patent period for a life-saving product might be permitted under Article 30.[52] Furthermore, Frederick M Abbott and Jerome H Reichmann have suggested that the *Canadian—Patent Protection of Pharmaceutical Products* case may not be followed by a future WTO panel, given the developments (discussed below) regarding the application of TRIPS to pharmaceutical products which arose after that case, such as the adoption of the Declaration on the TRIPS Agreement and Public Health in 2001.[53]

Under Article 6, TRIPS explicitly has no impact on the 'exhaustion' of IP rights. Exhaustion rules regulate the control a patent-holder has over patented goods after their original sale.[54] Once IP rights have been exhausted, the patent-holder has no control over subsequent sales. This means that TRIPS has no impact on parallel importation, which involves the importation of patented goods by one State from another State if the product was marketed in the latter State by the patent-holder.[55] Parallel importation can bring down the price of a product if the product is marketed in another country at a cheaper price.[56]

Article 31 permits States to issue compulsory licences in respect of the generic manufacture of patented goods for a particular purpose without the consent of the patent-holder. Such purposes might include a State's need to address a refusal by the patent-holder to licence sale of the product or a need to combat anti-competitive practices.[57] Compulsory licences may also be issued to ensure that a patented drug is made available at affordable prices in the case of a health emergency. The licence may prescribe that the government itself manufactures the product, or that a third party, such as a generic drugs manufacturer, is authorized to make and sell the

---

[51] WTO doc. WT/DS114/R (17 March 2000) (Report of the Panel).
[52] Robert Weissman, 'A long strange TRIPS: the Pharmaceutical Industry drive to Harmonize Global Intellectual Property, and the Remaining WTO Legal Alternatives Available to Third World Countries' (1996) 17 *University of Pennsylvania Journal of International Economic Law* 1069, 1111.
[53] Abbott and Reichmann, above n 20, 957–8, 986.   [54] McBeth, above n 50, 145.
[55] WTO, 'TRIPS and Pharmaceutical Patents' (WTO Fact Sheet, September 2006) 5.
[56] McBeth, above n 50, 145.
[57] Report of the Special Rapporteur on the Right to Health, above n 1, para 36.

product.[58] A State may only issue a compulsory licence when it has considered the individual merits of issuing such a licence (paragraph (a)). Under paragraph (b), the issuing of a compulsory licence must be preceded by genuine negotiations with the patent-holder to seek a voluntary licence on reasonable commercial terms. This condition is waived in times of 'national emergency or other circumstances of extreme urgency' or in the case of government manufacture and use. The patent-holder must nevertheless be notified as soon as possible in such circumstances. The scope and duration of a compulsory licence is limited to the purpose for which it is issued (paragraph (c)). Under paragraph (h), the patent-holder must receive 'adequate remuneration in the circumstances... taking into account the economic value of the authorization'. Finally, the decision to issue a compulsory licence, as well as the determination of the amount of remuneration, must be subject to judicial or other independent review (paragraphs (i) and (j)). It is uncertain how the 'adequacy' of remuneration should be calculated. The reference to 'economic value' seems logically concerned with the economic value to the licencee: the purpose of compulsory licensing would be defeated if adequate remuneration is based on the economic value of the patent to the patentee.[59]

Disputes over the extent of a WTO Member's compulsory licensing rights arose in the late 1990s and into the new century. A 1999 presidential decree in Brazil confirmed that compulsory licensing was a valid strategy for countering the high prices of anti-AIDS drugs under Brazilian law. At that time, Brazil did not actually issue any compulsory licences but the ever-present threat of doing so enabled it to negotiate deep price cuts with drug manufacturers[60] and consequently provide anti-retroviral treatment to all who needed it.[61] The greater availability of such drugs halved the number of deaths from HIV,[62] and also reduced the rate of infection due to the lower viral load in infected persons.[63] The costs of the programme were offset by savings in hospitalization rates, as well as incalculable savings to Brazil's society and economy.[64] Nevertheless, the US initiated a complaint against Brazil in the WTO, claiming that Brazil had breached TRIPS. This action was fairly typical of US policy at the time: it had threatened unilateral action against

---

[58] Ibid, para 37.   [59] Weissman, above n 52, 1114.

[60] Commission on Human Rights, 'The impact of the Agreement on Trade-Related Aspects of Intellectual Property Rights on human rights: Report of the High Commissioner', UN doc. E/CN.4/Sub.2/2001/13 (27 June 2001) (UNHCHR) paras 51–8. Note that Brazil did issue a compulsory licence in May 2007 after negotiations with the manufacturer Merck broke down in relation to an AIDS drug. See <http://ictsd.org/i/news/bridges/11643/>.

[61] Tina Rosenberg, 'Look at Brazil' *New York Times Magazine*, 28 January 2001; Gathii, above n 47, 734–5.

[62] Oxfam, 'Patients versus Patents: Five years after the Doha Declaration' (Oxfam Briefing Paper 95, 2006) <http://www.oxfam.org/sites/www.oxfam.org/files/Patents%20vs.%20Patients.pdf> accessed 27 October 2010.

[63] See Rosenberg, above n 61, 26; Consensus Statement of Members of the Faculty of Harvard University, Antiretroviral Treatment for AIDS in Poor Countries, March 2001, 14, <http://www.hsph.harvard.edu/hai/conferences_events/2001/consensus_aids_therapy.pdf> accessed 20 January 2003; Dirceu B Greco and Mariangela Samão, 'Brazilian policy of universal access to AIDS treatment: sustainability challenges and perspectives' (2007) 21 *AIDS* S37, S40.

[64] Joseph, above n 44, 444.

many States for seeking to use policies even though those policies were possibly compliant with TRIPS.[65]

In March 2001, a group of 39 pharmaceutical companies challenged the constitutionality of South African legislation, which was designed to facilitate access to cheaper drugs, in the High Court in Pretoria in March 2001, claiming that it breached their rights to property, namely their IP. The companies feared that the legislation expanded the government's powers to issue compulsory licences and import generic versions of patented goods. The companies urged the Court to interpret the legislation in light of TRIPS.[66] Notably, they did not urge the Court to interpret the legislation in light of any human rights treaties. No decision was ever made. The companies dropped the suit in April 2001 after a wave of global outrage. The spectre of 39 companies, whose combined profits outweighed the GDP of South Africa, moving to stop the provision of cheap drugs to a population with an appalling rate of HIV/AIDS did immeasurable damage to the companies' reputations.[67]

In 2001, developing States conducted a campaign within the WTO to clarify the scope of the compulsory licensing provisions.[68] Backtracking by opponents of compulsory licensing on this issue became evident. As noted, the South African pharmaceutical case collapsed. Furthermore, the US effectively backed away from its case against Brazil in 2001.[69] Indeed, the US's position was completely undermined by its own actions in October 2001. A few weeks after the September 11 terrorist attacks, a number of anthrax cases appeared in the US. In late October, the German company Bayer was forced to sell its anti-anthrax drug Cipro to both the US and Canada at a heavily discounted price after both States had threatened to issue compulsory licences. Such actions were astonishingly hypocritical: the US had suffered three deaths and Canada none, which hardly compared to the various medical emergencies, especially the alarming rates of HIV, being experienced in developing States.[70]

The battle over TRIPS and pharmaceuticals in the WTO culminated with the adoption of the Declaration on the TRIPS Agreement and Public Health[71] in December 2001. This Declaration asserted that TRIPS did 'not and should

---

[65] Ken Shadlen, 'Resources, Rules and international political economy: the politics of development in the WTO' in Sarah Joseph, David Kinley, and Jeff Waincymer (eds), *The World Trade Organization and Human Rights: Interdisciplinary Perspectives* (Edward Elgar, Cheltenham, 2009) 118–19. Eg, Shadlen notes at fn 22 that the US had withdrawn GSP preferences from States that failed to comply with higher IP standards than were required under TRIPS. See also McBeth, above n 50, 144.

[66] It seems unlikely that the Act actually breached TRIPS.   [67] Joseph, above n 44, 443–4.

[68] Shadlen, above n 65, 119.

[69] The complaint was settled on the basis that Brazil would consult with the US before issuing a compulsory licence due to a patent-holder's failure to work a patent locally: Duncan Matthews, 'Intellectual Property Rights, Human Rights and the Right to Health' in W Grosheide (ed), *Intellectual Property Rights and Human Rights: a Paradox* (Edward Elgar, 2010, forthcoming).

[70] Joseph, above n 44, 446–7; Joseph Stiglitz, *Making Globalization Work* (Penguin, London, 2007) 122. See also Abbott and Reichmann, above n 20, 939.

[71] WTO doc. WT/MIN(01)/DEC/2 (adopted on 14 November 2001). The following commentary is adapted from Joseph, above n 17, 364.

not prevent members from taking measures to protect public health'. Therefore, TRIPS 'can and should be interpreted and implemented in a manner supportive of WTO members' right to public health and, in particular, promote access to medicines for all'. In particular, the right of States to issue compulsory licences was reaffirmed, and 'public health crises, including those relating to HIV/AIDS, tuberculosis, malaria and other epidemics' were recognized as national emergencies for the purposes of issuing a TRIPS compliant compulsory licence. Finally, LDCs were given until 2016 before they are required to respect pharmaceutical patents.

The Doha Declaration clarified that the compulsory licensing provisions of TRIPS may be used to facilitate access to medicines to combat public health emergencies.

By the end of 2007, 52 developing States had issued post-Doha Declaration compulsory licences, indicating that the Declaration has had the desired effect of prompting needy States to make use of the Article 31 exception.[72] Most of these States are LDCs that do not have to provide patents for pharmaceuticals until 2016.[73] Use of compulsory licences has also been encouraged by some international donors, such as the Global Fund to Fight AIDS, TB and Malaria, the World Bank, and UNITAID.[74] The huge majority of these post-Doha compulsory licences relate to AIDS drugs, with only Thailand and Taiwan issuing compulsory licenses for drugs for other conditions.[75]

Another breakthrough arose within the WTO in 2003. One general restriction in TRIPS on compulsory licences is that the licence, under Article 31(f), must be issued 'predominantly for the supply of the domestic market'. This provision was problematic, as many developing States lack the capacity to manufacture generic pharmaceutical products, and therefore must import generics from countries which have such a capacity. Certainly, States may export compulsory licensed products so long as such exports are 'less than a predominant part of production':[76] India has legislated to routinely allow for export in such circumstances.[77] Nevertheless, the ability of States to import compulsorily licensed products is limited under Article 31(f) because other States are prohibited from producing such generic goods *primarily* for export.[78]

In 2003, the WTO's General Council waived the territorial restriction on compulsory licences for pharmaceutical products in certain circumstances.[79] The waiver

---

[72] 't Hoen, above n 18, 44.   [73] Ibid, 60.

[74] Ibid, 63–5. In contrast, the US President's Emergency Plan for AIDS Relief (PEPFAR) does not encourage implementation of the Doha Declaration.   [75] Ibid, 61.

[76] Abbott and Reichmann, above n 20, 958.   [77] 't Hoen, above n 18, 58–9.

[78] Howse and Teitel believe that the export of generics to impoverished States that lacked appropriate manufacturing capacity would have been permissible under Article 30: Robert Howse and Ruti Teitel, 'Beyond the Divide: the International Covenant on Economic Social and Cultural Rights and the World Trade Organization' in Joseph, Kinley and Waincymer (eds), above n 65, 61–2. See, for a similar argument, Abbott and Reichmann, above n 18, 957 and 986. At 958, Abbott and Reichmann also argue that generics can be exported to non-WTO members that lack capacity to manufacture their own products under Article 30.

[79] WTO, 'Implementation of Paragraph 6 of the Doha Declaration on the TRIPS Agreement and Public Health' (Decision of the General Council of 30 August 2003), WTO doc. WT/L/540 (30 August 2003).

remains in place, pending ratification of a formal TRIPS amendment (proposed Article 31bis) designed to enshrine the rules of the waiver.[80] Under the waiver, the territorial restrictions on compulsory licences may be lifted to facilitate the export of generic drugs to LDCs, or other States that notify the TRIPS Council of a desire to import due to a lack of manufacturing capacity, for the purposes of combating public health emergencies as specified in the Declaration. There are extensive procedural prerequisites concerning notice by both exporter and importer to the WTO's TRIPS Council regarding use of the waiver. Safeguards must be implemented to ensure that the compulsory licensed generics are not diverted to another market.

The waiver facilitates exports of generic drugs to LDCs and other vulnerable developing States to allow them to benefit from the compulsory licensing provisions. By March 2010, only Rwanda had notified the WTO of an intention to use the waiver as an importing State; Canada had agreed to export generic versions of the relevant anti-HIV drug. There are a number of possible explanations for this lack of use of the waiver.

First, some developing States with manufacturing capacity (as opposed to LDCs who generally lack such capacity) only had to fully comply with TRIPS with regard to pharmaceutical patents from 1 January 2005. Up until that time, such States could authorize generic production of patented goods, and supply such generics to other States: India in particular was a major supplier to the world of such generics. Therefore, the 2005 deadline delayed the need for some States to use the waiver provisions.[81]

Furthermore, the Doha Declaration and the waiver are likely to have prompted some pharmaceutical corporations, who feel threatened by compulsory licensing schemes, to make their products available to some developing States on a cheap or even cost-free basis. Indeed, numerous corporations have adopted such a strategy,[82] though these efforts are generally confined to drugs for AIDS, malaria, and a few other drugs, rather than the wide range of treatable killer diseases.[83]

Finally, Howse and Teitel bemoan the excessive formalities, suggesting that the requirements are too costly for generic manufacturers.[84] These formalities are discussed further below.

Does TRIPS permit States to comply with human rights duties regarding access to drugs?

In light of the flexibilities allowed under TRIPS, as well as the justification for patents in promoting future R&D, this section examines whether States are able

[80] WTO, 'Amendment of the TRIPS Agreement' (Decision of 6 December 2005), WTO doc. WT/L/641.
[81] Abbott and Reichmann, above n 20, 934, 949; 't Hoen, above n 28, 37.
[82] See, eg, <http://www.diflucanpartnership.org/en/welcome/Default.aspx> regarding Pfizer's initiatives. See also Abbott and Reichmann, above n 20, 948–9.
[83] Outterson, above n 18, 289–90.
[84] Howse and Teitel, above n 78, 62–3. See also Adam McBeth, 'When Nobody Comes to the Party: Why Have No States Used the WTO Scheme for Compulsory Licensing of Essential Medicines?' (2006) 3 *New Zealand Journal of International Law* 1, 23–30.

to simultaneously comply with TRIPS and their human rights duties regarding access to drugs.

In a 2009 report to the Human Rights Council, the Special Rapporteur on the Right to Health, Anand Grover, wrote extensively on TRIPS and the right of access to medicines. He did not explicitly find that TRIPS conflicted with the right. Instead he stressed that States had to take advantage of available TRIPS flexibilities if they are unable to independently facilitate access to patented goods. That is, States had to make full use of compulsory licensing, importation of generic goods under the 2003 waiver, parallel importation, the limited exceptions permitted under Article 30 TRIPS, and remaining transition periods.[85] States should also properly exercise their discretion over the standards for patentability to allow for opposition and revocation procedures and to combat anti-competitive practices. His comments on these issues are analysed below.

On timelines, Grover noted that many LDCs have already implemented TRIPS despite the 2013 deadline for general TRIPS implementation and the 2016 deadline for implementation of pharmaceutical patents.[86] This premature introduction of patent regimes deprived them of the ability to continue using generics, and also probably removed policy space that might have enabled the growth of local manufacturing capacity.[87]

Furthermore, while Article 27 of TRIPS provides that patents must be available for new inventions capable of industrial application, it does not specify particular criteria for patentability. Therefore, States are presumably able to apply strict criteria to prevent the 'evergreening' of patents. Evergreening 'refers to the practice of obtaining new patents on a patented medicine by making minor changes to it'.[88] Evergreening delays the introduction of generic competition. For example, Grover noted that India and the Philippines both refuse patents to 'new forms of known substances unless they [were] significantly more efficacious and new (or second) uses and combinations of new substances'.[89] India's high standard is evident in its refusal to patent new versions of Novartis's cancer drug Glivec, which was unsuccessfully challenged in local court proceedings by Novartis.[90]

Grover also noted that TRIPS did not prohibit States from adopting laws which allowed for the opposing and revocation of patents in appropriate circumstances. 'Oppositions' could help under-resourced patent offices make educated decisions over whether a product or process was truly patentable. India and Thailand both provide for oppositions, and civil society groups have been successful in both States in staving off patents for certain anti-HIV drugs. The right of 'opposition' should be extended to public interest groups and civil society organizations, rather than being limited to business competitors and government bodies.[91]

---

[85] Special Rapporteur on the Right to Health, above n 1, para 27.   [86] Ibid, para 30.
[87] Ibid, para 31.   [88] Ibid, para 34.   [89] Ibid, para 35.
[90] *Novartis v India* W.P. Nos 24759 of 2006 and 24760 of 2006, High Court of Madras (India), 6 August 2007. See also Abbott and Reichmann, above n 20, 959.
[91] Special Rapporteur on the Right to Health, above n 1, paras 50–2. On the provision for opposition in India, see 't Hoen, above n 18, 77–8.

On compulsory licensing, the language of the Doha Declaration arguably restricts compulsory licensing in respect of health crises beyond epidemics. Does its wording recognize the right to issue compulsory licences to facilitate access to drugs for sufferers of cancer, diabetes, heart disease, or other lethal non-communicable diseases? The US, for example, has behaved as if it does not, by threatening trade sanctions against Thailand in 2007 for its proposal to issue compulsory licences for medication for heart disease and cancer.[92] Canada, in enacting legislation to permit exports of compulsorily licensed drugs under the waiver, restricted such exports to AIDS drugs and off-patent medicines.[93]

However, it seems clear that the Doha Declaration is meant to list examples of relevant diseases, and is not an exhaustive list thereof: it does not limit its application to specific diseases.[94] The Declaration therefore reflects the reality of the global disease burden: 'the number one cause of death' in developing States is in fact heart disease.[95] In any case, the Doha Declaration did not change TRIPS law (beyond extending the deadline for compliance by LDCs with respect to pharmaceutical patents): it essentially clarified one aspect of TRIPS in order to stave off unwarranted pressure from pharmaceutical companies and developed States, particularly the US.[96] There is no reason to assume that Article 31 itself does not permit licences for such diseases.[97] However, many developing States may not wish to risk litigation or other consequences to find out.

Furthermore, Grover calls upon States to streamline their domestic legal provisions regarding compulsory licensing, which are often cumbersome.[98] In particular, the 'complex administrative procedures' entailed in the 2003 waiver have been exacerbated by further requirements imposed by the domestic laws of potential exporting States.[99]

Indeed, red tape requirements are probably a key reason for the lacklustre response thus far to the 2003 waiver. The waiver stipulates that exporting and importing States must notify the TRIPS council of the types and quantities of drugs involved in use of its scheme. The notification requirements needlessly expose vulnerable States to possible political pressure by alerting the world of their intentions.[100] Crucially, the requirements dictate that exporters can only export on a 'drug-by-drug, case-by-case, country-by-country' basis.[101] An importing country may not be able to provide enough of a market to enable a generics exporter to develop the economies of scale needed to make its venture economically viable.[102] In this respect, Abbott and Reichmann have suggested that groups of developing countries act jointly to seek imported generics, so as

---

[92] Outterson, above n 18, 282.   [93] Ibid, 281–2.

[94] Abbott and Reichmann, above n 20, 937; 't Hoen, above n 18, 32.

[95] Outterson, above n 18, 283; see also 't Hoen, above n 18, 86.

[96] Shadlen, above n 65, 121; see also James Harrison, *The Human Rights Impact of the World Trade Organisation* (Hart, Oxford, 2007) 165.

[97] Grover confidently proclaims that Article 31 allows compulsory licensing of drugs to combat such diseases at Special Rapporteur on the Right to Health, above n 1, para 37.

[98] Ibid, para 39.   [99] Ibid, para 41.   [100] 't Hoen, above n 18, 36–7.

[101] Ibid, 36.   [102] Ibid, xvii; Abbott and Reichmann, above n 20, 943.

to provide a viable market for offshore generic suppliers.[103] Nevertheless, Ellen 't Hoen, a former policy and advocacy director for Médecins sans Frontières and now a senior policy adviser with UNITAID, has concluded that the system is 'highly unlikely [to] provide sufficient economic incentive to keep the generic medicines sector in business'.[104]

Grover recommends that States adopt laws which give them the greatest flexibility to use parallel importation as a mechanism to bring down prices. In particular, States should adopt the principle of 'international exhaustion', dictating that IP rights are exhausted once a product is marketed anywhere in the world, thus allowing for parallel importation. South Africa, Kenya, and Honduras are examples of States which have adopted the principle of international exhaustion. In contrast, a principle of 'national exhaustion', which is adopted for example by Brazil and Morocco, only exhausts IP rights for the purposes of further sale inside a country, and does not permit importation of a product without the patent-holder's consent.[105]

Article 40 of TRIPS recognizes that IP rights-holders can abuse their position and unduly restrict competition by, for example, imposing unreasonable conditions of licence for use. Grover cites with approval the practice of the South African Competition Commission, which has held that the failure by a pharmaceutical company to grant a licence to a generics manufacturer was an abuse of its dominant position. Such measures could be repeated across the world to ease anticompetitive practices in the pharmaceutical industry.[106]

Finally, technical incapacities hamper the ability of some States, particularly LDCs, to utilize TRIPS flexibilities.[107] In this respect, they may receive technical assistance under Article 67 of TRIPS. Unfortunately, such technical assistance has often prompted developing States and LDCs to implement TRIPS before they were required to, and indeed to adopt IP laws that extend protection beyond that required under TRIPS.[108]

The implication from Grover's report is that TRIPS obligations do not conflict with the right of access to medicines, though he does conclude that TRIPS has 'had an adverse impact on prices and availability of medicines'.[109] It is up to States to utilize all available flexibilities, as needed, in order to ensure access to medicines domestically. The common failure to do so amounts to a violation of the right to health by the States concerned.

Similarly, the placement of pressure on weaker States by stronger States to forego such flexibilities constitutes an extraterritorial breach of human rights obligations by the latter States.[110] Despite the 2001 Doha Declaration and the 2003 waiver, such pressure continues. Thailand has been pressured by both the US and the

---

[103] Abbott and Reichmann, above n 20, 943, 972–7.
[104] 't Hoen, above n 18, 39; see also 42.
[105] Special Rapporteur on the Right to Health, above n 1, para 44.
[106] Ibid, paras 53–5. See also European Union Directorate-General for Competition, *Pharmaceutical Sector Inquiry-Preliminary Report*, 28 November 2008.
[107] Special Rapporteur on the Right to Health, above n 1, para 65.   [108] Ibid, para 63.
[109] Ibid, para 94.   [110] See Chapter 8 on extraterritorial obligations.

European Commission for its issuance of compulsory licences in 2006–2007.[111] Thailand has however made clear that it will 'bring a claim for WTO dispute settlement if trade sanctions are wrongfully imposed' against it in respect of those licenses, which are almost definitely TRIPS compliant.[112] Thailand's calling of the bluff of the North is an excellent development from a human rights point of view.

Pressure also comes from pharmaceutical companies: an example is Novartis's court challenge to India's failure to patent new versions of Glivec. After Novartis lost its case in the Madras High Court, it announced that it would 'redirect its research and development programs away from India to more receptive environments'.[113] While India seems robust enough to resist pressure from Novartis, the same is not necessarily true of more vulnerable developing States.

Therefore, despite the Doha Declaration and the waiver, pressure has been applied by the North and pharmaceutical companies, somewhat unsuccessfully, to attempt to dissuade States with emerging economies, such as Thailand, from making use of compulsory licensing. In contrast, such pressure has not been overtly applied to LDCs, such as the many from sub-Saharan Africa which have issued compulsory licences.[114] LDC markets are possibly too small to mobilize a backlash from pro-IP States and lobbies. More importantly, LDCs lack the capacity to manufacture their own generics so they must import them. If pressure is successfully applied to prevent States such as Thailand, India, and Brazil from manufacturing generics, import-dependent LDCs will lack suppliers outside the rubric of the scheme outlined in the waiver. As discussed above, that scheme is highly problematic.[115]

McBeth has also suggested that TRIPS does not directly conflict with the right to health. Rather:

the greater impediment to the realisation of the right to health in the context of access to essential medicines is not the framework of international trade law, but the conduct of governments and pharmaceutical corporations under cover of the sympathetic or at least ambiguous intellectual property provisions of the WTO system.[116]

At the least, however, TRIPS might be deemed to be an unfortunate development for the protection of human rights. Even the World Bank has deemed it 'inequitable' with regard to its impact on the developing world.[117]

E. A Reconsideration of the Justification for Intellectual Property

The diluting of IP rights via the extensive use of flexibilities, as advocated by Special Rapporteur Anand Grover, would presumably diminish the benefits of IP. For example, incentives for future R&D and technology transfer to developing

---

[111] Abbott and Reichmann, above n 20, 953–6; 't Hoen, above n 18, 49.
[112] Abbott and Reichmann, above n 20, 956.   [113] Ibid, 959.
[114] 't Hoen, above n 18, 65.   [115] Ibid, 66–7.   [116] McBeth, above n 50, 150.
[117] World Bank, *World Development Report 2006: Equity and Development* (World Bank, Washington DC, 2006) 215.

States might be jeopardized. Therefore, it is now necessary to revisit the justifications for IP.

First, one may note that Grover's recommendations are essentially aimed at developing States. While patented goods are expensive in developed States, those States generally have the capacity to provide many patented medicines to those who need them. Therefore, the real question is whether the adoption of flexibilities by developing States will have consequences for future innovation.

In response, one may note that the pharmaceutical industry reaped huge profits and engaged in significant levels of R&D long before TRIPS mandated the global extension of its patents. Furthermore, the developing world component of the patented pharmaceutical market is so small that it would make little difference to pharmaceutical profits, and therefore its well of R&D resources. For example, Africa constituted only 1.3 per cent of the pharmaceutical market at the turn of the century, prior to any possible impact of the Doha Declaration.[118] In 2006, the World Bank cited a study indicating that the extension of patent protection for drugs in the developing world by 20 years would equate, for the purposes of calculating profits, to a two-week extension for patents in the North.[119] Therefore, compulsory licensing or deep discounts per se in the developing world do not threaten pharmaceutical R&D.[120] Indeed, pharmaceutical companies could potentially benefit by basing their businesses on a 'high volume-low margin' basis in developing States, as opposed to virtually no profits due to a lack of sales.[121]

However, there is the danger of low price drugs in the developing world being re-imported back into Northern markets, which would undercut profits, and therefore pose a danger to existing levels of R&D. In response, one may note that parallel importation must have been a similar threat prior to TRIPS, yet the pharmaceutical industry managed to consistently reap exceptional profits. Secondly, Northern States are free under TRIPS and should be encouraged to pass laws that prevent parallel importation, if such measures are needed to preserve the feasibility of low prices in the developing world.[122]

Of course, Northern consumers might object to paying more than the developing world for the same pharmaceutical products. However, the level of need in the developing world regarding access to essential drugs is so comparatively great as to justify differential pricing or patent systems and the effective subsidization of third world drug prices by Northern governments.[123] In any case, as noted above, the third world market for pharmaceutical products is presently too small to greatly impact on the industry's pricing policies in the developed world. Insistence on the payment of full price simply shrinks that market even more.[124] More radical

---

[118] Rosenberg, above n 61.

[119] World Development Report 2006, above n 117, 214, citing Jean O Lanjouw and William Jack, 'Trading Up: How Much Should Poor Countries Pay to Support Pharmaceutical Innovation?' (2004) 4 *CGD Brief* 1, 6.   [120] World Development Report 2006, above n 117, 224.

[121] Abbott and Reichmann, above n 20, 970–1.   [122] UNHCHR, above n 60, para 47.

[123] See also Chapter 8; Stiglitz, above n 70, 120.

[124] See also World Development Report 2006, above n 117, 224–5.

solutions will be needed to reduce the huge outlays paid by Northern consumers, usually via their governments or insurers, to pharmaceutical companies.[125]

As noted above, there is an economic argument that developing States ultimately benefit from IP laws through increased domestic innovation and technology transfer. However, the evidence of technological transfer in the pharmaceutical sector is 'not compelling'.[126] Abbott and Reichmann explain:

> The major multinational pharmaceutical companies do not 'out-license' newer products for manufacture and distribution in developing country enterprises; research and development is concentrated in the home countries of major producers; and manufacturing facilities are shuttered and relocated as a matter of economic convenience.

> The evidence suggests that the wealthy OECD nations are little inclined to promote the development of world-class pharmaceutical producers in poor countries, which might eventually compete with the existing originators.[127]

One may recall the argument from Chapter 5 that the now-developed States freely used many policies, such as infant industry protection, to facilitate their own development, which are now denied to developing States. A similar argument may be made regarding IP protection. Robert Wade notes that developed States did not face global IP laws during their development processes: Japan, Taiwan, and South Korea were all previously known as 'counterfeit capitals', while the US in the nineteenth century was a 'bold pirate of intellectual property'.[128] The economist Ha-Joon Chang states that 'even the most advanced countries were still routinely violating the [IP rights] of other countries' citizens well into the twentieth century'.[129] Professor Daniel Gervais also notes that developed States '*gradually* increased their level of [IP] protection over several decades',[130] a far cry from the mere decade in which most developing States were given to jump from minimal protection to full TRIPS compliance. Finally, Chang has stated that economic development is essentially about 'absorbing advanced foreign technologies', so '[a]nything that makes it more difficult... is not good for economic development'.[131] While TRIPS might encourage greater technology transfer, it still restricts the ability of underdeveloped States to borrow (or steal) more advanced technologies, a tactic blatantly used by the now developed States while they were developing.

Furthermore, Professor Drahos has noted that 'the empirical evidence' that patents encourage innovation and invention is not 'clear cut'.[132] Strong IP rights

---

[125] See below, text at notes 173–8.

[126] Abbott and Reichmann, above n 20, 986.   [127] Ibid, 986.

[128] Robert Wade, 'What Strategies are Viable for Developing Countries Today? The World Trade Organization and the Shrinking of Policy Space' (2003) 10 *Review of International Political Economy* 621, 626, citing, *inter alia*, the grievances of Charles Dickens. See also Yong-Shik Lee, *Reclaiming Development in the World Trading System* (Cambridge University Press, Cambridge, 2006) 127.

[129] Ha-Joon Chang, *Kicking Away the Ladder: Development Strategy in Historical Perspective* (Anthem Press, London, 2003) 57; see also 84–5.

[130] Daniel J Gervais, 'Trips 3.0: Policy Calibration and Innovation Displacement' in Chantal Thomas and Joel P Trachtman (eds), *Developing Countries in the WTO Legal System* (Oxford University Press, New York, 2009) 363, 391 (emphasis added).

[131] Ha-Joon Chang, *Bad Samaritans: the Myth of Free Trade and the Secret History of Capitalism* (Bloomsbury Press, New York, 2008) 127.

[132] Peter Drahos, 'The Rights to Food and Health and Intellectual Property in the Era of "Biogopolies"' in Stephen Bottomley and David Kinley (eds), *Commercial Law and Human Rights* (Aldershot, Ashgate, 2002) 227.

may restrict the use of innovations and ideas, either legally or practically via the threat of expensive patent litigation.[133] Indeed, certain previously success-ful industries have been stunted by the introduction of patents. The granting of drug patents in Italy, which began in 1978, has not reportedly generated any real increase in R&D expenditure and drug innovation by Italian drug companies. Rather, the most noticeable result has been a sharp drop in Italy's drug export market, which had relied on generic copies.[134] India made full use of its tran-sition period under TRIPS (delaying implementation until 2005) and became 'a global supplier of affordable generic medicines'.[135] Indeed, India's abolition of pharmaceutical patents in the 1970s catalysed its generic drug industry and transformed it from a drug importing country into a major generic exporter.[136] The World Bank has cited a report indicating that the gain to the Indian econ-omy was $450 million, with consumers benefiting from $400 million of that gain, and drug producers sharing the rest. The loss to foreign producers was only $53 million.[137]

Gervais has suggested that the development rationale for TRIPS, that is that it will prompt innovation in the developing world, was based more on belief rather than actual data: 'TRIPS put the policy cart before the empirical horse'.[138] Nevertheless, he finds that there is evidence of significant R&D underway in the developing world, particularly India and China. However, Northern companies might simply be using these countries as 'new export markets and possibly lower-cost production centers, while maintaining the technological superiority in the West [or North], and hence, continued economic dominance'.[139]

Then again, it is questionable the extent to which such companies can prevent their technology from ultimately being exploited by these recipient countries for their own benefit. For example, India's computer and software industry has evolved considerably from the basic coding and call centre functions initially transferred to the country at the beginning of the century.[140] However, as noted above, India's pharmaceutical industry flourished prior to implementation of TRIPS, largely because of its abandonment of product patents 30 years earlier. Of course, India's pharmaceutical industry might now evolve to innovate and capture the massive profits available from new technologies and patents. Unfortunately, that strategy

---

[133] Gathii, above n 47, 758–9; see also Tom G Palmer, 'Are Patents and Copyrights Morally Justified? The Philosophy of Property Rights and Ideal Objects' (1990) 13 *Harvard Journal of Law and Public Policy* 817, 849; Roger E Meiners and Robert J Staaf, 'Patents, Copyright, and Trademarks: Property or Monopoly' (1990) 13 *Harvard Journal of Law and Public Policy* 911, 914; UNHCHR, above n 60, para 40.

[134] FM Scherer, 'The Pharmaceutical Industry and World Intellectual Property Standards' (2000) 53 *Vanderbilt Law Review* 2245; see also Drahos, above n 132, 192, at 230.

[135] Special Rapporteur on the Right to Health, above n 1, para 29.

[136] Ibid, para 29.

[137] World Development Report 2006, above n 117, 214, citing Chaudhuri, Shubham, Pinelopi K Goldberg, and Panle Jia, 'Estimating the Effects of Global Patent Protection in Pharmaceuticals: A Case Study of Quinolones in India' (World Bank: Washington, DC, 2004), <http://www.econ.yale.edu/~pg87/TRIPS.pdf> accessed 20 June 2010.

[138] Gervais, above n 130, 370.   [139] Ibid, 382.

[140] Much of the initial outsourcing of computer coding to India arose due to the Y2K bug crisis: see Thomas Friedman, *The World is Flat: the Globalized World in the Twenty-First Century* (Penguin, 2005) 131–6.

would be bad news for its impoverished customers in the developing world who have long relied on the 'pharmacy of the developing world'.[141] While India's drug companies might benefit from new business strategies catalysed by TRIPS, the poor probably will not.

Of course, most developing States lack the capacities of India and China. They have not yet reached a point where the increased costs generated by TRIPS and IP protection in general are outweighed by innovation benefits.[142] Such 'graduation' is not inevitable given that most States lack certain unique characteristics of India and China, such as geopolitical importance and massive manpower.

At this point, it is worth noting briefly another human rights and development problem generated by IP laws. Copyright laws obstruct access to educational materials by raising their price. The trade-focused NGO 3D has, for example, documented the difficulties in primary education in the Philippines caused by copyrights in textbooks, jeopardizing that State's compliance with human rights obligations regarding the right to education under the ICESCR and Article 28(1) of the Convention on the Rights of the Child.[143] Robert Wade reports that research libraries paid 66 per cent more for scientific monographs in 2001 than they did in 1986, yet they received 9 per cent fewer monographs for that money. They paid out 210 per cent more for 5 per cent fewer journals. He concludes that those 'price escalations widen the North-South gap in access to scientific knowledge'.[144] One can imagine the price escalations have become worse since many States implemented TRIPS after 2001. I will not embark upon a thorough examination of the potential clash between the right to education and TRIPS.[145] Suffice to note that any obstacles to basic education are completely counterproductive to a State's aspirations for economic, institutional and social development.

LDCs are a long way from achieving any benefits from IP. In 2005, the WTO Council on TRIPS extended the transition period for full compliance with TRIPS for LDCs to 2013.[146] However, that extension forbids the roll-back of laws to make them less TRIPS compliant, which renders the extension largely useless for many LDCs. Furthermore, it seems doubtful that that extension of time will be enough to permit LDCs to attain a position where IP laws are at all beneficial to them: further extensions will almost inevitably be needed. Nothing in these decisions affects the right of LDCs to delay TRIPS implementation with regard to pharmaceutical

---

[141] 't Hoen, above n 18, 78. Also see Report of the Special Rapporteur on the Right to Health, above n 1, para 30, n 34.

[142] See also Gervais, above n 130, 390.

[143] 3D, 'The Philippines: Impact of copyright rules on access to education' (July 2009) <http://www.3dthree.org/pdf_3D/3DCRC_PhilippinesJun09.pdf> accessed 20 September 2010.

[144] Wade, above n 128, 624.

[145] See, generally, Andrew Rens, Achal Prabhala, and Dick Kawooya, 'Intellectual Property, Education and Access to Knowledge in Southern Africa' (2006) Trade Law Centre for Southern Africa Working Paper No 13/2006 <http://www.tralac.org/unique/tralac/pdf/20061002_Rens_IntellectualProperty.pdf> accessed 20 September 2010); Margaret Chon, 'Intellectual Property from Below: Copyright and Capability for Education' (2006–2007) 40 *UC Davis L Rev* 803.

[146] WTO Doc. IP/C/40, 30 November 2005.

products until 2016. However, even that deadline is beginning to loom large as one which will need extending.

Problems regarding patents in the pharmaceutical industry

The most obvious argument against pharmaceutical patents is that they artificially raise prices and therefore restrict access to a product, which can be crucial for the enjoyment of rights to life and health. The following commentary focuses on other arguments against current levels of patent protection in the pharmaceutical industry. First, it is arguable that the pharmaceutical industry is unduly exploiting its patent monopolies, given the consistently massive level of profits in the industry. Second, concerns may be raised about the type of innovation currently occurring in the pharmaceutical industry.

The pharmaceutical industry has consistently, for many decades, been an extraordinarily profitable sector.[147] Furthermore, there is evidence that the amount reinvested into R&D is small compared to certain non-R&D outlays. For example, pharmaceutical companies tend to spend much more on marketing than they do on R&D.[148] These large marketing budgets indicate that prices can be trimmed without cutting R&D budgets.

Moreover, it has been suggested that pharmaceutical companies have routinely overstated their R&D costs.[149] For example, much of the R&D that contributes to the creation of new drugs is undertaken at public expense in government or university laboratories.[150] Indeed, public bodies may sometimes hold the initial patent on a drug, and then assign that patent to a drug company.[151] Publicly funded researchers

---

[147] For an overview of recent revenues and profits enjoyed by the pharmaceutical industry (2009 figures), see <http://money.cnn.com/magazines/fortune/global500/2009/industries/21/index.html>. See also Marcia Angell, 'The Pharmaceutical Industry: To Whom is it Accountable?' (2000) 342 *New England Journal of Medicine* 1902.

[148] See, eg, the figures quoted in the respective annual reports of 2009 for Merck <http://www.merck.com/finance/annualreport/ar2009/pdf/Merck_form_10-k.pdf> accessed 20 June 2010, 62 (US$8,543.2m for 'marketing and administrative expenses' and US$5,845m for R&D in 2009); 2009 Annual Report (Form 10-K) of Pfizer, filed 26 February 2010 for the fiscal year ended 31 December 2009, <http://media.pfizer.com/files/annualreport/2009/form10k_2009.pdf> accessed 20 June 2010, 46 (US$14,875m for 'selling, informational and administrative expenses' and US$7,845m for R&D in 2009. See also Harrison, above n 96, 152.

[149] See generally, Bob Young et al, 'Rx R&D Myths: The Case Against Drug Industry's R&D "Scare Card"' *Public Citizen's Congresswatch*, July 2001, <http://www.citizen.org> accessed 20 January 2003.

[150] Ibid, 7–10, App C thereto (National Institute of Health, NIH Contributions to Pharmaceutical Development: Case Study Analysis of the Top Selling Drugs, February 2000). See also James Packard Love, Affidavit (signed 9 April 2001) in the matter between *Pharmaceutical Manufacturers' Association of South Africa and Others v The President of the Republic of South Africa and Others* (2000) (3) BCLR 241 (South Africa Constitutional Court) <http://www.cptech.org/ip/health/sa/loveaffidavit/> accessed 21 September 2010. See also 't Hoen, above n 18, 80; Stiglitz, above n 70, 111, and Chang, above n 129, 31.

[151] Assignment of patents arising out of publicly funded research is permitted in most countries. In the US, under the Bayh-Dole Act of 1980, publicly funded researchers are required to keep their patents, but may licence another to act as the exclusive marketer of a patented product; the rights of an exclusive licensee in such situations generally mirror those of a patentee. Bayh-Dole Act of

may often perform the basic research into a drug, which is the most risky phase as future marketability is at its least predictable.[152] However, public funds are also often used at the later stages of a drug's development, such as in clinical trials.[153] Furthermore, reported R&D costs do not necessarily take into account the generous tax deductions available in many countries to the pharmaceutical industry.[154] Finally, increasing funding for R&D is coming from philanthropic organizations such as the Bill & Melinda Gates Foundation.[155] The pharmaceutical industry fought a nine-year battle in the US to prevent the disclosure of its R&D costs to congressional investigators, culminating in victory in the Supreme Court in 1983 in *Bowsher v Merck*.[156] The questions raised regarding the 'real' cost of pharmaceutical R&D suggest that prices could be lowered without sacrificing R&D outlays.

Finally, the differences in cost between patented drugs and generic competition are enormous. Special Rapporteur Grover reported that first generation antiretrovirals for treating HIV dropped from $US10,000 per person per year to US$350 per person per year for the generic product.[157] If pharmaceutical companies will not freely release the figures on R&D costs, one is entitled to be sceptical of the notion that R&D costs justify a 3,000 per cent markup.

Serious questions may also be raised regarding the current level of innovation in the pharmaceutical industry. The pharmaceutical industry spends much of its R&D money on 'me-too' or 'copycat' drugs, which are innovative enough to attract patent protection in many States (via 'evergreening'), but which in fact add little therapeutic value to existing medical treatments. These 'me-too' drugs are the fruits of 'safe' R&D, entailing only slight variations on themes already known to be profitable.[158] Indeed, 'me-toos and line extensions typically take up around 80 per cent of R&D spending',[159] so there is arguably a 'wasteful concentration of research on problems whose solution in the near future can be foreseen'[160] or has in fact already eventuated. One possible benefit of patented 'me-toos' is to provide price competition to the original patented drug.[161] However, the cost of patented drugs continues to escalate,

1980, Pub. L. No. 96-517, 94 Stat. 3015-28 (codified as amended at 35 U.S.C. §§ 200–11, 301–07 (1994)).

[152] Young et al, above n 149, 10.   [153] Ibid, 10.   [154] Ibid, 15–16.
[155] Outterson, above n 18, 287.
[156] 460 US 824 (1983) (Supreme Court of the United States). Congress could subpoena the documents (the power of subpoena was distinguished from the right of access in *Inspector General v Banner Plumbing Supply*, 34 F. Supp. 2d 682 (N.D. Ill. 1998)), but has thus far chosen not to do so. Note also that one of the reasons why a consortium of pharmaceuticals dropped action against the South African government in respect of new proposed drug laws (see above, note 150) was possibly because the relevant court may have ordered disclosure of R&D costs: see Nick Mathiason, 'The Pretoria Court Case: Drugs Round One to Africa' *Observer*, 22 April 2001, Business, 3.
[157] Special Rapporteur on the Right to Health, above n 1, para 20. Price drops of 99% have even been reported.
[158] 't Hoen, above n 18, 81; Angell, above n 147, 1903; Young et al, above n 149, 13–14.
[159] Jeffrey Robinson, *Prescription Games* (Simon & Schuster, London, 2001) 12. See also UNHCHR, above n 60, para 39.
[160] Friedrich A von Hayek, *The Fatal Conceit: The Errors of Socialism* (W.W. Bartley III edn, 1988) (quoted in Gathii, above n 47, 135).
[161] Singham, above n 46, 370–1; see also Edmund W Kitsch, 'Elementary and Persistent Errors in the Economic Analysis of Intellectual Property' (2000) 53 *Vanderbilt Law Review* 1727, 1729–38.

unlike patented goods in other industries, such as information technology, where computer products drop in price soon after their placement on the market.[162]

Finally, the incentives prompted by patent protection can create problems regarding the creation of needed drugs.[163] Lots of R&D is put into drugs which deal with chronic, ongoing conditions, like heart disease or high cholesterol, as opposed to cures and vaccines, which do not have the same ongoing market potential.[164] Disproportionate research is put into drugs to combat lucrative problems like obesity, cellulite, and impotence. These are distressing conditions but they are rarely life-threatening.[165] Comparatively little research is conducted into third world killers like malaria, tuberculosis, or sleeping sickness.[166] Perhaps it is arguable that the historically weak patent protection offered in the developing world has caused the industry's indifference to its diseases.[167] However, it is extremely doubtful that the pharmaceutical industry will significantly increase its R&D on diseases in the poorest States which cannot pay big money, regardless of the relevant standard of patent protection.[168]

A 'high volume, low margin' marketing strategy, if adopted, might mean that a company which successfully engages in such R&D could recoup significant economic returns with regard to new drugs for those neglected third world diseases which afflict huge numbers like malaria. Such a company would also benefit from the boost to its reputation.[169] However, the present conservatism within the business models of pharmaceutical companies is sending them down the tried and true route of R&D, including 'me-too' R&D, into diseases and conditions which afflict the affluent.[170] Nothing in the TRIPS model of global compulsory patents encourages pharmaceutical companies to diverge from that path.[171] The World Health Assembly, in adopting a 'Global strategy and plan of action on public health, innovation and intellectual property' in 2008, similarly concluded that IP rights alone do not provide sufficient incentive for development of new products to 'fight diseases where the potential paying market is small or uncertain'.[172]

A radical proposal?

Given these issues of excessive profit and innovation deficit, perhaps all States, including developed States, should control health budgets, and thus increase their

---

[162] See Robinson, above n 159, 89. Singham concedes that the 'key criterion [for price reduction in the pharmaceutical sector] appears to be the number and weight of off-patent chemical entities', rather than competition from patented 'me-toos' at above n 46, 370.

[163] World Development Report 2006, above n 117, 224.

[164] Anna-Marie Tabor, 'Recent Developments: AIDS Crisis' (2001) 38 *Harvard Journal on Legislation* 514, 524.

[165] Of course, morbid obesity is life-threatening, and obesity per se can lead to chronic health problems.

[166] See, generally, Médecins sans Frontières (MSF), *Fatal Imbalance: The Crisis in Research and Drugs for Neglected Diseases* (Médecins Sans Frontières, Geneva, 2001); UNHCHR, above n 60, para 38; Harrison, above n 96, 152.

[167] Singham, above n 46, 392–3.   [168] Drahos, above n 132, 229.

[169] Abbott and Reichmann, above n 20, 982.   [170] 't Hoen, above n 18, 82–3.

[171] Outterson, above n 18, 293.   [172] WHO doc. WHA 61.21, 24 May 2008, para 7.

'available resources' for the purposes of ICESCR, by imposing price caps on the pharmaceutical industry.[173]

Reduction of patent rights or the imposition of price caps would of course reduce profits. Despite high levels of profit in the pharmaceutical industry, *any* reduction in profits will probably lead to a reduction in R&D expenditure, given that it will be the corporations themselves that determine how to absorb the consequent revenue loss. Thus, any move to reduce prices could lead to a drop in R&D. Notwithstanding the present 'innovation' flaws in pharmaceutical R&D, it is still important not to jeopardize the possibility of breakthrough R&D, such as that which has produced the new generation HIV-AIDS therapies. Perhaps therefore, current government action in developed States which facilitates patents and high prices within their own territories is justifiable in international human rights law as a necessary means of ensuring ongoing innovation in the pharmaceutical industry.

In this regard however, it is worth noting that the biggest purchasers of patented prescription drugs are government healthcare programmes in the developed world.[174] Indeed, the high percentage of government trade within the total trade enjoyed by the pharmaceutical industry may not be comparable to any other industry except the armaments sector. Therefore, taxpayers' money constitutes the majority of the patent-generated profits of the pharmaceutical industry. While it may be reasonable for taxpayer money to largely subsidize pharmaceutical R&D costs, it may not be reasonable for taxpayers to largely subsidize marketing costs, executive salaries, and very large profits. Given the high percentage of government custom in the pharmaceutical industry, it seems that there is scope for interventionist public sector solutions to the problem of high pharmaceutical costs.

It must be noted that the predominance of government custom in pharmaceutical sales is not the case in the largest market, the US, where pharmaceutical benefits are largely funded by private rather than public health insurers.[175] Nevertheless, taxpayers in the US still largely subsidize pharmaceutical costs, as most taxpayers obtain health insurance, either personally or through their employer, to cover their potential health costs. Prescription drugs in the US are subsidized by taxpayers in their guise as consumers of health insurance rather than as taxpayers per se. Furthermore, tax subsidies are available for most private purchases of medicines.[176]

If there were weaker patent rights, those taxpayer costs would be considerably smaller. The consequent public savings could be redirected from the purchase of drugs at inflated prices to government-funded R&D into pharmaceutical products

[173] See UNHCHR, above n 60, 64; see also General Comment 14, above n 21, para 51.

[174] Outterson, above n 18, 285–6; S Jacobzone, 'Pharmaceutical Policies in OECD Countries: Reconciling Social and Industrial Goals' *OECD Labour Market and Social Policy Occasional Papers*, No 40, (OECD Publishing, Paris, 2000) 4, 9, 94.

[175] US public funds do however make up a sizeable proportion of pharmaceutical purchasers, due to safety net schemes for the poorest people.

[176] Outterson, above n 18, 285–6.

in universities and government research bodies.[177] Public savings on patent-inflated prices could pick up the shortfall into R&D that might eventuate from any reduction in patent rights. Such a plan might not lead to more net R&D, but it may lead to cheaper drugs for all without a diminution in R&D. Such a plan might also lead to more consistently useful innovation, as publicly funded scientists are hopefully more concerned with Nobel prizes than profits.[178]

This 'public sector' solution to the problem of access to drugs could well cause a plunge in pharmaceutical profits to the detriment of its many shareholders. Furthermore, sceptics would undoubtedly question the capacity of the public sector to be as innovative as the private sector. It is recognized that such a solution is unlikely to presently garner much political support. I include it, however, to show that IP regimes are challengeable as the preferable means of promoting innovation in certain industries. To that end, I turn to two other proposals regarding IP alternatives.

Other alternatives to IP

As noted above, a problem with the current structures and incentives (largely based on IP) of the pharmaceutical industry is that they do not incentivize research in drugs for neglected diseases, that is those that overwhelmingly afflict people in the developing world but not people in the developed world. Furthermore, patents incentivize research into symptom relief rather than cures and vaccines. In response, Thomas Pogge has proposed an alternative scheme for incentivizing pharmaceutical research. He has proposed that States contribute to a Health Impact Fund from which pharmaceutical innovators are paid according to the positive health impact of their products. Such funding would incentivize products which cure diseases, including those which exclusively afflict the poor, and would also encourage lower prices so that the health impact of a drug is increased. The details of this proposal are beyond the scope of this book.[179] It is mentioned to demonstrate that there are probably feasible alternatives to IP protection in order to incentivize much-needed medical innovations.

The NGO, Knowledge Ecology International (KEI), has put forward a proposal for a new treaty to be included under the rubric of WTO commitments, which would contain binding commitments offered on a voluntary basis on the GATS

---

[177] Due to the idiosyncratic public/private divide of pharmaceutical expenditure in the US, it is likely that any plan to increase publicly funded R&D in the US would result in an increase rather than a mere redirection of public expenditure. However, due to likely decreased costs of private health insurance in the US, it might not lead to increased expenditure by actual taxpayers (who are simultaneously consumers of health insurance).

[178] Note that by July 2001, publicly funded scientists had won 90 Nobel Prizes compared to four from private industry; see Young et al, above n 149, 8.

[179] See Thomas Pogge, 'Medicines for the World: Boosting innovation without obstructing free access' (2008) *Revista Internacional de dereitos humanos* 8, 5–6 <http://www.yale.edu/macmillan/igh/files/SUR.pdf> accessed 17 April 2010, 11–14. For more details, see Aidan Hollis and Thomas Pogge, *The Health Impact Fund: Making New Medicines Accessible to all* (Incentives for Global Health, 2008) <http://www.yale.edu/macmillan/igh/#> accessed 20 September 2010.

model, by WTO Members to fund and support 'the provision of global public goods involving knowledge'.[180] The KEI has chosen the WTO as an appropriate domain for such a treaty due to its current existence[181] and its strong enforcement mechanisms.

A 'public good' is not a commodity as such. It is 'non-rival', in that one or more people can use or consume it at the same time without diminishing its availability. For example, hammers and apples are 'rival' whereas a scenic view, clean air and public safety are non-rival.[182] Public goods are also non-excludable in that no one can be excluded from using it. Examples of public goods include environmental preservation, security, and knowledge. A 'global public good' addresses an issue of global importance which cannot be addressed adequately by one State acting alone, and must therefore be addressed multilaterally.[183] The tackling of climate change is an example of a global public good. There is a deficit in global public goods because States do not have sufficient incentives to contribute to the global public good compared to their own national public good. At the same time, there has been a growth of private sector interest in global public goods such as Wikipedia and other knowledge based products available freely via the web. Examples of knowledge-based global public goods which need greater resources are: the funding of the development of an AIDS vaccine and drugs for neglected diseases, patent or copyright buy-outs of products that are valuable for the enjoyment of human rights, the running of clinical trials, and digitization of publications in the public domain.

It is beyond the scope of this book to discuss the pros and cons of the KEI's proposal. At this stage, KEI states that a proposal will be made within the WTO itself 'in the not too distant future'. The KEI's proposal is an interesting challenge to the WTO's paradigmatic approach of promoting private enterprise and private ownership of knowledge under IP laws. There are clearly many goods and services which are best provided on a public and open access basis rather than on a profit basis: surely not everything should be commodified, packaged, and sold. It is also an interesting counterpoint to the IP regime promoted by TRIPS, recognizing that private ownership of certain desirable knowledge goods is problematic because there are not enough incentives for the private sector (for example, in the case of drugs for neglected diseases) or because private ownership restricts access too much (for example, in the case of goods which are essential for the enjoyment of human rights).

The WTO's cart is currently hitched exclusively to the private sector horse, backed by an assumption that private sector initiatives are more efficient and preferable. Yet private markets do not and may not be able to address certain 'public goods'

---

[180] Knowledge Ecology International, 'KEI Proposal: A WTO Agreement on the Supply of Knowledge as a Global Public Good' (June 2008) via <http://www.keionline.org/wtoandpublicgoods> accessed 23 January 2010. The following commentary summarizes a presentation on the topic by James Love at the WTO Ministerial in Geneva on 1 December 2009.

[181] It is easier to utilize an existing institution rather than create another international institution.

[182] See <http://en.wikipedia.org/wiki/Rivalry_(economics)> accessed 29 January 2010.

[183] Stiglitz, above n 70, 281.

problems, such as the need for low-cost medicines for poor people.[184] Furthermore, there is no particular reason why the WTO should continue to ignore the need for the facilitation of access to public goods. Indeed, such facilitation represents perhaps a fruitful new direction for its work, especially when one considers that it is proving very difficult to reach agreement on the further liberalization of private trade.

Certainly, initiatives that diverge from traditional IP protection are on the global agenda. For example, the World Health Assembly, in its 'Global strategy and plan of action on public health, innovation and intellectual property', has suggested that, where appropriate, the costs of R&D and the price of health products should be de-linked,[185] which would 'break the vicious cycle of financing R&D through high drug prices'.[186] The Strategy also calls for intergovernmental talks to explore the utility of new instruments and mechanisms, including 'an essential health and biomedical R&D treaty'.[187] The Strategy document clearly recognizes that TRIPS, 'today's predominant global R&D treaty',[188] does not adequately address global needs regarding rights to adequate standards of health.

F. The IP Maximalist Trend

Despite serious and justified misgivings about the desirability of global IP laws and the promotion of a human rights approach of permitting States to utilize TRIPS flexibilities as much as possible to facilitate access to medicines, an IP maximalist approach is taking hold in global trade negotiations.

To be sure, there are no serious proposals to strengthen IP protection in the WTO. However, as noted in Chapters 3 and 9, bilateral free trade agreements have proliferated in the last decade while Doha round negotiations have stalled. 'TRIPS-plus' provisions, which impose even stricter IP obligations than TRIPS on States, have been included in numerous bilateral agreements, particularly those concluded by the US. TRIPS-plus obligations have also been imposed as conditions on States that have acceded to the WTO, such as China, Jordan, and Cambodia.[189] Typical 'TRIPS plus' provisions include longer patent terms, a guarantee of patentability for second uses, a guarantee of data exclusivity, further conditions on compulsory licensing, bans on parallel imports, and stronger enforcement mechanisms.[190]

Under TRIPS, the 20 years of patent protection is deemed to run from the date of filing for a patent. Thus, the term of effective protection is reduced if a State's determination of patentability takes a long time. Article 62(2) of TRIPS states,

---

[184] Abbott and Reichmann, above n 20, 987.
[185] WHO doc. WHA 61.21, 24 May 2008, para 4.   [186] 't Hoen, above n 18, 93.
[187] WHO doc. WHA 61.21, 24 May 2008, para 30(2.3)(c).   [188] 't Hoen, above n 18, 93.
[189] Eg, Cambodia's WTO accession provides for data exclusivity: see United Nations Development Program, *Asia Pacific Human Development Report 2006: Trade on Human Terms* (Colombo, UNDP, 2006) 133. On Jordan, see 't Hoen, above n 18, 72.
[190] Special Rapporteur on the Right to Health, above n 1, para 78; Jean-Frédéric Morin, 'Tripping up TRIPS debates IP and health in bilateral agreements' (2006) 1 *Journal of Intellectual Property Management* 37, 39.

vaguely, that national procedures permit the granting or registration of patent within a 'reasonable' time. US bilateral agreements now oblige parties to extend a patent term in case of unreasonable curtailment of the patent period caused by the marketing approval process.[191]

As noted above, Article 27 of TRIPS seems to leave significant room for States to impose strict patentability standards, as has occurred in India. US bilateral agreements with a number of States, including Morocco, Bahrain, and Australia dictate that patents must be available for 'new uses and methods of using a known product', thus narrowing State discretion with regard to patentability requirements.[192]

Provisions mandating protection of data exclusivity are contained in US bilateral agreements with Chile, Morocco, Bahrain, Australia, and Singapore.[193] Depending on the term of such protection, data exclusivity may prevent a generic competitor from relying on the clinical data gathered by a patent-holder in bringing the drug to market: it must therefore conduct its own clinical trials. Data exclusivity delays the introduction of generic competition and raises costs for generic competitors. It also raises ethical concerns, as it prompts the conduct of unnecessary human trials.[194]

Some US bilateral trade agreements contain restrictions on compulsory licensing beyond the restrictions imposed by Article 31 of TRIPS. First, data exclusivity may significantly delay the impact of a compulsory licence.[195] Secondly, provisions in US bilaterals concluded with Australia and Singapore might restrict the ability of those States to sign up to the 2003 waiver as exporting countries.[196]

Some US bilaterals also demand that the parties adopt the principle of national exhaustion, thus effectively prohibiting parallel importation. So far, this provision has only affected States that already follow that principle.[197] Nevertheless, such provisions prohibit such States from altering their law.

Finally, stronger enforcement mechanisms may provide greater obligations to impose criminal sanctions for pirating, and mandatory expansions of powers of subpoena in IP infringement cases. Stronger enforcement provisions could have a greater 'chilling impact' on potential competitors.[198] These provisions are troubling as IP infringement cases are often lost, indicating that overambitious infringement claims are often made. It is unfortunate if entities are discouraged from testing where the limits of an IP right might lie due to the increased consequences of losing an infringement case. Furthermore, stronger enforcement mechanisms may result in seizures of suspect goods even in transit, as occurred when the Netherlands seized generic drugs sent from India to Brazil, and returned them to India.[199] Such actions could frustrate use of the 2003 waiver.

---

[191] Morin, above n 190, 43–4.   [192] Ibid, 41.   [193] Ibid, 42.
[194] Special Rapporteur on the Right to Health, above n 1, para 78.
[195] Ibid, para 82; Morin, above n 190, 47.   [196] Morin, above n 190, 47.
[197] Ibid, 48.   [198] Special Rapporteur on the Right to Health, above n 1, para 91.
[199] Indeed, India and Brazil have now launched a WTO dispute against the EU in respect of that seizure. See, eg, International Centre for Trade and Sustainable Development, 'EU Challenged on Generics Seizures", *Bridges*, Vol 14, No 3, September 2010.

The TRIPS plus provisions of the US bilateral agreements, which are nego-tiated under conditions of an asymmetric balance of power,[200] contravene the spirit of cooperation engendered by the Doha Declaration and the waiver.[201] To that end, the US has faced criticism, such as that from the (then) French President Jacques Chirac who accused the US of 'immoral blackmail'.[202] However, while the EU has been less aggressive than the US in terms of raising IP standards in bilateral trade agreements, it has pursued various TRIPS plus outcomes. For example, under the European Partnership Agreements (EPAs) currently being concluded or negotiated with African, Caribbean, and Pacific States, the EU has pushed for TRIPS plus provisions. EPAs with Caribbean States mandate stronger protection of digital content than is required under TRIPS, with likely impacts for the right to education in those States.[203] The EU is also pushing for inclusion of a requirement that its EPA partners adopt the IP system devel-oped by the International Union for the Protection of New Varieties of Plants (UPOV)[204] as the standard for protecting IP in new plant varieties. The prob-lems with the UPOV standard with regard to the right to food are discussed in Chapter 6.[205]

The sting in the tail of TRIPS plus provisions is that those bound by them may have to offer those same TRIPS plus protections to all other States in the WTO. While GATT and GATS contain exceptions permitting some departure from MFN provisions for bilateral and regional free trade deals,[206] TRIPS contains no such exception. Therefore, TRIPS plus protection might have to be offered to all other States in the WTO on the basis of MFN obligations.[207]

Despite some 'wins' for those who wish to alleviate the potential human rights impacts of TRIPS in the form of the Doha Declaration and the 2003 waiver, IP maximalists are successfully recasting and strengthening the global IP landscape via the conclusion of WTO accessions, bilateral and regional agreements. In fact, the Pharmaceutical Research and Manufacturers of America (PhRMA) has been quite open about this strategy. In 2004, it stated:

PhRMA recognises that the current impasse in the Doha Development Round negotia-tions as well as in the deliberations in the TRIPS Council call into question the current value of the WTO as a venue for improving the worldwide protection of intellectual prop-erty. Free Trade Agreements thus provide a logical approach to gaining improved intellec-tual property protection.[208]

[200] World Development Report 2006, above n 117, 215. See Chapter 3, Part E.
[201] Morin, above n 190, 51.
[202] Ibid, 51, citing Jacques Chirac, *Message à la Quinzième Conférence Internationale sur le Sida*.
[203] Oxfam, 'Partnership or Power Play? How Europe should bring Development into its trade deals with African, Caribbean, and Pacific countries' (Oxfam Briefing Paper 110, 21 April 2008) 33.
[204] UNGA, 'Report of the Special Rapporteur on the Right to Food, Olivier de Schutter: Seed policies and the right to food: enhancing agrobiodiversity and encouraging innovation', UN doc. A/64/170 (23 July 2009) para 16.   [205] See Chapter 6, Part E, especially at notes 234–9.
[206] Article XXIV GATT and Article V GATS.
[207] Abbott and Reichmann, above n 20, 963–4.
[208] Pharmaceutical Research and Manufacturers of America (PhRMA), 'Special 301 submission', 12 February 2004, as cited in Morin, above n 190, at 40.

G. Conclusion

The TRIPS agreement has probably given rise to the most vociferous human rights criticisms of the WTO, especially with regard to its impact on the right to food (as discussed in Chapter 6) and the right to health. The above commentary has largely focused on the impact of TRIPS on access to pharmaceuticals. It is possible that TRIPS in fact allows sufficient flexibility to permit States to comply with their obligations regarding the right to health, but it makes that task more difficult, particularly for poorer States. Furthermore, the traditional justifications for global patent protection are challengeable. The development rationale for global IP protection is highly suspect, especially given that Northern States did not respect such rights during their own paths to development. Specific concerns beyond high prices arise with regard to the pharmaceutical industry, such as an innovation deficit and queries about the real cost to the private sector of pharmaceutical R&D. Despite challenges to the desirability of global patent protection under TRIPS, explicit recognition of important TRIPS flexibilities in the Doha Declaration and the 2003 waiver, the trend in current regional and bilateral trade negotiations is, unfortunately, to drive up standards of IP protection. A rollback of TRIPS for many developing States (not only LDCs) would be a preferable policy trajectory.[209]

---

[209] Stiglitz, above n 70, 119.

8

Extraterritorial Human Rights Duties

In Chapters 5 to 7, serious iniquities within the WTO system for developing States are identified. Some WTO rules are simply unsuitable for such States. That unsuitability can generate harm to human rights, as developing States are deprived of their capacities to discharge their human rights obligations. An overhaul of the WTO is recommended in order to better cater for the needs of developing States. A lopsided Doha deal, shrinking protectionist opportunities for the North yet increasing policy space for poorer States, is needed.

What, if any, are the duties of a State to the persons outside its own territory, that is the people in other States? This question is very relevant in the context of the WTO, given the arguments regarding unfair rules, and a need for a new bargain which addresses that unfairness. Is there any relevant obligation owed under international human rights law by the Northern States to the people of the South to 'even out' the deal? Similarly, is there any obligation of Northern States to refrain from concluding and/or enforcing rules which undermine a developing State's capacity to implement human rights?

A. Extraterritorial Obligations under International Human Rights Law

Do States have 'diagonal obligations' to the people in other States under international human rights law?[1]

Article 1(3) of the UN Charter specifies that one of the purposes of the UN is:

To achieve international co-operation in solving international problems of an economic, social, cultural, or humanitarian character, and in promoting and encouraging respect for human rights and for fundamental freedoms for all without distinction as to race, sex, language, or religion...

Article 56 of the UN Charter obliges States to take '*joint* and separate action' (emphasis added) to achieve the purposes set out in Article 55. Article 55 requires

---

[1] Vertical obligations refer to the obligations owed by a State to its population with regard to its own conduct. Horizontal obligations refer to a State's duty to apply human rights in the private sphere ('horizontally') so as to protect people from harm to their rights from other people or other non-State actors. Diagonal obligations refer to a State's duty to the people of another State.

the promotion of:

(a) higher standards of living; full employment, and conditions to enable social progress and development;
(b) solutions of international, economic, social, health, and related problems, and international cultural and educational cooperation; and
(c) universal respect for, and observance of, human rights and fundamental freedoms for all without distinction as to race, sex, language, or religion.

Furthermore, Articles 22 and 28 of the UDHR imply the existence of extraterritorial obligations. Article 22 focuses on the economic sphere:

Everyone, as a member of society, has the right to social security and is entitled to realization, through national effort and international co-operation and in accordance with the organization and resources of each State, of the economic, social and cultural rights indispensable for his dignity and the free development of his personality.

Article 28 states:

Everyone is entitled to a social and international order in which the rights and freedoms set forth in this Declaration can be fully realized.

Furthermore, Articles 16 to 18 of the Articles on State Responsibility of the International Law Commission[2] prescribe that State responsibility can rest with a State in regard to the internationally wrongful actions of another State. Articles 16 to 18 clearly envisage instances of extraterritorial State responsibility.[3] Such responsibility arises if the former State aids and abets the latter in the commission of a wrongful act (Article 16), if the former State directs or controls the commission of the wrongful act by the latter State (Article 17), or if the former State coerces the latter State to commit a wrongful act (Article 18). An example of such coercion could be the pressure placed by States on LDCs not to take advantage of TRIPS flexibilities in relation to pharmaceutical products, causing the latter to breach their obligations regarding the right to health under Article 12 of the ICESCR.

These provisions of the UN Charter, the UDHR, and the Articles of State Responsibility, which are often accepted as part of customary international law, lay a strong foundation from which one might identify relevant extraterritorial duties under customary international law.[4] Furthermore, States must take regard of the extraterritorial impacts of their activities under general international law.[5]

---

[2] Articles on Responsibility of States for Internationally Wrongful Acts (2001) UN doc. A/Res/56/83.
[3] See also Olivier De Schutter, 'A Human Rights Approach to Trade and Investment Policies' in FIAN and others, *The Global Food Challenge: Towards a Human Rights Approach to Trade and Investment Policies* (FIAN, Germany, 2009) 18–19.
[4] Margot Salomon, *Global Responsibility for Human Rights* (Oxford University Press, Oxford, 2007) 64–75.
[5] *Trail Smelter Case (US v Canada)* (1941) 3 RIAA 1905 (International Arbitration), 1905, and *Corfu Channel Case (UK v Albania)* (ICJ Judgment) (1949) ICJ Rep 1949, 4 at 18.

The Declaration on the Right to Development and Millennium Development Goals

A duty to fulfil human rights in other States is evident in the words of the Declaration on the Right to Development 1986 (DRD). Article 3 states:

States have the duty to co-operate with each other in ensuring development and eliminating obstacles to development. States should realize their rights and fulfil their duties in such a manner as to promote a new international economic order based on sovereign equality, interdependence, mutual interest and co-operation among all States, as well as to encourage the observance and realization of human rights.

Article 4 states:

1. States have the duty to take steps, individually and collectively, to formulate international development policies with a view to facilitating the full realization of the right to development.
2. Sustained action is required to promote more rapid development of developing countries. As a complement to the efforts of developing countries, effective international co-operation is essential in providing these countries with appropriate means and facilities to foster their comprehensive development.

Of course, the legal status of the DRD is debatable given that it is not a treaty. Its potential status as customary international law is supported by its mandatory language, its adoption with only one vote against (the US) and six abstentions in 1986, consensus support by 171 States (including the US) for the DRD in Article 10 of the Vienna Declaration and Programme of Action of 1993, and the existence of numerous procedures within the UN designed to advance the implementation of the right to development.[6] On the other hand, there must be doubts over whether sufficient State practice and *opinio juris* exist to bed down the customary status of the DRD. Nevertheless, its norms add to the long list of evidence of extraterritorial duties to fulfil human rights.

Finally, the Millennium Development Goals (MDGs) set out a number of targets in the socio-economic field to be achieved by 2015, such as halving extreme poverty and hunger. Goal 8 relates to the development of a 'global partnership for development', including a target (Target 12) of developing further 'an open, rule-based predictable, non-discriminatory trading system' and another target (Target 13) of addressing the special needs of LDCs. The MDGs have been reiterated on numerous occasions,[7] which lays the platform for 'a strong argument that some such obligation has crystallized into customary law'.[8]

---

[6] Salomon, above n 4, 89.

[7] See, eg, United Nations Millennium Declaration (2000) (Resolution Adopted by the General Assembly) UN doc. A/RES/55/2 (Millennium Declaration), the Report of the Johannesburg World Summit on Sustainable Development, UN doc. A/CONF.199/20, and the Monterrey Consensus, The International Conference on Financing for Development, 18–22 March 2002, Monterrey, Mexico (Monterrey Consensus).

[8] Philip Alston, 'Ships Passing in the Night: The Current State of the Human Rights and Development Debate seen through the Lens of the Millennium Development Goals' (2005) 27 *Human Rights Quarterly* 755, 778.

B. Treaties

Numerous human rights bodies, as well as the International Court of Justice (ICJ), have confirmed the existence of extraterritorial obligations under human rights treaties. The analysis below will be largely confined to the legal situation regarding extraterritoriality under the two International Covenants.[9]

ICCPR

Article 2(1) of the ICCPR requires States to respect and ensure ICCPR rights 'to all individuals within its territory and subject to its jurisdiction'. The Human Rights Committee (HRC) has confirmed that the reference to 'jurisdiction' extends a State's ICCPR responsibilities beyond its own territory. For example, the HRC (and other UN human rights treaty bodies) has confirmed that Israel has obligations with regard to human rights in the Occupied Territories,[10] and the same for the US regarding its military base in Guantanamo Bay in Cuba.[11] In numerous cases, such as *Montero v Uruguay*, States have been held responsible for the actions of their overseas consulates in unreasonably refusing to renew a citizen's passport.[12] In *Montero*, the relevant refusal by the Uruguayan consulate in Germany breached Montero's rights under Article 12(2), the right to leave any country. In *Lopez Burgos v Uruguay*, Uruguay was held responsible for the kidnap in Argentina of a man by its agents.[13] In General Comment 31, the HRC described the extraterritorial impact of the ICCPR as follows:

[A] State party must respect and ensure the rights laid down in the Covenant to *anyone within the power or effective control* of that State Party, even if not situated within the territory of the State Party.... This principle also applies to those within the power or effective control of the forces of a State Party acting outside its territory, regardless of the circumstances in which such power or effective control was obtained.[14]

Therefore, the HRC has taken the view that a State has human rights obligations to a person overseas who is under the effective control of its agents even if the person is outside its territory. The State's extraterritorial responsibility is limited by the

[9] Much of the following commentary is adapted from Sarah Joseph, 'Scope of Application' in Daniel Moeckli, Sangeeta Shah, and Sandesh Sivakumaran (eds), *International Human Rights Law* (Oxford University Press, Oxford, 2010) 150–70.
[10] See, eg, HRC, 'Concluding Observations of the Human Rights Committee: Israel', UN doc. CCPR/CO/78/ISR (21 August 2003). See also *Legal Consequences of the Construction of a Wall in the Occupied Palestinian Territory (Advisory Opinion)* ICJ Rep 2004, 136.
[11] See, eg, HRC, 'Concluding Observations of the Human Rights Committee: US', UN doc. CCPR/C/USA/CO/3 (15 September 2006).
[12] CCPR/C/18/D/106/1981 (31 March 1983) (HRC).
[13] CCPR/C/13/D/52/1979 (29 July 1981) (HRC). See also *Celiberti de Casariego v Uruguay*, UN doc. CCPR/C/13/D/56/1979 (29 July 1981) and *Domukovsky et al v Georgia*, UN docs. CCPR/C/62/D/623, 624, 626 & 627/1995 (29 May 1998) (both HRC).
[14] HRC, 'General Comment 31: Nature of the General Legal Obligation Imposed on States Parties to the Covenant', UN doc. CCPR/C/21/Rev.1/Add.13 (26 May 2004), para 10 (emphasis added).

extent to which that control impacts on the person's enjoyment of a right under the ICCPR. For example, the US is responsible for the full range of human rights of the Guantanamo Bay detainees, given its total control over the lives of those people. On the other hand, the consulate in *Montero* attracted Uruguayan responsibility over the relevant person's right to freedom of movement under Article 12(2) of the ICCPR; it seems, however, that that consulate had no control over Montero's other ICCPR rights so Uruguay, at the relevant time, had no responsibility with regard to those other rights while Montero remained in Germany.[15]

The view of extraterritorial responsibility taken by the HRC is similar to that taken by the organs of the Inter-American system of human rights.[16] Its approach was also endorsed by the ICJ in its advisory opinion on the *Legal Consequences of the Construction of a Wall in the Occupied Palestinian Territory*.[17]

The HRC's approach to extraterritorial obligations seems broader than the view of the European Court of Human Rights. The Grand Chamber of the European Court in *Bankovic et al v Belgium et al*[18] suggested that extraterritorial responsibility extended only to territories (rather than people) over which a State exercised effective control.[19] This approach is more conservative, and it seems to permit the perpetration of human rights abuses abroad by an agent of a High Contracting Party to the ECHR without recourse, so long as the High Contracting Party does not control the territory in which the act arises.[20] The *Bankovic* interpretation however has been subjected to numerous exceptions, and seems to have been contradicted in a later decision by a single chamber of the European Court in *Issa v Turkey*.[21]

ICESCR

The ICESCR does not contain a provision relating to jurisdictional or territorial scope.[22] Article 2(1) does however say that States must progressively realize ICESCR rights through steps taken individually 'and through international

---

[15] See also *Munaf v Romania*, UN doc. CCPR/C/96/D/1539/2006 (21 August 2009) (HRC).
[16] See *Coard et al v United States* (1999) Inter-Am Comm HR, Case 10.951, Rep No 109/99; *Armando Alejandre Jr., Carlos Costa, Mario de la Pena y Pablo Morales v Republica de Cuba* (1999) Inter-Am Comm HR, Case 11.589, Report No 86/99; *Victor Saldano v Argentina* (1998) Inter-Am Comm HR, Petition, Report No 38/99.
[17] *Legal Consequences of the Construction of a Wall in the Occupied Palestinian Territory (Advisory Opinion)* ICJ Rep 2004, 136, paras 104–14.
[18] *Bankovic et al v Belgium et al* (2007) 44 EHRR SE5, para 59.
[19] *Bankovic* was also decided on the basis that the ECHR did not extend beyond its 'espace juridique', that is the legal space of the Council of Europe. The case concerned alleged violations perpetrated by NATO troops in Serbia and Montenegro, which was outside the Council of Europe at that time. The 'espace juridique' argument does not logically extend to the UN treaties, which have global coverage. See also Damira Kamchibekova, 'State Responsibility for Extraterritorial Human Rights Violations' (2007) 13 *Buffalo Human Rights Law Review* 87, 145–6.
[20] See also Ralph Wilde, 'Legal "Black hole"? Extraterritorial State action and international treaty law on civil and political rights' (2005) 26 *Michigan Journal of International Law* 1, 25–8.
[21] (2005) 41 EHRR 27.
[22] The new Optional Protocol to the ICESCR states in Article 2 that communications may be received on behalf of people 'under the jurisdiction of a State party'.

assistance and cooperation'.[23] Those words seem to imply that States should at least refrain from actions which harm those rights abroad, as such measures are decidedly uncooperative.

The ICJ confirmed in its advisory opinion on the *Legal Consequences of the Construction of a Wall in the Occupied Palestinian Territory* that States have duties under the ICESCR to 'territories over which a State party has sovereignty and to those over which that State exercises territorial jurisdiction.'[24] Ultimately, the Court found that Israel had violated a number of rights in the ICESCR by building part of a security wall in the Occupied West Bank which, for example, hindered access to educational facilities, places of employment, health services, agricultural land, and sources of water. In *Democratic Republic of Congo v Uganda* the ICJ found that States are responsible under international human rights treaties for acts done in the exercise of jurisdiction outside their territory, especially (but not necessarily exclusively) in occupied territories.[25] The *Wall* standard focused on territorial control (which Israel exercised over the West Bank), at least in respect of the ICESCR,[26] while the *Congo* standard seemed to focus on extraterritorial acts with regard to all human rights treaties. Notions of territorial control were also absent in Judge Weeramantry's dissent in *Legality of the Use by a State of Nuclear Weapons in Armed Conflict*, when he stated, in regard to Article 12 on the right to health in the ICESCR, that 'each state is under an obligation to respect the right to health of all members of the international community'.[27]

Given that premier international court, the ICJ, believes that some form of extraterritorial jurisdiction under the ICESCR exists, it is safe to assume that States are required to *respect* ICESCR rights outside their borders, that is, to refrain from harming such rights. The Committee on Economic, Social and Cultural Rights has confirmed its belief in the existence of such duties on a number of occasions. For example, regarding the right to water (an aspect of the right to an adequate standard of living in Article 11 of the ICESCR), it has stated:

> To comply with their international obligations in relation to the right to water, States parties have to respect the enjoyment of the right in other countries. International cooperation requires States parties to refrain from actions that interfere, directly or indirectly, with the enjoyment of the right to water in other countries. Any activities undertaken within the

---

[23] See also Convention on the Rights of the Child (adopted 20 November 1989, entered into force 2 September 1990) 1577 UNTS 3 (CRC), Articles 4, 24, 28; Convention on the Rights of Persons with Disabilities (adopted 13 December 2006, entered into force 3 May 2008) UN doc. A/RES/61/106 (CPRD), Article 32.

[24] *Wall*, above n 17, paras 111–13.

[25] *Armed Activities on the Territory of the Congo (Democratic Republic of the Congo v Uganda) (Judgment, Merits)* ICJ Rep 2005, 168, para 216.

[26] As noted above, the ICJ endorsed the HRC's approach with regard to the ICCPR, which does not require control over territory. See John Cerone, 'Human Dignity in the Line of Fire: The Application of International Human Rights Law during Armed Conflict, Occupation, and Peace Operations' (2006) 39 *Vanderbilt Journal of Transnational Law* 1446, 1474–8, commenting on the apparent different standard adopted by the ICJ in *Wall* regarding extraterritoriality under, respectively, the ICCPR and the ICESCR.

[27] *Legality of the Use by a State of Nuclear Weapons in Armed Conflict* (Dissenting Opinion, Judge Weeramantry) (1996) ICJ Rep (1996), 66, 144.

State party's jurisdiction should not deprive another country of the ability to realize the right to water for persons in its jurisdiction. . . . [28]

. . . With regard to the conclusion and implementation of other international and regional agreements, States parties should take steps to ensure that these instruments do not adversely impact upon the right to water. Agreements concerning trade liberalization should not curtail or inhibit a country's capacity to ensure the full realization of the right to water.[29]

The most important aspects of a duty to respect economic, social, and cultural rights may arise with regard to intra-territorial acts which have an extraterritorial effect, rather than with extraterritorial acts as such. For example, the adoption by a State of protectionist measures within its territory might cause harm to the enjoyment of the right to work and to an adequate standard of living of those in relevant export industries outside its territory. The comparable analysis is arguably that of cases regarding refoulement rather than the cases concerning extraterritorial obligations as such. Under the ICCPR and the CAT, States have duties not to deport a person to a State where he or she might face torture or other irreparable harm to his or her human rights (for example, arbitrary execution) if such harm was foreseeable at the time of the deportation.[30] Those cases do not concern extraterritorial actions by the sending State, but rather, intra-territorial actions with extraterritorial consequences. By analogy, a State's intra-territorial decisions, actions and policies breach its ICESCR obligations if they cause reasonably foreseeable harm to ICESCR rights outside its territory.[31] However, the connection between the State and the expelled person is clearer than in the case of an external person who suffers harm from economic measures, as the impugned act of refoulement initially occurs while the person is within the State's territory, and the act is clearly aimed at that person such as to cause harm to his or her rights. There will normally be a clearer causal link in the case of refoulement. However, if a causal link can be established, the refoulement analysis is appropriate in analysing the human rights law implications of an economic policy.

Indeed, it is arguable that certain trade policies of some Northern States foreseeably harm the enjoyment of economic, social, and cultural rights in the South. Examples of such policies might be export subsidies, cotton subsidies, tariff escalation, and the enforcement of intellectual property rights over goods which are essential to the enjoyment of human rights. All of these policies are allowed or encouraged by WTO rules. Furthermore, a State should not seek to conclude trade deals which, if implemented, would undermine another State's capacity to fulfil its

---

[28] CESCR, 'General Comment No. 15: The right to water (arts. 11 and 12 of the International Covenant on Economic, Social and Cultural Rights)' UN doc. E/C.12/2002/11 (20 January 2003) para 31.

[29] Ibid, paras 34–5.

[30] See, eg, *Agiza v Sweden*, UN doc. CAT/C/34/D/233/2003 (24 May 2005) (Committee Against Torture); *Alzery v Sweden*, UN doc. CCPR/C/88/D/1416/2005 (10 November 2006) (HRC); *Judge v Canada*, UN doc. CCPR/C/78/D/829/1998 (5 August 2002) (HRC); HRC, General Comment 31, above n 14, para 12; *Soering v UK* (1989) 11 EHRR 439.

[31] See also *Trail Smelter Case (US v Canada)*, above n 5, 1965.

human rights duties.[32] In this respect, the (then) Special Rapporteur on the Right to Health, Paul Hunt, stated in 2004:

States should respect the enjoyment of the right to health in other jurisdictions, and ensure that no international trade agreement or policy adversely impacts upon the right to health in other countries.[33]

A year later, the Special Rapporteur on the Right to Food, Jean Ziegler, stated:

States should also refrain from taking decisions within the WTO . . . that can lead to violations of the right to food in other countries. It is evident that decisions taken by a Ministry of Agriculture or a Ministry of Finance within WTO . . . are acts of the authorities of a State that can produce effects outside their own territory. If these effects lead to violations of the right to food, then these decisions must be revised.[34]

If the effects of a State's trade policy are not so direct as to contravene an extraterritorial duty to respect human rights, or a causal link is impossible to prove, they could come within an extraterritorial duty to fulfil human rights. The potential existence and ramifications of such a duty are discussed below.

The Committee on Economic, Social and Cultural Rights has indicated that States parties also have duties to *protect* ICESCR rights in other States.[35] For example, it stated in General Comment 15 on the right to water that States should take steps 'to prevent their own citizens and companies from violating the right to water of individuals and communities in other countries'.[36] On the other hand, experts at a series of workshops convened in 2006 under the auspices of the UN Special Representative on the issue of Human Rights and Transnational Corporations concluded that the existence of such extraterritorial duties remained an open question.[37]

International trade law indirectly empowers private traders, particularly multinational corporations (who are the main engines of international trade), and yet provides for no corresponding duties.[38] This is so even if the behaviour of multinational corporations might distort trade, as is the case with the monopolistic

---

[32] See also De Schutter, above n 3, 20.

[33] Commission on Human Rights, 'The right of everyone to the enjoyment of the highest attainable standard of physical and mental health: Report of the Special Rapporteur on the Right to Health, Paul Hunt: Mission to the World Trade Organization', UN doc. E/CN.4/2004/49/Add.1 (1 March 2004).

[34] Commission on Human Rights, 'Report of the Special Rapporteur on the right to food, Jean Ziegler', UN doc. E/CN.4/2005/47 (24 January 2005) para 52.

[35] Ibid, paras 53–5. See also Chapter 1, text between notes 61 and 65.

[36] CESCR, General Comment No 15, above n 28, para 33. See also CESCR, 'General Comment No. 19: The right to social security (art. 9)', UN doc. E/C.12/GC/19 (4 February 2008) para 54.

[37] See Human Rights Council, 'Report of the Special Representative of the Secretary-General on the issue of human rights and transnational corporations and other business enterprises: Corporate responsibility under international law and issues in extraterritorial regulation: summary of legal workshops', UN doc A/HRC/4/35/Add.2 (15 February 2007) 15.

[38] See, eg, Human Rights Council, 'Report of the Special Rapporteur on the right to food, Olivier De Schutter: Mission to the World Trade Organization', UN doc. A/HRC/10/5/Add.2 (25 June 2008) para 46.

practices of agribusiness companies in the food industry.[39] In enhancing corporate power, WTO law adds to a systemic human rights problem, in that the power of many multinationals is enormous and perhaps on occasion greater than that of some (particularly developing) States, rendering it difficult for those States to appropriately regulate those entities.[40] Given such circumstances, perhaps it is desirable that home States, which are normally developed States, be required to close accountability gaps by regulating the offshore activities of their companies and protecting offshore people from corporate practices that harm human rights.[41] In the trade context, implementation of such a duty could involve, for example, constraining the global monopolistic behaviour of a company. It could also involve negotiating WTO amendments which allow for the multilateral control of global monopoly and monopsony power.[42] It could also involve prevention of export dumping by private actors.[43]

The most controversial aspect of potential extraterritorial duties under the ICESCR relates to *fulfilling* ICESCR rights in other States, or, in the words of Jean Ziegler, when he was the Special Rapporteur on the Right to Food, a duty to 'support the fulfilment' of ICESCR rights.[44] Such a duty would imply that rich States are obliged to provide aid to assist poorer countries. Rich States predictably resist such a characterization of their ICESCR duties. However, numerous human rights bodies have suggested otherwise. As noted in Chapter 1,[45] the duty to fulfil is split into three further duties: to 'facilitate' (for example, to 'provide an enabling environment' for the fulfilment of ICESCR rights);[46] to 'promote' (for example, to disseminate information and raise awareness of a right); and to 'provide', namely to furnish direct assistance to those people who need such assistance in order to enjoy a particular right.[47] While the greatest controversy concerns duties to 'provide', Ziegler locates the formulation of 'equitable trade rules' within the duty to 'facilitate' ICESCR rights.[48] Examples of a relevant duty to 'provide' might include the provision of aid to industries and farmers in the poorest States to increase their capacities to benefit from liberalized trade.[49]

---

[39] See Chapter 6, text at notes 116–44.

[40] See the discussion of this point in David Kinley, *Civilising Globalisation* (Cambridge University Press, Cambridge, 2009) 160–6. See also Caroline Dommen, 'Raising Human Rights Concerns in the World Trade Organization: Actors, Processes and Possible Strategies' (2002) 24 *Human Rights Quarterly* 1, 14.

[41] See Report of the Special Rapporteur on the right to food, above n 34, para 54.

[42] See also Olivier De Schutter, *International Trade in Agriculture and the Right to Food* (Dialogue on Globalization Occasional Paper No 46 (Friedrich Ebert Stiftung, Geneva, 2009) 45–6.

[43] See Armin Paasch, 'World Agricultural Trade and Human Rights: Case Studies on Violations of the Right to Food of Small Farmers' in FIAN and others, above n 3, 39, 46, discussing the dumping of poultry on Ghanaian markets by EU companies.

[44] Report of the Special Rapporteur on the right to food, above n 34, para 57. Ziegler makes this distinction in recognition of the fact that a duty to completely fulfil the right could not realistically be imposed on an extraterritorial basis, as such a duty might imply that the territorial State has no such duties: para 47.

[45] See Chapter 1, text at notes 62–3.

[46] Report of the Special Rapporteur on the right to food, above n 34, para 57.

[47] Ibid, paras 57–8.   [48] Ibid, para 57.   [49] De Schutter, above n 42, 20.

The Committee has indicated that States have an extraterritorial duty to fulfil ICESCR rights when they are in a position to do so.[50] The Committee, in its General Comment 3, on 'the nature of States parties' obligations' stated:

in the absence of an active programme of international assistance and cooperation on the part of all those States that are in a position to undertake one, the full realization of economic, social and cultural rights will remain an unfulfilled aspiration in many countries.[51]

Regarding the right to health, it has stated:

[The] Committee [has drawn] attention to the obligation of all States parties to take steps, individually and through international assistance and cooperation, especially economic and technical, towards the full realization of the rights recognized in the Covenant, such as the right to health. In the spirit of article 56 of the Charter of the United Nations, the specific provisions of the Covenant (articles 12, 2(1), 22, and 23) and the Alma-Ata Declaration on primary health care, States parties should recognize the essential role of international cooperation and comply with their commitment to take joint and separate action to achieve the full realization of the right to health. In this regard, States parties are referred to the Alma-Ata Declaration which proclaims that the existing gross inequality in the health status of the people, particularly between developed and developing countries, as well as within countries, is politically, socially and economically unacceptable and is, therefore, of common concern to all countries.[52]

Regarding the right to water, the Committee has stated:

Depending on the availability of resources, States should facilitate realization of the right to water in other countries, for example through provision of water resources, financial and technical assistance, and provide the necessary aid when required. In disaster relief and emergency assistance, including assistance to refugees and displaced persons, priority should be given to Covenant rights, including the provision of adequate water. International assistance should be provided in a manner that is consistent with the Covenant and other human rights standards, and sustainable and culturally appropriate. The economically developed States parties have a special responsibility and interest to assist the poorer developing States in this regard.

States parties should ensure that the right to water is given due attention in international agreements and, to that end, should consider the development of further legal instruments.[53]

---

[50] See, eg, CESCR, 'General Comment 3: The Nature of States Parties' Obligations (Art. 2, Para. 1, of the Covenent)', UN doc. E/1991/23 (14 December 1990) para 14; CESCR, 'General Comment 12: Right to adequate food (Art. 11)', UN doc. E/C.12/1999/5 (12 May 1999) para 35; CESCR General Comment 15, above n 28, para 38.

[51] CESCR, General Comment 3, above n 50, para 14.

[52] CESCR, 'General Comment 14: The right to the highest attainable standard of health (article 12 of the International Covenant on Economic, Social and Cultural Rights)', UN doc. E/C.12/2000/4 (11 August 2000) paras 38–40.

[53] General Comment 15, above n 28, paras 34–5.

The Committee has expressed similar views regarding the right to food[54] and the right to work.[55]

C. Responsibility and Causation in a World of Inequality and Neediness

In a world of global economic interdependence, where many States are incapable of making serious progress towards the fulfilment of economic, social, and cultural rights beyond minimalist protections without international assistance and cooperation of some sort, extraterritorial duties are arguably necessary to give such rights meaning. The ICESCR recognizes rights for all, but clearly is most concerned with the rights of the poorest and most marginalized. Yet a denial of extraterritorial duties would deprive such people of meaningful avenues to claim redress: the 'have-nots' in the developing world would have no claim upon the 'haves' of the developed world, who are in the best position to provide assistance. The economic incapacities of their own State might shield that State from ICESCR liability so long as it is utilizing available resources in good faith, and the vast resources available outside the country would be irrelevant in the calculus of whether rights had or had not been violated. There would be a 'disjunction between the proclamation of rights...and the contingent conditions for their fulfilment'.[56]

At this point it is necessary to remind the reader that we live in a world with an astonishingly inequitable distribution of income, resources, and influence. Even minor levels of redistribution would make an enormous difference to the extreme poor, at very little cost to the comparatively wealthy.[57] Using 2004 World Bank figures, Professor Thomas Pogge calculated in 2005 that only 1.3 per cent of global product was consumed by the bottom 44 per cent of the world's population, with the top 15 per cent consuming 81 per cent. He calculated that the transfer of just 1 per cent of global product from the top to the bottom would be enough to lift those at the bottom out of extreme poverty. Pogge's figures are older and slightly more extreme than the poverty statistics from the World Bank cited in Chapter 5,[58] but the argument can still be made that the transfer of a tiny portion of Northern wealth to the Southern poor could have a massive impact on poverty rates in the latter at little cost to the former. Furthermore, the affordability of such an adjustment is evident in light of the massive bailouts of Northern financial institutions that materialized in the wake of the global economic crisis of 2008–2009.[59] The

---

[54] General Comment 12, above n 50, para 36. See also Chapter 6, text after n 6.
[55] CESCR, 'General Comment 18: The right to work (art. 6),' UN doc. E/C.12/GC/18 (6 February 2006) para 30.
[56] Matthew Craven, 'The Violence of Dispossession: Extraterritoriality and Economic, Social and Cultural Rights' in Mashood A Baderin and Robert McCorquodale (eds), *Economic Social and Cultural Rights in Action* (Oxford University Press, Oxford, 2007), 83.
[57] Thomas Pogge, 'World Poverty and Human Rights' (2005) 19 *Ethics and International Affairs* 1, 1.
[58] See Chapter 5, text at notes 154–67.
[59] Eg, during the Bush Administration, the Emergency Economic Stabilization Act of 2008 authorized the spending up to US$700 billion. Similarly, during the Obama Administration,

equitable adjustment of WTO rules would go some of the way towards realizing that redistribution. Other measures of assistance which would have an undoubted impact, such as Northern States actually fulfilling their long-standing and repeated commitment to devoting 0.7 per cent of Gross National Income in overseas development aid, are beyond the scope of this book.

As noted in Chapter 5, the causes of poverty and inequality are complex, and it is difficult to isolate precise causes thereof. However, the global international economic system developed over many years, preceding and including the WTO system along with contemporaneous developments, has tolerated and probably contributed to this system of radical inequality between haves and have-nots, with the former disproportionately located in the North and the latter disproportionately located in the South.[60] This radical inequality entails, for the many at the bottom, real deprivation in terms of access to the necessities of human rights and even death from poverty-related causes, while those at the top bask in comparatively absurd luxury.[61]

Pogge argues that any global order which tolerates, for as long as ours has, this level of inequality and poverty is by definition unjust, and its perpetuation without compensation or reform in fact harms human rights in the South, thus amounting to a failure to respect their human rights.[62] Pogge thus frames the extraterritorial duties of North to South in the language of negative duties, rather than the more controversial positive duties. He has gone further by outlining how the global order has generated massive inequity, giving rise to a duty to reverse that trend:[63]

There are at least three morally significant connections between us and the global poor. First, their social starting positions and ours have emerged from a single historical process that was pervaded by massive grievous wrongs . . . including genocide, colonialism and slavery, [which] play a role in explaining both their poverty and our affluence. Second, they and we depend on a single natural resource base, from the benefits of which they are largely, and without compensation, excluded. The affluent countries and the elites of the developing world divide these resources on mutually agreeable terms without leaving

the American Recovery and Reinvestment Act of 2009 authorized the spending of up to US$787 billion.

[60] Salomon, above n 4, 62.

[61] Thomas Pogge, 'Growth and Inequality: Understanding Recent Trends and Political Choices' (2008) *Dissent*, 7–8 <http://www.dissentmagazine.org/article/?article=990> accessed 20 September 2010.

[62] Pogge, above n 57, 5; see also Thomas Pogge, 'Severe Poverty as a Violation of Negative Duties' (2005) 19 *Ethics and International Affairs* 55, 68.

[63] Even the renowned political philosopher John Rawls might agree with such an argument. John Rawls, *The Laws of Peoples* (Harvard University Press, Cambridge, 2001) is often misinterpreted as implying that the peoples of one State have no moral obligation to the peoples of another. Rawls does countenance a 'duty to assist', which would presumably arise in cases of extreme poverty. See generally, Patrick Emerton, 'International Economic Justice: is a Principled Liberalism Possible?' in Sarah Joseph, David Kinley, and Jeff Waincymer (eds), *The World Trade Organization and Human Rights: Interdisciplinary Perspectives* (Edward Elgar, Cheltenham, 2009) 133–61. See also Frank J Garcia, *Trade, Inequality and Justice: Towards a Liberal Theory of Just Trade* (Transnational Publishers, Ardsley Park, 2003) Chapters 2 and 3, esp 137–44. Compare Joel Trachtman, 'Legal Aspects of a Poverty Agenda at the WTO: Trade Law and "Global Apartheid"' (2003) 6 *Journal of International Economic Law* 3, 7.

'enough and as good' for the remaining majority of humankind. Third, they and we coexist within a single global economic order that has a strong tendency to perpetuate and even to aggravate global economic equality.[64]

Harms have undoubtedly been inflicted on the South, which have generated ongoing legacies with economic impact, such as colonialism as well as the design of the current global order.[65] However, Mathias Risse, in a direct response to Pogge, points out that we cannot know what would have happened in the counterfactual situation. For example, ex-colonies could conceivably be worse off now if they had never been colonized.[66] However, the reverse proposition—that colonialism has indeed caused more harm than had it not happened—cannot be disproved either. All we do know is that colonization caused harm and generated inequality, and has a direct link to the identity and location today of those at the top and those at the bottom.[67] Furthermore, colonizers forced certain economic policies on colonies for many decades which hampered their industrial development,[68] providing strong evidence that colonization has played a major role in underdevelopment and associated harms.[69]

Finally, colonialism is not the only relevant historical wrong inflicted by the North upon the South, as noted in the above quote from Pogge. The slave trade, for example, inflicted enormous economic harm (along with the obvious physical and psychological harm) on the people of the African continent, by removing large numbers of able-bodied people from societies.

Risse has also pointed out that current poverty rates are far lower than those in previous centuries. 'In 1820, 75% of the world population lived on less than $US1 a day, appropriately adjusted.' Indeed, 'almost everybody was poor'.[70] There have also been great improvements across the world in life expectancy and literacy.[71] Therefore, perhaps one can argue that '[h]istorically speaking, the global order seems to have greatly benefited the poor'.[72] However, these historical aggregate figures neglect the fact that 25 per cent remain in extreme poverty today, millions die from poverty-related causes, people go hungry when there is enough arable land to feed us all,[73] and their misery could probably be cured by a small readjustment in

---

[64] See T Pogge, 'Priorities of Global Justice' (2001) 32 *Metaphilosophy* 6, 14–15. See also J Hunter, 'Broken Promises: Agriculture and Development in the WTO' (2003) 4 *Melbourne International Law Journal* 299, 301.

[65] See also Garcia, above n 63, 210.

[66] Matthias Risse, 'Do we owe the global poor assistance or rectification?' (2005) 19 *Ethics and International Affairs* 1, 12–14.   [67] Thomas Pogge, above n 62, 56.

[68] See Mehdi Shafaeddin, 'Does Trade Openness Favour or Hinder Industrialization and Development?', *Third World Network Trade & Development Series No. 31* (TWN, Malaysia, 2006), 24, for a case study on how colonial policies harmed the Indian textile industry throughout the 1800s.

[69] See also Megan Davis, 'International Trade, the World Trade Organisation, and the Human Rights of Indigenous Peoples' (2006) 8 *Balayi* 5, 7–9, discussing how the trading activities of indigenous peoples were disrupted by colonizers.

[70] Risse, above n 66, 9.

[71] See also Martin Wolf, *Why Globalisation Works* (Yale Nota Bene, London, 2005) 164–6.

[72] Risse, above n 66, 12.

[73] See Chapter 6, text at notes 18–23.

the sharing of global income. Risse's historical statistics do not provide an acceptable answer to 'the complaint of those who avoidably suffer and die against those who confine them to a life of grinding poverty'.[74] The historical decline in poverty cannot justify the 'continued imposition of global order that is designed so that it foreseeably reproduces avoidable severe poverty on a massive scale'.[75]

As another response to Pogge, it may be argued that poverty is largely the result of poor domestic policies. After all, many poor States have been plagued for decades by incompetent and predatory governments, as well as local armed conflict. There is no doubt that local governance plays a major role in, respectively, generating, exacerbating or, alternatively, redressing poverty. On the other hand, Pogge is correct to point out that that does not mean that global factors play no role.[76] Such is particularly the case with the WTO, where the rules are almost universally recognized as unfair to developing States,[77] even by high level bureaucrats within the WTO itself.[78] Pogge also points out the connivance of the North with corrupt governments in the South by way of the global resource privilege: Northern companies and governments have knowingly bought resource rights from corrupt and illegitimate governments, knowing that that money will probably be squandered with no benefit for the people of the relevant States.[79] Due to the global borrowing privilege, Northern banks and international institutions dominated by Northern governments have lent money to such rulers, in circumstances where the lenders know or should know that the money will be wasted on arms and palaces. Such transactions foreseeably increase the wealth of the corrupt elites, with little benefit and indeed active harm for those that they govern (in the form of lost future wealth and the repayment of squandered loans with interest), and the North has been entirely complicit in them.[80] Furthermore, Northern States have benefited from arms sales to developed States, knowing that those arms will be used for the purposes of human rights abuse, to fan the fires of civil or regional conflict, and/or to deplete the already poor coffers of those client States.[81] Local corruption is not a purely local phenomenon divorced from the global economy which absolves global economic arrangements from responsibility for ongoing poverty and inequality.

Trade liberalization and other measures which remove government control over the economy are sometimes thought to reduce the scope for corruption in a State. However, neo-liberal market reforms can on occasion increase corruption. The loss of public resources might increase the temptation for corrupt practices in the public sector. Public officials might be tempted to curry favour to increase future private sector employment opportunities. Neoliberal reforms can be undertaken in such a way as to favour the rich, as noted in Chapter 2 regarding the introduction of land titling in Cambodia.[82] Another infamous example was the process of

---

[74] Pogge, above n 62, 57.   [75] Ibid, 58.
[76] Pogge, above n 57, 6. See also Pogge, above n 62, 64–5.
[77] World Bank, *World Development Report 2006: Equity and Development* (World Bank, Washington DC, 2006) 210; Pogge, above n 57, 6.
[78] See Chapter 5, text at notes 15 and 105.
[79] See also Joseph Stiglitz, *Making Globalization Work* (Penguin, London, 2007) 138–44.
[80] Pogge, above n 57, 7.   [81] Stiglitz, above n 79, 286.
[82] See Chapter 2, text at note 19.

liberalization and privatization in 1990s Russia. In any case, private sector corruption clearly exists in the absence of public sector dishonesty, and can have devastating consequences, as evinced by episodes such as the demises of Enron and Worldcom.[83]

Finally, Ha-Joon Chang argues that the impact of corruption on underdevelopment is possibly overstated and is at the least not well understood. He points out that Mobutu's Zaire and Suharto's Indonesia were both notoriously corrupt, yet the latter fared quite creditably in the economic arena while the former languished disastrously. While corruption cannot be good for the States in question, Chang posits that corruption is used 'as a convenient justification' by the North, perhaps to divert attention from other possible causes of poverty and underdevelopment, such as iniquities in the global trading system.[84] At the least, an emphasis on local corruption is used to deflect awareness of the level of Northern responsibility for Southern poverty.

D. Practical Operation of Extraterritorial Duties

How could extraterritorial duties, whether to respect or fulfil, be operationalized? When, for example, would State X have a duty to a person in State Y to take positive actions to fulfil his or her rights? And when could that person's socio-economic deprivation be held to come within the responsibility of a particular external State?

In this respect, Dr Margot Salomon has drawn attention to the distinction between obligations of conduct and obligations of result in delineating extraterritorial duties.[85] Whereas it is difficult to maintain that an external State has a duty to ensure that a certain level of socio-economic prosperity is enjoyed in another State, it is less difficult to argue that States should adhere to processes which are likely or more likely to generate appropriate outcomes.[86] In the context of the WTO, developed States might be required to drop prohibitive barriers to goods from developing States, which is likely to generate greater prosperity in the latter States but cannot be guaranteed to do so, given that other factors may come into play (for example, natural disasters, local corruption).[87] It might also entail good faith negotiation in the Doha round, with a view to redressing the inequities of the Uruguay round.

Salomon has also drawn attention to the familiar human rights principle of due diligence,[88] which applies to determine a State's responsibility in cases of human rights harms perpetrated within its territory by non-State agents. The State's responsibility is engaged when it fails to take reasonable actions which would avert foreseeable harm by a non-State actor. For example, States must take measures to

---

[83] See generally, Ha-Joon Chang, *Bad Samaritans: the Myth of Free Trade and the Secret History of Capitalism* (Bloomsbury Press, New York, 2008) 168–71.

[84] Ibid, 160–1.   [85] Salomon, above n 4, 184–9.

[86] Ibid, 102–3, 133–9, 143.   [87] Pogge, above n 62, 77.

[88] Salomon, above n 4, 184–9.

protect persons, most often women, from domestic violence.[89] Similarly, a State's failure to adopt reasonable actions within the context of the WTO foreseeably perpetuates ongoing poverty, and thus constitutes a breach of its extraterritorial human rights obligations.

Finally, Salomon has devised criteria for allocating global responsibilities to States in creating a just institutional economic order.[90] Her four indicators for determining responsibility are: (1) the contribution a State has made to the emergence of a problem (for example, poverty exacerbated by resource depletion under colonization); (2) the relative power wielded by a State at the international level (for example, its influence within the WTO); (3) whether it is in a position to assist (for example, its levels of wealth); and (4) the extent to which that State benefits from the distribution of global wealth and resources (for example, the extent to which the State has benefited from WTO rules, and other relevant rules of the global economy).[91] Such criteria do not confine responsibilities to developed States, though they would bear the most extensive responsibilities under this framework. Criteria 2 and 4 imply some responsibilities for the States with the most successful emerging economies, such as China and Brazil.

The existence of extraterritorial duties to the people of other States must not be seen to diminish the duties of those other States towards their own people. Extraterritorial duties are complementary and supportive: the primary duty to implement human rights rests with the territorial State. Its failure to implement its obligations in good faith, for example by wasting resources through corrupt or frivolous expenditure, or simple bad governance, will violate its human rights duties, regardless of the fulfilment (or existence) of extraterritorial duties by other States.

A difficult question arises, with regard to rights for people in the South for assistance in poverty alleviation from the North, over whether the North can justifiably attach conditions to aid to guard against the squandering of redistributed resources.[92] Such issues are more relevant in a bilateral context rather than in the global multilateral context which is the subject matter of this book. Conditionality is not so relevant in the context of a duty to reform WTO rules and domestic trade policies to more equitably accommodate the development needs of the South by allowing greater policy space for developing States according to their level of industrialization while permitting greater market access in the North.

Issues regarding conditionality are more relevant to the distribution of foreign aid and to debt forgiveness. Foreign aid will be needed to assist developing States to bring their economies to a position where they can actually benefit from

[89] See, eg, *A.T. v Hungary*, UN doc. CEDAW/A/61/38/2006 (26 January 2005) (CEDAW Committee); *Goekce v Austria*, UN doc. CEDAW/C/39/D/5/2005 (6 August 2007); *Yildirim v Austria*, UN doc. CEDAW/C/39/D/6/2005 (6 August 2007) (all CEDAW Committee).
[90] Salomon's arguments go beyond WTO reform into reform of global financial and economic architecture beyond the field of trade.
[91] Salomon, above n 4, 193.
[92] See, in support of such conditionality, Trachtman, above n 63, 20–1.

liberalization. Such aid would contrast with current trade aid commitments, which are generally designed to alleviate the burden of liberalization; trade aid is granted after rather than before extensive liberalization. Such aid also goes beyond aid for trade in helping the poorest States develop essential institutional infrastructure, such as welfare safety nets for globalization losers, which should be in place *prior* to major liberalization in order to preserve the human rights of those losers. Discussion of the mechanics of such aid is beyond the scope of this book.

There are strong arguments in favour of both positive and negative duties for richer States to assist poorer States in implementing human rights, including economic, social, and cultural rights. It may therefore be legitimately argued that the Northern States have a duty under international human rights law to agree to a new WTO deal which addresses the unfairness of the Uruguay deal and facilitates economic development in the South.[93]

E. Balancing Human Rights in North and South

A new lopsided deal which allows greater market access for the South, yet allows the South to retain or even be restored certain policy space, would clearly impact on traders in the North, including their enjoyment of human rights.[94] For example, the main political justification for continued agricultural protection in the North is to protect livelihoods in the Northern farming sector. Northern farmers, like their Southern counterparts, also wish to protect their livelihoods and communities.[95] They would (and do) question why their rights to work or rights to enjoy their own culture should be sacrificed to help out people in the South.[96]

The losers from liberalization in the North are more likely than those in the South to receive compensation from the winners through, for example, social security payments and public health care funded by tax revenues. Indeed, taxpayers in many Northern States are currently subsidizing the farming sector, so it arguably makes sense to transform those subsidies into welfare payments or retraining schemes, while simultaneously allowing agricultural competition which benefits not only Southern farmers but also Northern consumers.[97]

However, political imperatives encourage States to shift losses offshore rather than contain them within their own populations. For example, it is more politically palatable for EU governments to subsidize their farmers and hurt the poor in developing countries, rather than provide social welfare to their farmers and to adopt policies that might destroy local rural communities.[98]

---

[93] See also, generally, Garcia, above n 63.   [94] See also Trachtman, above n 63, 13.

[95] Christine Breining-Kaufman, 'The Right to Food and Trade in Agriculture' in Thomas Cottier, Joost Pauwelyn, and Elizabeth Bürgi (eds), *Human Rights and International Trade* (Oxford University Press, Oxford, 2005) 370.   [96] See also Hunter, above n 64, 320–1.

[97] Ibid, 321; Trachtman, above n 63, 13.

[98] Joel R Paul, 'Do International Trade Institutions Contribute to Economic Growth and Development?' (2003) 44 *Virginia Journal of International Law* 285, 303.

Subsidies are more justifiable from a human rights point of view if they help to underpin the livelihoods and cultures of individual farmers, particularly those in financial need. To be sure, the elimination of certain protections in the developed world will have to be graduated, in order to allow for adjustment by the former beneficiaries of those protections, especially when those beneficiaries are not wealthy, such as unskilled workers in the developed world who will lose from the reduction of tariff peaks.[99] However, the fact is that most Northern agricultural subsidies go to large agribusiness farmers rather than individual farmers in need.[100]

There is no doubt that Northern States that are party to the ICESCR have a duty to promote the economic, social, and cultural rights of people within their territories, and that these duties must somewhat offset any duties they have to people outside their borders in the South. However, the extraordinary inequitable distribution of wealth in the world signals that these local duties cannot entirely offset extraterritorial duties. At some point, the right of a person in the North to a subsidized job instead of a welfare payment (or another job) cannot override the right of a person in the South to an adequate standard of living which could be earned in the absence of distorting trade measures.[101] The balance between local and extraterritorial duties could be determined by a standard of reasonableness or proportionality.[102] While such tests might be imprecise, there are some clear instances of unreasonable promotion of local interests at the expense of extraterritorial interests: some Northern trade measures are completely unjustifiable in terms of protecting local people, given the level of intrusion into the rights of those offshore.[103] An example is the overproduction of sugar by the EU, which protects local markets for local producers, but also distorts offshore markets to the detriment of sugar producers in their home markets.[104] Indeed, the scale and distorting effects of EU farm subsidies is illustrated by the fact that in 2003, each EU cow was said to be worth a net subsidy of $2.50 a day, an amount that would double, at least, the average daily income of half the world's population![105] Germany's (then) Minister for Development Cooperation, Heidemarie Wieczorek-Zeul, conceded in 2008 that export subsidies breach the right to food if they cause hunger in the developing world.[106] Another example could be protectionism in the textiles industry, whereby each job saved in the North in 2002 costs 35 jobs in low-income States.[107] That job lost is unfortunate, but the relevant person is more likely than

---

[99] Joseph E Stiglitz and Andrew Charlton, *Fair Trade for All* (Oxford University Press, New York, 2005) 122–3.

[100] See Chapter 6, text at notes 242–51. See also Yong-Shik Lee, Reclaiming Development in the World Trading System (Cambridge University Press, Cambridge, 2006) 113.

[101] See also Pogge, above n 62, 72.

[102] Wouter Vandenhole, 'Third states obligations under the ICESCR: a case study of EU sugar policy' (2007) 76 *Nordic Journal of International Law* 73, 93–4.

[103] Olivier De Schutter, above n 42, 45.   [104] Vandenhole, above n 102, 93.

[105] See also Wolf, above n 71, 215; Stiglitz, above n 79, 85.

[106] As quoted in Paasch, above n 43, 41.

[107] These figures come from remarks made by World Bank Chief Economist, Nicholas Stern, in a speech in 2002: a report of the speech is available at <http://web.worldbank.org/WBSITE/EXTERNAL/NEWS/0,contentMDK:20076497~menuPK:34457~pagePK:34370~piPK

the 35 to have access to social security (which might be more remunerative if public funds lost through protectionism were recouped) to tide him or her over until he or she found another job. Cotton subsidies in the US and EU are totally undermining the economic capacities of some of the world's poorest people in the C4 countries of Western Africa in order to benefit comparatively few farmers in the North:[108] that balance seems highly disproportionate when less money might suffice to shift those farmers to more efficient industries. As a final example, the need to protect the interests of innovators via the enforcement of lucrative patent rights is probably outweighed by the need to permit access to a life-saving invention by poor people who otherwise cannot afford it.

The 'balancing' of the rights of Northern and Southern traders may sound suspiciously like a utilitarian analysis, a theory which underpins free trade but not human rights.[109] However, the proposed balancing takes into account notions of global justice rather than mere economic efficiency. Furthermore, while arguments that the North should drop trade barriers (such as agricultural subsidies) might align with free trade arguments, the argument that developing States should retain policy space does not.

There are also undoubted benefits for the North in helping the South, beyond lower prices for their consumers. Magnanimity (or rather, fairness) in the Doha round by the North may inject life into the present moribund state of multilateralism, which is largely caused by intractable North/South divisions, and has impacted detrimentally not only the Doha round but also negotiations on tackling climate change.[110] Furthermore, the alleviation of poverty has a positive economic impact,[111] by helping to transform the poor into viable consumers, opening up marketing possibilities for both Southern and Northern markets.[112]

Certain rights for people in the North should however be preserved or even enhanced, despite opposition from the South. There are, in particular, legitimate concerns about advantages flowing to Southern industries due to severely inadequate regulations, such as poor or non-existent environmental and labour standards.[113] At some point, those standards can be so low as to be genuinely trade distorting. The labour rights debate is examined in Chapter 4.

:34424~theSitePK:4607,00.html> accessed 20 September 2010. Since 2002, quantitative restrictions in the textiles sector have been phased out in accordance with WTO timetables under the WTO Agreement on Textiles and Clothing.

[108] See also Chapter 5, text at note 117.   [109] See also Chapter 1, text at notes 65–9.

[110] See, eg, Saliem Fakir, 'Was Copenhagen the Death of Multilateral Environmental Agreements?' (12 January 2010) *The South African Civil Society Information Service* <http://www.sacsis.org.za/site/article/408.1> accessed 20 September 2010. See also International Centre for Trade and Sustainable Development, 'Trade and Climate: Joined at the Hip?' (2010) 14 *Bridges Monthly Digest*.

[111] Dani Rodrik, *The Global Governance of Trade: As if Development Really Mattered* (UNDP, New York, 2001) 12.

[112] See generally, CK Pralahad and Stuart L Hart, 'The Fortune at the Bottom of the Pyramid' (2002) 26 *Strategy + Competition Magazine*. See also World Development Report 2006, above n 77, 206. See also Chang, above n 83, 220.

[113] Robert Wai, 'Countering, Branding and Dealing: Using Economic and Social Rights in and Around the International Trade Regime' (2003) 14 *European Journal of International Law* 35, 49–50.

F. Conclusion

There are sound legal and moral arguments in favour of the recognition of extraterritorial human rights duties. Of relevance to the WTO/human rights debate is the notion that richer States have human rights duties to help alleviate poverty in poorer States. Such duties help to underpin arguments that WTO obligations should be recast so as to be fairer to developing States, and to boost their capacity to abide by their human rights obligations to their own populations.

9

WTO Reform, the Doha Round, and Other Free Trade Initiatives

In this chapter I summarize potential WTO reforms in light of the human rights deficiencies within, or that are likely to be prompted by, WTO rules and processes, which are identified in Chapters 3 to 7. These proposals are evaluated, and then compared with current proposals on the table during the Doha round. Finally, the phenomenon of bilateral and other free trade agreements outside the auspices of the WTO, focusing on the example of European Partnership Agreements, is discussed.

Chapter 3 and democratic deficit

Chapter 3 identifies processes within the WTO which inherently favour certain constituencies over others. Those disadvantaged constituencies are social justice advocates and interest groups, and developing States. Chapter 4 examines the extent of substantive disadvantages which accrue for social justice interest groups, while Chapters 5 to 7 examine substantive disadvantages for developing States which impact on human rights.

One solution to the democratic deficiencies identified in Chapter 3 is that WTO processes be amended to permit greater participation by those disadvantaged constituencies, which would improve the legitimacy and perhaps the quality of its input. Social justice NGOs are exercising greater indirect power over the Doha round processes compared to the Uruguay round processes, but those efforts are yet to translate generally into identifiable concrete outcomes.[1] Furthermore, greater direct inputs by NGOs would complicate an already complex and gridlocked negotiation process. That fact does not mean that major input reform is a bad idea, but it means that it is unlikely to happen in the foreseeable future.

Regarding developing States, it is unquestionable that such States are exercising greater negotiation muscle in the current round. Future WTO rounds will not come to a close without satisfying key developing States such as India, China, and Brazil. This does not mean however that final agreements will be in the interests of

---

[1] Some exceptions arise, such as with respect to the important initiatives on TRIPS and access to medicines, on which see Chapter 7.

all developing States, as the interests of such States are not uniform. Furthermore, the tougher negotiation stance by the South, coupled with intransigence from the North, means that the Doha round is currently stalled, and the unfair Uruguay round rules prevails. Again, this is not an argument for the South to give in: a bad Doha deal is not necessarily better than no deal.

Another response to democratic deficit is for the powers of the WTO to be diminished, or the rules diluted. If the consequences of its outputs are defused, there will not be such a discrepancy between its output power and its input legitimacy. Therefore, many of the reform options discussed below focus on limiting the WTO's mandate to override national decision-making power.

Chapter 4 and human rights trade measures

Chapter 4 addresses the human rights issues that have traditionally dominated the discourse of trade and human rights,[2] that is the extent to which WTO rules limit the capacity of States to impose trade measures, including trade sanctions, for human rights purposes.

Early debates on the linkage between trade and human rights focused on 'outward measures', the extent to which a State can express disapproval, or attempt to coerce human rights change in an abusive State, by way of trade sanctions. It is submitted that this issue is in fact one of the least important within the WTO/human rights debate due to the questionable desirability and efficacy of such sanctions from a human rights point of view, and the fact that States are rarely required under international human rights law to implement outward measures.[3] It was concluded that outward measures will rarely be permissible under WTO law, except to the extent they are justified under Article XXI GATT (and Article XIV bis GATS) or are allowed under a waiver, as is the case with regard to the global bans on trade in conflict diamonds.[4]

Trade measures can also constitute 'inward measures', whereby trade is restricted for the purpose of protecting the human rights of a State's own population, such as perhaps the ban on asbestos building products by the EC in *Asbestos*, the ban on retreaded tyres in *Brazil—Tyres*, or the ban on hormone-treated beef in *Beef Hormone*. Some inward measures are undoubtedly required under international human rights law. Given the dearth and varying approaches of relevant WTO cases, it is uncertain the extent to which such measures are accommodated under WTO law. There remains the real possibility of direct conflicts between WTO

---

[2] James Harrison, *The Human Rights Impact of the World Trade Organisation* (Hart, Oxford, 2007) 126 and 176.

[3] Furthermore, the Security Council and some States seems more intent these days on imposing 'smarter', targeted sanctions on States, rather than comprehensive economic embargoes: many smart sanctions regimes do not raise WTO issues.

[4] As noted at Chapter 4, text at note 29, the contribution of the trade in conflict diamonds to breaches of human rights and humanitarian law in Western African civil wars was so direct and serious that it was possibly a situation where outward measures were in fact mandated by international human rights obligations.

law and human rights law in this respect. Certainly, the broad interpretation given to WTO obligations (for example, regarding 'like goods', 'discrimination', and quota/market access obligations in Article XI GATT and Article XVI GATS) coupled with strict interpretation of relevant exceptions in Article XX GATT and Article XIV GATS may overly restrict the scope for States to enact appropriate inward measures.

Chapters 5 and 6: developing States and the WTO

In Chapter 5, the inherent bias within the Uruguay round bargain, whereby the greatest winners are developed States and the greatest losers are some of the world's poorest States, is discussed. Furthermore, the downside of free trade in economic terms, which impacts on the capacities of a State to implement human rights obligations, is discussed. In Chapter 6, the flaws in the Agreement on Agriculture are analysed. Furthermore, the merits of free trade in the agricultural arena are questioned, given unique problems in agricultural markets, and the coincidence between hungry people and vulnerable smallhold farmers, who are disadvantaged within the global trade arena.

In both chapters, it is suggested that the Doha round should yield a lopsided bargain which benefits developing States more than developed States. While the latter should be required to further open up their markets and eliminate destructive protectionism such as certain agricultural subsidies (for example, regarding cotton in the US and sugar in the EU), the former should preserve and even regain policy space in order to pursue more tailored development policies. Such a lopsided agreement would accord with the notion of the North having extraterritorial obligations to take measure to facilitate the right to development and the alleviation of poverty in the South, as discussed in Chapter 8. The extent to which Doha proposals reflect these recommendations is discussed below.

Chapters 6 and 7: TRIPS and human rights

The impact of TRIPS on the human rights to food and health is discussed, respectively, in Chapter 6 and Chapter 7. It is possible that TRIPS provides sufficient room for States to discharge their human rights obligations, so long as TRIPS flexibilities and exceptions are interpreted broadly. Nevertheless, TRIPS shrinks a State's options and also constrains development policy in ways that were not experienced by the richest States during their own transformations into industrialized countries. Furthermore, the benefits of intellectual property protection in terms of the promotion of creative endeavour, research, and development are possibly overstated. Even if those benefits are accepted, TRIPS probably grants overly generous rights to intellectual property rights holders at the expense of the enjoyment of countervailing human rights. It is submitted therefore that a rollback of TRIPS, for example in the form of the granting of greater flexibility in implementation for developing States, is desirable.

A. Potential Reforms in Light of the Issues
Raised in Chapters 3 to 7[5]

Deferential doctrines

Perhaps the WTO dispute settlement bodies should make greater use of deferential doctrines like the margin of appreciation. For example, Winickoff et al argue that States should be given significant leeway under the SPS agreement, perhaps akin to a margin of appreciation, when they are applying standards in areas where there is low certainty regarding potential risks, and low consensus on those risks (such as in the case of GMOs).[6]

The interpretation of limitations to WTO obligations could be loosened: for example the intense scrutiny of Article XX exceptions could be replaced by applying a more lenient standard of reasonableness.[7] Only the most unreasonable trade restrictions would be clearly disallowed, whereas 'borderline' restrictions would generally be acceptable. More decision-making power would be restored to national levels. Of course, more trade restrictions would inevitably be allowed under such a system.

Perhaps greater deference should be given to national decisions when the WTO deals with inward measures, those designed to protect national populations, compared to outward measures, those aimed at protecting other people or somehow changing behaviour overseas. States should have more discretion regarding the imposition of inward measures, as they have considerable international obligations to protect their own people and comparatively few if any obligations to impose trade sanctions in order to protect people in other States.[8] Examples of relevant types of inward measures could be measures to protect health by limiting imports of goods that are harmful, or, more controversially, those which might be harmful to health. Indeed, States are already likely to have greater scope under WTO law to impose inward measures compared to outward measures.

Obligations of non-discrimination rather than minimum standards

Perhaps the WTO should return to its humbler GATT roots, and only target discriminatory protectionism, rather than branching out into the realm of minimum standards as in the TRIPS, the SPS, and TBT agreements.[9] Furthermore, the

---

[5] The following commentary is adapted from Sarah Joseph, 'Democratic deficit, Participation and the WTO' in Sarah Joseph, David Kinley, and Jeff Waincymer (eds), *The World Trade Organization and Human Rights: Interdisciplinary Perspectives* (Edward Elgar, Cheltenham, 2009) 313–43.

[6] David Winickoff, Shiela Jasanoff, Lawrence Busch, and Robin Grove-White, 'Adjudicating the GM Food Wars: Science, Risk, and Democracy in World Trade Law' (2005) 81 *Yale Journal of International Law* 81, 86, 107–8.

[7] See Chapter 3, text prior to and at note 160; and Chapter 4, text between notes 148 and 149.

[8] United Nations High Commissioner for Human Rights, *Human Rights and World Trade Agreements: Using General Exception Clauses to Protect Human Rights* (OHCHR, New York and Geneva, 2005) 16–17. See also generally, Harrison, above n 2, Chapters 5–8 and 212.

[9] See David M Driesen, 'What is Free Trade? The Real Issue Lurking behind the Trade and Environment Debate' (2001) 41 *Virginia Journal of International Law* 279, 327–9. See also Deborah

interpretation of 'quota' or 'market access' provisions could be rolled back so as to clearly cover only discriminatory provisions.[10]

Ultimately, as Professor Robert Hudec stated, the removal of 'minimum standards' requirements and a retreat to non-discrimination involves a value judgement that the danger of excessive protectionism is not as bad as the danger of inadequate or inappropriate minimum standards in the relevant areas.[11] From the point of view of economic efficiency, the former danger is probably more concerning than the latter. However, from the point of view of many non-trade lobbies and possibly consumers, that equation is probably reversed.

Respecting consumer choice

Given that free trade is partly designed to enhance consumer choice, perhaps consumer choices should be respected, at least with regard to their perceptions of their own welfare. For example, if Europeans do not want hormone-treated meat to be imported into Europe, why force it on them? Why insist that consumer choice be 'rational', or, as required under the SPS, based on science?[12] As consumers are effectively the people of a State in a commercial guise, the respecting of consumer choices arguably equates with respecting the democratic choices of a State, thus enhancing participatory rights.[13]

Such a proposal assumes that consumer choice can actually be established. Dr Caroline Foster has concluded that while such evidence would be difficult to ascertain, it would still be possible to do so.[14] She notes, for example, that States are already required to seek the views of interested parties prior to imposing anti-dumping measures or countermeasures against subsidies. She concludes:

Further thought should be given to whether the practical difficulties associated with consulting the public constitute a good reason to hold back from pursuing such a development [that is, the explicit conferral of greater weight on national public opinion in WTO dispute resolution] if it is otherwise sound in principle.[15]

Of course, the forced import of goods under WTO rules does not force a consumer to actually consume those goods. The GMO example, however, demonstrates that

Z Cass, *The Constitutionalization of the World Trade Organization* (Oxford University Press, New York, 2005) 213–16; Harrison, above n 2, 248.

[10] See Chapter 4, text at notes 59–68.

[11] Robert Hudec, ' "Circumventing" Democracy: the Political Morality of Trade Negotiations' (1993) 25 *NYU Journal of International Law and Politics* 311, 321.

[12] See also Driesen, above n 9, 319. See generally, Caroline E Foster, 'Public Opinion and the interpretation of the World Trade Organisation's Agreement on Sanitary and Phytosanitary Measures' in Joseph, Kinley, and Waincymer (eds), above n 5, 285–311.

[13] Indeed, consumer choice has been relevant in some aspects under WTO law. Eg, it was relevant in the determination of 'like products' by the Appellate Body in *European Communities—Measures Affecting Asbestos and Asbestos-Containing Products*, WTO doc. WT/DS135/AB/R (00-1157) AB-2000-11 (5 April 2001) (Report of the Appellate Body) paras 130 and 139. See Chapter 4, text at notes 34–43.

[14] Foster, above n 12, 302–3.

[15] Ibid, 303. Foster does not advocate that consumer choice be decisive, unlike the proposal discussed here.

consumer choice is not necessarily easy to exercise. Concerns have been raised, regarding GMOs, of uncontrolled cross-contamination, meaning that it might become impossible to guarantee that a certain type of food is in fact GM-free. Furthermore unsuspecting consumers may not be aware of GMOs in meals that are not home-cooked, or of what their children might consume outside the home.

In this regard, it is reiterated that mandatory labelling requirements should be allowed to ensure that consumers are able to make an informed choice about whether they wish to consume certain goods.[16] Full disclosure would let market forces 'decide' if it is acceptable for goods to have certain characteristics (for example, contain GM ingredients) or be manufactured by an undesirable process (which, for example, hurts labourers or the environment). At the moment, the compatibility of labelling systems with the TBT cannot be presumed.[17]

A caveat regarding the first three reform proposals

These first three reform proposals involve weakening the impact of WTO rules, so as to allow more policy space for Member States, thus enhancing their capacities to implement their human rights obligations, particularly regarding economic, social, and cultural rights. It has been argued in this book that developing States need the restoration of such policy space. However, a dilution of the impact of WTO rules would also restore policy space to the North. In that case, the ability of Northern States to abuse protectionist measures in the agricultural field which, as discussed in Chapter 6, can detrimentally impact on the right to food by devastating the livelihoods of Southern farmers, would be enhanced. Even non-discriminatory SPS or TBT requirements (including, perhaps, even some types of labelling requirements) could impose intolerable burden on exporters from developing States lacking relevant technical capacities. Consumer choice might be manipulated for protectionist or nationalistic ends: for example it may not be so difficult to whip up consumer hysteria over a very minor or virtually non-existent health threat, which may be an apt description of the EU's concern over aflatoxins.[18]

Therefore, there are dangers in implementing any of the above three mooted reforms. The interests of developing States have to be secured by a new lopsided deal, rather than by the dilution of WTO rules alone. The negative impact of such dilution on developing States (by weakening constraints on Northern trade policies) should then be more than offset by the restoration of their own policy space (through dilution and a favourably assymetric Doha deal), and the imposition

---

[16] See Chapter 4, text at notes 212–14.

[17] In *European Communities—Measures affecting the approval and marketing of biotech products*, WTO docs. WT/DS291/R, WT/DS292/R and WT/DS293/R (29 September 2006) (Report of the Panel) ('*EC—Biotech*'), the Panel alluded to the possibility that EC regulations on the labelling of GMOs breached the SPS agreement at [7.392]. See also, eg, Carlos Lopez-Hurtado, 'Social Labelling and the WTO' (2002) 5 *Journal of International Economic Law* 719; Nick Covelli and Viktor Hohots, 'The Health Regulation of Biotech Foods under the WTO Agreements' (2003) 6 *Journal of International Economic Law* 773.

[18] See Chapter 4, text at notes 192–3. Note that Foster, above n 12, has suggested methods of constraining the abuse of any justification of trade measures by reference to consumer choice: see Chapter 4, text at notes 183–4.

of more obligations through a new deal on the North. Furthermore, it must be remembered that the restoration of some policy space for developed States will also give the North greater scope to implement justifiable trade measures which implement their own human rights obligations, a desirable outcome from a human rights point of view.

A human rights exception and a social clause

The merits of a labour rights or social clause are discussed in Chapter 4. Such measures could have both an outward purpose (that is, to induce labour rights compliance in delinquent States) and an inward purpose (protection of local workers from unfair competition from States 'benefiting' from poor labour rights standards). It was concluded that there is merit in reviving the discussion of such a clause. However, there are no current proposals within the WTO in this respect.

An alternative mechanism is for a human rights clause, such as a new Article XX exception allowing for trade measures which protect human rights, to be incorporated into WTO agreements. While some have argued that the public morals exceptions can effectively operate as human rights clauses, it is far from certain that such an interpretation will be adopted by the dispute settlement bodies.[19] A human rights clause would remove ambiguity in this respect. However, the introduction of such an exception has not been formally discussed within the Doha round.

In any case, it is not satisfactory, from a human rights point of view, for human rights to operate as a mere exception within the WTO. As noted in Chapter 4, the prohibitions on trade measures under WTO law are very broad. Once a prima facie breach is established, the burden of proving the applicability of an exception lies with the State relying on that exception. Therefore, once a prima facie breach of WTO law is established, the burden of proving the permissibility of a human rights trade measure would always lie with the State imposing that measure.[20] Hence, in any process of balancing trade impact versus human rights impact, the human rights side of the equation is disadvantaged. Under international human rights law, adverse trade impacts per se are not recognized as a qualification to human rights. The balancing of human rights considerations against trade impacts is not countenanced, let alone the outweighing of human rights considerations by trade considerations.

An alternative is for a treaty mandating the positive protection of human rights to be passed as a part of the WTO package. Such a treaty would be a human rights version of TRIPS. This reform might sound very attractive from a human rights point of view. After all, the sharp 'teeth' of the WTO would become available to enforce human rights obligations. However, there are numerous obstacles to and issues with such a proposal. Most obviously, political will for such a development

---

[19] See Chapter 4, text at notes 97–100.
[20] See WTO, *Dispute Settlement System Training Module,* Chapter 10.6, 'Legal Issues arising in WTO dispute settlement' <http://www.wto.org/english/tratop_e/dispu_e/disp_settlement_cbt_e/c10s6p1_e.htm> accessed 19 October 2010; Harrison, above n 2, 215–16.

is completely lacking: such a treaty would massively stretch the mandate of the WTO far beyond the field of trade. Such a development would essentially render the WTO a type of world governing body, with significant enforcement power in both the commercial and the social justice realms. Unless there is a radical change in the internal culture of the WTO, which is dominated by commercial and trade values, such a pre-eminent role for the WTO would be highly unsatisfactory for human rights advocates. There would be a serious danger of the WTO entrenching the subordination of human rights values to trade values rather than improving human rights protection.[21] A far preferable measure would be the strengthening of human rights norms through existing or new improved human rights bodies, rather than through a trade organization, while simultaneously enhancing the likelihood of rights-sensitive interpretations of existing WTO provisions through deferential doctrines and approaches such as those discussed above.

Human rights impact assessments

Presently, 'there is no effective monitoring of the human rights implications of the Marrakesh decision'.[22] Perhaps the impact of WTO rules, as well as new WTO proposals, should be subjected to human rights impact assessments. The NGO 3D has defined human rights impact assessments (HRIAs) as tools which:

> measure the gap between legal human rights standards and a current or proposed action, with the objective to enhance the knowledge of decision makers and stakeholders and to limit the adverse effects of governmental and corporate activities.[23]

Ideally, such assessments should take place in advance of the implementation of trade agreements so as to influence modification before human rights damage is done. Indeed, States undoubtedly have duties under human rights treaties to take their human rights obligations into account while negotiating trade treaties, and not to undertake trade obligations which undermine their ability to fulfil their human rights obligations.[24] *Ex ante* HRIAs would assist States to fulfil due diligence obligations in that respect.

Realistically however, certain human rights impacts may be unforeseen, or their magnitude may be underestimated (or overestimated). Therefore, there will be an inevitable need for *ex post facto* assessments. In this regard, the Special Rapporteur on the Right to Food has recommended that trade agreements be adopted provisionally with sunset clauses so as to allow for modification in case

---

[21] See, generally, Philip Alston, 'Resisting the Merger and Acquisition of Human Rights by Trade Law: A Reply to Petersmann' (2002) 13 *European Journal of International Law* 815, esp at 836. See also Harrison, above n 2, 218–19, discussing the problems of subjecting human rights arguments to the WTO legal system. Indeed, the same problem would probably arise if human rights were included as a new express exception to WTO obligations, as suggested in the previous paragraph.

[22] Harrison, above n 2, 228.

[23] 3D, 'Insights on Human Rights Impact Assessments of Trade Policies and Agreements' (3D, Geneva, undated) 2 <http://www.3dthree.org/pdf_3D/HRIAsbackgroundinformation.pdf> accessed 20 September 2010.

[24] See, eg, Chapter 2, text at notes 137–9. See also Chapter 8, text at notes 29–34.

their implementation is found by independent assessments to be generating human rights violations.[25]

HRIAs as applied to the trade area are in their relative infancy. In late 2009, 3D reported that only three such assessments, formally focusing on human rights, had been undertaken of trade agreements.[26] Unsurprisingly, such a small sampling has not generated an 'overall approved methodology',[27] despite the extensive additional scholarship, NGO, and public examination of the specific impacts of various trade agreements. Indeed, although good practices and templates are increasingly being identified, it is not possible to outline a single, fixed model or methodological framework given the range of circumstances which might give rise to HRIAs: '[n]o methodology will fit every situation without some modification'.[28]

Only the European Union carries out systematic Sustainability Impact Assessments (SIAs) on WTO proposals, which examine social and environmental impacts.[29] Unfortunately, as outlined by Dr James Harrison, they currently suffer from a number of deficiencies. For example, the EU's SIAs do not presently refer explicitly to human rights, though they do address indicators which are within the realm of economic social and cultural rights.[30] The analysis of the impact on potential losers from the proposals is underwhelming. For example, one analysis of WTO agricultural proposals acknowledged the adjustment costs for smallhold farmers, but noted that the same adjustment costs might also fall on large farmers. There was no appreciation of the more devastating impact those costs would have on the smaller farmers, due to their lesser capacity to adjust as needed.[31] Furthermore, echoing the common or even dominant response to complaints about the adverse impact of trade law and policy on human rights, the solution advocated to any problems tends to be the adoption of mitigating measures, often SDT type measures such as the granting of aid, rather than reconsideration of the overall policy.[32] Finally, governments often fail to respond adequately to SIAs.[33] Despite these considerable flaws, one must acknowledge that the EU's SIAs are only about a decade old, and could still represent a 'laudable first step' towards systemic human rights impact assessments.[34]

The methodological parameters for HRIAs can be expected to concretize as they become more common. HRIAs will also be assisted by the ongoing work

[25] Human Rights Council, 'Report of the Special Rapporteur on the Right to Food, Olivier De Schutter: Mission to the World Trade Organization', UN doc. A/HRC/10/5/Add.2 (25 June 2008) para 37.
[26] 3D, above n 23, 3, reporting on HRIAs on the likely future impacts of the Thailand-US Free Trade Agreement, and assessments of the past human rights impacts on particular rights by international trade and financial agreements on Ghana, Honduras, and Indonesia; and on the right to health of the US-Dominican Republic-Central American Free Trade Agreement.
[27] Ibid, 3   [28] Ibid, 4.   [29] Harrison, above n 2, 229.   [30] Ibid, 229.
[31] Ibid, 231, citing Overseas Development Institute, Sustainability Impact Assessment of Proposed WTO Negotiations, Final report of the Agricultural Sector Study, 22 April 2005, 33.
[32] Ibid, 231.
[33] Ibid, 233. See, eg, the EU's continuing pursuit of MFN clauses in European Partnership Agreements, despite the fact that such a clause will undermine regional unity in relevant regions, contrary to the advice in an SIA. See below, text at notes 80–2.
[34] Ibid, 229 and 232.

being done, for example within the UN's Office of the High Commissioner for Human Rights, on delineating human rights indicators which aid in the measurement and assessment of human rights impacts and levels of compliance.[35] There is also great potential for relevant lessons to be learnt from the increased attention given to HRIAs in the corporate sector as an element of the due diligence required under the framework for business and human rights promulgated by the UN Special Representative on Business and Human Rights.[36] HRIAs represent a route for providing for greater legitimacy for trade policies, greater consistency between human rights and trade policies, and greater human rights accountability in the implementation of trade policies.[37]

A Human Rights Declaration

James Harrison has also suggested that the WTO might adopt a Declaration, like the Doha Declaration on TRIPS and Public Health, which signals the Members' intention that WTO obligations not be interpreted, implemented, or enforced in a way that undermines their abilities to comply with their human rights obligations.[38] Such a Declaration could act as a green light to the dispute settlement bodies to adopt, as far as possible, a human rights compliant interpretation of WTO measures. Alternatively, and perhaps more importantly, the existence of such a Declaration, adopted by a consensus of WTO members, would act as a political and moral barrier for States that might otherwise seek to challenge measures that can be reasonably justified on a human rights basis.

Deferring to expert opinion

WTO bodies could regularly defer to other experts when an issue concerns serious non-trade issues, such as the Office of the High Commissioner for Human Rights or the human rights treaty bodies if human rights issues should arise, or the International Labour Organization (ILO) in respect of labour issues.[39] The WTO's current mandate could be maintained, but other international expert bodies could

---

[35] See, eg, Office of the High Commissioner for Human Rights, 'Report on Indicators for Promoting and Monitoring the Implementation of Human Rights', UN doc. HRI/MC/2008/3 (6 June 2008).

[36] See, eg, Human Rights Council, Report of the Special Representative of the Secretary-General on the issue of human rights and transnational corporations and other business enterprises, John Ruggie, 'Business and Human Rights: further steps toward the operationalization of the "protect, respect and remedy" framework', UN doc. A/HRC/14/27, paras 79–86.

[37] 3D, above n 23, 5. See also generally James Harrison and Alessa Goller, 'Trade and Human Rights: What does "Impact Assessment" have to offer?' (2008) 8 *Human Rights Law Review* 587 and 'Human Rights Assessments for Trade and Investment Agreements', Report of the Expert Seminar, 23–24 June 2010, at <http://www.srfood.org/images/stories/pdf/otherdocuments/report_hria-seminar_2010_eng.pdf> accessed 19 December 2010.

[38] Harrison, above n 2, 240–1. Therefore, such a Declaration would not apply to most outward measures. See Chapter 4, text at notes 25–30.

[39] See Daniel C Esty, 'The World Trade Organization's legitimacy crisis' (2002) 1 *World Trade Review* 7, 17–18; Harrison, above n 2, 219–21.

be integrated into WTO processes regarding issues that clearly straddle the trade and non-trade divide. In extreme cases, the resolution of relevant disputes could effectively be ceded to that other body. This suggestion was raised with regard to a labour rights clause and the ILO in Chapter 4.

Conclusion

None of the above proposals are the subject of serious negotiation within the WTO at the moment. However, some of the above proposals, in particular those regarding interpretation of WTO obligations, could be independently implemented by WTO dispute settlement bodies.[40] Indeed, WTO dispute settlement bodies could consistently utilize human rights obligations to interpret WTO obligations, minimizing inconsistency to the extent possible within the words of the text of WTO treaties. As noted in Chapter 2, the Appellate Body used environmental treaties to interpret Article XX(g) in *Shrimp I* even though not all parties to that case were parties to the relevant environmental treaties.[41] Such interpretations could arise with regard to the WTO exceptions and also with regard to the interpretation of concepts such as non-discrimination, 'like goods', 'public morals', and 'public order'.

To be sure, the use of such interpretative techniques would be controversial, and would seem to depart from the strict letter of the text of WTO treaties.[42] At least two conflicting values are at play here: the protection and promotion of human rights and strict legalism. From a human rights point of view, the former value is more important.[43]

History indicates that developing States would be unhappy with such interpretations.[44] However, as noted in Chapter 3, the divergence between the interests of developing States and the goal of human rights promotion in a WTO context has been overstated, and overly influenced by the early focus of WTO/human rights debate on the issue of trade sanctions. In fact, it is submitted that the most important human rights issues within the WTO concern the extent to which WTO obligations work against the interests of the people of developing States. Developing States would probably not be unhappy, for example, if their own WTO obligations, such as those under TRIPS, were interpreted in light of the ICESCR.

---

[40] Harrison, above n 2, 242.   [41] See Chapter 2, text at notes 123–35.

[42] Jagdish Bhagwati, 'Afterword: the Question of Linkage' (2002) 96 *American Journal of International Law* 126, esp at 131–4.

[43] The dispute between 'certainty' and strict legalism in legal interpretation, and dynamic interpretation in light, eg, of social justice considerations is hardly unique to the discussion of WTO law. This debate routinely arises in the context of both domestic law and international law, and will not be extensively examined here. As an example in the Australian context, compare the differing interpretative philosophies adopted by the two respective judges in M Kirby, 'The Australian Use of International Human Rights Norms: Form Bangalore to Balliol—A View from the Antipodes' (1993) 16 *University of New South Wales Law Review* 363 and D Heydon, 'Judicial Activism and the Death of the Rule of Law' (2003) 47(1) *Quadrant* 363. Both authors were appointed to the High Court of Australia after they had written their respective pieces.

[44] See, eg, Eric Neumayer, 'The WTO and the Environment: Its Past Record is Better than Critics Believe, But the Future Outlook is Bleak' (2004) 4 *Global Environmental Politics* 1 <http://ideas .repec.org/a/tpr/glenvp/v4y2004i3p1-8.html> accessed 21 September 2010.

In any case, interpretative innovation by dispute settlement bodies can only go so far in redressing human rights concerns regarding the WTO. Such innovation would have to be well entrenched before it could remove any chilling impact of WTO rules, which may be largely driven by apprehension over the meaning of the rules rather than actual WTO interpretations. The ability of WTO panels and (to a lesser extent) its Appellate Body to adopt such interpretative techniques in a satisfactory manner is doubtful, given that their personnel are trade experts, not human rights experts. Furthermore, no amount of sympathetic interpretation, other than a blatant abandonment of the current WTO text, would permit some of the policies advocated in this book, such as the permissibility of adequate infant industry protection for developing States.

B. The Doha Development Round: The Story So Far

The first post-Uruguay round of negotiations got off to a false start in Seattle in 1999, where the Ministerial Conference collapsed amid protests in the streets and major splits inside the WTO between North and South. The ball got rolling in Doha in 2001 with the launch of the Doha Development round. The round's name firmly points to a focus on Southern issues. However, progress in the Doha round has been very disappointing. Talks collapsed again in Cancún in 2003. The Ministerial Conference in December 2005 in Hong Kong yielded only modest progress. Expectations were so low by the time of the Ministerial Conference in Geneva in late 2009 that the Ministerial was not designed to be a meeting for negotiation. While most States expressed a commitment to try to bring the Doha round to a successful conclusion, serious doubts remain at the time of writing as to whether that will be possible in the short term.

The title of the Doha Development round seems to promise that the promotion of 'development' is the main goal of the Doha round of negotiations. However, development has, disappointingly, taken a back seat to a Uruguay-like focus on opening up markets across the world on a 'give and take' basis.[45] Alternatively, it has simply been assumed by certain powerbrokers within the WTO, wrongly, that trade liberalization is somehow synonymous with development.

Developing States are generally most interested in rectifying the imbalances in the AoA, as that agreement was an important part of the Northern side of the Uruguay bargain, and yet it has not yielded outcomes which justify the concessions made by the South in the Uruguay round. However, agricultural negotiations will not be concluded unless negotiations on non-agricultural market access (NAMA) are also concluded: the two sets of negotiations are now coupled. As the promise of further agricultural negotiation is mandated in Article 20 of the AoA, developing States view the coupling of NAMA negotiations with AoA negotiations as a

---

[45] Joy Kategekwa, 'Empty Promises: What happened to "development" in the WTO's Doha round?' (Oxfam International Briefing Paper 131, 16 July 2009).

concession on their part.[46] The adding of NAMA to the mix of negotiations has contributed to the delay in the round's conclusion.

Agricultural negotiations

As discussed in Chapter 6, world agricultural trade is severely distorted by continuing subsidies. Unfortunately, Doha round proposals do not go very far in eliminating those subsidies. In Hong Kong, Northern States proposed to phase out export subsidies by 2013.[47] 'Amber box' subsidies will also be cut. However, these cuts will be undermined by continued use of the 'blue' and 'green' boxes, which will not apparently be disciplined in the Doha round. Retention of these loopholes in the same form will essentially allow developed States to maintain their trade distorting spending levels.[48]

Tariffs across the board will be significantly reduced though States will be permitted to maintain very high tariffs (of over 100 per cent) on certain 'sensitive products'.[49] While the tariff cuts from developed States would be welcome, the cuts for developing States, and the limitation of the notion of sensitive products, limits the policy space which is probably needed to protect food security and vulnerable farmers.

Cotton has been described as the litmus test for the bona fides of the North in the Doha Round.[50] At Hong Kong, Northern government had promised to eliminate export subsidies in cotton by 2006.[51] Of course, that deadline has long passed, as it was dependent on the conclusion of the Doha round. In any case, Oxfam has argued that the US agreed to do no more than had been mandated under the dispute settlement system in *United States—Subsidies on Upland Cotton*, and probably 'fell short' of those findings in delaying implementation.[52] At Hong Kong, it was also agreed that cotton subsidies would be reduced by a greater level than for other agricultural goods.[53] However, since Hong Kong, little headway in cotton negotiations has been made, so the devastating impacts of subsidies continue.[54]

---

[46] Muchkund Dubey, 'An Appraisal of the WTO's Hong Kong Ministerial Outcome' (Third World Network Briefing Paper 31, February 2006).

[47] WTO, 'Ministerial Declaration' (Adopted on 18 December 2005, Hong Kong) WTO doc. WT/MIN(05)DEC (22 December 2005) para 6.

[48] Kategekwa, above n 45.

[49] Martin Khor, 'Analysis of the new WTO Agricultural and NAMA texts of 6 December 2008' *Third World Network Trade & Development Series 37* (TWN, Malaysia, 2009) 11.

[50] Joel P Trachtman, 'Developing Countries, the Doha round, Preferences, and the Right to Regulate' in Chantal Thomas and Joel P Trachtman (eds), *Developing Countries in the WTO Legal System* (Oxford University Press, New York, 2009) 111, 124.

[51] Hong Kong Ministerial Declaration, above n 47, para 11.

[52] Oxfam, 'What happened in Hong Kong? Initial Analysis of the WTO Ministerial' (Oxfam Briefing Paper 85, December 2005), 12 <http://www.oxfam.org/en/policy/bp85-hongkong> accessed 19 September 2010.

[53] Trachtman, above n 50, 125. See also Hong Kong Ministerial Declaration, above n 47, 11–12.

[54] 'Cotton-4 (C4) countries to intensify campaign against US, EU', *StockMarketsReview.com*, 27 July 2009 at <http://www.stockmarketsreview.com/commodities/cotton_4_countries_to_intensify_campaign_against_us_eu_20090727/> (16 January 2010).

Negotiations in July 2008 broke down largely due to disagreements over a new 'Special Safeguard Mechanism' to protect the livelihoods of farmers in developing States. This issue is discussed in Chapter 6.

Overall, current agricultural proposals indicate that Northern protectionism might be reduced, but will not be adequately restrained after the new Doha round. It seems likely that Northern subsidies, protected by arbitrary designations under the blue and green boxes, will continue to harm agricultural industries in the South. At the same time, adequate policy space will not be preserved or restored to the South. While much of the current policy constraints have been largely caused by factors outside the WTO, such as IFI conditionality and bilateral or other free trade agreements, Doha proposals would shrink the flexibility officially available for such States within the WTO.

Non-Agricultural Market Access (NAMA)

NAMA negotiations are aimed at increasing liberalization in non-agricultural trade. One battle between North and South concerned the formula under which cuts would be made. The South favoured a linear cut, which would mean that States basically cut tariffs by the same amount. However, the North favoured the Swiss formula, under which higher tariffs are cut by higher rates. As the highest tariffs are generally in the South, that formula leads to deeper cuts from the South than the North. The Swiss formula was endorsed at Hong Kong, representing a 'win' for the North. The adoption of the Swiss formula breaks the promise of the Doha Ministerial Declaration, whereby 'less than full reciprocity' would be demanded from developing States.[55]

The exact rates of application of the Swiss formula remain under negotiation. Current proposals would reduce most tariffs for developing States to around 11–12 per cent, with very few tariff lines exceeding 15 per cent.[56] SVEs would be permitted greater flexibility, but would still be required to cut tariffs as dramatically as they did in the Uruguay round. LDCs would not be required to cut tariffs.[57] Developed States under Doha proposals would have much lower average tariff rates (around 2 per cent on average or less). However, given their tariffs are currently around 3 per cent on average, the cut, whilst big in percentage terms, is small in quantitative terms. Such cuts will not affect Northern industries as much as the proposed cuts for developing States and SVEs.[58]

An 'anti-concentration' clause is contained in current draft proposals, whereby higher tariffs cannot be concentrated in a particular sector. This clause, if adopted, would limit the possibilities for selective infant industry protection.[59]

---

[55] WTO, 'Ministerial Declaration' (Adopted on 14 November 2001, Doha) WTO doc. WT/MIN(01)/DEC/1 (20 November 2001) para 16.

[56] Khor, above n 49, 6.   [57] Ibid, 4.

[58] Ha-Joon Chang, 'Developing Countries need to wake up to the Realities of the NAMA negotiations' (Third World Network Briefing Paper 26, June 2005) 2.

[59] Khor, above n 49, 2.

Certainly, the policy space for LDCs will not be shrunk under current proposals. Furthermore, developed countries have agreed to permit duty-free and quota-free (DFQF) market access to the LDCs of 97 per cent of 'products originating from LDCs, defined at the tariff line level'.[60] The exemption from this commitment of 3 per cent of tariff lines allows developed countries to exclude the most important sectors. An ActionAid spokesperson has wryly observed that 'Bangladesh will be able to export all its non-existent nuclear submarines to the US, but not the textiles that make up 80% of what it sells overseas'.[61] This decision is a departure from the 100 per cent DFQF target flagged in the Doha Ministerial Declaration in 2001.[62]

As an historical comparison, the economist Ha-Joon Chang has referred to the average tariff rates for manufactured goods in developed States throughout the first half of the twentieth century, at a time when they probably had stronger economies than many developing States today. The average tariff rate in 1950 was 23 per cent in the UK and 14 per cent in the US.[63] Those rates are significantly higher than the average rates proposed for most developing States under current Doha proposals. Furthermore, he argues that the productivity gap between developed and developing States these days is so great that higher tariffs are needed by the latter in order to provide equivalent protection for industries.[64]

Overall, NAMA proposals preserve policy space only for LDCs, and no policy space is restored. Other developing States will lose significant policy space. Developed States will, however, reduce their tariff peaks, which will have beneficial effects for Southern exports. The conferral of 97 per cent DFQF status on LDCs sounds generous, but is in fact an unfortunate retreat from original Doha proposals. Current NAMA proposals are not generally geared towards optimal outcomes for development in the South.

Other

Further Southern concessions were made regarding GATS at the Hong Kong Ministerial. WTO Members must consider taking part in plurilateral negotiations on services liberalization if requested to do so,[65] which may open the way for greater political pressure to be placed on weaker countries to prise open their services markets. There are certainly no proposals for the introduction of greater safeguards into GATS to alleviate its potential impact on the enjoyment of essential services which are necessary for the enjoyment of human rights.[66]

---

[60] Hong Kong Ministerial Declaration, above n 46, Annex F, Decision 36.

[61] Larry Elliott, 'WTO summit: No easy way out as an encore looms: After a week of trench warfare, the idea of a spring trade pact looks far-fetched' *The Guardian*, 19 December 2005. See also Sukarmar Muralidharan, 'Pitfalls on the Road from Hong Kong' *All Africa*, 21 December 2005.

[62] See Doha Ministerial Declaration, above n 55, para 42, which mentions no limit to DFQF commitments for the least developed countries. See also UN World Summit 2005 Outcome, UN doc. A/Res/60/1, 24 October 2005, para 29.

[63] Chang, above n 58.

[64] Ha-Joon Chang, *Kicking Away the Ladder: Development Strategy in Historical Perspective* (Anthem Press, London, 2005, first published 2003) 67.

[65] Hong Kong Ministerial Declaration, above n 47, Annex C, para 7.

[66] See Chapter 5, text at notes 45–57.

Regarding TRIPS, there are no serious proposals to reduce commitments despite its deleterious impact on developing States. Negotiations are underway regarding the relationship between indigenous knowledge, the Convention on Biological Diversity, and TRIPS, as mentioned in Chapter 6. Those negotiations seem unlikely to be resolved in the near future.[67] The resolution of that issue is not a prerequisite for conclusion of the Doha round. In effect, that issue is on the back-burner, so TRIPS will continue to pose an apprehended obstacle to the enjoyment of relevant cultural rights.

Increased commitments regarding 'trade aid' are on the table. However, there is little sign that the delivery of increased aid will be an enforceable duty under a Doha deal, thus continuing the trend of SDT consisting of voluntary rather than obligatory provisions.[68] The aid will also be contingent upon States committing to further open their economies, which could generate premature liberalization, the dangers of which were discussed in Chapter 5.[69]

The Doha round was also intended to address issues related to investment and competition. However, developing States, which have signalled their opposition to the extension of the WTO into these areas since the Singapore Ministerial of 1997, successfully killed these issues with their refusal to negotiate on them at the Cancún Ministerial. Global investment rules would have been of the greatest benefit to the major foreign investors, namely Northern multinationals.[70] While a global competition policy to curb cartel behaviour by major multinationals would be beneficial for all States, particularly in the agricultural arena, the (now aborted) competition proposals were mainly aimed at breaking up local monopolies to ensure access for foreign competitors.[71] Again, the biggest beneficiaries would have been Northern multinationals.

Current Doha proposals would dictate a mix of trade policies which are far from optimal in assisting development and poverty alleviation in developing States, and could well be counterproductive. They will not improve the capacities of developing States to discharge their human rights obligations and could harm them. They do not represent a bona fide attempt by the North to fulfil relevant extraterritorial obligations to the people of the South.

Most States at the Geneva Ministerial called for a swift end to the Doha round. At the time of writing, nearly a year after that meeting, such sentiments seem to be wishful thinking or empty rhetoric.

---

[67] Martin Khor, 'Behind the July failure of the WTO's Doha talks' (Third World Network Briefing Paper 50, September 2008) 8.

[68] Hong Kong Ministerial Declaration, above n 47, para 57.

[69] See also Valentine Sendanyoye-Rugwabiza, 'Is the DDA a Development Round' (Address at the London School of Economics, 31 March 2006) 6 <http://www2.lse.ac.uk/PublicEvents/pdf/20060331-WTO.pdf> accessed 20 September 2010. See also Frank J Garcia, *Trade, Inequality and Justice: Towards a Liberal Theory of Just Trade* (Transnational Publishers, Ardsley Park, 2003) 188.

[70] See Ken Shadlen, 'Resources, Rules and international political economy: the politics of development in the WTO' in Joseph, Kinley, and Waincymer (eds), above n 5, 119, 127–9 on the short-lived Doha investment negotiations.

[71] See Chapter 6, text at note 141.

Other free trade agreements

The moribund Doha round has coincided with an explosion in bilateral and regional free trade agreements (FTAs) concluded outside the WTO structure. Such agreements are a permitted departure from MFN provisions under Article XXIV GATT and Article V GATS, so long as certain conditions are followed. Notably, such agreements must provide for the elimination of 'duties and other restrictive regulations of commerce' on 'substantially all' trade between the parties to the agreement. Therefore, an FTA will only comply with Article XXIV if it provides for extensive liberalization in respect of most of the parties' economies with regard to each other. Necessarily, FTAs provide for a much higher level of liberalization than is required under WTO rules and under Doha proposals. FTAs therefore shrink the economic policy space of their parties with respect to each other more than WTO rules. Furthermore, they are often concluded between parties with a greater power imbalance than arises within the multilateral context of the WTO.[72]

At the time of writing, extensive negotiations on FTAs known as European Partnership Agreements (EPAs) were being conducted between the EU and States in Africa, the Caribbean, and the Pacific (ACP countries). Current draft EPAs, if adopted, will radically alter economic relations between Europe and the ACP. The EU historically offered preferential treatment to certain ACP countries, but those preferences did not comply with GSP requirements as they were not offered on the same terms to all similarly situated developing States. The WTO waived MFN requirements in respect of these preferences until 31 December 2007, by which time new trading arrangements should have been concluded.[73] The EU had three options in order to comply with WTO rules. It could extend its GSP preferences to all like developing States, it could drop its ACP preferences, or it could conclude FTAs with the ACP countries. The EU chose to pursue the latter strategy.

EPAs are based on reciprocity, so ACP countries are required to open up their economies to EU exports under EPA provisions. The EU has interpreted the Article XXIV requirement that 'substantially all trade' be liberalized under an FTA to mean that at least 80 per cent of trade between itself and ACP countries should be tariff free within 15 years.[74] The EU itself would open up all of its sectors. However, the impact on the ACP would nevertheless be more dramatic, given average EU tariffs are already very low, and ACP tariffs are comparatively high. Furthermore, the EPAs will permit the continuation of European agricultural

---

[72] See Chapter, Part E.
[73] See WTO, 'European Communities—the ACP/EC Partnership Agreement' (Decision of 14 November 2001), WTO doc. WT/MIN(01)/15 (14 November 2001).
[74] Tobias Reichert, 'A Human Rights Approach to Trade and Investment Policies' in FIAN and others, *The Global Food Challenge: Towards a Human Rights Approach to Trade and Investment Policies* (FIAN, Germany, 2009) 29, 37; Stephen JJ Dearden, 'A review of EU Development Policy' (Manchester Metropolitan University 2006) 5 <http://e-space.mmu.ac.uk/e-space/bitstream/2173/13642/2/dearden%20EUSAnl1.pdf> accessed 20 September 2010.

subsidies. Subsidies would be allowed for ACP countries too, but they cannot afford them.[75]

The EU apparently believes that such reciprocity is needed in order to integrate ACP countries into the global economy:[76] the arguments against such thinking, in respect of developing and vulnerable economies are outlined in Chapter 5. A 2007 study on EPAs for the UN Human Rights Council concluded that the treaties would 'result, at least in the short run, in huge losses in revenue and restricted access to the EU market making it highly likely that the social and economic human rights of millions will be adversely affected'.[77] The European Commission's own sustainability impact assessments of EPAs by PricewaterCoopers (PwC) have warned of the consequences for ACP countries from lost tariff revenue and increased competition from EU exports. Without adequate safeguards and some continued asymmetry, PwC warn that the resultant '[d]amage to local production could disproportionately threaten the livelihoods and food security of rural populations'.[78] Oxfam also reports that '[e]conomic models showed that Europe would be the real winner, with most ACP countries... left worse off'.[79] At the end of 2007, ACP Ministers expressed 'serious concern' over the EPA process, claiming that European 'mercantilist interests have taken precedence over the ACP's developmental and regional integration interests'.[80]

Regarding those regional interests, the EU is insisting on inclusion of an MFN provision in EPAs. Such a clause would hinder possibilities for regional integration and South-South cooperation, as any liberalization within ACP regions must be accompanied by similar concessions to the comparatively gargantuan EU market. After all, the EU comprises 25 per cent of the ACP export market, but the ACP constitutes only 2 per cent of the EU's import markets.[81] Indeed, PwC stressed the importance of regional integration *within* ACP regions as an essential means for ACP countries to develop 'more integrated and competitive markets' and to enable them to take greater advantage of EPA benefits.[82]

[75] Oxfam, 'Partnership or Power Play? How Europe should bring Development into its trade deals with African, Caribbean, and Pacific countries' (Oxfam Briefing Paper 110, 21 April 2008) 17.
[76] Human Rights Council, 'The Cotonou Partnership Agreement between the European Union (EU) and the African, Caribbean and Pacific Countries (ACP countries) (Report by Dr Maria van Reisen, High Level Task Force on the Right to Development)', UN doc. A/HRC/12/Wg.2/TF/CRP.3/Rev.1 (5 May 2009) para 31; Dearden, above n 74, 6–7.
[77] Human Rights Council, 'Application of the criteria for periodic evaluation of global development partnerships—as defined in Millennium Development Goal 8—from the right to development perspective: the Cotonou Partnership Agreement between the European Union and ACP Countries (Report by Prof James Thuo Gathii), UN doc. A/HRC/8/WG.2/TF/CRP.6 (21 December 2007) 2.
[78] PricewaterhouseCoopers, 'Sustainability Impact Assessment of the EU-ACP Economic Partnership Agreements' (2007) 10.
[79] Oxfam, above n 75, 6.
[80] ACP Council of Ministers, 'Declaration of the ACP Council of Ministers at its 86th Session Expressing Serious Concern on the Status of the Negotiation of the Economic Partnership Agreements', Brussels, 13 December 2007, ACP/25/013/07.
[81] Oxfam, above n 75, 5.
[82] PwC, above n 78, 7. For a contrary view on the wisdom of regional trade agreements for poor States, see Paul Collier, *The Bottom Billion* (Oxford University Press, New York, 2008) 164–6.

Economic integration between reasonably 'like' economies does not pose the same danger of the large-scale destruction of industries by new competition. Rather, such integration offers opportunities for larger markets and greater efficiency. The MFN requirement would severely limit the abilities of ACP countries to negotiate beneficial arrangements with similarly sized markets, or with the stronger developing countries, such as China and India, 'where their exports are growing most rapidly'.[83] The conclusion of bilateral EPAs with different terms with ACP countries in a particular region in fact promotes regional fragmentation: in Africa only the East African Community contains States which have the same interim EPA commitments.[84] The MFN provision may instead reinforce the 'historical dependence' of former colonies on the EU,[85] which has been based on a 'vicious cycle' of the ACP exporting primary low-cost goods and importing high-value goods.[86]

Oxfam has argued that the EU used the expiry of the waiver in 2007 to pressure ACP countries to conclude EPAs.[87] Nevertheless, at the time of writing, most ACP States were resisting pressure to ratify EPAs. For example, LDCs feel they have little incentive to ratify such agreements as they already benefit from extensive market access to the EU under the Everything but Arms scheme.[88] Instead, numerous interim EPAs were initiated in order to cater for the expiry of the waiver.[89] To date, only one EPA has been finalized, between the EU and the Forum of Caribbean States.

Despite the potential detrimental impacts of EPAs, Tobias Reichert, an economist specializing in agricultural trade, has described EPAs as the 'softest' form of FTAs: other FTA negotiations are flagging greater restrictions on policy space. For example, the EU is striving for greater reciprocal market access in its FTA negotiations with India, China, and ASEAN, while the US commonly requires greater market access commitments in its bilateral negotiations.[90] The growth of FTAs is depriving developing States of needed policy space, with potentially catastrophic impacts on their capacity to combat poverty, to fulfil the right to development, and to generally discharge their human rights obligations. It will also hinder their capacity to retain bargaining power in the Doha round, which is crucial if the flawed Uruguay bargain is to be fixed.

C. Conclusion

The reforms suggested from the analysis in Chapters 3 to 7 are not reflected in the Doha round proposals. Indeed, despite its designation as a development round, it seems that the Doha round will turn out to be a pale successor to the Uruguay round, when (and if) it is concluded. The focus of negotiations is on 'business as usual' bargaining, rather than on development as such. Certainly, the right

[83] Oxfam, above n 75, 9.　　[84] Ibid, 17.　　[85] Ibid, 9.　　[86] Ibid, 5.
[87] Ibid, 7.　　[88] Dearden, above n 74, 4. See Chapter 5, text at notes 26–7.
[89] Van Reisen, above n 76, para 31.　　[90] Reichert, above n 74, 37.

to development, and human rights in general, are absent from serious Doha proposals.

Meanwhile, the 'action' in the free trade arena is taking place in bilateral and regional contexts. These agreements have served to exacerbate problems of democratic deficit,[91] and to impose more inappropriately onerous obligations on developing States than are likely to arise from the Doha round.[92]

---

[91] See Chapter 3, Part E.
[92] See also Chapter 7, Part F.

10

Conclusion

Despite idealistic proclamations by free trade enthusiasts which equate the promotion of free trade with the promotion of human rights,[1] the goals of the WTO regime and the international human rights regimes are very different, as outlined in Chapter 2. The WTO regime is geared towards the promotion of free trade in goods and services, along with the protection of intellectual property rights (perhaps anomalously, given the constraints they place on free trade). Only a narrow range of freedoms is promoted by the WTO, and those freedoms, such as freedom of contract or right to trade, are not recognized in the formal legal pantheon of international human rights. An exception may arise in the case of the right to intellectual property, which may partially correlate with an international human right (for example, Article 15(1)(c) of the ICESR), though the scope of intellectual property protection in TRIPS is far broader than that demanded by any human right regarding intellectual property. Though WTO rights belong to and are enforced by States, the rights essentially serve their private export interests, most obviously multinational corporations. Of course, protection of the commercial interests of foreign corporations can have beneficial effects on the enjoyment of human rights, for example by corporate employees and consumers with access to cheaper and better services or goods. However, the elevation of the interests of foreign traders over countervailing interests, such as those of local traders, entailed in WTO rules does not gel well with international human rights law, where no such priority is afforded. Similarly, the non-discrimination provisions of the WTO are designed to ensure non-discrimination between foreign traders, and to prohibit discrimination against foreign traders. Discrimination against local traders is allowed, and arguably encouraged by certain WTO decisions.[2] The human rights principle which allows and occasionally mandates the unequal treatment of unequals in the form of positive discrimination in favour of disadvantaged persons is not recognized under the WTO. Non-discrimination obligations under WTO law can therefore serve to entrench rather than address inequality. Finally, the rationale for the WTO is premised on utilitarian principles of economic efficiency. In contrast, human rights principles are essentially deontological; the rights of each human being regardless of his or her economic or other utility are cherished. Furthermore, as noted in Chapters 5 and 6, and also below, the utilitarian economic benefits of WTO rules are challengeable.

---

[1] See Introduction, text at notes 1–4.   [2] See Chapter 4, text at notes 141–3.

It has not been established in this book that human rights law prevails over WTO law as a matter of international law in the case of conflict, though it is more likely that human rights law prevails over trade law than vice versa.[3] In any case, any conflict is clearly undesirable and damages both regimes, the rule of law in the broadest sense, as well as the States that are subjected to divergent obligations. From a human rights point of view, any conflict is particularly debilitating as the stronger enforcement mechanisms within the WTO, compared to the global human rights regime, may lead to the *de facto* prioritization by States of their WTO obligations over their human rights obligations.

A number of human rights deficiencies within WTO rules and processes are identified in this book. There are inadequate avenues for participation in the rule making and rule enforcement processes, as outlined in Chapter 3. Those inadequacies disadvantage two particular constituencies: social justice (including human rights) interests and the people of developing States. Those processes, which undermine participatory rights (such as those in Article 25 of the ICCPR), help to generate unsatisfactory substantive outcomes, which again work to the disadvantage of those two constituencies. Democratic deficit is arguably a problem which arises with regard to all international organizations, given the remoteness of such organizations from individuals, and the fact that avenues for political participation are largely local and national rather than global. However, the power of, and lack of inclusiveness within, the WTO, as well as certain unique features of the regime such as the single undertaking, lead to the conclusion that its democratic deficit is more problematic than that which pervades international institutions in other areas, such as those within the international human rights framework.

So-called 'non-trade interests', such as labour rights interests or public health interests, are disadvantaged under WTO rules when they clash, or potentially clash, with free trade rules, despite the existence of exceptions to WTO rules, such as those in Article XX GATT. The ambit of WTO rules is very broad, as explained in Chapter 4, while the ambit of the exceptions is narrow and is subjected to a very high degree of scrutiny. The 'promotion of countervailing free trade interests' is not a recognized qualification to human rights. Yet a human rights measure, whether inward or outward, which is inconsistent with such interests will often be illegal under WTO rules, and thus expose a State to economic punishment. Indeed, a *perceived* conflict with WTO rules may well discourage States from enacting relevant human rights measures in the first place.[4]

It is true that some constraint on protectionist measures is welcome from a human rights point of view, notably where protectionist measures cause harms to the enjoyment of human rights by people in offshore industries. This scenario is most likely to arise where a developed State is protecting its industries from competitors in developing States, as explained in Chapter 4. Another area where WTO law might promote human rights concerns the extent to which it compels the import of good or services that facilitate the enjoyment of human rights, as discussed in Chapter 4 in the context of internet censorship. However, the detrimental

---

[3] See Chapter 2, text at notes 107–9.   [4] See Chapter 4, text at notes 219–20.

'human rights' impact of a protectionist measure, or a measure which obstructs foreign trade, is not a yardstick against which WTO compliance of that measure is assessed.[5]

WTO rules are unfair to developing States, as detailed in Chapters 5 to 7. In this respect, the political philosopher Thomas Pogge has issued a scathing critique of WTO rules:

The reality is that WTO globalization is opening markets where this serves important corporate interests in powerful countries, is preserving barriers to free exchange where this serves important corporate interests in powerful countries, and is shutting down free and open markets where this serves important corporate interests in powerful countries. The third type is exemplified by the [fact that] large pharmaceutical corporations have won the right to use monopoly patents to block free trade in vital medicines worldwide. The second case is exemplified by the uneven fortunes of protectionism: while poor WTO members are forced to open their markets, wealthier members maintain their tariffs and anti-dumping duties as well as their huge export credits and subsidies to domestic producers. To be sure, these protectionist measures are often theoretically illegal under WTO rules. But less developed countries usually lack the resources to bring and win cases against the US or EU. Moreover, such a country has little to gain from winning as affluent members typically continue their Treaty contraventions even in the face of clear-cut WTO rulings, confident that the weaker member will prudently refrain from imposing the retaliatory measures such rulings may entitle them to and that these retaliatory measures would, in any case, not seriously hurt them.[6]

Ha-Joon Chang echoes Pogge's sentiments by stating that WTO trading rules 'favour free trade in areas where the rich countries are stronger but not where they are weak'.[7]

Furthermore, WTO rules probably obstruct the capacities of developing States to implement their human rights obligations by closing off legitimate and well-established avenues of development and economic growth. Indeed, observance of WTO rules could on occasion generate human rights abuses. For example, TRIPS rules may compel States to adopt retrogressive measures with regard to the right to health. While arguments may be made to reconcile TRIPS and the right to health, as outlined in Chapter 7, the fact remains that the scope and therefore the constraints imposed upon States by TRIPS are uncertain due to the lack of authoritative interpretation of its terms. Moreover, enforcement of certain unfair WTO rules by States against other States, particularly by the North against the South, could constitute breaches of extraterritorial human rights obligations. Extraterritorial breaches may also be manifested in the maintenance of certain protectionist measures, which are allowed under WTO rules, particularly in the agricultural field.

---

[5] See Chapter 4, text between notes 153–5.
[6] Thomas Pogge, 'Medicines for the World: Boosting Innovation without Obstructing Free Access' (2008) *Revista Internacional de dereitos humanos* 8, 15–16 <http://www.yale.edu/macmillan/igh/files/SUR.pdf> accessed 17 April 2010.
[7] Ha-Joon Chang, *Bad Samaritans: The Myth of Free Trade and the Secret History of Capitalism* (Bloomsbury Press, New York, 2008) 13.

A. Free Trade Fundamentalism

The WTO prescribes free trade rules as a means to desirable ends, as is made clear in the preamble to the Marrakesh Agreement. Free trade is not an end in itself. If WTO rules do not in fact lead to those ends, any negative impact of WTO rules on human rights is unjustifiable from any point of view. In fact, one of the key reasons for the WTO's mission is undermined. And yet there are plausible arguments that WTO rules hamper economic growth and development in developing States, as outlined in Chapter 5.

The fervour with which free trade advocates continue to promote their cause is astonishing. Joseph Stiglitz and Andrew Charlton have stated that it 'is difficult to identify the evidentiary source of the bullishness for unqualified trade liberalization'.[8] Mehdi Shafaeddin gives an example of slavish adherence to free trade theory from the World Bank in 2005.[9] In that year, the World Bank published a *mea culpa* of sorts,[10] and conceded that free trade policies had not produced the expected economic outcomes in developing States. Shafaeddin highlights some of the extraordinary admissions in the report, including that means (free trade reforms) were mistaken for ends (economic growth) and that the 'one size fits all' policies dictated by global trade rules were ill conceived and inappropriate.[11] Despite those concessions, the World Bank report nevertheless concluded that protectionism was 'not good for economic growth', while 'trade openness' was described as 'a key element of a successful strategy'.[12]

Similarly, Armin Paasch, a senior adviser on agriculture and trade for the German NGO, FIAN, has noted how the possible negative links between trade rules and food security were ignored during major intergovernmental meetings convened in the wake of the World Food Crisis of 2007–2008, including those of the Food and Agricultural Organization (FAO) and the G8.[13] Indeed, all of the cited meetings called for a quick conclusion to the Doha round including major agricultural liberalization.[14] As noted in Chapter 6, liberalization from

---

[8] Joseph E Stiglitz and Andrew Charlton, *Fair Trade for All* (Oxford University Press, New York, 2005) 34.

[9] Mehdi Shafaeddin, 'Does Trade Openness Favour or Hinder Industrialization and Development?' *Third World Network Trade & Development Series No. 31* (TWN, Malaysia, 2006) 16–17.

[10] World Bank, *Economic Growth in the 1990s: Learning from a Decade of Reform* (World Bank, Washington DC, 2005) <http://www1.worldbank.org/prem/lessons1990s/> accessed 19 September 2010; see also Dani Rodrik, 'How to Save Globalisation from its Cheerleaders' (2007) 1 *The Journal of International Trade and Diplomacy* 1 <http://dev.wcfia.harvard.edu/sites/default/files/Rodrick_HowToSave.pdf> accessed 20 September 2010.

[11] Shafaeddin, above n 9, 17, quoting World Bank, above n 10, at 11–12.

[12] Shafaeddin, above n 9, 17, quoting World Bank, above n 10, at 137 and 18, respectively.

[13] Armin Paasch, 'World Agricultural Trade and Human Rights: Case Studies on Violations of the Right to Food of Small Farmers' in FIAN and others (eds), *The Global Food Challenge: Towards a Human Rights Approach to Trade and Investment Policies* (FIAN, Germany, 2009) 41.

[14] Ibid, 41.

the North is desirable but must be undertaken with care to avoid consequences for the right to food: further liberalization by much of the South is likely to harm smallholders, who make up about half of the global population of hungry people, and thus exacerbate problems regarding the right to food. The conclusion of the Doha round cannot be treated as an end in itself which will magically improve enjoyment of the right to food. While States within the Human Rights Council have acknowledged that trade agreements must be scrutinized and their implementation monitored to ensure that they do not jeopardize the right to food,[15] those same States seem blind to the potential failings of free trade agreements with regard to the right to food when acting in other forums, such as other UN organizations, the WTO, and international financial institutions.[16]

Professor Robert Driskill has also commented on the overwhelming tendency of economists to support free trade as a policy:

Unfortunately, most economic writing on the welfare implications of trade are not a balanced weighing of the evidence or a critical evaluation of the pros and cons of arguments, but rather are more akin to a zealous prosecutor's advocacy of a point of view.[17]

The economist Ha Joon Chang, a strident critic of WTO rules and current global free trade rules, argues that the institution is essentially supported by an 'army of ideologues'.[18] However, in his view, free trade advocates are not consciously promoting policies which harm developing States. The problem is more entrenched than that: they truly believe what they are saying. As Chang states:

But what is more worrying is that many of today's Bad Samaritans [promoters of global free trade] do not even realize that they are hurting the development countries with their policies.[19]

Unfortunately, self-righteous zeal is more stubborn, and harder to budge, than self interest.[20]

Of course, the above arguments are not meant to deny the need for rules for the global governance of trade. Otherwise 'the law of the jungle' and 'the survival of the fittest' would prevail. As noted in Chapter 3, the WTO serves the important purpose of putting some constraints on the economically powerful States which would otherwise not exist.[21] The 'peace dividend' from globally accepted trade rules enforced by peaceful means is also important. Explicit published rules of course are more transparent and predictable than 'no rules'. However, we should not accept rules that are not good, or which could be much better.

[15] Ibid, citing UN Human Rights Council, 'The right to food (revised draft resolution)', UN doc. A/HR C/7/L.6/Rev.1 (26 March 2008) para 17.
[16] Ibid, 42.
[17] Robert Driskill, 'Deconstructing the Argument for Free Trade' (First draft, February 2007) 2, available at <http://www.vanderbilt.edu/econ/faculty/Driskill/Deconstructing2008Feb09.pdf> accessed 20 September 2010.
[18] Chang, above n 7, 13.　　[19] Ibid, 16.　　[20] Ibid, 17.　　[21] See Chapter 3, Part E.

B. The Purported 'Neatness' of Free Trade Rules

The WTO has a reputation for being an efficient international organization which 'works'. Unlike many other international organizations, its enforcement procedures have real teeth. The human rights system is, in contrast, quite cumbersome and messy.[22] Trade practitioners are keen to shield their 'comparatively functional legal system' from 'what seems to be a far more politicized and legally uncertain system'.[23] However, while the politicization within the human rights regime is undeniable,[24] it is a fallacy to suggest that free trade is not itself an equally politicized issue. The stalemate within the Doha round, largely on North/South lines, bears witness to that fact.

From a legal point of view, it is true that human rights are vague at their margins, where judgements must be made as to whether a particular interference with a right is proportionate or reasonable, or whether a State is fulfilling its progressive obligations under ICESCR. However, the vagueness of human rights can be overstated. Often it is quite clear that a human rights abuse has taken place: not all human rights cases concern issues at the margins of rights. Furthermore, a wealth of domestic and international case law, as well as other instruments such as General Comments, aids in clarifying the meaning of rights.

Trade law is itself beset with uncertainties. The boundaries of 'discrimination' for the purposes of the chapeaus in Article XX GATT or Article XIV GATS, the scope of GATS and the TBT, the legal ramifications of the removal of the peace clause in the AoA, and the boundaries of the compulsory licensing exception in TRIPS are just a few examples of important unresolved issues of WTO law. Furthermore, it is likely that the uncertainties in WTO law have a more debilitating impact on government capacities than uncertainties in human rights law. While governments commonly test the boundaries of human rights law, governments are probably less willing to test the boundaries of WTO law and risk economic repercussions.

To reiterate an apt quote from Frank Garcia, 'there is no such thing as a pure trade issue'.[25] Given that trade law spills over into other areas of law, a desire for certainty per se cannot legitimately quarantine trade rules from supposed non-trade considerations such as human rights. Certainty in the law does not justify injustice or unfairness in the law. Certainty in the law is a virtue, but it does not justify bad rules.

---

[22] See, eg, Carlos Manuel Vázquez, 'Trade sanctions and human rights—past, present, and future' (2003) 6 *Journal of International Economic Law* 797, 803–7.

[23] James Harrison, *The Human Rights Impact of the World Trade Organisation* (Hart, Oxford, 2007) 35; see also Joseph Weiler, 'The Role of Lawyers and the Ethos of Diplomats: Reflections on the Internal and External Legitimacy of Dispute Settlement' in R Porter and others (eds), *Efficiency, Equity and Legitimacy: The Multilateral Trade System for the Millennium* (Brookings Institute Press, Washington DC, 2001) 337.

[24] See, eg, Yvonne Terlingen, 'The Human Rights Council: A New Era in UN Human Rights Work?' (2007) 21 *Ethics and International Affairs* 167.

[25] Frank Garcia, 'The Global Market and Human Rights: Trading away the Human Rights Principle' (1999) 7 *Brooklyn Journal of International Law* 51, 65.

C. Global Free Trade: Efficiency and Distribution

WTO rules compel States to liberalize their trade regimes. Trade liberalization undoubtedly creates winners and losers. WTO rules do not demand that States take measures to compensate the losers, nor do they require States to ensure that the gains from free trade are equitably distributed. Those matters are left to the discretion of Member States. Therefore, the WTO is mandating that States adopt policies that harm certain people, and does nothing to ensure recompense for those who are harmed. Yet the treatment of losers from trade liberalization is crucial from a human rights point of view. This does not mean that there can be no losers. Rather, it means that appropriate measures must be taken to alleviate the detrimental human impact of free trade reforms.[26]

Why are obligations regarding the dismantling of free trade obstacles felt to be worthy of explicit internationalization within the free trade agenda, while measures regarding redistribution and other social welfare issues associated with trade, such as labour protections and fair distribution of the gains of trade, are omitted? As noted by Andrew Lang, 'what we currently think of as "trade issues" and "trade values" are not predetermined but are in part a matter of choice'.[27] The very meaning of 'free trade', and therefore what 'should be' within and what 'should be' outside the mandate of a global trade organization, has changed over time.[28] James Gathii has stated that 'social issues are congealed into the very essence of the trade regime's history as well as its rules and praxises'.[29] The exclusion of the 'welfare' side of the 'embedded liberal' bargain from the WTO[30] is a political choice, rather than an incontestable given.

Margot Salomon explains that 'the dominant view remains that economics should focus on efficiency and growth alone and that distribution should be left to actors within the political domain'.[31] While confidently proclaiming the utilitarian benefits of free trade, which are challenged in Chapter 5, economists generally fail to 'stress the income distribution effects of trade'.[32] The absence of the latter within the WTO reflects a tendency in the economic realm to 'overstate the benefits of the rules [of the international trading framework] for economic progress' and to 'understate the distributional outcomes of the rules'.[33] Indeed, Driskill has

---

[26] See Chapter 2, text at notes 49–56.

[27] Andrew TF Lang, 'Reflecting on 'Linkage': Cognitive and Institutional Change in the International Trading System' (2007) *Modern Law Review* 523, 545.

[28] Ibid, 525–30. See also Robert Howse, 'From Politics to Technocracy-and back again: the Fate of the Multilateral Trading Regime' (2002) 96 *American Journal of International Law* 94, 104–6, and 112.

[29] James Thuo Gathii, 'Re-Characterizing the Social in the Constitutionalization of the WTO: A Preliminary Analysis' (2001) 7 *Widener Law Symposium Journal* 137, 173.

[30] See Chapter 2, text at notes 60–1.

[31] Margot Salomon, 'Global Economic Policy and Human Rights: Three Sites of Disconnection' (25 March 2010) *Carnegie Ethics Online* <http://www.cceia.org/resources/ethics_online/0043.html> accessed 20 September 2010.

[32] P Krugman and M Obstfeld, *International Economics*, 7th edn (Addison-Wesley, Boston, 2006) 70, quoted by Driskill, above n 17, at 20.

[33] Gathii, above n 29, 142.

criticized the economics profession for failing to identify the 'implicit criterion' that is being applied in concluding that free trade is good for a nation if it is known that it is not good for some people within the nation.[34] After all, people can reasonably disagree on whether a GDP figure, which lacks any information on the economic situation of actual human beings within a State, is the appropriate measure of the welfare of the nation.[35]

The inevitable consequence of the current structure of WTO rules is that the losers from free trade will often, if not always, be left behind. As explained by Gathii:

[W]hen a rule of international trade operates to liberalize trade, it operates simultaneously to create advantages and vulnerabilities not only in the states involved, but to companies, labour, consumers and individuals as well. In essence, the pursuit of freer trade has a corresponding distributional impact on stakeholders in international society, which the rules of the international trading regime do not capture.[36]

WTO rules are thus imbalanced because the 'costs of shifting production are assumed away rather than conceptualized as intrinsic to the working of the trading regime'.[37] As noted in Chapter 2, the WTO Director-General Pascal Lamy has conceded that many States currently lack the capacity to respond to these adjustment costs.[38]

The problem is exacerbated by the adoption of prevailing WTO rules in an era where neo-liberal economic theories predominated.[39] Neo-liberalism has also influenced the contemporaneous policies of other key economic bodies such as the IMF and World Bank.[40] Neoliberalism upholds the invisible hand of the market as the appropriate guiding force for economies with minimal State intervention. Given that redistribution and compensation for 'the losers from trade' normally requires State intervention, neoliberalism does not ideologically support the capacities of States to unilaterally assist those losers. Indeed, some relevant measures may well breach WTO rules, such as certain measures which would facilitate access by the poor to water.[41] Neoliberalism, whilst perhaps adorned with the recognition of some need for government regulation in discrete areas, may continue to dominate economic thinking, though, at the time of writing, the world is still working out its response to the Great Financial Crisis of 2008–2009.[42]

Neoliberal thinking dictates that the market should be cordoned off from politics and be left to its own devices. '[D]emocracy is acceptable to neo-liberals only in so far as it does not contradict the free market.'[43] However, such a demarcation of

---

[34] Driskill, above n 17, 6.   [35] Ibid, 15.   [36] Gathii, above n 29, 147.
[37] Ibid, 148.   [38] See Chapter 2, text at note 57.
[39] See Chapter 2, text at notes 62–4.
[40] See, eg, Gathii, above n 29, 152–3; Joseph Stiglitz, *Freefall: Free Markets and the Sinking of the Global Economy* (Allen Lane, London, 2010) 220.   [41] See Chapter 5, text at notes 52–7.
[42] The death of the neoliberal 'Washington consensus' has been proclaimed by many since the advent of the Global Financial Crisis in late 2008. Eg, the (then) UK Prime Minister Gordon Brown declared the 'old Washington consensus over' on 2 April 2009 at the conclusion of the G20 summit: see <http://www.number10.gov.uk/Page18934> accessed 22 April 2009. Of course, it remains to be seen whether such proclamations are premature.
[43] Chang, above n 7, 176; Gathii, above n 29, 169.

economics and politics *is* a political position: state abstention has consequences just like state intervention.[44] There is no natural division between politics and economics, just as there is no natural pre-ordained division between 'trade' and so-called 'non-trade' issues. As colourfully stated by Garcia, the 'efficiency model' promoted by the WTO and most economists needs to be 'flushed ... out of its assumed neutrality and into the mud pit of normative brawling, where it belongs'.[45] If the market is left unregulated by public power, market forces may be distorted by imbalances of private power.[46] The 'market' does not form a neutral baseline. Rather, nonintervention 'assumes that the existing distribution of wealth and entitlements is legitimate'.[47] Furthermore, intervention can be necessary to generate greater market efficiency. For example, as noted in Chapter 6, global agricultural markets are plagued by cartelization, which is anathema to a competitive market: further deregulation will only add to the power of monopolistic agribusinesses if it is not accompanied by measures to combat their concentrated power.

Furthermore, the inclusion of TRIPS within the WTO exposes neoliberals to charges of hypocrisy. TRIPS of course mandates considerable State intervention in the economy in one particular area. It seems to be no coincidence that this area happens to be one which generates huge benefits for corporate interests.

A final argument may be put against the current separation of efficiency and distribution within the global trading regime. The global trading system is not distributing gains equally or fairly between States, let alone between people. While free trade has probably been good for the aggregate welfare of richer States, it does not seem that it is presently serving the interests of poorer States. Distributional fairness between States, which is instrumentally related to distributional fairness between individuals within States, and is directly related to extraterritorial obligations regarding human rights, cannot be generated unilaterally at the national level.[48]

D. Equalizing the Regimes

A key problem with current international governance is its imbalance. Economic governance via institutions such as the WTO, the IMF, and the World Bank, is strong. Social justice governance, via bodies such as the international human rights institutions and the ILO, is weak. Furthermore, there is little coordination between the two sets of institutions.[49] The inevitable consequence is that States tend to take their global economic responsibilities more seriously than those concerning

---

[44] Gathii, above n 29, 168–9.

[45] Frank Garcia, *Trade, Inequality, and Justice: Toward a Liberal Theory of Just Trade* (Transnational Publishers, New York, 2003) 17.

[46] As Gathii, above n 29, notes at 168, enormous power is *de facto* delegated to multinational corporations in the absence of State intervention.

[47] Ibid, 168.   [48] See also Garcia, above n 45, 212.

[49] See also World Commission on the Social Dimension of Globalisation, *A Fair Globalization: Promoting Opportunities for all* (ILO, Geneva, 2004) para 607.

social justice. Indeed, this 'consequence' may in part be the 'cause' rather than the 'effect' of the lopsidedness in international governance. Governments perceive less self interest in fulfilling their human rights obligations compared to their trade obligations.[50] Similarly, they perceive less self interest in demanding compliance by other States with their human rights obligations compared to their reciprocal trade obligations.

In contrast, at the regional level, significant progress has been made in moving forward on both human rights and free trade. The most outstanding example of this phenomenon is in Europe, where the ECHR exerts significant influence alongside the most advanced free trade regime, the EU. Of course, the EU has now evolved far beyond its free trade origins into other areas of integration, including foreign policy and immigration. The organs of the EU have also begun to develop their own human rights competencies.[51] Indeed, at the time of writing, the EU was on the cusp of becoming a party to the ECHR in its own right.[52] In the Americas, the human rights regime actually predates significant regional trade liberalization in the form of MERCOSUR, NAFTA, and CAFTA. Similarly, regional courts in Africa, which began as trade courts, have begun to exercise human rights jurisdiction.[53] Furthermore, some new regional and bilateral trade treaties are paying more attention to human rights issues, such as labour rights and corporate social responsibility, unlike the WTO treaties.[54]

It is not proposed that the WTO play a major role in enforcing human rights, as has occurred with trade courts at the regional level.[55] Rather, the WTO should ensure that its rules and initiatives are compatible with the need for significant progress on and the strengthening of global governance regarding social justice concerns. To that end, it would be highly desirable for it to work with other organizations, such as the ILO, the World Health Organisation (WHO), the UN Development Program, the UN Conference on Trade and Development and human rights bodies to ensure coordination of policies, and to avoid incompatibility of rules and goals. Such cooperation should be substantive rather than token.[56] Given that trade affects on so many other areas of international concern, and on the work of so many other international organizations, the WTO must be open to cooperation and collaboration with such bodies.

---

[50] Vázquez, above n 22, 807–8.   [51] See, eg, Chapter 2, text at notes 20 and 96.
[52] Such accession is a requirement under Article 6(2) of the Treaty of Lisbon.
[53] See, eg, Solomon T Ebobrah, *A Critical Analysis of the Human Rights Mandate of the ECOWAS Community Court of Justice*, Research Partnership 1/2008: Danish Institute for Human Rights (Danish Institute for Human Rights, Copenhagen, 2009).
[54] See, eg, Michael Kerr, Richard Janda, and Chip Pitts in Chip Pitts (ed), *Corporate Social Responsibility: A Legal Analysis* (Lexis-Nexis, Markham, Ontario, 2009) at, eg, 317–18.
[55] See Chapter 1, text at notes 44–45.
[56] See also Robert O Keohane and Joseph S Nye, Jr, 'The Club Model of Multilateral Cooperation and Problems of Democratic Legitimacy: Problems of Democratic Legitimacy' (Working Paper No 4, John F. Kennedy School of Government, undated) 25–8 <http://www.ksg.harvard.edu/visions/publication/keohane_nye.pdf> accessed 19 September 2010. While a report by the Consultative Board to the Director General, *The Future of the WTO* (WTO, 2005), endorsed in Chapter IV 'coherence and coordination with intergovernmental organizations', it makes no mention of how cooperation with intergovernmental social institutions might influence WTO policies. At para 168, the report states bluntly that 'the WTO legal system … cannot be changed from the outside by other international organizations'.

An example of this approach *not* being advocated arose in discussions within the WHO concerning the facilitation of global access to drugs. The US and the European Commission argued (unsuccessfully) that it was inappropriate for the WHO to consider matters related to intellectual property as they claimed that the proper forums for such debate were the WTO and the World Intellectual Property Organization (WIPO).[57] Yet it is absurd to argue that such matters should be excluded from WHO discussions, given the impact of intellectual property rights on the abilities of States to maintain adequate supplies of necessary medicines.[58] It is difficult to avoid the conclusion that the US and the EC were 'trying to prevent discussion [of such matters] in a forum that might actually give some weight to global health' over the countervailing interests of intellectual property rights holders.[59] The WHO carried on with its work in that area, concluding with the adoption by the World Health Assembly of a Global Strategy and Plan of Action on Public Health, Innovation and Intellectual Property in May 2008.[60] A promising sign for this author, in light of the recommendation for greater cooperation between the WTO and relevant 'non-trade' bodies above, was the convening of a technical symposium on pricing and procurement practices regarding access to medicines in July 2010 under the joint auspices of the WHO, the WTO, and WIPO.[61]

The relative strengths of the respective global trade and social justice systems should be evened out. The diversity of the economic needs and capacities of States indicates that the 'one size fits all' ethos of the WTO should be abandoned, and more flexibility built into the system. For example, as argued in previous chapters, certain policy space should be restored to developing States. New flexibilities should clearly account for human rights obligations, including labour rights, though it is not proposed that the WTO become a human rights body. In regard to the actual enforcement of human rights, the ideal reform is for the international human rights regime to be strengthened.[62] It is beyond the scope of this book to discuss proposals for the strengthening of the human rights regime. Suffice to reiterate that the international legal order should be reformed so as to reflect at least an equal commitment to human rights as to economic matters. Such a change would require States to take their own human rights obligations, as well as the enforcement of the obligations of other States, far more seriously than they currently do. Unfortunately, political will

---

[57] See Frederick M Abbott and Jerome H Reichmann, 'The Doha Round's Public Health Legacy: Strategies for the Production and Diffusion of Patented Medicines under the Amended TRIPS Provisions' (2007) 10 *Journal of International Economic Law* 921, 968, and Kevin Outterson, 'Should access to medicines and TRIPS flexibilities be limited to specific diseases?' (2008) 34 *American Journal of Law and Medicine* 279, 297–9.

[58] Abbott and Reichmann, above n 57, 968.   [59] Outterson, above n 57, 298.

[60] WHO doc. WHA 61.21, 24 May 2008.

[61] See 'Joint WHO, WIPO, WTO Technical Symposium on Access to Medicines: Pricing and Procurement Practices', Geneva, 16 July 2010, at <http://www.who.int/phi/phi_symposium/en/index.html>, accessed 27 October 2010. As another example of collaboration between the WTO and a relevant 'non-trade' body, see WTO and ILO, *Trade and Employment: Challenges for Policy Research* (WTO secretariat, Geneva, 2007), a collaboration between the WTO and the ILO on the trade/labour relationship.

[62] See also Harrison, above n 23, 250.

in that regard is currently missing. Equalization between regimes is therefore more likely in the short term to entail weakening of the WTO rather than significant strengthening of the human rights system.[63]

E. Final Thoughts

From a human rights point of view, there are problems with both the WTO's processes and some of its substantive rules. Regarding the latter, problems arise with regard to their interpretation and their chilling effect in the absence of authoritative interpretation. The WTO's mission of promoting free trade and intellectual property rights should take more account of countervailing rights beyond those of foreign traders and intellectual property rights holders, the marked differences between States, and problems within the agricultural arena. Clearly, this book ultimately calls for major changes to the thinking which currently dominates the WTO. It is recognized that such changes are unlikely to occur in the short term, not least because the promotion of free trade (at least in certain areas) is being driven by more powerful actors than those promoting human rights.[64] However, the 'contemporary ascendancy of the pro-trade position' is not inevitable or unassailable.[65]

It is hoped that this book achieves its purpose of explaining why there are criticisms of the WTO from a human rights point of view, and that many if not all of those complaints are in fact valid. The WTO is not the demon organization it is portrayed to be by some of its most vociferous critics.[66] In some areas, such as agricultural protection in the North, the WTO is perhaps less culpable than the international financial institutions in promoting unfair rules,[67] though it may be fairly criticized for doing little to redress that unfairness. Some of its rules may on occasion assist in the enjoyment of human rights.[68] Finally, some trade issues give rise to complex human rights issues which, it must be conceded, are not easily resolved. For example, strict interpretation of the SPS agreement has been criticized for hindering the ability of States to protect the health of their populations, as evidenced in the *Beef Hormone* dispute. However, overly strict SPS standards, epitomized perhaps by the EU standard on aflatoxins in nuts and grains, can have devastating impacts on the livelihoods of some of the world's poorest people.[69]

For too long it has been assumed by dominant global policy-makers that progress on free trade per se will inevitably result in progress in other areas such as poverty alleviation and development. There has been a tendency to treat free trade as inherently beneficial or as a hermetically-sealed issue that has only benign or neutral effects. There is insufficient acknowledgment of the bad consequences of

---

[63] See also Sarah Joseph, 'Democratic Deficit, Participation and the WTO' in S Joseph, D Kinley, and J Waincymer (eds), *The World Trade Organization and Human Rights: Interdisciplinary Perspectives* (Edward Elgar, Cheltenham, 2009) 342–3.

[64] See also Ha-Joon Chang, *Kicking Away the Ladder: Development Strategy in Historical Perspective* (Anthem Press, London, 2003) 136.

[65] Gathii, above n 29, 152.   [66] See eg, Introduction, text at notes 5–6.

[67] See, eg, Chapter 6, text at notes 44–7 and 77.

[68] See, eg, Chapter 4, Part G. See also Chapter 4, text between notes 153–5.

[69] See Chapter 4, text at notes 192–3.

WTO rules, such as unwarranted constraints on the development policies of developing States; the chilling impact of WTO rules on the adoption of trade measures designed to enhance human rights; rising pharmaceutical and educational costs for poor people; social dislocation caused by jobs wiped out in 'inefficient' industries and the consequent generation of social inequality, exclusion, and resentment; and an increased if misguided desire amongst governments to ratchet down labour standards.[70] The WTO has a way to go before it can be deemed to be a true 'friend' of human rights.

---

[70] See also Joost Pauwelyn, 'The Sutherland Report: A Missed Opportunity for Genuine Debate on Trade, Globalization and Reforming the WTO' (2005) 8 *Journal of International Economic Law* 329, 335.

Bibliography

BOOKS, CHAPTERS, AND ARTICLES

Aaronsen, Susan, 'Seeping in slowly: how human rights concerns are penetrating the WTO' (2007) 6 *World Trade Review* 413

Abbott, Frederick M, 'Distributed Governance at the WTO-WIPO: an evolving model for open-architecture integrated governance' (2000) *Journal of International Economic Law* 63

Abbott, Frederick M and Reichmann, Jerome H, 'The Doha Round's Public Health Legacy: Strategies for the Production and Diffusion of Patented Medicines under the Amended TRIPS Provisions' (2007) 10 *Journal of International Economic Law* 921

Actionaid, 'Meals per Gallon: The Impact of Industrial Biofuels on People and Global Hunger' (Actionaid, London, 2010)

Alston, Philip, 'Making Space for New Human Rights: The Case of the Right to Development' (1988) 1 *Harvard Human Rights Year Book* 3

——, 'Resisting the Merger and Acquisition of Human Rights by Trade Law: A Reply to Petersmann' (2002) 13 *European Journal of International Law* 815

——, 'Ships Passing in the Night: The Current State of the Human Rights and Development Debate Seen Through the Lens of the Millennium Development Goals' (2005) 27 *Human Rights Quarterly* 755

Alvarez, Jose E, 'How not to Link: Institutional Conundrums on an Expanded Trade Regime' (2001) 7 *Widener Law Symposium Journal* 1

Angell, Marcia, 'The Pharmaceutical Industry: To Whom is it Accountable?' (2000) 342 *New England Journal of Medicine* 1902

Arda, Mehmet, 'Global Mechanisms Relevant to Small-Scale Farmers in Liberalised Trade Environment' in Tiina Huvio, Jukka Kola, and Tor Lundström (eds), *Small Scale Farmers in Liberalised Trade Environment: Proceedings of the Seminar on October 2004 in Haikko Finland* (University of Helsinki, Helsinki, 2005)

Atik, Jeffery, 'Democratizing the WTO' (2000–2001) 33 *George Washington International Law Review* 451

Attaran, Amir, 'How Do Patents And Economic Policies Affect Access To Essential Medicines In Developing Countries?' (May/June, 2004) *Health Affairs* 155

Avonius, Leena and Kingsbury, Damien, 'Introduction' in Leena Avonius and Damien Kingsbury (eds), *Human Rights in Asia: A Reassessment of the Asian Values Debate* (Palgrave MacMillan, New York, 2008)

Bardhan, Pranab, 'Globalisation and human rights: an economist's perspective' in Sarah Joseph, David Kinley, and Jeff Waincymer (eds), *The World Trade Organization and Human Rights: Interdisciplinary Perspectives* (Edward Elgar, Cheltenham, 2009)

Bartels, Lorand, 'Trade and Human Rights' in Daniel Bethlehem and others (eds), *Oxford Handbook of International Trade* (Oxford University Press, Oxford, 2009)

Baunsgaard, Thomas and Keen, Michael, 'Trade Revenue and (or?) Trade Liberalisation' (2005) *IMF Working Paper No 05/112*

Bedjaoui, Mohammed, 'The Right to Development' in Mohammed Bedjaoui (ed), *International Law: Achievements and Prospects* (Martinus Nijhoff Publishers, Boston, 1991)

Ben-David, Dan, Nordström, Håkan, and Winters, Alan, 'Trade, Income Disparity, and Poverty' (WTO Special Studies 5) (WTO, Geneva, 1999)

Bentham, Jeremy, 'Anarchical Fallacies' reprinted in Jeremy Waldron (ed), *Nonsense upon Stilts: Bentham, Burke and Marx on the Rights of Man* (Methuen, London, 1987)

Bhagwati, Jagdish, 'Afterword: the Question of Linkage' (2002) 96 *American Journal of International Law* 126

——, 'Challenges to the Doctrine of Free Trade' (1993) 25 *New York University Journal of International Law and Politics* 219

——, *Free Trade Today* (Princeton University Press, Princeton, NJ, 2002)

Breining-Kaufman, Christine, 'The Right to Food and Trade in Agriculture' in Thomas Cottier, Joost Pauwelyn and Elizabeth Bürgi (eds), *Human Rights and International Trade* (Oxford University Press, Oxford, 2005)

Bugalski, Natalie and Pred, David, 'Land Titling in Cambodia: Formalizing Inequality' (2010) 7 *Housing and ESC Rights Law Quarterly* 1

Cadot, Olivier and de Melo, Jaime, 'Why OECD Countries should reform Rules of Origin' (2008) 23 *World Bank Research Observer* 77

Carmody, Chi, 'When "Cultural Identity was not at Issue": Thinking about Canada— Certain Measures concerning Periodicals' (1999) 30 *Law and Policy in International Business* 231

Cass, Deborah Z, *The Constitutionalization of the World Trade Organization: Legitimacy, Democracy, and Community in the International Trading System* (Oxford University Press, Oxford, 2005)

Cassimatis, Anthony E, *Human Rights Related Trade Measures under International Law* (Martinus Nijhoff, Leiden, 2007)

Cerone, John, 'Human Dignity in the Line of Fire: The Application of International Human Rights Law during Armed Conflict, Occupation, and Peace Operations' (2006) 39 *Vanderbilt Journal of Transnational Law* 1446

Chan, Anita and Ross, Robert JS, 'Race to the Bottom: international trade without a social clause' (2003) 24 *Third World Quarterly* 1011

Chang, Ha-Joon, *Bad Samaritans: The Myth of Free Trade and the Secret History of Capitalism* (Bloomsbury Press, New York, 2008)

——, 'Developing Countries need to wake up to the Realities of the NAMA negotiations' (Third World Network Briefing Paper 26, June 2005)

——, *Kicking Away the Ladder: Development Strategy in Historical Perspective* (Anthem Press, London, 2003)

Chapman, Audrey, 'Approaching intellectual property as a human right (obligations related to Article 15(1)(c))' (2001) XXXV *Copyright Bulletin* 4

Charney, Jonathan I, 'The Persistent Objector Rule and the Development of Customary International Law' (1985) 56 *British Yearbook of International Law* 1

Charnovitz, Steve, 'Labor in the American Free Trade Area' in Philip Alston (ed), *Labour Rights as Human Rights* (Oxford University Press, Oxford, 2005)

——, 'The (neglected) employment dimension of the World Trade Organization' in Virginia A Leary and Daniel Warner (eds), *Social Issues, Globalisation and International Institutions* (Martinus Nijhoff, Leiden, 2006)

——, 'The WTO and Cosmopolitics' (2004) 7 *Journal of International Economic Law* 675

Chen, Shaohua and Ravallion, Martin, 'The developing world are poorer than we thought, but no less successful in the fight against poverty' (World Bank Policy Research Working Paper No 4703) (World Bank, Washington DC, August 2008) <http://siteresources.worldbank.org/JAPANINJAPANESEEXT/Resources/515497 -1201490097949/080827_The_Developing_World_is_Poorer_than_we_Thought .pdf> accessed 22 September 2010

Chon, Margaret, 'Intellectual Property from Below: Copyright and Capability for Education' (2006–2007) 40 *UC Davis L Rev* 803

Choudhury, Barnali, 'The Façade of Neutrality: Uncovering Gender Silences in International Trade' (2008) 15 *William and Mary Journal of Women and the Law* 113

Chua, Amy, 'The Paradox of Free Market Democracy: Rethinking Development Policy' (2000) 41 *Harvard International Law Journal* 287

——, *World on Fire: How Exporting Free Market Democracy Breeds Ethnic Hatred and Global Instability* (Doubleday, New York, 2002)

Cohen, Marc et al, *Impact of Climate Change and Bioenergy on Nutrition* (FAO and IFPRI, Rome, 2008) <http://www.fao.org/docrep/010/ai799e/ai799e00.HTM> accessed 22 September 2010

Cohn, Marjorie, 'The World Trade Organization: Elevating Property Interests above Human Rights' (2001) 29 *Georgia Journal of International and Comparative Law* 427

Colbran, Nicola and Eide, Asbjørn, 'Biofuel, the Environment, and Food Security' (Fall 2008) *Sustainable Development Law & Policy* 4

——, 'Indigenous Peoples in Indonesia: at risk of disappearing as distinct peoples in the rush for biofuel?' (2010) *International Journal for Minority and Group Rights*, forthcoming, paper on file with the author

Collier, Paul, *The Bottom Billion* (Oxford University Press, New York, 2008)

Cottier, Thomas, 'From Progressive Liberalization to Progressive Regulation' (2006) 9 *Journal of International Economic Law* 779

——, 'Preparing for Structural Reform of the WTO' (2007) 10 *Journal of International Economic Law* 497

Covelli, Nick and Hohots, Viktor, 'The Health Regulation of Biotech Foods under the WTO Agreements' (2003) 6 *Journal of International Economic Law* 773

Craven, Matthew, *The International Covenant on Economic Social and Cultural Rights* (Oxford University Press, Oxford, 1995)

——, 'The Violence of Dispossession: Extraterritoriality and Economic, Social and Cultural Rights' in Mashood A Baderin and Robert McCorquodale (eds), *Economic Social and Cultural Rights in Action* (Oxford University Press, Oxford, 2007)

Darrow, Mac, *Between Light and Shadow* (Hart, Portland, 2003)

Davidson, Scott, 'Introduction' in Alex Conte, Scott Davidson, and Richard Burchill, *Defining Civil and Political Rights: The Jurisprudence of the United Nations Human Rights Committee* (Aldershot, Ashgate, 2004)

Davis, Megan, 'Indigenous Struggles in Standard-setting: The United Nations Declaration on the Rights of Indigenous Peoples' (2008) 9 *Melbourne Journal of International Law* 439

——, 'International Trade, the World Trade Organisation, and the Human Rights of Indigenous Peoples' (2006) 8 *Balayi* 5

Davis, Michael H and Neacsu, Dana, 'Legitimacy, Globally: The Incoherence of Free Trade Practice, Global Economics, and the Governing Principles of Political Economy' (2001) 69 *University of Missouri Kansas City Law Review* 733

Deakin, Simon, 'Social Rights in a Globalized Economy' in Philip Alston (ed), *Labour Rights as Human Rights* (Oxford University Press, Oxford, 2005)

Dearden, Stephen JJ, 'A review of EU Development Policy' (Manchester Metropolitan University 2006) <http://e-space.mmu.ac.uk/e-space/bitstream/2173/13642/2/dearden%20EUSAnl1.pdf>

Defeis, Elizabeth F, 'Treaty of Lisbon and Human Rights' (2009–2010) 16 *ILSA Journal of International and Comparative Law* 413

Department of Foreign Affairs and Trade (DFAT), *Globalisation: Keeping the Gains* (Commonwealth of Australia, Canberra, 2003)

De Schutter, Olivier, 'A Human Rights Approach to Trade and Investment Policies' in FIAN and others, *The Global Food Challenge: Towards a Human Rights Approach to Trade and Investment Policies* (FIAN, Germany, 2009)

——, *International Trade in Agriculture and the Right to Food* (Dialogue on Globalization Occasional Paper No 46) (Friedrich Ebert Stiftung, Geneva, 2009)

Dillon, Sara, 'A Farewell to "Linkage": International Trade Law and Global Sustainability Indicators' (2002) 51 *Rutgers Law Review* 87

Dollar, David and Kraay, Aart, 'Growth is Good for the Poor' (World Bank Policy Research Working Paper No 2587) (World Bank, Washington DC, April, 2001) <http://wdsbeta.worldbank.org/external/default/WDSContentServer/IW3P/IB/2001/05/11/0 00094946_01042806383524/Rendered/PDF/multi0page.pdf> accessed 22 September 2010

——, 'Trade, Growth and Poverty' (World Bank Policy Research Working Paper No 2615) (World Bank, Washington DC, June, 2001) <http://wdsbeta.worldbank.org/external/default/WDSContentServer/IW3P/IB/2002/08/23/000094946_02082304142939/Rendered/PDF/multi0page.pdf> accessed 22 September 2010

Dommen, Caroline, 'Raising Human Rights Concerns in the World Trade Organization: Actors, Processes and Possible Strategies' (2002) 24 *Human Rights Quarterly* 1

Donnelly, Jack, 'Human rights and Asian values: A Defense of "Western" Imperialism' in Joanne R Bauer and Daniel A Bell (eds), *The East Asian Challenge for Human Rights* (Cambridge University Press, New York, 1999)

——, *Universal Human Rights in Theory and Practice*, 2nd edn (Cornell University Press, Ithaca, 2002)

Donoho, Douglas Lee, 'Relativism versus Universalism in Human Rights: the Search for Meaningful Standards' (1991) 27 *Stanford Journal of International Law* 345

Drahos, Peter, 'The Rights to Food and Health and Intellectual Property in the Era of "Biogopolies"' in Stephen Bottomley and David Kinley (eds), *Commercial Law and Human Rights* (Ashgate, Dartmouth, 2002)

Driesen, David M, 'What is Free Trade? The Real Issue Lurking behind the Trade and Environment Debate' (2001) 41 *Virginia Journal of International Law* 279

Driskill, Robert, 'Deconstructing the arguments for free trade' (February 2007) <http://www.vanderbilt.edu/econ/faculty/Driskill/DeconstructingfreetradeAug27a2007.pdf> accessed 22 September 2010

Duffy, Helen, 'Hadijatou Mani Koroua v Niger: Slavery Unveiled by the ECOWAS Court' (2009) 9 *Human Rights Law Review* 151

Dunoff, Jeffrey L, 'The Death of the Trade Regime' (1999) 10 *European Journal of International Law* 733

——, 'The misguided debate over NGO participation at the WTO' (1998) 1 *Journal of International Economic Law* 433

Ebobrah, Solomon T, *A Critical Analysis of the Human Rights Mandate of the ECOWAS Community Court of Justice*, Research Partnership 1/2008: Danish Institute for Human Rights (Danish Institute for Human Rights, Copenhagen, 2009)

Edwardson, Shelley, 'Reconciling TRIPS and the Right to Food' in Thomas Cottier, Joost Pauwelyn, and Elizabeth Bürgi (eds), *Human Rights and International Trade* (Oxford University Press, Oxford, 2005)

Emberland, Marius, *The Human Rights of Companies: Exploring the Structure of ECHR Protection* (Oxford University Press, New York, 2006)

Emerton, Patrick, 'International Economic Justice: is a Principled Liberalism Possible?' in Sarah Joseph, David Kinley, and Jeff Waincymer (eds), *The World Trade Organization and Human Rights: Interdisciplinary Perspectives* (Edward Elgar, Cheltenham, 2009)

Esty, Daniel C, 'The World Trade Organization's legitimacy crisis' (2002) 1 *World Trade Review* 7

Ewing-Chow, Michael, 'First do no harm: Trade sanctions and human rights' (2007) 5 *Northwestern Journal of International Human Rights* 153

Fakir, Saliem, 'Was Copenhagen the Death of Multilateral Environmental Agreements?' (12 January 2010) *The South African Civil Society Information Service* <http://www.sacsis.org.za/site/article/408.1> accessed 20 September 2010

Finger, J Michael and Schuler, Philip, 'Implementation of Uruguay Round Commitments: the Development Challenge' (World Bank Policy Research Working Paper No 2215, September 1999)

Ford, Sara, 'Compulsory Licensing Provisions under the TRIPS Agreement: Balancing Pills and Patents' (2000) 15 *American University International Law Review* 941

Foster, Caroline E, 'Public Opinion and the Interpretation of the World Trade Organisation's Agreement on Sanitary and Phytosanitary Measures' in Sarah Joseph, David Kinley, and Jeff Waincymer (eds), *The World Trade Organization and Human Rights: Interdisciplinary Perspectives* (Edward Elgar, Cheltenham, 2009)

Friedman, Thomas, *The World is Flat: The Globalized World of the Twenty-First Century* (Penguin, New York, 2005)

Garcia, Frank, 'The Global Market and Human Rights: Trading away the Human Rights Principle' (1999) 7 *Brooklyn Journal of International Law* 51

Garcia, Frank J, *Trade, Inequality and Justice: Towards a Liberal Theory of Just Trade* (Transnational Publishers, Ardsley Park, 2003)

Gathii, James Thuo, 'Construing Intellectual Property Rights and Competition Policy Consistency with Facilitating Access to Affordable AIDS Drugs to Low-End Consumers' (2001) 53 *Florida Law Review* 727

——, 'Re-Characterizing the Social in the Constitutionalization of the WTO: A Preliminary Analysis' (2001) 7 *Widener Law Symposium Journal* 137

Gervais, Daniel J, 'Trips 3.0: Policy Calibration and Innovation Displacement' in Chantal Thomas and Joel P Trachtman (eds), *Developing Countries in the WTO Legal System* (Oxford University Press, New York, 2009)

Gifford, Daniel J and Kudrle, Robert J, 'Trade and Competition Policy in the Developing World' in Chantal Thomas and Joel P Trachtman (eds), *Developing Countries in the WTO Legal System* (Oxford University Press, Oxford, 2009)

Ginbar, Yuval, 'Human Rights in ASEAN—Setting Sail or Treading Water?' (2010) 10 *Human Rights Law Review* 504

Glendon, Mary Ann, *A World Made New: Eleanor Roosevelt and the Universal Declaration of Human Rights* (Random House, New York, 2001)

Goode, Walter, *Dictionary of Trade Policy Terms*, 5th edn (Cambridge University Press, Cambridge, 2007)

Greco, Dirceu B and Samão, Mariangela, 'Brazilian policy of universal access to AIDS treatment: sustainability challenges and perspectives' (2007) 21 *AIDS* S37

Griffin, Gerard, Nyland, Chris, and O'Rourke, Anne, 'Trade Unions and the Social Clause: A North South Union Divide?' (National Key Centre in Industrial Relations, Monash University, Working Paper No 81, December 2002) <http://www.buseco.monash.edu.au/mgt/research/working-papers/nkcir-working-papers/nkcir-workingpaper-81.pdf> accessed 20 September 2010

Griswold, Daniel T, 'Trading Tyranny for Freedom: How Open Markets Till the Soil for Democracy' (2004) *Trade Policy Analysis no 26* <http://www.freetrade.org/node/37> accessed 20 September 2010

Grossman, Ciel, Herrick, Amy, and Shao, Ting, *From Gas Masks to Chocolate Fountains: The Emerging Influence of NGOs in the WTO and the Implications for Global Trade Governance*, February 2006 (prepared for Charles Leopold Foundation for the Progress of Humankind and the Institute for a New Reflection on Governance)

Harrison, James, 'Incentives for Development: the EC's Generalized System of Preferences, India's WTO Challenge and Reform' (2005) 42 *Common Market Law Review* 1663

——, *The Human Rights Impact of the World Trade Organisation* (Hart, Oxford, 2007)

—— and Goller, Alessa, 'Trade and Human Rights: What does "Impact Assessment" have to offer?' (2008) 8 *Human Rights Law Review* 587

Hausman, Daniel M and McPherson, Michael S, 'Taking Ethics Seriously: Economics and Contemporary Moral Philosophy' (1993) 31 *Journal of Economic Literature* 671

Helfer, Laurence R, 'Regime Shifting: The TRIPS Agreement and the New Dynamics of International Intellectual Property Lawmaking' (2004) 29 *Yale Journal of International Law* 1

Hepple, Bob, *Labour Laws and Global Trade* (Hart, Oxford, 2005)

Heydon, D, 'Judicial Activism and the Death of the Rule of Law' (2003) 47 *Quadrant* 363

Hindley, Brian and Lee-Makiyama, Hosuk, 'Protectionism Online: Internet Censorship and International Trade Law' (2009) *ECIPE Working Paper No 12/2009*

Hoekman, Bernard, 'Operationalizing the Concept of Policy Space in the WTO: Beyond Special and Differential Treatment' (2005) 8 *Journal of International Economic Law* 405

't Hoen, Ellen FM, *The Global Politics of Pharmaceutical Monopoly Power: Drug patents, access, innovation and the application of the WTO Doha Declaration on TRIPS and Public Health* (AMB Publishers, the Netherlands, 2009)

Hollis, Aidan and Pogge, Thomas, *The Health Impact Fund: Making New Medicines Accessible to all* (Incentives for Global Health, 2008) <http://www.yale.edu/macmillan/igh/#> accessed 20 September 2010

Howard, Rhoda, 'The Full-Belly Thesis: Should Economic Rights take Priority over Civil and Political Rights? Evidence from Sub-Saharan Africa' (1983) 5 *Human Rights Quarterly* 467

Howse, Robert, 'Back to Court After Shrimp/Turtle? Almost but not quite yet: India's short-lived challenge to labour and environmental exceptions in the European Union's generalized system of preferences' (2003) 18 *American University International Law Review* 1333

——, 'From Politics to Technocracy—and back again: the Fate of the Multilateral Trading Regime' (2002) 96 *American Journal of International Law* 94

——, 'Human Rights in the WTO: Whose Rights, What Humanity? Comment on Petersmann' (2002) 13 *European Journal of International Law* 651

——, 'The World Trade Organization and the Protection of Workers' Rights' (1999) 3 *Journal of Small and Emerging Small Business Law* 131

—— and Teitel, Ruti, 'Beyond the Divide: the International Covenant on Economic Social and Cultural Rights and the World Trade Organization' in Sarah Joseph, David Kinley, and Jeff Waincymer (eds), *The World Trade Organization and Human Rights: Interdisciplinary Perspectives* (Edward Elgar, Cheltenham, 2009)

——, Langille, Brian, with Burda, Julien, 'The World Trade Organization and Labour Rights: Man bites Dog' in Leary and Warner (eds), *Social Issues, Globalisation and International Institutions* (Martinus Nijhoff, Leiden, 2006)

Hudec, Robert, '"Circumventing" Democracy: The Political Morality of Trade Negotiations' (1993) 25 *NYU Journal of International Law and Politics* 311

Hunt, Paul, 'Reclaiming Economic, Social and Cultural Rights' (1993) 1 *Waikato Law Review* 141

Hunter, J, 'Broken Promises: Agriculture and Development in the WTO' (2003) 4 *Melbourne International Law Journal* 299

International Centre for Trade and Sustainable Development, 'Brazil slams EU for seizure of generic drugs' (2009) 13 *Intellectual Property Programme* <http://ictsd.org/i/news/bridgesweekly/39772/> accessed 23 January 2009

International Commission of Jurists (ICJ), *Report of the ICJ Expert Legal Panel on Corporate Complicity in International Crimes: Corporate Complicity & Legal Accountability* (2008) Vols 1–3

Jacobzone, S, 'Pharmaceutical Policies in OECD Countries: Reconciling Social and Industrial Goals' *OECD Labour Market and Social Policy Occasional Papers*, No 40, (OECD Publishing, Paris, 2000)

Joseph, Sarah, 'Civil and political rights' in Mashood Baderin and Manisuli Ssenyonjo (eds), *International Human Rights Law: Six Decades after the UDHR* (Ashgate, Surrey, 2010, forthcoming)

——, 'Democratic Deficit, Participation and the WTO' in Sarah Joseph, David Kinley, and Jeff Waincymer (eds), *The World Trade Organization and Human Rights: Interdisciplinary Perspectives* (Edward Elgar, Cheltenham, 2009)

——, 'Denouement of the Deaths on the Rock: the Right to Life of Terrorists' (1996) 14 *Netherlands Quarterly of Human Rights* 5

——, 'Pharmaceutical Corporations and Access to Drugs: the "Fourth Wave" of Corporate Human Rights Scrutiny' (2003) 25 *Human Rights Quarterly* 425

——, 'Scope of Application' in Daniel Moeckli, Sangeeta Shah, and Sandesh Sivakumaran (eds), *International Human Rights Law* (Oxford University Press, Oxford, 2010)

——, 'Trade and the Right to Health' in Andrew Clapham and Mary Robinson (eds), *Realizing the Right to Health* (Swissbook, Geneva, 2009)

——, 'Trade to Live or Live to Trade: The World Trade Organization, Development, and Poverty' in Mashood Baderin and Robert McCorquodale (eds), *Economic, Social and Cultural Rights in Action* (Oxford University Press, Oxford, 2007)

—— and Kyriakakis, Joanna, 'United Nations and Human Rights' in Sarah Joseph and Adam McBeth (eds), *Research Handbook on International Human Rights Law* (Edward Elgar, Cheltenham, 2010)

——, Schultz, Jenny, and Castan, Melissa, *The International Covenant on Civil and Political Rights: Cases, Materials and Commentary*, 2nd edn (Oxford University Press, Oxford, 2004)

Kacsur, Charles J, 'Economic Sanctions Targeting Yugoslavia: An Effective National Security Strategy Component' (2003) *Storming Media*

Kapoor, Ilan, 'Deliberative democracy and the WTO' (2004) 11 *Review of International Political Economy* 522

Kaufmann, Daniel, 'Human Rights and Governance: The Empirical Challenge' in Philip Alston and Mary Robinson (eds), *Human Rights and Development: Towards Mutual Reinforcement* (Oxford University Press, New York, 2005)

Kaukob, Rashid S, 'Development Effects of the Doha Round on Small and Vulnerable Economies [SVEs]' (CUTS CITEE Working Paper 1/2009) <http://www.cuts-citee.org/pdf/WP09-01.pdf> accessed 20 September 2010

Kelsey, Jane, 'World Trade and Small Nations in the South Pacific Region' (2004–2005) 14 *Kansas Journal of Law and Public Policy* 248

Keohane, Robert O and Nye Jr, Joseph S, 'The Club Model of Multilateral Cooperation and the World Trade Organization: Problems of Democratic Legitimacy' (Working Paper No 4, John F Kennedy School of Government, undated) <http://www.ksg.harvard.edu/visions/publication/keohane_nye.pdf> accessed 19 September 2010

Kerr, Michael, Janda, Richard, and Pitts, Chip in Chip Pitts (ed), *Corporate Social Responsibility: A Legal Analysis* (Butterworths/Lexis-Nexis, Canada, 2009)

Khor, Martin, 'Analysis of the new WTO Agricultural and NAMA texts of 6 December 2008' *Third World Network Trade & Development Series 37* (TWN, Malaysia, 2009)

——, 'Implications of some WTO rules on the Realisation of the MDGs' *Third World Network Trade & Development Series 26* (TWN, Malaysia, 2005)

Kinley, David, *Civilising Globalisation* (Cambridge University Press, Cambridge, 2009)

—— and Martin, Penny, 'International Human Rights Law at Home: Addressing the Politics of Denial' (2002) 26 *Melbourne University Law Review* 466

Kirby, Michael, 'The Australian Use of International Human Rights Norms: From Bangalore to Balliol—A View from the Antipodes' (1993) 16 *University of New South Wales Law Review* 363

Kitsch, Edmund W, 'Elementary and Persistent Errors in the Economic Analysis of Intellectual Property' (2000) 53 *Vanderbilt Law Review* 1727

Kurtz, Jürgen, 'A Look Behind the Mirror: Standardization, Institutions and the WTO SPS and TBT Agreements' (2007) 30 *University of New South Wales* 504

Kurwijila, Rosebud V, 'Small-scale farmers' role and challenges in developing Africa's agriculture sector' in Tiina Huvio, Jukka Kola, and Tor Lundström (eds), *Small Scale Farmers in Liberalised Trade Environment: Proceedings of the Seminar on October 2004 in Haikko Finland* (University of Helsinki, Helsinki, 2005)

Kwa, Aileen, 'African Countries and EPAs: do Agricultural Safeguards afford Adequate Protection?' (2008) 25 *South Centre Bulletin: Reflections and Foresights*

Nordås, Hildegunn Kyvik, 'The Global Textile and Clothing Industry post the Agreement on Textiles and Clothing' (Discussion Paper No 5) (WTO, Switzerland, 2004)

Lang, Andrew, 'Inter-regime Encounters' in Sarah Joseph, David Kinley, and Jeff Waincymer (eds), *The World Trade Organization and Human Rights: Interdisciplinary Perspectives* (Edward Elgar, Cheltenham, 2009)

——, 'Reflecting on "Linkage": Cognitive and Institutional Change in the International Trading System' (2007) 70 *Modern Law Review* 523

——, 'The GATS and regulatory autonomy: a case study of social regulation of the water industry' (2004) 7 *Journal of International Economic Law* 801

——, *Trade Agreements, Business, and Human Rights: the case of export processing zones* (Corporate Responsibility Initiative, Working Paper no 57) (April 2010)

Langford, Malcolm, 'The Justiciability of Social Rights: From Practice to Theory' in Malcolm Langford (ed), *Social Rights Jurisprudence: Emerging Trends in International and Comparative Law* (Cambridge University Press, New York, 2008)

Lee, Yong-Shik, *Reclaiming Development in the World Trading System* (Cambridge University Press, Cambridge, 2006)

Lendle, Andreas and Schaus, Malorie, 'Sustainability Criteria in the EU Renewable Energy Directive: Consistent with WTO Rules?' ICTSD Information Note No 2, September 2010

Leskien, Dan and Flinter, Michael, *Intellectual Property Rights and Plant Genetic Resources: Options for a Sui Generis System* (Issues in Genetic Resources no 6) (International Plant Genetic Resources Institute, Rome, Italy, 1997)

Lim, CL, 'The *Amicus* Brief Issue at the WTO' (2005) 4 *Chinese Journal of International Law* 85

Locke, John, 'The Second Treatise of Government' reprinted in Peter Laslett (ed), *Locke, Two Treatises of Government*, 2nd edn (Cambridge University Press, Cambridge, 1988)

Lopez-Hurtado, Carlos, 'Social Labelling and the WTO' (2002) 5 *Journal of International Economic Law* 719

Marceau, Gabrielle, 'WTO Dispute Settlement and Human Rights' (2002) 13 *European Journal of International Law* 753

Matthews, Duncan, 'Intellectual Property Rights, Human Rights and the Right to Health' in W Grosheide (ed), *Intellectual Property Rights and Human Rights: A Paradox* (Edward Elgar, 2010, forthcoming)

Mazoyer, M, 'Protecting Small Farmers and the Rural Poor in the Context of Globalisation' (FAO, Rome, 2001)

McBeth, Adam, 'Human rights in economic globalisation' in Sarah Joseph and Adam McBeth (eds), *Research Handbook on International Human Rights Law* (Edward Elgar, Cheltenham, 2010)

——, *International Economic Actors and Human Rights* (Routledge, Oxford, 2010)

——, 'When Nobody Comes to the Party: Why Have No States Used the WTO Scheme for Compulsory Licensing of Essential Medicines?' (2006) 3 *New Zealand Journal of International Law* 1

McCorquodale, Robert, 'An Inclusive International Legal System' (2004) 17 *Leiden Journal of International Law* 477

——, 'Self Determination: a Human Rights Approach' (1994) 43 *ICLQ* 857

McEvoy, Kieran, 'Law, Struggle, and Political Transformation in Northern Ireland' (2000) 27 *Journal of Law and Society* 542

McGoldrick, Dominic, *The Human Rights Committee: Its Role in the Development of the International Covenant on Civil and Political Rights*, 2nd edn (Oxford University Press, New York, 1994)

Médecins Sans Frontières (MSF), *Fatal Imbalance: The Crisis in Research and Drugs for Neglected Diseases* (Médecins Sans Frontières, Geneva, 2001)

Meiners, Roger E and Staaf, Robert J, 'Patents, Copyright, and Trademarks: Property or Monopoly' (1990) 13 *Harvard Journal of Law and Public Policy* 911

Meléndez-Ortiz, Ricardo, Bellmann, Christophe, and Hepburn, Jonathan (eds), *Agricultural Subsidies in the Green Box* (Cambridge University Press, Cambridge, 2009)

Morin, Jean-Frédéric, 'Tripping up TRIPS debates IP and health in bilateral agreements' (2006) 1 *Journal of Intellectual Property Management* 37

Morsink, Johannes, 'The Philosophy of the Universal Declaration' (1982) 4 *Human Rights Quarterly* 391

Mueller, John and Mueller, Karl, 'Sanctions of Mass Destruction' (1999) 78 *Foreign Affairs* 43

Murphy, Sophia, *Concentrated Market Power and Agricultural Trade* (Heinrich Boell Stiftung, Berlin, 2006)

——, 'WTO Agreement on Agriculture: Suitable Model for a Global Food System?' (2002) 7 *Foreign Policy in Focus* 3

Narlikar, Amrita, *The World Trade Organization: A Very Short Introduction* (Oxford University Press, New York, 2005)

Neumayer, Eric, 'The WTO and the Environment: Its Past Record is Better than Critics Believe, But the Future Outlook is Bleak' (2004) 4 *Global Environmental Politics* 1

Newland, Kathleen, 'Workers of the World, Now What?' (1999) 114 *Foreign Policy* 52

Oloka-Onyango, J, 'Beyond the Rhetoric: Reinvigorating the Struggle For Economic and Social Rights in Africa' (1995) 26 *California Western International Law Journal* 1

Orford, Anne, 'Beyond Harmonization: Trade, Human Rights and the Economy of Sacrifice' (2005) 18 *Leiden Journal of International Law* 179

——, 'Locating the International: Military and Monetary Interventions after the Cold War' (1997) 38 *Harvard International Law Journal* 443

Otsuki, Tsenuhiro, Wilson, John S, and Sewadeh, Mirvat, 'A Race to the Top? A Case Study of Food Safety Standards and African exports' (World Bank Policy Research Working Paper No 2563) (World Bank, Washington DC, February 2001)

Outterson, Kevin, 'Should access to medicines and TRIPS flexibilities be limited to specific diseases?' (2008) 34 *American Journal of Law and Medicine* 279

Oxfam, *Rigged Rules and Double Standards* (Oxfam, London, 2002)

——, *What happened in Hong Kong? Initial Analysis of the WTO Ministerial*, (Oxfam Briefing Paper 85, December 2005)

——, *Patients versus Patents: Five years after the Doha Declaration* (Oxfam Briefing Paper 95, 2006)

——, *Partnership or Power Play? How Europe should bring Development into its trade deals with African, Caribbean, and Pacific countries* (Oxfam Briefing Paper 110, 21 April 2008)

Paasch, Armin, 'World Agricultural Trade and Human Rights: Case Studies on Violations of the Right to Food of Small Farmers' in FIAN and others (eds), *The Global Food Challenge: Towards a Human Rights Approach to Trade and Investment Policies* (FIAN, Germany, 2009)

Palmer, Tom G, 'Are Patents and Copyrights Morally Justified? The Philosophy of Property Rights and Ideal Objects' (1990) 13 *Harvard Journal of Law and Public Policy* 817

Paul, James A and Wahlberg, Katarina, *A new era of world hunger?—the Global Food Crisis Analyzed* (Friedrich Ebert Stiftung, New York, August 2008)

Paul, Joel R, 'Do International Trade Institutions Contribute to Economic Growth and Development?' (2003) 44 *Virginia Journal of International Law* 285

Pauwelyn, Joost, *Conflict of Norms in Public International Law: How WTO law relates to other norms of International Law* (Cambridge University Press, Cambridge, 2003)

——, 'The Role of Public International Law in the WTO: How Far Can We Go?' (2001) 95 *American Journal of International Law* 535

——, 'The Sutherland Report: A Missed Opportunity for Genuine Debate on Trade, Globalization and Reforming the WTO' (2005) 8 *Journal of International Economic Law* 329

——, 'The Transformation of World Trade' (2005–2006) 104 *Michigan Law Review* 1

Petersmann, Ernst-Ulrich, 'The Human Rights Approach Advocated by the United Nations High Commissioner for Human Rights and by the International Labour Organisation: is it relevant for WTO law and Policy?' (2004) 7 *Journal of International Economic Law* 605

——, 'Time for a United Nations 'Global Compact' for integrating human rights into the law of worldwide institutions: lessons from European integration' (2002) 13 *European Journal of International Law* 621

Pitts III, Joe W (Chip), 'Corporate Social Responsibility: Current Status and Future Evolution' (2009) 6 *Rutgers Journal of Law and Public Policy* 334

——, 'The First U.N. Social Forum: History and Analysis' (2002) 31 *Denver Journal of International Law* 297

Pogge, Thomas, 'Growth and Inequality: Understanding Recent Trends and Political Choices' (2008) *Dissent* <http://www.dissentmagazine.org/article/?article=990> accessed 20 September 2010

——, 'Medicines for the World: Boosting innovation without obstructing free access' (2008) *Revista Internacional de dereitos humanos* 8 <http://www.yale.edu/macmillan/igh/files/SUR.pdf> accessed 17 April 2010

——, 'Priorities of Global Justice' (2001) 32 *Metaphilosophy* 6

——, 'Recognized and Violated: the Human Rights of the Global Poor' (2005) 18 *Leiden Journal of International Law* 717

——, 'Severe Poverty as a Violation of Negative Duties' (2005) 19 *Ethics and International Affairs* 55

——, 'World Poverty and Human Rights' (2005) 19 *Ethics and International Affairs* 1

Powell, Stephen, 'The place of human rights law in World Trade Organization rules' (2004) 16 *Florida Journal of International Law* 219

Pralahad, CK and Hart, Stuart L, 'The Fortune at the Bottom of the Pyramid' (2002) 26 *Strategy + Competition Magazine*

Raustiala, Kal, 'Rethinking the sovereignty debate in international economic law' (2003) 6 *Journal of International Economic Law* 841

Ravallion, Martin, Chen, Shaohua, and Sangraula, Prem, 'Dollar a Day Revisited' (World Bank Policy Research Working Paper No 4620) (World Bank, Washington DC, May 2008)

Reardon, Thomas and others, 'The Rise of Supermarkets in Africa, Asia and Latin America' (2003) 5 *American Journal of Agricultural Economics* 1140

Reddy, Sanjay G and Pogge, Thomas W, 'How *not* to count the poor' (Columbia University paper, version 6.2) (2005) <http://www.columbia.edu/~sr793/count.pdf> accessed 22 September 2010

Reichert, Tobias, 'Agricultural Trade Liberalization in Multilateral and Bilateral Trade Negotiations' in FIAN and others, *The Global Food Challenge: Towards a Human Rights Approach to Trade and Investment Policies* (FIAN, Germany, 2009)

——, 'A Human Rights Approach to Trade and Investment Policies' in FIAN and others, *The Global Food Challenge: Towards a Human Rights Approach to Trade and Investment Policies* (FIAN, Germany, 2009)

Rens, Andrew, Prabhala, Achal, and Kawooya, Dick, 'Intellectual Property, Education and Access to Knowledge in Southern Africa' (2006) Trade Law Centre for Southern Africa Working Paper No 13/2006 <http://www.tralac.org/unique/tralac/pdf/20061002_Rens_IntellectualProperty.pdf> accessed 20 September 2010

Restatement of the Law Third, Foreign Relations Law of the United States (American Law Institute, St Paul, 1987)

Risse, Matthias, 'Do we owe the global poor assistance or rectification?' (2005) 19 *Ethics and International Affairs* 1

Robertson, Robert E, 'Measuring State Compliance with the Obligation to Devote the "Maximum Available Resources" to Realizing Economic, Social, and Cultural Rights' (1994) 16 *Human Rights Quarterly* 693

Robinson, Jeffrey, *Prescription Games* (Simon & Schuster, London, 2001)

Rodrik, Dani, 'How to Save Globalisation from its Cheerleaders' (2007) 1 *The Journal of International Trade and Diplomacy* <http://dev.wcfia.harvard.edu/sites/default/files/Rodrick_HowToSave.pdf> accessed 20 September 2010

——, *One Economics, Many Recipes: Globalization, Institutions, and Economic Growth* (Princeton, Princeton University Press, 2008)

——, *The Global Governance of Trade: As if Development Really Mattered* (UNDP, New York, 2001)

——, 'Trading in Illusions' (March/April 2001) *Foreign Policy* 55

Ruggie, John, 'International Regimes, Transactions and Change: Embedded Liberalism in the Postwar Economic Order' (1982) 36 *International Organization* 379

Salomon, Margot, 'Global Economic Policy and Human Rights: Three Sites of Disconnection' (2010) *Carnegie Ethics Online* <http://www.cceia.org/resources/ethics_online/0043.html> accessed 22 September 2010

——, *Global Responsibility for Human Rights* (Oxford University Press, Oxford, 2007)

Sapra, Seem, 'The WTO System of Trade Governance: The Stale NGO Debate and the Appropriate Role for Non-State Actors' (2009) 11 *Oregon Review of International Law* 71

Save the Children, *Freedom from Hunger for Children under Six* (Save the Children, India, 2009)

Scherer, FM, 'The Pharmaceutical Industry and World Intellectual Property Standards' (2000) 53 *Vanderbilt Law Review* 2245

Schnepf, Randy and Womach, Jasper, 'Potential Challenges to US Farm Subsidies in the WTO: a Brief Overview', *CRS Report for Congress* (25 October 2006)

Schultz, Jennifer, 'The demise of "green" protectionism: the WTO decision on the US Gasoline rule' (1996) 25 *Denver Journal of International Law and Policy* 1

Schultz, Jenny and Ball, Rachel 'Trade as a weapon? The WTO and human rights-based trade measures' (2007) 12 *Deakin Law Review* 41

Schwartz, Bryan, 'The Doha Round and Investment: Lessons from Chapter 11 of NAFTA' (2003) 3 *Asper Review of International Business and Trade Law* 1

Sell, Susan K, *Private Power, Public Law: The Globalization of Intellectual Property Rights* (Cambridge University Press, Cambridge, 2003)

Sen, Amartya, 'Human Rights and Asian Values: What Lee Kwan Yew and Le Peng Don't Understand about Asia' (1997) 217 *The New Republic* 33

——, 'Human rights and economic achievements' in Joanne R Bauer and Daniel A Bell (eds), *The East Asian Challenge for Human Rights* (Cambridge University Press, Cambridge, 1999)

——, *Inequality Re-Examined* (Oxford University Press, Oxford, 1995)

——, 'Poor, Relatively Speaking' (1983) 35 *Oxford Economic Papers* 153

Sengupta, Arjun, 'On the Theory and Practice of the Right to Development' (2002) 24 *Human Rights Quarterly* 837

Shadlen, Ken, 'Resources, Rules and international political economy: the politics of development in the WTO' in Sarah Joseph, David Kinley, and Jeff Waincymer (eds), *The World Trade Organization and Human Rights: Interdisciplinary Perspectives* (Edward Elgar, Cheltenham, 2009)

Shafaeddin, Mehdi, 'Does Trade Openness Favour or Hinder Industrialization and Development?' *Third World Network Trade & Development Series No. 31* (TWN, Malaysia, 2006)

——, 'Is Industrial Policy Relevant in the 21st Century?' *Third World Network Trade & Development Series 36* (TWN, Malaysia, 2008)

——, 'Towards an Alternative Perspective on Trade and Industrial Policies' (2005) 36 *Development and Change* 1143

Shaffer, Gregory C, *Defending Interests: Public Private Partnerships in WTO Litigation* (Brookings Institution Press, Washington DC, 2003)

Shell, G Richard, 'Trade Legalism and International Relations Theory: An Analysis of the World Trade Organization' (1995) 44 *Duke Law Journal* 829

Shelton, Dinah, 'Normative Hierarchy in International Law' (2006) 100 *American Journal of International Law* 291

Shue, Henry, *Basic Rights* (Princeton University Press, Princeton, 1980)

Singham, Shanker A, 'Competition Policy and the Stimulation of Innovation: TRIPS and the interface between Competition and Patent Protection in the Pharmaceutical Industry' (2000) 26 *Brooklyn Journal of International Law* 363

Sivakumaran, Sandesh, 'The International Court of Justice and Human Rights' in Sarah Joseph and Adam McBeth (eds), *Research Handbook on International Human Rights Law* (Edward Elgar, Cheltenham, 2010)

Skogly, Sigrun, *Human Rights Obligations of the World Bank and the International Monetary Fund* (Cavendish, London, 2001)

Skogstad, Grace, 'International Institutions and Food Safety Regulation: Values in Conflict' in Ian Holland and Jenny Flemings (eds), *Government Reformed: Values and New Political Institutions* (Ashgate, Dartmouth, 2003)

Smaller, Carin and Murphy, Sophia, *Bridging the Divide: a human rights vision for global food trade* (Institute of Agriculture and Trade Policy, Geneva, 2008)

Sohn, Louis, 'The Human Rights Law of the Charter' (1977) 12 *Texas International Law Journal* 129

——, 'The new international law: protection of the rights of individuals rather than States' (1982) 32 *American University Law Review* 1

Spieldoch, Alexandra, *A Row to Hoe: the Gender Impact of Trade Liberalization on our Food System, Agricultural Markets and Women's Human Rights* (Friedrich Ebert Stiftung, Geneva, 2007)

Steiner, Henry, Alston, Philip, and Goodman, Ryan, *International Human Rights Law in Context*, 3rd edn (Oxford University Press, New York, 2008)

Stiglitz, Joseph, *Globalization and its Discontents* (Penguin, London, 2002)

——, *Making Globalization Work* (Penguin, London, 2007)

——, 'Social Justice and Global Trade' (2006) 169 *Far Eastern Economic Review* 18

——, *Freefall: Free Markets and the Sinking of the Global Economy* (Allen Lane, London, 2010)

—— and Charlton, Andrew, *Fair Trade for All* (Oxford University Press, New York, 2005)

Tabor, Anna-Marie, 'Recent Developments: AIDS Crisis' (2001) 38 *Harvard Journal on Legislation* 514

Terlingen, Yvonne, 'The Human Rights Council: A New Era in UN Human Rights Work?' (2007) 21 *Ethics and International Affairs* 167

Tesón, Fernando R and Klick, Jonathan, 'Global Justice and Trade: a Puzzling Omission' (2007) *FSU College of Law, Public Law Research Paper No 285, FSU College of Law, Law and Economics Paper No 07-24* <http://papers.ssrn.com/sol3/papers.cfm?abstract_id=1022996> accessed 22 September 2010

Thomas, Chantal, 'Poverty Reduction, Trade, and Rights' (2003) 18 *American University International Law Review* 1399

——, 'The WTO and labour rights: strategies of linkage' in Sarah Joseph, David Kinley, and Jeff Waincymer (eds), *The World Trade Organization and Human Rights: Interdisciplinary Perspectives* (Edward Elgar, Cheltenham, 2009)

Toulmin, Camilla and Guèye, Bara, 'Is there a future for family farming in West Africa?' in Tiina Huvio, Jukka Kola, and Tor Lundström (eds), *Small Scale Farmers in Liberalised Trade Environment: Proceedings of the Seminar on October 2004 in Haikko Finland* (University of Helsinki, Helsinki, 2005)

Trachtman, Joel P, 'Developing Countries, the Doha round, Preferences, and the Right to Regulate' in Chantal Thomas and Joel P Trachtman (eds), *Developing Countries in the WTO Legal System* (Oxford University Press, New York, 2009)

Trachtman, Joel P, 'Legal Aspects of a Poverty Agenda at the WTO: Trade Law and "Global Apartheid"' (2003) 6 *Journal of International Economic Law* 3

——, 'The Role of International Law in Economic Migration' (2008) (Society of International Economic Law Inaugural Conference 2008 Paper) <http://papers.ssrn.com/sol3/papers.cfm?abstract_id=1153499> accessed 19 September 2010

Trubek, David M and Cottrell, M Patrick, 'Robert Hudec and the Theory of International Economic Law' in Thomas and Trachtman (eds), *Developing Countries in the WTO Legal System* (Oxford University Press, New York, 2009)

Van den Bossche, Peter *The Law and Policy of the World Trade Organization* (Cambridge University Press, Cambridge, 2005)

Vandenhole, Wouter, 'Third states obligations under the ICESCR: a case study of EU sugar policy' (2007) 76 *Nordic Journal of International Law* 73

van Dijk, Pieter, van Hoof, Fried, van Rijn, Arjen, and Zwaak, Leo (eds), *Theory and Practice of the European Convention on Human Rights,* 4th edn (Intersentia, Antwerp, 2006)

Vázquez, Carlos Manuel, 'Trade sanctions and human rights—past, present, and future' (2003) 6 *Journal of International Economic Law* 797

von Braun, Joachin, 'Small-Scale Farmers in Liberalised Trade Environment' in Tiina Huvio, Jukka Kola, and Tor Lundström (eds), *Small Scale Farmers in Liberalised Trade Environment: Proceedings of the Seminar on October 2004 in Haikko Finland* (University of Helsinki, Helsinki, 2005)

Wade, Robert, 'What Strategies are Viable for Developing Countries Today? The World Trade Organization and the Shrinking of Policy Space' (2003) 10 *Review of International Political Economy* 621

Wahl, Peter, 'The Role of Speculation in the 2008 Food Price Bubble' in FIAN and others (eds), *The Global Food Challenge: Towards a Human Rights Approach to Trade and Investment Policies* (FIAN, Germany, 2009)

Wahlberg, Katarina, 'Food Aid for the Hungry?' (2008) *Global Policy Forum* <http://www.globalpolicy.org/component/content/article/217-hunger/46251-food-aid-for-the-hungry.html> accessed 22 September 2010

Wai, Robert, 'Countering, Branding and Dealing: Using Economic and Social Rights in and Around the International Trade Regime' (2003) 14 *European Journal of International Law* 35

Wallensteen, Peter, 'A century of economic sanctions: a field revisited' *Uppsala Peace Research Paper No 1* (Department of Peace and Conflict Research, Uppsala University, Sweden, 2000) <http://www.pcr.uu.se/pcr_doc/uprp/UPRP_No_1.pdf> accessed 14 December 2008

Waltz, Susan, 'Universalizing Human Rights: the Role of Small States in the Construction of the Universal Declaration of Human Rights' (2001) 23 *Human Rights Quarterly* 44

War on Want, 'Trading away our jobs: How free trade threatens employment around the world' (2009) <http://www.waronwant.org/attachments/Trading%20Away%20Our%20Jobs.pdf> accessed 5 February 2011

Weiler, Joseph, 'The Role of Lawyers and the Ethos of Diplomats: Reflections on the Internal and External Legitimacy of Dispute Settlement' in R Porter and others (eds), *Efficiency, Equity and Legitimacy: The Multilateral Trade System for the Millennium* (Brookings Institute Press, Washington DC, 2001)

Weissman, Robert, 'A long strange TRIPS: the Pharmaceutical Industry drive to Harmonize Global Intellectual Property, and the Remaining WTO Legal Alternatives Available to Third World Countries' (1996) 17 *University of Pennsylvania Journal of International Economic Law* 1069

Weston, Burns, 'Human Rights' (1984) 3 *Human Rights Quarterly* 257

Wilde, Ralph, 'Legal "Black hole"? Extraterritorial State action and international treaty law on civil and political rights' (2005) 26 *Michigan Journal of International Law* 1

Winickoff, David and others, 'Adjudicating the GM food wars: Science, Risk, and Democracy in World Trade Law' (2005) 81 *Yale Journal of International Law* 81

Wolf, Martin, *Why Globalisation Works* (Yale Nota Bene, London, 2005)

Wolfrun, Rüdiger, Stoll, Peter-Tobias, and Seibert-Fohr, Anja, *WTO: Technical Barriers and SPS Measures* (Martinus Nijhoff, Leiden, 2007)

Wright, Shelley, 'Women and the Global Economic Order: a Feminist Perspective' (1995) 10 *American University International Law Review* 861

Wu, Tim, 'The World Trade Law of Censorship and Internet Filtering' (3 May 2006) <http://papers.ssrn.com/sol3/papers.cfm?abstract_id=882459> accessed 22 September 2010

Xu, Yi-Chong and Weller, Patrick, *The Governance of World Trade: International Civil Servants and the GATT/WTO* (Edward Elgar, Cheltenham, 2004)

Young, Margaret A, 'The WTO's use of relevant rules of international law: an analysis of the *Biotech* case' (2007) 56 *International and Comparative Law Quarterly* 907

DOCUMENTS FROM INTERNATIONAL ORGANIZATIONS

CEDAW, 'General Recommendation No. 23: Women in political and public life (Article 7)', UN doc. A/52/38/Rev.1 (31 January 1997)

CERD, 'General Recommendation No. 21: Right to self-determination', UN doc. A/51/18 (23 August 1996)

CESCR, 'Concluding Observations of the Committee on Economic, Social and Cultural Rights: Israel', UN doc. E/C.12/1/Add.90 (23 May 2003)

——, 'General Comment No. 3: The Nature of States Parties' Obligations (Art. 2, Para. 1, of the Covenant)', UN doc. E/1991/23 (14 December 1990)

——, 'General Comment 6: The economic, social and cultural rights of older persons', UN doc. E/1996/22 (8 December 1995)

——, 'General Comment No. 8: The relationship between economic sanctions and respect for economic, social and cultural rights', UN doc. E/C.12/1997/8 (12 December 1997)

——, 'General Comment 12: Right to adequate food (Art. 11)', UN doc. E/C.12/1999/5 (12 May 1999)

——, 'General Comment No. 14: The right to the highest attainable standard of health (article 12 of the International Covenant on Economic, Social and Cultural Rights)', UN doc. E/C.12/2000/4 (11 August 2000)

——, 'General Comment No. 15: The right to water (arts. 11 and 12 of the International Covenant on Economic, Social and Cultural Rights)', UN doc. E/C.12/2002/11 (20 January 2003)

——, 'General Comment No. 17: The right of everyone to benefit from the protection of the moral and material interests resulting from any scientific, literary or artistic production of which he or she is the author (art. 15, para. 1(c))', UN doc. E/C.12/GC/17 (12 January 2006)

——, 'General Comment 18: The right to work (art. 6)', UN doc. E/C.12/GC/18 (6 February 2006)

——, 'General Comment No. 19: The right to social security (art. 9)', UN doc. E/C.12/GC/19 (4 February 2008)

CESCR, 'General Comment No. 20: Non-Discrimination in Economic, Social and Cultural Rights (art. 2, para. 2)', UN doc. E/C.12/GC/20 (2 July 2009)

——, 'General Comment No. 21: Right of everyone to take part in cultural life (art. 15, para. 1(a), of the International Covenant on Economic, Social and Cultural Rights)', UN doc. E/C.12/GC/21 (21 December 2009)

——, 'Human Rights and Intellectual Property: Statement by the Committee on Economic Social and Cultural Rights', UN doc. E/C.12/2001/15 (14 December 2001)

——, 'Poverty and the International Covenant on Economic Social and Cultural Rights', UN doc. E/C.12/2001/10 (10 May 2001)

——, 'Statement on Globalization and its impacts of economic, social and cultural rights', UN doc. E/1999/22 (11 May 1998)

Commission on Human Rights, 'Analytical study of the High Commissioner for Human Rights on the Fundamental Principle of Non-Discrimination in the Context of Globalization', UN doc. E/CN.4/2004/40 (15 January 2004)

——, 'Analytical Study of the High Commissioner for Human Rights on the fundamental principle of participation and its application in the context of globalization: Report of the High Commissioner', UN doc. E/CN.4/2005/41 (23 December 2004)

——, 'Liberalization of Trade in Services and Human Rights: Report of the High Commissioner on Human Rights to the Economic and Social Council', UN doc. E/CN.4/Sub.2/2002/9 (25 June 2002)

——, 'Mainstreaming the right to development into international trade law and policy at the World Trade Organization (paper prepared by Robert Howse)', UN doc. E/CN.4/Sub.2/2004/17 (9 June 2004)

——, 'Realization of economic, social and cultural rights: Second progress report prepared by Mr. Danilo Türk, Special Rapporteur', UN doc. E/CN.4/Sub.2/1991/17 (18 July 1991)

——, 'Report of the Special Rapporteur on adequate housing as a component of the right to an adequate standard of living, Miloon Kothari: Summary of communications sent and replies received from Governments and other actors', UN doc. E/CN.4/2006/41/Add.1 (23 December 2005)

——, 'Report of the Special Rapporteur on the right of everyone to the enjoyment of the highest attainable standard of physical and mental health, Paul Hunt', UN doc. E/CN.4/2006/48 (3 March 2006)

——, 'Report of the Special Rapporteur on the right to food, Jean Ziegler', UN doc. E/CN.4/2005/47 (24 January 2005)

——, 'The impact of the Agreement on Trade-Related Aspects of Intellectual Property Rights on human rights: Report of the High Commissioner', UN doc. E/CN.4/Sub.2/2001/13 (27 June 2001)

——, 'The Realization of Economic, Social and Cultural Rights: Final report submitted by Mr. Danilo Türk, Special Rapporteur', UN doc. E/CN.4/Sub.2/1992/16 (3 July 1992)

Commission on Human Rights, 'The right of everyone to the enjoyment of the highest attainable standard of physical and mental health: Report of the Special Rapporteur, Paul Hunt: Mission to the World Trade Organization', UN doc. E/CN.4/2004/49/Add.1 (1 March 2004)

European Union Directorate-General for Competition, *Pharmaceutical Sector Inquiry-Preliminary Report* (28 November 2008)

FAO, *The State of Food and Agriculture: Agricultural Trade and Poverty—Can Trade Work for the Poor?* (FAO, Rome, 2005)

——, *Voluntary Guidelines to support the progressive realization of the right to adequate food in the context of national food security* (FAO, Rome, 2005)

GATT, 'Ministerial Decision on Measures Concerning the Possible Negative Effects of the Before Program on Least Developed and Net Food-Importing Developing Countries', GATT doc. LT/UR/D-1/2 (1993)

HRC, 'Concluding Observations of the Human Rights Committee: Israel', UN doc. CCPR/CO/78/ISR (21 August 2003)

——, 'Concluding Observations of the Human Rights Committee: US', UN doc. CCPR/C/USA/CO/3 (15 September 2006)

——, 'General Comment No. 6: The right to life (art. 6)' Sixteenth session, 1982 (30 April 1982

——, 'General Comment No. 18: Non-discrimination', UN doc. HRI/GEN/1/Rev.1 (10 November 1989)

——, 'General Comment 23: The rights of minorities (Article 27)', UN doc. CCPR/C/21/Rev.1/Add.5 (8 April 1994)

——, 'General Comment 25: The right to participate in public affairs, voting rights and the right of equal access to public service (Article 25)', UN doc. CCPR/C/21/Rev.1/Add.7 (12 July 1996)

——, 'General Comment No. 27: Freedom of Movement (Art. 12)', UN doc. CCPR/C/21/Rev.1/Add.9 (2 November 1999)

——, 'General Comment No. 28: Equality of rights between men and women (article 3)', UN doc. CCPR/C/21/Rev.1/Add.10 (29 March 2000)

——, 'General Comment No. 31: Nature of the General Legal Obligation Imposed on States Parties to the Covenant', UN doc. CCPR/C/21/Rev.1/Add.13 (26 May 2004)

——, 'General Comment No. 33: The Obligations of States Parties under the Optional Protocol to the International Covenant on Civil and Political Rights', UN doc. CCPR/C/GC/33 (5 November 2008)

——, 'Application of the criteria for periodic evaluation of global development partnerships—as defined in Millennium Development Goal 8—from the right to development perspective: the Cotonou Partnership Agreement between the European Union and ACP Countries (Report by Prof. James Thuo Gathii)', UN doc. A/HRC/8/WG.2/TF/CRP.6 (21 December 2007)

——, 'Access to Medicine in the context of the right of everyone to the enjoyment of the highest attainable standard of physical and mental health', UN doc. A/HRC/RES/12/24 (12 October 2009)

——, 'National Report Submitted in Accordance with Paragraph 15(A) of the Annex to Human Rights Council Resolution 5/1: China', UN doc. A/HRC/WG.6/4/CHN/1 (10 November 2008)

——, 'Report of the Special Rapporteur on the right of everyone to the enjoyment of the highest attainable standard of physical and mental health, Anand Grover', UN doc. A/HRC/11/12 (31 March 2009)

——, 'Report of the Special Rapporteur on the right of everyone to the enjoyment of the highest attainable standard of physical and mental health: Preliminary note on the mission to Ecuador and Colombia', UN doc. A/HRC/7/11/Add.3 (4 March 2007)

——, 'Report of the Special Rapporteur on the Right to Food, Olivier De Schutter: Agribusiness and the Right to Food', UN doc. A/HRC/13/33 (22 December 2009)

——, 'Report of the Special Rapporteur on the right to food, Olivier De Schutter: Building resilience: a human rights framework for world food and nutrition security', UN doc. A/HRC/9/23 (8 September 2008)

——, 'Report of the Special Rapporteur on the right to food, Olivier De Schutter: Mission to the World Trade Organization', UN doc. A/HRC/10/5/Add.2 (25 June 2008)

HRC, 'Report of the Special Rapporteur on the Right to Food, Olivier De Schutter: Large-scale land acquisitions and leases: A set of minimum principles and measures to address the human rights challenge', UN doc. A/HRC/13/33/Add.2 (28 December 2009).

——, 'Report of the Special Representative of the Secretary-General on the issue of human rights and transnational corporations and other business entities: Business and human rights: mapping international standards of responsibility and accountability for corporate acts', UN doc. A/HRC/4/35 (19 February 2007)

——, 'Report of the Special Representative of the Secretary-General, John Ruggie, on the issue of human rights and transnational corporations and other business enterprises: Corporate responsibility under international law and issues in extraterritorial regulation: summary of legal workshops', UN doc. A/HRC/4/35/Add.2 (15 February 2007)

——, 'Report of the Special Representative of the Secretary-General on the issue of human rights and transnational corporations and other business enterprises, John Ruggie, Business and Human Rights: Further steps toward the operationalization of the "protect, respect and remedy" framework', UN doc. A/HRC/14/27 (9 April 2010)

——, 'Report to the General Assembly on the Fifth Session of the Council', UN doc. A/HRC/5/21 (7 August 2007)

——, 'The Cotonou Partnership Agreement between the European Union (EU) and the African, Caribbean and Pacific Countries (ACP countries) (Report by Dr Maria van Reisen, High Level Task Force on the Right to Development)', UN doc. A/HRC/12/WG.2/TF/CRP.3/Rev.1 (5 May 2009)

International Assessment of Agricultural Knowledge, Science and Technology for Development (IAAKSTD), *Agriculture at the Crossroads* (IAAKSTD, Washington DC, 2009)

International Law Commission, 'Articles on Responsibility of States for Internationally Wrongful Acts' (2001) UN doc. A/Res/s6/83

——, 'Fragmentation of International Law: Difficulties Arising from the Diversification and Expansion of International Law. Report of the Study Group of the International Law Commission: Finalised by Martti Koskenniemi', UN doc. A/CN.4/L.682 (13 April 2006)

OECD, *Trade, Employment and Labour Standards* (OECD, Paris, 1996)

——, *International Trade and Core Labor Standards* (OECD, Paris, 2000)

OHCHR, 'Report on Indicators for Promoting and Monitoring the Implementation of Human Rights', UN doc. HRI/MC/2008/3 (6 June 2008)

——, 'The Human Rights Impact of Economic Sanctions on Iraq' (Background paper prepared by the Office of the High Commissioner for Human Rights for the meeting of the Executive Committee on Humanitarian Affairs) (5 September 2000) <http://www.casi.org.uk/info/undocs/sanct31.pdf> accessed 22 September 2010

Oloka-Onyango, J and Udagama, Deepika, 'The Realization of Economic, Social and Cultural Rights: Globalization and its Impact on the Full Enjoyment of Human Rights', UN doc. E/CN.4/Sub.2/2000/13 (15 June 2000)

Report of the Johannesburg World Summit on Sustainable Development, UN doc. A/CONF.199/20

Report of the Secretary-General on the Work of the Organization, UN GAOR 53rd Sess., Supp. No 1, UN doc. A/53/1 (1998)

UN, *Millennium Development Goals Report 2009* (DESA, New York, 2009)

——, Commission on the Private Sector and Development, *Unleashing Entrepreneurship: Making Business work for the Poor* (UNDP, New York, 2004) via <http://www.undp.org/cpsd/report/index.html> accessed 22 September 2010

UNCTAD, *The Least Developed Countries Report 2006: Developing Productive Capacities* (UN, New York and Geneva, 2006)
——, *World Investment Report 2002, Transnational Corporations and Export Competitiveness*, UN doc. UNCTAD/WIR/2002 (UN, Geneva, 2002)
UNDP, *Asia Pacific Human Development Report 2006: Trade on Human Terms* (UNDP, Colombo, 2006)
——, *Human Development Report 2004: Cultural Liberty in Today's Diverse World* (UNDP, New York, 2004)
——, *Human Development Report 2005: International Cooperation at a Crossroads: Aid, Trade and Security in an Unequal World* (UNDP, New York, 2005)
——, *Human Development Report 2007/2008. Fighting climate change: Human solidarity in a divided world* (Palgrave Macmillan, Hampshire/New York, 2007)
——, *Poverty Reduction and Human Rights: A Practice Note* (2003)
UNECOSOC, 'Report of the United Nations High Commissioner for Human Rights', UN doc. E/2007/82 (25 June 2007)
——, 'Report of the High Commissioner for Human Rights on implementation of economic, social and cultural rights, UN doc. E/2009/90 (8 June 2009)
UNGA, 'Human Rights and Unilateral Coercive Measures', UN doc. A/RES/63/179 (18 December 2008)
——, 'Report of the Independent Expert on the Question of Human Rights and Extreme Poverty', UN doc. A/63/274 (13 August 2008)
——, 'Report of the Special Rapporteur on the right of everyone to the enjoyment of the highest attainable standard of physical and mental health, Paul Hunt', UN doc. A/61/338 (13 September 2006)
——, 'Report of the Special Rapporteur on the right to food, Jean Ziegler', UN doc. A/62/289 (22 August 2007)
——, 'Report of the Special Rapporteur on the Right to Food, Olivier De Schutter', UN doc. A/63/278 (21 October 2008)
——, 'Report of the Special Rapporteur on the Right to Food, Olivier de Schutter: Seed policies and the right to food: enhancing agrobiodiversity and encouraging innovation', UN doc. A/64/170 (23 July 2009)
——, 'We the Peoples: Civil Society, the United Nations and Global Governance: Report of the Panel of Eminent Persons on United-Nations Civil Society Relations', UN doc. A/58/817 (11 June 2004)
United Nations Human Settlements Programme, *Global Report on Human Settlements 2006: The Challenge of Slums* (UN Habitat, London, 2006)
United Nations Office of the High Commissioner for Human Rights, *Human Rights and World Trade Agreements: Using General Exception Clauses to Protect Human Rights* (Office of the High Commissioner for Human Rights, New York and Geneva, 2005) <http://www.fao.org/righttofood/kc/downloads/vl/docs/AH311.pdf> accessed 20 September 2010
World Bank, *Economic Growth in the 1990s: Learning from a Decade of Reform* (World Bank, Washington DC, 2005) <http://www1.worldbank.org/prem/lessons1990s/> accessed 19 September 2010
——, *World Development Report 2002: Building Institutions for Markets* (World Bank, Washington DC, 2002) via <http://www.worldbank.org/wdr/2001/fulltext/fulltext2002.htm> accessed 20 September 2010
——, *World Development Report 2006: Equity and Development* (World Bank, Washington DC, 2006)

World Bank, *World Development Report 2008: Agriculture for Development* (World Bank, Washington DC, 2008)

World Commission on the Social Dimension of Globalisation, *A Fair Globalization: Promoting Opportunities for all* (ILO, Geneva, 2004)

World Health Organization, *The World Medicines Situation* (WHO, 2004) <http://apps .who.int/medicinedocs/en/d/Js6160e/9.html> accessed 20 September 2010

——, 'Global Strategy and Plan of Action on Public Health, Innovation and Intellectual Property', WHO doc. AHA 61.21, 24 May 2008

——, 'Integrated Framework For Trade-Related Technical Assistance to Least Developed Countries', WTO doc. WT/MIN (96)/14, 7 January 1997

WTO, 'Accession of Least-Developed Countries' (Decision of 10 December 2002), WTO doc. WT/L/508

——, 'Amendment of the TRIPS Agreement' (Decision of 6 December 2005), WTO doc. WT/L/641

——, 'Declaration on the TRIPS Agreement and Public Health' (Adopted on 14 November 2001), WTO doc. WT/MIN(01)/DEC/2 (20 November 2001)

——, 'European Communities—the ACP-EC Partnership Agreement' (Decision of 14 November 2001), WTO doc. WT/MIN(01)/15 (14 November 2001)

——, 'Guidelines for arrangements on relations with Non-Governmental Organizations', WTO doc. WT/L/162 (Decision adopted by the General Council on 18 July 1996) (23 July 1996)

——, 'Implementation of paragraph 6 of the Doha Declaration on the TRIPS Agreement and public health' (Decision of the General Council of 30 August 2003), WTO doc. WT/L/540

——, 'Kimberley Process Certification Scheme for Rough Diamonds' (Decision of 15 December 2006), WTO doc. WT/L/676 (19 December 2006)

——, 'Ministerial Declaration' (Adopted on 13 December 1996, Singapore), WTO doc. WT/MIN(96)/14 (18 December 1996)

——, 'Ministerial Declaration' (Adopted on 14 November 2001, Doha) WTO doc. WT/MIN(01)/DEC/1 (20 November 2001)

——, 'Ministerial Declaration' (Adopted on 18 December 2005, Hong Kong) WTO doc. WT/MIN(05)/DEC (22 December 2005)

——, Report by the Consultative Board to the Director-General, *The Future of the WTO: Addressing Institutional Challenges in the New Millennium* (WTO, Geneva, 2004)

——, *The Future of the WTO: Addressing Institutional Challenges in the New Millennium* (Report by the Consultative Board to the former Director-General Supachai Panitchpakdi) (WTO, Geneva, 2004) ('Sutherland Report')

WTO, 'The Relationship between the TRIPS Agreement and the Convention on Biological Diversity (Council for Trade-Related Aspects of Intellectual Property Rights', WTO doc. IP/C/W/368/Rev.1 (8 February 2006)

——, 'Waiver Concerning Kimberley Process Certification Scheme for Rough Diamonds' (Decision of 15 May 2003), WTO doc. WT/L/518 (27 May 2003)

—— and ILO, *Trade and Employment: Challenges for Policy Research* (WTO Secretariat, Geneva, 2007)

Index